PRAISE FOR

EVERY CANADIAN'S GUIDE
TO THE LAW

"A most significant accomplishment. [The] book does indeed represent a very successful effort to 'demystify the law for the average person.' An excellent handbook for Canadians and . . . a very important reference for high school law classes."

The Honourable R. Roy McMurtry,
Chief Justice of Ontario and former Attorney General

"This is a superior product. It is wonderfully accessible, with beautiful brevity and clarity. . . . I am now as fully informed as a person can get. . . . [This book] is a glorious achievement."

June Callwood, author, journalist and activist

"Once again the wise and bracing Linda Silver Dranoff cuts through legal jargon to tell us all what we really need to know to take charge of our legal affairs. I'll keep this indispensable book within easy reach until she writes her next one."

Rona Maynard, former editor, *Chatelaine*

"Thanks not just for the book but for keeping up the good fight all these years in . . . taking law to the people."

Harry W. Arthurs, President Emeritus, York University,
and former Dean, Osgoode Hall Law School

LINDA SILVER DRANOFF

EVERY CANADIAN'S GUIDE TO THE LAW

THIRD EDITION

Collins

Every Canadian's Guide to the Law, Third Edition
© 1997, 2001, 2005 by Linda Silver Dranoff. All rights reserved.

Published by HarperCollins Publishers Ltd

First edition by HarperCollins Publishers Ltd as *Everyone's
Guide to the Law: A Handbook for Canadians*: 1997
Revised Edition: 2001
Third edition: 2005

HarperCollins books may be purchased for educational,
business, or sales promotional use through our Special
Markets Department.

HarperCollins Publishers Ltd
2 Bloor Street East, 20th Floor
Toronto, Ontario, Canada
M4W 1A8

www.harpercollins.ca

Library and Archives Canada Cataloguing in Publication

Dranoff, Linda Silver
Every Canadian's guide to the law / Linda Silver Dranoff. –
3rd ed.

Previous eds. published under title: Everyone's guide to the
law : a handbook for Canadians

Includes index.

ISBN-13: 978-0-00-639546-1
ISBN-10: 0-00-639546-5

1. Law – Canada – Popular works. I. Dranoff, Linda Silver.
Everyone's guide to the law. II. Title.

KE447.D72 2005   349.71   C2004-907090-8
KF387.D72 2005

HC 9 8 7 6 5 4 3 2 1

Printed and bound in the United States
Set in Utopia

CONTENTS

⚖

11. PLANNING FOR THE FUTURE 331

12. ACCESS TO THE LEGAL SYSTEM 364

ACKNOWLEDGEMENTS

⚖

This book is dedicated to my husband, Jack Marmer. I am grateful for his stalwart support and depth of understanding while I laboured countless evenings and weekends writing this book, in its three editions. He has been a perceptive and knowledgeable sounding board.

I extend my sincere thanks to my law partner, Judith Huddart, who gave me unstinting support and solid and painstaking research assistance throughout. I also appreciate the careful research help provided for the various editions by Sandra Schnurr, Maryellen Symons and Beth Dranoff.

The HarperCollins group has been exceptional: a special thank-you to Iris Tupholme, Publisher and Editor-in-Chief, for her editorial vision and perceptive suggestions; Rebecca Vogan for her respectful and helpful copy-editing; Nicole Langlois, Noelle Zitzer and Jim Gifford for their efficiency in steering the project through the editorial production process.

Thanks also to my literary agent, Beverley Slopen, for her enthusiasm for the project and her help in seeing it come to life. As always, my large and loving family have provided cheerful encouragement.

CHAPTER 1

INTRODUCTION

⚖

This book is an attempt to demystify the law for the average person. In my over 30-year career as a practising lawyer, legal columnist for 25 years with *Chatelaine* magazine, speaker, television and radio guest and on-air legal advisor, I have been asked all kinds of questions by people who need to know the right, the *legal*, thing to do in all sorts of circumstances.

No two cases presented to me have been exactly alike. But whether or not individuals are involved in or considering a lawsuit, they need plainly stated information and practical advice. They want to know their rights and obligations. Sometimes, people do not have an immediate problem; they are just curious about the law generally or the legal implications of something that happened to someone they know or have heard about. People are interested in a broad range of legal issues, and this book canvasses as many of them as possible. At the same time, with the increasing lack of affordable legal services and cuts to legal aid, more people are forced to represent themselves. They need basic information to help them do so, and to recognize when they should stretch their limited resources and retain a lawyer.

To understand the law, and how the legal system applies the law in practice, I believe that we must know how it evolved and continues to evolve.

The law is a living thing. The tree of law is composed of many branches and roots: *legislation*, to which legislators and government committees contribute; *court rulings*, to which lawyers and judges add their interpretations; *lobbying* and "friend of the court" submissions, by which the public gets its voice heard; *royal commissions*, which inquire into issues that may not be before the courts (for example, the Romanow Commission on the Future of Health Care in Canada, which reported in 2002; *public hearings and task forces* by legislative committees or appointed individuals; and *law reform commissions*, in which academics and reformers have their say.

The common law, as we know it outside Quebec (Quebec has a civil code containing, in effect, a complete legislative code), has grown and evolved to meet the new needs of every society and community. It is an intermeshing of *statute law*—legislation passed by elected officials in legislative assemblies—and *interpretive law*—rulings on the meaning of the law applied to individual situations by individual judges, and sometimes juries, in particular cases. Judgments that interpret or extend the law to resolve a unique problem in a specific case can have a major impact on other individuals with legal problems. When the judge makes a ruling that sets a precedent, this precedent helps future litigants.

The interrelationship between the legislature and the courts has changed since the passage of the Charter of Rights and Freedoms in 1982. Before the Charter, their roles were clear: The legislature passed statute law, and the courts interpreted that law in individual cases. Sometimes, the court extended the meaning of the statute law and set a precedent, which means that the court changed the law for other cases. But after the Charter came into effect (1982 for all but the equality provisions, which came into force in 1985), judges had the authority to invalidate statute provisions that were contrary to the Charter's protection of individual rights. This authority gave the courts final say, which they had never had before.

Their final say was subject only to the right of the legislatures to invoke Section 33 of the Charter, the "notwithstanding clause." In what were expected to be rare cases, legislatures were permitted to pass a law saying that "notwithstanding" the court's decision that the government had breached the Charter, the legislature had the right to do so. This power has been used infrequently.

The ongoing tension between the courts and legislators has been well described by Mr. Justice Gérard La Forest, writing for the minority in a case at the Supreme Court of Canada. In his statement, he clarified the difference between their roles:

> ... the fundamental institutional distinction between the legislative and judicial functions ... lies at the very heart of our political and constitutional system. ... Courts are specialists in the protection of liberty and the interpretation of legislation. ... However, courts are not specialists in the realm of policy-making, nor should they be. This is a role properly assigned to the elected representatives of the people, who have at their disposal the necessary institutional resources to enable them to compile and assess social science evidence, to mediate between competing social interests, and to reach out and protect vulnerable groups. ...

Who *should* have the final say? An appointed, unaccountable judge or an elected legislator? At first blush, it appears that elected representatives would bring about the more democratic process. But politicians make decisions based on party discipline. When the political party in power has the majority of seats in Parliament, the prime minister and Cabinet usually dictate how the individual politicians will vote (unless they are free to vote as they wish on a particular issue, such as capital punishment). Maybe it is just as well that our system allows both judges and legislators to have the final say in different cases.

Legislation does not state every possible rule of human interaction, nor have the judges in their courtrooms dealt with all the permutations of human conduct. But statute law and interpretive law form the bone and tissue of the legal skeleton, which lawyers use to negotiate for their clients. When a new situation arises, lawyers and judges apply the basic legal principles and the case law to help resolve the conflict; they add more tissue to the skeleton.

When legal principles do not settle a problem, then either the combatants compromise and avoid court, with its high cost and uncertain outcome, or they choose court and hope that they will get what they want from a judge.

Access to Justice

If combatants choose court, they must have access to the justice system and confidence in the process and the result. Access to justice has become one of the most important challenges facing society. Access does not simply mean that the door to the courthouse is open, or that anyone can issue a writ in civil court to right a wrong done to him or her. It does not simply mean that people can register a complaint in criminal court or call in the police to bring the criminal justice system to bear if a crime is committed against them or their neighbours. It is much more complicated.

To get access to justice, you must be able to afford legal advice and assistance, because without a lawyer it is difficult to properly advocate your interests. Before going to court in a civil case, consider whether retaining a lawyer to fight your case is cost effective. At the end of the process, you want to end up with more than just the ability to pay your legal fees. You can represent yourself in Small Claims Court, but note that the maximum for which you can sue in this court is usually less than $10,000. If you cannot afford representation and cannot represent yourself, legal aid is supposed to be available, particularly in criminal cases. But the problem is that legal aid underfunding and cuts threaten access and quality of service in many parts of Canada. When legal aid is not available, many people are representing themselves. This may be risky especially in criminal cases and serious civil cases.

The legal system is becoming unaffordable for the average person for a number of reasons. Two stand out in my experience.

First, the process is sometimes unduly complex. Additional steps to the process that were meant to (and often do) expedite and facilitate conflict resolution have also added to the cost to the litigant and the time it takes to resolve disputes. These added steps include case management, pre-trials, mediation, arbitration, case conferences, and the opportunity to ask for summary judgment. In criminal matters the courts now require the Crown to provide full disclosure of its evidence to the defence. While the intention was to resolve disputes or abbreviate the issues for trial, these new steps have added time and cost to the process.

Second, some litigants with deep pockets abuse the system. If you are unlucky, you will be up against an opponent and his or her lawyer who absolutely refuse to settle on any reasonable basis. They may bring nuisance motions, for example, or deliberately lengthen examinations for discovery. When your opponent wants absolute victory and wants you to suffer total defeat, expect an expensive battle. The law has been limited in its ability to curb these abuses.

I believe that the legal system *must* be made to work for the average person, and that unreasonable litigants must not be allowed to get away with abusive tactics. I believe that the law is our best and only real tool for ensuring that individuals are treated fairly, and that the legal system contributes to a civilized society.

As a practising lawyer, I have experienced

first-hand the multi-faceted, complex nature of the concept of justice and the legal system charged with the task of achieving it. I am elated when the system works and equity is achieved, when opponents behave decently, and when judges not only resolve individual disputes, but use these cases to clarify and interpret the law, and in the process set helpful precedents. And I must persist despite frustration when opponents use "win-at-all-costs" strategies and when litigants do not achieve a clear-cut resolution. I have experienced first-hand the tension that arises when a system formulated to resolve disputes must also deliver justice.

After more than 30 years, I still wish that the legal system worked at all times in an efficient, fair and affordable manner. But even when it is cumbersome, expensive and sometimes inequitable, I would not replace it with a different system, but I might modernize and streamline its procedures to improve access at a more acceptable cost to litigants. Our dispute resolution system is based on rule of law, not rule by force. Rules of evidence and procedural safeguards have evolved in an attempt to ensure fair results. Generally, there is respect for this legal system, and so judicial pronouncements are obeyed.

Chapter 12 provides help in accessing the legal system if you must represent yourself, guides you in hiring a lawyer, examines legal aid, and discusses alternatives such as mediation and arbitration, hiring a paralegal, using Small Claims Court and joining with others in class-action suits.

The Evolution of the Law: New Trends

This book also aims to provide the reader with insight into how laws change over time. Many legal issues contained in this book did not exist or were never contemplated when I started practising law. Evolving social trends have focused legal attention on such issues as common-law and same-sex relationships, pay and employment equity, women who choose to have children alone, sexual harassment and victims of crime. Animal rights law is a coming thing. It is an effort to protect animals as more than mere property and give them increased rights. The recession of the 1990s brought with it a keen interest in wrongful dismissal actions and bankruptcy, and the legal implications of contract, as compared to traditional employment relationships. The arrival of AIDS in the early 1980s created legal as well as medical problems. Many legal issues have arisen out of the escalating rates of divorce and remarriage and the increasing number of common-law and same-sex relationships. The changing nature of the family is having its impact on law. With the emergence in recent years of more sophisticated technology and medical advances, issues such as surrogate motherhood, abortion rights, breast implants, pacemakers, and air quality and other environmental concerns have taken on legal significance. Long-buried issues such as same-sex relationships, sexual abuse, incest, wife battering and sexual harassment demand public and therefore legal attention.

The law continues to evolve. Watch for these new trends: Aboriginal justice systems and their effect on our legal system; morality issues intersecting with legal issues; interest in the rule of law, especially as it applies to government actions; an increase in the number of proven wrongful convictions, focusing public attention on the problem and possible solutions; specialized courts requiring specialized staff to deal, for example, with domestic violence and mental health issues and alternate dispute resolution methods—such as mediation and collaborative law—that replace adversarial trials and are gradually privatizing the legal system, which potentially erodes the emphasis on rule of law. New laws protect whistle-blowers whose jobs may be in jeopardy because they put the public interest ahead of their employers' interests.

But the law does not only evolve. It can also devolve. Governments have abandoned or reduced their responsibility for governance in areas in which they formerly acted as guardians of public health and welfare.

Each of these trends is examined in greater detail below, except mediation and collaborative law, which is examined in Chapters 10 and 12.

Aboriginal Justice: The First Nations communities in Canada are seeking to reclaim not only their historic land and contractual rights from the government, but also their right to make and interpret laws for their own people. Although the cultural wellspring of First Nations law is different from common law and civil law, the Aboriginal system can teach us much. Some Aboriginal communities are reintroducing ancient solutions such as sentencing circles, in which community leaders and elders sit in a circle with perpetrator and victim. They review why the crime happened and consider what can be done to make reparations, all with a view to healing the community and

avoiding repeat offences. Aboriginal leaders express dissatisfaction with the punitive forms of criminal law, and prefer solutions that achieve prevention and protection. In 1996, the Criminal Code was amended, and sentencing principles were changed to take into account Aboriginal offenders and the role of their communities in their rehabilitation. The Supreme Court of Canada in 1999 noted that as Aboriginal people comprise 12 percent of the prison population, judges should consider restorative justice programs for native offenders.

Law and Morality: The law has also evolved to include what many would consider moral issues. A commercial case between two mining companies began the trend. International Corona Resources disclosed a confidential "find" and exploration results to Lac Minerals in the course of discussions about a possible joint venture. Lac Minerals then quickly bought the property before International Corona was able to complete its purchase of the site. The lawsuit that followed ended up in the Supreme Court of Canada, which ruled in 1989 that Lac Minerals had breached its "fiduciary duty" and its "confidence." Even though Lac Minerals had no contractual obligation to keep the information confidential, it was in a position of trust and was *morally* bound to behave as a fiduciary. The receipt of confidential information in circumstances of confidence establishes a duty not to use that information for any purpose other than that for which it is conveyed.

This case has been widely applied to a variety of situations. For example, a B.C. man followed the advice of his accountant to invest in certain MURBS (Multi-Use Residential Buildings), only to find later that the accountant also acted for the developers of the MURBS. Following the Lac Minerals case, the Supreme Court of Canada in 1994 found the accountant in breach of fiduciary duty. Fiduciaries have an obligation not only to act with skill and competence, but also, considering the power imbalance in their relationship, to use their discretion in the best interests of the vulnerable person, and to behave in such a way as to merit the special trust, loyalty and confidence placed in them. The Court said that a person seeking advice should not need to protect himself or herself from the abuse of power by the independent professional advisor. This case could be applied to other professional advisors as well. In 2000, the Supreme Court of Canada ordered a stockbrokerage to pay a client $925,000 for losses he suffered in the mismanagement of his portfolio; the company had speculated with funds that should have been managed conservatively.

Fiduciary duty is not the only incursion of morality into law. Since about 1991, the trend has been towards an increasing judicial willingness to enforce a duty to negotiate and perform contracts in good faith, a duty that requires self-interested parties to have regard for each other's legitimate interests, even in transactions with strangers. For example, in 1993 in Ottawa, an employer was found to have a duty of good faith to warn a long-standing employee that his performance was unsatisfactory, and to give him an opportunity to correct it rather than to just summarily dismiss him. An employee also has an obligation to act in good faith: In a 1991 Newfoundland case, a real estate agent who promised to remain with her employer for two years left after a few months, unscrupulously taking a listing with her. The court found that the employee

acted in breach of a duty to act in good faith.

In a 1994 Ontario case, a bank was found to owe a cosigner of a debt a duty to protect the cosigner from herself. A mother, using her home as collateral, cosigned a loan for her daughter and her spouse, which they failed to repay. When the bank tried to take the mother's home, she went to court. The judge invalidated the loan because the mother had not received independent legal advice, saying that the bank should not have given the loan without it. This case shows that even a bank has a duty to behave in a way that protects and does not take advantage of a person.

In 2000, a B.C. court overturned a mayoralty election because the winner had knowingly spread lies about his opponent and therefore won by fraudulent means.

Rule of Law Applied to Governments: The rule of law is the basis of our constitutional order, and protects us from arbitrary acts of public officials. For example, Manitoba's government was found by a court to have breached its contract with four First Nations students when it unilaterally reduced funds for an affirmative action university program. The Manitoba Court of Queen's Bench issued a ruling that said the province had no right to alter the terms of a program at the University of Manitoba known as "ACCESS," which the province began funding jointly with Ottawa in 1991. The program was designed to provide an opportunity for members of certain disadvantaged groups to obtain a postsecondary education that would otherwise be unavailable to them because of social, economic, cultural or linguistic barriers, or through lack of formal education. The government had agreed to pay a partial living allowance to students in the ACCESS program, who were mostly single parents of First Nations and Métis ancestry, and to pay for their tuition fees, books and transportation. The government was ordered to keep its word to these students. The trial decision was upheld by the Manitoba Court of Appeal in 1997. As one of the few cases on record that required a government to maintain a promised program, this case can be a useful precedent in similar situations.

In 1996, the Ontario government tried to terminate the services of eight directors of Ontario Hydro, around the time Hydro's board of directors was to make critical decisions about the corporation's future. The legal rule was that directors of Ontario Hydro could be terminated only "for cause," and not just because the government wanted to change control of the board. No cause was suggested in the Cabinet order-in-council that purported to dismiss the directors; in fact, gratitude was expressed for their contributions. Four directors applied to a court for reinstatement, which was granted. In effect, the Cabinet was not permitted to make an arbitrary decision, but had to abide by the "rule of law" that directors could be dismissed only for cause.

The rule of law is threatened in Canada by the anti-terrorism legislation rushed into law without the usual parliamentary scrutiny after the terrorist attacks on the Pentagon and the World Trade Center on September 11, 2001. Civil liberties are not adequately protected by the law, which, for example, permits detention for long periods of time without trial and arbitrary arrests based on racial profiling.

Recently, a new legal claim has been evolving in which a person hurt by a decision or action of a public official, who can prove that the official acted intentionally and with targeted malice, can allege the "intentional tort of abuse of public office."

The rule of law will be available in more cases in future if a 2004 decision of the Supreme Court of Canada is applied widely. In the case of *British Columbia (Minister of Forests)* v. *Okanagan Indian Band*, the government was ordered to pay interim costs to four Indian bands in a logging/land dispute with the British Columbia government. The court said, in cases of public importance and merit, trial judges should award court costs to poor litigants to enable them to bring their cases to trial, where the litigation would be unable to proceed if the order was not made.

Wrongful Convictions: Canadians have read of travesties of justice in the wrongful conviction and incarceration of Donald Marshall of Nova Scotia, Guy Paul Morin of Ontario, David Milgaard of Saskatchewan and others. Circumstantial evidence, incorrect assumptions of police officers and juries, and inadequate forensic evidence are only some of the factors that have contributed to great injustices done to some individuals. Loud proclamations of innocence have not gained them vindication and freedom; it has been scientific advances, especially DNA evidence, that have been able to prove with certainty their innocence.

For example, an inquiry held in 1997 heard that when Guy Paul Morin was accused of murder in the 1984 death of the next-door child who disappeared, it was because the police assumed guilt from his failure to join in the search for her and his failure to attend her funeral when she was found. The report of the commissioner, Fred Kaufman, a former judge of the Quebec

Court of Appeal, was a damning indictment of the shoddy, unreliable and negligent conduct of many of those involved in the case, including the police, forensic scientists and Crown prosecutors.

Morin was acquitted at trial, but the appeal court reversed the decision and sent him to be retried, and he was convicted at the retrial. He was not exonerated until 1995 as a result of DNA evidence. He received compensation from the Ontario government of $700,000 for himself and $550,000 for his parents because they had exhausted their life savings to pay for his first trial and the appeal.

Some have received compensation from the government for wrongful incarceration, but only after a long struggle. For example, Donald Marshall served 12 years for a first-degree murder he was later proven not to have committed; the Nova Scotia government agreed to pay him and his parents annual allowances amounting to over $1 million. Susan Nelles was charged with the first-degree murder of babies at Sick Children's Hospital in Toronto and was exonerated at a preliminary inquiry; she received $60,000 in compensation.

The Criminal Code allows convicts who have exhausted all other avenues of appeal to ask the Department of Justice for a review. For example, Steven Truscott asked the minister of justice in 2004 for a review of his 1959 murder conviction. Justice Minister Irwin Cotler found there was a reasonable chance that there had been a miscarriage of justice, and he referred the case for an open-ended (and final) review to the Ontario Court of Appeal, to be heard as if it were an appeal, to determine if there's a reasonable chance the fresh evidence that had emerged in the case could have affected the verdict.

An organization formed in 1993, the Association in Defence of the Wrongly Convicted (AIDWYC), is pressing for the establishment of an independent commission outside government called the Wrongful Conviction Board to be composed of former and current judges, lawyers and members of the public. If the commission is given the power to access all documents, investigate fresh evidence, compel witnesses to testify and refer cases back to the court system, this, AIDWYC hopes, will reduce the number of wrongful convictions. In the meantime, the organization has been instrumental in overturning several convictions and raising serious doubts about others.

The Environment: Governments have been abandoning or reducing their role as guardians of public health and welfare.

In Ontario, the government had relinquished its role as protector of the environment by, for example, eliminating many environmental regulations without public consultation, moving towards privatization of such essentials as drinking water, and slashing funding for environmental programs, including tests of drinking water. Ontario charges against polluters fell by about 50 percent from 1992 to 1997. This resulted in a number of public tragedies, including, in 2000, an outbreak of E. coli bacteria in Walkerton, Ontario, that caused seven fatalities. Ontario had more than 1900 water protection law violations in 2000, with only four of the nearly 200 violators actually facing charges. This meant that 98 percent of violators got away with their conduct, according to a 2002 Sierra Legal Defence Fund report.

This may change. In late 2004, following a change of government a year earlier,

Ontario introduced "you spill you pay" legislation to crack down on polluters. The proposed law shifts enforcement away from courts and into the hands of bureaucrats with authority to act within days of a spill, triples fines and creates a community cleanup fund. Penalties can be imposed of up to $20,000 a day for individuals and $100,000 a day for corporations.

Federal environmental charges against polluters dropped 78 percent between 1992 and 1998. No one was jailed in the ten-year period between 1988 and 1998 under Canada's Environmental Protection Act or Fisheries Act. And statistics released in 2000 reveal that Canadian imports of hazardous waste are rising sharply and a growing proportion of it is being dumped without treatment rather than being recycled. The volume of hazardous waste imported in 1999 exceeded all hazardous waste produced within Canada that year. The budget for Environment Canada has been reduced by about 40 percent over the past few years.

The federal government passed a revised Canadian Environmental Protection Act in 1999, which many experts denounced as too weak to protect Canadians from toxic pollution. It replaced 1988 legislation intended to eliminate toxic pollution in Canada but which had only assessed 31 out of 32,000 chemicals in its 11 years. The 1999 legislation was revised in 2003 with the stated intention of strengthening it. But the experts were still right to be concerned. According to a 2004 report by the Canadian Environmental Law Association, the most recent statistics (for 2002) show that the amount of toxic pollutants reported released and transferred had increased by 49 percent over a seven-year period. Ninety percent of companies report no change projected for 2003–2005. Fines remain low, and even those who do face fines deduct them as a business expense.

There is some cause for hope. A relatively new area of law permits citizens to individually or in class actions join together to sue governments for "regulatory negligence" when a government fails to adequately enforce its own rules and regulations. For example, lawsuits can be brought against both the polluter and the government for harm to drinking water if it can be proven that the government has not enforced its antipollution rules. A homeowner who is not warned by health authorities that her house has been built on radioactive soil can sue the government. So can drivers involved in accidents on icy highways that should have been sanded.

And in 2000, the Supreme Court of Canada ruled in favour of a Toronto homeowner who sued the city (as well as the contractor) when the city inspectors did not inspect a critical aspect of construction that was part of its mandate but approved a building permit anyway; when the work proved defective (the underpinnings were inadequate and the basement flooded), the owner sued the city for negligent inspection and won. The contractor and the city were ruled jointly and severally liable for damages in the amount of $49,368.80 plus interest.

Ontario and the Territories have all adopted laws permitting citizens to sue if they believe the standards set in the regulations are not high enough. Some federal environmental legislation also permits civil suits.

Specialized Courts: A trend has begun in the establishment of specialized courts with specially trained judges, lawyers and support staff. So far, these courts have been established to deal with criminal charges of domestic violence (see Chapter 8), drug addiction and mental health, and there is talk of specialized courts for impaired driving charges. What these have in common is the effort to add mental health professionals to assist in the rehabilitation of people with personal problems of drug and alcohol use, and to help them avoid incarceration, which seldom aids in prevention of future offences. Domestic violence courts also have behavioural specialists on staff to help perpetrators learn how to handle their anger and stop taking it out on their spouses. Provincial family courts have been specialized courts for some time. The trend is towards therapeutic jurisprudence, which sees the law as a healing agent and not just a punitive instrument.

Whistle-Blower Protection: Employees who act to warn the public of improper conduct by government and corporations are described as "whistle-blowers" and there is a trend to provide job protection for them. For example, the federal Liberal government enacted legislation in 2004 to protect from reprisal most federal bureaucrats who blow the whistle on wrongdoing. The law provides that public servants will not be demoted, fired or otherwise disciplined for calling attention to waste, corruption or mismanagement, and that a public service integrity commissioner will be appointed to investigate their confidential complaints.

The contents of this book were, to the best of my knowledge, accurate at the time of writing. However, the law does evolve and it may not be precisely the same on the day you read a particular section. This book is intended to give general information and advice. If you have a particular legal problem, you should consult a lawyer for advice on dealing with your unique circumstances.

If you have a lawyer or are about to hire one to assist you with a legal problem, this book will help you know what questions to ask and what information your lawyer needs in order to advise you. The information in this book can assist a self-represented litigant to have a basic understanding of the law. I hope this book also contributes to a citizen's greater general knowledge of the law. I believe that knowledge of the law and its application is empowering, and should be part of every person's perspective on the world.

CHAPTER 2

BIRTH ISSUES

⚖

Introduction

The issues now facing men and women who contemplate having and raising families together are very different from those facing earlier generations.

Before 1967, it was illegal to sell or distribute contraceptives, and before 1969 abortion was considered a criminal act and legally available only under narrowly prescribed circumstances. In 1988, abortion was decriminalized, and left as a matter of choice between a woman and her physician. Control over childbirth has evolved to the point where some people consider having a surrogate bear their child, babies are conceived in test tubes and a Royal Commission developed policies, which were eventually transformed into law, to deal with such futuristic reproductive technologies as sex selection, fetal surgery and stem-cell research. Today, women can and do choose to have a child on their own. Their sperm donors sometimes demand access; sometimes the recipients of the sperm seek support.

Some issues have come full circle. Centuries ago, for example, midwives were the professionals who delivered babies. Once medical science took over with the specialty of obstetrics, midwives were relegated to the background. In recent years, midwifery has been recognized in some jurisdictions as a self-governing profession.

A. THE CHOICE TO HAVE A CHILD OR NOT

1. Fetal Rights

The law does not grant the rights and duties of a legal "person" to a baby until she or he sees the light of day. The Criminal Code of Canada says that a child becomes a human being after having "completely proceeded in a living state" from his or her mother's body, whether or not the child has taken a breath, has an independent circulation, or has been separated from the umbilical cord.

Although an unborn child has no legal identity independent of the mother before birth, the law does acknowledge, in a limited sense, that the baby previously existed as a fetus in the mother's womb. For example, an unborn child has the right to inherit property after birth; a bequest in a will "to my children" will include a posthumous child born to the deceased man's wife if she was pregnant at the time of his death.

There is no right to sue on behalf of the fetus for a miscarriage or stillborn birth arising from an injury to the mother during pregnancy. However, if injury occurs to a baby while in the womb, and the baby survives to be born alive (rather than stillborn), the child or her parents or legal guardian may sue after birth and after the nature and extent of the injury have been determined. Courts have awarded compensation to children for prenatal injuries from car and other accidents in which third parties are at fault. In a 1999 Supreme Court of Canada decision, a child born with pre-natal injuries suffered in a car accident caused by his mother could not collect compensation from his mother or her insurance company. The Court ruled as a matter of public policy that courts should not impose a duty of care on a pregnant woman towards her fetus or subsequently born child.

Before birth, the laws are applied in a variety of ways:

ABORTION

Anti-abortion groups, arguing that life begins at conception, have unsuccessfully tried to claim for the fetus the same legal rights enjoyed by a person already born, including the right to live. In 1979, an Ottawa lawyer sued two local hospitals, allegedly on behalf of all unborn children, to prevent any more abortions at the hospitals. The Ontario Supreme Court said not only that a fetus is not a person, but also that the lawyer had no right to represent all unborn children since he had no personal, proprietary or parental rights at stake, and could not represent the public interest.

But, in 1981, the Supreme Court of Canada gave former Manitoba Cabinet minister Joe Borowski the right to challenge the federal government, on behalf of the unborn, for allowing abortions. He went ahead with his lawsuit, arguing that abortions violated the right-to-life guarantees in the Charter of Rights and Freedoms. Section 7 of the Charter promises that everyone has the right to "life, liberty and security of the person." Unsuccessfully, he tried to claim those rights for a fetus from the instant of conception.

The Saskatchewan Court of Queen's Bench in 1983 and the Court of Appeal in 1987 concluded that Canada's abortion law of the time was valid. (During this time, Section 251 of the Criminal Code stated that a woman needed the approval of a hospital abortion committee that was composed of at least three doctors, and that agreed that termination of the pregnancy was medically necessary to protect a woman's life or health, either physical or psychological.) The Courts also ruled that a fetus was not a legal person, and therefore was not protected by the 1982 Canadian Charter of Rights and Freedoms.

In the period between the Saskatchewan Court of Appeal hearing in 1987 and the Supreme Court of Canada hearing between October 1988 and March 1989, the abortion sections of the Criminal Code of Canada were struck down as unconstitutional by the Supreme Court of Canada in early 1988 in the case of *R.* v. *Morgentaler*. After many years of struggle and constitutional challenges by Dr. Henry Morgentaler and his supporters, abortion was decriminalized.

As a result, the Supreme Court of Canada dismissed Borowski's appeal in 1989, deciding not to make a decision in the case because the matter had become "moot"— that is, since the case raised a hypothetical or abstract question, a decision would not resolve a live and concrete controversy affecting the rights of parties. The law stood that a fetus has no legal standing as a person before birth. See also section A3, "Abortion," later in this chapter.

CHILD WELFARE

Child-welfare legislation does not specifically protect a fetus. As a result, the general law applies, which states that a fetus is not entitled to the same protection as a living person. However, there are times when judges have been faced with troublesome cases of pregnant women who jeopardize the health of their unborn child. Judges have responded by stretching the law to protect the fetus. When the court order is not appealed, these judges may succeed. In other cases, judges have refused to make any order affecting the fetus.

For example, in a 1987 B.C. case, a pregnant woman was required by court order to undergo a Caesarean section (surgical delivery of a baby through the abdomen) against her will, to save the baby's life. In 1987, an Ontario Children's Aid Society secured a court order making an unborn child a temporary ward of the CAS, so the CAS could take steps to protect the fetus prior to birth. And, in 1990, the New Brunswick Ministry of Health and Community Services was granted an order permitting it to supervise the mother and fetus.

But a 1988 B.C. court decided that an unborn child was not a "child" within the meaning of the child-welfare legislation, and

that therefore the court could not intervene. And in 1996, Winnipeg judge Perry Schulman's effort to protect the fetus of a pregnant, glue-sniffing 22-year-old woman was overturned by the Manitoba Court of Appeal. Judge Schulman had ordered the woman into the custody of the Director of Child and Family Services, who was given the power to have her treated during her pregnancy. The woman had damaged herself and three other children (all Crown wards) by her addiction. The Director was specifically permitted to have her committed under mental health legislation if she failed to take treatment. The judge relied on the "parens patriae" jurisdiction of judges to act beyond the scope of statute or interpretive law to protect the weak, vulnerable, and mentally incompetent.

The Manitoba Court of Appeal reversed the order on the basis that the fetus was not a person under law, and the courts should not be in the position of choosing between the rights of the mother and the fetus. This court said that the lower court had no jurisdiction to require the mother to undergo treatment, when a psychiatrist gave evidence that she was not mentally ill as defined by law, and therefore competent to make her own decisions.

The case was sent to the Supreme Court of Canada, which agreed to hear the appeal of Winnipeg's Child and Family Services agency. The Supreme Court of Canada decided in 1997 that the Manitoba Court of Appeal was right.

RIGHTS OF THE MOTHER

The conflict between fetal and maternal rights has almost always been resolved in favour of the mother. To put fetal rights ahead of maternal rights would create obligations that would be impossible to enforce legally, such as defined pre-natal care of the mother. If fetal rights were put first, a defective child might have the legal right to sue the mother for negligence in caring for herself. For example, if the mother smoked, drank or took drugs during pregnancy, these acts might be regarded as negligent care of the fetus. Taken to extremes, a mother might be forced to have pre-natal surgery, and a doctor might be sued by someone on behalf of a dead fetus for negligence during the performance of fetal surgery. These examples suggest some of the implications of putting fetal rights ahead of maternal rights.

MOTHER'S WORK

Sometimes a mother's working conditions may affect the fetus. Only the province of Quebec, however, protects pregnant working women employed in hazardous working conditions by reassigning them to safe job tasks or giving them paid preventive leave. If the employee raises the issue, the onus is on the employer to prove the safety of the working conditions. More than 20,000 Quebec women annually exercise their right to preventive reassignment or paid leave to avoid reproductive health hazards.

The Canada Labour Code was amended in 2000 to permit a pregnant or nursing woman to stop performing her job if it poses a risk to her health or the health of the fetus or child. The employer may reassign her to other duties but must continue her wages and benefits at the same level. The Canada Labour Code applies to the federal government, Crown corporations and federally regulated companies such as Air Canada and banks.

In the rest of Canada, there is no legislation that specifically addresses safety issues for pregnant employees. There are occupational health and safety laws that apply to all employees, but the onus is on the employee to prove that refusing to work is reasonable. In Ontario, for example, any employee can complain about unsafe working conditions and refuse to work, triggering a government safety inspection, but then he or she must show that it is reasonable not to work under those conditions.

An Ontario case, initiated in 1985 and finally resolved in 1992, addressed this issue. A pregnant spray painter asked her employer to accommodate her obstetrician's concern that the paint fumes could cause damage to the fetus. When she requested that the employer move her, during her pregnancy, from spray painting duties into packing duties, a position that was available, the employer put up roadblocks, wanted more proof from the doctor and put her on an involuntary nine-month leave of absence without pay. The employee complained to a board of inquiry established by the Ontario Human Rights Commission. The board found, and was sustained on appeal, that the employer had behaved in a "paternalistic, patronising and unreasonable" manner. The employer was told it had a duty to accommodate the employee's request, especially since it involved neither undue interference in the operation of the business nor undue expense to the employer.

CITIZENSHIP

A fetus is not a citizen of Canada just because it was conceived here; it must be born in Canada. A pregnant woman unsuccessfully tried to have her deportation from Canada delayed by arguing that the fetus was a Canadian citizen. The court ruled that a citizen is a person already born in Canada or who has chosen to become a Canadian citizen.

INHERITANCE RIGHTS OF AN UNBORN CHILD

A child "en ventre sa mère" (in the mother's womb) can inherit only after birth. If, for example, a person dies leaving bequests to "all my grandchildren," and the person's daughter is then pregnant, the bequest must be held until the child is born. If the woman miscarries or aborts, or the child is born dead, then the bequest goes back into the estate to be shared among the other beneficiaries.

REPRODUCTIVE TECHNOLOGIES

In recent years, the expanding technological ability to control the childbirth process has focused more closely on the fetus. After hearing from about 40,000 individuals and 400 organizations, Canada's Royal Commission on New Reproductive Technologies released in 1993 a lengthy and detailed report entitled *To Proceed with Care*. In it, the Commission recommended that the government outlaw the sale of eggs, sperm, embryos and fetal tissue, ban surrogate motherhood, control in vitro fertilization, ban the donation of eggs in exchange for in vitro services and close sex-selection clinics. (It was already illegal to sell babies.)

Soon after the Commission's report, a procedure was developed to surgically extract sperm from the body of a dead man. The cases were brought to light when several widows asked for the procedure after their husbands died suddenly.

The government's initial response to the Commission's report was in 1995 when the federal health minister called for "voluntary restraint" in the commercial use of reproductive technologies. In 1996, the federal government introduced, but did not pass, the Human Reproductive and Genetic Technologies Act, intended to prohibit practices that commercialize reproduction or are inconsistent with principles of human dignity.

In 2004, the federal government passed the Assisted Human Reproduction Act to finally establish public policy to deal with reproductive technologies. The new law banned human cloning, commercial (but not volunteer) surrogacy contracts, the sale of human sperm and eggs, sex selection, genetic alteration, creation of artificial wombs and retrieval of eggs from fetuses and cadavers. It set standards for in vitro fertilization and embryonic stem-cell research, allowing scientists to work with surplus embryos created in the course of infertility treatments, but not to clone embryos for research purposes. A federal agency was to be established to oversee fertility clinics, and a national registry of donor health records was to be set up. The law is to be reviewed after three years.

The dangers inherent in modern reproductive technologies were highlighted in newspaper reports in 1995 about a Dutch couple who had twins as a result of in vitro fertilization, supposedly using the wife's ovum and the husband's sperm. One twin was black and the other white because, when the technician failed to clean an instrument used in the insemination process, the mother's eggs were accidentally inseminated with a black donor's sperm as well as with her husband's. As the child's complexion darkened during his first year of life, the parents had tests taken that confirmed he had a different biological father from his sibling. In a tightly knit homogeneous Dutch village, the black child of a white mother created quite a sensation.

2. Choice and Consent

In a nutshell, a man and a woman decide whether to have intercourse and whether to use contraception. After that, it is up to fate and the procreative powers of the couple to determine whether the woman gets pregnant. It is then up to the woman alone to determine whether she chooses to see the pregnancy through to completion. Her partner's opinion and moral support will be important. Normally, she will consult with her doctor and perhaps secure a second opinion. But the woman is in charge of her own life, and the final decision over her body is hers.

The role of the man in childbirth decisions can create difficulties because he may want a say. When the couple have a good relationship, and can communicate and make joint decisions for their mutual well-being, they do so, and the law does not get involved. But when they cannot agree about completing or terminating a pregnancy, the man has sometimes sought legal intervention to demand that his wishes be considered or that the abortion be stopped.

Lawsuits have been brought by husbands and boyfriends to stop the plans of a wife or girlfriend for an abortion, even though Canadian law never required the man's consent or even required that he be consulted. In fact, there was no law about the man's consent at all. The law was silent, and a consent requirement cannot be assumed; it must be stated.

A series of cases reached the courts between 1979 and 1989. One example stands out.

In the case of *Tremblay* v. *Daigle*, the Supreme Court of Canada finally put an end to the question of consent. Jean-Guy Tremblay went to a Quebec court to prevent his ex-girlfriend, who was 18 weeks pregnant, from having an abortion. They had just separated after five months of cohabitation. In the court documents, 21-year-old Chantal Daigle explained why she wanted the abortion. She described her 25-year-old boyfriend as jealous, possessive and physically abusive to the extent that police assistance was required.

The Quebec court issued an injunction to stop Daigle's planned abortion on the basis that the fetus was a human being under the Quebec Charter of Human Rights and Freedoms and therefore had a "right to life." Daigle appealed, and the Quebec Court of Appeal upheld the injunction. She appealed again to the Supreme Court of Canada, which heard the case on short notice. By this time, some organizations had joined the battle, including the Canadian Abortion Rights Action League (CARAL), the Women's Legal Education and Action Fund (LEAF), the Canadian Civil Liberties Association, the Campaign Life Coalition and the attorneys general of Canada and Quebec.

In the meantime, Daigle had gone ahead with her abortion, as her lawyer announced during the argument of her case before the

Supreme Court. News reports suggested that it had taken place outside Quebec because she was said to be in her twenty-second or twenty-third week of pregnancy and Quebec hospitals would not perform abortions over 20 weeks into the pregnancy. The Supreme Court of Canada decided to render judgment anyway. It allowed the appeal and approved the abortion, ruling that the fetus is not a person in law, and the man has no legal right of veto over the woman's decision regarding the fetus she is carrying.

The consent issue may also arise in connection with medical operations affecting childbirth, such as hysterectomies and vasectomies. A husband's consent is not required for his wife's hysterectomy, and a husband has no legal right to prevent a hysterectomy if the wife chooses to have one. Marriage does not give a husband the legal right to a fertile wife or control of his wife's reproductive organs. It is the woman's decision, and before the operation can be performed, the doctor and hospital require only her voluntary informed consent. If the physician uncovers a condition during surgery that may prove fatal if he or she waits, or if a procedure is necessary to save the woman's life and she is incapable of communicating her decision (if she is unconscious, for example), then the physician can proceed without consent.

Some wary doctors and hospital boards used to make it a policy—and some still do—to try to secure the husband's consent to his wife's sterilization, abortion or any operation that affects her child-bearing capacity. But a hospital or doctor cannot indirectly confer a right on a husband or potential father by asking for his consent when the law does not grant him that right.

A married woman who wants children, but whose husband had a vasectomy without her knowledge and approval, also has no rights. From the law's point of view, a vasectomy is a private matter between a man and his doctor. A married man has no legal obligation to consult his wife about undergoing the procedure because, although it may terminate his ability to impregnate her, it does not affect his ability to have sexual relations.

3. Abortion

There is no longer any valid federal law preventing or criminalizing abortion, or requiring anyone's consent to the procedure other than the pregnant woman's.

In 1988, the Supreme Court of Canada ruled that the law on abortion was unconstitutional because it restricted a woman's right to control her own reproductive life, and thus infringed her constitutionally protected guarantees to security of the person, liberty and freedom of conscience. The Court thus invalidated the consent requirements in the Criminal Code and decriminalized abortion. It also unanimously determined that the civil law in Quebec, the Quebec Charter, and the common law do not protect fetal life or interests.

The chief justice at the time, Brian Dickson, summed it up:

> Forcing a woman by threat of criminal sanction to carry a fetus to term unless she meets certain criteria unrelated to her own priorities and aspirations is a profound interference with a woman's body and thus a violation of security of the person.

Madam Justice Bertha Wilson went further and ruled that the constitutional right to liberty guarantees freedom of conscience and personal autonomy over important decisions intimately affecting private lives. She was blunt in saying that only a woman could understand the dilemma:

It is probably impossible for a man to respond, even imaginatively, to such a dilemma not just because it is outside the realm of his personal experience (although this is, of course, the case) but because he can relate to it only by objectifying it, thereby eliminating the subjective elements of the female psyche which are at the heart of the dilemma.

The Court, as a whole, effectively decriminalized abortion (although the law is still in the Criminal Code), and made it a private matter between a woman and her physician, thus respecting the rights of individual women to control their reproductive lives and bodies. The rights of pregnant women were considered more important than the rights of a fetus. And in 2004, the federal government made it easier for drugstores across Canada to provide the morning-after pill—a kind of retroactive birth control—without prescription.

DR. HENRY MORGENTALER

The struggle to remove abortion from the Criminal Code had been spearheaded by Dr. Henry Morgentaler, who urged the repeal of abortion laws that, he said, "compelled the unwilling to bear the unwanted."

When Morgentaler started his campaign, abortion was regulated in the Criminal

Code. The law stated that a woman could legally have an abortion only if the procedure was approved by a three-member hospital committee because it was necessary to protect the woman's life and health.

Morgentaler opened an abortion clinic in Montreal in 1968, and in 1973 announced that he had performed more than 5,000 abortions over this five-year period. The Quebec government prosecuted him and—despite jury acquittals and an appeal court win—continued to do so until 1976, when Quebec's newly elected Parti Québécois government abandoned all proceedings against him and eventually permitted abortion clinics in the province. Over the next 20 years, Morgentaler continued his fight for easier access by women to abortion services in the other Canadian provinces. His long battle to decriminalize abortion ended in victory in the 1988 case bearing his name, when the Supreme Court of Canada ruled that the abortion law was unconstitutional. Since then, he has opened clinics across Canada and challenged provincial governments that have tried to close him down or deny health plan coverage to women for abortion services. See the next section on Access to Abortion Services.

CURRENT STATUS

So, with abortion removed from the Criminal Code, what rules *do* apply?

- The decision to terminate a pregnancy becomes a medical and moral choice. An abortion is legal if the woman chooses to have it and if a doctor agrees to perform it. Neither the woman nor her doctor can be accused or convicted of a criminal offence.

- It is no longer illegal for a woman to have an abortion in a specialized clinic or a doctor's office.

It appears that no federal government will attempt to legislate abortion back into the Criminal Code. One government tried in 1989, the year after the Supreme Court decision, when it proposed a law to replace the one that was struck down. The proposed law would have recriminalized abortion and reinstated a requirement that a doctor must consent to the abortion. But after much public and parliamentary debate, the proposed anti-abortion prohibitions in the Criminal Code resulted in a tie vote of senators in January 1991, and so the federal government decided to abandon further lawmaking on the subject.

4. Access to Abortion Services

When abortion was decriminalized, access to abortion became the key issue, one in which the courts were also involved. Because health care is a provincial responsibility, policies on funding and facilities vary from province to province. Once the Supreme Court of Canada ruled that abortion was legal, the focus of attention shifted to the provinces, which had to decide whether they would pay for abortions and whether abortions would be permitted outside hospitals in clinics. Once again, Dr. Henry Morgentaler carried the fight, setting up clinics across the country and challenging the provincial governments, often in court cases, to approve and fund them. Some jurisdictions tried to limit the avail-

ability of abortion by exempting clinic-performed procedures from coverage by government-paid health insurance, or by trying to ban the existence of freestanding abortion clinics outside hospitals.

Currently, every province but Saskatchewan and Prince Edward Island has at least one private abortion clinic (there are none in the Territories), and most provinces and territories provide funding for abortions, although some insist that funded abortions be carried out in hospitals. However, as of 2003, only 17.8 percent of all "general" hospitals actually did abortions—some provinces didn't offer any in-hospital abortion services. Actual numbers: only 123 hospitals nationally, or one in five, will do the procedure. In the 1990s, the number of hospitals performing abortions dropped and more were performed in private clinics. In 1990, clinics accounted for 22 percent of abortions. By 1998, clinics were doing one-third of all abortions. Clinic abortions are more likely to be unfunded by government. A Manitoba judge ruled in December 2004 that the province's Health Services Insurance Act that forces women to pay for abortions at private clinics is unconstitutional, and breaches their Charter rights to liberty and security of the person.

Rural and non-urban women find access much more difficult and often have to travel into major urban areas to locate abortion services.

Government "restructuring" of hospitals has led to some forced mergers between those hospitals that do offer abortion services and those that do not, including Catholic facilities. In some cases, the hospitals that do not permit abortions have dictated future policy for the merged hospital. For example, when Toronto's St. Michael's

Hospital was merged with Wellesley Hospital in 1998, the merged facility did not offer abortions, vasectomies, contraception and most tubal ligations. Before the merger, Wellesley Hospital had performed between 1,000 and 1,500 abortions a year.

Now that some of these access issues have been resolved, some members of the anti-choice lobby have shifted their attention to the local level, harassing doctors and patients, bombing and setting fire to clinics, issuing death threats to doctors, and making attempts on their lives, picketing doctors' homes and offices and lobbying politicians to stop funding abortions. In response, police announced in 1998 a joint unit to investigate shootings of doctors in British Columbia, Hamilton and Winnipeg.

Following is a snapshot of the issues associated with abortion access in each province.

British Columbia: After Gary Romalis, a Vancouver doctor who performed abortions, was shot through his kitchen window in 1994, British Columbia passed a law called the Access to Abortion Services Act, which prohibited picketing within 50 metres of an abortion clinic, 10 to 20 metres of a doctor's office and 160 metres of a doctor's home. When a person was accused of breaching this law in January 1996, however, a B.C. provincial court said the Act violated the Charter. The B.C. government appealed this ruling successfully and two appeal courts upheld the Act, in 1999 and again in 2003. However, in July 2000 the same doctor was stabbed in the back in the lobby of his clinic by a lone male attacker, who has not been found. Dr. Romalis fortunately recovered.

Under a former government, British Columbia initially refused to pay for abortions through its health insurance plan unless a hospital committee approved and the woman's life was in danger. That refusal was struck down by the courts, and British Columbia now provides full funding for hospitals and clinics performing abortions. The province has 37 hospitals and three clinics that perform this procedure. As of 2003, 22 percent of the province's hospitals performed abortions.

Alberta: In 1995, the Alberta government decided to discontinue funding for abortions unless they were "medically necessary." But their plan foundered when Alberta's doctors, represented by the College of Physicians and Surgeons, refused to define "medically necessary." Now Alberta's public health insurance plan continues to pay the doctor's fee in a hospital and private clinic. As of 2003, Alberta had four hospitals and one clinic that performed abortions—only 5 percent of the province's total hospital count. Abortions are performed in hospitals and clinics to varying gestational cut-offs: as low as 12 weeks in one hospital and up to 20 weeks in another facility.

Saskatchewan: The Saskatchewan government covers the cost of abortions only in hospitals, and is opposed to clinics. In 2003, only 3 percent of the province's hospitals performed abortions. This number represented two hospitals total willing to provide this service. Of those hospitals willing to perform abortions, the procedure is available up to 12 weeks in one hospital and up to 14 weeks in the other. A 1996 reciprocal billing plan between Alberta and Saskatchewan means that women who can afford the travel costs can have their procedures out of province as a back-up option as well.

According to the Saskatchewan Hospital Standards Act, parental consent is required for all surgical procedures performed on patients under the age of 18.

Manitoba: Manitoba covers the entire cost of abortions carried out at its four hospitals that perform this procedure. In 1992, the Manitoba Court of Queen's Bench ruled that the province must also pay for abortions at private clinics. The government appealed the ruling, but lost in 1993. Manitoba then passed a law that excluded payment for non-hospital abortions. This legislation was successfully appealed by Dr. Henry Morgentaler, who has since sold his Winnipeg clinic to local women and it is now known as Jane's Clinic.

As of 2003, only 4 percent of the province's hospitals performed abortions with gestations up to 14 weeks and the province did not cover the full costs of abortions performed at private clinics. According to Childbirth by Choice Trust research, as of 2003 access was concentrated in Winnipeg, where there were only eight doctors willing to perform the procedure. Although parental consent is required at one of the two provincial hospitals willing to perform abortions, some doctors will not ask for proof of that consent if the minor has been referred by a private doctor. Morgentaler's clinic did not require parental consent.

Ontario: Ontario funds abortions, but fewer than half of its hospitals offer abortion services, and only five clinics perform abortions.

Fewer hospitals were offering abortions in 2003 than in 1992. In 1992, only 83 of Ontario's 217 hospitals offered therapeutic abortions. In 2003, only 44—or 23.4 percent—of 188 hospitals polled in Ontario would perform them. Real access continues to be concentrated in Ottawa, Toronto and southwestern Ontario. Toronto's five abortion clinics perform about one-quarter of all abortions in Ontario. When the Conservative Ontario government restructured the province's health care system, abortion services were withdrawn or reduced in many communities. Continued harassment and assaults have caused a number of doctors to stop performing abortions.

As of 2003, only five hospitals in the province would provide abortions past 20 weeks—if there was a severe fetal anomaly, or if the pregnancy put the life or health of the woman at risk—although it is regarded as safe to conduct an abortion even 20 weeks into the pregnancy.

Quebec: Quebec has had the best access to abortion services in Canada since the late 1970s, when Morgentaler's challenges to the law succeeded in removing restrictions. The province continues to allow abortions to be performed in government-funded community and women's health centres, hospitals and private clinics. Quebec pays the doctor's fee in private clinics, but the patient pays a facility fee. In hospitals, the province covers all costs. As of 2003, 34.8 percent of the province's hospitals were performing abortions. About 70 percent of all Quebec abortion facilities are located in or around Montreal, with private clinics covering approximately 50 percent of all abortion services offered in the city. As of 2003, Quebec was still not paying the full costs of abortions handled by private clinics.

New Brunswick: New Brunswick will pay only for abortions deemed medically necessary by two doctors and performed by a gynecologist in an approved hospital; it does not pay for clinic care. As of 2003, only two hospitals and one private clinic performed abortions in this province. Of those hospitals, one will provide abortions only in "exceptional circumstances," which total approximately 28 such operations per year. Dr. Henry Morgentaler challenged the government's refusal to pay for New Brunswick women to have out-of-province clinic abortions and won in 1989, but the government continued to deny payment. The New Brunswick government temporarily shut down the Morgentaler clinic in 1994 but Dr. Morgentaler won again in court and in 1998 reopened the clinic, which is still not government funded. He launched another lawsuit in 2003 against the New Brunswick government over access to private clinic abortions. The case is still before the courts. Morgentaler's clinic in Fredericton provides abortions up to 16 weeks, and they are performed by two out-of-province doctors who fly in every two weeks.

Nova Scotia: In 1989, Nova Scotia passed the Medical Services Act, which required all abortions to be performed in a hospital. Morgentaler defied the law and opened Nova Scotia's first abortion clinic that year. In 1990, Morgentaler was acquitted of 14 charges, but the province still refused to extend health insurance coverage to abortions performed at private clinics, pending its appeal to the Supreme Court of Canada. The province lost its appeal; the Court ruled that the province had no right to legislate in an area that was basically criminal law. Nova Scotia's public health scheme now pays all fees in a hospital, but only the doctor's fee in a private clinic, where the patient pays a facility fee.

Seven hospitals (10 percent) and one private clinic perform abortions in Nova Scotia, as of 2003. Eighty-five percent of abortions performed in Nova Scotia as of 2003 were done out of one hospital (Queen Elizabeth II Health Sciences Centre) in Halifax. Hospitals and Morgentaler's clinic will perform abortions up to 16 weeks, and neither form of facility requires minors (under age 19) to have parental consent.

Prince Edward Island: Prince Edward Island attempted to restrict public funding of abortions by passing regulations to cover only abortions performed in a hospital, provided they were medically required as determined by a committee of five doctors. In fact, the island hospitals did not perform this procedure at all, and so the regulations effectively prohibited abortions in the province. In 1995, Morgentaler challenged this state of affairs in the courts and won. The court held that the regulations were inconsistent with the policy of the statute, which was to provide universal funding for basic health services, and that the government had no justification for restricting eligibility for payment of hospital abortions. The court decison was overruled in 1996 by the Prince Edward Island Court of Appeal, authorizing the government to make regulations denying payment for an abortion unless the patient medically required it and it was performed in a hospital. Abortions are not available in Prince Edward Island and P.E.I. women have no access to publicly funded care at hospitals in Atlantic Canada except in a medical emergency. As of 2003, there continued to be not one hospital in Prince Edward Island that would perform abortions, nor did the province cover the full cost of an abortion performed in a private clinic. The Childbirth by Choice Trust, in their 2003 report on the state of access to abortion in Canada, estimated that approximately 200 P.E.I. women per year must travel to New Brunswick or Nova Scotia to receive private-clinic abortions for fetuses between eight and 16 weeks, and to Montreal, Toronto or Boston if the fetus is more than 16 weeks.

Newfoundland and Labrador: In 1990, the city council in St. John's made a short-lived effort to prevent Morgentaler from opening an abortion clinic. The councillors revoked the occupancy permit for the clinic within hours of its official opening, but when Morgentaler announced his intention to defy city council and begin court proceedings, a newly elected city council overturned the earlier council's decision and allowed the clinic to remain open. Both hospitals and private clinics are now government funded.

As of 2003, 14 percent of hospitals in Newfoundland and Labrador perform abortions. However, this number represents two hospitals in the entire province, only one of which actually performs abortions on a regular basis. That hospital will undertake an abortion provided the woman's pregnancy has not advanced beyond 15 weeks and she has obtained a referral from her doctor. The Morgentaler clinic in St. John's performs the same number of abortions as the hospital, despite being open only one day per week. There are no hospitals in Labrador that will perform an abortion on demand; the Western General Hospital in Cornerbrook will give a woman an abortion only in extremely urgent medical cases.

Yukon Territory: The government covers all fees for abortions if they take place in hospital. As of 2003, one hospital in Whitehorse performs abortions up to the twelfth week of pregnancy. The territory's health insurance covers abortion after 12 weeks in a Vancouver hospital, as long as the pregnant woman has been referred by a Yukon doctor. The services are covered by a reciprocal agreement between British Columbia and the Yukon, so that a pregnant woman does not need to pay for the service in advance and then wait for reimbursement. However, if a woman wants a clinic abortion (available in either British Columbia or Alberta), medical insurance will pay only the physician fee and not the clinic fee. Medical practitioners need to contact the parent(s) or guardian(s) of a minor (under the age of 19) only if they believe that minor's life is in danger.

Northwest Territories: The government pays all fees for abortions that take place in a hospital up to the thirteenth week of pregnancy. As of 2003, two hospitals (representing 67 percent of the territories' facilities) perform abortions.

Nunavut: When Nunavut became a territory in 1999, there was one abortion provider, who worked out of the Baffin Regional Hospital in Iqaluit. This provider left Nunavut in 2003, effectively leaving the territory with no hospitals that would perform abortions. The government of Nunavut covers the costs for a woman to travel to facilities in Ottawa or Montreal where abortion is available, and also covers the costs of the procedure, as long as it is performed in a hospital.

Generally speaking, access to and funding for abortion has improved, but whether or not it has improved for an individual woman now depends on the woman finding a doctor and hospital or clinic where she lives to carry out the procedure.

5. Single Unattached Mother by Choice

For a variety of reasons, some women decide to have a child alone.

The path considered by these women involves many social, personal and legal questions: Are they ready for the emotional and financial responsibility of raising a child alone? What would they tell the child about the father? Who would raise the child if something happened to the mother? Should the woman use artificial insemination or a trusted male friend as a sperm donor? Is custody or access likely to be an issue? A woman considering this option would be wise to consult a lawyer to review how local laws affect her situation.

From a legal viewpoint, the woman's simplest course is to be artificially inseminated by an anonymous sperm donor. This method leaves the woman truly on her own as a parent, free from interference.

The alternative is to have a trusted male friend consent to be the sperm donor, either through intercourse or artificial insemination, provided that his future role in the child's life, if any, is negotiated in advance and that the woman can rely upon him to keep his word. It is unlikely that the courts would enforce a written agreement because it might be considered against public policy. "Public policy" is a term applied to considerations of what is best for society. In this case, public policy would likely prefer that a father have access to his child if that is best for the child.

In a 1997 Alberta case, a woman sought to avoid access by her child's out-of-province father, claiming they had an agreement that he would only be the sperm donor and source of financial support. She said she chose to create a fatherless family unit. The court ruled it was in the child's best interests to know his father.

If the sperm donor wants a relationship with the child, the man and the woman should reach an understanding on child support, visiting rights, whether true paternity will be reflected on the birth certificate and whose surname the child will carry.

Getting pregnant without the man's consent—by lying to him about contraception, for example—is not wise. If he later finds out the child is his, he can seek a court order declaring his paternity, as well as access to the child or even custody.

In all cases where the biological father knows of the child's existence, several issues may arise.

CUSTODY

Historically, the law once guaranteed custody to the mother of a child born out of wedlock, unless she was unfit or had abandoned the child. Now, however, the laws of many provinces say that the father of a child born in or out of wedlock has an equal right to make a claim for custody. If there is a dispute, the courts decide custody based on the best interests of the child. If the claim for custody is made at birth, one of the deciding factors is whether the mother plans to breast-feed the child. If she does not, the father has a chance at custody.

The situation is different in British Columbia, Alberta, Manitoba and Saskatchewan, where an unmarried mother is automatically entitled to custody, provided she has never lived with the man. See also the section on Custody and Access in Chapter 10.

ACCESS

The father is normally entitled to see the child, unless there are compelling reasons against it. His choice not to marry the child's mother is not relevant to access decisions.

FINANCIAL SUPPORT

Any mother, married or single, has the right to obtain financial support from the father. The amount is based on the parents' relative incomes and the child's needs, and is not affected by the circumstances of the pregnancy. In fact, court cases have ruled that the biological father must pay child support even if the mother became pregnant against the father's wishes, or duped him into getting her pregnant by saying that she was using contraceptives. If a woman is on welfare, the welfare authorities usually have the right to pursue the father for support on behalf of the mother, and to reimburse themselves for the amount of the welfare payments.

A single mother will probably have to cope with employers who may fear that she will not be able to fulfil her duties, and with landlords who may assume that she will be unable to manage the rent alone. Human rights legislation everywhere prohibits discrimination in employment and housing on the basis of marital status and sex, and in some places on the basis of family status. However, proving discrimination under these circumstances may be difficult.

6. Midwives

Midwifery is part of the modern struggle by women for choice and control over childbirth and reproductive matters—not only whether to give birth, but how to give birth. Many women value midwifery's approach, which treats pregnancy and childbirth as normal and healthy, and emphasizes education, counselling and continuous supportive care. Some midwives describe themselves as specialists in normal birth.

Up until the eighteenth century, the European tradition practised in Canada was that only women were present at a birth. The medical profession started taking over this responsibility in the nineteenth century, and eventually only licensed doctors were allowed to attend births in Canada and in other Western countries, even though elsewhere in the world midwives delivered most babies. Some midwives continued to practise in Canada in response to a demand for their services.

Since the 1970s, there has been a renewed interest in natural childbirth with less medical intervention. People have become concerned over high rates of Caesarean sections, routine use of forceps during delivery, over-medication and induced births. Increasing numbers of pregnant women have demanded the midwife's specialized assistance, often in addition to their doctor's care, whether they plan to give birth in a hospital or at home. With a midwife in attendance, a woman and her partner often find the course of the pregnancy less stressful.

In many provinces, midwifery still exists in a legal vacuum: It is neither expressly illegal, nor officially recognized. Therefore, midwives risk prosecution if anything goes wrong during the delivery.

THE LEGALIZATION
OF MIDWIFERY

When Ontario recognized and licensed mid-wives in 1992, implementing many of the recommendations of the 1987 Ontario Mid-wifery Task Force, chaired by Mary Eberts, it became the first province or territory to for-mally legalize midwifery. As a result, mid-wives in Ontario were legitimized as an autonomous profession.

Ontario's law designates midwives as self-governing professionals under the Regulated Health Professions Act, just like doctors, nurses and others in the health care field. In much the same way that nurses are governed by the College of Nurses of Ontario, mid-wives are regulated by the College of Mid-wives. The college grants licences, ensures members are qualified and maintains stan-dards of professional ethics. Anyone dissat-isfied with care can lodge a complaint with the college, which will investigate the case and rule on it. In cases of misconduct or incompetence, the college may suspend or revoke a midwife's licence to practise.

The Ontario Midwifery Act authorizes midwives to conduct "spontaneous normal vaginal deliveries" at home or in hospitals or birthing centres; to care for, assess and monitor women during pregnancy, labour, childbirth and the postpartum period; to perform certain procedures, including epi-siotomy (a surgical cut to enlarge the vaginal opening and facilitate birth); and to admin-ister and prescribe certain drugs. The cost of a midwife's services is covered by Ontario's health insurance plan.

Prospective midwives (who can be women or men) are required to complete an approved four-year postsecondary degree program to earn certification. A shorter upgrading course is available for midwives already practising.

Many midwives previously trained as nurses, but they must still meet the certifica-tion requirements. The only practitioners who do not have to fulfil the education and certification requirements are Aboriginal midwives, who are defined as Aboriginal persons who provide traditional midwifery services. They are entitled to use the title *midwife* and present themselves as qualified to practise traditional midwifery.

Only members of the College of Midwives may identify themselves as midwives. But an adjunct profession of childbirth educa-tors, called *doulas,* are also available to sup-port, guide and comfort the mother through labour and/or the postpartum period. Doulas are not legally licensed in the same way as midwives, and have no authority to perform clinical tests or prescribe drugs. They are often called in when midwives are not available, but are not covered by provin-cial health insurance plans.

Other provinces have brought in laws similar to Ontario's. British Columbia, in 1995, designated midwifery a health profes-sion and regulated midwives under its Health Professions Act; a College of Mid-wives was established, which began regulat-ing midwifery (and paying for it) in 1998. Alberta's law was passed in 1999, but mid-wives are neither publicly funded nor do most of them have hospital privileges. Que-bec's law was passed in 1999, and Mani-toba's came into force in 2000.

In the Northwest Territories and Nunavut, a limited form of midwifery has been legal-ized by allowing midwives to practise at birthing centres as part of a pilot project, provided they take government examina-tions and become licensed. Saskatchewan passed legislation in 1999 to make midwifery legal and allow licensed midwives to deliver babies in hospitals as well as homes. Nova Scotia had planned to permit midwifery to be a self-governing profession but the government changed its mind in 2000.

Newfoundland and Labrador has a law on the books (passed in 1919) that permits a midwifery board to license midwives, who are then allowed to use the title and charge fees for their services. However, no board has been appointed for many years. Nurse-midwives do practise in the northern part of Newfoundland, but only by agreement among health agencies.

In those provinces where midwifery is not legislated, the laws usually make no reference to midwives and clearly state that only licensed doctors may practise obstetrics. At the same time, there are no laws that prohibit the use of a midwife for a home delivery, or prevent a woman from asking a hospital to permit a midwife to be present in addition to the doctor. Since many hospitals allow spouses and friends to be present for support, a midwife may be engaged to help with the labour process and, if the doctor is co-operative, assist with the birth.

Most health insurance plans outside Ontario, British Columbia and Manitoba do not cover payment of midwives' services.

Canadian midwives are internationally recognized as leaders in the struggle for woman-centred childbirth. Nevertheless, some continue to operate without specific legal sanction and are therefore vulnerable to prosecution. In the past, if a midwife presided over a birth in which mother or child was injured, the authorities were quick to blame the midwife. As a result, there were many coroner inquests into such cases. In provinces where midwifery continues to be unregulated, midwives may still be vulnerable to criminal prosecution for such charges as manslaughter or criminal negligence; to civil suits for compensation for personal injury arising from alleged negligence; or to charges of practising medicine without a licence.

7. Paternity Suits and Financial Support

If a woman becomes pregnant and has the child, the man who impregnated her must support that child. In fact, both parents have a legal responsibility to support any child they bring into the world, whether or not they intended or wanted the birth to occur. This obligation exists even if the birth results from contraceptive failure, intentional or not.

PROVING PATERNITY

Before the mother can claim support from the father, paternity must be either acknowledged or proven. If the partners are married, the law presumes that any child born to them while they live together is the product of their union.

If the partners were not married at the time of conception (regardless of whether or not they lived together), and the man denies that he is the father, the mother may have to go to court to prove paternity. It is best to start the legal proceeding for a declaration of paternity as soon as possible after the birth.

In all provinces and territories, the mother can seek a declaration of paternity based on a presumption made by the law. The law presumes that the man must have fathered the child if he was living with the mother at the time of conception or birth, especially if he has acknowledged paternity (perhaps by signing a statement to that effect) or has since married the mother. But the father can still dispute the allegation. If he does, the courts decide whether or not he is the father, based on what he and the mother say and other evidence they present.

Today, blood tests and DNA tests provide the best evidence. Blood tests can be used almost everywhere as evidence to determine a child's parentage. In some cases, the man may refuse to give blood if he thinks there is a possibility that he is the father. But this tactic can backfire: A judge may conclude that the man knows he is the father if he refuses to co-operate. DNA tests are almost 100 percent accurate.

A court may consider other evidence as well as, or instead of, blood tests. There may be evidence of sexual relations at the time of conception or proof that the man encouraged or offered to pay for an abortion. Perhaps others knew that the man and woman had an exclusive liaison, so it was unlikely that she became pregnant by another man.

If the blood tests do not exclude the possibility that the man is the father (he is called the putative father or alleged father), and circumstantial evidence points to his paternity, the judge may declare him to be the legal father and order that he pay support. He may also have a duty to support the woman to the extent that he can, particularly if they lived together. If they never set up a household together, his obligation may be limited to child support.

FINANCIAL SUPPORT

If paternity is established, the father must support the child until the age and in the amount specified by provincial law. All provinces except Alberta have passed laws to mirror the federal child-support guidelines, which will determine the amount of child support the father must pay (see Chapter 10). In Alberta, the child support payment will be determined the way support was calculated everywhere before the guidelines were legislated. The amount will be based on the child's needs, the father's ability to pay and, generally, the mother's ability to contribute to the child's support. A court has the power to order the father to pay periodic support or even a lump sum, to transfer property to the mother or place it in trust for the child, and to pay for the mother's prenatal care and birth expenses.

As a last resort, if a father fails to support the child, he may be charged with a criminal offence for shirking his parental duty to provide the basic necessities of life to a child under 16.

8. Surrogate Pre-Conception Agreements

A woman who agrees to be a surrogate mother allows her body to be impregnated, usually by artificial insemination, to carry the child of another. The insemination can be with the husband's sperm and the surrogate's egg, or the egg may be from the wife, fertilized with the husband's sperm and then implanted in the surrogate mother.

This issue came to the fore in the early 1980s when a number of cases of surrogate pregnancy hit the news, mostly because, in each case, the woman who carried the child to term changed her mind and wanted to keep the child as her own. The surrogate mother's reconsideration opened the agreement to legal scrutiny.

In one case, a surrogate bore a child for an Ontario couple. After the birth, the hospital refused to hand the baby over to the biological father, or even acknowledge him as the father. Instead, the hospital turned the baby over to the Catholic Children's Aid Society. To get the baby he had contracted for, the father had to go to court with a custody claim and prove paternity.

In 2004, the federal government passed the Assisted Human Reproduction Act to finally establish public policy in this matter; the law banned commercial surrogacy contracts, but permitted volunteer surrogacy agreements.

Some existing laws may be applied to surrogacy arrangements. For example, there are laws against selling babies (once born), or human tissue, or a body part for transplant purposes. If a prospective father pays a surrogate mother a fee, he may find himself dealing with the law against selling babies. It is currently legal to cover the surrogate's expenses. In a British Columbia case, the court did not regard payment of medical, travel and legal expenses as illegal.

For the hospital records and the birth certificate, the father and the surrogate mother should be registered as parents, but the surrogate should not be registered as the father's wife. The father's wife is not allowed to register herself as the birth mother; if she does, she will face a penalty for falsifying birth records.

During the pregnancy and again after the birth, the surrogate mother will be required to consent to the father's wife's adoption of the baby. Provincial authorities must be notified so that they can conduct their normal investigation and prepare a report. This procedure is mandatory before most adoptions to determine whether prospective parents can provide proper care.

If the surrogate is married, there may be further complications. Until the father and his wife legally adopt the baby, the law presumes that the surrogate's husband is the father of the child and will give the baby his surname. If the surrogate has sexual intercourse with her husband or sexual partner during the artificial insemination period, there is a risk that the child may biologically be his.

It would be wise to have the surrogate's husband sign a consent as well. If he refuses or objects to her plan to be a surrogate mother, it would be best to cancel the arrangement, since he might claim paternity.

A contract should be signed by the father, his wife, the surrogate and her husband, if she is married; however, it may still not be enforceable. The surrogate may back out after the child is born because a mother is allowed a period of time after birth within which to change her mind about giving her baby up for adoption. The contract can state that the surrogate will not claim child support or pre-natal expenses if she decides to keep the baby, but this clause may not protect the father from an obligation to pay long-term child support. On the other hand, if the child is born with a mental or physical disability, the surrogate risks raising the child alone.

If, despite the significant risks, a surrogacy arrangement is agreed upon, then some of the following terms for the agreement should be considered. The couple should require the surrogate mother to do the following:

- Undergo psychological, medical and genetic tests before artificial insemination
- Forgo sexual intercourse with her husband or lover for at least two weeks before and two weeks after artificial insemination
- Follow specified nutritional guidelines, get proper rest, not smoke, not drink alcohol, not take drugs or expose herself to other possible hazards and provide information on her medical condition during pregnancy
- Attempt another artificial insemination or terminate the contract if the first artificial insemination does not work or if she miscarries involuntarily
- Seek the father and his wife's permission if she wants to abort, either because of medical problems or second thoughts
- Acknowledge the father's paternity, register the child with his surname, direct the hospital to release the baby to him and consent to the father and his wife's adoption of the baby

The surrogate mother should require the father and his wife to do the following:

- Acknowledge paternity
- Accept responsibility for the child, even if the baby is born with health problems
- Agree to pay the surrogate's expenses as she incurs them

The ethical and emotional aspects of surrogate mothering are as new and unexplored as the legal aspects, so anyone considering this kind of arrangement should decide carefully whether or not it is worth the risks.

9. Rights and Duties of Sperm Donors

Whether or not a sperm donor has any rights and duties to the child that results depends on the manner in which the sperm was "donated." If he was an anonymous donor of sperm *without sexual intercourse* for the purpose of artificially inseminating an unidentified woman, he is regarded as a *sperm donor*.

However, if the means of transferring sperm was sexual intercourse with a woman he knew, which resulted in a child being born to them, he is the *biological father*, even if they had an agreement that the sexual intercourse was solely for the purpose of helping the woman to get pregnant. This is so even if the man did not realize that the woman was using him in order to help her get pregnant, and even if she lied that she was using contraceptives.

A biological father has all the responsibilities of a father, including liability for child support under the Child Support Guidelines in accordance with his income. He can also ask for access to the child.

In a 1997 Alberta case, a woman arranged a rendezvous with a male friend and asked if he would provide the sperm for her to conceive. He agreed, and they had sexual intercourse over a period of months until the woman got pregnant; he even agreed to pay child support. But when he asked for access to the child, she said she wanted to raise the child alone. The court ordered that he be given access on the basis that this was in the the child's best interest. The court also made it clear that he was the biological father and not a simple "sperm donor," as the woman had assumed.

Few Canadian laws currently deal with

sperm donors. In Newfoundland and the Yukon, for example, the law clearly states that a man whose semen is used to artificially and anonymously inseminate a woman other than his wife or common-law partner is *not* the father of the resulting child. In addition, as long as the woman is living with her legal or common-law spouse *and* the spouse has consented to the insemination, that person is legally considered the father of the child conceived. This paternity by consent is also included in Quebec's Civil Code. Whether or not other provinces specify these concepts in their laws, they are common practice. A recent federal law states that reimbursement of donors will be strictly limited to their receipted expenses incurred in the course of providing sperm.

Regulation of sperm donations has been left to the medical profession. Doctors have traditionally kept the identity of sperm donors confidential, and sperm recipients have relied on doctors to ensure the sperm meets acceptable standards and has been tested for diseases. If an issue arises regarding diseased sperm, such as AIDS-infected sperm, the doctor, not the donor, is the one sued for negligence or breach of contract.

There is no reported case in Canada, to my knowledge, where a woman or child tried to identify a true sperm donor as a parent, even though the identification of paternity has become almost foolproof with advances in DNA testing. There is a tradition of confidentiality between the donor and the recipient of the sperm, and usually a mutual desire for anonymity. The donor does not wish to have any legal obligations for the child. And the mother and her partner consider assisted contraception a private matter between them and their doctor. They may not even plan to tell the child a donor was involved.

B. TEEN SEXUALITY

1. Teens and Contraception

There is no law preventing anyone—a parent, teacher, friend, pharmacist or doctor—from giving birth control information or selling non-prescription items, such as condoms or contraceptive foams, to anyone, including a child under 16. But the law is not clear-cut about a doctor's legal position if, without parental consent, a girl requests a prescription for birth control pills or wants to be fitted for a diaphragm or intrauterine device, or a boy seeks a vasectomy.

Generally speaking, parental consent is required for non-emergency medical treatment of any child. However, there are times when a mature child wishes to make her own choices against a parent's wishes, and that is when the law can help the doctor to know when to accept a child's consent.

The general law of consent concerning any form of medical treatment applies to contraception, but it is not easy to define how the law in any province will apply to a particular case. First, there is no nationally agreed-on age of consent (for example, Quebec says 14, New Brunswick says 16 and Saskatchewan says 18), just as there is no nationally agreed-on age of majority. Second, not all provinces have specific laws defining when and under what circumstances a child may consent without parental involvement. Third, in provinces with legislation the rules are often complex and internally inconsistent. Some examples: A child under 16 may not be able to give consent to treatment in a hospital, but may be able to in a doctor's office. In some places, a doctor must first try to get a parent's consent; in others, the parent must be informed if the child is to remain in treatment for more than a brief time. In some places, a child under 16 who is married is permitted to consent; in others, a child under 16 can consent to anything but sterilization. In New Brunswick, for example, a child under 16 *can* consent to medical treatment if, in the opinion of a doctor, the minor is capable of understanding the nature and consequences of the treatment and it is in her best interests.

But provincial legislation is not all that applies. Some common-law rules will apply in provinces without specific legislation, and will also stand alongside provincial legislation to complicate matters further. The common law states that an individual may consent to treatment as long as she can understand the nature and quality of the act, its likely results and its possible complications. The doctor must therefore make a decision about the intelligence and maturity of the individual in each case, gauging the patient's ability to understand the benefits and risks of the medical procedure, and therefore to give informed consent.

In some places, the common-law rules are beginning to be incorporated into provincial legislation. For example, British Columbia updated its law in 1993 that a person under the age of majority, without parental involvement, may consent to medical treatment if the health care professional explains the procedure to the child and is satisfied that he or she understands the nature and consequences, reasonably foreseeable benefits and risks of the procedure; and if the health care professional has made reasonable efforts to determine and has concluded that the procedure is in the child's best interests.

To my knowledge, no doctor in Canada has ever been sued by a parent or charged with contributing to juvenile delinquency for providing birth control information or devices to a child under 16. If a parent were to sue a doctor and win the lawsuit (an unlikely event), the compensation awarded would be minimal because a child is not the parent's property; in other words, a parent should not be compensated for "damage to property."

If a parent were to seek an injunction to prevent a child from receiving birth control information or devices, the court would probably hesitate to enforce a parent's determination to control a child against her wishes. Consent requirements are meant not to punish or to assert parental power over the child, but to protect the child until he or she is old enough to give informed consent.

A teenager who seeks contraception may be acting out of a sense of personal responsibility, an ability to comprehend the nature, procreative implications and health risks of the sexual act.

2. Teens and Abortion

A girl under 16 who gets pregnant and wants an abortion normally needs her parent's consent if she lives in a province with legislation or regulations that require parental consent for any medical treatment of minors. For example, a girl in Quebec who is 14 or older can have an abortion without parental consent. In Ontario, Manitoba and New Brunswick, a girl must be 16 for her own consent to be valid. In Saskatchewan and Prince Edward Island, the age of consent for abortion is 18. Generally speaking, where Morgentaler clinics or similar facilities exist, a girl under the age of 16 can provide her own consent after pre-abortion counselling, provided she is capable of understanding the nature and consequences of this medical treatment, and that it is in her best interests. See also the previous section on Teens and Contraception.

Where no specific rules exist, the common law applies to permit a doctor to perform an abortion on a teen, provided the doctor believes the girl is mature enough to fully understand the nature and consequences of the procedure, and can give informed consent.

If the doctor refuses to perform the procedure without a parent's consent, then the girl can report to the child-welfare authorities that she is being denied necessary medical treatment. She can ask to be made a Crown ward, in the hope that the Children's Aid Society will consent in the place of her parents. Here are three such cases.

In 1991, a 14-year-old Ontario girl, with her doctor's recommendation, decided to abort an unwanted pregnancy. A psychologist testified the girl was intelligent and knew what she was doing. The girl gave evidence that she could not finish school and become a nurse if she had a child to look after and support. She also told the court that she had consulted medical and social work experts for advice.

Her parents refused consent, saying they believed, according to their religion, that abortion was murder. They even offered to take responsibility for the child if their daughter carried the fetus to term, but that statement did not tip the scales in their favour. The judge said the Supreme Court of Canada had made it clear that the fetus had no legal status. Therefore, the Court designated the girl a temporary ward of the local Children's Aid Society, which consented to the abortion in place of the parents. The judge ruled that the best interests of the girl took precedence over the wishes of her parents.

In 1985, a 15-year-old Ontario girl wanted to terminate a pregnancy that her medical advisors concluded would not be good for her health. Her parents would not consent, nor would the Catholic Children's Aid Society of Metropolitan Toronto. When the girl said she wanted to change her religious faith, she was successful in getting the court to make her a ward of the non-sectarian Children's Aid Society in order to receive the abortion she wanted.

According to Ontario legislation, the court could consider the wishes of the child regarding religious faith. The judge said the girl no longer wished to be a Roman Catholic because the church would not let her have the abortion she needed, and he credited the girl with making a decision that was not "sham, insincere or flip."

In 1987, a 16-year-old Alberta girl had a bitter legal battle with her parents, who got an injunction preventing her from having an abortion. When she appealed to the Alberta Court of Appeal, it supported her right to make the decision for herself.

In most provinces, including British Columbia, Saskatchewan, Alberta, Manitoba, Prince Edward Island and Newfoundland and Labrador, the government allows child-welfare authorities to authorize medical treatment for children in their care, but only on condition that a medical doctor has recommended treatment.

Elsewhere (Ontario, Quebec, New Brunswick, Nova Scotia, and the Territories), the child-welfare legislation does not specifically require the medical treatment to be recommended by a doctor. But in the Northwest Territories and Nunavut, the treatment must be necessary "to preserve the child's life."

The legal ages of children covered under child-welfare legislation vary from 16 to 19 years, province to province, with some legislation even extending to an older age in certain cases. Once a child has reached the designated age of majority in a jurisdiction, parental consent should not be an issue.

Legal procedures involving intervention by child-welfare authorities vary from province to province. Because court applications take time and cost money, they can endanger the girl by delaying the procedure; in the 1991 Ontario case, the girl was already 17 weeks pregnant when she decided she wanted an abortion.

In every case, the best interests of the pregnant girl are supposed to be paramount, and she must show she is mature enough to know what she is doing. Her decision should be based on information and counselling; the earlier she receives them, the better.

3. Teens and Pregnancy

A pregnant teen does not legally require her parent's consent to carry through with her pregnancy. Although an unmarried girl under the age of consent (which varies from province to province) may require her parent's consent to have an abortion, this does not mean that the parent can insist on the teen having an abortion. If a parent forced a daughter to abort against her will, the parent and the doctor who performed the operation could probably be sued for assault.

If the parent asked a judge to order the abortion to take place, the judge might grant permission if the court agreed that the abortion was essential to the daughter's survival and that she could not consent to the abortion herself, perhaps because she was mentally incapable. But if the abortion were for

contraceptive purposes only, the court would probably disapprove.

In 1979, a precedent-setting court ruling in Prince Edward Island would not even allow the mother of a mentally retarded 24-year-old woman to consent to sterilization on her daughter's behalf. The judge accepted the evidence of the woman's widowed 60-year-old mother that her daughter did not understand that pregnancy and birth could result from sexual intercourse, that her daughter was not capable of informed consent and that her daughter was not able to use other means of preventing birth. The young woman was allegedly incapable of following any contraceptive regimen or of caring for any child she might bear. The judge said, however, that the law could not authorize the violation of the daughter's person, and that sterilization should not be used as a method of contraception.

The judge may have made an exception if sterilization had been strictly therapeutic and necessary to the daughter's health, and if its contraceptive effect had been incidental. However, the court felt it could not allow the parents to consent to sterilization on behalf of a child unless the legislature had passed a law saying so.

The P.E.I. Court of Appeal approved the sterilization, but it was postponed pending a further appeal. The Supreme Court of Canada did not hear the appeal until 1985; by then, the Charter of Rights and Freedoms was in effect, and so the Court was in a position to accept constitutional arguments. The young woman's lawyer argued that Section 15 of the Charter, in effect since April 17, 1985, gave guarantees of equality to the mentally handicapped, and Section 7 guaranteed her "security of the person," which should protect her from non-medical sterilization.

When the Supreme Court of Canada's decision was released in 1986, the Supreme Court agreed with the trial decision: Sterilization should never be authorized for non-therapeutic purposes, and the court should only permit the procedure if it benefits the person in need of protection and not someone else. (In this case, the mother feared that she would end up responsible for raising the child if her daughter got pregnant.) Prince Edward Island subsequently put this rule into its law.

Courts continue to follow this ruling. In fact, Ontario also has a specific rule to this effect: The Ontario Public Hospitals Regulations expressly states that surgery for the purpose of sterilization on a patient under the age of 16 is prohibited unless it is medically necessary to protect the physical health of the child. Therefore, a parent is not allowed to consent to sterilization on behalf of a mentally disabled child under 16.

Although parents may believe that it is in the best interests of the fetus not to be born, and in the best interests of their teen not to have the baby, they do not have the right to present themselves as the legal representative of their daughter's unborn child.

4. Teen Sex and Criminal Consequences

A teenager may be surprised to learn that criminal consequences are possible when he or she has sexual relations with another teen. While the law used to punish only the boy for taking sexual advantage of the girl, legal prohibition has been stated in a gender-neutral fashion since 1985. This amendment may have resulted from a 1985 Ontario case in which a 16-year-old boy was charged with the statutory rape of his consenting 13-year-old girlfriend. The judge ruled that the statutory rape provisions of the Criminal Code violated the equality provisions of the Canadian Charter of Rights and Freedoms because the Criminal Code prohibited girls under the age of 14 from consenting to sexual activity, but did not prohibit boys. The equality issue being ignored was whether girls *need* more protection than boys.

In any event, this law now applies to all persons everywhere in Canada, since criminal law is a federal statute.

The specific consequences of teen sexual behaviour depend on the participants' ages and the nature of their relationship. A person under 14 cannot be tried for certain sexual offences, such as touching someone else for a sexual purpose, unless the person under 14 is in a position of trust or authority in relation to the other person, or if the other person is in a relationship of dependency. In a 1996 decision, a 13-year-old foster brother was accused of breaching a position of trust through sexual relations with his foster mother's own daughter, who was almost two years younger than he was. The Ontario Court of Appeal acquitted the young man on the basis that he was not in a position of trust, was less than two years older and was between age 12 and 16.

If the teen is between 14 and 18, he or she will normally be sentenced under the Young Offenders Act. If the teen is over 18, he or she will suffer adult consequences under the Criminal Code. However, irrespective of his or her age and the nature of the relationship, a teen can still be charged with sexual assault, a more serious crime.

If a person is 16 or more years of age, and engages in sexual intercourse with a teenager who is between 12 and 14, he or she may be guilty of an indictable offence with a maximum sentence of ten years in jail. If the older one is the boy, as is usually the case, he cannot use the excuse that he believed the girl was over 14. He must be found to have taken "all reasonable steps" to determine the age of the girl.

If the complainant is less than 14 years of age, the Criminal Code says her consent is irrelevant because she is not legally permitted to consent to intercourse. The accused can use her consent as a defence only if he is over 12 and under 16 years of age, less than two years older than the complainant and not in a position of trust or authority. As well, the complainant must not be in a relationship of dependency.

If the older teen is between 14 and 16, it is possible that he or she will not be charged or convicted, depending on circumstances. The courts are clear that the purpose of the law is to protect children from sexual exploitation and premature sexual relations. The attitude of a 1977 Canadian court would probably still be persuasive: The court had ruled that sexual intercourse between two juveniles was not immoral and that "sexual activity resulting from high spirits, exuberance, curiosity or healthy affection of the young is no concern of the courts."

While a teen who breached these rules would no doubt be convicted if intercourse were proven, the sentence would be tailored to the circumstances. For example, in 1979 an Ontario judge convicted a 17-year-old of getting his consenting 12-year-old girlfriend pregnant, but gave him a suspended sentence and put him on probation. However, if the older of the two is in his or her late teens or twenties and in a position of authority over the younger one, he or she may get close to the maximum possible sentence (ten years to life), especially if he or she were found to have abused a position of trust for sexual gratification, threatened the younger person or assaulted her or him. A 1997 Statistics Canada study revealed that 54 percent of the babies born to mothers aged 17 or younger had fathers who were 20 or older at the time of the birth, suggesting that it is not just youthful enthusiasm that sends girls astray but the seduction of an older man.

CHAPTER 3

WORKING LIFE

⚖

Introduction

The law affects everyone's working life, often in unexpected ways.

People may come up against legal issues when looking for their very first job, and they will have to decide how to respond. For example, a young person looking for a job should not be surprised if a prospective employer asks about the use of illegal drugs such as cocaine or marijuana, or asks the candidate to take a test to confirm drug status. Young women must also be prepared to deal with questions about their use of birth control or their intentions about having children. They should also find out their rights if they get pregnant. In addition, child labour laws may affect a teen's job search.

Everyone needs to know about laws dealing with vacation, overtime and sick pay, employment insurance and Canada Pension Plan. Working conditions such as air quality also have legal ramifications.

Things can go wrong on the job. A worker can feel wronged by less-than-equal pay and less-than-equal opportunity, which remain intractable problems. Sexual and other forms of harassment are often part of

the job scene. In each of these situations, there are legal protections.

The issues discussed in this chapter reflect our times. Our parents had fewer legal rights in relation to employment and were often happy simply to have work that paid them a living. Employees today have enforceable rights, although their willingness to use them may depend on their sense of security in their job and on their ability to find another. Many of today's workers do not expect to stay with one employer for their entire working life.

A. GETTING THE JOB

1. Interview Questions and Personnel Records

It is against the law to discriminate against an employee or would-be employee. The information that an employer asks for in an interview or on an application form and keeps in personnel records should not express or imply an intention to discriminate, unless the information is relevant to determining the applicant's ability to do the job. If the information is not relevant to job qualifications and appears discriminatory, the employer's reasons for seeking the information may be suspect, and the job applicant may have reason to complain to a human rights commission. Here are some examples:

- Discrimination on the basis of race, colour, religion or creed, physical or mental handicap or disability is prohibited everywhere in Canada, and so questions irrelevant to job qualifications may not be asked.
- Discrimination on the basis of age is prohibited. Employers may ask only if the applicant is between 18 and 65, but may not ask the precise age. Laws in the federal jurisdiction, Manitoba, Quebec, Ontario, New Brunswick, Nova Scotia Prince Edward Island and the Territories do not specify at which age an applicant can be refused. Other laws protect particular age groups; for example, Saskatchewan protects a person between the ages of 18 and 64, and British Columbia and Newfoundland and Labrador protect those between 19 and 65. If a precise age is required for a benefits plan or another reasonable use after a candidate is hired, the employer can ask the question then.
- Discrimination on the basis of sex and marital status is against the law everywhere in Canada. A person cannot be refused a job for being female, single, married or divorced. An employer should not ask whether to address a woman as Mrs. or Miss, since the neutral title Ms can be used without asking the question. If the employer does ask, the applicant can avoid the issue by stating a preference to be called Ms.

Employers should not ask about an applicant's living arrangements or a spouse's employment. Information about a spouse should be recorded only after the employee is hired if, for instance, it relates to coverage under a company benefits plan. Questions about whom to contact in case of an emergency, or the name of an insurance beneficiary, are inappropriate before the candidate is hired.

- Discrimination on the basis of pregnancy or childbirth is prohibited in all provinces and territories and in the federal jurisdiction. For example, a female applicant should not be asked whether she is pregnant or plans to have children, or what kind of child-care arrangements she has made. She should simply be asked whether she is available to work the required hours, and if she is able to meet the job's travel or relocation requirements. Once she is hired, information about pregnancy and childbirth should be recorded in her personnel file only if, for instance, she takes maternity leave or her employer covers part of her medical costs.
- Discrimination based on family status ("civil status" in Quebec) is forbidden everywhere except New Brunswick and Newfoundland and Labrador. For example, a single parent may not be asked in a job interview about the number of children or dependants she has.
- Discrimination based on sexual orientation is prohibited everywhere except the Northwest Territories and Nunavut. While Alberta's legislation does not state this prohibition specifically, the Supreme Court of Canada read it into Alberta's legislation in 1998.

- Discrimination based on national or ethnic origin is prohibited in the federal jurisdiction and elsewhere, except in British Columbia and Alberta, and may be discerned in questions about birthplace and immigration status. It is reasonable, however, for an employer to ask if a job applicant is legally entitled to work in Canada, and, *after* the person is hired, to request proof of landed immigrant status or a valid work permit.

On the other hand, employers have a duty to be careful in choosing whom to hire, or they may potentially be found vicariously liable, particularly when the employee is in a position of trust or dealing with vulnerable third parties. For example, it is reasonable for an employer to do background checks on employees who will be caring for children or handling money.

2. Drug Testing

No law in Canada states that it is illegal for an employer to insist, before or after hiring, that an employee take a test to confirm the absence of drug use. Furthermore, human rights codes do not appear to forbid drug testing as a prerequisite for employment. However, some jurisdictions do protect drug users against discrimination in employment.

The Canadian Human Rights Act, which is applicable to federal government employees, Crown corporations and companies in the federal jurisdiction such as banks and airlines, specifically prohibits discrimination based on alcohol or drug dependency. As a matter of policy, the human rights commissions everywhere but in the Yukon, the Northwest Territories and Quebec accept complaints of discrimination on the basis of alcohol or drug dependency. The Canadian Human Rights Commission instituted in 1999 a policy on drug testing. The Commission stated that, normally, drug testing cannot be justified unless safety is an issue. Usually, any drug test requirement by employers in the federal jurisdiction will be considered discriminatory.

There is also no constitutional protection against drug testing. The Charter of Rights and Freedoms is intended to protect an individual only from discrimination in legislation and possibly from discrimination in administrative acts of government. The Charter has not been interpreted as dealing with matters of private rights between individuals or between individuals and corporations.

If an employer requests a drug test and the job applicant refuses, the applicant cannot then complain if he or she does not get the job. If the applicant takes the test and it reveals drug use, the applicant may have no legal remedy if he or she does not get the job. It all depends on whether freedom from drug use is a reasonable requirement of the job, and therefore whether human rights protections are infringed.

Once hired, if the employee is thereafter fired because a test indicates drug abuse, the employee can allege wrongful dismissal if he or she can prove an error in the test results. Urine samples, the standard method of testing for non-prescription drug use, can identify traces of drugs but not a habitual drug user. Some opponents of drug testing fear that innocent employees may become victims of labelling errors; others worry about the accuracy of the tests. An employee's use of prescribed or over-the-counter medication may affect the results.

However, if a drug test is accurate and the employee does, in fact, abuse drugs, the employer is probably legally justified in terminating the employee, assuming the employer can prove that drug use affected the employee's job performance or was liable to affect it, and that freedom from alcohol or drug dependency is a bona fide occupational requirement.

If drug testing indicates drug abuse, an employer is not obliged to keep the information confidential unless he or she has promised to do so in advance and in writing. Nor is the employer obliged to report illegal drug use to the police.

Although drug testing is uncommon as a condition of employment in Canada, it is used in some cases—for prospective employees of Air Canada, for example. In 1992, Imperial Oil's drug and alcohol testing policy for "safety-sensitive" positions was challenged by four employees who filed complaints with the Ontario Human Rights Commission. One employee was demoted for drinking, even though he had given up alcohol eight years earlier and had participated in a company-sponsored substance-abuse program.

His complaint of discrimination went to a one-person board of inquiry in 1995 set up by the Ontario Human Rights Commission. The board of inquiry determined not only that alcoholism is a handicap protected from discrimination under the Ontario Human Rights Code, but that the employer has a duty to accommodate the employee. In this case, Imperial Oil had moved the employee to a different job and was told that it had a duty to reinstate him in his former position, even though the employer had designated the job as "safety-sensitive." He was awarded damages of $21,241. Imperial Oil lost its appeal to the Divisional Court, which in 1998 ruled that pre-employment and random drug-testing policies imposed by employers to monitor previous and current substance abuse by employees are unlawful. The case was then sent to the Ontario Court of Appeal, which in 2000 allowed the appeal in part, and ruled that Imperial Oil's alcohol and drug testing policies were discriminatory. The Court ruled that blood tests for drugs were not a bona fide occupational requirement but Breathalyzer tests for alcohol were reasonable. The Court held that the employee could not be automatically dismissed as the employer had a duty to accommodate and tailor sanctions to the employee's circumstances.

In another case in 1996, the Federal Court quashed a Canadian Human Rights tribunal finding of non-discrimination. The human rights tribunal had decided that the Toronto Dominion Bank policy since 1991 of mandatory drug testing for new and returning employees was *not* discrimination on the basis of disability. The Canadian Human Rights Act defines a disability as "any previous or existing mental or physical disability and includes disfigurement and previous or existing dependence on alcohol or a drug." Instead the Federal Court ruled that the bank policy had in fact amounted to "adverse-effect discrimination." The decision was appealed to the Federal Court of Appeal, which upheld it in 1998.

The meaning of this form of discrimination was well defined in 1990 by then Supreme Court of Canada justice Bertha Wilson as "a rule that is neutral on its face but has an adverse discriminatory effect on certain members of the group to whom it applies." Madam Justice Wilson went on to clarify that "where a rule has an adverse discriminatory effect, the appropriate response is to uphold the rule in its general application and consider whether the employer could have accommodated the employee adversely affected without undue hardship."

To prove that a duty of accommodation applies, the employer must show that the policy was rationally connected to the performance of the job.

3. Discrimination because of Pregnancy

It is against the law of every jurisdiction for employers to discriminate against pregnant women. A pregnant woman is entitled to be hired, to receive benefits and to be reinstated after the pregnancy, usually without loss of seniority.

In 1989, the Supreme Court of Canada ruled that discrimination against pregnant women in employment is the same as discrimination on the basis of sex, and is a violation of human rights protection under the law.

The case that set the precedent involved several women who worked as part-time cashiers for a Manitoba Safeway store and complained of discrimination on the basis of sex under the store's accident and sickness plan. The company plan paid sick employees a maximum of two-thirds of regular salary for 26 weeks, but covered pregnant employees for only nine weeks, even if the cause of illness was unrelated to the pregnancy.

The plan also exempted pregnant women from receiving sickness benefits during the period in which they were eligible to receive unemployment insurance. During this time, pregnant women were not entitled to any compensation under the company plan, even if they suffered from an ailment that was totally unrelated to the pregnancy.

One cashier, who had to stop work because of anemia, pointed out that, had she suffered anemia for any reason other than pregnancy, she would have been entitled to collect sickness benefits. The Supreme Court agreed with her that the plan's terms gave a pregnant woman fewer benefits than a non-pregnant person, and concluded that the plan discriminated on the basis of sex and therefore breached Manitoba's human rights legislation.

If a pregnant woman is discriminated against in employment because of pregnancy, she should first talk to her employer and advise her or him of the law as she understands it and the potential for a human rights complaint. If there is a union in the workplace, she could discuss the possibility of filing a grievance against the employer with the local steward. If the grievance does not succeed, a complaint to a human rights commission would be the next step.

4. Independent Contractors

Contract arrangements, in which employers engage staff "on contract" for a specified period or indefinitely, are becoming more common.

Contract workers do not have the same rights as permanent employees, and contractors do not have the same obligations as employers.

EMPLOYMENT STANDARDS LAWS

Employees generally are protected by employment standards legislation, and are entitled to two weeks vacation with pay for every year of employment, a ceiling on the hours of weekly work required in exchange for regular pay, pay for statutory holidays, a contribution by the employer to each employee's Canada Pension Plan and Employment Insurance premiums, and a mandatory minimum notice period for dismissal. Some employees also receive benefit plans for extended health care and disability insurance. The employer pays various payroll taxes for each employee, such as CPP, EI, and Workers' Compensation.

CONTRACT TERMS

Contract workers are generally limited to the rights spelled out in the contract, which will specify the term of the contract, rate of pay and notice (usually minimal) required for termination. They usually get little or no paid vacation and statutory holidays; they must pay both the employer and employee CPP contribution (that is, double what an employee contributes); they may not be entitled to employment insurance; they frequently do not receive health, disability and other insurance benefits.

Independent contractors may prefer this way of working, and when they do, it is usually because they are running their own business and can take advantage of certain tax deductions available to small business owners. They also have more control over their time and their method of working.

The Canadian Council on Social Development reported in 2000 on the changing face of the self-employed. It reported that in 1998, there were more than 2,525,000 self-employed workers in Canada, including incorporated and non-incorporated work-

ers, those with and without paid employees, and unpaid workers in family businesses. The proportion of self-employed women increased from 1990 to 1998 by more than 50 percent, from 591,000 to 891,000. In 1998, 13.7 percent of women in the Canadian labour market were self-employed, and more than 35 percent of self-employed people were women. The majority of these (59 percent) were between the ages of 20 and 45. Seventy-five percent of jobs created from 1990 to 1998 were non-incorporated businesses without paid employees. One of the consequences is that many young women of child-bearing age do not have the benefit of paid maternity leave through employment insurance. Public policy has not caught up to these facts.

CONTRACT WORKER OR EMPLOYEE: WHICH IS IT?

Sometimes, the worker wants the protection of employment standards legislation and believes the contract is a thinly disguised employment relationship. If a contract worker complains to an employment standards office, that government agency must determine whether the worker was an employee and entitled to its protection by assessing the precise relationship between the parties. The Ontario legislation, for example, applies to every contract of employment, oral or written, express or implied, where the employment is for work or services to be performed in Ontario. The act defines an employee as a person who performs any work for or supplies any services to an employer, who does work at home for an employer or who receives any instruction or training in the activity, business, work, trade, occupation or profession of the employer.

The case law is clear that the courts are to give the term "employee" a broad and liberal interpretation. In one case, for example, an individual contracting with a company to be the owner-manager of a convenience store was found to be an employee for purposes of employment standards legislation. In another case, a person operating and managing an electronics store under a franchise agreement with the owner was found to be an employee.

The employment standards people and the courts have evolved a way of determining whether a person is an employee or independent contractor. Employees are told what work to do, when to do it and how to do it; their work is an integral part of the employer's business; they use the employer's tools and equipment; they devote their entire work time to the duties given them by the employer; they have no risk of loss and no chance of profit.

Contractors, on the other hand, have control of their time and their place of work, and ownership of their tools; they are given a task to do and exercise a certain amount of judgment over its manner of completion; they work for more than one person; they have a chance of profit and a risk of loss.

In the end, there are numerous factors to consider, and the issue will always be determined according to the facts of the individual case. But those workers who want to be sure of their rights should call their local employment standards office for advice.

B. EMPLOYEE BENEFITS

1. Sick Pay

There is no law anywhere in Canada that requires employers to pay their employees for the time they are away from work due to illness. Some employers provide sick pay for defined periods as a voluntary benefit of employment; others do so as part of a union-negotiated collective agreement; and others arrange for contributory or noncontributory disability insurance coverage. But if an employer refuses to provide sick pay, an employee has no legal right to demand it.

Employers in most jurisdictions are also not required by law to permit time off for illness, even without pay. However, illness may not be just cause for dismissal either. For all practical purposes, a short-term period off work due to illness has no consequences to the employee beyond loss of pay.

2. Overtime Pay

All provinces, territories and the federal jurisdiction have laws setting standard hours of work, and require overtime pay or compensatory time instead of pay.

Standard weekly hours of work range from 40 in British Columbia, Manitoba, Saskatchewan, Newfoundland and Labrador, the Northwest Territories, Nunavut, Quebec, the Yukon and the federal jurisdiction, to 44 hours per week in Alberta, Ontario and New Brunswick, and to 48 hours per week in Nova Scotia and Prince Edward Island. Almost all jurisdictions set the rate for overtime pay at a one-and-a-half-times formula: one-and-a-half times an established minimum rate in some places, and one-and-a-half times the employee's regular wage in others.

Certain industries and types of employment may be exempt. For example, in many places domestic workers, students, supervisory, managerial and professional personnel are excluded. In some provinces, seasonal industries may be exempt, and in some places, emergency situations in companies free employers from paying for overtime work.

The choice of compensatory time off or overtime pay is at the discretion of the employer, as is the decision about when the compensatory time will be taken.

3. Maternity, Paternity, Parental and Adoption Leave

It is an established legal right everywhere in Canada for pregnant salaried women to have at least an unpaid maternity leave of absence. Those salaried women who have paid Employment Insurance premiums are also entitled to payments at prescribed levels and for prescribed periods through the Employment Insurance Commission. Paid and unpaid leave for fathers and for adoptive parents are also available in some places, as is an additional period of child-care leave for mothers.

These rights are a marked improvement for employed families. As recently as the 1950s, a woman was expected to quit her job when she got pregnant, or at least shortly before delivery. Fathers received no leave at all because there was no expectation that they would share in child care. The needs of adoptive parents were simply ignored. But now, laws require employers to provide a specified minimum period of maternity

leave, and some generous employers may make more time available. In all jurisdictions, both prospective parents can now count on parental or child-care leave to allow the second parent to take a leave of absence without pay to help care for the newborn. The law now recognizes that many fathers want an early and sustained opportunity to bond with their children.

Part-time employees are covered by the same rules, since the legislation in every jurisdiction makes no distinction between full- and part-time employees. Some employees are not covered; professionals and domestics, for example, are not protected by most employment standards legislation. Nor are independent contractors or self-employed persons. Doctors are not covered by employment standards legislation and may not be entitled to Employment Insurance payments. However, in Ontario and Nova Scotia there are now paid maternity benefits for women doctors. Ontario's plan was instituted in 2000 and the government pays 50 percent of average weekly earnings up to $880 a week for a maximum of 17 consecutive weeks. The Quebec and Nova Scotia law societies are providing some maternity benefits for lawyers, starting in 2005. Quebec's plan allows fathers some parental-leave pay.

The laws and rules differ across the country, and are changed from time to time. The local employment standards department or Ministry of Labour will be able to verify the current situation.

The employer is entitled to ask for a medical certificate verifying the pregnancy and the estimated due date.

MATERNITY LEAVE FOR MOTHERS

The "qualifying period" is the minimum period a pregnant woman must work continuously for one employer before her estimated delivery date in order to qualify for an unpaid leave of absence. Its requirements depend on the province:

- No minimum qualifying period in British Columbia, Quebec or New Brunswick
- 13 weeks in Ontario
- 20 weeks in Saskatchewan, Prince Edward Island and Newfoundland and Labrador
- Six months in the federal jurisdiction
- 12 months in Alberta, Manitoba, Nova Scotia, the Northwest Territories and Nunavut and Yukon Territory

Pregnant women must provide "required notice" to their employers of commencement of leave (which may be abbreviated for medical reasons) as follows:

- Two weeks in Alberta, Newfoundland and Labrador, New Brunswick (which also requires four months' notice of intent to take leave) and Ontario
- Three weeks in Quebec
- Four weeks in British Columbia, Manitoba, Nova Scotia, Prince Edward Island, Saskatchewan, the Northwest Territories and Nunavut, Yukon Territory and the federal jurisdiction

The permitted length of leave is:

- 18 weeks of unpaid leave in Quebec and Saskatchewan
- 17 weeks of unpaid leave in British Columbia, Manitoba, New Brunswick, Newfoundland and Labrador, Nova Scotia, Ontario, Prince Edward Island, the federal jurisdiction, the Northwest Territories and Nunavut and the Yukon
- 15 weeks of unpaid leave in Alberta

Unpaid leave can be extended for medical reasons relating to the pregnancy or birth only in some places, on medical certification, and for only a limited period.

PARENTAL/CHILD-CARE LEAVE

Parental or child-care leave is a defined period of time available to the mother or father after the baby is born. The qualifying period is the same as for maternity leave, and so is the required notice, except for New Brunswick's four-week notice period.

Permitted length of parental/child-care leave is as follows:

- 35 weeks in Newfoundland and Labrador, and in Prince Edward Island
- 37 weeks in the federal jurisdiction, Alberta, British Columbia, Manitoba, New Brunswick, the Northwest Territories, Nunavut, Ontario, Saskatchewan and the Yukon
- 52 weeks in Quebec and Nova Scotia

ADOPTION LEAVE

Adoption leave is the same as parental leave in those jurisdictions that have it, except that Newfoundland and Labrador, Prince Edward Island and Saskatchewan allow more time off for adoptive parents than for parental leave—52 weeks in each case.

JOB AND BENEFITS PROTECTION

In every jurisdiction, the laws guarantee an employee reinstatement after the leave period to at least a comparable job with the same or similar wages and benefits, without loss of seniority. The vacation pay must be the same as it would have been if the employee had worked the maternity or parental leave.

PARTIALLY PAID LEAVE THROUGH EMPLOYMENT INSURANCE

Maternity benefits through employment insurance are available for 15 weeks in every province and in the federal jurisdiction, provided the employee was employed in insurable employment for at least 600 hours over the last qualifying period (usually 52 weeks) before the leave, contributed by paying Employment Insurance premiums, ceased working because of pregnancy, and her regular weekly earnings decreased by more than 40 percent. She can expect to be paid 55 percent of her insurable income up to a maximum of approximately $413 per week.

Maternity benefits are payable beginning eight weeks before actual or expected delivery, and eligibility ends 17 weeks after actual or expected delivery. If the baby is hospitalized after birth, the employee may claim benefits during a 52-week period, but at the most the employee will receive 15 weeks of additional benefits.

Employment Insurance also pays for a maximum of 35 weeks of parental leave to either natural or adoptive parent, payable up to one year after the new child is brought home.

Maternity and parental benefits can both be claimed from EI, with a maximum combined claim of 50 weeks.

Adoptive parents were limited to ten weeks of parental leave benefits until a May 1996 court decision ruled that this legislation discriminated against adoptive parents. The court stated that adoptive parents needed the same period as biological parents for bonding and family integration after bringing the baby home, and gave the government one year to change the law, which it did effective December 31, 2000.

A "Record of Employment" from the employer must be submitted to the local EI office in order to make the claim; the first cheque can take two weeks to arrive.

Employment insurance benefits are not available to the self-employed or independent contractors.

FULLY PAID LEAVE

Fully paid leave is not mandated by any legislation. However, some unions have negotiated a period of fully paid leave into collective bargaining agreements.

4. Vacation Pay

Every Canadian jurisdiction has legislation entitling employees to two weeks of paid vacation per year, except Saskatchewan, which requires three weeks. In addition, Alberta, British Columbia, Manitoba, New Brunswick, Newfoundland and Labrador, Quebec, Saskatchewan, the Northwest Territories, Nunavut and the federal government provide for longer vacations after a specified period of employment. For example, Alberta, British Columbia and Manitoba entitle workers to three weeks of vacation after they complete five years of continuous employment with one employer. The most generous jurisdiction is Saskatchewan, which provides four weeks of annual vacation after ten years of employment.

An employee must complete a year of employment to become eligible for vacation with pay. She or he continues to earn the right to paid vacation while on maternity or parental leave. If a public holiday falls during the vacation period, the employee is entitled to take an extra day of holiday.

Employees are not entitled to take their vacations whenever they wish. Nor is an employer required by law to accommodate the employee's preference as to when vacations will be taken. In most provinces, however, employees are entitled to take their vacation time all at once, rather than having to break it up into smaller periods.

Vacation pay is calculated as a percentage of the gross earnings paid during the year in which the vacation right was earned. Generally, an employee who is entitled to two weeks of paid vacation receives 4 percent of his or her yearly wages. Depending on the province, commission payments, discretionary bonuses, overtime pay and vacation pay itself may not be included in the annual wages, upon which vacation pay is calculated. A part-time employee is entitled to vacation with pay on the same basis.

If an employer sells, merges or otherwise transfers the business to another employer, the earned vacation entitlement of the employee is unaffected.

An employee who is terminated before having used up the earned vacation time must be paid for all accumulated vacation pay entitlement.

Only employees covered by the Employment Standards Act in their province or territory are protected; for example, certain professionals and domestics are usually not covered by the legislation. However, these employees may have employment contracts to protect them, or unions to apply a collective bargaining agreement that may provide more vacation pay than the minimum required by law.

5. Employment Insurance

What used to be called Unemployment Insurance (UI) is now called Employment Insurance (EI) in what the federal government described as a "fundamental restructuring" of the program in 1996. The changes were phased in over an extended period ending in 2001.

Overall, the changes lengthened the qualifying period, penalized repeat users, lowered benefits for most people and reduced premiums. At its inception, the previous Unemployment Insurance Plan was touted as an insurance scheme that should entitle insured employees to a fixed and predictable benefit over time. However, successive governments have treated the plan as a form of social assistance, and the 1996 changes continued the tradition of governments' tinkering with contribution levels and benefits according to overall government budgets and regional planning needs. By 2004, the accumulated surplus in the EI fund was $46 billion, which the government diverted to other purposes rather than pay the unemployed or retrain them. According to the auditor general, this surplus is three times the estimated reserve needed to cover the expenses for the unemployed.

Employees and employers are still required to pay premiums to the plan. Since 1994, the government has been gradually reducing the contribution required of employees and employers; in 2005 the employee pays $1.95 for every $100 of insurable earnings, and the employer pays $2.73 for every $100 of insurable earnings per employee. The maximum contribution to the plan in 2005 is $761 for an employee and $1065 for an employer. An employee is currently able to insure earnings of up to $750 per week, or $39,000 per year. For repeat users, benefits drop by up to five percentage points.

Eligibility is based upon hours worked, rather than weeks worked. The qualifying period is 420 to 700 hours in a year, depending on the regional unemployment rate. Although this system allows part-time workers who work less than 15 hours a week to qualify, it reduces eligibility for most part-timers. For example, a worker in a lower unemployment area, such as Toronto, who works 14 hours a week would need to work for almost 40 weeks to qualify, rather than 17 weeks under the current system.

A qualifying period of 910 hours applies to new entrants or re-entrants into the work force, regardless of regional unemployment rates. Full-time homemakers who return to the work force therefore have to work for 26 weeks full-time, at 35 hours per week, or for 52 weeks on a half-time basis, at 17.5 hours per week.

Benefits are calculated at 55 percent of the maximum insurable earnings, resulting in a maximum EI benefit of approximately $413 per week. An eligible recipient may continue to receive EI for up to 45 weeks. While eligibility is not based upon a means test, "high" income earners do not get to keep all the benefits they receive. When the recipient's tax return is filed, the EI benefits are subject to a clawback for those with 20 or more weeks of claims over the previous five years. Since 1999, the clawback was applied to those whose income exceeded $39,000 a year. From 1996 to 1998, it was only when income exceeded $48,750 that EI benefits were reclaimed. Prior to 1996, EI recipients were allowed to earn $63,570 a year before having any benefits clawed back. Claimants are allowed to earn up to $50 a week without having their benefits reduced.

Under the first year of the revised EI structure, only 43 percent of unemployed Canadians received benefits, compared to 83 percent in 1989 under the former Unemployment Insurance plan. Cash benefits fell in the first year of the new Employment Insurance structure by $2 billion from $12 billion to $10 billion, at the same time as the surplus substantially increased. The government promised to use some of its savings to fund direct employment assistance programs, but these benefit only the (fewer) workers who are eligible for EI. At the same time, the government has made it clear that a lot of the surplus would not go towards unemployment but towards deficit and tax reduction.

In 2004, the government promised that expected premium revenues should correspond to expected program costs, and that premium rates should be relatively stable over time. At the same time, the government's chief actuary, reporting on the outlook for 2005, noted that an additional $1.3 billion would be added to the EI surplus in 2004, so that by the end of 2004, the cumulative surplus was expected to be $46.2 billion.

In 2004, the federal government made up to 6 weeks of employment insurance benefits available to those workers who must take time off to provide compassionate care or support to a gravely ill family member at risk of dying within 26 weeks. To be eligible, a person must show that her regular earnings from work have decreased by more than 40 percent and she has accumulated 600 insured hours in the prior 52 weeks or since the start of the last claim. These are the persons considered family members: your child or the child of your spouse or common-law partner; your wife/husband or common-law partner; your father/mother; your father's wife/mother's husband; the common-law partner of your father/mother. Common-law partner means a person who has been living in a conjugal relationship with that person for at least a year. Care or support is defined as providing psychological or emotional support, or arranging for care by a third party, or directly providing or participating in the care.

6. *Canada Pension Plan*

Since 1966 when the Canada Pension Plan (CPP) was established, everyone over 18 employed in Canada for wages has been required to contribute to the plan, and the employer has been required to contribute an equivalent amount. Quebec residents have their own affiliated plan known as the Quebec Pension Plan (QPP).

The Canada Pension Plan is not like a private pension plan. Private plans are required by law to keep the contributions in trust, invest them in a cautious manner and pay pension benefits from employer and employee contributions and interest earned on the contributions. CPP, in contrast, is operated as a "pay as you go" scheme, where outgoing benefits in any one year are financed by incoming contributions to the plan in that same year.

CPP used to keep a contingency fund with about two years of pension payments in reserve, which it used to loan out to the provinces at beneficial interest rates. The assumption has been that future contributions by employers and employees would be more than adequate to pay pensioners. But, in fact, the CPP and its sister plan, the Quebec Pension Plan, together have an unfunded liability that is larger than the federal public debt, although the government does not include this liability in its accounts.

CPP has been under enormous pressure as, according to the federal government, an aging population, more pensioners and fewer workers, slower economic growth and the increasing costs of CPP disability pensions threaten to strain the system to its limit.

In 1998, the federal government took steps to improve the financial health of the Canada Pension Plan using essentially two means. The system changed to permit investment in stock market equities, instead of low-rate loans to provinces. And the contributions by workers and their employers were significantly increased, and continued to increase annually until 2003. The government said this will result in a much larger reserve fund to eventually provide for about five years of benefits.

In 2004, employee contributions were calculated as 4.95 percent of annual earnings between $3,500 (the basic exemption) and $40,500, the maximum pensionable earnings. Thus the most an employee paid in 2004 was $1,831.50. This has been increasing annually, and compares to a contribution rate in 1996 of 2.8 percent of annual earnings based on a lower maximum with the highest contribution being $893.20. This is a significant increase. Employers are required to match the employee's contribution on the employee's behalf. A self-employed person pays both the employee's and employer's share when she files her tax return, which is 9.9 percent or $3,663.00.

CPP benefits are payable only if contributions have been made for certain minimum qualifying periods. Different qualifying periods apply to benefits payable on retirement, death and disability.

Orphan's benefits are payable to dependent children of deceased contributors up to the age of 18 or, if the child is attending school full-time, up to the age of 25. If the child has a disability, there is no age maximum. In 2005 the orphan's pension was $195.96 per month.

A disability pension is payable to a contributor who suffers from a severe and prolonged mental or physical disability that prevents him or her from pursuing any substantially gainful occupation. In 2005, the maximum monthly disability pension was $1,010.23. The disability pension ceases at age 65, when it is replaced by a retirement pension. To be eligible for disability benefits, workers must have made contributions in four of the prior six years instead of the previous requirement of two of the prior three years or five of the prior ten years. Retirement pensions for disability beneficiaries are now based on maximum pensionable earnings at the time of disability and are indexed annually.

7. Workers' Compensation

Every province and territory has workers' compensation legislation. While the main features of workers' compensation legislation are similar, the details vary from one jurisdiction to another. Some jurisdictions include all industries except those that are specifically excluded by the legislation or the regulations. Others (for example, Ontario) list only the industries that are covered. In any event, most workers are covered by workers' compensation schemes. Participation is mandatory for employers in the included industries, and there is generally an opt-in provision for employers not covered and for independent contractors. Workers' compensation is administered by a board or commission, and disputes are heard by a specialized tribunal. There may be a workers' advisor to assist claimants.

Workers' compensation provides benefits to workers injured on the job by accidents or by deliberate actions of another worker, and to workers who contract an occupational disease. If the worker is injured through his or her own wrongdoing, benefits are not provided unless death or permanent disability results. If a worker is killed, benefits are provided to her or his dependent spouse and minor children. Stress is generally not covered, unless it results from a single traumatic event. The legislation takes away the right to sue the employer and fellow employees for work-related injuries and occupational diseases. The right to sue others who may have caused a work-related injury is not taken away, but the board or commission may stand in the worker's place and exercise his right to sue if benefits have been paid.

Employers pay into an injury fund. The levy is determined by the industry group to which the employer belongs and the size of the employer's payroll. Employers may not charge employees or make deductions from their wages to offset the compensation levy. Employees are not permitted to waive compensation benefits.

Injured employees are compensated for lost earning capacity and receive medical aid. If the worker is off work, benefits are paid until she can return to work. If she cannot return to her previous job and can only work at a lower-paying occupation, benefits to compensate for the difference are paid. The compensation rates are fixed by the Acts and regulations in each jurisdiction. Compensation continues for as long as the injury or disability continues. If it is permanent, regular compensation generally stops at age 65 and the worker begins receiving an annuity funded out of a portion of her or his benefits. Rehabilitation and retraining services are part of the compensation scheme.

Employers are not permitted to dismiss or penalize a worker for being injured or for claiming compensation under the legislation. They must permit the worker to return to work when he is able to do so. Workers are required to report injuries and occupational diseases, to submit to medical examinations and take medical treatment, to co-operate with rehabilitation and retraining and to return to work when able. Some jurisdictions provide retraining services for spouses of workers killed in a job-related accident or by a job-related illness.

C. ON-THE-JOB RIGHTS

1. Equal Pay for Women

Women have had "rights" to equal pay since the early 1950s, but only on paper. The first legislation in Canada to require employers to pay women the same as men for identical work was enacted in 1951, when Ontario passed Canada's first equal pay laws. Unfortunately, these laws stated lofty principles but did not have the programs and enforcement to give them teeth and bite. Nor did these laws result in fair wages, because many women were segregated into female occupations, such as nursing or secretarial jobs, and few men were doing precisely the same work.

In the mid 1970s, the laws of some provinces were improved to require that women be paid the same for performing "substantially the same" work. However, many employers successfully justified their unequal wages by giving reasons other than sex. Enforcement was not effective. An individual had to register a complaint about unequal pay that did not address systemic discrimination.

With women earning only 65 cents on average for every dollar a man earned, and research showing that part of this wage gap was unquestionably due to discrimination, the legislation was improved again. In the mid 1980s, some governments amended the law to say that women should be paid equally for "work of equal value"; this amendment required employers to compare the pay rates between women and men working in dissimilar jobs that involved the same skills, effort, responsibility and working conditions.

Manitoba: In 1985, Manitoba became the first province in Canada to require its public sector to be pro-active and develop plans to secure for provincial government employees what "equal pay for work of equal value" came to be called—"pay equity."

Ontario: Ontario came next in 1988 when the innovative Pay Equity Act took effect, which surpassed all previous legislative attempts to promote equal pay for women in Canada. Ontario was the only Canadian jurisdiction to require public-sector employers and private-sector employers with ten or more employees to take the initiative in adjusting pay patterns and to work to solve unfair pay scales in the female job ghettos.

The Act required equal pay for women who perform jobs of equal value to men in the same establishment. Women's and men's jobs were compared on the basis of skill, effort, responsibility and working conditions to determine their value; for example, a secretary's duties may be compared with a truck driver's. Allowances were permitted for wage differences arising from such factors as seniority and merit.

The employers with 100 or more people on staff were required to develop pay equity plans in conjunction with their employees or unions, and post them for employees to see. Firms with ten or more employees were expected to establish and maintain compensation practices to result in pay equity.

A Pay Equity Commission was established to monitor the law's effectiveness, hear complaints and make rulings on pay equity disputes. If an employer did not implement a pay equity plan or contravened the Act in some other way, a complaint to the Pay Equity Commission might invoke an order for a plan to be prepared for the employer. It might also lead to retroactive wage adjustments for an entire female job classification.

A company found guilty of pay equity violations could be fined up to $25,000. Any company or union official who authorized or acquiesced in a breach of the Act could be liable to a $2,000 penalty, whether or not the company itself had been prosecuted or convicted.

When the government in Ontario changed in 1995, the money available to ensure pay equity within the public service was cut back by the Conservatives in power, although the law remained in place.

In 1995, the government tried to withdraw funding for pay equity aimed at increasing the salaries of some of the lowest-paid women in its jurisdiction, such as workers in nursing homes and women's shelters. The move was challenged by the Service Employees International Union, Local 204, and the Ontario Court (General Division) struck down the Conservative government's changes on the basis that they violated the equality guarantees under the Charter of Rights and Freedoms.

The court ruling was in September 1997, and many of the women waited for their money for a long time. By 2001, the government owed the women an estimated $140 million, and the union mounted another legal case, this time with five unions taking the offensive. It was not until 2003 that the case was settled and the 100,000 women were paid $414 million over three years.

Quebec: Pro-active legislation came into force in Quebec on November 21, 1997, and covered employers whose enterprises have ten or more employees. The law required all employers covered by the Act to have a pay equity plan in place by November 21, 2001, and to rectify differences in compensation by November 21, 2005.

Elsewhere: Pay equity is now official policy in almost all Canadian jurisdictions (the exceptions are Alberta, Newfoundland and Labrador, and Saskatchewan), although provisions and the nature of legislation, if any, vary widely. In British Columbia, when the Liberals took office in 2001, they repealed private sector pay equity legislation that had been introduced by the previous New

Democratic government. Outside Ontario, Quebec and Manitoba, the remedy for a woman who suffers discrimination in pay is a complaint to her provincial human rights commission (in the Northwest Territories, to a Fair Practices Officer) or, if in the federal jurisdiction, to the Canadian Human Rights Commission.

Federal Law: The Canadian Human Rights Commission responds to complaints from individuals and may also initiate its own complaints where it suspects systemic discrimination. Since 1978, the Canadian Human Rights Act has specifically prohibited discrimination by an employer between male and female employees who perform work of equal value. Value is defined as a composite of skill, effort, responsibility and working conditions. There are Equal Wage Guidelines under the Canadian Human Rights Act that describe how the rules are to be implemented.

In 1980 the Canadian Human Rights Commission settled its first complaint involving equal pay for work of equal value by securing $14,262 in back pay for a former director of nursing of a federally operated Montreal hospital. She had been paid $10,000 a year less than the assistant director-general, whose job was of roughly equal value to hers.

In the same year, the Commission also settled a case of systemic discrimination by awarding back pay to government librarians (63.5 percent of them female) because they had been paid unequally compared to historical researchers (74.6 percent of them male). The historical researchers earned more than the librarians, even though librarians must have graduate qualifications in library science while researchers need only an undergraduate degree. This case—

the first settlement of a complaint comparing entire occupational groups whose members performed dissimilar services—set the pattern for subsequent complaints.

The most significant award was confirmed in 1999. Determining a complaint registered in 1984, a federal human rights tribunal in 1998 had ruled that pay inequities suffered by numerous federal government employees, including secretaries, hospital clerks and library workers, had to be corrected. The great majority of the workers earned less than $30,000 a year. The federal government appealed the decision, saying the cost was too high and arguing that the methodology used to determine the wage gap between men and women was faulty. The tribunal's decision was upheld by the Federal Court in 1999, ending what was by then the longest and largest human rights case in North America. The court ordered 13 years of back pay to workers. In 2000 the government started making lump-sum payments for back amounts; the increases were regularized in pay adjustments that took effect in 2000 and a series of adjustments implemented throughout 2000 and 2001. The award amounted to about $3.5 billion to be distributed among about 230,000 former and current federal government employees, more than 85 percent of whom are women.

Men can apply for pay equity increases as well. For example, a male rate clerk in a national trucking company alleged that he was paid unequally as compared to two women in the same job. The complaint was dismissed in 1989 because the company voluntarily raised his salary, and the Canadian Human Rights Commission was persuaded that discrimination was not the cause of the differential; rather, the inconsistencies in compensation practices were caused by a lack of formal procedures.

Under human rights laws, wage differences may be justified under certain circumstances. For example, guidelines under the Canadian Human Rights Act include a list of factors considered reasonable in justifying male/female wage differences, including seniority, formalized performance rating and sex, where it is a bona fide occupational requirement (washroom attendant, for example).

The federal complaint-based model is being challenged by the federal Pay Equity Task Force, whose report, released in May 2004, recommended the adoption of legislation that will require all federally regulated employers to proactively develop pay equity plans and timetables, and to provide mechanisms that will ensure effective monitoring and enforcement. Proactive legislation has been found to be more effective than a complaints-based model.

The Charter of Rights and Freedoms and Pay Equity: In 2004, the Supreme Court of Canada dealt with a Charter-based appeal by the Newfoundland Association of Public Employees, which was supported by the Women's Legal Education and Action Fund ("LEAF"). The Newfoundland and Labrador government had signed a pay equity agreement in favour of 5,000 female health care sector employees, and subsequently introduced the Public Sector Restraint Act, which had deferred the pay equity increase for three years. The government claimed that it had to do so to reduce its deficit due to a financial crisis. The union challenged the government's action, and an arbitration board ruled that the Act discriminated against the employees in violation of the equality rights provisions of the Charter of Rights and Freedoms. The board ordered the government to comply with the pay equity agreement. The case was appealed all the way up to the Supreme Court of Canada, which unanimously agreed that Newfoundland and Labrador's government had discriminated against women and breached the Charter equality rights. However, the Court then held that this discriminatory treatment of women was justified under Section 1 of the Charter as reasonably necessary because of the Newfoundland and Labrador government's fiscal deficit. This analysis threatens pay equity for women everywhere, as governments and employers can always argue financial distress, but surely that would also justify reducing pay for everyone, not just for women. The fact is that women historically have been the ones to take the brunt of these kinds of arguments.

Despite these concerted efforts to bridge the gap between male and female wages, inequity remains, and appears to be entrenched. Statistics Canada reported that in 1995 women working full-time received on average 73.1 cents for every dollar earned by a man, and that at least one-third of the differential resulted from discrimination. By 1998, women working full-time received on average 72.2 cents for every dollar earned by a man, indicating a slight erosion in the numbers, and a trend in the wrong direction. The 2001 Census revealed that the wage gap had continued to deteriorate; it was 70.9 percent in 2001. For visible minority women in relation to visible minority men, this was 75.9 percent and for Aboriginal women in relation to Aboriginal men, the wage gap was 77.2 percent.

2. Discrimination in Employment on Diversity Grounds

While the pay equity laws serve only to rectify the wage differential between men and women, members of disadvantaged groups who are concerned that they are not paid equally with others, or who suffer discrimination in hiring because of disability, race, religion or other differences, should consider registering a complaint of discrimination under provincial or federal human rights legislation. Everywhere in Canada, human rights laws provide that no one is to be discriminated against in employment on the basis of his or her race or colour, religion or creed, disability, marital status, sex, age, sexual orientation, family status, ancestry or place of origin; or, in some places, political beliefs, dependence on alcohol or drugs, pardoned conviction or source of income (Ontario bans discrimination in accommodation on the grounds of receipt of public assistance); or (only in Quebec) language.

A study by the federal Heritage Department, released in 1995 and based on data gathered during the 1991 Census, revealed that Canadian men who are members of a visible minority earn significantly less than similarly qualified white Canadians, even after taking into account that some of the visible-minority Canadians may not have the same education or language skills. The disparity existed not just for immigrants but also for Canadian-born members of minorities. The difference in pay worked out to substantial dollars: the mean earnings of men self-described as Canadian or British were $37,000 to $40,000, while men identifying themselves as black, Chinese or another visible minority earned $21,000 to $31,000. Aboriginal men earned a mean income of $23,000.

The 2001 Census showed that the average full-time job for all working Canadians paid $43,298, whereas members of visible minorities working full-time earned $37,957 and Aboriginals $33,426.

In 1995, a Canadian Human Rights Commission tribunal found that two employees of the Department of National Health and Welfare were not hired solely because of their race, colour and ethnic or national origin (they were both raised in India). The two were highly qualified research scientists with long-time Canadian experience who had been seconded to the immunology division; while there, they received good performance reviews. But when they applied for permanent employment, they were not seriously considered for the jobs. Relying partly on the evidence of subjective and perfunctory interviews, and on the fact that a continued search was made for similarly qualified individuals to fill the positions, the tribunal ruled that the men were discriminated against.

3. Discrimination in Employment due to Disability

Discrimination in employment on the basis of physical or mental handicap or disability is prohibited everywhere in Canada. It is discrimination when working conditions appropriate for an able-bodied person have an adverse impact on a person with a disability.

There are important qualifiers. If the "ability" is not a reasonable and bona fide qualification for the job, then it is discrimination to fail to hire a person with a disability. For example, a Newfoundland and Labrador human rights board of inquiry found that a student with partial hearing loss in his right ear suffered discrimination on the basis of disability when he was refused summer employment by a mining company as a surveyor's assistant. The mining company made no suggestion that he would be unable to perform the duties of the job, and gave him no opportunity to show that he could. The company was ordered to compensate the student for lost wages and give him a chance to be assessed for ability to do the job; if he proved capable, the mining company had to give him a spot the next summer.

However, in certain situations, it may be acceptable and *not* discriminatory to fail to hire or to fire the person with a disability. For example, the Federal Court approved a Canadian Human Rights tribunal ruling that a person with a disability was not discriminated against when he was dismissed from his job. The complaint was brought by a 35-year-old longshoreman who was disabled by a childhood brain injury that left him with a speech impediment, awkward gait and lack of co-ordination of the left extremities. The tribunal heard evidence that he could not perform certain tasks in this hazardous employment and ruled that it was reasonable to require a degree of co-ordination for this kind of work.

Under certain circumstances, an employer might have a duty to accommodate the person with a disability, when the disability does not affect job performance or when modifications in the working conditions or the job description can be made without undue hardship.

In 1990, then Supreme Court justice Bertha Wilson made law by identifying the critical issue in such cases: whether the employer can accommodate the employee without undue hardship. Since then, judges have tried to define when it is reasonable to impose that duty to accommodate and what constitutes undue hardship.

For instance, in a 1997 case against the Department of National Defence, a hearing-impaired employee alleged discrimination based on the department's failure to accommodate her disability. After 12 years as a clerk sorting mail and filing, she was transferred to a job where the supervisor also expected her to answer telephones. She could not communicate effectively on the telephone despite the use of hearing aids and a telephone amplifier. She argued that the employer could have accommodated her by having other employees answer telephones while she concentrated on her other duties. The tribunal found that the employer had discriminated against the clerk, and ordered the department to pay lost wages, some legal costs and $3,000 compensation for injury to feelings.

In 1998, the Canadian Human Rights Act was amended to define the duty of employers in the federal jurisdiction to accommodate and protect the needs of Canadians who work for federally regulated companies like banks or for the federal government. Employers in the federal jurisdiction now have a duty to accommodate the needs of individuals with disabilities unless that would cause undue hardship on the employer, "considering health, safety and cost," even if the ability would otherwise be a bona fide occupational requirement or bona fide justification.

The largest number of new complaints to the Canadian Human Rights Commission in recent years has been claims of discrimination based on disability—in 2003, these represented 37 percent of 1,320 signed complaints to the federal commission. The Ontario Human Rights Commission in its

2003–2004 annual report found the same trend; disability represented 57.3 percent of total complaints filed. Manitoba's Human Rights Commission reported that in 2003, 40 percent of all complaints filed were based on disability. Saskatchewan reported 41.1 percent for the same period.

Much of the systemic discrimination complained of arises from inaccessible workplaces and public services such as public transit. But the first landmark case in disability rights (Eldridge) was in 1997 when the Supreme Court of Canada ruled that the B.C. government's refusal to supply sign language interpreters for deaf people receiving medical care infringed their right to equal treatment under the Charter. The words of Mr. Justice Gérard La Forest led the way when he said, "people with disabilities have too long been excluded from the labour force, denied access to opportunities for social interaction and advancement, subjected to invidious stereotyping and relegated to institutions." Subsequent cases (see Chapter 7, A1) raise the hope that removal of barriers to participation will be built into policies, services and programs rather than being addressed after the fact through accommodation.

4. Employment Equity

HUMAN RIGHTS REMEDIES

In every province and territory and in the federal jurisdiction, human rights laws exist to prohibit discrimination in employment and to order remedies when discrimination occurs. These remedies can include affirmative action programs. In addition, the federal government has an employment equity law in place to pro-actively promote equal opportunity, sometimes by way of affirmative action programs. These days affirmative action is more often called employment equity, having been renamed by the 1984 federal Royal Commission on Equality in Employment chaired by Madam Justice Rosalie S. Abella, now a judge of the Supreme Court of Canada.

Employment equity programs require the employer to undertake approved programs to improve employment opportunities and remedy inequities for all disadvantaged groups. These programs benefit groups that have been historically disadvantaged. Laws are in place in most jurisdictions and in the Charter of Rights and Freedoms to protect the programs from charges of "reverse discrimination."

The programs aim to deal with systemic discrimination, which is often unintentional but based on faulty assumptions ingrained in the structure of the workplace. While some employers' regulations appear neutral and seem to apply equally to everyone, they can have an adverse impact on non-traditional applicants. For example, unnecessary height and weight requirements for some jobs, such as a security guard or an orderly, may exclude women or members of certain visible minorities who may be small and short but still have the capacity to perform the job. A requirement that an employee not wear a hat may adversely affect a Sikh, whose culture requires him to wear a turban.

Timing of work shifts may also have an adverse impact on a member of a religious group. Larry S. Renaud, a school custodian in British Columbia who observes the Seventh Day Adventist faith, refused to work

Friday afternoon shifts because his religion forbade him to work from sundown Friday to sundown Saturday. The employer was willing to accommodate him with a Sunday to Thursday shift, but the union objected to Renaud's departing from the schedule in the collective agreement, partly because he did not have the seniority for the Sunday to Thursday shift.

When Renaud was fired in 1985 for failing to turn up for work on a Friday afternoon, he registered a complaint with the B.C. Council of Human Rights, which awarded him damages to be paid by both the employer and the union. The union and employer appealed (and won) at both the B.C. Supreme Court and the B.C. Court of Appeal. But when Renaud appealed to the Supreme Court of Canada, it reinstated his victory in 1992, and ruled that the employer and the union both had a duty to accommodate an employee under these circumstances by taking reasonable measures up to the point of undue hardship.

Affirmative action/employment equity programs have been court-approved since 1987. In a class action, 155 women had lodged complaints against the Canadian National Railroad (CN) that CN's recruitment, hiring and promotion policies discouraged women from working in non-traditional jobs. The tribunal agreed, and also pointed out that CN did not employ as many women in non-traditional jobs as other companies did. CN was required to establish a special employment program to aim for 13 percent female participation in specified jobs, with at least one of every four job openings going to women until the quota was reached. The Supreme Court of Canada concluded that CN's policies and practices were discriminatory, and upheld the tribunal-imposed

employment equity program. Human rights legislation in any province may be applied in a similar way.

ROYAL COMMISSION ON EQUALITY IN EMPLOYMENT

In 1984, the Abella Commission inquired into "the most efficient, effective and equitable means of promoting employment opportunities, eliminating systemic discrimination and assisting all individuals to compete for employment opportunities on an equal basis." The Commission was directed to focus on women, Aboriginals, visible minorities and the disabled, and concluded in 1984 that the obstacles to their full equality were "so formidable and self-perpetuating that they cannot be overcome without intervention."

Voluntary programs were dismissed as ineffective in countering pervasive discrimination. Instead, employment equity programs were recommended, obliging employers not to meet quotas, but to develop and maintain practices designed to eliminate discriminatory barriers in the workplace, including inadequate child care, absence of training programs and inaccessible workplaces.

EMPLOYMENT EQUITY ACT 1985

In 1985, the Commission's recommendations were partially implemented by the federal Employment Equity Act, which applied to private-sector employers with 100 or more employees that did more than $200,000 worth of business with the federal government. The legislation stated that these employers had to have employment equity plans or they would lose government contracts. Similar plans were required of the federal public service and federally regulated companies such as banks and Crown corporations.

This law was designed to redress discrimination against women, people with disabilities, Aboriginal people and visible minorities, and to require employers to make a plan, set out goals and target dates, and file annual progress reports.

As stated in the legislation, the goal was "to achieve equality in the workplace . . . by giving effect to the principle that employment equity means more than treating persons in the same way but also requires special measures and the accommodation of differences." But the Act was toothless—while employers were required to implement employment equity and file progress reports, the only penalty that existed was for failure to file reports.

EMPLOYMENT EQUITY ACT 1996

The federal government toughened the Employment Equity Act and widened its scope by enacting legislation that came into force on October 24, 1996.

In the 1996 amendments, the disadvantaged groups that are protected remain the same, but they are more precisely defined. "Members of visible minorities" means "persons, other than Aboriginal peoples, who are non-Caucasian in race or non-white in colour." "Persons with disabilities" means "persons who have a long-term or recurring physical, mental, sensory, psychiatric or learning impairment and who (a) consider themselves to be disadvan-

taged in employment by reason of that impairment, or (b) believe that an employer or potential employer is likely to consider them to be disadvantaged in employment by reason of that impairment. . . ." Aboriginals are defined as persons who are Indian, Inuit or Métis.

Employers are required to identify and eliminate employment barriers. They also have to institute positive policies and practices by collecting information, and by preparing a plan that defines short-term programs (less than three years) and long-term goals, and establishes a timetable. All employees in the federal public sector, including the Canadian Armed Forces, the Royal Canadian Mounted Police and the Canadian Security Intelligence Service are covered under this legislation, bringing the total number of people whose employment equity claims are assisted and protected by the law to about 1 million, including 300,000 on Ottawa's payroll. Any private-sector employer of 100 or more employees on, or in connection with, a "federal work, undertaking or business" must comply. With these amendments, employment equity joins the merit standard as a determining factor of employment in the federal civil service.

The Canadian Human Rights Commission enforces the legislation and has the authority to conduct compliance audits of the approximately 350 public and private employers covered under the Federal Contractors' Program to ensure that "numerical goals" (not quotas) are met, to hold tribunals and to levy fines of up to $50,000 for non-compliance with the law.

An elaborate procedure protects the rights of employers if they do not agree with the result of the compliance audit. First, the compliance officer has to negotiate with the employer for an undertaking to comply. If the negotiation fails or if the employer breaches the undertaking, the Commission will get involved and may appoint an employment equity review tribunal, with similar powers to those of a court. The Commission and tribunal are limited in their orders, however; the law states that no order can be made that "causes undue hardship on an employer," "require[s] an employer to hire or promote unqualified persons," "require[s] an employer to create new positions in its workforce" or "impose[s] a quota on an employer." Quota is helpfully defined as "a requirement to hire or promote a fixed and arbitrary number of persons during a given period."

Penalties, which are at the discretion of a government minister, shall not exceed $10,000 for a single violation and $50,000 for repeated or continued violations.

The Employment Equity Act provides for a review of its effectiveness every five years. The government committee consulted widely for the 2001 review, and made a series of recommendations, primarily that the Employment Equity Act should continue but be strengthened. The government undertook to do so.

ELSEWHERE

Ontario had employment equity legislation in place between 1993 and 1995. It affected more than 17,000 companies and 75 percent of all Ontario workers, including all public service employees and businesses with more than 50 employees.

This law was misunderstood as a quota system although it was similar to the 1996 federal law which was not challenged as a quota system. When the Ontario government changed in 1995, the Conservative government repealed the law, and went so far as to require companies that had already complied with the 1993 legislation to destroy information they had secured. The Alliance for Employment Equity appealed the repeal of this law. The Ontario Court of Appeal dismissed their appeal in 1998 on the basis that courts as a matter of policy are reluctant to interfere with the legislative authority of governments. A subsequent appeal to the Supreme Court of Canada in 1999 was refused, effectively ending the matter.

Ontario residents seeking employment equity now have a single option: they can make a complaint of systemic discrimination to the Ontario Human Rights Commission, which may impose a remedy of an employment equity plan. Employers who wish to please their work force may still choose to implement an employment equity plan voluntarily.

Seven provinces (British Columbia, Manitoba, Saskatchewan, Quebec, Nova Scotia, New Brunswick and Prince Edward Island) have employment equity policies. Of these, only British Columbia has legislation. Only Quebec extends employment equity beyond the public service. In fact, Quebec combines it with a contract compliance program, whereby any public or private sector employer with more than 100 employees and receiving provincial funds of $100,000 or more is required to implement particular employment equity programs.

Nova Scotia's policy, in place since 1975, was tested in the courts. In a 1996 case, the Nova Scotia Court of Appeal ruled that the city of Dartmouth had an approved affirmative action program for police officer trainees and dismissed the complaint of a white male applicant that he had been discriminated against on the basis of race, sex and colour. The eight advertised trainee positions were filled by six females and two black males. The complainant argued unsuccessfully that he should have been selected on the basis of objective criteria.

The federal agency Status of Women Canada, completed in 2000 an interprovincial comparative study of employment equity policy in Canada. The authors of the study concluded that the employment equity impasse possesses two extremely difficult aspects. First, the barriers are deeply embedded in historic oppressions that affect society in general, but are expressed in subtle ways, even among those most dedicated to overcoming barriers and implementing equity. Second, the problems need to be addressed by political rather than policy initiatives, to take account of provincial and regional differences and needs. These are among the report's recommendations: Clear guidelines and targets should be legislated; targets should increase progressively rather than remain static; positive reinforcement should be built into the system; detailed annual reports on employment equity achievements should be mandatory.

THE CHARTER

The Charter of Rights and Freedoms also justifies both affirmative action and employment equity programs. The Charter protects every person's right to equality without discrimination. While it does not create an enforceable remedy or a methodology to create change, the Charter does contain a statement of principle that an individual can raise before a court in the context of a lawsuit. The Charter states that affirmative action programs are immunized from charges of discrimination, and do not add up to reverse discrimination. For the first time, in 2000, the Supreme Court of Canada ruled that this Charter provision does not insulate affirmative action programs from judicial scrutiny. In *Lovelace* v. *Ontario,* the Court, in reviewing this section of the Charter, signalled that governments have constitutional leeway to create targeted affirmative action programs that assist some disadvantaged groups but not others.

EMERGING ISSUES

With Canada's increasingly diverse society, there are emerging issues that equity-seekers will have to resolve. First, what is the solution when there are competing equality claims between individuals from different socially disadvantaged groups, or between one individual and other members of the same socially disadvantaged group? Historically, discrimination has been imposed by the advantaged against the disadvantaged; how can equity be achieved when the disadvantaged are in conflict with each other?

Second, some people have misunderstood and misapplied the intention of employment equity. For example, several years ago the Ontario College of Art in Toronto announced that it would hire only members of historically disadvantaged groups in order to implement employment equity principles. The criticism that followed highlighted the problem with this approach: It ignores the merit claims of individuals just because they are members of groups that have been advantaged historically, even if the individuals themselves have not benefited. Historically, the purpose of affirmative action and employment equity programs has been to ensure that a person who is different in ways that are irrelevant to the needs of the job (non-Caucasian or non-Anglican, for example), but who is at least as meritorious as other candidates, will not lose the opportunity because of her or his difference.

Third, women are not breaking through to the positions of power and influence in the workplace, despite assumptions to the contrary. Studies show that women face an impermeable "glass ceiling" in seeking to improve their position in the workplace. According to the International Labour Organization, "the higher the position, the more glaring the gender gap." Women are placed in personnel and administrative sectors rather than professional and line positions that lead to the top. The rate at which women are promoted to senior posts has lagged behind their participation in the work force and the speed at which they upgrade their qualifications. Not surprisingly, more women are leaving large professional firms and large corporations and becoming entrepreneurs.

Increasing numbers of working people are self-employed independent contractors, with few laws providing protection and support. Policy-makers should be paying attention to this growing area of need.

The legislatures and the courts will be called upon to deal with these issues.

OTHER OPTIONS

If a person cannot prove discrimination or prefers not to complain to a human rights commission, there are more informal but potentially effective options:

- Working through unions to negotiate for inclusion of an affirmative action or employment equity program in the next contract
- Organizing a workers' committee to approach the employer with positive suggestions for retraining and promoting members of disadvantaged groups
- Expressing interest to the human resources department in existing programs or in instituting new ones for employees
- Ensuring that workplaces are accessible to workers with disabilities
- Using the "contract compliance" rules as an opportunity to pressure for change (federal jurisdiction only)
- Encouraging companies to include members of historically disadvantaged groups on their board of directors. For example, a study in 2000 of the Canadian Policy Research Network revealed that very few companies had a woman as chief executive officer or director, or in top management. In fact, women made up only 6 to 9.4 percent of board members and 3.4 percent of the highest ranks of senior management in leading Canadian companies, even though women comprised 37 percent of all managers nationally in 1998.

5. Part-Time Work

Employment standards legislation exists in all provinces and territories and in the federal jurisdiction to provide workers with minimum standards of protection. While the specific rules vary, a part-time worker generally has less legal protection than a full-time employee but more than a casual or seasonal worker. Statistics Canada defines a part-time worker as someone who usually works less than 30 hours a week. As of 1999, part-time workers in Canada made up 18.5 percent of all workers. Seventy percent of all part-timers were women. Any questions about laws in a particular province or territory can be answered by the local employment standards office.

Here is where matters stand on key employment issues related to part-time workers.

RATE OF PAY

There is no law requiring an employer to pay the same rates to full- and part-time employees; part-time employees doing the same work can expect not only to earn less as a result of working fewer hours, but also to earn less per hour than full-time employees. However, minimum wage laws apply equally to part-time and full-time employees.

STATUTORY HOLIDAYS

Part-timers are generally entitled to paid statutory holidays, as long as they meet the eligibility requirements. To qualify, an employee must usually work a certain number of regularly scheduled work days immediately before the holiday (often at least 15 days during the 30 calendar days preceding the holiday). An employee who worked three days a week or fewer, therefore, would usually not qualify for statutory-holiday pay. However, in Ontario, the right to a paid holiday applies to an employee who has earned wages on at least 12 days during the four work weeks immediately preceding a public holiday, that is, three days a week.

MINIMUM NUMBER OF HOURS

Labour laws in most provinces require employees to be paid "call-in pay," a minimum entitlement when an employee reports for work only to be sent home for lack of work. Employers are required to guarantee at least three hours of pay per day.

MATERNITY LEAVE

A part-time employee has the same right to unpaid maternity leave as a full-time employee, which usually means that she must have worked continuously for the same employer for 12 months in the year before the pregnancy to qualify.

PAID SICK LEAVE

No law requires employers to provide sick pay, and most jurisdictions do not give an employee rights to unpaid sick leave. Studies have shown that 65 percent of part-timers do not get paid sick-leave benefits.

PAID VACATIONS

In all Canadian jurisdictions, a part-timer is entitled to a paid vacation after completing one full and uninterrupted year's employment. A part-time employee would receive less vacation pay than a full-timer because the amount is calculated as a percentage of the employee's annual earnings.

PRIVATE PENSION PLANS

In almost all the provinces, and under federal law, part-time employees have the right to join their employer's private pension plan after completing 24 months of continuous employment, as long as they have earned at least 35 percent of the year's maximum pensionable earnings as established by the Canada Pension Plan. As an alternative, some provinces, including Saskatchewan, Ontario, Quebec and Prince Edward Island, consider employees eligible if they have worked 700 hours in each of two prior consecutive calendar years.

CANADA PENSION PLAN

Part-timers may contribute to the Canada Pension Plan on earnings over $3,500 and will receive a reduced pension at retirement in proportion to their contribution of premiums.

BENEFITS

Saskatchewan is the forerunner in providing part-time employees with benefits. Its legislation requires employers to provide part-time workers with the same benefits offered to full-timers, including dental care, group life insurance and prescription drugs.

EMPLOYMENT INSURANCE

Part-time workers can insure their income under the federal Employment Insurance program. However, changes made in 1996 have reduced eligibility for most part-timers.

Although a part-timer can work less than 15 hours a week to qualify, the number of hours a part-time employee needs to work in a year has increased. The qualifying period is 420 to 700 hours in a year, and varies depending on the regional unemployment rate.

ADVANCE NOTICE OF TERMINATION OF EMPLOYMENT

When an employer wishes to terminate a part-time worker's employment, the amount of notice required is usually determined by the length of service. It can vary from no advance notice for workers employed less than three months to one or two weeks' notice for those employed more than three months.

6. Unions and the Legal Right to Unionize

Labour laws protect the right of most workers to organize unions to bargain with employers for a contract regulating pay and work conditions. Each province has its own laws to control and protect unionization, and the Canada Labour Code covers federal workers in federally regulated and interprovincial businesses, such as banks, airlines and broadcasting. In 1998, the federal government amended the Canada Labour Code to (a) provide more protection for workers during the period between certification and ratification of a first collective agreement and during bargaining for a new agreement, and (b) prohibit the use of replacement workers.

Some occupational groups, however, are not guaranteed the legal right to unionize. Labour laws in some provinces do not apply to domestics, farmers, gardeners, architects, dentists, lawyers, doctors, managers, police or hospital workers.

UNFAIR LABOUR PRACTICES

Most other occupations have the right to organize, and laws against unfair labour practices prohibit employers from interfering. For instance, it is illegal for an employer to fire an employee because of union involvement or to refuse to hire a person who will not agree to approve a union. After the union has applied for certification as the employees' official bargaining agent, an employer is forbidden to change wages or working conditions without consulting it.

Unions are also prohibited from unfair labour practices, such as organizing on the employer's time or interfering with the formation of an employers' organization.

If an employer is acting contrary to law, a complaint may be registered with the provincial or federal labour relations board. The board may hold a public hearing; if it finds that the employer has engaged in an unfair labour practice, the board can order that the practice be stopped, levy a fine against the employer or compensate or reinstate an aggrieved employee. The union can ask to be certified automatically if the board determines that the employer has used undue influence to discourage employees from unionizing—for example, by offering to raise wages if workers resist forming a union.

CERTIFICATION

Otherwise, to obtain certification, the union must apply to the board. In most jurisdictions, a union needs to sign up a certain percentage of dues-paying members before applying for certification—for example, a "clear majority" in Saskatchewan, a majority in Quebec and the federal jurisdiction, more than 50 percent in New Brunswick and Nova Scotia, 55 percent in Ontario and British Columbia and 65 percent in Manitoba. After the union applies for certification, the board informs the employer, who must notify all workers that the union proposes to become their bargaining agent. The board holds a hearing to give the employer and any worker an opportunity to raise objections (1) to the union, (2) to the categories of workers that the union proposes to include in the bargaining unit, or (3) to unfair labour practices. After hearing all sides, the board decides whether or not the union truly represents the majority of employees and should be certified. The board also decides which workers will be included in the bargaining unit.

If the union is unable to sign up the required number of members to entitle it to automatic certification, the board will order a representation vote. The union will be certified in most jurisdictions if there is a majority vote in favour.

COLLECTIVE AGREEMENTS

Once the union is certified, the employer must bargain with it in good faith to reach a collective agreement. The union is legally obligated to represent all workers in the bargaining unit, whether or not they belong to the union. The union may try to negotiate a contract clause requiring all employees in the bargaining unit to pay union dues, regardless of whether they are union members, or a clause making union membership a condition of continued employment.

TRENDS

In 1995, the Ontario government tried to limit the power of Ontario unions and changed the procedures for union certification to make rules that let the government or any private company avoid keeping the collective bargaining agreements with the public service through privatization, if they took over responsibility for a government service. So, if a public servant's job is privatized, he or she may not only lose the job, but also seniority, benefits, previous wage level and the union itself. By way of contrast, public service workers are protected if their jobs are privatized in British Columbia and Saskatchewan.

In 1998, the same Ontario government passed a law, without public hearings, limiting the right of the Ontario Labour Relations Board to certify a union where the certification vote is less than 55 percent due to the fact that the employer was proven to have intimidated the employees from voting.

Other trends affecting unions are a result of changing times and social and economic upheaval. The extensive restructuring of the economy with downsizing, outsourcing and layoffs affects unionized workers, whose unions can often propose alternatives to layoffs such as job-sharing, a reduced work week and voluntary retirement. Where job losses are unavoidable, a union can negotiate for retraining and adjustment programs, and help ensure some protection for employees with seniority.

Unions can also help deal with cases of discrimination. Human rights commissions have become overburdened, understaffed and underfinanced. A union member who is a victim of discrimination may have speedier remedies available through the union, many of which have their own procedures and remedies for handling such cases. For example, a harasser may be required to apologize, undergo special training, or be suspended, transferred or demoted.

The changing nature of the workplace can affect the role of the union as well. Many workers now work from their homes, accessing their employer through computer, fax and electronic mail. If a union is in place before homeworkers are added to a company's work force, the union may be able to protect the rights of these employees, called "teleworkers," who are at risk when it comes to fair benefits, overtime and holiday pay.

7. Dismissal

An employee is not entitled to a job; an employer is entitled to hire and fire at will. However, an employee *is* entitled to either proper notice or pay for the notice period if the employer has no *legal* justification for dismissing the worker, and provided that the employer follows the laws and any union agreements in place to protect employees' rights.

There are minimum rights to notice or pay in provincial and territorial employment standards acts. Sometimes, the collective bargaining agreements deal with the issue. If the dismissal resulted from discrimination, a complaint to a human rights commission might be appropriate, and can usually proceed at the same time as a civil suit for dismissal. As there are strategic considerations for determining how to proceed, it is wise to have a strategy discussion with an employment lawyer, who will consider whether sufficient notice or pay in lieu of notice was offered, and whether a remedy is available under the common law of wrongful dismissal.

EMPLOYMENT STANDARDS LEGISLATION

Minimum legislation for statutory notice exists everywhere in Canada; in the provinces, it is usually called employment standards laws, and the federal government has the Canada Labour Code. Every province has different mandatory notice requirements.

For example, the law in Ontario provides that an employer must give written notice or salary for the notice period to an employee who has worked for the employer for more than three months. During the standard three-month probationary period, a person can be dismissed without notice or pay. When the period of employment is more than three months and less than one year, one week's notice is mandatory; when the period of employment is between one and three years, two weeks of notice; between three and four years, three weeks of notice; and so on, on the basis of one week a year up to eight years, when eight weeks of notice are required.

Notice is not required under employment standards laws in certain cases: if the employee is guilty of willful misconduct, neglect of duty or disobedience; if the layoff is temporary; if the occupation is excluded from the law; or if the job is for a limited term or task.

In Ontario, employees are entitled to collect their pay for working during the notice period and their vacation pay in lieu of time off (4 percent of wages in Ontario) within seven days of termination. Government investigators will enforce an employee's rights.

Additional obligations may apply to mass terminations. Ontario, for example, entitles employees who number 50 or more but less than 200 who are terminated all at once to at least eight weeks of written notice; if 200 or more but less than 500 are terminated, 12 weeks of written notice must be given; if more than 500 are terminated, 16 weeks of notice must be given. Ontario also requires substantial severance pay benefits for long-time employees of large employers: In addition to the standard termination pay, an employee who has worked at least five years for an employer with a payroll of $2.5 million or more is entitled to receive a week's pay for each year worked, up to a maximum of 26 weeks' pay.

An employer who does not meet her or his legal obligation, or who intimidates an employee who has complained about a breach of the Employment Standards Act of Ontario, may be penalized with a fine of up to $50,000 and/or six months in jail.

An employee in any Canadian jurisdiction except Ontario may complain under an employment standards act and, at the same time, sue in court for breach of contract and wrongful dismissal under the common law. Ontario amended its law in December 1996, to take away the right of employees to complain under the Employment Standards Act and also sue for breach of contract and wrongful dismissal under the common law. Although that government has been replaced, the rule remains enshrined in law. The ban on pursuing both remedies applies even if the amount of money owed to the employee is greater than the amount that can be ordered under the Act. The courts applying the common law usually expect employers to give longer periods of notice and more generous severance pay than is provided under employment standards legislation.

An employer often does not offer notice or severance pay according to the common-law standard without the intervention of a lawyer or the courts. These matters are often settled out of court.

UNION GRIEVANCE

A union collective agreement may include guarantees of job security, except for those fired for "just cause," as defined in the collective agreement. Employees should follow established union grievance procedures before deciding whether to approach employment standards investigators, who may otherwise refuse to prosecute. In most cases, a union grievance and a lawsuit for wrongful dismissal can happen at the same time.

HUMAN RIGHTS LAWS

If an employee's dismissal results from discrimination on a prohibited ground, the employee can complain to a human rights commission without the assistance of a lawyer. If a commission's investigators confirm discrimination, a commission may order the payment of wages the employee would have earned had the dismissal not occurred, and the employee's reinstatement in the job if requested and appropriate. In some cases, monetary compensation may include an award for mental anguish. An employer who has contravened a human rights code or who does not go along with a commission's board of inquiry order may be found guilty of an offence and on conviction be liable to a fine.

A complaint to a human rights commission may have to be disposed of before a civil suit for wrongful dismissal can be brought.

THE COMMON LAW OF WRONGFUL DISMISSAL

A lawsuit for wrongful dismissal may be necessary if an employee is advised by a lawyer that he is entitled to more notice (or severance pay in lieu of notice) than his employer is offering. This lawsuit is available only if the employee is sure that his employer had no "just cause" (as it is legally defined) to fire him.

An employer who has just cause may dismiss an employee without notice or severance pay, but must prove just cause—not always an easy or straightforward thing to do.

The most common reason for firing an employee is poor job performance. But mere dissatisfaction with the employee's work is not enough to justify dismissal for cause. The employer must show that the employee is incompetent or that the work is persistently and significantly substandard.

Even then, the employer must give the employee a clear written warning that she or he will be terminated if his or her performance does not improve. The warning must spell out the required standards of performance, explain what the employee can do to improve, provide a reasonable opportunity to do so and leave no doubt that the job is in jeopardy if the employee fails to measure up.

An employer is usually expected to provide a series of increasingly serious warnings.

Chronic lateness or excessive absenteeism may justify dismissal, except if it is due to a temporary, even if lengthy, illness. Dismissal is justified, however, if an illness is permanent and keeps an employee off the job.

Persistent serious misconduct (rather than a single, isolated incident) may also justify dismissal. Examples of this kind of behaviour include insolence, willful refusal to obey a proper order, arguments with customers and alcohol or drug abuse that affects job performance. Again, the employee must be warned that if the misconduct continues, the job will be in jeopardy.

In a 1997 B.C. case, an employer was justified in firing a 17-year employee because he repeatedly slept on the job and lied about it. His dishonesty did him in; the lying was considered a breach of his duty of faithful service to his employer.

Immediate dismissal without warnings is justified when an employer discovers that the employee is stealing, or engaging in other forms of fraud or dishonesty—such as breaching rules of confidentiality, carrying on a business in competition with the employer or taking part in some other conflict of interest. The employer need not have enough evidence to support a criminal conviction where the standard of proof is "beyond a reasonable doubt," but need only establish the facts on a "balance of probabilities"—a less stringent standard of proof.

An employee found to have sexually harassed another employee may be fired on the spot for cause.

There are a number of cases when an employee is entitled to notice or severance pay even when dismissed: if the employee has been dismissed because of a negative attitude or personality conflict, so long as the employee's work and the employer's business have not been adversely affected by the employee's behaviour; if a corporate reorganization has caused redundancy or lack of work; if the employee has refused to accept a unilateral change in important working conditions, such as a geographical transfer, change of position or reduction in pay or hours of work, and his or her refusal is considered reasonable.

Extra-marital affairs with co-workers may not be grounds to fire an employee, even if the employee is given warnings that they are unacceptable. An Ontario court awarded a lothario 12 months' salary instead of notice, ruling that his employer had no cause to fire him, that there was no evidence the affairs adversely affected the man's job performance or the company and that the affairs were "consensual," private, and not on company time.

Sometimes, an employee's refusal to accept a change in pay or hours of work may be regarded as insubordination and may mean the employee can be fired for cause. In a recent decision, an employee who quit because he had trouble adjusting to changes in his work environment and working for a manager 25 years his junior sued for "constructive dismissal" (which means the change in working conditions was so unacceptable that it was the same as being fired). He was refused compensation. The judge commented that ". . . employers, facing the market conditions that now prevail, must be able to expect flexibility from employees."

On the other hand, an employee may be justified in considering such changes tantamount to dismissal. In the Supreme Court of Canada's first ruling on constructive dismissal in 1997, a former sales manager was given $150,000 compensation for wrongful dismissal because the essential terms of his employment contract were changed when his employer, as part of a major reorganization, demoted him and changed his method of pay from salary plus commission to straight commission.

If the employee resigns, there is no severance pay. But the resignation must be unequivocal and be accepted by the employer. If the employer responds to the resignation with "You can leave now," he will have, in the eyes of the law, fired the employee, who may then be entitled to severance pay. In a 1986 Ontario case, an employee quit, giving six months' notice. The employer tried to have the resignation take effect in two months. The employee sued and got an order for six months' pay.

WHAT IS REASONABLE NOTICE AND REASONABLE SEVERANCE PAY?

Unless the employer is justified in dismissing an employee without notice or severance pay, the employer must provide reasonable notice, or severance pay in lieu of notice. To determine "reasonable notice" or severance pay in lieu of notice, the courts have developed guidelines based on the nature of the job and level of responsibility, length of service, the age of the employee and the availability of similar employment, and the employee's experience and qualifications. These guidelines mean that the higher up a person is on the executive ladder, the more highly skilled the occupation or the better the employment contract, the greater the severance pay. The most a court usually gives is about 24 months' pay. But a court has been known to go higher on rare

occasions. For example, in 1996, the New Brunswick Court of Appeal ruled that pay for 28 months' notice was appropriate when a 57-year-old executive editor with 36 years' service was unjustly dismissed.

A case in Ontario tested whether a clerical worker should receive the same severance rights as an executive. The worker, a 55-year-old insurance underwriter with a Grade 12 education and 29 years of service, was offered nine months' salary when she was dismissed as redundant. She sued successfully for 20 months' pay—what a senior manager might get—and the trial judge sympathized that "the loss of a job is almost always a devastating experience, financially and emotionally, for any employee." The employer appealed to the Ontario Court of Appeal, which disagreed with the trial judge and reduced the award to 12 months. But in a different Ontario Court of Appeal decision, the Court clarified that there is no 12-month ceiling on awards for non-managerial employees.

If an employer induced an employee to leave a previous job to work for her or him, and soon after, or even several years later, dismisses the employee, this "inducement" factor may lengthen the notice period. Important factors are whether the employer actively pursued the employee, who perhaps had not applied for the job; what promises the employer made; whether the employee's prior job was secure; whether the employee relocated; and what the employee's future job chances are.

The leading case on this issue has become abbreviated as "the Wallace Factor" for the name of the person who took the case forward. Jack Wallace had taken on a sales job at a company when he was 45 years old, only after the company promised him a job until retirement. The company nevertheless fired him when he was 59 and tried to argue just cause, which it never proved. The case went to the Supreme Court of Canada, which in 1997 ordered payment for 24 months' pay in lieu of notice instead of the 15 months' ordered by the Manitoba Court of Appeal, because of the bad faith shown by the employer.

WHAT IS REQUIRED OF THE EMPLOYEE?

An employee's claim for severance pay is based on the actual loss suffered within the appropriate notice period. Employees have a duty to mitigate their damages and make their best efforts to find new employment. If an employee is legally entitled to six months' notice, and succeeds in finding another job at similar remuneration after four months, then the claim is limited to the four months of actual unemployment. If, however, the new job pays less than the old one, the employee will not only be entitled to severance pay for the four-month period of unemployment, but may also seek the difference in remuneration between the two jobs for the remaining two months of the notice period.

OTHER ENTITLEMENT BESIDES NOTICE

Not only lost pay is at stake. Claims can also be successfully made for the value of lost benefits such as medical coverage, pension contributions and vacation pay for the notice period, missed bonuses and overtime if they were routine, and prejudgment interest.

However, an employee is usually not able to get continued coverage of premiums for short- and long-term disability insurance. Some employers offer terminated employees what has come to be called "outplacement counselling" to assist them in locating alternate employment and in dealing with any psychological distress from the termination.

Several 1995 decisions of the B.C. Court of Appeal have ruled that workers who are fired while receiving disability pay from insurance can continue to collect this disability pay on top of severance pay. Another B.C. case ruled that employees can collect pension benefits on top of severance pay if they are fired and choose to take early retirement.

Normally, an employee is compensated only for loss of pay. But if, for example, a wrongfully dismissed employee was publicly humiliated by her employer, or falsely accused of theft, then she may be entitled to damages for emotional stress.

In extreme cases, punitive and exemplary damages have been ordered in addition to severance. A B.C. court in 1993 awarded a fired employee the sum of $75,000 punitive damages and $50,000 exemplary or aggravated damages to punish the employer for its malicious conduct. The employer had publicly lied in saying the employee was being fired for cause when the employer had (and knew it had) no just cause. The case sent a message to employers that the courts would not condone frivolous allegations of just cause for dismissal.

A dismissed employee would be wise to speak to a lawyer before accepting a severance package. A lawyer can help assess the fairness of the package and the likely outcome of a lawsuit compared to the legal costs. If the employee does not like the offer, he should not delay; his strongest claim is while he remains unemployed. His lawyer may be able to negotiate a settlement with his employer or, if that fails, start a lawsuit. Most wrongful dismissal suits are settled out of court.

If an employee accepts a severance package and signs a release without being given time to consider, and without seeking independent legal advice, the release may not be binding on the employee in certain cases: if the terms are unconscionable, if an inequality of bargaining power existed between the employer and employee or if the employee was not allowed to get independent legal advice (ILA). In an Ottawa case in 1995, a severance agreement was set aside because the employer pressured the employee to sign the deal right away or the terms would change, and the employee had no opportunity to get ILA. A sensible employer will expect an employee to get ILA.

An employee may not be able to collect severance if she lost her job because the employer went bankrupt. Decisions of both the Ontario and Alberta courts in 1995 ruled that an employee in these circumstances cannot make a claim against the Trustee in Bankruptcy for severance pay. Ontario has in place a fund to provide employees laid off by bankrupt companies with limited termination pay and wages of up to $5,000 each.

People who work on contract—an increasingly common form of working relationship—may well wonder to what extent they are protected by wrongful dismissal laws. Often the fact of a contract relationship will protect the employer from wrongful dismissal claims because workers will not challenge the meaning of this relationship. They assume that the contract places them outside employment standards laws and common-law rules affecting "employees."

But this is not always so. Sometimes contract workers are entitled to notice of termination or pay in lieu thereof, no matter what the contract stipulates. It all depends on the reality of the working relationship: If the boss controlled how the work was done, if he owned the tools of work, if he took the risk of loss and chance of profit and if he completely integrated the worker into the organization, the law would likely regard the worker as an employee, and require legal notice provisions to be followed during the term of the contract. For example, in 1999, an Ontario court ruled that when a person working full-time for 15 uninterrupted one-year contracts was fired, she was entitled to 12 months' salary in lieu of notice.

8. Forced Retirement

Retirement became a critical issue in the early 1990s as the economy and the job market worsened. Some workers voluntarily took early retirement, sometimes accompanied by financial incentives and buy-out packages. Some were forced into early retirement because, after a layoff, they could not find another job. Others planned to use the inflationary wealth they assumed would continue uninterrupted to pay for their retirement, but no longer had the means to stop working.

With a relatively improved economy, and higher employment more recently, some older people are deferring retirement. According to a 2003 report from Statistics Canada, the median retirement age was about 65 from the mid-1970s to the mid-1980s, and then it dropped quickly until

1997, when it stabilized at a median of age 61. In 2003, this changed direction. The median retirement age for men became 63.3 and for women 60.4.

Many people want to continue working longer than their employer wants them to, and are forced out by either mandatory retirement policies or pressure from the employer. The question is, does the law give them a choice?

Quebec Law: Quebec law protects its people best from forced retirement. The Quebec Labour Standards Act prohibits compulsory retirement based on age or number of years of service, regardless of what is stipulated in other Quebec legislation, a collective agreement, the employee's contributory retirement plan or "the common practice of his employer." If an employee is eligible to retire but wants to continue working, he or she may do so for as long as his or her abilities allow. If the person earns less money than before, perhaps because of a decision to switch to part-time work, he or she may still claim the company pension, as long as the total income received is not more than his or her salary was before the new arrangement took effect.

Elsewhere: In every jurisdiction in Canada, there are human rights laws protecting a worker from discrimination based on age, including harassment because of age. Manitoba, Quebec, Nova Scotia, Prince Edward Island, the Northwest Territories and Nunavut, Yukon Territory, and the federal jurisdiction do not specify the age that is protected, but elsewhere the age is defined. In Alberta, Saskatchewan and Ontario, a person must be over 18 to rely on this law and (except in Alberta) under 65; in British Columbia and Newfoundland and Labrador, between 19 and 65; and in New Brunswick, over 19.

This means that in British Columbia, Saskatchewan, Ontario, and Newfoundland and Labrador, policies requiring retirement at age 65 are not considered discrimination based on age. In 2004, the Ontario government announced that it is considering abolishing mandatory retirement.

If a person can prove age discrimination in employment, she or he should register a complaint with the local human rights commission.

The Canadian Human Rights Act—which applies to employees of the federal government, Crown corporations and federally regulated private enterprises such as airlines and banks—permits certain exceptions to the prohibition of discrimination on the basis of age. It allows employers to force workers to retire at the normal age of retirement for employees in similar positions, on the basis that it is a bona fide occupational requirement, or at a maximum age limit for the position that has been set by a law or regulation.

WHEN IS MANDATORY RETIREMENT LEGAL?

When is it reasonable for laws to intervene and require a worker to retire, whatever the age? It is undesirable to risk keeping people in jobs if they have become less competent, particularly if public safety is at stake. The question is whether all workers should be forced to retire at a certain age or whether each individual should be judged on his or her own health and capabilities. For example, under the federal law some workers, such as pilots, have been forced to retire at 60 regardless of their physical or mental capabilities.

In one case, the Supreme Court of Canada ruled that firefighters in a Toronto suburb could not be forced to retire at 60. The court did not find sufficient risk among some 60-year-old firefighters to warrant retirement of all 60-year-old firefighters; the policy was declared discriminatory.

However, the Supreme Court of Canada in 1995 overruled the Ontario Human Rights Commission, the Ontario Divisional Court and the Ontario Court of Appeal, and ruled that a mandatory retirement policy of age 60 in the Stratford, Ontario, police force was a "bona fide occupational requirement"—meaning that the rule was not adopted for a discriminatory reason, but to enforce a legitimate policy to require police officers to be less than 60. The Court stated that testing each officer on an individual basis was not feasible.

In 1994, ten members of the Canadian Armed Forces were reinstated and the armed forces were told they could not automatically retire people at age 55. The Federal Court upheld a decision of a Canadian Human Rights Commission tribunal, ruling that individual testing of fitness for duty was not only feasible, but already taking place routinely.

Many of the cases that come before human rights hearings deal with group discrimination against employees such as firefighters, police, pilots and soldiers because of mandatory retirement policies. Individual complaints are different, and a 1994 Quebec case is typical of the problems faced by older workers in our downsizing, restructuring job world.

Mr. Georges Blais was fired at the age of 59 by the Quebec mining company for which he had worked for 29 years. The given reason was that the company was restructuring. In fact, Blais was able to show the Quebec human rights tribunal that he suffered age discrimination, and that other management employees aged 52 and older were dismissed from their employment in disproportionately higher numbers than younger employees. The tribunal stated that the company could have relocated Blais elsewhere within the company if restructuring were the real issue, and ordered the company to pay him $112,000 in lost wages. But that was not all. The tribunal pointed out that Blais had dedicated an important part of his life to the company as a competent and energetic employee, and that he suffered serious harm to his dignity and psychological well-being; in light of this consideration, the tribunal ordered the company to pay $15,000 for what they called "moral damages."

However, not all decisions made because of age will be ruled discriminatory. For example, in 1995 a 60-year-old applied to the Ottawa-Carleton Regional Transit Commission to be hired as a bus driver and was rejected. When he alleged age discrimination to the Ontario Human Rights Commission, it dismissed his complaint, saying that the Transit Commission was justified. It ruled that requiring a new employee to be younger was a bona fide occupational requirement, and that hiring a 60-year-old was a safety and economic risk.

Under the equality rights provisions of the Charter of Rights and Freedoms, it is unconstitutional not to give every individual equal protection and benefit of the law without discrimination based on age.

Any workers who feel victimized by age discrimination should complain to the human rights commission in their province or territory, or to the federal commission if they are under its jurisdiction.

D. WORKING CONDITIONS

1. Air Quality in the Workplace

An employee has the basic legal right to safe working conditions. The federal government and all provinces and territories have health and safety laws to keep certain pollutants at a nonhazardous level. These pollutants include some contaminants contained in tobacco smoke, such as carbon monoxide. In fact, tobacco smoke is the largest source of indoor air pollution, and contains more than 50 known cancer-causing substances. Other pollutants include ozone from photocopiers, asbestos fibre from building insulation and formaldehyde from construction materials. Building ventilation systems are rarely adequate to clean the pollutants from the indoor air.

In some provinces and federal agencies, employees facing health hazards may be legally entitled to refuse to work or ask for a change of assignment. In one instance, an Air Canada employee refused to work in a smoke-filled job site; the airline was ordered under the Canada Labour Code to provide proper ventilation and to enforce a no-smoking ban. The Canada Labour Code was amended in 1999 to improve occupational health and safety in workplaces under federal jurisdiction. It established three fundamental employee rights: to know about hazards in the workplace, to participate in correcting those hazards, and to refuse dangerous work. Employees should check the laws applicable to their own province or workplace before they refuse to work.

A 2004 amendment to the federal Criminal Code makes clear the responsibility of an organization's executives to provide a safe and healthy workplace. It establishes rules for criminal liability of organizations for the acts of their representatives. It establishes a legal duty for all persons who direct work to take reasonable steps to ensure the safety of workers and the public, and provides sentencing and probation options.

Twenty years ago, I wrote that no province banned smoking in the workplace. There have been significant changes in this area as more and more people have become aware of the effects of smoking and other pollutants on indoor air quality and on the workers' health. To combat the problem of second-hand smoke, by-laws that limit smoking in the workplace now govern many cities. Many provinces have passed smoking-in-the-workplace laws. Manitoba in 2004 passed the strictest law in the country, banning smoking in *all* public places and indoor workplaces. New Brunswick has a similar law and Ontario is planning to follow suit by 2007. Saskatchewan has plans to do so in 2005. Partial smoking bans were legislated in 2003 by Nova Scotia, Prince Edward Island and British Columbia.

Many employers are voluntarily establishing smoke-free workplaces and permitting employees to smoke only in certain non-work areas. But restricting rather than banning smoking may not be entirely effective; according to some U.S. studies, it takes over three hours to rid the air in an entire office building of the smoke of one cigarette. If existing laws do not help reduce pollutants such as cigarette smoke, an employer may decide to eliminate the source by hiring only non-smokers or people who will not smoke on the job. This prerequisite for employment does not contravene existing human rights legislation.

Many workplaces have health and safety committees, made up of employer and employee representatives, which monitor and implement policies to provide better air quality in the workplace.

A person who becomes ill as a direct and provable result of a polluted work environment may be eligible to receive disability pay if covered by workers' compensation, or may be able to sue the employer for compensation. Workers' compensation may help if the non-smoker has an allergy so severe that he or she is unable to work. The Ontario Workers' Compensation Board paid the claim of a woman who developed bronchial asthma because of concentrations of tobacco and dust in her work area that her employer's ventilation system could not handle.

On May 1, 2004, the Workers' Compensation Board for the Northwest Territories and Nunavut banned smoking in all enclosed businesses and work sites in both territories, including bars. This took precedence over and went further than the law passed by Nunavut's legislature six months earlier, which had banned smoking in all public places.

See also the section on Mother's Work in Chapter 2.

2. Sexual Harassment

Sexual harassment has developed into a serious and persistent workplace issue.

The Supreme Court of Canada defined sexual harassment in the workplace "as unwelcome conduct of a sexual nature that detrimentally affects the work environment or leads to adverse job-related consequences" for its victims. The Court ruled that legal prohibitions against sexual discrimination include sexual harassment.

The case was a landmark when it was decided in 1989, and has been followed as a precedent or mentioned as a guide in at least 153 later cases across Canada. The Women's Legal Education and Action Fund (LEAF) was the intervenor.

In the case in question, two waitresses in a Winnipeg restaurant had complained that a supervisor made persistent unwelcome sexual advances to them. This harassment caused one of the women to quit her job, while the other was fired for objecting to the supervisor's behaviour. Their employer did not take the women's complaints seriously and tolerated the supervisor's conduct.

In its ruling, the Supreme Court affirmed the responsibility of the employer if he or she allows one employee to harass another employee sexually. Then Chief Justice Brian Dickson stated, "When sexual harassment occurs in the workplace, it is an abuse of both economic and sexual power," and ordered the employer to pay one waitress $480 in lost wages and $3,500 in damages, and the other $3,000 in lost wages and $3,000 in damages.

In stating the reasons for the decision, Mr. Justice Dickson also said:

Sexual harassment is a demeaning practice, one that constitutes a profound affront to the dignity of the employees forced to endure it. By requiring an employee to contend with unwelcome sexual actions or explicit sexual demands, sexual harassment in the workplace attacks the dignity and self-respect of the victim, both as an employee and as a human being.

In most jurisdictions, sexual harassment is prohibited; where it is not specifically proscribed, the prohibition against sexual discrimination would, in light of this Supreme Court ruling, be interpreted to include sexual harassment.

Sexual harassment may include the following behaviour by an employer, manager, supervisor or co-worker: the demand for and expectation of sexual relations; intimidation with verbal abuse or threats, jokes and innuendos; leering and other gestures; unwelcome invitations or suggestive photographs; touching, patting, pinching, or other unwanted physical contact, including physical assault.

An innocent bid for social contact that does not threaten employment is not interpreted as sexual harassment. In one case, a human rights adjudicator put it succinctly when he said that "an invitation to dinner is not an invitation to a complaint."

Most cases heard by human rights boards of inquiry have been ones in which the complainants were directly or indirectly led to believe that their continued employment or promotion depended on sexual services, and often the employees were fired or denied promotions when they refused.

If an employee submits to sexual acts out of personal fear or fear of losing the job, there may still be a case against the boss. The authorities will have to be convinced that the employee's participation was involuntary. In one such case, a female supervisor of a team of cleaners with the Department of National Defence was sexually harassed by her foreman while she was on probation. She told him to stop and said his advances were unwelcome, but he persisted and threatened her job. Although she gave in, the human rights tribunal found that she did so out of fear and intimidation. The parties settled the cleaner's claim for lost wages out of court at a reported $80,000 for three years of paid leave and tuition. A tribunal added $5,000 for pain and suffering (the maximum available for pain and suffering under the Canadian Human Rights Act) and ordered a written apology to be posted for other employees to see. It took 14 years for the woman's complaint to be finally resolved.

Verbal harassment can amount to sexual harassment. A clerk in a federal department was harassed by her supervisor—he repeatedly invited her for drinks, asked for dates, telephoned her at home and made sexual comments and suggestions. When she refused his advances, he became abusive and threatened to demote her, yelled at her constantly and even went so far as to tell co-workers that he was having an affair with her and she was not doing her job properly. He was dismissed as a result of her complaint, but she had had to use sick leave, take unpaid leave and eventually quit because of the harassment. She was awarded $20,000 in compensation for lost wages, pain and suffering.

A deck hand on a tugboat was sexually harassed by the skipper, who grabbed the deck hand's genitals several times. When he complained to the corporation that owned the tugboat, it did nothing, and the complainant was eventually fired. He was awarded $2,000 for hurt feelings and $1,760 for lost wages.

A 1990 Ontario case extended the prohibition against sexual harassment to include remarks implying sexual unattractiveness. The case concerned an office worker who had been subjected to relentless taunts and insults by a male co-worker over a 14-year period. The co-worker frequently disparaged her heavyset figure by making neighing sounds or commenting, as she walked about the office, "Waddle, waddle, waddle." Often he would say, "Swish, swish, swish," imitating the sound of her pantyhose when her legs rubbed together as she walked. He would refer to her as a "fat cow," and called the complainant and another female co-worker the "fridge sisters." Sometimes, he whistled the tune to the line, "Slow down, you move too fast," from a song, to sarcastically imply that she worked too slowly. On one day, she counted 36 such instances.

The woman frequently complained to her supervisor about the co-worker's behaviour. Since both employees did their work satisfactorily, however, the supervisor dismissed the problem as simply a personality conflict.

It was a personality conflict that reduced her at times to tears, but she could not afford to leave her job. When the situation deteriorated to the point where she developed migraine headaches, she finally resigned and registered a complaint of sexual harassment with the Ontario Human Rights Commission.

The Ontario Human Rights Code declares that everyone has the right to freedom from sexual harassment by co-workers, supervisors or employers. In the Ontario law, harassment is defined as vexatious comment or conduct that is known, or ought reasonably to be known, to be unwelcome.

The co-worker admitted to "bugging" and "teasing" the complainant but insisted he was simply trying to make her more productive. The Commission's board of inquiry rejected his argument. It decided that gender-based insults about an employee's personal appearance constitute sexual harassment just as much as unwanted sexual advances do. Furthermore, because of the harasser's often-stated opinion that women belonged at home with their children, his apparent bias against other women in the office and the absence of any other possible motive, the board was convinced that he harassed her because she was a woman.

She was awarded $48,273 in compensation, which included $43,273 for her lost earnings and $5,000 for her hurt feelings. The co-worker, the company and the supervisor who had done nothing to stop the harassment were all held liable to pay this amount.

In a unique B.C. case in 1997, the parents of a 13-year-old boy who masturbated in front of his live-in nanny had to compensate her because they did not provide a harassment-free workplace.

REMEDIES

If an employee receives unwelcome propositions from someone who is in a position of authority, she or he should say "No" immediately and unambiguously. To prove that the answer was No at an early stage, it may be advisable for the employee to send a formal written protest to the harasser, by registered mail for proof of receipt, and to keep a copy. If sexual advances persist, and it is clear that the employee's refusal puts some aspect of employment in jeopardy, she or he should tell the harasser's supervisor or another supervisor. The employer is required by law in most jurisdictions to investigate and prevent further harassment. Indeed, an employer has a duty to provide a harassment-free workplace.

If the employer does not conduct an investigation, or the employee is dissatisfied with the results, she or he should complain without delay to the appropriate human rights commission. A board of inquiry may hold a hearing, and if the complaint is verified, the board has the authority to order that the harassment stop, and the harasser and/or the harasser's boss pay a fine. Few harassers have been ordered fired. Sometimes, a board of inquiry has recommended that the offender be transferred and/or required to attend a training session on sexual harassment; sometimes, the harasser is required to apologize to the complainant.

A board may also order the employer to compensate the complainant for lost wages or mental anguish. To determine compensation for mental anguish, the board considers the psychological impact of the sexual harassment and whether the harassment was verbal or physical, short- or long-term, frequent or sporadic.

Other avenues of complaint include a grievance to the union in unionized employment, or a lawsuit against the employer or boss. A wrongful dismissal suit may be fitting if the employee was forced to leave the job due to the harassment, and a proven harasser can be fired for cause.

3. Other Harassment

Harassment on any prohibited ground is considered a form of discrimination. Human rights codes generally prohibit discrimination in employment, accommodation and the provision of goods, services and facilities based on race or colour, religion or creed, sex (including pregnancy or childbirth), age, disability, marital status, sexual orientation, family status, ancestry or place of origin and, in some places, political belief, dependence on alcohol or drugs, pardoned conviction, source of income (Ontario bans discrimination in accommodation on the grounds of receipt of public assistance), and (only in Quebec) language. Accordingly, people who are harassed on any of these grounds may register a complaint with the provincial, territorial or federal human rights commission.

Harassment can take the form of threats, intimidation, verbal abuse, or unwelcome remarks or jokes about such subjects as race, religion, disability or age. It can be the display of racist or other offensive pictures or posters. The harasser can be a boss, a landlord or someone providing a service.

Here are some examples.

A black employee of Canadian Pacific Rail complained of harassment because of his race and colour. Among the incidents he reported was one in which his locker and its contents were destroyed with black paint. When CP Rail became aware of the incident, the supervisor did everything possible to investigate, but was unable to discover the culprit. CP Rail had a clear policy in place to prevent discrimination, and publicly regarded the incident as reprehensible and criminal. The Canadian human rights tribunal that investigated the complaint held that the employer had met the requirements of the Canadian Human Rights Act, and was not responsible for the harassment in that case.

A black part-time store cashier in a "racially poisoned work environment," where the manager made inappropriate jokes and comments based on racial stereotyping, received $3,000 compensation for pain and suffering and injured feelings.

A native Canadian who was subjected to racial harassment over a ten-year period in the form of frequent slurs, jokes and differential treatment was awarded $2,500 for injury to his feelings and self-respect.

Two Métis passengers were asked by the driver of a long-distance bus they were boarding whether or not they had been drinking. The driver also searched their hand baggage. There was no indication that the two men had been drinking, and other passengers were not searched or asked this question. The bus company agreed that the driver had used bad judgment, and a settlement was reached with the help of the Canadian Human Rights Commission. The passengers received letters of apology and travel vouchers, and the driver got counselling on dealing with passengers.

An individual with a mental disability, who was able to do his work well in a baking facility, was harassed by his foreman, who called him "stupid" and "dummy," criticized his work unjustifiably in front of other employees and threatened to fire him. The Ontario board of inquiry ruled that the foreman engaged in the harassing conduct because the employee was mentally disabled, and found both the company and the foreman liable to pay $3,889 in compensation.

In 2004, Quebec became the first province to outlaw workplace bullying, which was described as a corporate form of schoolyard bullying. The amendment to the Quebec Labour Standards Act prohibits "vexatious behaviour" that takes the form of repeated insults, vulgar remarks or gestures that are offensive, demeaning and undermine a person's self-esteem. The law applies only to non-union employees in provincially regulated businesses. The law gives the province's labour standards board the

authority to order fines, punitive damages and the reinstatement of employees.

4. Working and Child Care

Working parents need care for their children during their working hours. Employers and government policy-makers, however, have operated on the assumption that this fact of life was not their problem. The law's involvement in child care is generally confined to setting provincial standards of care required for child-care facilities and programs, both in the larger day-care centres and, in almost all provinces, in regulated family (home) day care.

There are various types of child care: *group day-care centres* that are inspected and licensed by provincial governments; *licensed home day care*, where caregivers are supervised in their own homes by licensed agencies or by provincial or municipal agencies; *informal care* in unlicensed and unsupervised homes with a friend, relative or neighbour; *nanny care* by a person who is hired as an employee to live in or live out, but who cares only for the children in the home.

The provincial standards of care establish the maximum children-to-caregiver ratio at various ages that a facility is able to take in. For example, in Ontario a caregiver may look after no more than three babies 18 months or younger, or five toddlers aged 18 months to two-and-a-half years, or eight preschoolers aged two-and-a-half to five years.

The provinces also regulate training of day-care workers, the amount and type of food served to children, the toys, equipment and space needed, both indoors and outdoors. If a parent is concerned about the standards in his or her child's day care, he or she should contact the provincial child-care branch responsible for supervision.

Governments also have a system of subsidies for parents of children in licensed day care who cannot afford to pay day-care fees. Depending on the province, parents must meet an income or needs test. The federal government, which at one time contributed substantially to the provinces for the provision of day-care services, reduced transfer payments in the 1990s; some provinces handled this reduction by passing on the day-care problem to the municipalities, which in some provinces represent the level of government most directly involved in providing actual child-care services. The end result was a reduction in subsidies to families. Only 31 percent of child-care spaces were subsidized in 1998.

Governments have been asked for many years to establish universal, accessible, quality day care for the welfare of children in Canada. However, people who set social policy for governments acted on their belief that a mother is "employed" solely in the care of her own children. As long ago as 1970, the Royal Commission on the Status of Women took exception to this view: "The time is past when society can refuse to provide community child services in the hope of dissuading mothers from having their children and going to work."

It is an indisputable fact that most parents are employed outside the home these days. In 2000, 60 percent of women aged 15 and over were in the labour force, up from 42 percent in 1976 and 24 percent in 1951.

Sixty-five percent of all children under 13 had mothers in the paid labour force in 1998, an increase from 57 percent just six years earlier. In 1998, 61 percent of women with their youngest child under age six and 71.9 percent of those with their youngest between age six and 15 were employed in the paid labour force. An even more significant fact for policy-makers is the *growth* in the labour force participation rate of women with young children. Between 1976 and 1999, the participation rate of women with a youngest child aged three to five grew from 37 to 66 percent. When the youngest child was under age three, the rate more than doubled—from 28 percent in 1976 to 61 percent in 1999.

Moreover, dual-earner families have supplanted the "traditional" family composed of a breadwinning husband and a stay-at-home wife. Since 1976, when 57 percent of the families were traditional and 36 percent were dual earners, society has changed; in 1997, traditional families comprised only 26 percent of families, while dual earners had increased to 62 percent.

Despite lobbying efforts by parents and child-care activist groups, and despite convincing research from experts proving that good quality day care enhances a child's development and gives the child a better chance of becoming a successful, well-adjusted adult, successive governments have left a trail of broken promises over more than 20 years, to provide significantly more day-care places than currently exist.

However, it is also true that the availability of day care has improved significantly since statistics began being collected in 1971; in that year, there were 17,391 regulated day-care spaces in Canada for children under 13 years of age compared to 394,291 in 1994, 516,734 in 1998 and 593,430 in 2001.

But there are still not enough spaces. Compare this to the fact that 3,308,700 children under age 13 in Canada in 2001 had mothers in the paid labour force, and it is clear that most of the children of full-time working parents are not in regulated (that is, centre-based or family day care) facilities. ("Full-time working parents" includes two-parent families in which both parents work full-time as well as families with a lone parent who works full-time.)

The number of day-care places does not meet the need because not only has the amount of each subsidy been decreased, but the overall number of subsidies has been reduced. It is questionable whether parents can cope with paying the full cost of day care, since many of them are also facing the economic consequences of government and corporate downsizing in their jobs.

Quebec is the exception. Quebec provides universal day care for seven dollars a day for all children under age 13, and offers the most generous government-subsidized plan in North America. The plan is publicly funded, rather than subsidized on an individual basis.

The trend elsewhere, where funding is available, is for governments to put money in the hands of parents and expect them to find and pay for child care with it, instead of supporting child-care programs and creating day-care spaces in the accredited facilities.

A good day-care experience serves the interests of both children and parents. Research is clear that quality child care offers children from families that have suffered severe economic, social and psychological deprivation what may be their only chance of overcoming these obstacles. U.S. studies have concluded that one dollar spent on quality preschool care saves seven dollars in the long term on police, welfare, social services and prisons. But even for ordinary families with minimal levels of dysfunction, a day-care facility can give a child opportunities for learning and socialization that cannot be matched in the home.

Parents can urge their employers to set up workplace day-care centres and their schools to set up child-care programs. They can also participate in community-run day-care co-operatives, and can pressure governments to create more day-care spaces.

In 2004 the federal Liberal government promised a significant change in policy and funding in the platform on which it won re-election. It pledged to invest $5 billion over five years for a national system of early learning and child care. Moreover, the ministers of social development across Canada agreed in principle that there should be a high-quality system that is universal, inclusive and accessible, with strong accountability, measurable goals, provincial-territorial flexibility and that focuses on helping children reach developmental objectives. While this country is among the wealthiest nations on earth, a 2004 study by the Organization for Economic Cooperation and Development pointed out that Canada (with the exception of Quebec) has an inadequate, fragmented and underfunded patchwork of early learning and child-care services, which compares extremely unfavourably with many other developed nations.

Dr. Marie Bountrogianni, Ontario's minister for services of children and youth, herself a child psychologist and former child-care director, announced in 2004 an ambitious "Best Start" plan that would revolutionize child care in Ontario. The plan attempts to integrate the education and care of young children. The preliminary goal is to create a full day of learning and care for four- and five-year-olds, with 50,000 new spots by 2007, and the long-term goal is to provide full day care for all children from age two and a half upwards, within 15 years. Ontario intends to develop a college of early childhood educators to self-regulate and provide professional development for child-care workers. It also plans to overhaul the Day Nurseries Act, which now focuses primarily on health and safety guidelines, to add guidelines for an early-learning curriculum.

5. Taxation of Child-Care Costs

Tax law allows the parent with the lower net income before child-care expenses to deduct from income the lowest of three amounts: the actual amount spent on child care; two-thirds of earned income (which is generally employment or business income); or the total of $7,000 for each child six years and under (or over six if disabled) on December 31 of that year, and $4,000 for each eligible child aged seven to 16. The actual amount spent on day care is not deductible.

In addition, there is a child tax benefit in the form of a tax-free cheque to help working parents, or the parent primarily responsible for the children. The amount varies with income. The child tax benefit amount payable for the first child as of July 2004 is $2,719. The actual amount of benefit per child is reduced for working parents with a higher income.

A businessperson cannot deduct child-care costs from taxable income and thereby reduce taxes. The Supreme Court of Canada ruled in 1993 that mothers who are also self-employed businesswomen cannot claim their child-care costs as a tax deduction, even if they incurred these costs to earn income. Seven judges produced this majority decision; the Court's two female judges—Claire L'Heureux-Dubé and Beverley McLachlin—dissented.

The ruling was the result of a court chal-lenge by Elizabeth Symes, a self-employed Toronto lawyer who had hired a nanny to care for her two children. She deducted the nanny's salary as a business expense for the taxation years of 1982 through 1985.

To understand why her self-employed status was an issue, it is necessary to know the basic rules about deductions. Under the federal Income Tax Act, a self-employed person can generally deduct any reasonable expenses incurred to earn income. Certain expenses are necessary and deductible with-out question, such as office rent, employees' salaries, leased office equipment and tele-phone bills. But other expenses are subject to certain maximums. For example, if a busi-nessperson takes a client to lunch, only 50 percent of the meal's cost is deductible.

Some expenses are ambiguous, and the rules do not list all of them, so if taxpayers think a certain expense was necessary to earn income, they can claim it on their tax return. If the tax department challenges the claim, the courts must decide whether the expense was necessary.

Child-care costs have not been consid-ered a business expense in the tax rules. The standard child-care tax deduction makes no distinction between an employed and self-employed person for the purpose of claiming child-care expenses. In Elizabeth Symes's case, the minister of national rev-enue disallowed her deductions, reasoning that the nanny's salary was merely a per-sonal or living expense rather than a cost of earning income. Symes was allowed only the standard child-care deduction based on the then-applicable ceilings of $1,000 for 1982, $2,000 for each of 1983 and 1984, and $4,000 for 1985.

Symes appealed to the Federal Court, Trial Division, and won. But the minister of national revenue then appealed to the Federal Court of Appeal, which ruled against her and sided with the tax department. Undeterred, Symes appealed to the Supreme Court of Canada, which, as we have seen, ruled against her.

The judges who rendered the majority decision agreed that Symes incurred child-care expenses because of her law practice, but also concluded that she would have needed child-care help regardless of her self-employment status. They relied on customary accounting practice and tax analysis, which do not accept the cost of child care as a business expense. And they gave short shrift to Symes's argument that refusing her the right to deduct child-care expenses infringed on her right to equality, guaranteed by the Charter of Rights.

In the end, the majority ruled that the Income Tax Act already provides specifically for limited deductibility of the cost of child care, so Symes could not rely on the provisions of the act that allow for the deduction of business expenses.

The dissenting opinion, delivered by Madam Justice L'Heureux-Dubé, suggested that tax laws should be adapted to reflect the changing role of women in the workplace and family, just as those laws have evolved to adapt to changing business practices. She noted that women tend to bear the cost of child care, and that women, unlike most men, often cannot work without it.

The majority of the court argued that such a change would give self-employed women an advantage over women with jobs. But as Madam Justice L'Heureux-Dubé pointed out, the Income Tax Act already gives the self-employed an advantage: they can claim a variety of business deductions, while employees cannot.

6. Child Labour Laws

If a child or teen wants to find a job, he and his parents should be aware of relevant laws. Governments try to protect children in a number of ways: by requiring them to attend school, usually until the age of 16, by setting minimum ages for most employment, and by limiting the times they can work and the jobs they can do. In cases where these rules are breached, the law generally holds the employer responsible. However, parents could also be liable—if, say, a child under 16 skips school in order to work.

SCHOOL ATTENDANCE

Children of school age—generally defined as under 16—must attend school under provincial law. In Ontario, for example, anyone who employs a child during school hours may be fined up to $200. Ontario announced in 2004 that it was considering raising this to age 18.

MINIMUM AGE FOR WORK

The minimum age for work varies by province and territory, and often depends on the specific job, industry and situation. Most provinces and territories specify a minimum age for a child to hold even a part-time job. The age ranges from 14 to 17, with additional restrictions and exemptions in each jurisdiction. In several provinces, for example, the minimum age can be waived with written permission from the child's parents and the province's minister of labour or director of employment standards.

Sometimes, employers try to get around

the rules. In a 1988 Alberta case, a man whose business was direct sales of chocolate bars was charged with eight counts of employing individuals under 15. He argued that since he paid commissions, he was not strictly employing the children; the court disagreed and found him guilty.

WORK HOURS

Some jurisdictions limit the number of hours a child can work during a school week. Alberta's laws, for example, say that school-children under 15 can work only two hours on school days and up to eight hours on other days. In Newfoundland and Labrador, a schoolchild's hours of work, when added to the hours in school, cannot total more than eight hours in any day. Many jurisdictions also prohibit children from working during certain periods of the day, such as between 10 p.m. and 6 a.m.

TYPES OF JOBS

Some provincial laws specify the jobs that children are allowed—or not allowed—to do. In Alberta, for example, a child from 12 to 15 years of age may deliver small wares for a retail store, deliver newspapers and flyers or be an office clerk, messenger or retail clerk. In Newfoundland and Labrador, a child under 16 may be a messenger, newspaper vendor or shoe shiner, or may set pins in a bowling alley. Most jurisdictions also bar children from certain jobs, generally those that could injure a child's health, education, welfare or morals. In Ontario, for example, youths under 16 cannot work in construction or logging.

EXEMPTIONS

Children working in a family business or on a farm may be exempt from some of these regulations. Exemptions may also be allowed in other circumstances, sometimes with the consent of a parent and/or supervision by an adult.

CHAPTER 4

MARRIAGE

⚖

Introduction

The institution of marriage has been transformed in our times. It is no longer regarded as the binding contract it once was. The goal of marriage today is not always to have children. Most people no longer assume that the man will take sole responsibility for supporting a family. Some men are full-time "househusbands," or share part-time responsibility for the children. Some women are choosing to raise children without known fathers. Many women are forced to raise children alone as a result of divorce or absent fathers. Some people choose not to marry but otherwise live a married life. Some are in same-sex unions, and a few of these couples are entering into formal marriages, where laws permit.

The number of families made up of married couples with children declined from 55 percent in 1981 to to 44 percent in 2001; the number of common-law couples doubled between 1981 and 1995 to nearly 1 million common-law couples—by 2001 this number had risen to 1,158,400. There were 1,311,200 single parent families in 2001, and the number of never-married single parents increased from one in ten single parents in 1981 to one in four in 1995, all according to recent information from Statistics Canada.

The law regulates marriage and makes rules for what happens if a marriage breaks down. It does not regulate relationships outside marriage in the same way, but has evolved law, mostly through case law, to help those who have disputes within those relationships. In Chapter 4, we look at the legal implications of marriage; in Chapter 5, we examine common-law relationships; and in Chapter 7 and elsewhere (see Index), we focus on same-sex relationships.

A. MAKING THE DECISION TO MARRY

1. Legal Factors

Men and women today are conflicted over the decision to marry, not only due to possible lingering doubts about the prospective mate, but also out of concern at being enmeshed in the legal implications of the marriage institution. For marriage is certainly more than a relationship or a personal bond. As an institution, it embodies age-old customs, expectations, and assumptions with legal and economic consequences.

While modern attitudes about marriage have adapted to current economic and social circumstances, many people yearn to live according to traditional ways. Research studies have shown the ambivalent dreams of teenaged girls, who long for a prince charming to take care of them while they raise children, and at the same time wish for a prestigious career—with no apparent understanding of how they will manage both.

Implicit in the traditional institution of marriage was the idea that a woman was dependent on her husband, who agreed to provide her with economic security. The fact that some men never supported their families and some women worked outside the home as sole breadwinners did not affect conventional expectations.

Cynics used to view the economic aspect of marriage as an exchange—the woman selling her exclusive child-bearing capacity and her sexual, personal and housekeeping services for the permanent right to support. Some provincial laws applicable to separation used to institutionalize this so-called exchange by depriving a spouse of financial support for not being sexually faithful. The only province today that specifically refers to adultery is Alberta, which still has a law on its books that a spouse who has committed adultery cannot apply for support under provincial legislation. In 1999, Alberta provided an alternative avenue that effectively circumvents its own law. This law permits a married or common-law spouse to apply for support after separation, and this right is not contingent on acceptable conduct. In certain other provinces and territories, namely New Brunswick, Nova Scotia, the Northwest Territories and Nunavut and Yukon Territory, "conduct" (which may include adultery) is a factor in determining support eligibility. Ontario has a law that is rarely applied: It says the amount of support ordered may be affected by conduct that is "so unconscionable as to constitute an obvious and gross repudiation of the relationship."

If the couple are choosing to live a traditional lifestyle in which they expect the woman to be at home and financially dependent, it makes sense for them to be married. She will have better legal protection to share property, share legal possession of the matrimonial home and be entitled to spousal support, for example, provided she does not enter into a marriage contract that releases some of these rights. The same is true for any man who agrees to live the non-traditional lifestyle of a "house-husband."

On the other hand, two childless, independent people with their own economic security and social status may choose not to marry because they feel they do not need the protection of the law. If the couple have or plan to have children, they will likely want to marry for the children's sake. Deeply held religious convictions may also motivate marriage.

Marriage itself may not require sharing of all property but in most provinces, when they separate or divorce, a person is required to share property or its value with a mate; the extent and manner of sharing depends on the laws of the jurisdiction in which the couple reside. This legislation is particularly applicable when a home is brought into the marriage and becomes the matrimonial home: The laws in British Columbia, Saskatchewan, Ontario, New

Brunswick, Nova Scotia, Newfoundland and Labrador, the Northwest Territories and Nunavut and Yukon Territory all make special provision for sharing the matrimonial home under certain conditions. Alberta still has dower rights in its legislation, which can give a spouse a life interest in the "homestead" and the right to consent to sale. Unmarried partners have greater control over their own assets, but may still be required to share with a partner in certain circumstances, usually in proportion to financial contribution (see Chapter 5).

2. Legal Requirements

Once a couple makes the decision to marry, there are legal requirements to be considered. All of these requirements assume the standing legal definition of marriage, first articulated in 1866 by Lord Hyde: "Marriage is the voluntary union for life of one man and one woman to the exclusion of all others."

STATUS

A person must be a free agent and have the right to marry. Otherwise, if a person is already married, a second marriage ceremony without an intervening divorce makes him or her a bigamist. A divorced person does not have the right to remarry unless the divorce is valid under the laws of his or her province or territory. The provincial issuer of marriage licences will want to see the previous divorce papers in order to issue a marriage licence. A widow or widower may have to show his or her late mate's death certificate.

CHOICE OF MATE

There are laws preventing marriages based on consanguinity (blood relations) and affinity (related by marriage); a breach of these laws makes the marriage void. For example, a man would breach the consanguinity rules if he married his grandmother, aunt, mother, daughter, sister, granddaughter or niece. A woman would breach the affinity rules if she married her grandmother's husband, aunt's husband, husband's uncle, stepfather, husband's son, daughter's husband or husband's brother.

CONSENT

The marriage must be voluntary to be valid. Only duress that amounts to an absence of free will is sufficient to invalidate a marriage. Any social pressures that impel an individual to go through with a wedding do not fit within the legal definition of duress.

MENTAL COMPETENCE

Both parties must be able to understand the marriage ceremony, and understand their rights and responsibilities as spouses to live together in an exclusive sexual relationship and to provide financially for one another. If a person lacks mental competence, or was drugged or drunk and did not understand what he or she was doing, the marriage might be annulled as though it never happened. The law calls it "void ab initio."

AGE

The age when a person can marry without parental consent varies across the country, and depends on the age of majority, but is usually 18 or 19. A person generally cannot marry below the age of majority without parental consent or court order.

FORMALITIES

The formalities of the civil part of the marriage ceremony are prescribed by law and are the same across Canada. Sometime before the ceremony, the couple must get a marriage licence or, in some places, have the "banns published" (that is, have the marriage announced) in a local church.

NON-TRADITIONAL MARRIAGES

There are people today who do not fit into the traditional definition of marriage, but still want to consider themselves married.

These include people who are separated from their spouses, but not divorced from them, and want to live with another person in a state of marriage. These couples often live common-law, which, according to the traditional definition, means a man and woman who present themselves to the community as husband and wife, but were never legally married. The special legal rules for common-law partners are discussed in the next chapter.

Some homosexual and lesbian couples wish to live together in committed unions or marriages, where they are legal (see Chapter 7). Some couples create rituals akin to marriage ceremonies for the purpose of declaring to the community their permanent commitment to each other, and sign agreements to clarify their financial obligations and rights.

BROKEN ENGAGEMENTS

If the engagement is broken, the ring must be returned by the person who broke the engagement, but not by the person who was "jilted." Wedding gifts are usually regarded as conditional on the marriage, and sent back if the wedding is called off.

An engagement to marry is considered a contract, and some jurisdictions still allow lawsuits for breach of promise of marriage to compensate the injured party for suffering and any financial losses, such as the catering deposit and other costs. Ontario has specifically abolished this lawsuit.

3. Legal Rights and Duties of Spouses

The legal rights of spouses within marriage are defined as much by custom as by law; in many ways, our legal institutions assume that a couple will work out the details of their personal relationship without the legal system getting involved. As a result, married couples end up with fewer legal rights during their working marriage than if they separate or divorce, when society often has to step in and regulate the dissolution of their relationship.

Some of the legal issues a married or about-to-be-married person may wish to know about follow. While a married person may choose not to insist on these rights, they are still available to her or him.

INDEPENDENCE

The law no longer considers a married couple "one person." Each person is free as an individual to do as she or he wishes without the spouse's permission, and to maintain her or his own personal identity. A woman does not become her husband's property upon marriage. Spouses have no right to abuse each other physically or mentally. Each person has the sole right to consent to medical operations on her or his own body.

LIFELONG COMMITMENT

Marriage vows exchanged in religious ceremonies—to love, honour, cherish and be faithful "until death do us part"—are promises that the law cannot and will not enforce.

NAME

A woman does *not* have to change her surname upon marriage—although some wives choose to assume their husband's surname. Most men do not even consider whether to change their surname to that of their wife, although some create a family name that represents a combination of both surnames.

IDENTIFICATION

A new bride or groom may need to inform credit-granting agencies, such as banks, of a change in status and/or name if she or he has any loans with them. Employers may also need to be told so that they can update human resource records.

SEXUAL RELATIONS

Sexual relations between spouses are a reasonable and normal expectation of the marital state, and a marriage is not considered legally consummated unless sexual intercourse takes place. Neither spouse can enforce this point in a court of law, although refusal of sexual relations for extended periods can be grounds for divorce on the basis of cruelty, and a marriage that is not consummated may be annulled. No one is expected to live within a sexless marriage unless he or she wants to do so. At the same time, married persons cannot force sex on each other; any attempt to do so may be considered sexual assault and a criminal offence.

CONSENT TO ABORTION AND VASECTOMY

A wife does not need to secure her husband's consent for an abortion. A husband does not need to secure his wife's consent for a vasectomy. While both operations affect a person's ability to procreate, a person is in charge of his or her own life, and the final decision is his or her own.

Legally, a married person need not even consult his or her mate about these decisions. However, spouses should probably discuss any important choice that affects both of them.

CITIZENSHIP AND RESIDENCE

If a person marries someone from another country, her or his citizenship does not automatically change to that of the spouse, but she or he is likely to have an easier time becoming a citizen of that country. If either spouse wants to move to another city or country, the other is not legally required to go along.

PASSPORT

Newly married people must advise the passport office of their marital status when they apply for a passport. However, they may request that the passport be issued in a maiden name or accustomed name.

MEDICAL BENEFITS

Family plans that cover medical and dental care, drug plans and extended health coverage usually cover a spouse as well. If a person is entitled to coverage under a spouse's plan, the second person's name should be registered on it. If the other spouse's plan gives better coverage, of course, the couple should choose to be registered under it.

INCOME TAXES

Marriage can affect tax status. To calculate tax deductions, an employer will probably ask for an up-to-date TD1 form to find out whether the employee is single or is claiming a spouse as a dependant (the couple's choice). When there are children, the employer must be advised which spouse will claim the child tax benefit for them. Marriage may also have other tax implications, such as attribution of income. In most instances, as prescribed by the Income Tax Act, property may pass between husband and wife without tax consequences.

BENEFICIARY DESIGNATIONS

Beneficiary designations for life insurance, pension and registered retirement savings plans should be up to date. While one spouse may decide to designate the other or the other's estate as the beneficiary of insurance or RRSP plans in his or her will, it is better to change the beneficiary directly with the insurance company or the institution that manages the RRSP. Pension plans usually require notification according to their rules, and will likely not accept a designation by will.

FINANCIAL SUPPORT

In most provinces, wives and husbands have a mutual obligation to support each other in accordance with their own financial ability and the extent of the other spouse's needs during marriage. However, a court is unlikely to enforce this obligation during the marriage.

Furthermore, one spouse cannot be forced to provide the other with luxuries. A spouse is obliged only to provide the basic necessities of life—modest shelter, food, clothing, medical treatment and expenses. Failure to provide minimal support is a criminal offence, but charges are rarely laid.

PROPERTY OWNERSHIP

If either spouse owned property separately when single, ownership is not automatically shared upon marriage. However, in Newfoundland and Labrador, a marriage creates a joint tenancy in the matrimonial home, and in New Brunswick, each spouse is normally entitled to one-half the net proceeds of sale of any matrimonial home, irrespective of how title is held.

Elsewhere, each spouse continues to own his or her separate property, although the other spouse may legally claim part ownership if she or he contributes to it financially. Homemaking and child-rearing work, however, does not legally entitle a spouse to a share in ownership during marriage. Each spouse's wages are his or her own, although the couple may need to share wages to maintain the basic necessities when living together.

LIVING IN THE FAMILY HOME

Under family law, the home in which a married couple lives is the matrimonial home, and the husband and wife have an equal right to live there during the marriage, even if only one spouse owns the home. In some jurisdictions, a couple can own more than one matrimonial home, such as a city home and a country cottage. Neither spouse can force the other out without a court order, which a judge is unlikely to grant unless the unwanted spouse is seriously harming the family.

Even if one spouse has sole ownership of the family home, generally she or he cannot sell or mortgage it without the other's consent.

DEBTS

There is no law making a married person automatically responsible for his or her spouse's debts, unless he or she cosigns or acts as guarantor. But banks and other creditors may require both spouses to sign for a debt if a loan is made to either spouse on the strength of the couple's total earnings. Creditors may also arbitrarily decide to give spouses a joint credit rating; there is little legal recourse if the husband and wife prefer separate ratings. A spouse should be careful about requesting and using a second card on the other spouse's credit facility because doing so may make him or her jointly liable for all obligations against the card. Husbands and wives should also get independent legal advice before cosigning or guaranteeing their spouse's loan.

CHILDREN

Parents automatically share custody of their children. This means that they jointly provide daily care—both parents have a legal duty to provide their children with the necessities of life—and they jointly make decisions about the children. Although in some provinces the father is legally allowed to decide the children's religion, courts would be unlikely to enforce this law and would be reluctant to intervene if the parents disagreed on the decision during an ongoing marriage.

When making their wills, parents should each appoint the same guardian for the children in the event that both parents die in a common disaster or around the same time. If parents name different guardians, a court would be forced to decide which of the two guardians to appoint.

LAST WILL AND TESTAMENT

On marriage, a previous will is automatically invalidated, unless the will specifically states that it was made in contemplation of marriage. If a married person should die after the marriage but before a new will has been prepared, her or his property would be distributed according to legal rules of intestacy (a distribution scheme which identifies who receives the estate of someone who dies without a will).

QUEBEC

Quebec's Civil Code states specifically the rights and duties of spouses, which apply no matter what a marriage contract says. The Civil Code stipulates that each spouse has the same rights and obligations in marriage as the other, and that they "owe each other respect, fidelity, succour and assistance." They "are bound to live together ... [and they] together take in hand the moral and material direction of the family, exercise parental authority and assume the tasks resulting therefrom." The Code says that the couple choose the family residence together and are expected to contribute to the marriage in accordance with their means, which may include a spouse contributing by her or his activities within the home. They are responsible for each other's debts incurred for the current needs of the family. They are expected to use their own surnames after marriage. Only married persons have a mutual obligation of support.

4. Marriage Contracts

It used to be that when a couple made the commitment to marry, whether in a traditional or non-traditional ceremony, they were convinced that the marriage was for a lifetime. This is no longer the case; the divorce rate has escalated, and couples today are more aware that they can end the marriage if it fails to work for them.

But they often have an unrealistic expectation that the laws will remain the same as they were on the day they married. Family law has gone through an exceptional number of significant changes in the past 30 years. As a result, if a person wants certainty in the event of marriage breakdown or the death of a spouse, it is wise to negotiate a marriage contract.

The courts will not enforce the promises in the marriage vows as a binding legal contract. Even though people at a wedding witness vows such as, "with all my worldly goods I thee endow," the courts dismiss these statements as part of the mating ritual. When a dispute arises out of a marriage, the courts do not take the vows seriously in determining the nature of the marital contract. For example, even when the exchange of vows has implied that marriage represents an equal partnership, the courts have not applied the wedding statements to require equal division of assets. Those who hear a spouse say words such as, "everything I have will be yours, darling" should not expect a judge to take this promise literally.

Furthermore, no one should assume that the laws or the way the courts interpret them will remain the same when the marriage comes under legal scrutiny—that is, in the event of divorce or death. But a marriage contract offers a couple the opportunity to make their own custom-tailored law, and guarantees them some measure of predictability if the laws do change.

Therefore, a couple planning to marry who want to ensure that their expectations and assumptions are not only mutual, but binding and legally enforceable, must have a marriage contract. And if they want to be extra cautious, they may wish to consider marriage contract insurance. Specialty insurance companies offer insurance to protect both lawyers and their clients against the possibility the marriage contract is challenged in court and any provision is set aside. The insurance company pays the insured client his losses, relieves the lawyer of any financial responsibility arising from the drafting and execution of the contract, and pays the legal costs of the lawsuit. As an example of the cost of the coverage, one company charges a flat $2,500 for ten years of minimum coverage, which protects a person with $2.5 million against a loss of 50 percent of his assets. There can be significant exceptions to coverage. For example, this same company does not protect against claims in connection with child and spousal support and claims to assets arising from changes in legislation.

WHAT IS A MARRIAGE CONTRACT?

A marriage contract is an agreement between two persons who plan to marry or are already married that sets out rights and obligations within the marriage and/or upon separation and/or upon death. It must be negotiated openly with full and complete disclosure of all assets and liabilities of each partner. Complete disclosure is important for legal reasons, but the discussion can also be used as an opportunity to enhance and deepen the marital relationship.

A couple must execute a marriage contract properly according to the requirements of the law, and must enter into it voluntarily and freely, with each person seeking independent legal advice on the implications and meanings of the agreement for both spouses. The agreement states that the parties will be bound by their promises. The courts in all provinces will enforce such an agreement.

WHAT DOES A MARRIAGE CONTRACT INCLUDE?

A marriage contract usually includes the following sections:

- **Property:** The agreement establishes a formula for the division of present or future property owned by the couple separately or together. It is best to refer only to categories of property, rather than to specific items. For example, an agreement should say "matrimonial home" instead of "9500 Main Street." The contract should include a formula for dividing business and investment assets, too, especially if the couple are in a business partnership.
- **Support:** The agreement should state whether or not spousal support will be paid by one partner to the other if the marriage breaks down. Much, of course, will depend on the family's circumstances. If both spouses are income-earners at a similar level and expect to have no children, then they may choose to opt out of support duties and rights. Few couples, however, are in this position. The care of children is an important factor in determining support obligations and needs. If one spouse will stay home to take responsibility for the children and the home, with consequential

loss of employability, seniority, pension and general financial potential, then the income-earning spouse must pay reasonable spousal and child support. If the spouse who cares for the children and home also works outside the home part-time or full-time, he or she will earn less because of the dual responsibilities; therefore, his or her income would have to be supplemented by the major income-earner in the event of separation.

If the spouses waive all claims to support, or include support terms that result in unconscionable circumstances, a court has the discretion to disregard the support provisions in the marriage contract and make its own order, even if the provision was fair and reasonable when it was negotiated. An unconscionable circumstance might be the destitution of a spouse forced onto social assistance. In any event, spouses cannot waive child support, as a matter of public policy.

- **Household Expenses:** Some couples want the agreement to specify their arrangement for sharing responsibility for household expenses during the marriage. For instance, one couple might say that they will deposit all separate income into a joint account and pay all family expenses from it, or they might agree that the husband will pay the cottage mortgage but will not thereby be entitled to more than one-half of the cottage. Alternatively, they might decide that the wife's wages will be invested for the benefit of both.
- **Children:** Remarried partners with children from previous unions may want to clarify future support of these children in the event of separation. A step-parent may find himself or herself

with the responsibility of financially supporting his or her mate's children from a prior marriage or relationship because he or she behaved like a parent in assuming actual financial obligations. This relationship is called "in loco parentis" (in the place of a parent).
- **Religion:** If the couple are from different cultural and/or religious backgrounds, they might want to agree in advance on the religious upbringing of the children.
- **Effect on a Will:** The marriage contract may have provisions that come into effect on the death of one party, or the couple may decide to leave these provisions to their wills. However, a marriage contract will be legally binding and enforceable, and can be worded to take precedence over a last will and testament. Furthermore, one spouse should not depend on the other to provide protection in his or her last will and testament, because that will is revocable and can be changed from time to time.
- **Inheritances:** Most couples prefer to specify that inheritances are to remain the property of the heir and are not to be shared with the family as of right. A couple should be careful to include the matrimonial home in this category if it has been or will be bought with inherited funds.
- **Gifts:** The contract should refer to the disposition of gifts to either or both parties; it should specify how to define them, how to prove they exist, and who should be entitled to share their increase in value.
- **Wedding Gifts:** It is appropriate to share wedding gifts, but the agreement should state how to divide them, perhaps

according to who is more attached emotionally to certain items or according to a strict division of financial value. In one case that went to court over the division of wedding gifts, the judge resolved the issue by ordering that the person who invited the giver to the wedding be the one to receive the gift upon breakdown of the marriage.

UNENFORCEABLE TERMS

Some terms in marriage contracts may not be enforceable in some jurisdictions:

- Provisions that limit the right of a spouse to live in the matrimonial home, or consent to the mortgaging or encumbrancing of it.
- Decisions as to custody or the manner of exercising access to children after marriage breakdown. However, an agreement can say that both spouses will co-operate in working out what is in the best interests of the children, and that, if agreement cannot be reached, mediation or conciliation will be used to resolve the dispute without litigation, if possible.
- Terms in a contract deciding who will do the housework, or how many children to have, or who will take out the garbage, or who will do the dishes. Courts cannot monitor such agreements.

SETTING ASIDE AN ENTIRE CONTRACT

It is very difficult to set aside a properly executed and witnessed marriage contract in which the parties had independent legal advice and provided full financial disclosure. However, there are two possible ways:

- **Duress:** If the agreement was signed under duress—which means that a signatory was physically forced to sign, or that the signatory's well-being and perhaps his or her family's well-being were threatened—it may be set aside.
- **Undue Influence:** If an agreement is signed when a party has been unduly influenced by his or her spouse, it may be set aside. Undue influence does not necessarily involve physical violence, but it does mean that someone has used improper pressure, causing the other person to act against his or her better judgment. Allegations of undue influence are not easy to prove. To charge undue influence, a person cannot simply say, "he/she pressured me into it."

By the Supreme Court of Canada decision in *Hartshorne* v. *Hartshorne* in 2004, the court demonstrated an unwillingness to tamper with the terms of a marriage contract, even if the result turned out to be unfair to one of the parties. In that B.C. case, the couple, both lawyers, lived together for 13 years, 9 of these as married partners subject to a marriage contract. The wife remained at home to care for their two children, one of whom had special needs. The B.C. trial and appeal courts thought that the result was unfair to the wife, and awarded her a greater interest in the family's assets than the marriage contract required. The law in British Columbia actually permits the court to reapportion property if the marriage contract terms turn out to be unfair.

However, the Supreme Court of Canada

disagreed, opining that the courts should respect the deals people make, and be reluctant to second-guess them. While the court's job is to determine whether the outcome arising from the marriage agreement is fair, the main issue is whether the parties likely contemplated what their personal circumstances would be if they separated. In the Hartshorne case, the court determined that things unfolded as anticipated for them in that they were living independent of each other as far as property was concerned and there was no commingling of funds, and they had planned that the wife would stay at home to raise the children. The court ruled that any inequities would be corrected through spousal support.

B. RIGHTS AND RESPONSIBILITIES BETWEEN SPOUSES

1. Name

While it has been customary in many cultures, including Canada, for a married couple to share the same surname, it is not a legal requirement. However, many married couples prefer to do so, and when they do decide to share a surname, they usually choose the husband's. Quebec is the exception in Canada; the Quebec Civil Code actually stipulates that husbands and wives keep their own surnames after marriage. When same-sex couples choose to marry, they sometimes agree to share the same name.

A person who wants to keep his or her own name should just do so. They do not need anyone's permission. And no one—be it employer, bank or any authority that insists on attaching legal significance to a purely social custom—has a right to make it difficult for a person to continue to be identified by her own name. Even though a person is married, she has the right to choose whether to keep or change her name.

But to avoid practical problems, a person should make her choice before saying, "I do," or at least before changing any official identification records to her married name. If a woman takes on her husband's surname, and later changes her mind and decides to use her maiden name exclusively, she may come up against administrative roadblocks wherever she lives—although the roadblocks are far fewer than formerly and she will eventually be able to get past them.

This is another area of the law that has experienced significant change over the years. Thirty years ago, a married woman was assumed to share her husband's surname. Twenty years ago, a married woman in some provinces was allowed to apply for a court change-of-name order to use her maiden name, but she had to apply to change her husband and children's surname to her maiden name as well—the assumption then was that members of a family had to bear the same name. While the law in Newfoundland and Labrador still makes this assumption, the legislation elsewhere has been revised to permit a married person to change his or her own name without his or her spouse and children changing theirs.

Divorced women generally can resume their maiden names without formal court order.

Passport policy also shows the change in the social and legal climate. Thirty years ago, Canadian government policy required a married woman's passport to be in her husband's name. Twenty years ago, she was able to obtain a maiden-name passport if she showed that she had never used her husband's name. Once having assumed her husband's name, however, she could receive a passport in a different name only if she proved she was known by that name in the community. The passport would usually include the words, "The married name of the bearer is. . . ." These days, it is easier to get a maiden-name passport, even after having had a married-name passport. All a woman needs to do is reapply to the passport office for another passport. And today, some same-sex couples are choosing to share the same surname.

2. Planning for Support

When a husband and wife plan to start a family, they must decide who will care for the children and how this care will be paid for. While traditionally women have stayed home to care for the children or have accommodated child-care duties in their work outside the home, more men today choose to stay home and look after their children. If a person who has been employed outside the home and has built a career plans to remain at home for a period of time after the birth of a child, she or he may feel particularly vulnerable because of lost opportunities, seniority, pension rights and other benefits of employment.

Existing laws may not provide sufficient protection. For example, there are no laws setting guidelines for the amount of support to be paid by a spouse for spousal or child support *during* marriage. Indeed, there are no laws ensuring that any support at all is paid—except for the rarely applied criminal law that spouses cannot leave their partner

and children destitute of the basic necessities (food and shelter, for instance).

If the couple ever separates or divorces, a court may rule on the amount of support, but this amount is usually not enough to meet either needs or expectations for child support. The law expects a spouse to contribute to his or her own support.

Prospective parents, who may be worried about their spouse's financial and personal support after the children are born, would be wise to negotiate a legal, enforceable contract, ideally before the woman becomes pregnant. The contract should be in effect during the marriage and also if the marriage ends due to separation, divorce or death. While this is not a common form of marital contract, it will be useful in some circumstances.

Both spouses should have separate lawyers to advise them with respect to the terms and wording, and ensure that the contract is properly witnessed and signed. Here are some suggested terms:

- The contract should take effect upon pregnancy or disability (for example, if the woman must stop working outside the home because of a difficult pregnancy and needs financial support). If the couple already have a child, the contract should be effective immediately.
- The contract should state the amount of child support—preferably a percentage of the employed partner's income or a proportion of a predetermined budget for the child. This percentage or proportion should yield an amount sufficient to maintain the same lifestyle for the child if the marriage breaks down; otherwise, the courts may not order enough.

- The contract should contain a formula for spousal support and an agreement on how long the support will continue, depending on the family's means and notwithstanding any law to the contrary. If the woman is not employed outside the home during pregnancy and/or child-rearing, she should negotiate for a percentage of her spouse's income, at least for a specified period. If she later works outside the home, financial arrangements could acknowledge her additional child-care and home responsibilities.
- The contract should establish how the child-care responsibilities will be shared—perhaps equally or in a different proportion, based on the job responsibilities of each spouse outside the home and whether the couple receive any hired or family help with child-care and household duties. Although these arrangements may not be enforceable in a court of law, they will at least clarify the couple's mutual understanding and, in the event of a breach of contract, suggest the amount of damages to be calculated.
- The couple may want to agree that, if their marriage breaks down, sole ownership or at least occupancy for a predetermined period of time of the family home will go to the parent with whom the children are living.
- To ensure that the surviving partner retains the family home if one spouse dies, both should be named as joint tenants with survivorship rights to the entire home. The couple should not only state this joint tenancy in the contract, but should register both their names on the title to the home.

- The contract should establish the extent to which each spouse will contribute to the financing of the children's postsecondary education.
- The contract should stipulate that both partners will have sufficient life insurance to help support the family if either one dies. It is wise to ensure that the policy names the other spouse irrevocably, and that both spouses have a commitment to pay the premiums. Both should also draw up wills that financially protect the family.
- If all of the couple's retirement savings are currently in a registered retirement savings plan in one spouse's name, half of the savings should be put in a plan in the other's name. The savings can be transferred by way of a tax-free spousal rollover.

3. Residence

Married persons have a mutual obligation of support that includes at least modest shelter. They also have a joint right to live in their matrimonial home, and have their consent sought to any sale or encumbrancing. Most people regard the matrimonial home as a special type of property that represents a family's emotional as well as financial security, and no spouse can evict his or her mate, no matter whose name is on title.

OWNERSHIP

Most Canadian provinces continue to apply the traditional "separation of property" rules to determine who owns property during marriage. Under these rules, each spouse continues to own separately the property that belonged to him or her before the marriage, and property bought during the marriage belongs to the person who paid for it. Notwithstanding whose name is on the title to the property, a person who makes a financial contribution to someone else's property can ask a court to award a right of ownership in proportion to the financial contribution.

The same rules have applied to marital homes during the marriage. If title to the home is in one spouse's name, then the other spouse has no right to claim a share of ownership unless that spouse helped with the down payment or mortgage payments, or earned wages that contributed to the family pot out of which the mortgage was paid. If that spouse's contribution to the marriage was not financial but was as a homemaker and child nurturer, that spouse would not be entitled to claim a share of ownership of the matrimonial home without registered ownership.

While all provinces have modernized their property laws, they have almost all chosen to divide property only on marriage breakdown and/or death of a spouse, rather than to reapportion equities of ownership from day one of the marriage.

Except for Newfoundland and Labrador and New Brunswick, the provinces that have tried to protect the wife during cohabitation in an ongoing marriage have not given her any right to share the ownership of the matrimonial home or indeed any matrimonial property. The right to live in and sometimes to control the disposition of the home is the only protection most married women in Canada have.

Newfoundland and Labrador, however, presumes that every matrimonial home is jointly owned by the spouses with the same rights of possession and survivorship. New Brunswick provides that when a matrimonial home is sold, each spouse is entitled to one-half of the net proceeds, subject to any court order or contrary terms in a domestic contract.

POSSESSION AND CONTROL

Neither husband nor wife may sell or mortgage the matrimonial home without the other's signed consent. This requirement has tactical as well as monetary significance. The fact that a spouse needs the other's signature on documents gives some control and may even provide leverage to ensure receipt of the financial benefit to which the spouse is entitled.

But whatever province or territory a married person lives in, genuine long-term financial security lies in sharing actual ownership of the family home or being on title as a joint tenant. A marriage contract may also help.

4. Sex

The law views sexual relations as implicit in the marital relationship. If a marriage has not been consummated, then a court may be able to dissolve it. However, a marriage is considered consummated if sexual intercourse takes place even once; subsequent impotence is not grounds for annulment.

In the legal definition of non-consummation, one of the spouses must be unable to perform the act of sexual intercourse—defined as full and complete penetration—with the other spouse. Ejaculation, the possibility of procreation and the achievement of sexual satisfaction are not necessary. The inability to consummate must exist at the time of marriage and be incurable. If a woman has borne a child by her husband, this does not conclusively prove that he is not impotent, as long as the couple can prove that the child was conceived without penetration or by artificial insemination.

The cause of impotence can be either physical or psychological. A repugnance towards the sexual act itself is considered a form of mental impotence.

To prove non-consummation, medical evidence may be offered to show that the woman is still a virgin. If this evidence is not available or appropriate, the court evaluates the uncorroborated testimony of the spouse.

If one spouse is capable of consummating the marriage but has wilfully refused to do so for at least one year, even though the other spouse is willing, then divorce, rather than annulment, is the only legal recourse.

A decree of nullity declares that a marriage did not exist from the beginning and nullifies it on the basis of a situation that existed at the time of marriage. The parties are restored to their original status as if they had never been married. In contrast, a divorce decree terminates an existing valid marriage because of events arising after the marriage took place.

Either spouse may seek an annulment. If the spouse seeking the annulment is the impotent one, he must either show that he was not aware of his impotence at the time of marriage, or that his spouse was aware of it and married him anyway.

If the applicant has not proved her or his case, or if the applicant has accepted the marriage for a substantial length of time on the basis of the other spouse's impotence, the annulment might not be granted. If the court decides that impotence is not the real reason for seeking an annulment, then annulment will be refused on the grounds that the applicant is not "sincere." Sincerity is particularly important when the impotent party is seeking the annulment. The court wants to ensure the parties are acting in good faith.

5. Debts

Married people are not automatically responsible for the repayment of their spouse's debts. In fact, no creditor can even ask a spouse to pay his or her spouse's debts, unless that spouse signed documents accepting responsibility.

A married person may be asked to sign one of two types of documents for his or her partner. If a spouse signs a guarantee on a loan, firms owed money will first seek payment from the main borrower. If the main borrower cannot or will not pay, the guarantor will be responsible. If, on the other hand, a spouse co-signs a loan, he or she becomes jointly liable for the debt. A creditor who is owed money can go after both signatories and all their assets to repay the entire debt. The holder of a second card on a spouse's credit card may thereby become jointly liable to pay for anything charged on the card by either person.

A married person is not obligated to advise his or her partner about debts, or ask for consent to borrow, although it is wise to do so.

Sometimes, a spouse is asked to do more than co-sign or guarantee a loan, especially when money is being raised for a business.

The lender may request that the matrimonial home serve as collateral security for the loan. If a spouse agrees to this request and the primary borrower fails to maintain payments, the house can be lost or significantly reduced in equity. The bank can seek to foreclose on the mortgage and take over or sell the home to receive the money it is owed. If the bank forecloses, it receives all proceeds from the sale. Alternatively, if the home is taken over by "power of sale," any money remaining after the bank is paid is available to the owners or another creditor.

If a married person is willing to co-sign or act as guarantor, but does not want to risk losing equity in the home if the marriage breaks down, the wise course of action is to first negotiate a side agreement between spouses. Such an agreement might at least ensure that if the marriage ends, the primary borrower will have the obligation to repay the debt from his or her share of the family's assets. The agreement should also limit the extent of any bank guarantee to a specified amount.

Matters of debt become more complex if a couple separate and/or divorce. Without ever co-signing or acting as guarantor for their spouse's loan, ex-spouses can be left penniless if the other spouse's debts wipe out his or her assets. In Ontario, for example, spouses deduct their debts from their assets before determining what they owe the other spouse.

A few years ago, a 61-year-old farm woman in Ontario found herself in exactly this position. After the separation, she lost her rightful share of the $5-million farm business that she and her estranged husband had both struggled to build. Her husband had sole title to the farm. While still married to the woman and without ever telling her, the husband pledged it as security for a $3.5-million bank loan. He invested the money in the stock market and lost it. After the marriage breakdown, the woman vied with other creditors for rights to the farm, but the court gave the bank priority.

Laws about dividing debts and property after a marriage breakdown vary from province to province. Ownership of property remains the best way for people to protect themselves from partners who may go into debt.

Since spouses can do whatever they want with their own property during the marriage, including borrowing against it (except, in some jurisdictions, the matrimonial home), non-titled spouses would be smart to get their name on title as owner or part-owner to as many of the family's assets as possible. That way, their consent would be required in order to sell or mortgage the property.

CHAPTER 5

COMMON LAW

⚖

1. Legal Rights and Responsibilities of Common-Law Partners

Twenty years ago, I wrote that Canadian law "took little notice of a union known as a 'common-law' marriage." This is no longer the case; more and more rights and obligations of marriage are being transferred to common-law couples. Some may have thought they were avoiding all that by living together "without benefit of clergy." Others assumed they got the same benefits, but the law did not agree.

In fact, an increasing number of couples choose to live together without a legal marriage. According to the most recent census statistics (2001), 14 percent of all families are living common-law (compared to 6 percent in 1981). About 732,900 children, or 13 percent of the total number of children, lived with common-law parents in 2001 (20 years earlier, this was 3 percent.)

Quebec has the highest proportion of common-law marriages, according to the 2001 Census—508,500 common-law families accounted for 30 percent of all couple families, and almost 29 percent of children were living with common-law parents in Quebec, more than double the national average.

By way of comparison, fewer marriages are occurring. The statistics show that 70 percent of families in 2001 were living within a legal marriage (reduced from 73.7 percent in 1996 and 80.2 percent in 1986).

The large majority of lone-parent families (83 percent in 1996) are headed by women. In 1996, there were 945,000 female-headed lone-parent families in Canada, representing 19 percent of all families with children at home (any age). This figure is almost double that of 1971, when 10 percent of families with children were headed by female lone parents. Lone-parent families headed by men totalled 192,000 in 1996, representing 4 percent of families with children, up from 3 percent in 1971.

It is getting more difficult even to define a common-law relationship because definitions differ for different purposes. Traditionally, this relationship was legally defined as an alliance between parties who passed themselves off in the community as married, consummated their union by living together in a sexual relationship and were free to marry each other. Although they did not possess a marriage licence, they did have a commitment akin to traditional marriage.

Today, the laws vary. For example, the

support laws in some provinces have been extended from common-law partners to include live-in partners, where there is no pretense of a long-term relationship. In another change, the federal government's Old Age Security program now states that public representation is no longer used to determine whether a common-law relationship exists. Since the trend in the law is towards greater recognition of the rights of common-law spouses, and legal treatment of the couple as married partners, the law in this area is subject to particular continual change. Moreover, in most places, the law for opposite-sex common-law partners is being extended to same-sex unmarried partners. See Chapter 7, Section A4.

Here is how cohabitation may affect a person's interests.

THE HOME

If the partners live in a home owned on title by the two of them, they are protected by their registered interest, just as anyone would be; in fact, a name on the title is the best assurance of ownership. In many provinces, a person who lives with the registered owner but is not registered as owner has no ownership interest. However, if the non-titled partner makes a contribution to purchase, renovate, pay off the mortgage or participate in some other way with work, money or money's worth (labour) to the home, then he or she may make a claim in court for a share of the value of the home. The non-titled partner will be required to prove his or her claim with evidence of contribution, and will not be able to secure his or her rights until the lawsuit is over.

In the meantime, while the claim is pending, the person's lawyer will probably bring a motion to court for an order that the home not be sold or encumbered until the litigation is over. If this motion is granted, the court order will be registered on title to the property and will warn any potential purchasers or mortgagers to deal with the owner at their peril unless the non-owner's rights are first resolved.

If one partner wants or needs to have sole registered ownership, but the couple acknowledge that their true ownership is shared, they should put this mutual intention in writing. A lawyer should draw up a written agreement, which should be properly and legally witnessed, stating that one partner owns the property partially in trust for the other, and to what extent. Then, if the property is real estate, the trust agreement should be registered on the title if there is concern that the partner may use his or her sole ownership to the non-owner's disadvantage. Unless a person's interest is registered on title, which gives notice of a claim, the titled owner may sell or mortgage the property.

There are recent exceptions: the Northwest Territories, Nunavut, Saskatchewan and Manitoba now automatically include cohabitants in their matrimonial property laws. In British Columbia, Quebec and Nova Scotia, common-law couples are now able to register their relationship or civil union, which allows them to take advantage of the relevant provincial matrimonial law on the breakdown of the relationship. Elsewhere, property ownership would still have to be proven in a court of law by title or contribution.

SUPPORT

Most provinces provide for a mutual obligation of support between unmarried couples if certain criteria are met. For example, in Ontario, Saskatchewan, Manitoba, New Brunswick and Prince Edward Island, a man and woman who live together continuously for three years or more are entitled to claim support from each other, particularly if a dependency has been created by the relationship, or if they live in a relationship that is defined as having "some permanence" because they are the natural or adoptive parents of a child. In Nova Scotia, support obligations only apply after one year (or if the couple have a child together). Most other provinces have varying minimum periods.

But the definition of cohabit was stretched by an Ontario judge in 1996 to rule that a man was still a "spouse" to a woman with whom he had never lived, although they spent four or five nights a week together. According to him, they had a seven-year "affair"; according to her, he had made promises of permanence and fidelity. The judge ruled that "he had given the woman every reason to believe that she was in a permanent relationship with him. He told her he loved only her and intended to be faithful. He never told [her] she was just a girlfriend and it was his intention to be free, independent and carry on affairs with a number of other women. . . . The court cannot condone fraud and deceit."

NAME

It is not necessary for a common-law couple to be known by the same surname, although some couples may prefer to share one. Gen-erally speaking, one partner may simply assume the other's surname without anyone's consent.

A person does not need to use a common-law partner's name in order to receive spousal benefits such as support, workers' compensation, criminal injuries compensation and Canada Pension Plan.

In the end, the duration and nature of the relationship, not the surname used, will determine whether the law should treat two people as a common-law couple.

CHILDREN

The children of a common-law relationship normally use their mother's surname, unless she wants to register them in the father's name and he agrees in writing, or a court declares him to be the father of the children. All provincial laws oblige both parents to support their children.

PENSION PLANS

A common-law spouse may be able to receive the benefits of a spouse from certain private pension plans and the Canada Pension Plan, provided that the partner has no legal mate to take priority. The Canada Pension Plan now defines spouse generally to include a person who has been cohabiting in a conjugal relationship with the contributor for a continuous period of at least one year.

SPOUSAL BENEFITS

More and more benefit plans are being extended to common-law couples on the same basis as married partners. A 1995 Supreme Court of Canada case began the trend to put common-law partners on the same legal footing as married couples.

The case of *Miron* v. *Trudel* concluded that the exclusion of heterosexual cohabitants from the accident benefits available to married spouses under Ontario's car insurance law was a breach of the equality guarantees of the Charter of Rights and Freedoms. While the Charter does not state that marital status is one of its protected grounds, the Supreme Court took the issue under its wing by concluding that marital status was an "analogous ground."

This case has had a widespread impact and helped to extend to heterosexual common-law partners the same rights and obligations as married partners.

SOCIAL ASSISTANCE

A woman on social assistance who lived with a man who did not support her has always had to contend with assumptions that if she lived with him, he was contributing financially and the government need not help out. The courts have ruled time and time again against governments on what has come to be called "the spouse in the house" rule, but governments continue to try to cut off women on social assistance if they get a hint that she is living with a man, whether or not he is providing for, or even has the means to provide for, her financially. The most recent legal challenge was by the Ontario government, which was told by the Ontario Divisional Court in 2000 that it could not refuse welfare benefits to a woman who had a man in her home on a temporary basis; refusal was legitimate

only after they were together three years and so demonstrated some permanence. The Court wrote that the government was acting on "false stereotypes and myths . . . [which] appears to owe a good deal to the view of some in society that a woman on social assistance should refrain from intimacy with a man." The Ontario government in 2002 lost its appeal, but secured leave in 2003 to further appeal to the Supreme Court of Canada. After a change in government in Ontario, the appeal was discontinued in 2004.

INCOME TAX LAWS

Income tax law has caught up to common-law spouses, who used to pay tax as if they were single. Since January 1, 1993, the law gives common-law spouses a new status for tax purposes: They have the same rights and are subject to the same liabilities as legally married spouses. Since 2000, this has been extended to same-sex couples. As defined for tax purposes, a taxpayer's "spouse" includes a person who cohabits with the taxpayer in a conjugal relationship throughout a 12-month period, or for a shorter time if both are the natural or adoptive parents of the same child.

The implications of this change in tax law depend on the common-law couple's personal circumstances. The new status helps some and hurts others. Some examples:

- Common-law partners lose the equivalent-to-married deduction they were entitled to claim for a child of a former marriage.
- Payments and benefits through the tax system that are connected to family

income have been reduced because such benefits as GST rebates and the child tax benefit system are related to family income, rather than individual income.

- A family can have only one "principal residence" for tax purposes. Therefore, unmarried partners who each have a "principal residence" will have to choose which one is the family principal residence for tax purposes.
- Common-law and same-sex couples are now entitled to the tax-free rollovers previously available only to married couples. With concern to RRSPs, this change is helpful because these couples will be able to "income split" (the higher-income spouse takes the RRSP deduction in the year the contribution is made, and the lower-income spouse includes the payments in income when the RRSP is transferred to an annuity or collapsed).
- Unmarried couples can transfer between themselves unused tuition, and age, education, pension and disability credits, thereby reducing their total federal tax payable.

INHERITANCE RIGHTS

Live-in partners have no automatic right to inherit each other's property upon death. But support is possible if one partner was dependent on the other financially at date of death, and the will failed to provide adequately for the dependent person. Support—usually a monthly allowance from the estate—is currently available with certain limitations in almost every province and territory.

Generally speaking, if a couple want to ensure that they have rights not provided by law, or ensure that they agree on the mutual rights and expectations they do want, then they should have a cohabitation contract.

2. Cohabitation Contracts

A cohabitation contract protects a couple who live together outside marriage. It has traditionally been an agreement between a man and woman who plan to live together as husband and wife, but without the marriage vows. This contract is valid in Ontario, Quebec, Manitoba, Alberta, Saskatchewan, New Brunswick, Prince Edward Island, Newfoundland and Labrador, British Columbia and all the Territories.

Where the province or territory recognizes same-sex unions and also recognizes cohabitation contracts, the contracts would be enforceable when entered into by a same-sex couple.

Alberta's law is an interesting example. Enacted in 2002, Alberta's Adult Interdependent Relationships Act permits agreements between adult interdependent partners, defined as persons in a "relationship of interdependence" outside marriage in which any two persons "share one another's lives, are emotionally committed to one another, and function as an economic and domestic unit." The label of "spouse" is limited to meaning the husband or wife of a married person. The legislation specifies how to determine whether such a relationship exists, and states that all the circumstances of the relationship must be considered, and identifies the following relevant factors: whether or not the persons have a conjugal relationship; the degree of exclusivity of the relationship; the conduct and habits of the persons in respect of household activities and living arrangements; the degree to which the persons hold themselves out to others as an economic and domestic unit; the degree to which the persons formalize their legal obligations, intentions and responsibilities towards one another; the extent to which direct and indirect contributions have been made by either person to the other or to their mutual well-being; the degree of financial dependence or interdependence and any arrangements for financial support between the persons; the care and support of children; the ownership, use and acquisition of property.

Their legal rights do not take effect however, unless they have lived together in this kind of relationship for at least three years, or sooner if there is a child by birth or adoption.

The contract sets out the rights and duties within the relationship and in the event of separation and/or death. Partners must honestly disclose their assets and liabilities and, to be certain the contract is enforceable, each partner should have independent legal advice. The contract represents evidence of the agreement between the parties; if one partner fails to abide by it, the other partner will have proof of their intentions.

Some or all of the following terms might be included in a cohabitation contract.

PROPERTY

If one partner is the titled owner of the home, the law does not state that the other partner automatically becomes a joint owner. Therefore, unless both parties agree to have both names on title as part owners,

they must deal with the issue in the cohabitation agreement. If the non-titled partner made or plans to make a specific contribution, that contribution should be reflected in the agreement. For example, if the house remains in one partner's name, but the other pays for all groceries and household expenses, the contract should state that these contributions entitle the other partner to receive compensation according to a specified formula if the relationship ends. If one partner is a full-time homemaker, the contract should state that this position represents an equal contribution to the relationship.

It is also wise to specify that both partners have the right to live in the home. Otherwise, by law, only married persons and those named on the title have that right.

It is advisable to deal with property ownership in a cohabitation contract; the law treats the property rights of common-law and same-sex couples differently from property rights of married partners.

The Nova Scotia Court of Appeal in *Walsh* v. *Bona* ruled in 2000 that the province's legislation, which protected the property rights only of married spouses, was unconstitutional. The appeal court temporarily suspended the law for 12 months to permit the legislature to change the law to treat common-law partners equally with married partners. The case went to the Supreme Court of Canada, which decided that the Nova Scotia Court of Appeal got it wrong. The Supreme Court of Canada in 2002 stated that it was not discriminatory under the Charter to treat unmarried cohabiting persons differently than married persons when it came to property rights arising out of their relationship. The Court said that the distinction does not affect the dignity of these persons and does not deny them access to a benefit or advantage available to married persons. Madam Justice Claire L'Heureux-Dubé dissented.

Nevertheless, the Northwest Territories, Nunavut, Saskatchewan and Manitoba automatically include cohabitants in their matrimonial property laws. In British Columbia, Quebec and Nova Scotia, common-law couples are able to register their relationship or civil union, which allows them to take advantage of the relevant provincial matrimonial law on the breakdown of the relationship.

Elsewhere, property ownership would have to be proven in a court of law by title or contribution. Some direction has been given in the 2003 Ontario Court of Appeal decision in *Wylie* v. *LeClair*. The Court made it very clear that common-law partners would not be treated the same as married partners when it came to property division. The Court reversed the decision of the trial judge, whom, they noted with disapproval, had made an order that effectively gave a common-law spouse the equivalent property rights as if she had been married.

In that case, the couple had been together for 15 years and had two children. The trial judge said the male partner had been unjustly enriched by the domestic and child-raising services of the female partner, and ordered a payment to her of $150,000, basically half of the assets. The appeal court disagreed with the analysis, and said the way to calculate it was to assess the value of the services that he received. The Court decided that $70,000 represented this value.

SUPPORT

The matter of support must be dealt with if one party is expected to be a wage earner and the other a homemaker and/or child caregiver. If one will earn less because of the relationship by staying home to raise children, for example, or by working part-time, that person will suffer loss of employability, seniority, pension and earning potential. The contract should include a clause that states the two partners are mutually dependent and will support each other during the relationship and if it breaks down. Without such a clause, a common-law or same-sex spouse might have to prove that the couple lived together for a specified prerequisite period.

DEATH

If one partner dies before the other, the contract should include protection for the survivor. This protection can include the right to live in the home, the right to be a beneficiary of the other's RRSP and the right to income from his or her estate. The agreement should acknowledge that the law allows the couple to share each other's Canada Pension Plan credits earned during the cohabitation. The couple should also ensure that the survivor and/or the children are named the beneficiary of any life insurance. Finally, the couple should provide at least what their contract requires for each other in their individual wills. But since a will can be revoked at any time, the contract should take precedence over the will unless the will provides more than the contract does.

CHILDREN

The contract can mention whether the couple have children together, but it cannot spell out enforceable provisions for custody or access should they separate. Whether or not parents are married, the law states that children's care and support is decided based on their best interests—which cannot be anticipated in the contract. The contract cannot specify the amount of support because a decision will be made based on the circumstances when the need arises.

3. Legal Rights of Children Born Outside Marriage

Traditionally, a child born outside marriage was regarded in law as no one's child, because the father failed to give not only legal acknowledgement, but also status and financial protection that, formerly, only men could give. Legally, an "illegitimate" child had been considered to belong to the mother.

Over the past 30 years, most provinces and territories have enacted legislation to dispense with the distinction between children of married and unmarried parents; now all children in these jurisdictions generally have the same rights.

Here are examples of how children born outside marriage are treated in law.

INHERITANCE

In the territories and in most provinces, the law specifically states that there is no legal distinction between a child born inside or outside marriage, and if a parent's will states that property is to be left to the "children," it applies to children born inside and outside the marriage. If the parent dies without a will, children born inside and outside the marriage are entitled to a share of the estate.

FINANCIAL SUPPORT

All provinces have laws that entitle children born outside marriage to be regularly supported by both their natural parents. If the father does not admit paternity, the mother may have to prove it through blood tests, DNA tests or other corroborated evidence, such as testimony from witnesses to whom he admitted that he was the father. The mother or another person who is caring for the child (for example, a grandparent) can make the application for support on behalf of the child. The court will fix an amount based on the father's ability to pay, the child's reasonable needs and the mother's ability to contribute to the child's support.

A biological father cannot argue that he should not have to pay child support because the mother misrepresented her use of contraceptives. If she had a child and his sperm was involved (DNA tests are almost foolproof), he must pay according to the child's needs and his means.

CUSTODY

With a few exceptions, custody disputes between unmarried parents are decided on the basis of the child's best interests, which is the same rule applied to children of married parents.

RIGHT TO GIVE THE CHILD UP FOR ADOPTION

Historically, giving up a child for adoption has been the right of an unwed mother, but in rare cases a biological father tries to prevent this from happening. If the biological father brings an application for custody of the child so that the child cannot be given up for adoption, he must prove that he is the child's father and that his care will serve the best interests of the child.

SURNAME

A child born of unmarried parents usually bears the mother's surname. The child can be given the father's surname, however, if he acknowledges paternity, or paternity is declared, and the mother agrees that the child take his name.

In the first case of its kind in Canada, the Supreme Court of Canada in 2003 ruled unanimously that it was discriminatory for mothers to have the sole power to decide their children's surnames. In the case, *Trociuk* v. *British Columbia (Attorney General)*, the father wanted triplets of a common-law relationship to bear his name in hyphenated form with that of the mother. He was refused by the B.C. Supreme Court as well as the B.C. Court of Appeal, but the Supreme Court of Canada decided that not to do so would be unconstitutional and breach the equality rights section of the Charter on the basis of sex. The Court noted that the birth registration document was not just a means of identification, but was the formal recognition of the biological ties between parent and child, and a way of affirming those ties.

4. Rights and Obligations on Separation

If the couple have a cohabitation contract, the contract will determine the rights and duties of the couple on separation. If they have no contract, and they are unable to agree by themselves or through mediation on how to resolve matters arising out of the breakdown of their relationship, then the court will have to decide on application by either party. In that event, ownership of property will be determined by title or court claims mostly based on trust law, support will be determined by provincial family law, and custody and access will be determined by the best interests of the children. However, when a common-law partner gives up paid employment to live in a common-law relationship and care for children, he or she still takes legal risks because the caregiver partner does not receive the same legal protection given to married people. Fortunately, he or she still has some rights to support.

SUPPORT

Our laws recognize that financial dependency is sometimes created or fostered by the unmarried relationship. This dependency is usually present when the couple have a child and one partner loses income, seniority and perhaps marketable skills by devoting herself or himself to child care. But dependency can also be created when one of the partners works for the other without pay, and then asserts entitlement to a fair reward.

In most provinces and territories today, a common-law partner has the right to claim financial support, usually so long as an application to court is made within one year of separation. Most provinces specify the number of years of cohabitation that will require a mutual obligation of support. For example, Ontario and Manitoba specify three years. If the couple have children together, that usually reduces the period.

CHILDREN

Child support as well as custody and access laws are generally the same as for married partners.

BENEFITS

Unmarried partners have certain other rights, depending on whether their relationship fits into the definition of a common-law relationship in the applicable legislation. For instance, a provincial workers' compensation scheme may allow common-law spouses to claim benefits, as may criminal injuries compensation boards where they exist.

PROPERTY

It used to be that no legislation in Canada provided for automatic sharing of property between common-law spouses.

However, in the last couple of years, the Northwest Territories, Nunavut, Saskatchewan and Manitoba passed laws that automatically included cohabitants in their matrimonial property laws. And in Quebec, British Columbia, Manitoba, Nova Scotia, common-law couples are able to register their relationship or civil union and take advantage of the relevant provincial matrimonial law on the breakdown of the relationship.

Elsewhere, the traditional rights and remedies remain. Property in a common-law partner's name will continue to belong to him or her, unless the other partner has made a contribution (preferably financial) to the property. Regardless of where a person lives in Canada, the claim to a rightful share of property registered in the name of another must be based on a contribution to the property and put forward by an argument called "constructive trust." According to constructive trust, it is unfair to let one person profit at another's expense; therefore, the court should construct a trust relationship and rule that one partner hold part of his or her interest in the property in trust for the other.

Rosa Becker used this remedy in a landmark case on the rights of common-law spouses. She was a common-law wife who successfully claimed a one-half share of the beekeeping business that she and her common-law partner had run together for 20 years, even though the legal title was in his name. The Supreme Court of Canada said her efforts entitled her to a one-half share in the Ontario beekeeping farm and business. The 1980 ruling established the property rights of common-law wives who contributed financially to property.

The Supreme Court of Canada went further in a 1986 ruling that gave Mary Sorochan of Alberta one-third of her partner's land because she had contributed to the preservation, maintenance and improvement of that property during their 42-year common-law relationship.

Then, in 1988, these rights were further extended to non-financial homemaking contributions in a decision of the Ontario Supreme Court. The case was brought by Marlene Crisp, a common-law wife who had lived with her electrician partner Thomas Banton for 13 years and had provided what the court termed "spousal services," without which he would not have been able to have a family, pursue further education and buy and improve a home. Banton had put the property in his name, although Crisp had expected him to list both their names on documents identifying ownership.

The Court ordered Banton to give his homemaker common-law wife an unprecedented 40 percent of the home, the main asset accumulated during their 13-year relationship. As a result of this decision, a common-law partner who was exclusively involved with household management and child care, and made no direct financial contribution to the relationship, can successfully assert a claim to share in the property accumulated during the relationship.

Common-law spouses continue to bring these claims to court. An Ontario woman had to persist as far as the Ontario Court of Appeal in her battle for her share of a farm property from her late common-law partner's estate. In 1997, that court ruled that he had held the farm partly in trust for her. She had left her job to work on his farm and take care of his home. They lived together for 30 years, and she nursed him through a stroke until he died. Without legislation requiring common-law spouses to share their property, the non-titled spouse is left only with the remedy of a court proceeding.

Property claims of common-law partners can be expensive to take to court, and in some cases a litigant can "win the battle but lose the war." The Rosa Becker case is a tragic example of the legal system's inade-

quacy in some cases. Rosa Becker never got a penny of the $150,000 the court awarded. After further legal efforts, she eventually collected only $68,000, and all of that money went towards her legal fees. After the case ended in the courts, Rosa Becker committed suicide and left a note saying that she considered her death to be a protest against the legal system, which had not helped her to collect her award.

This sad story raises an issue that litigants know all too well. Once a litigant gets a judgment, that judgment must still be enforced, and legal fees are required to do so. The court system does not generally enforce its own orders and further legal proceedings may be needed.

There are various enforcement methods:

- A certificate may be registered against the title of the property to warn of pending litigation.
- An injunction may be sought to prevent someone from disposing of any assets.
- The judgment may be registered with a sheriff, who may seize and sell almost any property, including real estate, cars, shares, term deposits, mortgages and furniture.
- Through the court or a sheriff, a lawyer may arrange garnishment of bank accounts, salary or income from private pension plans.
- The court may order the appointment of a receiver to manage any funds to be received by the person who owes the money.
- If there is a cohabitation contract, it can be registered against the title of all real estate in the partner's name to provide notice to any potential purchaser or mortgagee.

Common-law property rights are changing rapidly, and a person's rights today depend on her place of residence and whether the provincial or territorial government has already changed or plans to change its laws, or whether a recent Supreme Court of Canada decision prevails.

Here is how events unfolded. In 2000, the Nova Scotia Court of Appeal ruled in the case of *Walsh* v. *Bono*, a common-law couple who separated after a ten-year relationship and two children, that the Nova Scotia Matrimonial Property Act was unconstitutional in excluding common-law spouses from the right to share property. While the appeal to the Supreme Court of Canada was pending, Walsh and Bono had settled their property issues, and Nova Scotia changed its law to allow common-law couples to register a domestic partnership after two years of cohabitation to secure the same property rights as married couples. Quebec and British Columbia followed suit with similar voluntary registration schemes. Laws passed in Saskatchewan, Nunavut, the Northwest Territories and Manitoba went even further to provide, in addition to voluntary registration, mandatory sharing of property after a specified period of cohabitation, even if the couple did not register, unless they signed a cohabitation contract saying otherwise. For example, Manitoba's law specifies that if a couple does not register but lives together for at least three years, they will be required to share property accumulated during their relationship.

In the meantime, the Nova Scotia case of *Walsh* v. *Bono* proceeded on appeal to the Supreme Court of Canada, which ruled that people should be permitted to choose whether or not to marry and take on the property-sharing obligations of matrimony, and a decision not to marry should be respected. The Court held that it was constitutional and did not breach the equality rights of the Charter of Rights and Freedoms to fail to require property sharing after the breakdown of a common-law relationship. In a dissenting opinion, Madam Justice Claire L'Heureux-Dubé, examining the issue in the context of people's everyday lives, pointed out that married and common-law relationships are really the same except as to the formalities, and the initial intentions of the parties when they get together are less important than dealing with the equities at the end of the relationship. She held that the freedom to choose is often illusory, and one of the partners may be exploited by their failure to consider the legal consequences of the nature of their relationship, and if they then seek to prove their claim in court, it can be onerous and very expensive.

The consequence of the Supreme Court of Canada decision is to keep the law in Alberta, Ontario, New Brunswick, Prince Edward Island, Newfoundland and Labrador, and the Yukon the way it used to be. This means that in these jurisdictions, a common-law partner has no *automatic* right, as married couples do, to share property just because of their relationship. If they live together in a manner resembling marriage, but are not legally married, they are governed by a different set of rules than married spouses. They have to *prove* their entitlement by proving a contribution in work, money or money's worth. For example, they can assert a claim if they did the physical labour of painting or landscaping ("work"), if they paid money towards the mortgage or for renovations ("money"), or did all the housekeeping so a cleaning person did not have to be hired ("money's worth"). Unless such couples come to an agreement, they will have to prove their contributions in court, with evidence.

RIGHTS ON DEATH

There is no right to inherit the property of a common-law spouse, although there may be a right to claim support as dependants under certain conditions in most places in Canada. Most government pension plans allow a common-law spouse to assert a claim to her partner's pension, and give government agencies discretion to consider a person in an informal living relationship as legally married for the purpose of receiving a pension. Usually the spouse must prove that the relationship had a measure of permanence. The Canada Pension Plan deems a common-law partner to be the "surviving spouse" if the common-law or same-sex couple were living together in a conjugal relationship at the time of death and had so cohabited for a continuous period of at least one year.

Most legislation concerning provincial pension benefits includes reference to common-law spouses. In some provinces, a common-law partner is entitled to status as a spouse only if the pension member has no legal spouse at the time of her or his death.

Whether these rights of common-law spouses, where they exist, will be granted also to same-sex couples will depend on the jurisdiction and when the claim is made, as the courts and legislatures are trying to keep up with the rapid changes in this area of law.

CHAPTER 6

PARENTS AND CHILDREN

⚖

Introduction

Society has an interest in the well-being of children, and there are protective laws in place to enforce proper treatment. At the same time, the community prefers that parents take full responsibility for their children and assumes that they make the right decisions for them, unless facts to the contrary come to public attention. Child-welfare legislation therefore walks a fine line between intruding in the private affairs of families and ensuring society's legitimate responsibility to care for its children properly.

The protective laws currently in place combine several kinds of legislation; laws that codify people's reasonable assumptions about the role of parents to provide care, supervision, discipline and financial support; laws that provide for the protection of vulnerable children and facilitate their removal to a place of protection; and criminal prohibitions to deter bad behaviour towards children and exploitation of children's vulnerability. The United Nations Convention on the Rights of the Child, to which Canada is a signatory, adds a strong voice on children's rights.

1. Responsibilities of Parents and the Community

Parents are expected to take responsibility for the proper care and supervision, love and devotion, nurturing and education of their children. Only when they fail to do so does the community wish to become involved.

CHILD-WELFARE LAWS

All provinces have child-welfare laws that prohibit the physical and emotional abuse of children. They delegate to Children's Aid Societies (CAS) the obligation of dealing with children confirmed by the courts to be in need of protection.

A child may be defined as in need of protection for many reasons. Physical harm and emotional abuse are key indicators. Physical harm may be obvious, but emotional abuse is more difficult to prove, and the CAS may find it difficult to intervene in those cases. Failure to provide essential shelter, food and medical care or a pattern of neglect are other reasons the CAS may intervene.

The CAS has the duty and obligation to

bring parents before the courts in order to get authorization from the court to take continuing action in the particular case, subject to some short-term emergency powers. A CAS worker may recommend that parents be supervised until they show that it is safe to leave children in their care, or that a temporary homemaker be placed in the home, at public expense, to help the parents improve their parenting skills. In extreme cases, in which the parents are deemed incapable of providing proper care, welfare authorities may recommend that the children be permanently removed from the family home and placed in foster care.

For the purpose of CAS intervention, a child is defined as being either under the age of majority or under age 16 or 18, depending on the particular jurisdiction.

CRIMINAL LAW

The federal Criminal Code has something to say about the care of children as well. The Code considers it a crime for parents or guardians (defined as anyone who, in law or in fact, has custody or control of a child) not to provide "necessaries of life" for a child under 16. The parent or guardian who fails to perform that duty, endangering the life or health of a child, is liable to punishment ranging from a fine to up to two years in jail.

These are the essential laws on child welfare and most parents do not come into contact with them. However, the intersection between the duties of parents and the responsibility of the community comes increasingly to the fore when governments unilaterally reduce their budgetary commitments to Children's Aid Societies, child-care centres, school breakfast and lunch programs, children's recreational programs and other programs by which the community shares the burden with the parents. In fact, these programs enable some parents to keep their children with them.

The cuts by some provincial governments to their welfare programs have affected the ability of some parents to hold their families together at all. Some families have lost their place to live, some have lost their food and others have lost the ability to care for their children. In these cases, often an underfunded and overstretched CAS has had to step in to provide foster care for the children.

The laws protecting children seem to exist to prevent the worst from happening. But they have little power to promote increased spending on programs because spending decisions are part of the political process. Those who want governments to invest in universal, accessible child-care programs, early childhood education, nutrition programs for the poor and malnourished, shelter for the growing number of homeless children, literacy and training programs, social work and psychologist assistance for preventive care must lobby politically.

INTERNATIONAL LAW

International law may be a persuasive reminder of government commitments. In 1989, Canada signed the United Nations Convention on the Rights of the Child. This document states that "childhood is entitled to special care and assistance," and that although parents have primary responsibility for children, the governments of the signatory countries shall assist them and ensure the development of institutions, facilities and services for the care of children, including child-care services for the children of working parents. The Convention affirms the right of a child to social assistance, an education and a standard of living adequate for the child's physical, mental, spiritual, moral and social development.

2. Parental Care and Supervision

A parent is responsible to make reasonable provision for a child's supervision and safety until the child is old enough to take care of himself or herself. Leaving a child alone for an unreasonable length of time is an offence in most provinces. In almost all provinces, the age depends on the circumstances of the particular child. However, the federal Criminal Code states that anyone who abandons or exposes a child under ten to danger, and thus endangers the child's health or life, is liable to a two-year prison sentence. A person who "abandons or exposes" is "leaving the child to its fate," as one judge put it. A baby-sitter or anyone else who undertakes the care of a child is under the same legal obligation as a parent.

The responsibilities of the Children's Aid Societies include situations in which a parent leaves a child alone without making reasonable arrangements for supervision and care. Charges may be laid under provincial child-welfare laws.

In most provinces and territories, parents will not be challenged for leaving a sensible child aged 10 to 12 to cope for a limited period in safe conditions.

Ontario provides an example of how these laws apply. In Ontario, a parent must provide a child under 16 with reasonable supervision, but only when the child is younger than ten is the onus on the parent to prove

that the care provided was reasonable in the circumstances.

The question of supervision most often arises in cases where parents leave children alone, and the child is injured. In 1991, a Toronto single mother left her two children, aged two years and six months, and her three-year-old nephew alone for almost five hours while she went shopping. While she was gone, one of the children turned on a gas stove. Fortunately, a neighbour smelled smoke, broke down the door and found the children alone but unhurt. The mother was convicted of child abandonment, sentenced to three years' probation and ordered to seek psychiatric counselling.

On the other hand, in a 1990 case in Winnipeg, a single mother left her two sleeping children, an eight-month-old baby and a 21-month-old toddler, while she went to a nearby laundromat. The toddler awoke, climbed up onto the stove and turned on an element, which melted the rubber sole of his running shoe and trapped him on the burner. When the mother returned less than an hour after she had left, she found the toddler on the stove, burnt but basically unharmed. The mother was acquitted of the charge of child abandonment on the basis that she was a devoted mother who had simply made a serious error in judgment.

Parents can be found guilty of abandonment even if they are at home. For example, some parents leave a child unattended in the bathtub. In a 1995 Ontario case, a father and mother were convicted of criminal negligence for the death of their seven-month-old son, whom they left alone to splash in the bath while they watched television. Their method of checking on him was to press the mute button on the television control from time to time to listen for the splashing. The court ruled that they showed "wanton or reckless disregard" for the child's life and safety.

In these cases, subject to court approval, CAS may recommend that parents be supervised, or that a temporary homemaker be placed in the home or that the children be put into foster care.

There are few statistics on cases involving lack of supervision because authorities only crack down on the ones they hear about—the accidents and needless deaths. But it is a safe bet that too many parents take chances, sometimes because they see no choice: They have to work to support their families, and they have no one to mind the kids. Often the lack of supervision is the result of inadequate support services for parents, a symptom of the dearth of emergency baby-sitting services, overnight child-care centres for emergency and shift worker use, and more affordable and accessible child care for all working parents.

The law deals with other kinds of supervisory problems as well. For example, the B.C. Court of Appeal ruled that a father had not taken proper care of his children and was partly liable when two of his children were seriously injured and two killed when the car in which he had permitted them to be passengers skidded off an icy road into a power pole. The father had insisted that his 16-year-old son drive the car against the boy's wishes, knowing his son was a driving risk because he was a new driver and suffered mental disabilities caused by brain damage. Moreover, the mother, a driving instructor herself, had warned the father not to let the son drive.

In the late 1990s, a new trend surfaced to legislate parental responsibility for their children's misdeeds. Manitoba, Ontario and British Columbia enacted legislation to make parents civilly liable for their children's actions. Ontario's legislation goes so far as to assume that any damage or loss resulting from a child's actions was intentionally caused, unless the parent can persuade the judge otherwise and prove that he or she made reasonable efforts to prevent or discourage the child from engaging in the kind of activity that resulted in the loss or damage—a tall order indeed.

The new laws make parents generally liable for the misdeeds of their children just by the fact of parenthood. To avoid liability, parents must show they were exercising reasonable supervision and control of their child and made reasonable efforts to prevent or discourage the child from engaging in the kind of activity that caused the loss or damage, or that the action causing the damage was not intentional. In evaluating this, a court can consider such factors as the age and prior conduct of the child; the potential danger of the activity; whether the child was under the supervision of the parent at the time or the parent made reasonable arrangements for the supervision of the child; any psychological or medical disorders of the child and whether the parent has sought professional assistance for the child; the physical or mental capacity of the child; and whether the parent has sought to improve her parenting skills by attending parenting courses.

The legislation covers claims for property loss and has monetary limits on recovery. In Ontario and Britiah Columbia, you cannot collect more than $10,000, plus interest and costs. Few legal actions have been brought under these laws to date.

This new "get-tough" approach goes beyond the previous common-law rule, which allowed an injured party to sue the parent of a child wrongdoer, but be compensated only if the parent was proven negligent. At common law, the mere fact of a parent–child relationship does not automatically make a parent liable for the wrongful acts of their child.

3. Parental Discipline

A parent is permitted to discipline his or her child, and even to use force, if the corrective discipline is appropriate to the circumstances. Appropriateness is the critical issue. When the court has believed that the parent went too far, it has on occasion criminally charged the parent with common assault.

A tourist passing through London, Ontario, several years ago spanked his son outside a restaurant and was charged with assault by a bystander. The court dismissed the charge, finding that the parent's discipline was appropriate to the offence and that he was not acting in a fit of rage.

In another case, a stepfather slapped his 13-year-old stepson on the mouth with an open hand, and was found not guilty of assault. The court ruled in 1995 that the child's behaviour warranted corrective action, that the parent was in control of his emotions and that he had used reasonable force towards the boy while exercising parental discipline.

On the other hand, a stepfather was found guilty of three counts of common assault for striking the two children of his common-law wife. He had boxed the ear of an 11-year-old and put his arm across the boy's throat, making it difficult for the child to breathe. He had grabbed another boy, pulled him down the stairs and forced him to the floor, where he placed his knee on the boy's back to keep him there. He had taken this boy to the wall and simultaneously shoved him at the wall while slamming the wall, full force, with his fist in front of the boy's face. The parent acknowledged to the court that nothing the boys did was so serious as to warrant this kind of behaviour.

The court concluded that the assaults were capricious and unreasonable, carried out in a state of anger, and that the father's goal was to instil fear in order to engender respect, rather than to correct the minor behaviour lapses of the boys.

Parents who physically abuse a child may not only have that child removed from their care by the CAS, but may also be punished by criminal law. For example, the Ontario Court of Appeal handed down an eight-year prison sentence for the attempted murder of a three-month-old baby by her father, who, tired of her crying, threw her on the floor and left her brain-dead.

In 2000, an Ontario judge upheld the constitutional validity of Section 43 of the Criminal Code, loosely referred to as "the spanking law," which allows parents and teachers to use reasonable force to correct a child's behaviour, and in fact enables parents and teachers to carry out their responsibilities. The trial judge cautioned that in each case "reasonable" force must be determined by the courts through an objective test based on contemporary community standards, including the nature of the offence calling for correction, the age and character of the child and the likely effect of the punishment on this particular child, the degree of gravity of the punishment, the circumstances under which it was inflicted, and the injuries, if any, suffered.

The case was appealed. The Ontario Court of Appeal in 2002 dismissed the appeal, with a comment that the Criminal Code exemption for parents and teachers did not mean that physical punishment of children was acceptable, but ". . . criminalization is often too blunt and heavy-handed an instrument with which to address many of the problems concerning the welfare of children."

In 2004, the Supreme Court of Canada agreed with both lower courts that the law did not contradict the Charter.

Bystanders have a legal duty to report cases of ill-treated children everywhere except in the Yukon, where reporting is discretionary. Doctors must usually report suspicious cases even if doing so breaches the professional privilege attached to doctor/patient communications. In all provinces except Newfoundland and Labrador and Nova Scotia, lawyers do not have to report if doing so would divulge confidential solicitor/client communications. Normally, the identity of the informant is not revealed.

In a 1995 Ontario case, a baby-sitter reported suspicious bruises on a four-year-old to the Children's Aid Society, whose social workers had been making regular supervisory visits to the home for five weeks. The baby-sitter made further frantic calls, but despite a return CAS visit, the baby-sitter found the child dead the next morning and the autopsy confirmed internal injuries. This tragic case shows that it is not always easy for a bystander to step in and make a difference.

4. Religious and Moral Upbringing and Health Care

Parents have considerable freedom from government intervention in giving their children a religious and moral education and, within limits, determining their health care. However, federal criminal and provincial child-welfare laws still have a role to play to protect children in case their parents or others responsible for their care act in ways that could potentially harm them.

As noted earlier, parents or guardians may be regarded as criminals for failing to provide necessities to a child under 16. Necessities can include medical treatment needed to preserve life, even if the method of treatment contravenes the parents' religious beliefs. Therefore, a parent who denies treatment on religious grounds, thereby causing harm to the child or accelerating the child's death, may be convicted of criminal negligence. While the Canadian Charter of Rights and Freedoms contains guarantees of religious freedom, it does not extend to parents the right to risk a child's life or health on religious grounds.

The Supreme Court of Canada ruled in 1995 that parents could not invoke the Charter of Rights as an excuse for refusing a blood transfusion for their infant daughter. The Court held that it was reasonable to grant a Children's Aid Society temporary wardship so that the CAS could consent to the blood transfusion for the child, whose parents belonged to the Jehovah's Witnesses faith. The parents had argued that the Charter right of "liberty" meant that they had unconstrained freedom and the right to make decisions of fundamental personal importance, which included the right to nurture a child and make decisions about the child's welfare and medical care. The Court did not disagree, but ruled that intervention can be justified when parental conduct falls below a socially acceptable standard, and when children's lives and well-being are in jeopardy.

In another case involving "necessaries," a father and mother were sentenced to a jail term of two years less a day (one day less than the maximum sentence) for failing to provide a proper diet and medical treatment for their 16-month-old daughter, who died of malnutrition and bronchopneumonia. The parents had stopped taking the child to a medical doctor and were following the advice of an herbalist, who recommended a diet without meat or dairy products, and herbal remedies to treat a rash and weight loss.

Some parents not only do not trust in the efficacy of vaccinations, but also believe that they are potentially harmful. There are few laws dealing with this matter; usually it arises as a public health issue in connection with school attendance. Rules often exist that children are not permitted to attend school unless they have received certain customary vaccinations.

The law is clear that no one can force a child to be vaccinated without consent, which is why schools send home permission forms to be signed by a parent or guardian. On the other hand, schools have a right to make rules to keep safe all the children under their supervision, and may ask parents who don't give permission to keep their children out of school.

Many jurisdictions in Canada now provide free mass immunizations to children, particularly when there is a threat of the spread of diseases such as meningitis or hepatitis B. In Ontario, the law goes farther and states par-

ents are duty-bound to have their child immunized for designated diseases, but a parent's written consent is still required before the immunization can be given. Ontario's Immunization of School Pupils Act also provides for exemptions with a medical certificate from a doctor, or a statement filed by a parent who states that vaccinations are contrary to their conscience or religious belief. Without an exemption, a student in Ontario who cannot provide proof of required immunizations may be excluded or suspended from school for up to 20 days. And a parent who contravenes the Act may be found guilty and fined up to $1,000.

In a 2001 B.C. case, a nurse was carrying out a program of hepatitis B immunization of Grade 6 children at an elementary school. She sent each child home with a pamphlet and a consent form. When one girl did not return a signed form, the nurse testified that she followed her standard practice of calling the child's parents. She had a note that she secured verbal consent, but the parents denied this, and the nurse admitted she could not recollect the actual call.

The 11-year-old girl told the nurse that her parents did not want her vaccinated. The nurse testified that children sometimes say this as a delaying tactic, and that is how she interpreted this child's comment. The nurse told the child that she had spoken with her parents, that they *did* want her to have it, and she proceeded with the immunization. When the parents found out, they sued for damages.

The judge believed that the nurse acted in good faith, sure that she had the parents' verbal consent, but ruled that the nurse should not have acted without checking with the parents, in view of the child's statement. The judge stated that a vaccination without parental consent, even though there was no evidence of any harm being caused to the child, constituted battery (the intentional infliction of unlawful force). The court ordered the community health nurse and her employer, the South Fraser Health Region, to pay general damages of $1,000. The judge noted that health care providers must respect the fundamental principle that all individuals control access to their bodies.

Generally, courts have viewed immunization to be in a child's best interests. In considering an application under Alberta's Child Welfare Act in 2002, a mother's failure to ensure her child had medication and immunizations contributed to a finding that she was placing her child at risk. Parents with differing views on immunization should work this out if they separate. If they do not, then a court must decide, usually with professional help, whether this would be in their child's best interests.

In two recent family law cases, one in Alberta and the other in Ontario, the judges preferred the evidence of the children's doctors and other specialists, generally supporting vaccinations over a parent's worries about allergies or unverified articles opposing vaccinations from magazines and off the Internet. Before such articles could be admissible as evidence, both courts held that the authors must not only be identified, but evidence of their qualifications must be provided.

Sometimes, the parents are not battling the state but each other over who should control the children's upbringing. The only legal guide in these cases is the rule that the "best interests of the child" must prevail over the wishes and needs of either parent.

How judges interpret "best interests" depends on the facts of each case. Although the courts try to set guidelines for interpreting best interests, they sometimes establish conflicting rules. The matter of spiritual upbringing has come before the courts. In 1994, the Supreme Court of Canada dealt with two cases in which fathers wanted to expose their children to the tenets of their religious faith—in both cases Jehovah's Witnesses—and ruled in opposite ways on the same day. In one case, the Court said best interests means what is shown to benefit the child; in the other, the Court interpreted best interests more broadly to mean what is shown not to harm the child. Even though both cases arose in separation situations, any court dealing with the rights of parents within an ongoing marriage will likely be guided by one of these decisions.

The Criminal Code contains other prohibitions against behaviour related to religious and moral upbringing. For example, the Code states that anyone in control of premises who knowingly permits a child under 18 to be there for the purpose of engaging in sexual activity prohibited by the Criminal Code, or a parent or guardian who promotes prohibited sexual activity by a child under 18, is subject to imprisonment for up to five years if the child is under 14, and two years if the child is 14 or more but less than 18. It is also a crime to participate in "adultery or sexual immorality or indulge in habitual drunkenness or any other form of vice" in the home of a child who is "or appears to be" under age 18, and thereby endanger the child's morals. The maximum sentence is two years. Finally, anyone who gives a child under 18 unsupervised access to a firearm is subject to punishment of up to two years in jail, unless the child has a permit. There are other issues dealing with the exploitation of children in Chapter 8.

5. Naming Children

The traditional expectation has been that a child will bear the surname of the father, and that everyone in the family will have the same surname. Many families continue this pattern, but many others have chosen a different way.

Currently, many women keep their own surnames after marriage and after the birth of their children. Some women have or raise children on their own. In these cases, the legal surname of the children depends on the laws of the province in which the children are born. Most provinces have modified their laws to take into account individual circumstances and preferences by allowing parents to choose the surname of their child.

In Ontario, for example, when both parents consent, the child can be given the surname or former surname of either parent, or a surname consisting of one surname or former surname of each parent, hyphenated or combined. If the parents cannot agree, the child must be given either the parents' surname if they use the same one, or, if they have different surnames, a surname consisting of both parents' surnames hyphenated or combined in alphabetical order.

Until the traditional requirements changed, if a married woman was separated from her husband and conceived a child by someone else, she was still legally required to give the child her husband's surname. Now, most jurisdictions allow a married but separated woman the same choices as an unmarried woman. Generally, she can give the child her surname or, with the natural father's consent, she can choose his surname or a hyphenated combination of her and his surnames.

6. Adoption

Adoption of children is a time-honoured way for adults to expand their family, express their love for children and provide a home for youngsters whose parents have not been able to care for them. The consent of both biological parents (if known) is required, but these consents generally cannot be signed until after the child is born. Even then, they can usually be withdrawn within a specified period of time (depending on the province's rules).

An adoption order permanently changes a child's status: She or he becomes the child of the adoptive parents for all purposes, the same as if she or he had been born to them. Once adopted, the child is entitled to take the adoptive family's surname, be financially supported and have the same inheritance rights as a natural child.

The natural parents have no further obligations and rights with respect to the child. In most cases, this used to mean that the child was completely separated from her or his biological parents, but in the past few years this rule has been softened to some extent. Recently, the biological mother and father have occasionally sought and been granted continuing rights of access, even if the child was made a Crown ward, and even if a step-parent adopts the child.

There have been several reported cases of siblings successfully claiming access. For example, a Canadian woman brought two orphaned Mexican children to live with her in Canada, but decided, after two years, to adopt only the girl; the boy was made a Crown ward. When the woman would not let this ten-year-old contact his half-sister, he successfully applied to the court for an access order. The appeal by the woman and the CAS did not succeed.

DOMESTIC ADOPTIONS

Every province and territory has its own rules. Most jurisdictions will deal with an adoption if either the person applying to adopt or the child to be adopted lives within its boundaries; in some jurisdictions, such as Ontario, both the child and the applicant must reside in the province. Adoption hearings are relatively informal and are normally arranged to protect the anonymity of the parties.

Fees: All jurisdictions prohibit the charging of fees to arrange adoptions, beyond the basic actual costs to handle the procedure, and require an investigation by a provincial agency and an official report regarding the applicant(s) and child before an adoption order is made. They may make an exception in some cases where the child welfare agency is itself placing the child for adoption (rather than simply conducting the investigation), or where a relative or step-parent is adopting the child. Most jurisdictions require the child to live with the adoptive parent for a period of time, usually six months, before making the adoption order.

Crown Wards: Provincial and territorial adoption legislation deals with adoptions of Crown wards (children already in the custody of a provincial child welfare agency), private adoptions (often through licensees regulated by the province) and private relative and step-parent adoptions.

Step-Parent Adoptions: The qualifications in step-parent and relative adoptions may be less stringent, especially if a husband and wife make the application jointly and the child to be adopted is the natural son or daughter of one of them.

Qualifications: Generally speaking, prospective adoptive parents are not required to be married. However, since the applicant's spouse is required to consent before the adoption will be approved, both partners must agree to the adoption.

It is a significant change in social policy that in all provinces a single adult may now apply to adopt a child, although the circumstances of the single adult will be reviewed by the court. For example, an Alberta court refused an application for adoption by a widow, who was the guardian of a two-and-a-half-year-old child. The birth mother had left the child with this woman and then disappeared. The birth father could not be located; he had left the mother when he learned of her pregnancy, saying he did not care if the child was aborted or adopted.

The widow appealed the decision, and the Alberta Court of Appeal in 1995 ruled that, except for being single, the woman met all reasonable criteria: She was the only parent the child had known since birth; she had two children of her own, aged 11 and 13; she was a good parent; she had a strong extended family who lived in close proximity. The Court granted the adoption order.

Same-sex couples can now adopt children in Alberta, British Columbia, Ontario, Saskatchewan, Manitoba, Quebec, Nova Scotia, New Brunswick, Newfoundland and Labrador, and the Northwest Territories, and on a case-by-case basis in some other provinces and territories.

In some cases, grandparents apply to adopt a child. The Northwest Territories and

Nunavut laws specifically state that when a child is a Crown ward and is placed for adoption, preference will be given to the grandparents if they apply. Sometimes the application of grandparents who have been involved with the child's care is preferred over the application of strangers; sometimes it is not. For example, in one case the Ontario Court of Appeal in 1994 upheld a lower court's refusal to let grandparents adopt a child when the birth parents had consented to an adoption by strangers. However, in another case the grandparents were allowed to claim custody or access after the adoption order went through to strangers. Although the child was formally adopted by strangers, the grandparents were still able to prove that it was in the child's best interests to be in their custody or to have access to them.

Consents Required: Depending on the particular circumstances, provinces and territories often require written consents from both biological parents or guardians of the child, the child welfare agency (if the child is a Crown ward), the child (generally if aged 12 or over) and the spouse of the applicant. Some provinces and territories require the consent of the biological mother only if the parents are not married or the mother's husband did not father the child. The rules vary among the provinces and territories, depending on whether the father signed the birth registration or formally acknowledged paternity, whether the father has custody or access rights and with whom the child is actually living.

Heritage Factor: Some provinces, namely, British Columbia, Saskatchewan, Ontario and Prince Edward Island, specifically recognize that it is in children's best interests to consider such factors as their cultural, racial, linguistic and religious heritage. Certain provinces (British Columbia and Ontario) also recognize the importance of maintaining an Aboriginal child's heritage. The Northwest Territories and Nunavut have passed legislation to recognize adoptions that have taken place according to Aboriginal custom, to ensure that these children are granted birth certificates and social insurance numbers and have official status under provincial legislation.

Secrecy and Disclosure: Historically, adoption records have been kept secret because secrecy was considered better for everyone. In recent years, however, some adopted children, now adults, have exerted increasing pressure to learn their biological background and to contact parents and siblings. Secrecy is no longer the rule in many places. Since 1996, new legislation has been passed in many provinces to change the assumptions and allow adopted children and birth families the freedom to find each other; "confidentiality unless interested parties consent otherwise" has given way to an assumption of "disclosure unless an interested party registers a veto."

Still, all provinces and territories have some form of adoption disclosure registry. Typically, adult adoptees and birth parents must consent before information identifying them will be released. Most provinces also provide for counselling to ease the disclosure process.

Newer legislation loosens the identification process. Saskatchewan's law allows the release of birth records for adoptions that took place after April 1, 1997, without anyone's consent, although a veto may be registered. Similarly, British Columbia's adoption legislation, which applies to adoptions that occurred after November 4, 1996, provides for "openness agreements" to be made by prospective adoptive parents and others who have established a relationship with the child. An adopted person over 19 may apply to the director of vital statistics for a copy of the original birth registration and adoption order, unless a party has filed a disclosure veto. The person who placed the child for adoption can find out the child's adoptive name.

Alberta's 1999 legislation stated that if both an adopted person and his or her biological parents or siblings have applied to the adoption registry, the identity of any person who has not filed a veto will be disclosed. Information from the birth registration and adoption record may be disclosed to an adopted person if the biological parents consent. For adoptions that took place after January 1, 2000, disclosure of adoption record information to the adopted person and the biological parents is automatic on request unless a veto has been filed. In 2004 Alberta opened up its adoption records without veto power for all adoptions occurring after January 1, 2005. For adoptions that took place before January 1, 2005, a specified period of time for filing a veto was stated.

Manitoba's 1999 legislation allows for openness agreements between adoptive and birth parents. A disclosure or contact veto may be registered. Information will be provided on request unless a veto is registered.

In the Northwest Territories and Nunavut since 1998, the adoption registry must not only provide the name of the adoptee and birth parent or parents but also the names of all other children, parents and grandparents of the adopting parent and natural parent.

Once the adoptee reaches age 19—the age of majority—this information can be released, on request, to any of the above persons. This disclosure policy applies only to adoptions that took place since 1998.

Quebec provides that an adopted person aged 14 or over is entitled to information enabling him or her to find his or her birth parents if they have consented; similarly the adoptee must consent if his parents want to find him. If the child is under 14 both birth and adoptive parents must agree before the child is given any information or even the fact of the application for information.

In 2003 Newfoundland and Labrador enacted legislation to provide for openness agreements, an adoption registry, a disclosure veto and a no-contact declaration. It also provided that people adopted after April 30, 2003, upon reaching age 19, will be able to apply for copies of their original birth registration and adoption information.

FOREIGN ADOPTIONS

For some time, the supply of born-in-Canada children available for adoption has not met the demand. As a result, a number of Canadian families have adopted children from other countries, such as Romania, Paraguay, China, Guatemala, El Salvador, India, Ukraine and Georgia.

All jurisdictions have legislation to recognize foreign adoptions. In 2002, there were 1,891 foreign adoptions in Canada; the greatest number by far were from China (771) with the next most popular countries being Russia (146), India (126) and South Korea (97). Generally, if the adoption is made pursuant to the laws of the foreign jurisdiction, it will have the same force and effect as if made in Canada. Proof of compliance with the laws of the foreign country is required.

All provinces except Quebec and Newfoundland and Labrador have also adopted the Intercountry Adoptions Act of the Hague Convention, an attempt to promote a system of co-operation between member states. The purpose of the Act is to protect the interests and rights of children involved in intercountry adoptions by establishing standards and criteria regarding issues such as eligibility of a child for adoption and suitability of adoptive parents. A specific goal is to prevent the abduction, sale or traffic in children. The consent of the mother must be freely given after the birth of the child. The preamble assumes that the foreign adoption is occurring only because there is no suitable family to take the child in the country of birth.

Newspapers report that some children in poor countries are sold and others are stolen from their parents for sale to unscrupulous adoption agents.

Romania used to provide significant numbers of babies from its overpopulated state-run orphanages, a product of the years when both contraception and abortion were illegal. In 2002, Romania provided only 15 children for adoption. Reports of these adoptions revealed that some children had developmental problems arising from inadequate pre-natal care and/or impersonal post-natal institutionalized care.

Chinese orphanages are providing babies for adoption. Almost all the Chinese babies available for adoption are girls, abandoned by families who want to meet China's one-child-per-family policy with a son.

Regardless of the child's country of origin, if the adoption is finalized in Canada, Canadian laws generally require the freely given consent of the natural mother—unless the child is a ward of the state. The father's consent is also required if the father is known or named on the birth certificate. The father's consent may be dispensed with in some circumstances by some courts, but the mother's consent is always required. Health inspections of the child by the immigration department, and in-home visits by Canadian social workers, are usually part of the process. Ontario levies a fee of $925 to process a foreign adoption. The agency that provides the adoption services will also need to be paid; note that agencies in Ontario must be licensed specifically for intercountry adoption services.

It is wise to ensure that lawyers both in the foreign country and in Canada have reviewed the documentation to make certain the laws of the place of adoption were observed.

Most Canadian provinces require either the applicant or child to be a resident of the province for a specified period before allowing an application to be made to validate a foreign adoption order. However, Ontario requires both the child and the applicant to be resident in the province before the court will accept jurisdiction to make an adoption order; therefore, Ontario will not make an adoption order dealing with a foreign resident. A number of provinces specifically provide in their legislation for the adoption of children who reside in other countries. In rare cases, an adoptive parent may persuade a Canadian judge that, in the best interests of the child, the Canadian court should make the adoption order rather than just recognize the foreign order, but this strategy is a last resort.

7. Financial Support

A parent's duty of financial support is more than a moral imperative; it is a legal rule. Provincial and federal laws unequivocally require parents to support their children.

The term "parent" includes both mother and father. Parents of a child born outside marriage, adoptive parents and legal guardians all have an obligation to provide support. In some cases, a person who has treated the child as his or her own, and has stood *in loco parentis* (in the place of a parent), may have the same obligation.

CRIMINAL LAW

The Criminal Code, which applies across Canada, states that it is the legal duty of a parent to provide the "necessaries" of life for a child under 16 years of age, which include shelter, clothing, food, education and training, medical treatment and medicines. It also states that anyone, including a parent, who has assumed an obligation to provide the necessities of life to a person who is dependent because of illness, disability or other cause must continue to do so, regardless of the dependant's age.

Failure to provide these necessities is punishable by up to two years in prison. When passing sentence on what he called "one of the worst cases of abuse of a poor helpless child that I have ever seen," an Ontario judge in 1985 criticized the short maximum penalty allowed by law. He was sentencing a mother for severely beating and starving her ten-year-old child, to the extent that the child had the weight of a three-year-old and the height of a five-year-old. The sentence was two years for failing to provide the necessities and three years for assault, to be served concurrently.

PROVINCIAL LAW

Every province also has laws requiring child support, but the issue does not normally come before the courts unless the parents are separated and the custodial parent seeks support. The maximum age to which a child is entitled to support differs from province to province, and ranges from 16 to 19; at the specified age, the support ends, regardless of a child's circumstances.

If a child leaves home while under the age of majority and in some cases under age 16, and needs financial assistance, the child or the Children's Aid Society may seek financial aid from the parents. Generally, a child aged 16 or older cannot be forced to live at home or under the care of the CAS. However, a child who leaves voluntarily to live independently may be required to be self-supporting. If the child leaves involuntarily, parents may be required to support an unmarried child up to age 19. Most other provinces have similar laws.

If the child applies for financial support, the court will determine whether the departure was voluntary or not. If the judge decides that the child was driven away by an intolerable situation at home, perhaps physical or emotional abuse, and had no choice but to leave, the parents will have to support the child while she or he lives away from home.

Ontario courts have heard a number of cases of teenagers who left home around the age of 16, often because new stepfathers had made them feel unwelcome in their own home. The courts ordered the mothers and stepfathers to support these children so that they could continue high school while living away from home.

If both parents work, the court may order both to support the child according to their income. The child cannot usually get welfare while the parents are still legally required to support her or him and are able to do so. Like the child, welfare authorities may go to court to enforce the parents' support.

SUPPORT FOR OLDER CHILDREN

In New Brunswick, Quebec and the Yukon, parents are required to support minor children only. The Yukon specifies "minor and unmarried."

Elsewhere, most provinces and territories require support for adult children under certain circumstances. Ontario requires parents to support a child who is a minor and unmarried, or is in a full-time (not necessarily postsecondary) program of education. British Columbia, Alberta, Manitoba, Newfoundland and Labrador, Nova Scotia, Prince Edward Island, the Northwest Territories, Nunavut and Saskatchewan require parents to support a child over the age of majority who is unable to support himself or herself because of illness, disability or "other cause." Among these jurisdictions, Newfoundland and Labrador, the Northwest Territories, Nunavut and Saskatchewan explicitly include "reasonable pursuit of education" as a basis for requiring support. Prince Edward Island includes enrolment in a full-time program of education. Nova Scotia excludes postsecondary students over age 24.

A child of divorced parents whose support has been ordered under the Divorce Act has the right to be maintained up to and past age 16 if he or she is in the custody of a parent and cannot support himself or herself due to illness, disability or "other cause." "Other cause" has been interpreted to include attendance at a postsecondary school, when appropriate. It has also included unemployment because of the economy's lack of jobs, in the case of a 20-year-old unemployed daughter. For example, a court would expect university-educated parents to support their children through university. A student will generally receive support appropriate to the parents' status and income, but usually not past age 23 or the completion of the first university undergraduate degree. There is no upper age limit to which a disabled child of divorced parents can get support. A Divorce Court may refuse to grant a divorce if reasonable maintenance arrangements have not been made.

WHAT HAPPENS IF THE PAYER DIES?

If a dependent child receives support payments ordered by a court under provincial support or divorce law, the parent's estate would likely be required to continue the payments after the parent's death, even if the child is an adult. If the adult child is needy but does not already receive court-ordered payments, the child or someone representing the child may be able to apply for support from the parent's estate under the law's dependants' relief provisions. Most provinces have these laws, which allow dependent children of any age to apply for support. However, in Ontario, for example, a parent's estate will not be required to pay support unless a legal obligation of support or payments existed immediately before the parent's death.

In some rare cases, the court may order the estate of a parent who dies without providing for adult children to pay where there is no actual dependency, because of a moral obligation. In a 1994 New Brunswick case, the two grown (and retired) children of the deceased sought a share of their father's estate, instead of the five dollars he left them in his will. The court ruled that he had a moral obligation to them; because he deserted them as children, they did not have the means to get a good education and therefore never had the skills for a well-paying job. The court overruled the will, which had left everything but the five-dollar bequests to a long-time friend of the deceased, and instead ordered the estate shared equally among the three—the two children and the friend.

8. Support of Parents by Adult Children

Adult children may have a moral obligation to support a parent in need. Under certain circumstances, they may also have a legal obligation. Much depends on the history of the parent/child relationship.

Under the Criminal Code of Canada, an adult child is required to provide the basic necessities of life, such as food, shelter and medical treatment, for a parent who is in the child's charge—for example, living with the child—and unable to provide the necessities for herself or himself due to age, illness, insanity or other cause. The child can be prosecuted for failing to provide the necessities for the parent.

Most of the provinces and territories have legislation obligating an adult child to pay support to a needy parent, to the extent the child is capable, if the parent has supported or cared for the child. Some jurisdictions limit parental support to disabled or destitute parents, and some specifically direct the court to keep in mind the child's own needs and other responsibilities.

Under provincial and territorial laws, it is likely that a parent's request for support will be upheld by the court only if the parent cared for the child or contributed to the child's support during childhood. Applications would likely be rejected from a parent who deserted the family and made no support payments or from a biological parent who gave up a child for adoption; on the other hand, the adoptive parent who raised the child would be entitled to seek support.

A court can order parental support only from an adult child who is over the age of majority (the age varies from province to province) and only if the adult child has the financial means, considering other obligations. Before deciding how much support to order, the court reviews the parent's circumstances and needs and the child's ability to pay.

While there have been few reported cases in which parents have had to go to court for an order to enforce a child's duty of parental support, they do exist.

In one such case in 1982, an Ontario mother sought support from her son because her husband had failed to support her and had given all his property to the son, who was supporting the father. The court ordered the son to pay his mother a monthly allowance as well. In another Ontario case, a son who had sponsored his parents' immigration to Canada from Guyana was ordered to pay each parent $175 a month.

In an Ontario case, a 58-year-old mother succeeded in her suit, even though she had been a far from perfect parent. It was enough for her to show that she had provided both financial support and personal care, however minimal. In 1993, the provincial court ordered her four adult children, aged 34 to 39, to pay her interim support of $1,000 a month, pending trial, retroactive to the date in 1990 that she launched her suit. The mother had represented herself in the proceedings.

The mother was primarily a homemaker until she separated from her abusive alcoholic husband in 1973, when the children were teenagers. The family lived on social assistance for a while, and three of the children worked their way through university, all eventually building successful careers.

Meanwhile, the mother completed a two-year high-school upgrading program and then earned a psychology degree. She began a business administration course but couldn't afford to complete it. The only job she could get—live-in caregiver to an elderly woman—paid a salary of $150 per week. With her widow's pension, her total income was $848 per month. She wanted support from her children so she could live on her own, get dental and chiropractic treatment and pay for car repairs.

The four children argued that their mother was not entitled to support under Ontario's Family Law Act because she had not provided them with sufficient care or support and had no financial need. In their view, entitlement required an exceptional contribution over and above the minimum support she was legally obliged to provide. They also said that she did not deserve support because of her serious flaws as a parent—lack of empathy, frequent use of harsh physical punishments and failure to protect her daughters from sexual abuse. Her care fell below parenting norms, they maintained, as established by a social work expert who gave evidence.

The court rejected both arguments, finding that the mother had provided financial support as well as moral support. The fact that the family lived on welfare when the children were young should not defeat a parental claim. The court decided a parent need only prove that either support or care was provided. As for the mother's parenting skills, the court concluded that they had to be judged in the context of her time. Her frequent use of physical discipline, which was said to be more common in the 1950s and 1960s, did not negate her entitlement to support. The judge also observed that the mother's care "was somehow influential" in producing four well-educated and worthy adults.

The children got a stay of the interim order for a while and appealed it twice. An interim order of the Ontario Court of Appeal in 1995 ruled that the children must pay the $1,000 per month pending the hearing of the appeal. When the appeal was heard in 1996, the three appeal-court judges ruled that the children must support the mother and pay towards her court costs, and referred the matter back to the lower court to determine whether the amount was appropriate.

Another court case showed that parents are not entitled to support from children who were never dependent on them. In 1987, an Ontario widow lost her case for interim support against her two adult stepsons. She claimed that she had provided moral and financial support for them by assuming day-to-day responsibility for their late father and mentally disabled sister. At the time of her marriage, however, the stepsons were 28 and 34 and living independently, which they continued to do. The judge refused her claim.

A Quebec court in 1997 ordered a woman who won a $2.1 million lottery to pay a $1,000 monthly allowance for three years to her estranged, poverty-stricken parents who were on welfare.

In some provinces, persons other than parents, such as step-parents, foster parents and grandparents, are allowed to seek support in court. Sometimes, nursing homes or government assistance programs may want a child to take primary responsibility for an infirm parent's care. Laws in Ontario and Prince Edward Island clearly forbid creditors from applying for support on a parent's behalf, but some provinces consider these requests.

CHAPTER 7

HUMAN AND CIVIL RIGHTS

⚖

Introduction

The right to live one's life free of discrimination is a basic human right. Our society has been establishing laws to protect individuals from discriminatory treatment since the 1950s when the first human rights code was legislated in Canada. Since then, every province and territory, as well as the federal government, has established human rights laws and human rights commissions, whose job it is to ensure that the lofty principles in the laws are carried out.

The laws are periodically reviewed. In 2003, the Canadian Human Rights Commission announced steps to improve resolution of human rights disputes, by expanding the availability of non-adversarial alternative dispute resolution to promote the settlement of cases fairly and quickly. This followed the success of its pilot project, which was launched in 1999; by 2002, 64 per cent of the cases that went this route were mediated successfully. Starting in 2003, the CHRC offered alternate dispute resolution at all stages of the complaint process, instead of its previous availability only at the initial stage or just before the case went to tribunal.

Discrimination can be direct and obvious; if someone says you cannot rent an apartment because you are black, or have a child, or wear a turban, you know you are suffering discrimination. Discrimination can also be indirect and systemic—when the employer's rules appear neutral but have an adverse impact on a specific group. One example is a height requirement that excludes most women and members of certain racial groups. Another is inflexible working hours that include a day set aside for religious worship by certain groups. The Supreme Court of Canada in 1999 removed the distinction between the remedies for direct and indirect discrimination.

Social attitudes towards human rights issues have changed dramatically. For example, it is now against the law to ask job applicants or prospective tenants questions that would require them to admit they fall into one of the protected human rights groups, such as race. Simply asking such questions is seen as engaging in discriminatory conduct.

Nevertheless, for both the 1996 and 2001 Censuses, Statistics Canada itself decided to ask Canadians to identify themselves according to race in its census questionnaire. According to the stated reason for the request, the federal government wanted data to support programs that promote equal opportunities to share in the social, cultural and economic life of Canada. Despite opposition from some Canadians, the federal privacy commissioner did not seem to consider the question as invading the privacy of citizens.

The 2001 question offered the following options: "White, Chinese, South Asian (e.g., East Indian, Pakistani, Sri Lankan), Black, Arab, Filipino, Southeast Asian (e.g., Cambodian, Indonesian, Laotian, Vietnamese), West Asian (e.g., Afghan, Iranian), Latin American, Japanese, Korean, Other."

The census questionnaire also asked to which ethnic or cultural group the person's ancestors belonged, and offered some examples: "Canadian, French, English, German, Scottish, Canadian, Italian, Irish, Chinese, Cree, Micmac, Métis, Inuit (Eskimo), Ukrainian, Dutch, East Indian, Polish, Portuguese, Filipino, Jewish, Greek, Jamaican, Vietnamese, Lebanese, Chilean, Somali, etc."

And it asked about religious affiliation. The options offered were "Roman Catholic, Ukrainian Catholic, United Church, Anglican, Lutheran, Baptist, Greek Orthodox, Jewish, Islam, Buddhist, Hindu, Sikh, etc."

In addition to human rights legislation, Canada has had the Charter of Rights and Freedoms since 1982, which entrenched in our Constitution certain protections and guarantees as individuals against government. People who believe that their Charter rights have been infringed upon have no commission to complain to, but can raise the issue in a lawsuit.

This chapter presents some examples of specific issues of human rights violations that have arisen over the years, and describes how our legal system has dealt with them. Some discrimination issues are also discussed in other chapters. If a person thinks that he or she has suffered or is suffering discrimination, he or she should consult a local human rights commission office and/or a civil liberties lawyer.

A. HUMAN RIGHTS

1. How Human Rights Commissions Operate

If a person has reasonable grounds to believe he has suffered discrimination in a way that offends the human rights codes, he should register a complaint with a provincial human rights commission or, if in the federal jurisdiction, with the Canadian Human Rights Commission.

Human rights commissions are set up on a complaint model. This means that an individual must usually register a complaint in order to get help from a commission; the commissions do not normally go looking for lawbreakers. However, in some cases, a commission can take notice of "systemic discrimination" and lay a complaint itself. Systemic discrimination is bias within an organization's very structure that affects everyone in the organization, rather than bias that is focused on an individual.

Human rights codes generally prohibit discrimination in employment, accommodation and the provision of goods, services and facilities based on race or colour, religion or creed, sex (including pregnancy or childbirth), age, disability, marital status, sexual orientation, family status, ancestry or place of origin, and, in some places, political belief, dependence on alcohol or drugs, pardoned conviction, source of income (Ontario bans discrimination in accommodation on the grounds of receipt of public assistance), and (only in Quebec) language. Alberta added "poverty" to the list in 1996 so that welfare recipients can now complain to their province's human rights commission if they are turned down for housing or bank accounts because of their financial status.

How these grounds are defined has evolved over the years. For example, sexual discrimination now includes sexual harassment in most jurisdictions. Discrimination on the basis of sexual orientation is prohibited everywhere in Canada. In many places today, it is considered discrimination on the basis of disability to discharge a person from his or her job because he or she has AIDS. In some jurisdictions, the failure to build access ramps in public facilities is also considered discrimination against people with disabilities.

A person suspecting discrimination should gather together any available evidence to prove the claims and get written statements from any witnesses, if there are any. She should keep a written record of precisely what happened and who said or did what to whom. She should keep original documents in her possession for now, and provide photocopies to the human rights investigator. The investigator will make a report and either recommend that the complaint is well founded and that the commission should therefore proceed to establish a tribunal to hear the complaint in a procedure akin to a trial, or the investigator will try to conciliate the complaint and resolve it by agreement of the parties.

The advantage of a complaint to a human rights commission over a civil lawsuit is cost: The commission pays the cost of investigating the case. While in some cases the complainant might find it helpful and even advisable to consult a lawyer, she or he may not need to pay for private legal advice at all because the human rights commission, if it verifies that the complaint is reasonable, will pursue it for her or him. If the commission or an appointed hearing tribunal finds proof of discrimination, it has the authority to order remedies that will comply with the law's human rights protection. Remedies may include reinstatement, a fine, an affirmative action program for the workplace, compensation or punitive damages. Each jurisdiction has its own rules and policies.

In November 2000, the Federal Court (Trial Division) made a ruling that could have affected many cases before human rights commissions. In a pay equity case against Bell Canada, Bell persuaded the court that a tribunal appointed by a human rights commission lacks institutional impartiality. The Federal Court (Court of Appeal) disagreed in 2001; in 2003, the Supreme Court of Canada settled the issue by confirming that a tribunal established by the Canadian Human Rights Commission is independent and impartial and "being fettered by law does not render a tribunal partial."

At times, the commission will determine that a complaint does not merit intervention; at other times, it will decide that the otherwise discriminatory behaviour was justified. For example, the Canadian Human Rights Act states that it is not a discriminatory practice for an individual to be denied access to, or occupancy of, or differentiated adversely with respect to any good, service, facility or accommodation, or any commercial premises or residential accommodation, if there is a "bona fide justification" (BFJ) for that denial or differentiation. Similarly, a practice may not be discriminatory if it is based on a "bona fide occupational requirement" (BFOR). The Canadian Human Rights Commission has detailed policy guidelines based on court interpretations to ensure that this justification or occupational requirement is objectively based and reasonable in the circumstances.

The Supreme Court of Canada interpretations in two significant cases removed the previous distinction between the remedies for direct and indirect discrimination.

A female firefighter, Tawny Meiorin, with two satisfactory years' service in an elite B.C. government firefighting unit, lost her employment after she failed new aerobic fitness tests. It was proven that most women could not meet the test standard even with training, and that the newly prescribed aerobic capacity was not necessary to do the work safely and well. The Court ruled in 1999 that the B.C. government failed to provide credible evidence that her inability to meet the standard created a safety risk, and so failed to justify the new tests as a bona fide occupational requirement. The Court also ruled that the government had not discharged its burden of showing that it had accommodated the claimant without undue hardship. The duty to accommodate means that employers are required to ensure that each person is evaluated according to his or her own personal abilities rather than presumed group characteristics.

Shortly afterwards, in 1999, the Court extended the new principle in the Meiorin case to people with disabilities. Although Terry Grismer had passed British Columbia's driving tests a number of times, he was denied a licence because generally people with his particular visual impairment (loss of most of his left-side peripheral vision in both eyes) were denied licences in British Columbia even though many other countries granted licences to people with that problem. The Court ruled that people with disabilities should be judged by what they are actually able to do, and not by abstract or general standards.

Both these cases require federally regulated employers and service providers to ensure that their standards promote real equality. They emphasize the need for systemic accommodation to ensure equal opportunity rather than individual exceptions on a case-by case basis.

Once a commission rules that a person has suffered discrimination, various remedies are available, depending on the jurisdiction. For example, a commission can issue an order to cease discriminatory conduct, make available the rights or opportunities denied due to the violation, compensate the complainant for lost wages and expenses and mental anguish, or implement an affirmative action program to remedy systemic discrimination in the workplace. A commission may also levy a penalty, ranging from a low of $100 for an individual and $500 for a corporation or trade union in the Northwest Territories, Nunavut, and Newfoundland and Labrador to a high of $5,000 for an individual and $50,000 for an employer in the federal jurisdiction covered by the Canadian Human Rights Commission.

2. Discrimination in Accommodation

When a landlord rejects an application for tenancy on a basis that is prohibited under provincial or federal human rights laws, the prospective tenant has a right to complain. For example, if the application is rejected because the applicant is a sole-support parent, the landlord may be affecting the applicant's right to be free of discrimination on the basis of family status, sex and marital status with respect to accommodation. If the application is rejected because the applicant is black or a member of another visible minority, the landlord may be discriminating on the basis of race or colour. Other grounds such as religion and disability are also protected.

Let's look first at the example of discrimination against a sole-support parent with children. A complaint may be made to a human rights commission in most jurisdictions. The human rights laws specifically prohibit discrimination on the basis of family status, which means that landlords who refuse to rent accommodation to families with children are breaking the law.

In some situations, landlords can refuse to rent to families with children if reasonable circumstances exist to justify the refusal—if tenants will share facilities, such as a kitchen, bathroom or common entrance, with the owner's family, for example.

In any place where there is no specific prohibition of discrimination on the basis of family status, a case may be made that a landlord's refusal to rent to a parent discriminates on the basis of age (young children), marital status (families) or possibly sex (young mother).

Discrimination against single parents is prohibited in every province and territory on the basis of sex and on the basis of marital status. Both sex and marital status are prohibited grounds in the federal jurisdiction covered by the Canadian Human Rights Act.

Once a complaint is registered, and the commission or tribunal hears the case, it has the authority to order remedies. These may include the provision of alternate rental accommodation or advance notice of future vacancies, compensation for out-of-pocket expenses, moving expenses, additional costs of alternative rental accommodation elsewhere or, in some cases, injured feelings.

Legislation usually stipulates a maximum fine (paid to the government). For example, Ontario's maximum is $25,000 for an individual or corporation. Most other provinces have a maximum fine of $500 to $2,000 for individuals or corporations.

Some provinces also award monetary compensation in exceptional circumstances.

The Canadian Human Rights Commission has the discretion to order that the victim of discrimination be compensated for additional costs of obtaining alternative accommodation, as well as for any expenses incurred. The Commission can also order the perpetrator to pay the victim up to $5,000 in cases where the landlord has been willful or reckless, or where the complainant has suffered humiliation.

Furthermore, any of the commissions will probably order the landlord to provide the disputed accommodation, if the prospective tenant still wants to live in it. However, this may not be realistic, because human rights complaints currently take two years or more to be adjudicated.

It is worth keeping in mind that 15 percent of families with children are headed by a lone woman, according to the 1996 Census. Even though this group represents a substantial proportion of the population, prejudice against single mothers in housing certainly exists, and the only real legal help available is through human rights legislation. Few cases have been brought forward by single mothers, but here is an example.

A 1993 Ontario board of inquiry reviewed a complaint by a woman who answered an advertisement for a basement apartment that was described as being suitable for "one lady." When she took her three-year-old with her to see the apartment, she was told that the owner did not want a child living there and was refused the apartment. The board found that the woman had been discriminated against on the basis of her family status, and required the owners to pay her $2,000 as compensation for her disappointment and embarrassment.

In a 1993 Nova Scotia case, a board of inquiry ruled that a landlord had discriminated against a black person on the basis of race in refusing to rent an apartment to her. The complainant inquired about the apartment over the telephone, but when she met with the owners she was informed that the apartment had already been rented. Her husband then phoned the owners to inquire about the apartment and was told it was still available. The board awarded the complainant $1,500 for hurt feelings and humiliation.

3. Discrimination in Public Services and Facilities

Private clubs and sporting associations, when they are public services and facilities, may be guilty of discrimination if they turn away people on one of the prohibited grounds in the human rights codes, such as sex, race, religion, disability, national or ethnic origin, sexual orientation or age. Most of these cases arise when women want to join men-only clubs or females want to play on male-only sports teams.

Men's clubs can legally exclude women, and women's clubs can legally exclude men, if the clubs are not legally defined as "public" groups. If they are considered public, clubs may claim legal exemptions that allow them to exclude members of the opposite sex for certain reasons specified in human rights codes.

SPORTS

The legal definition of a "public" facility or service is not straightforward, as the few known cases reveal. For example, the courts said human rights laws were not breached in the 1977 Ontario cases of local sports associations not allowing girls to play hockey or softball with boys. Although the games were played in arenas or parks to which the public was customarily admitted, the games were not legally considered to be services and facilities available to the public. On the other hand, in a later decision, an Ontario private school that received no public funds was defined as sufficiently public to be governed by human rights laws—it provided a public service in a place to which the public was customarily admitted.

In a 1993 decision, an Ontario board of inquiry ruled that the Ontario Soccer Association discriminated against two girls when it permitted them to be barred from playing soccer on a boys' team in a soccer tournament. The girls were 16 and 15 years old and had played soccer on a boys' team. However, they were told they could not play in the tournament because the team might be disqualified as a result. The board found that the association's rules violated the Ontario

Human Rights Code by discriminating on the basis of sex. The board of inquiry ordered the Ontario Soccer Association to pay each girl $3,500 as compensation for the humiliation she had experienced, and to ensure its rules did not bar girls and women from participating in boys' and men's teams in the future.

CLUBS

When a court is determining whether a club is private or public, access to club membership is relevant. Women's or men's clubs are not considered legally private just because they charge dues to their members (even if members fully fund the club) or have other barriers to entry. If a club advertises memberships to the public, it might thereby be offering services to the public and be required to abide by anti-discrimination laws. However, a club likely would not be considered public if new members could join only through sponsorship and personal invitation by current members, and if current members exercised substantial discretion and selectivity in screening new members.

Access to club premises is not relevant. For example, a private club that opened its restaurant to the public would not necessarily lose its private status.

Some provincial human rights codes allow public clubs to be exempted from sex discrimination laws for reasonable cause, providing the club is acting in good faith. For instance, the exemption might be claimed on grounds of "public decency" by a women's fitness club that has only one sauna and shower room or a men's squash club that has only men's washroom facilities.

Membership in clubs becomes an issue from time to time. In 1996, the Supreme Court of Canada heard a case involving a 74-year-old woman who wanted to join the Yukon Order of Pioneers, a historical society that was open only to men. The main issue was whether the organization provided a service to the public or was a private social club. The Court was divided along gender lines; the seven male judges outvoted their two female colleagues. The majority referred to a "Klondike brotherhood, founded upon moral values and male camaraderie," and ruled that the Yukon Order of Pioneers was a private club that was entitled to restrict its membership. The minority said that, apart from gender, the organization was not particularly selective in choosing members: "It is the members' common status and history as pioneers, rather than as men, which forms the common bond between them."

Anyone who reasonably believes that a club in his or her community is discriminating may contact the local human rights commission.

4. Discrimination in Sexual Orientation

Gays and lesbians were considered criminals and were beyond the protections and obligations of the law until a 1969 amendment to the Criminal Code ruled "homosexual acts" were no longer criminal offences. Through the 1970s and 1980s, the rights of homosexual individuals and couples were few and they continued to suffer discrimination in areas like employment, housing and immigration, and were excluded from the legal rights granted to heterosexuals.

This changed in the 1990s, when there was a significant expansion of same-sex legal rights and responsibilities, largely as a result of efforts from members of the lesbian and gay community. Many individuals and same-sex couples pressed their claims for equal treatment through courts and human rights tribunals, successfully using the equality provisions of the Charter of Rights and Freedoms to challenge unequal treatment. Governments have changed legislation and policies either because courts have ordered them to do so or because of threats of court cases.

The pace of change has been striking, as these highlights demonstrate.

In 1988 Michael Leshner, a Crown counsel with the Ontario Ministry of the Attorney General, complained to the Ontario Human Rights Commission that his job benefits plan was discriminatory. Because the plan covered only opposite-sex partners, Leshner's homosexual partner was not eligible to be a beneficiary. In 1990, prior to hearing the case, the Ontario government agreed to extend full coverage of supplementary health, hospital and dental benefits to same-sex partners of provincial government employees.

But when Leshner later wanted to designate his partner as beneficiary of his pension plan's survivor benefits, he was told this was impossible because the federal Income Tax Act limited the definition of "spouse" to an opposite-sex partner. He then took his complaint to an Ontario Human Rights Commission board of inquiry, which, in 1992, decided that the definition was discriminatory under the Ontario Human Rights Code and the Canadian Charter of Rights. The board ordered the Ontario government to provide equal survivor benefits to the partners of gay and lesbian employees.

In 1989 Timothy Veysey successfully challenged the federal penitentiary's refusal to allow him to visit his gay partner.

In 1991, the B.C. Supreme Court declared that the B.C. Medical Services Commission had violated Timothy Knodel's rights by refusing to provide benefits to his same-sex partner.

In 1992, the Canadian Armed Forces, facing a court challenge, agreed to stop discrimination against gays.

In 1993, an adjudicator ruled that the federal government had breached both its collective agreement and the Canadian Human Rights Act by refusing family-related leave so that a gay civil servant could look after his ailing partner and by refusing the employee's request for bereavement leave when his partner's father died.

In 1995, the federal government amended the Criminal Code to allow more severe penalties for crimes motivated by hatred on certain grounds, including sexual orientation. The same year, the federal government changed its policy regarding employees to provide that all leave-related benefits must be extended to same-sex spouses, including bereavement leave, leave for family-related responsibilities, leave for relocation of spouse, foreign service directives, isolated post directives and relocation directives.

In 1995, when a doctor refused to artificially inseminate a lesbian couple, he was found by the B.C. Council of Human Rights to be guilty of discrimination on the basis of sexual orientation.

In 1995, an Ontario provincial court judge ruled that homosexual couples have the right to apply to adopt a child under the Child and Family Services Act.

The year 1995 also saw an apparent defeat that turned out to represent an opening wide of the court's door to a flood of litigation relying on the Charter of Rights and Freedoms. A deeply divided Supreme Court of Canada rendered a 5–4 decision in *Egan & Nesbit* v. *Canada* that ultimately declined to order that same-sex partners can be considered "spouses" for the purpose of the spouse's allowance provision of the Old Age Security Act. The appellants, Jim Egan and Jack Nesbit, had been in a same-sex relationship for over 47 years when Egan applied for a spouse's allowance for his partner. The application was denied because of their same-sex relationship; the ruling was that only married or common-law partners were entitled to the benefit of the pension.

At the same time, there was agreement among most of the nine judges that "sexual orientation" can be read into the Charter of Rights as a ground of discrimination, even though the Charter did not say so in specific terms. This was the first Supreme Court of Canada case to accept that homosexuals were protected by the equality guarantees of the Charter of Rights and Freedoms.

In 1996, the Canadian Human Rights Act was expanded to prohibit discrimination on the basis of sexual orientation, and a human rights tribunal ordered the federal government to extend medical and dental benefits to the same-sex partners of its employees.

In 1996, both the trial and the Court of Appeal level in Ontario held M. was entitled to sue her former partner, H., for support on the same basis as heterosexual partners under Ontario's Family Law Act, striking down the opposite-sex definition of *spouse*.

In 1998, British Columbia passed changes to its Adoption Act and Family Relations Act to give same-sex couples who cohabited for two years the same rights and responsibilities as heterosexual couples, including pension rights, a right to contract into property and to inherit from their partner if they die without a will. That same year, the British Columbia and Nova Scotia governments introduced equal pension benefits for public sector employees with same-sex partners.

In 1998, the Ontario Court of Appeal ruled that the federal government's definition of "spouse" in the Income Tax Act was unconstitutional as it excluded same-sex survivor benefits from employers' pension plans. As a result of this decision, Nova Scotia became the first province in Canada to provide pension and medical benefits to same-sex partners of government employees.

In 1998, the Supreme Court of Canada declared to Alberta that its human rights legislation would be interpreted to include sexual orientation as a prohibited ground—whether or not it is specified in the legislation (*Vriend* v. *Alberta*). This marked the first time the Supreme Court of Canada amended legislation on constitutional grounds by reading into law new rights that elected politicians had expressly refused to grant.

In 1999, the Supreme Court of Canada dismissed an appeal by the attorney general of Ontario of the 1996 *M.* v. *H.* decision, and upheld the right of same-sex couples to claim spousal support in the same way as heterosexual common-law couples; the Court told the Ontario government it had six months to bring its unconstitutional legislation into compliance, before the ruling would take effect.

In 1999, Ontario passed an omnibus bill amending its laws to include same-sex couples. Rather than providing them with the rights of common-law heterosexual spouses, Ontario set up a separate class of "same-sex partners."

In 1999, Quebec also brought in legislation

to extend rights to same-sex couples (not including the right to marriage) in 39 different laws including, for example, workers' compensation and social assistance to give same-sex couples the same rights as opposite-sex couples.

In 1999, Alberta joined Ontario and British Columbia in permitting same-sex couples to adopt.

In 1999, the federal Parliament voted to preserve the heterosexual definition of marriage, but the rumblings of change were already moving across the country.

In 2000, the federal government enacted an omnibus bill to extend to same-sex couples who had cohabited for one year the same rights and responsibilities as those given to common-law heterosexual couples, with respect to income tax rules, Old Age Security, and Canada Pension Plan. All the rules on RRSPs that apply to married and common-law spouses would now also apply to same-sex partners, including allowing contributions to spousal RRSPs, and rollovers on death. In all, 68 pieces of legislation were amended.

In 2000, in separate legislation dealing with immigration, the "family class" provisions were also expanded to include same-sex couples.

In 2000, Nova Scotia introduced legislation to revise the definition of *spouse* in their family law to include common-law and same-sex partners who have lived together in a conjugal relationship continuously for one year. In 2001, same-sex couples in Nova Scotia were the first in Canada to be able to register their unions under new registered domestic partnership legislation. Quebec followed in 2001 by extending the definition of *spouse* in 39 laws to include same-sex couples in a "de facto union."

The 2001 Census conducted by Statistics Canada canvassed the number of same-sex families for the first time in the history of the census and released the results in 2002: Nearly 3 percent of all common-law couples declared themselves gay or lesbian. Of 11 million households surveyed, 34,200 couples said they were living in homosexual relationships, a figure that represents nearly 3 percent of the 1,158,410 common-law couples counted, or about 0.5 percent of all couples, both married and common law.

In 2001, Manitoba amended its Family Maintenance Act to comply with the Supreme Court of Canada decision in *M.* v. *H.* to extend support and certain pension and death benefit provisions applicable to persons in common-law relationships to those in same-sex partnerships. Newfoundland and Labrador also changed its family law to add a definition of partner as either one of two persons who have cohabited in a conjugal relationship outside marriage for a period of at least two years, or one year if they are together the adoptive or biological parents of a child.

In 2002, Prince Edward Island passed legislation to treat same-sex couples the same way as common-law couples.

In 2002, both an Ontario court and a British Columbia court authorized the first nationwide class-action suit over gay rights, in this case, to challenge the failure of the federal government to provide survivor Canada Pension Plan benefits to the partners of deceased homosexuals. The lawsuit alleged that the federal government discriminated, because while it collected CPP premiums from all Canadians, it denied survivor pensions to gays and lesbians whose partners died prior to January 1, 1998. The federal government had imposed that cutoff date in its 2000 legislation. The lawsuit sought benefits for all gay and lesbian survivors retroactive to April 17, 1985, the day equality guarantees were enshrined in the Canadian Charter of Rights and Freedoms. The Ontario court in 2003 ruled that survivors benefits should be paid back to April 17, 1985, because otherwise homosexual survivors were not treated equally with heterosexual survivors. The decision was upheld by the Ontario Court of Appeal in November 2004.

In 2003, Alberta passed a law giving same-sex couples the same rights as married couples, defining "adult interdependent partners" as a committed relationship that lasts at least three years or where there is a child by birth or adoption or where the couple signs a written agreement.

In 2003, same-sex couples in Ontario gained the right to marry when the Ontario Court of Appeal upheld a 2002 trial judgment and legalized same-sex marriage in Ontario. The Court ruled that the definition of the legal institution of marriage was not frozen in time but could be flexible, especially in view of the historical disadvantage and discrimination suffered by gays. The three appeal court judges changed the definition of marriage to "the voluntary union for life of two persons to the exclusion of all others." Moreover, the Court refused to suspend the application of the case to give Parliament an opportunity to act. Instead, it made the effect of its decision immediate and ordered that the marriage licence be issued to the appellants.

This was the first time that gays were allowed to legally marry and the right was instant. The Ontario Court of Appeal ruling was hailed as a landmark and the three Court of Appeal judges who wrote the deci-

sion (Chief Justice McMurtry, Justice MacPherson and Justice Gillese) were named by *The Globe and Mail* as "Nation Builders of the Year" in 2003.

The decision was handed down June 10, 2003, and was immediately followed by a flurry of marriages; the first marriage licence was granted to Michael Leshner, who had started it all, 15 years earlier, in 1988.

Soon after, the courts in other provinces were challenged to follow suit. In 2003, the British Columbia Court of Appeal had ruled to validate same-sex marriages but initially placed a one-year moratorium on the implementation of the ruling, to give the federal government a chance to act. However, once the Ontario Court of Appeal chose not to put a moratorium on its judgment, the B.C. Court of Appeal lifted its own. A Yukon court validated same-sex marriage later in 2003, and in 2004, Manitoba, Nova Scotia, Saskatchewan, Quebec, and Newfoundland and Labrador courts followed.

The federal government was more cautious than the provinces in the legitimization of same-sex marriage. In October 2004, it presented a "Reference re Same-Sex Marriage" to the Supreme Court of Canada, asking the nine judges to decide whether the opposite sex requirement for marriage for civil purposes was consistent with the Charter. By December 2004, the Supreme Court of Canada had responded, saying that the federal government had the power to change the definition of marriage, and its proposed legislation was constitutional. The Court pointed to our system of laws as a "living tree which by way of progressive interpretation, accommodates and addresses the realities of modern life." The judges went on to point out that the word "marriage" in the constitution "does not exclude same-sex marriage." The Court said that clergy could refuse to conduct same-sex marriage ceremonies as an expression of freedom of religion. The Court refused, however, to answer the question whether the traditional man–woman definition of marriage was constitutional. The federal bill to validate same-sex marriage had not yet been passed, when this book went to press.

With the recognition of the right to same-sex marriage came same-sex divorce, granted in 2004 by an Ontario court, which also declared that the opposite-sex definition of spouse in the Divorce Act is "unconstitutional, inoperative and of no force and effect" because it contravenes the equality rights guarantees of the Charter. That same-sex divorce case is believed to be a world first.

In 2004, the federal Parliament further extended the hate crimes protection in the Criminal Code to homosexuals by approving a private member's bill brought in by New Democratic MP Svend Robinson.

As it stands at this writing, the legal position of gays and lesbians in and out of same-sex relationships has been significantly improved.

Discrimination on the basis of sexual orientation is prohibited by the human rights laws in all jurisdictions in Canada, except the Northwest Territories and Nunavut, and a complaint may be registered with the federal or a provincial human rights commission if discrimination is suffered in employment, accommodation or use of public services and facilities. The Criminal Code protects homosexuals from hate crimes. The equality rights in the Charter of Rights and Freedoms apply to gays and lesbians.

Canada Pension Plan and Old Age Security Survivor Benefits are now available to survivors of same-sex unions, where the pensioner died after April 17, 1985. Many gays or lesbians who work for the federal government, or for provincial or territorial governments, may name their same-sex partner as the beneficiary of survivor pension benefits. Health benefit plan coverage is available to same-sex partners of provincial government employees in many jurisdictions.

Family laws will generally apply to same-sex couples. Same-sex marriage is now legal in Ontario, Quebec, British Columbia, the Yukon, Manitoba, Nova Scotia, and Saskatchewan, and test cases are pending elsewhere at this writing. Where same-sex marriage has been recognized, and the couple do marry, the laws of spousal support, property and divorce applicable to married couples will generally apply. Where it has not been recognized or where the couple do not marry, the rules applicable to common-law couples will often apply.

Custody and access orders are available to members of same-sex unions, and, as with heterosexual unions, the best interests of the children apply. Same-sex couples can adopt children in Alberta, British Columbia, Ontario, Saskatchewan, Manitoba, Quebec, Nova Scotia, New Brunswick, Newfoundland and Labrador, and the Northwest Territories as well as on a case-by-case basis in some other provinces and territories.

The laws continue to be amended to bring them into line with the decided cases and the legislation.

B. CIVIL RIGHTS

1. Access to Government Information and Privacy Laws

A citizen who wants to get information in government records, including personal information, may be entitled to access some government files with the help of privacy and access-to-information laws. These laws now exist in the federal jurisdiction and many provinces.

Access to Information: The federal access-to-information law allows any Canadian citizen or permanent resident of Canada to get a look at and copy files of government activities and many public institutions and agencies. It prohibits disclosure of records containing information about an individual without consent, unless the information is already publicly available. Once the information is permitted to be disclosed, it can be used only in certain ways: to fulfil the purpose for which it was collected (for example, the income tax department may get information from an income tax return to assess taxes); to comply with the law or a subpoena; for archival, statistical or audit purposes; or for other reasons set out in the privacy law.

The federal government keeps a significant number of information banks on citizens. The information banks, with records culled from dealings with the federal government, are listed by government department or institution in the Index of Personal Information, which is available at public libraries, federal government information offices in major cities and some post offices in rural areas. The index lists available information sources, such as records about federal income tax, employment insurance, family allowances, Canada Pension Plan, customs declarations, passports and immigration.

A citizen also has the right to access information in government files, to see "any record under the control of a government institution" in order to know the documentary basis of the government's official decisions. This right even applies to records held by a government department as part of a contract to provide services to a non-government party.

To request a look at files in a federal department or institution, a person should use the formal application available at post offices and libraries, where a list is kept of the individuals in each department in charge of access-to-information requests. The department or institution is required to respond within 30 days and provide photocopies of its file contents or allow an applicant to inspect the originals at its office. If a person finds mistakes in the file, he or she may make a request to have the information corrected. If the government department refuses to change the records, the person involved has the right to have the errors noted as part of the file.

If the department or institution does not answer the application within 30 days or refuses the request for information, a complaint to the federal privacy commissioner in Ottawa may be made. The commissioner has no power to force disclosure but investigates the complaint. If he or she disagrees with the refusal but cannot persuade the department or institution to provide the information, an appeal may be registered with the Federal Court.

In 2000, the federal privacy commissioner

in his annual report to Parliament revealed with concern that Human Resources Development Canada has gathered in one place "an extraordinarily detailed" and "relatively invisible" database that contains personal and financial information on individual Canadians.

Technological advances have made access to government information and departments easier. Many of them can be reached through websites or by e-mail.

However, some files are closed by law. For example, if national security, police investigation and enforcement or a person's safety is involved, or if solicitor/client privilege might be breached, the files are not made available. Records of Cabinet meetings are kept confidential. In a ruling in 2004, Canada's information commissioner upheld a federal government decision to keep divorce records confidential.

Privacy: The federal privacy law, in effect since 1983, imposes obligations on about 150 federal government departments and agencies to respect the privacy rights of Canadians. It lets a person know what personal information is in government hands, and establishes rules for the individual to assert some control over its collection, use and accuracy. The law also protects privacy by preventing others from having this information; information provided for one purpose may not be used for an unrelated purpose. For example, income tax returns may not be used by the Employment Insurance Commission.

Every province and territory has privacy legislation governing the collection, use and disclosure of personal information held by government agencies. Newfoundland and Labrador has passed legislation, but it is not yet in force. All jurisdictions with personal data protection legislation provide Canadians with an opportunity to ensure the accuracy of their personal information. The process is monitored either by an independent commissioner or ombudsman authorized to receive and investigate complaints.

Personal Information Protection and Electronic Documents Act: The federal government passed the Personal Information Protection and Electronic Documents Act (PIPEDA), which established rules to govern the collection, use and disclosure of personal information by organizations in the course of commercial activity. On January 1, 2001, the law applied to federally regulated companies—banks, insurers, telecommunications and transportation companies. On January 1, 2002, the personal health information collected, used or disclosed by these organizations was also covered. On January 1, 2004, the law applied to private business activities.

The law encouraged the provinces and territories to develop their own privacy laws for private companies, and if their laws met the standard set by PIPEDA, that jurisdiction would be exempt from PIPEDA and subject to its own law instead. British Columbia, Alberta and Quebec passed their own privacy legislation similar to the federal law, so that their law would govern businesses in their province. Quebec's 1994 privacy laws governing Quebec (but not federal) businesses preceded the federal government's by ten years, and was in 2003 exempted from the application of PIPEDA as it is substantially similar to the federal act. However, the Quebec government responded by opposing PIPEDA and the exemption process to ensure that its jurisdiction over privacy and personal information was respected, and because it disagreed with the exemption process. The Quebec government challenged (by means of a reference to the Court of Appeal of Quebec) the constitutional validity of Part 1 of PIPEDA and the jurisdiction of the federal government to legislate it. The reference had not yet been heard at the time of this writing.

PIPEDA requires organizations that collect personal information to review their policies and procedures to ensure the protection of both customer and employee privacy. On January 1, 2004, private businesses as well were required to appoint an information officer (sometimes called a privacy officer). This officer is responsible for developing and publishing a privacy policy on the collection, use and disclosure of personal information; for establishing procedures to protect personal information; for ensuring that individuals can see and correct almost all personal information held about them; for implementing a retention and destruction of information policy; for training the firm's staff in privacy policy; for acting as a contact person for inquiries from the public or clients; and for putting in place a complaints process. The officer, who is also responsible for overseeing compliance, is expected to be a senior person in the firm.

Organizations will be held accountable in respect of their compliance with PIPEDA. The federal information and privacy commissioner monitors the implementation of PIPEDA and functions as an ombudsman. The commissioner has investigative and audit powers.

The impact of technology, particularly e-mail and the Internet, has increased the need for a review of privacy laws to protect individuals. Now employers must have in place workplace policies regarding personal-use access by employees to e-mail and the Internet.

Businesses must secure a customer's consent before they collect and use an individual's personal information, and the purpose for the collection of information must be reasonable and the information must be securely stored. Magazines, for example, can no longer sell names and addresses of subscribers to third parties without the consent of subscribers. But companies can still send customers marketing and promotional information.

The law gives individual customers and employees the right to see and ask for corrections to personal information an organization may have collected about them. It also applies to information sold across provincial and territorial boundaries. As of January 1, 2002, the personal health information collected, used or disclosed by these organizations was also covered.

The privacy commissioner of Canada is also authorized to receive and investigate complaints.

There are other laws that contain provisions that protect the privacy rights of Canadians. The federal Bank Act, for example, contains provisions regulating the use and disclosure of personal financial information by federally regulated financial institutions. Similar restrictions can be found in provincial statutes that regulate the activities of financial institutions, such as credit unions and insurance companies in provincial jurisdiction.

Various consumer-protection laws at federal and provincial levels offer some protections and recourse against business practices that may in fact be an invasion of privacy.

2. Access to Medical Records

A patient's right to access his or her own medical records arises from time to time, particularly if the doctor dies, moves away or stops practising.

The hospital's and doctor's notes and files about a patient belong to the doctor and hospital, although, as a matter of practice, many doctors have been willing to provide information from their files on request. Since a 1992 Supreme Court of Canada case, applicable across Canada, patients have had the legal right of access to their complete medical record, provided they pay any physicians a reasonable fee for their costs. In that 1992 case, a patient had requested a copy of her complete medical file. The doctor produced copies of the notes but not copies of the consultants' reports or records from the patient's previous physician because she felt it would be unethical for her to release them. The patient went to court and the trial judge ordered a copy of the complete file given to the patient, a ruling that was upheld by both the New Brunswick Court of Appeal and the Supreme Court of Canada.

Most professional licensing bodies also have something to say about the matter. In Ontario, for example, it is considered professional misconduct for a doctor to fail to provide a medical report requested by a patient, unless the doctor can prove that there is good reason not to do so.

Under some circumstances, hospitals have the power to withhold information about a patient's hospital record, including laboratory x-rays and other test results. In Ontario, for example, hospital medical records are considered hospital property, and hospitals are permitted to refuse to disclose information, if they consider that knowing this information would be contrary to the patient's best interests. However, the hospital must be prepared to justify its reasons for refusing. As every province has its own laws governing hospitals and doctors, a patient should check them for a specific problem.

Sometimes, the doctor believes the patient would not understand or might misinterpret the medical records, leading to unnecessary harm or anguish. This situation is especially true for written reports of a psychiatric disorder, which a patient might be unable to accept.

Doctors make notes and keep records as reminders to themselves, not as a medical history for the patient. They list the patient's symptoms, the tests undertaken, the treatment given, the medications that helped and other information. These notes are essential to proper medical care. In fact, doctors can be charged with professional misconduct in Ontario if they do not keep these records.

No one outside the hospital or doctor's office (for example, insurance companies, the police, lawyers) is allowed to see a patient's medical records unless the patient provides written authorization permitting disclosure, or the medical records are subpoenaed in a court proceeding.

A patient has a right to have records kept accurately. If a patient is suing for injury suffered at the hands of a doctor or a hospital, and can prove the injury was caused by negligence in keeping, reading or applying the information from the records, that evidence may assist in the lawsuit against the doctor or the hospital and its staff.

On the other hand, because doctors have an obligation to keep records accurately, they will not agree to omit or add something to the record at a patient's request. For example, a patient might wish the fact of testing positive for the HIV virus to be omitted, in case this information falls into the wrong hands. The doctor will not agree to this request, however, because she or he needs an accurate record for the file in order to give the individual proper medical care in future. In any event, doctors are obliged to protect a patient's confidentiality, unless they must take part in mandatory public health reporting for certain diseases or they must respond to a subpoena of medical records. In 1996, the Ontario College of Physicians and Surgeons added another exception to its list: the obligation of a doctor to reveal to police and the possible victim any admission by a patient that he or she planned to harm someone. This admission could include the threat of violence or the threat, by an AIDS carrier, of having unprotected sexual intercourse.

When a physician dies, medical records in his or her possession legally become part of the estate, and the doctor's executor has control of them. To learn the executor's identity, a patient may contact the Probate Court in the judicial district or county where the doctor lived. But if another physician takes over the practice, that doctor will become custodian of the files. The patient may choose to stay with the new doctor, or may ask that the medical file, or a copy of it, be forwarded to another physician.

If the doctor moves away or stops practising, it is the patients' responsibility to see that their records are transferred to another doctor.

3. Getting Help from an Ombudsman

The ombudsman's role was specifically designed to examine complaints from individuals who feel that they have been unfairly treated by government agencies, officials or employees. Every Canadian jurisdiction, except Prince Edward Island, Newfoundland and Labrador and the Northwest Territories and Nunavut, has an ombudsman who is appointed by the provincial or territorial government. The Ontario ombudsman's mission statement illustrates the goal of most ombudsmen: "to strive to ensure that people are served justly, equitably, and fairly by Ontario governmental organizations."

Depending on whether a provincial or federal agency is involved, people should complain to their provincial ombudsman or to one of four federal commissioners, who are limited to specialized roles: the privacy commissioner, the correctional investigator, the commissioner of official languages, and the information commissioner under the Access to Information Act. There is no federal ombudsman, although there have been calls for the establishment of a federal agency to deal with Employment Insurance, Canada Pension Plan, Immigration Board and federal garnishment problems. Municipal and local governments do not have ombudsmen either, but some provincial ombudsmen have jurisdiction over municipal agencies.

A person can complain to an ombudsman only if he or she has been affected personally and directly. In some provinces, a group of people may submit a joint complaint. In all provinces, the ombudsman may initiate investigations without receiving a specific complaint. There is no charge for the service, and no need to hire a lawyer.

When the ombudsman receives a complaint, the first question is whether or not the office has jurisdiction. If not, the ombudsman's office will usually advise about alternatives. An ombudsman does not have the jurisdiction to investigate a complaint until the person has exhausted every right to appeal or review provided by the government agency involved or the legislation. In the course of a preliminary investigation, the ombudsman's office often resolves the complaint. But if detailed investigation is required, the ombudsman has the authority to call all necessary witnesses and obtain files and documents.

Then, the ombudsman will decide whether the complaint is reasonable and, if so, will make recommendations to the minister of the department involved and the civil servants in charge. If the minister does not accept the recommendations, the ombudsman can report this to the premier and legislature but, unlike a judge, cannot make a binding or enforceable order on government.

The person chosen to be ombudsman is usually a high-level public official who is respected by the public for her or his independence from outside pressure. She or he will not act as an advocate, as a lawyer does, but as an impartial investigator. Although the ombudsman is often perceived as an omnipotent being who can provide perfect justice and right all wrongs, she or he can act only within the authority established by Parliament or a provincial legislature, to which she or he is responsible.

Nonetheless, the ombudsman fulfils a very persuasive role and can often correct abuse through diplomacy. Sometimes, in investigating several complaints against the same department, the ombudsman is in a position to recommend wide-ranging changes in procedures and practices that may prevent general bureaucratic abuses and help enact administrative changes.

The most common types of complaint to an ombudsman are wrong or unreasonable interpretations of criteria, standards, guidelines, regulations, laws, information or evidence; discriminatory consequences of a decision or policy on an individual or group; harassment, bias, mismanagement, or bad faith by a government official; and unreasonable delay.

The trend towards privatization, contracting-out and outsourcing of services could remove certain public services from the ombudsman's jurisdiction. The ombudsman's office is the agency best situated to view and comment on the effect on public services of downsizing within the public service.

In 2002, a Financial Services Ombuds Network was established by the financial services industry, composed of banks, life and health insurers, property and casualty insurers, investment dealers and mutual fund dealers, to deal with complaints by the public.

4. Non-Smokers' Rights

When I first wrote some 20-odd years ago about the legal right to ask smokers to put out their cigarettes, few people accepted the right of non-smokers to unsullied air. How far non-smokers' rights have come!

The dangers of second-hand smoke are now well known. Non-smokers can suffer nasal irritation, watery eyes and, if exposed frequently to smoke over a long period, health problems similar to those of smokers, including greater risk of lung damage and cancer, respiratory and cardiac diseases, and even infertility.

If a smoker has a non-smoking spouse, the non-smoker has double the risk of getting lung cancer than if she or he had a non-smoking partner. Children are also endangered and have been known to suffer respiratory damage from a parent's smoking. We now know, as well, that pregnant women exposed to cigarette smoke are more likely to miscarry or give birth to underweight and stillborn babies.

A 67-year-old Ontario woman had to get help from the courts to deal with the health consequences of her husband's chain-smoking habit. Although she had undergone surgery on a cancerous left lung, he would not stop smoking in their house. She was granted a court injunction ordering her husband to stop smoking at home.

The ability to provide a smoke-free home was the determining factor in a 2002 Ontario custody case. The court ruled that a four-year-old boy with breathing difficulties should live primarily with his non-smoking father, as his mother persisted in smoking and allowing others to do so in the boy's presence.

There are now laws in many jurisdictions that can force smokers to put out their cigarettes.

The federal Non-Smokers' Health Act, passed in 1988, regulates smoking in the federal workplace and on planes, trains, ships and buses. Smoking is banned on all domestic and international flights of Canadian airlines. Every employee in the federal workplace is entitled to a smoke-free environment. If someone smokes on a plane, for example, a fellow passenger has a perfect right to ask the flight attendant to take action.

Most provinces prohibit smoking in public places, including government buildings, banks and hospitals, and regulate the extent of smoking in restaurants and bars. Manitoba enacted the strictest provincial law, called the Non-Smokers Health Protection Act, in 2004, which made it the first province to ban smoking in *all* public places and indoor workplaces. Saskatchewan has promised a similar law by 2005 and Ontario by 2007. Such other provinces as Nova Scotia, Prince Edward Island, New Brunswick and British Columbia have enacted smoking bans, except that smoking is still allowed in specially ventilated smoking rooms in bars and restaurants. Currently, Ontario has a Health Protection and Promotion Act, passed in 1984, which allows non-smokers to complain to a board of health or the medical officer of health with the power to deal with the occupational and environmental health hazards to indoor air quality. The medical officer of health must investigate all complaints in conjunction with the provincial authority in charge, and report to the complainant on the results of the investigation. Complainants can ask not to be publicly identified.

Many municipal councils have passed non-smoking by-laws similar to the one spearheaded in Hamilton, Ontario, where the city council was the first to ban smoking in most public places and required restaurants to have no-smoking areas.

The most far-reaching city regulation on smoking was enacted in Vancouver in 1996, and it also focused on the dangers of smoke to children. All smoking in restaurants and in public places frequented by persons under age 18 was banned. The law was challenged twice in the courts in two separate cases and the legislation was upheld both times in 1998 and in 2000 by the B.C. Court of Appeal. Similar anti-smoking laws, which ban smoking in any indoor location where minors are present, were passed in Winnipeg, Manitoba, and St. John's, Newfoundland, in 2002. In 2001, Edmonton banned smoking in all public places where children are served, except for lounges.

In 2003, Alberta passed a law that allows police to seize the cigarettes of anyone under age 18 who is caught smoking or is found to be in possession of tobacco products. They can also fine offenders $100. And in 2001, Ottawa banned smoking in all workplaces and public spaces, with no allowance for designated smoking rooms. Victoria, British Columbia, and Waterloo, Ontario, have similar bans.

The federal Tobacco Products Control Act, passed in 1988, prohibited the advertising and promotion of tobacco products in Canada and regulated the labelling and monitoring of these products. It imposed a total ban on tobacco advertising and promotion, and required packaging to carry unattributed health warnings.

The tobacco industry mounted a legal challenge to this law, claiming that the law took away from its companies the Charter of Rights guarantee of freedom of expression. In 1995, by a narrow 5–4 vote, the nine judges of the Supreme Court of Canada struck down this law, agreeing with the companies that the ban offended the guarantee of freedom of expression. The Court ruled that the government had not proven, as it must under Section 1 of the Charter, that its attempt to limit freedom of expression was in fact reasonable and justified in a free and democratic society. The Court would not permit the government to simply limit Charter rights as it chose. The minority judges would have deferred to Parliament, because they believed the government had a rational basis for the legislation and was trying to achieve a social policy objective of widespread impact.

The tobacco industry then instituted a code of conduct, promising that self-regulation of advertising would be effective. However, after six months of the code, Health Canada reported that the code was unenforceable, illusory and weaker, in fact, than the one that was in effect before the government passed the 1988 law banning tobacco advertising.

The federal government enacted the Tobacco Act in 1997, most of which came into force on April 25, 1997; the restrictions on sponsorship of events came into force on October 1, 1998. The Act regulates promotional activities. It prohibits testimonials or endorsements, including the use of fictional characters to promote tobacco products. Lifestyle advertising and advertising that appeals to young persons are forbidden. Permitted forms of advertising may appear only in material that is addressed by name to an adult, is in publications with an 85 percent adult readership, or is in places from which young persons are excluded by law. Sponsorship of a "person, entity, event, activity or permanent facility" that appeals to young persons, or that is associated with a way of life that includes such elements as "glamour, recreation, excitement, vitality, risk or daring," is permitted. However, severe restrictions are placed on the sponsor's promotional materials.

Tobacco product–related brand elements may appear only on the bottom 10 percent of any promotional materials. The promotional materials may appear on programs and signs on the site of the event, and may be distributed subject to the same restrictions as advertising. No permanent sports or cultural facility may display a tobacco brand element or manufacturer's name, as part of the facility's name or otherwise. The sale and advertising of tobacco accessories and of non-tobacco products that display tobacco product–related brand elements is also restricted. Sponsorships that were already in place before the restrictions came into force on October 1, 1998, were not subjected to the new restrictions until October 1, 2000. Sponsorships were phased out by 2003.

In addition, the Tobacco Products Labelling Regulations were made law in 2000. They require that health warnings cover 50 percent of the principal display surface of tobacco product packages, except for cigars. In 2004, the government announced more stringent labelling requirements.

In 2004, an Ontario court denied certification of a class-action lawsuit. Four smokers were trying to sue three leading tobacco manufacturers for manipulating the amount of nicotine in cigarettes in order to create addiction and therefore increase sales. The judge ruled that the lawsuit was too broad and did not meet the requirements for certification. The plaintiffs had wanted not only damages but the establishment of nicotine-addiction centres.

Three provinces, Newfoundland and Labrador, Ontario and British Columbia, have passed laws permitting them to recover from the tobacco companies the costs of medical care for smokers. Ontario tried to sue for damages in courts in the United States, but the lawsuit was rejected, as U.S. law did not permit a foreign government to sue in the United States. In 2004, the B.C. Court of Appeal, in a unanimous decision, ruled the Liberal government's Tobacco Damages and Health Care Costs Recovery Act is constitutionally valid legislation and the government could proceed with a lawsuit that seeks to recover $10 billion in health care costs from tobacco companies. Statistics provided by the B.C. government say about 80 percent cent of the province's smokers started smoking before they were 19 years old, and about 50 percent of people who smoke die of smoking-related illnesses, including lung diseases, heart diseases and numerous forms of cancer. It alleges tobacco manufacturers failed to warn consumers of the dangers of smoking, marked light cigarettes as safe and targeted children in their advertising and marketing. The tobacco industry appealed to the Supreme Court of Canada.

In Newfoundland and Labrador, a class-action lawsuit was started in 2004 against Imperial Tobacco, claiming the company deceived its customers in its marketing for light and mild cigarettes. The lawsuit alleges the tobacco company used forbidden, deceptive trade practices. The suit will seek the refund of money made from the sales of light and mild cigarettes since their introduction in the 1970s.

In 2005 a Quebec court certified two class-action lawsuits against three tobacco companies, which will require them to stand trial.

Canada has become a world leader in its respect for non-smokers' rights and the abolition of second-hand smoke from public spaces or work environments. In 2001, Russia and Egypt enacted laws against tobacco advertising and Israel banned smoking in public places (except separately ventilated smoking rooms). In 2003, New York banned smoking in most bars and restaurants. The following year, Ireland instituted a total ban in all workplaces, including pubs.

5. Breathalyzer Tests

Individuals suspected of impaired driving are required to co-operate with the police and take a Breathalyzer test, provided the police officer has "reasonable and probable grounds" to suspect impairment. If the officer believes that the suspected person is in no physical condition to give a breath sample, he or she may require blood samples instead.

It is a criminal offence to operate a motor vehicle while impaired by alcohol or a drug, or with a blood alcohol level exceeding 80 milligrams of alcohol per 100 millilitres of blood. It is an offence for an impaired person even to have the care and control of a vehicle, whether or not it is in motion, and whether or not the person intends to drive.

Before administering a Breathalyzer test, the police officer must inform the person of the right to legal counsel, and provide him or her with an opportunity, before taking the test, to contact a lawyer and consult the lawyer privately. The consultation may take place in a confidential telephone conversation, not necessarily in person. The driver cannot use the right to counsel as a ploy to delay the test for an unreasonable length of time; doing so may be regarded as tantamount to refusing to take the test.

If the police officer wrongfully denies a person the right to counsel, this action does not provide a reasonable excuse for refusing to comply with the Breathalyzer demand. Instead, the person should seek to exclude the results of the Breathalyzer test under the Charter of Rights and Freedoms. However, in 1995 one drunk-driving suspect in Calgary was acquitted in a case of this kind. When the suspect could not find his lawyer's up-to-date telephone number, the arresting officer failed to call directory assistance for him, even though the officer knew the difficulty the accused man was facing.

If the suspect refuses to take a test for impaired driving, the refusal may be used as evidence against her or him at a trial, and the court may make the adverse inference that the suspect must have been impaired. Refusal to take the test is also a criminal offence, and brings a penalty of $600 for a first offence and a jail term ranging from 14 days to five years for subsequent offences.

In cases where it is not contrary to the public interest, Canada's Criminal Code permits a court to give impaired driving offenders a conditional discharge, provided they seek treatment for alcohol abuse. But repeat offenders will be punished more severely.

In 1999, the Criminal Code increased the length of the mandatory driving prohibition to one year minimum and three years maximum on a first offence, two years minimum and five years maximum on a second offence, and three years minimum, with no maximum, on subsequent offences. The prohibitions are in addition to any term of imprisonment. See also the section on sentencing for crimes in Chapter 8.

Alberta toughened its impaired driving rules in 1999 to permit the government to issue an automatic three-month driving suspension to those charged but not yet convicted of driving with a blood alcohol level over the legal limit, and to suspend drivers who refuse to provide a breath sample.

In 2000, British Columbia passed a law that drunk drivers would lose their drivers' licence for one year for a first offence, and three years for a second offence. Third-time offenders would lose their licence for their lifetime.

In Ontario, drivers who are accused of any Criminal Code driving-related offences will lose their driving privileges. Since 1998, drivers' licences are suspended for one year on a first conviction, three years on a second conviction, and for life on a third conviction. This lifetime suspension can be reduced to ten years if certain conditions are met. If, however, someone is convicted of a fourth offence, the lifetime suspension becomes absolute and there is no possibility of that person ever having an Ontario driver's licence again. A driving suspension is effective 24 hours a day until the licence is reinstated.

As of December 23, 2001, the Ontario government implemented a law requiring individuals who were convicted of an impaired driving offence to install an ignition interlock device in their vehicle before being allowed to drive again.

Before a licence will be reinstated, the driver cannot drive any motor vehicle that is not equipped with an approved ignition interlock device. Every time the driver gets in the car, he will have to blow into a tube that is attached to a device that sits under the dash and reads his blood/alcohol concentration. If he has been drinking, the car will not start.

6. Jury Duty

Everyone accused of a criminal offence is entitled to be judged by a jury of his or her peers, and a person involved in certain civil trials may also be able to request a jury.

Every citizen has a duty to serve on a jury if asked, unless the prospective juror has a personal interest in the case, has a relationship with the trial judge, prosecutor, accused, defence counsel or a possible witness, or will suffer personal hardship by serving. Personal hardship can be claimed, for example, by a sole proprietor whose means of livelihood will be jeopardized by a lengthy absence, or a mother who has no one with whom to leave her children. Most provinces exempt people who work in the legal system, some government officials and those whose job is considered essential to the province.

Jurors are usually selected by computer from voters lists. If a person gets a notice for jury duty, he or she must respond or risk contempt of court charges. If a juror becomes ill while serving on a jury, the judge may agree to excuse him or her, as long as there are at least ten jurors left to make the decision in the case.

Women used to be able to exempt themselves from jury duty simply because they were women. It was not until the 1950s that most provinces even permitted women to be jurors. In 1970, the Royal Commission on the Status of Women recommended the abolition of discriminatory exemptions, and now all provinces have cancelled women's automatic exemption for civil trials.

Women can no longer claim an exemption on gender grounds for criminal trials, either. Since 1972, the Criminal Code has stated that, for juries in criminal cases, "no person may be disqualified, exempted or excused from serving as a . . . juror in criminal proceedings on the grounds of his or her sex."

Some women accused of crimes, as well as some women in civil cases, have felt that unless a reasonable number of women was on the jury, they were not being judged by their peers. In 1972, an entire Ontario jury panel was challenged and dismissed, and the trial delayed, because the judge stated that the original list of jurors should have contained an equal number of men and women.

Once a person appears in response to a notice for jury duty, she or he may still be challenged as a juror either by the prosecutor or the defence lawyer. Rules have evolved in the courts for the use of challenges to jurors. For example, in a 1995 case the lawyer for an accused charged with committing assault on his wife was not allowed to challenge jurors with respect to their views, feelings or opinions about violence against women. His lawyer filed statistical data stating that 50 percent of women reported violence by men known to them, that 25 percent of women had experienced violence at the hands of a current or past marital partner and that approximately 17 percent of currently married women reported violence by their spouse—and then argued that he was entitled to an impartial jury. The judge disagreed, saying the statistics did not show that the jury was likely to be partial.

In 1996, however, the Ontario Court of Appeal ruled that trial courts should permit the screening of jurors for potential racial bias in any criminal trial in the province in which an accused person is black. The ruling stated that the court has to determine whether there exists a realistic potential for partiality on the part of a prospective juror. Also in 1996, an Ontario court ruled that potential homophobia is sufficient grounds to challenge jurors for cause. In the same year, the B.C. Court of Appeal ruled that prospective jurors need not be screened for racial bias in trials in which the accused is an Aboriginal person. This case was appealed to the Supreme Court of Canada, which ruled unanimously in 1998 that prospective jurors may be questioned about their racial views to root out those whose prejudices could destroy the fairness of a criminal trial.

Unfortunately, jurors are not paid commensurately with the important responsibility they fulfil in our society. The pay for jury duty is nominal; it varies from province to province and often depends on how long the trial lasts. For example, in Ontario a juror is paid $40 a day for trials running 10 to 49 days, and for the rare trials lasting longer than 50 days, $100 a day. In addition, jurors are ordinarily paid an allowance for mileage, and reimbursed on a modest scale for meals and lodging.

Some employers voluntarily continue to pay an employee her or his regular wage while on jury duty, and many unionized employees have had this protection negotiated into their contracts. Jurors on salary are usually required to give the jury pay to their employers.

Jurors are not allowed to talk about the case while evidence is being heard; nor are they allowed to later divulge how they reached their verdict. Any juror who reveals jury deliberations is guilty of a summary offence and liable to six months in prison.

7. Constitutional Rights

On April 17, 1982, the Canadian Charter of Rights and Freedoms became law. It is a document to which every jurisdiction in Canada but Quebec subscribes (Quebec passed its own charter). It provides for enshrined guarantees of fundamental freedoms, legal rights, equality rights, democratic rights, mobility and language rights. Because the Charter is said to be "entrenched," its provisions supersede and override every other law passed by a subscribing government.

Fundamental freedoms, which are Charter-guaranteed, include freedom of conscience and religion, belief, opinion and expression, freedom of the press, and freedom to meet together peaceably and with whom we wish.

The Charter guarantees legal rights, including the right to live our own lives, personal liberty, the right to individual security, the right not to be deprived of rights except by due process of law, the right to be free from unreasonable search, seizure or imprisonment, the right to be presumed innocent until proven guilty, and the right to specified treatment on arrest or in criminal court proceedings. These rights are usually invoked in the context of criminal cases.

Democratic rights are assured, such as the right to vote, and the obligation of the legislatures to sit annually and have a new election at least every five years. Mobility rights are also guaranteed—the freedom to move within and outside of Canada. So are language rights—equality of status, rights and privileges for both English and French as official languages of Canada.

The Charter of Rights and Freedoms guarantees equality in very specific terms in Sections 15 and 28:

15. (1) Every individual is equal before and under the law and has the right to the equal protection and equal benefit of the law without discrimination and, in particular, without discrimination based on race, national or ethnic origin, colour, religion, sex, age or mental or physical disability.

(2) Subsection (1) does not preclude any law, program or activity that has as its object the amelioration of conditions of disadvantaged individuals or groups including those that are disadvantaged because of race, national or ethnic origin, colour, religion, sex, age or mental or physical disability.

28. Notwithstanding anything in this Charter, the rights and freedoms referred to in it are guaranteed equally to male and female persons.

Equal rights, under Section 15, prohibit discrimination on the grounds of race, religion, national or ethnic origin, colour, age and mental or physical disability. Section 15 gives additional and special protection to women because it is enhanced with the extra power of Section 28, which is Canada's Equal Rights Amendment. This protection means that, even though there are limitations on the constitutional guarantees of fundamental freedoms, legal, democratic, mobility and language rights expressed in the other sections of the Charter, all the rights and freedoms referred to are nevertheless guaranteed equally to men and women.

The case law has interpreted equality rights as available not to every individual but only to members of chronically disadvantaged groups, an interpretation that leaves some worthy litigants without Charter protection.

The Charter can only be invoked to assure citizens that they will be treated properly in relation to government; that is, only government action is subject to Charter challenge. There is no right to challenge the unequal behaviour of another individual or a company on the basis of the Constitution. Human rights commissions still provide the remedy to complaints of discrimination by individuals and companies.

Since affirmative action programs to remedy inequality are clearly approved in the

Charter, special programs to remedy inequity for disadvantaged groups are not regarded as discriminatory.

The Charter replaced the 1960 Canadian Bill of Rights, which was a well-intentioned but inadequate effort to demonstrate Canada's commitment to ensuring the rights of Canadians. It expressed important principles, but because it was only another ordinary federal law that guaranteed constitutional rights within the federal jurisdiction, it did not affect provincial laws or override other federal laws, as the Charter does. Some of the court decisions interpreted the Bill of Rights narrowly and restrictively, giving it even less impact. It was these decisions, in fact, that highlighted the importance of Charter language.

The guarantees in the Charter can be limited basically in two ways: by the "reasonable limits clause" and by the "notwithstanding clause."

First, the limit must be proven to be reasonable. Section 1 introduces the Charter:

The Canadian Charter of Rights and Freedoms guarantees the rights and freedoms set out in it subject only to such reasonable limits prescribed by law as can be demonstrably justified in a free and democratic society.

Second, governments can invoke the notwithstanding clause (Section 33) in the Constitution to override a constitutional breach, as follows:

Parliament or the legislature of a province may expressly declare in an Act of Parliament or the legislature, as the case may be, that the Act or a provision thereof shall operate notwithstanding a provision included in Section 2 or Sections 7 to 15 of this Charter.

The notwithstanding clause was the compromise that enabled the Charter to become law. Parliament or a provincial legislature can expressly exempt a law for a five-year renewable term from the Charter guarantees of fundamental freedoms, legal rights and equality rights. In fact, this clause has rarely been invoked since the Charter was enacted in 1982. Only two provinces have invoked the notwithstanding clause: Quebec and Saskatchewan.

The Charter provides an opportunity for the judiciary to protect constitutionally granted civil liberties by standing as sentry over political decisions. Many significant cases in the last 20 years have called upon the courts to apply the Charter to protect individuals on the basis of an infringement of their fundamental freedoms, legal rights, equality rights, democratic rights, mobility and language rights.

As the Charter affects many areas of the law, many Charter cases are referred to throughout this book. But what the cases add up to is difficult to summarize. For example, a law prohibiting the operation of retail stores on Sunday was declared invalid as a breach of freedom of religion guarantees; however, a law that failed to permit a businesswoman to deduct her child-care expenses as a business expense was not found to be in breach of Charter equality rights. And in 2000, the Ontario Court of Appeal struck down the law making it a crime to possess marijuana because the law did not include exemptions for people who needed it for medical reasons. The Court ruled that forcing a person to choose between his health and imprisonment violates his constitutional right to liberty and security of the person, and gave the government one year to amend the law or lose it. The federal government announced that it would amend the law.

When the government responded in 2001 with its Marijuana Medical Access Regulations, it permitted those with medical need to possess and, in some cases, produce marijuana to treat symptoms of serious medical conditions. When these regulations came back before the court, the judge decided that the new rules were not a constitutionally acceptable medical exemption to the criminal prohibition against possession of marijuana. The Ontario Court of Appeal agreed, and so did the Supreme Court of Canada.

In 2004, the Supreme Court of Canada dealt with the difficult constitutional question of the right of the courts to tell parliamentarians how to spend public money, and analyze expenditures for their accord with the Charter. The case was brought by parents of autistic children against the government of British Columbia, alleging that its failure to fund applied behavioural therapy for autism violated the equality rights guarantees in the Canadian Charter of Rights and Freedoms. In the case of *The Attorney General of British Columbia* v. *Connor Auton,* the parents noted that the government acknowledged the importance of early intervention, diagnosis and assessment for autistic children, and funded a number of programs for autistic children but did not establish funding for applied behavioural therapy, known as ABA/IBI therapy, for all autistic children between the ages of three and six. The trial judge ruled that the failure to do so violated the children's equality rights, and directed the province to fund early ABA/IBI therapy for children with autism. The court even awarded $20,000 in damages to each of the parents. The Court of Appeal upheld the judgment, but made a change in requiring the treatment to be medically advised.

The Supreme Court of Canada unanimously reversed the decision, stating that the government's failing was in not meeting the "gold standard." The Court noted that the government did not deny to autistic people benefits that it gave to others in the same situation, that its approach to the provision of other comparable novel therapies was the same and so a finding of discrimination could not be sustained.

8. Gun Control

Gun control legislation passed in 1996 was a serious government effort to tighten laws affecting the possession and use of firearms, and thereby protect Canadian citizens.

The law now requires, for the first time, Canada's 3 million gun owners to register their 7 million firearms, including rifles and shotguns. The registration system was phased in gradually until it was fully implemented in 2003. It replaced firearms acquisition certificates with renewable five-year arms possession certificates. Before the new licence is issued, a police check must ensure that there is no court order prohibiting the applicant from having a firearm. Failure to register will carry a fine of up to $2,000 and six months in jail.

If a gun is used while committing a serious crime, such as murder, manslaughter, sexual assault, robbery, extortion or kidnapping, a minimum mandatory four-year jail sentence will be imposed. The maximum sentence is 14 years. The penalty is the same even if an imitation firearm is used, and applies whether or not the person causes or means to cause bodily harm to any person as a result of using the firearm. This penalty is in addition to the penalty for the crime itself.

The penalty for trafficking in firearms or possessing a loaded unregistered restricted weapon is up to ten years in prison.

It is an offence to carry or store a firearm or ammunition in a careless manner, and if convicted, the person faces a jail term of up to two years for a first offence and five years for a second or subsequent offence. A person who points a gun at another, even if the gun is not loaded, is liable to imprisonment for up to five years.

Women abused by men seeking gun permits will have an opportunity to register an objection with the police, to prevent the man getting a gun permit.

The intention of the legislation is to help ensure a more peaceful society. The government hopes that the results will justify the administrative costs of implementing and maintaining the registration system. The law was challenged in the courts and the Supreme Court of Canada unanimously upheld the constitutionality of the law in 2000.

9. Prostitution

Prostitution has never been illegal in Canada. However, laws have attempted to control solicitation of customers in public areas.

Residents of some neighbourhoods complain that prostitutes or men seeking their services impede the free flow of pedestrian or vehicular traffic or access to homes. When this happens, the police should be called.

In 1985, the Criminal Code was amended to help citizens and the police address this problem. The amendment made it an offence for a person in a public place to stop or try to stop any car, impede the free flow of pedestrians or traffic or access to premises, or stop or try to stop a person or "in any manner communicate" or try to communicate with a person for the purpose of engaging in prostitution or of obtaining the sexual services of a prostitute.

A Nova Scotia man who was charged with this crime challenged its constitutionality, saying that the law violated the Charter guarantees of freedom of expression when it made it an offence to "in any manner communicate" with a person for the purposes of prostitution.

The man was convicted of seeking to procure the services of a woman he thought was a prostitute but who was actually a plainclothes police officer. He then took his case to Nova Scotia's Court of Appeal, which reversed the conviction and dismissed the charge against him. The Court ruled that no matter how much one disapproves of a prostitute and her customer, the law preserves through Charter guarantees their right to live, sexually and otherwise, without interference by the law where no harm is done to anyone else.

The Court also felt that the Charter protections of freedom of association protect sexual association between consenting adults, "whether the consent is freely given or paid for."

The case was appealed to the Supreme

Court of Canada, which upheld the man's conviction and reversed the Court of Appeal ruling. The Court ruled that while the Charter protections of freedom of expression extended to the activity of communication for the purposes of engaging in prostitution, it was reasonable to infringe on that freedom under the circumstances.

CHAPTER 8

INJURY, ABUSE, VICTIMIZATION:
CRIMINAL CHARGES AND CIVIL REMEDIES

⚖

Introduction

A person who injures or causes harm to another without justification and with provable negligence can be sued in a civil court and, if found liable, be ordered to pay compensation to the victim for the cost of his or her injuries—for example, loss of income, cost of present and future care, counselling. The victim may also secure an amount for "pain and suffering" and, if subjected to high-handed, arrogant conduct in the litigation, possibly an additional amount called "punitive damages" or "exemplary damages," intended to punish the wrong-doer for his or her conduct.

This branch of the law is known as "torts" and the person who inflicts the harm is a "tortfeasor." The compensation is called "damages."

Personal injury can take many forms. It may be a physical injury brought about, for example, by a car accident, a medical operation, or the use of medications or medical devices. It may be the result of a beating. It may be an emotional injury, caused by sexual assault, for example, or by an attack on the victim's reputation, giving rise to a lawsuit for libel or slander. A person's life may be threatened by reckless sexual contact with an AIDS carrier. Dependants suffer damage and injury when a family member on whom they relied financially is fatally injured. All these are considered personal injuries, and if the victim can prove liability and prove that the injury was a reasonably foreseeable result of negligence, then compensation may be ordered by a court, or agreed upon by the parties or their insurers.

Personal injury law and criminal law frequently intersect. When an injury arises out of a criminal offence, the police may lay a charge. If convicted, the accused may serve time in jail, pay a fine or, in some cases, be required to pay restitution. At the same time, the victim may sue the perpetrator for compensation in a civil court.

The national crime rate, based on data reported by police and recorded by Statistics Canada, increased by 6 percent in 2003—the first sizeable jump in more than ten years. The good news is that the increase was not caused by a jump in violent crimes, the rate of which has fallen 11 percent since 1993 and remained more or less unchanged in 2003. Canada's homicide rate was down 7 percent (to 1.8 homicides for every 100,000 people) in 2003—its lowest level since 1967.

While 548 reported homicides in 2003 was a drop of 34 fewer than recorded the previous year, there were 32 more attempted murders during 2003. Although most violent crime categories were down, robberies were up 5.4 percent and attempted murder was up by 3.8 percent. Police reported just over 304,515 incidents of violent crime in 2003. This represented 12 percent of the overall number of Criminal Code offences reported by police in 2003. While the 2003 rate was 15 percent lower than in 1993, it was still 14 percent higher than the rate of 1978.

Most major categories of violent crime declined in 2002–2003, including homicide (down 6.6 percent), assault (down 0.7 percent), other assaults (down 2.1 percent), sexual assault (down 5.2 percent), other sexual offences (down 8.7 percent) and abduction (down 8.2 percent).

The presence of firearms in violent crime continues to diminish. In 1999, 4.1 percent of violent crimes involved a firearm, compared with 5.6 percent in 1995. Robberies with a firearm have been dropping since 1991; in 1999 the rate was 50 percent lower than in 1991. However, firearms continue to account for about one in three homicides.

Statistics Canada reported in 2004 that the national property crime rate rose 4 percent in 2003, after hitting a nearly 20-year low the year before. It was the first substantial rise since 1991. However, the rate is still 26 percent lower than it was a decade earlier. Rates rose for all major categories of property crime, particularly break-ins, which were up 2 percent, the first substantial increase in this area in more than a decade.

The youth crime rate is on the rise, having increased by 5 percent in 2003. The rate of youths charged with violent crime increased 3 percent, the third increase in four years. It is not clear whether or not this is as a result of increased police reporting under the 2002 Youth Criminal Justice Act.

From 1989 to 1999, female youth violent crime increased 81 percent, more than 2.5 times the rate of increase among male youths (up 30 percent). However, the male youth violent crime rate was still almost three times higher than the female rate. In 1999, the violent crime rate dropped for both male (down 4.6 percent) and female (down 6.5 percent) youths.

A 1999 Statistics Canada study reported that almost two-thirds of sexual assault victims are younger than 18 (62 percent) and close to one-third (30 percent) are under 12.

Crimes of sexual exploitation have come to the fore in the last few years, and some of the stories are truly shocking. What is even more shocking is that some of the courts seem reluctant to impose severe sentences on these perpetrators. Examples of cases and sentences are included in the sections that follow.

Solutions to the problems of abuse are gradually being tested and implemented. Saskatchewan's legislation, the Victims of Domestic Violence Act, was the forerunner because it assists the victim immediately with emergency intervention and court orders. It is described in greater detail in the section on Spousal Abuse: Criminal and Civil Options in this chapter.

Complainants and crime victims may also be negatively affected by the legal process. Victims must endure a long, complex and confusing process, and face arduous cross-examination by defence counsel. Serious efforts have been made in recent years to rectify the situation, and make the process more responsive to the reasonable needs of victims.

This chapter focuses on the many ways in which a person can be injured, abused and victimized, and on the remedies provided by criminal and civil law.

A. OF CHILDREN

1. Harming an Infant

The Criminal Code deals with harm to infants in different ways, depending on the circumstances and the nature of the impact on the child.

INFANTICIDE

The less punitive charge of infanticide is applied to murders of infants by their mothers, in cases where the mother proves, through her own testimony or perhaps medical evidence, that she was disturbed "from the effects of giving birth" or "the effect of lactation." The law is thereby acknowledging how postpartum depression affects some women. Infanticide carries a maximum of five years' imprisonment. If a baby's death occurred due to efforts to preserve the mother's life during birth, no one would be charged.

MURDER OR MANSLAUGHTER

Parents can be accused of murder or manslaughter, however, when infanticide is not the appropriate charge. Some cases have brought heavy sentences, with the most severe reported punishment meted out to a New Brunswick couple in 1995: 16 years for causing the death of their three-year-old son. Steven and Lorelei Turner were convicted of manslaughter after the court heard evidence that the child suffered two dislocated shoulders, was starved, bound in a leather harness, tied to his bed and gagged with a sock to muffle his cries, constantly belittled and cursed, left outside alone in the cold for hours on end and given no medical attention. The child weighed just over nine kilograms when he died. In handing down the sentence, Mr. Justice Thomas Riordan said it had to reflect the "revulsion of society for a crime committed on a vulnerable, innocent, totally dependent, helpless child." The couple's appeal was dismissed by the New Brunswick Court of Appeal, and leave to appeal further was denied by the Supreme Court of Canada.

In another case, a three-hour-old baby was found almost suffocated inside a tightly sealed plastic bag. If an abandoned baby dies and the death was intentionally or recklessly caused, either or both parents could be charged with murder and sentenced to imprisonment for a maximum of a lifetime.

LEAVING A CHILD TO BE FOUND UNHARMED

If a baby is left where she or he may be found unharmed, either or both parents will likely face a charge of abandonment, with up to two years in jail as punishment. For example, in one case a four-day-old baby was found on the steps of a Children's Aid Society office with a note from the mother: "I am sorry to do this. Please take her and look after her, see that she gets the good parents she deserves."

EXPOSING A CHILD
TO POSSIBLE HARM

It is against the law for a parent to abandon or expose a child's life or health to harm by leaving a child under ten alone for an "unreasonable" length of time. The definition of unreasonable depends on the age of the child; for example, a court would likely consider it unreasonable to leave an infant alone for *any* time. In one case, a woman locked her five-month-old son in her apartment for 22 hours while she went downtown to apply for a job. Under the Criminal Code, the punishment for such an offence is up to two years in jail.

FAILING TO PROVIDE
BASIC NECESSITIES

A parent who endangers the life of a child under 16 by not providing food, shelter and necessary medical care is liable to punishment ranging from a fine of up to $500 to a maximum of two years in prison.

CONCEALING A BIRTH

Regardless of the circumstance of the baby's death, anyone who intentionally conceals the delivery of a child is liable to a maximum of two years' imprisonment. If a mother fails to obtain assistance in childbirth in order to conceal the baby's birth, and the baby dies as a result, the mother is liable for up to five years' imprisonment. Finally, anyone who disposes of the dead body of a child, with the intention of concealing its birth, is liable for up to two years in prison.

Under child protection laws in most of the provinces, the Children's Aid Society may step in to supervise parental care or to put the child in a foster home. Anyone who sees suspicious circumstances regarding the welfare of a child has an obligation to report these circumstances to the Children's Aid Society.

2. Incest: Criminal Charges and Civil Remedies for Compensation

An adult victim of childhood sexual abuse is entitled to charge his or her abuser as a criminal as well as to sue for compensation. The victim must decide whether to charge the abuser in a criminal court, or sue in a civil court, or both.

The sentence imposed in a criminal court often seems inadequate compared to the harm caused to the victim, although sentences have seemed somewhat stiffer in the past few years. Criminal law focuses on punishing the abuser and deterring similar crimes by others. The advantage of a civil suit is that the victim can claim compensation from the perpetrator for personal injury, pain and suffering.

CRIMINAL CHARGES

Under the Criminal Code, it is a crime of incest to have sexual intercourse with any person who is known to be by blood relationship a parent, child, brother, sister, grandparent or grandchild. Incest carries a maximum 14-year jail sentence. The victim is protected from conviction on incest charges if participation in sexual acts was forced or if the victim acquiesced under duress. Most often, the complainant is a woman who had sexual relations as a child with her father and, as an adult, charges him with incest. However, there are a number of reported cases of young boys who were sexually abused by fathers or other male relatives. There is the rare case where a woman is the perpetrator. Sibling incest has also been reported.

Incest is not the only charge. If the perpetrator used force, he could also be charged with sexual assault, which carries a maximum ten-year sentence; sexual assault with threats, a weapon or causing bodily harm (maximum 14-year sentence); or aggravated sexual assault, if the perpetrator wounded the victim or endangered the victim's life (maximum life sentence). Judges rarely hand out maximum sentences, however. If the judge believes the victim's evidence at the trial, he or she is permitted to accept the victim's word without corroboration.

Although there is no time limit in criminal law for bringing charges, until about the last decade few reported cases reached the courts in which a victim charged a parent once she or he became an adult. However, a number of such criminal cases were heard in the 1990s. In 1995, the B.C. Court of Appeal sustained a trial court sentence of a father to 12 years in prison—two consecutive six-year terms for two counts of incest on his two daughters, and one count of sexual assault on his son, to be served concurrently. The Court regarded the case as one of the worst because the children were abused from an early age, and the abuse included manipulation, threats, violence and forced intercourse. One of the girls had become pregnant as a result and had borne a child. The Court believed that the total sentence imposed of 12 years for all offences was stringent; however, under the Criminal Code the Court could have awarded a maximum penalty of 14 years for each offence.

In another case before the B.C. Court of Appeal in 1995, described by the trial judge as a "worst case," a man pleaded guilty to four counts of incest with his daughter, beginning when she was ten after her mother died, and continuing for more than 25 years. She gave birth to five children, all fathered by him, and gave the first two up for adoption. She shared his bed and kept his house. He had stopped her from attending school during Grade 10, and had threatened her, using firearms, that he would kill her and the children if she failed to have sexual relations with him. After his arrest at age 63, he threatened her life, and she had to move away and hide from him. The appeal court upheld the trial judge's sentence of ten years on each of four counts, to be served concurrently. At the same time, he was ordered to serve at least one-half his sentence before being eligible for parole and was prohibited from using firearms for ten years. His total jail sentence, therefore, which could not exceed ten years, might be as little as five years if he were paroled. The maximum available sentence was 14 years on each of the four counts, to be served consecutively (56 years).

In a 1994 Prince Edward Island case, a 37-year-old father of four was sentenced to a total of only five years in jail for incest with one of his daughters, between the time she was 10 and 12. The incest stopped when her mother found out. The girl was so distraught by the abuse—sexual touching started when she was seven and progressed to sexual intercourse when she was ten—that she tried three times to commit suicide.

In a 1992 Newfoundland and Labrador case, a father who committed incest against his daughter for ten years, beginning when she was seven, and who employed threats, force and violence, and who had a prior conviction involving another daughter, was sentenced to only seven years' imprisonment.

In 1994, one father even tried to avoid criminal consequences by unsuccessfully arguing that incest was a victimless crime between consenting adults!

In a 1997 case of incest with three siblings, the B.C. Court of Appeal upheld a sentence of seven years for a 33-year-old man's sexual offences against his brother and two sisters, all younger than him, and one as young as age seven, which occurred from the time he was 17 until he was 24.

In a 1997 Alberta case of incest by a mother with her son while he was 11 to 14 years of age, a trial judge sentenced the mother to only one year in prison, stating that the principle of general deterrence was not a factor because mother–son incest is rare. The Alberta Court of Appeal increased the sentence to three years, saying female perpetrators should not be treated differently from male perpetrators because the effect on the victim is no different. The Court also took into account that while the mother was willing, she was motivated to please her common-law husband, who was also sentenced—to four years.

The courts seem to view these sentences as appropriate. In 2001, the British Columbia Court of Appeal sustained a sentence of four years for incest by father to daughter. In 2000, Manitoba's appeal court agreed with a sentence of six years in similar circumstances. And in 2004, the Saskatchewan Court of Appeal increased to five years from two years a trial judgment for incest—in this case by a grandfather on his granddaughter, resulting in a pregnancy.

A case of many years of brother-to-sister incest that came before the B.C. Court in

2003 resulted in a decision under the Youth Criminal Justice Act, as the boy was 15 at that time and the girl was 14. The court put him on probation for two years, and he was to stay away from his sister except with an adult supervising, report to a youth court worker and attend counselling.

CLAIMS FOR COMPENSATION IN CIVIL COURT

Civil cases used to be rare, and when they came forward, the most difficult obstacle was the statute of limitations. Provincial legislation required a victim of childhood assault to start legal action within a defined period after attaining the age of majority. In Ontario, for example, the defined period was four years; in most other provinces, it was two years.

The limitation rules, however, were modified in 1992, when a landmark decision by the Supreme Court of Canada confirmed that an adult who was a victim of childhood sexual abuse could sue her or his abuser for compensation even though the statutory limitation period had passed. The Supreme Court of Canada stated that the limitation rules did not take into account the fact that much of the damage from childhood sexual abuse is not manifested, and often does not come into awareness, until well into adulthood, during therapy.

It is also possible for victims to sue their abuser before they reach the age of majority, but there are a couple of disadvantages. First, as the extent of the harm to the child may not yet be apparent, the amount of compensation is difficult to measure. The court must therefore be persuaded as to the likelihood of long-term damage. Second, an adult must start the action on the victim's behalf as "litigation guardian."

In 1991, a girl of nine was awarded a total of $25,000 to be paid by a convicted child abuser. Her parents were also awarded a total of $6,000 for their suffering. In an earlier Manitoba decision, a 16-year-old girl was awarded $65,000 for sexual assaults committed over a period of six years by her mother's former common-law husband.

In determining the amount of compensation, the court considers the physical and especially the emotional impact on the victim. Expert evidence by mental health professionals who have treated the victim helps the court consider such factors as the victim's feelings of shame, vulnerability and guilt, her or his lack of self-esteem and difficulty in forming lasting relationships, and the likelihood of future antisocial behaviour. It is often difficult to set an appropriate level of compensation for economic loss; a clear test has not yet been established to determine how much income, past and future, a survivor of childhood sexual assault has lost.

The court may also award "aggravated damages" based on several factors: the conduct of the abuser; his relationship to the victim, such as relative or family friend in a position of trust; the type of assault, such as one involving intercourse as opposed to fondling; the vulnerability of the child, such as the age at which the abuse began; and the duration of the abuse.

The court may also order the abuser to compensate the victim for actual out-of-pocket losses or anticipated losses resulting from the abuse, which may include the cost of past and future therapy.

The amount of the awards varies widely, but are increasing. While they initially were in the range of $40,000 to $60,000, by 1992, a B.C. court awarded $190,000 for damages ($130,000 general and $60,000 punitive) in the case of a 19-year-old woman against her father. Then a judge awarded $284,000 in the 1992 case of a 23-year-old Ontario woman against her father. This amount included $225,000 for general, aggravated and punitive damages plus $59,000 for past and future therapy costs.

In 1995, also in Ontario, an uncle described as a "sexual predator" by the court was ordered to pay his four nieces, whom he had sexually molested throughout their childhood years, about $440,000. They had also charged him as a criminal, but he served only 89 days in jail.

In 1996, the B.C. Supreme Court awarded a 42-year-old woman the sum of $473,262 for years of sexual abuse suffered at the hands of her father, starting when she was three years old. The $473,262 included $150,000 in past lost wages, $150,000 for future lost wages, $12,000 for lost pension benefits, $6,262 for counselling expenses, $10,000 for future counselling costs and $145,000 for general and aggravated damages.

The awards continue to climb. A 2003 Alberta case is an indicator. In that case, a stepfather who went so far as to impregnate his stepdaughter, and caused her "catastrophic emotional damage," which made this bright woman unemployable, was ordered to pay a total of over $4 million dollars plus interest and costs for general and punitive damages, past and future loss of income, and counselling expenses.

In 1993, in what is believed to be the first Canadian case of its kind, a civil court in Cornwall, Ontario, ruled that a mother had a legal duty to protect her daughter from abuse by the girl's father, and that she had failed in this duty. The judge said the conclusion was "inescapable" that the mother knew of the ongoing sexual relationship between father and daughter. Both parents were ordered to pay the daughter $60,000 for general damages and $30,700 for future-care expenses. But only the mother was ordered to pay a further $45,000 for punitive damages. (There were no punitive damages awarded against the father because he was serving a prison sentence, and the law limits punishment to one or the other.)

In the past several years, an award for breach of fiduciary duty has evolved, recognizing the unique responsibility of parents to their children. In a 1999 Ontario case, a trial judge ordered a father to pay his five daughters $125,000 each, as compensation for his breach of fiduciary duty. He had terrorized, brutalized and violently and repeatedly sexually assaulted them during their childhood.

GOVERNMENT COMPENSATION

In most provinces, victims of sexual abuse can apply for compensation to a criminal injuries compensation board. Some jurisdictions may have a limitation period for applying. Usually, a woman does not have to secure a conviction against the perpetrator to be considered a victim of crime for the purposes of the compensation scheme. She may receive compensation from the board for some of the following: medical expenses, counselling, pain and suffering, and maintenance for a child born as a result of the sexual abuse.

In the only reported case of its kind, a daughter killed her abusive father after enduring 17 years of physical and sexual abuse, and being held a virtual prisoner in her own home. He supplied her with drugs and alcohol and played the role of pimp, forcing her to work as a prostitute. She pleaded guilty to manslaughter and was given a suspended sentence by Ontario judge Jack Nadelle, who compared her reaction and justification to that of a battered spouse.

Some imaginative defence counsel, in seeking to defend their clients against incest charges, allege that the victims are suffering "false memory syndrome," suggesting that the victims' memories are fictionalized or instilled by their counsellors. False memory syndrome has not been medically recognized. On the other hand, it is medically accepted that terrifying memories can be repressed for many years, until adulthood when they come gradually to awareness. The Ontario Court of Appeal in 1996 dismissed an appeal brought forward on the basis of the trial judge's alleged failure to identify the complainant's statements as a product of false memory syndrome.

3. Sexual Exploitation of Children: Molestation, Prostitution and Pornography

Children are over-represented among the victims of crime, and are particularly vulnerable to sexual exploitation. Statistics gathered in Canada for 2002 reveal that children and youth under the age of 18 represented 23 percent of the population but accounted for 61 percent of victims of sexual assault and 20 percent of all victims of physical assault. Girls represented 79 percent of victims of family-related sexual assaults. Rates of sexual offences were highest among girls between the ages of 11 and 14, with the highest rate at age 13 (165 per 100,000 females). Among boys, rates of family-related sexual assault were highest for those between the ages of 3 and 7. Rates of family-related physical assaults against girls and boys generally increased with age. The highest age-specific rate for girls was at age 17 (362 per 100,000 females) and the highest rate for boys was at age 15 (196 per 100,000 males).

In 1995, Statistics Canada reported that one-quarter of reported victims of sexual assault were children under 12; of these, one-third were boys and two-thirds were girls. Another one-third of sexual assault victims were between 12 and 17.

Canadians have become more aware of the vulnerability of children to sexual exploitation, and governments have responded with more effective laws to protect children.

MOLESTATION

In 1984, the federal Badgley Committee on Sexual Offences Against Children and Youths had exposed the widespread incidence of child molestation. Its researchers reported that one in two females and one in three males had been victims of an unwanted sexual act—ranging from unwanted touching of a sexual part of the body to sexual assault; four-fifths of the incidents occurred during childhood or youth. The members of the committee pointed out that because the legal framework in the Criminal Code was designed for adult sexual victims and dealt inadequately with the particular vulnerability of children, it was difficult to prove a case against child molesters. The Badgley Committee made recommendations for change, many of which have been implemented.

A CHILD'S EVIDENCE IN COURT

In 1988, the Criminal Code was amended to give youngsters, especially those under 14, increased protection and enable them to give evidence against abusers more easily. In 1999, the Criminal Code was amended further to provide increased protections for child witnesses.

In court, children's evidence no longer needs to be corroborated by another person or confirmed by evidence to justify a conviction. Judges must satisfy themselves that the child understands the nature of an oath or affirmation and is able to state what happened truthfully, and then it is up to the judge and/or jury to decide if the child's evidence is credible. A child who does not understand the nature of an oath or affirmation can still testify if he or she promises to tell the truth. The judge must be satisfied that the child understands the difference between telling the truth and telling a lie and understands the nature of a promise.

In order to secure a candid account, the judge has the option of allowing the child to testify away from the accused or outside the courtroom. This provision applies in cases of sexual offences, prostitution-related offences and all levels of assault and sexual assault. A videotape of the child's testimony can be admitted as evidence; this statement is taken reasonably soon after the alleged offence, and may be admitted at trial instead of the child testifying about the events. However, the child must take the stand for the purpose of adopting the statements in the videotape. The videotape is not automatically admissible; the judge must decide in a hearing away from the jury (a "voir dire"). Another alternative allows a child witness to testify behind a screen in the courtroom or outside the courtroom over closed-circuit television.

Witnesses under the age of 14 and witnesses who have a mental or physical disability may have a support person present in court and close to the witness while testifying, if the judge is of the opinion that the proper administration of justice requires it. The judge may order that the witness and the support person not communicate with each other while the witness is testifying.

If the person accused of sexual offences, assault or prostitution-related offences is representing himself, he is prohibited from personally cross-examining witnesses under 18 unless the judge makes an exception for good reason. Counsel must be appointed to conduct the cross-examination for him. This avoids allowing the accused person to terrorize a witness by the mere act of cross-examination.

The judge is obligated to inform persons under 18 that they can apply to the court to protect their identity from publication or broadcasting.

SEXUAL OFFENCES

Adults are prohibited from touching a child or encouraging the child to touch her or his own body or someone else's "for a sexual purpose." They are subject to fines and/or a potential maximum jail term of ten years. The same acts committed on a "young person" (defined as someone between 14 and 18 years of age) by an adult in a position of trust or authority, or on whom the youth is dependent, carry a five-year maximum jail sentence.

It is now a specific offence, punishable with a maximum $2,000 fine and up to six months in jail, for anyone to expose his or her genital organs to a child under 14 for a sexual purpose.

Children are protected from exploitation by their own parents. It is a specific offence for a parent or guardian to sell the sexual services of a child under age 18. An adult convicted of the crime becomes liable to a maximum five-year jail term if the child is under 14, and two years if the child is between 14 and 18. Householders who permit a child to be on their premises for a sexual purpose are similarly liable.

In 1993, a new law was passed to allow a court to order that people convicted of a sexual offence against a person under 14 be prohibited for a period as long as their entire lifetime from attending a public park, swimming area, schoolyard or playground, or from being employed or volunteering in a capacity that involves a position of trust towards those under 14. Breach of such an order carries a maximum of two years' imprisonment.

The sentencing principles stated in the Criminal Code include an open invitation to judges to increase sentences when the offenders abused their spouse or child, or abused a position of trust or authority in relation to the victim.

JUVENILE PROSTITUTION

Since 1988, more severe punishment has faced those who profit from or participate in juvenile prostitution. A person who lives on the avails of a prostitute under the age of 18 is liable to a maximum 14-year jail sentence. A customer who pays for the sexual services of a person under 18 may spend up to five years in jail.

In 1997 the Criminal Code was amended to further protect children from adult predators who seek children for sexual services or exploit young prostitutes for economic gain, or entice a young person under 18 into prostitution. The law will make it easier for police to apprehend customers of young prostitutes by making it illegal to attempt to procure the sexual services of someone who is under the age of 18. A new offence of "aggravated procuring" carries a five-year minimum sentence for those who, for their own profit and while living on the avails of child prostitutes, use violence or intimidation to force a youth to carry out prostitution-related activities. Other measures make it easier for young prostitutes to testify against their pimps.

The law allows proceedings to be instituted in Canada against Canadian citizens who engage in activities associated with child prostitution when they are out of the country. This effort to deal with child sex tourism permits police to charge tour operators or travel agents who make arrangements for child prostitutes for their clients. This move against child sex tourism is intended to send a strong signal worldwide that Canada will not tolerate the sexual exploitation of any country's children. In 2004, the apparent first prosecution under this law was commenced in British Columbia against a married father, alleging sexual interference, sexual touching and soliciting the services of a girl under the age of 18. All of these activities were alleged to have taken place in Asian countries.

Alberta passed a law in 1998, the Protection of Children Involved in Prostitution Act, which categorized prostitutes under age 18 as victims of sexual abuse and the johns as sexual abusers; authorized police to enter buildings without a search warrant if they thought child prostitutes were inside; and permitted police to temporarily lock up for three days in "safe houses" children suspected of working as prostitutes. In 2000, an Alberta provincial court struck down the law as an unconstitutional violation of the rights against unreasonable search and seizure.

FEMALE GENITAL MUTILATION

In 1997, the Criminal Code was amended to criminalize female genital mutilation, a practice that is promoted in some cultures, but that can cause severe and irreversible health problems to girls and women. This practice involves excising or mutilating the clitoris of female infants or children. The Criminal Code states that any consent given by the female is not regarded as valid except if she is over 18 and suffers no bodily harm, or if a qualified and licensed doctor performs the surgery for the benefit of the physical health of the woman. The law now defines female genital mutilation as aggravated assault, an indictable offence subject to as many as 14 years in jail.

CHILD PORNOGRAPHY

When the Badgley Committee presented its report in 1984, the remedies available under the Criminal Code to deal with child pornography were inadequate. Police could lay charges for "procuring the defilement" of a girl (maximum 14 years if the child were under 14 and five years if 14 or over); corrupting the morals of a child under 18 in their home (maximum two years); or publishing or distributing obscene photos or films (maximum two years and/or a fine of up to $500).

The Committee had recommended explicit and severe sanctions against persons involved in the making, distribution, sale or importation of child pornography that visually depicted explicit sexual conduct of persons under age 18, with a penalty of up to ten years. The members also recommended that postal, customs, broadcasting, film and video rules fall into line.

In 1985, legislation empowered customs officers to prevent obscene magazines, films and videotapes containing sexual violence and child pornography from entering Canada. The ban extends to any depiction of youngsters who are or appear to be under 18 in an "even slightly sexually suggestive" context.

In 1993, new legislation made it a criminal offence punishable by up to ten years in jail for a person to make, print, publish, possess for the purpose of publication, import or distribute any child pornography, which is defined as a photograph, film or videotape that shows a person who is or is shown to be less than 18 engaged in explicit sexual activity. In a 1995 case, a 20-year-old Toronto man was the first person in Canada to be convicted of distributing child pornography through computer bulletin board systems.

Another 1995 case decided by the Ontario Court of Appeal revealed how the courts viewed the sentencing provisions of the Code. The Court reduced sentences applied by the trial judge from ten years to five years for one offender and from 15 years to seven years for his accomplice. The two had filmed pornography involving three boys under the age of 14 and nine boys between 14 and 18, and were in breach of lifetime prohibition orders restricting their access to young boys.

In 1999, a B.C. Supreme Court judge struck down the section of the Criminal Code that outlaws the possession of child pornography when he acquitted 65-year-old John Robin Sharpe of possession. He believed that his constitutional rights to freedom of expression and privacy had been breached. On his return to Canada from a trip, his luggage was routinely searched by airport customs, who found stories he had written and photos of nude boys, all pornographic. The judge acknowledged that children suffer harm from posing for pornographic pictures, but gave Sharpe's constitutional rights higher importance. The B.C. Court of Appeal agreed with the trial judge but the B.C. government successfully appealed to the Supreme Court of Canada, which, in January 2001, ordered a new trial.

At that new trial in 2002, Sharpe was convicted of two counts of possession of child pornography, but was acquitted of the charge of distributing child pornography based on the defence of artistic merit. Sharpe was given a four-month conditional sentence. He spent no time in jail, but was required to have no one-on-one contact with anyone under age 18, and to remain in his home between 4 p.m. and 8 a.m. daily. The Crown chose not to appeal. The federal government immediately promised changes to the law to plug loopholes.

Later that year, Sharpe was again charged, this time with gross indecency, and indecent and sexual assault on one of the boys whose photo he had taken. The police had the picture in their possession as a result of the earlier charges. Sharpe is on bail and these charges are still making their way through the courts at this writing.

4. Violence in Schools

School violence is increasing. A report to the solicitor general of Canada in 1994, based on five years of data from 510 police forces and 125 school boards, concluded that violence and armed students are on the increase in schools. The trend is being fuelled, the report stated, by peer pressure, lack of parental supervision and guidance, a sense of status conferred by weapons use, violence in the media and an absence of consequences for violent behaviour.

When a school experiences violent incidents, causing children, their parents, teachers and the community to fear for the children's safety, the school seeks available legal and practical solutions.

Teachers have concerns for their own safety as well, because they are also in the line of fire. In 1993, a Manitoba teacher sued her school board for keeping a violent student in class and therefore failing to provide her with safe working conditions.

Provincial education acts permit suspension or expulsion of violent students, but not much else. In Ontario, for example, school principals can suspend a student for up to 20 school days for "conduct injurious to the moral tone of the school or to the physical or mental well-being of others in the school." School boards can expel a student for exceptionally intractable conduct after a hearing in which the student and his or her parents have a right to participate.

But expulsion is no panacea. Young people may turn to crime because their lack of education bars them from the job market. Or, they may enroll in a school under a different board's jurisdiction—where educators may not know the students' history of aggression.

Because school authorities have little power to deal with troubled students when suspension or expulsion is inappropriate, other methods have evolved.

SPECIAL CLASSES FOR VIOLENT STUDENTS

When an angry seven-year-old girl repeatedly disrupted her class, despite several short suspensions, one Ontario school board wanted to transfer her to a special class for difficult youngsters. The parents refused until the board suspended the child with the promise that she could return if her parents agreed to the plan, which they did within a month.

CRIMINAL CHARGES

In the past, many schools concealed student violence to protect their reputations. No longer able to handle the problem on their own, however, many now collaborate with the police, and routinely report student assaults and lay criminal charges.

The catch is that the Youth Criminal Justice Act protects young people under 18 from adult penalties and keeps their record confidential. The Ontario government has recommended that suspensions or expulsions for violence should be noted in students' records and these records should follow students within the school system.

INCREASED SECURITY

Some schools now have their corridors and playgrounds patrolled by police officers.

Others have installed electronic security systems and surveillance cameras.

Police involvement is even more likely in the future. For example, the Ontario government's policy requires schools to inform police of all serious violent acts by students aged 12 and older. Schools must also keep "violence records" for at least three years, which will follow students from school to school.

CITY BY-LAWS

In 2003, Edmonton passed a by-law making bullying illegal, and the police and teachers reported safer schools. The law is believed to be the first of its kind in Canada. It made a wide variety of behaviour, from physical force to intimidation and threats, punishable by a fine of up to $250.

PREVENTION

But surveillance and punishment will not ensure safe schools. Prevention deserves just as much attention—and prevention means addressing the causes of student aggression, such as family violence, violence-filled TV shows and parents who cannot meet children's need for nurturing. Here are some methods that some schools have tried with success:

- Provide parenting programs to help mothers and fathers cope with troubled youth.
- Strengthen media literacy in the curriculum to help students understand that violent acts on television should not be imitated.

- Train students in mediation and conflict resolution so that they can help peers resolve disputes peacefully.
- Introduce "school watch" programs that keep students involved in solutions to violence. One innovative program in St. Catharines, Ontario, since emulated by other schools, encourages students to report undesirable behaviour by peers. To reduce bullying, the program provides a buddy system and an escort service from the school to the parking lot.
- Introduce a student "crime-stoppers" program, as one Toronto school successfully did, whereby students can report information anonymously to a special hot line to help prevent and solve crimes in the school.

5. Responsibility for Injuries and Damages Caused by Children

Parents are not automatically liable for acts of their children that harm others. Parents are, however, obligated to exercise "reasonable care"—defined according to community standards—in the supervision and control of their child's activities.

Whether or not parents can be sued or sue other parents because of injuries inflicted by a child depends on a number of factors, but particularly on the child's age, his or her level of maturity and the nature of the injuries. In this context, some important questions need to be answered: Was it reasonable to expect the parents to know that their child might do what he or she did? If so, did they do anything to prevent the child's misbehaviour? Was it reasonable to expect them to be able to control their child under the particular circumstances?

A child's conduct is measured according to age, capacity, knowledge and experience. A court will try to determine whether the child exercised the degree of caution to be expected from an average child of the same age and intelligence.

The parents of a very young child will likely be held legally responsible for acts of the child that injure others. For example, if a toddler overturns a burning candle and starts a fire that harms people and property, the parents will be held liable because they should have been supervising the child more closely. If a one-year-old infant crawls into traffic, causing two cars to collide, with injuries to the drivers and passengers, the parent of the infant will likely be held responsible. Similarly, the parent of a five-year-old who injures someone while playing with a bow and arrow is also likely to be held responsible.

When a child reaches an age when adult standards of behaviour are reasonably expected, the child will be held responsible. There is no magic age when these adult standards can be assumed. Realistically, however, as a child becomes more independent, the parents have less opportunity to supervise, and so their duty to control the child's activities diminishes.

Parental-liability cases typically arise in instances where a child has access to a dangerous object, such as a gun. When parents permit a child to use such an object without providing adequate supervision and safety instructions, or without imposing restrictions on access, they have often been held liable for resulting injuries. A mischievous youngster can get parents into trouble legally if a court concludes that they should have been able to anticipate and prevent their child's misbehaviour. Allowing younger children to use peashooters, for instance, has been found to be reckless parental behaviour. In one case, an Alberta court concluded that no matter how thoroughly a child is trained in its use, the parent is not justified in allowing an average nine-year-old, for instance, to use a pellet gun unsupervised. A normally responsible 13-year-old, however, is unlikely to get his parents into trouble.

If the child acted out of character in causing an accident, the child and not the parent will be considered liable. For example, in one case that went to court a 13-year-old boy played with his father's rifle without permission and it went off, injuring another child. The rifle and ammunition had been stored separately. The intelligent, normally obedient boy had been taught how to use a gun, but forbidden to do so unsupervised. In this case, the father was not held responsible because he would have had no reason to anticipate his son's actions.

The court determined that it was not improper for a father to have confidence in his son and that his mistake in judgment did not constitute negligence.

When there is no weapon involved, it is more difficult to hold parents liable for harm caused by a child's wrongful actions. Proof would have to be available that the parents knew their child tended to misbehave in the particular way that caused harm (such as punching or tripping others), that the parents should have anticipated the misbehaviour, and that the parents could have taken some reasonable step to prevent the misbehaviour.

Parents who know their child has violent tendencies have a duty to act to prevent harm to others. In one case, when a father knew of his son's habit of throwing rocks but failed to punish the boy and warn him that this activity could harm others, the father was found liable when the boy injured another child. On the other hand, the parent may know that their daughter or son is a troublemaker but may not be able to anticipate the nature of the child's misbehaviour. If the only way to prevent the misbehaviour is to keep the child locked up, the parent will likely not be found liable.

An example of how difficult it is to determine liability in these cases arose in a case decided by the British Columbia Supreme Court in 1996. The parents of a 17-year-old boy who set fire to a neighbour's home were found not liable for the damage because, while the boy was prone to break and enter, he had never committed arson before, and the parents could not have foreseen that he would do that.

In Ontario, when children under the age of 19 are sued for compensation for damage to property, personal injury or death caused by their fault or neglect, the law puts the onus on the parents to prove that they exercised reasonable supervision and control over their children. Elsewhere, the burden of proof is on the person who brings the lawsuit forward to prove that the parents should be held liable.

Parents must take reasonable precautions to ensure that their children do not create an unreasonable risk of danger to themselves or to others.

Although the common law and case precedent is clear as to when a parent may be found liable for his child's misdeeds, the legislatures of some provinces have chosen to legislate in this area, including Manitoba and Ontario.

6. Youth Criminal Justice Act

The 2002 Youth Criminal Justice Act became law on April 1, 2003, replacing the Young Offenders Act, in effect since 1985. The YCJA applies to young people who are between the ages of 12 and 18 when they commit an offence. The minimum age of criminal responsibility under the Act is 12 years; children who have not reached their twelfth birthday cannot be charged with a criminal offence, but may be dealt with, if appropriate, through the provincial child-welfare system. When a person reaches his or her eighteenth birthday, he or she becomes an adult in the eyes of the law and is dealt with in the ordinary court system.

In some cases involving serious offences, such as murder, armed robbery or sexual assault, a young person who is 14 or over may receive an adult sentence if they have committed an offence for which an adult would be liable to imprisonment for more than two years. However, they are not ordinarily tried in adult court. The decision as to whether a young person should be sentenced as a youth or as an adult is made only after a youth court, or an adult court deemed to be a youth court, finds the defendant guilty. However, in order to be fair, any young person who is at risk of receiving an adult sentence will have the option to elect to be tried either by a youth justice court judge or by a judge in an adult court, with or without a preliminary inquiry and/or a jury.

The principles of the new youth justice system are to promote the protection of the public. In doing so, the law specifically ranks rehabilitation, reintegration, accountability and timeliness above incarceration and deterrence of the offender.

EXTRAJUDICIAL MEASURES

A key aspect of the new system is the opportunity to deal with young people who commit minor offences outside the formal criminal justice system, by permitting police and court officials to use out-of-court measures without laying a charge, to correct recalcitrant behaviour. These alternatives are available at the discretion of the officials, and are used particularly when the child has committed a non-violent offence and has not previously been found guilty of an offence. If subsequently, the child is brought before a youth justice court regarding another alleged offence, the fact that he was dealt with previously by an extrajudicial measure is not admissible as evidence of prior offending behaviour in the new proceeding.

EXTRAJUDICIAL SANCTIONS

These may be used after a formal charge is laid, to divert a child out of the formal criminal process, when extrajudicial measures are inadequate because of the seriousness of the offence, the nature and number of previous offences committed or other aggravating circumstances. The child must consent to the sanctions and accept responsibility for the offending behaviour. The law does not specify what extrajudicial sanctions may be imposed, but Ontario judges note that these can include essays, apologies to the victim, compensation or restitution, charitable donations, education sessions, community service and peer mediation.

RIGHTS OF YOUNG PEOPLE

If the authorities have decided to proceed with charges against a young person, they must follow strict procedural guidelines that are designed to protect the accused's rights. The young person's parents or other adult relative must be notified of all proceedings. If the parents refuse to attend, the court may make an order requiring them to do so, or be found in contempt of court. If the young person is found guilty of the offence, the parents are entitled to express their views before the judge passes sentence.

Like accused persons in adult court, young people have a right to retain and instruct counsel. They must be informed of that right by the police when they are arrested, and if they appear in court unrepresented, the youth court judge must inform them of their right to counsel. If young people wish to obtain counsel but are unable to do so, the judge must refer them to legal aid, if available, or appoint counsel to represent them. The young people themselves, rather than their parents, instruct the lawyer. A lawyer is available to a youth at any stage of the proceedings, including whether or not to accept extrajudicial sanctions.

If young people are detained in custody upon being arrested, they are entitled to seek bail pending their trial. However, the new law presumes that detention is unnecessary in most cases. Where detention is nevertheless ordered, the youth must be kept separate from adults. The youth court may release young people into the care of a responsible adult who can control them and ensure their attendance in court. Bail may be revoked if the young people breach any conditions imposed on their release.

Young offenders cannot be identified in

the media. The proceedings may be reported but the young people cannot be named and their photograph may not be published. An exception may be made if the young accused is a danger to the public and is being sought by the police.

The police can photograph and fingerprint young persons who are accused of committing an offence, just as they do adults. Samples for DNA testing can be taken from young persons as from adults. The youth has the right to have a parent or counsel present when the sample is taken. All youth-court records (except those related to an offence of murder), including fingerprints and photographs, are supposed to be destroyed following the expiration of specified crime-free periods. In effect, the young person is supposed to be given an opportunity to start fresh, with no criminal record. A record of murder, however, may be kept indefinitely.

SENTENCING

The new law sets out the principles for sentencing that a court is to apply. The purpose of sentencing is to "hold a young person accountable for an offence through the imposition of just sanctions that have meaningful consequences for the young person and that promote his or her rehabilitation and reintegration into society." The sentence must not result in a more severe punishment for the child than an adult would get. The court must consider all reasonable alternatives that impose the fewest restrictions but still are likely to rehabilitate the youth and promote in him a sense of responsibility.

A custodial sentence must not be ordered unless there is no reasonable alternative.

These factors must be considered: the extent of the youth's participation in the offence, the harm done, any reparation made, the criminal record, etc. A court must consider a pre-sentence report before imprisonment. The judge may impose the appropriate one of the following sentences:

- Grant a reprimand (warning)
- Grant an absolute discharge
- Give a conditional discharge with a reporting and supervision condition
- Impose a fine of up to $1,000, which may be used for victim assistance
- Make a restitution order for a payment of money
- Make a compensation order to the victim by way of personal service
- Sentence the young offender to community service
- Order probation for up to two years
- Impose a custody order of a maximum of three years for most crimes, but for first-degree murder ten years (maximum six years in custody), and for second-degree murder seven years (maximum four years in custody)
- Order intensive rehabilitative custody and supervision (for mentally disturbed individuals)

The court may order that the young person be prohibited from possessing any weapons if convicted of certain offences, mainly crimes of violence. The youth court judge must generally consider a predisposition report before committing a young person to custody. The report includes interviews with the young person, the parents and possibly the victim; the accused's prior record; information about the young person's attitude towards the crime and victim and whether he or she felt genuine remorse; relationship with her or his parents and the degree of control they exercise over her or him; and school and employment records. If the judge believes that the young person is suffering from a physical or mental disorder, he or she may order a medical, psychological or other assessment, either before sentencing or at any other stage of the proceeding.

A young person has the same right of appeal from the finding of guilt, or the disposition imposed, that an adult does.

7. Injuries at School

Both the teacher and the school board are responsible for the proper care of children in their custody. Generally, the law requires that a teacher and board behave the same as a "careful or prudent parent." This requirement applies even if a parent has signed a consent form for his or her child to play a particular sport.

How proper care is defined will depend on the circumstances. In all cases, though, the teacher is expected to take adequate safety measures, acquaint students with the dangers involved in the activity, and supervise properly, given the students' skill, age and experience.

Of course, even the most conscientious teacher is not able to avoid the possibility of an accident. When an accident occurs, the parents have sometimes sued, and so the courts have clarified under what circumstances it is appropriate to find the teachers and school boards liable. Here are some examples of cases that have reached the courts.

The standard of care required from a teacher and the teacher's school board was defined by the Supreme Court of Canada 23 years ago in the case of *Myers* v. *Peel County Board of Education* and remains the same to this day. In that case, a 15-year-old boy became paralysed after breaking his neck while using gym equipment. His teacher had allowed unsupervised students to use the equipment with insufficient mat protection. The teacher and board were found 80 percent liable for failing to provide adequate supervision. The other 20 percent was ruled the boy's fault, since he had failed to have another student act as a spotter to protect him. The boy was compensated for 80 percent of his damages.

On the other hand, the school board was found *not* liable in an Ontario case in which a 16-year-old boy's neck was broken in a routine tackle during an extra-curricular football game. The court ruled that the school board had fulfilled its responsibilities because the boy was an experienced player and knew the risks. He had been coached properly, had adequate equipment and his doctor had found him fit to play football.

Even if supervision and equipment are found lacking, the teacher or school board will not be found liable unless the injury was a foreseeable result of the activity. In the case of a 12-year-old Ontario student who was hurt by a snowball on school property after school, the court exonerated the school board, ruling that the incident could not have been foreseen. There was nothing inherently dangerous in the child's walking through the schoolyard, and supervision would not have prevented the accident.

Similarly, a 15-year-old boy in British Columbia was injured by a ball while lying on the grass watching a game during the school lunch break. The game was found not to be inherently dangerous. In applying the standard of care of a prudent parent, the court held that such a parent would not have hesitated to allow the game to proceed as it did.

However, when a 16-year-old boy in British Columbia was injured by a flying bat during an indoor baseball game, the court held that the supervising teacher was negligent because the bat lacked safety grips and the teacher failed to warn players of the danger of bats flying out of control.

In some cases, the duty owed by a teacher may extend beyond the classroom. In a 1993 Alberta case, a teacher in a vocational school for the learning disabled was held liable when, on a tour outside school, he allowed students to hike unsupervised up a mountain, instead of attending a movie with them as planned. One 19-year-old student fell, injuring himself. The court ruled that the teacher had breached his duty not to expose the student to an unreasonable risk of harm. But the student was found 25 percent liable for failing to take the proper steps to ensure his own safety.

All parents can help make school activities safer by working with teachers to ensure that children fully understand safety rules and accident prevention.

B. OF WOMEN

1. Abuse

Abuse of women can take many forms, including assault, threats, sexual assault, forcible confinement, criminal harassment, and even murder and attempted murder. No matter what form it takes and what it is called, abuse is against the criminal law. The perpetrator may be a spouse or an intimate friend, an acquaintance or a stranger, a colleague or an authority figure (for example, a doctor, teacher, priest). The remedy can be one or all of the following: a charge against the perpetrator under one of a number of criminal offences; a lawsuit in civil court for compensation for personal injuries suffered; an application to a government criminal injuries compensation board for compensation; a divorce; physical separation from the offender, preferably by way of a criminal and/or civil restraining order.

The Criminal Code defines any number of possible abuse offences. Assault, for example, is committed when a person applies force to another person without consent, or attempts or threatens by an act or gesture to apply force; conviction can lead to a penalty of up to five years in jail. Threatening to cause death or bodily harm to any person, or to burn, destroy or damage real property, is an offence punishable with up to 18 months in jail. Murder and manslaughter are offences that carry possible life imprisonment.

Offences against women often take the form of sexual assault, which is now the generic term in the Criminal Code for sexual offences against women. Rape was renamed and redefined as a sexual assault in order to emphasize that the offence is primarily violent rather than primarily sexual. There are three categories of sexual assault: sexual assault (assault of a sexual nature without a weapon or bodily harm), which carries a maximum jail sentence of ten years; sexual assault with a weapon, threatening or bodily harm, which can result in up to 14 years in jail; sexual assault aggravated by wounding or any life-endangering behaviour, which is subject to a maximum of life imprisonment.

Rape is the term that the public still prefers to describe sexual interference by a male with a female. Before 1983, the Criminal Code defined rape as forcible sexual intercourse, with any degree of penetration, by a man with an unwilling woman who was not his wife. At that time, even a wife who was separated but not divorced from her husband at the time the assault took place could not charge him with rape. Since 1983, however, the police have been able to charge husbands and ex-husbands with this crime. Furthermore, the definition of the offence no longer includes penetration or, indeed, any particular physical act.

Criminal harassment, otherwise known as stalking, which sometimes accompanies abusive relationships, has been added as a criminal offence in the past few years to deal with what appears to be an increasing problem. Stalking happens when a person repeatedly follows, communicates with, watches or threatens another person, and it is reasonable for the victim to fear for her or his safety. The penalty is up to five years in jail. If the stalker murders his victim in the course of stalking her, even if the murder is unintentional, he may be convicted of first-degree murder.

The Criminal Code states sexual offences in a gender-neutral manner. However, much of the sexual abuse that occurs in our society is directed at women by men. In addition, it is estimated that eight out of every ten women who are sexually assaulted are victimized by men they know. This kind of assault is also called spousal abuse, domestic violence, or date or acquaintance rape.

2. Spousal Abuse: Criminal and Civil Options

THE NATURE AND EXTENT OF THE PROBLEM

According to a 1994 Statistics Canada report of a 1993 survey into the problem of wife assault, an estimated 29 percent of Canadian women who have ever been married or lived with a man in a common-law relationship have been physically or sexually assaulted by their marital partner. Another contemporary Canadian study found that the women known to have been slain by their registered or common-law husbands between 1974 and 1990 constituted 15 percent of all solved homicides during this period and almost half of all women killed by men. A 2002 Statistics Canada report of the situation in 2001 showed little change. In 2001, one out of every five homicides that was solved had been committed by a current or ex-spouse and four out of five of these victims were women.

Between 1991 and 1994, 70 percent of female homicide victims were killed by their intimate male partners. Statistics Canada showed that in 2002 about 27 percent of all victims of violent crimes were also victims of family violence. Of all family violence victims included in the study, 62 percent "were victims at the hands of their spouse." Young women between 25 and 34 years of age experienced the highest rates of spousal violence.

While there have been cases in which a man was assaulted and abused by a woman, these cases are far less frequent; for convenience, therefore, in this chapter the abuser is referred to as the man and the victim as the woman.

Traditional laws and attitudes assumed that once a woman agreed to marry, she consented in advance to sexual relations whenever her husband wanted his "marital rights." Those laws were (and some still are) based on the legal fiction that when a man and a woman marry, they become one "legal personality"—the husband. As a result, the law (before 1983) stated, with questionable logic, that a man could not be charged with raping his own wife because rape cannot be self-inflicted.

Another legal relic was the idea that a woman's body became her husband's property on marriage. Even the famous English jurist Sir William Blackstone said in 1757 that a husband could give his wife "moderate correction." Some people speculate that severe penalties for rape were originally designed to protect the man's wife or daughter as his property, which society regarded as being devalued by sexual violation.

Unfortunately, these ideas continue to be relevant because many people still believe in them, even though the law is becoming more progressive. Those who still justify violent behaviour with cultural, religious, emotional or any reasons may need to be told that the law in Canada does not support their position.

The situation was well stated by Supreme Court of Canada Justice Bertha Wilson in 1990 in the Lavallee case, which accepted the battered woman's syndrome as a defence:

The gravity, indeed, the tragedy of domestic violence can hardly be overstated. Greater media attention to this phenomenon in recent years has revealed both its prevalence and its horrific impact on women from all walks of life. Far from protecting women, the law historically sanctioned the abuse of women within marriage as an aspect of the husband's ownership of his wife and his "right" to chastise her. One need only recall the centuries-old law that a man is entitled to beat his wife with a stick "no thicker than his thumb."

A COURSE OF ACTION

What is a woman to do? First of all, she must recognize that assault is against the law. Marriage or any intimate relationship is no excuse for assault or abuse, and unless the abuser agrees to effective counselling that stops the abuse, the woman has little choice but to end the relationship. If she stays in the hope that the man will change, she may endanger her life and her children's. Leaving is often very difficult but the woman must accept that it will never get easier. When the choice is between life and death, or between a life of torment and a life of tranquillity, the incentive to leave may be stronger.

The woman may choose to take her children either to the home of a family member or friend, or to a transition house, which accommodates women and their children for limited periods of time, helps them through the emotional and legal process and provides counselling strategies for change. Unfortunately, there are not enough shelters in every community to help abused victims. In 1999, there were only 508 shelters for abused women across Canada. More than 96,000 women and children across Canada spent time in shelters in during the 1999–2000 period, according to Statistics Canada. However, these statistics can be deceiving—a reflection more on the availability of space as opposed to the actual need for those spaces. During a single day (April 17, 2000), for example, 2,826 women and 2,525 children found places in shelters. On that same day, 254 women (9 percent of all admitted) and 222 children (also 9 percent) were turned away. Seventy-one percent of those were turned away because the shelters were full. (The rest were turned away because of drug/alcohol, mental illness or other problems.) As governments continue to cut back funding to shelters, this problem may only get worse.

The vast majority of these women, about 85 percent, were seeking shelter from someone with whom they had an intimate relationship. Just over one-third of these women (36 percent) were abused by their spouses, 32 percent by a common-law partner, 12 percent by a former spouse or partner, and about 5 percent by a current or ex-boyfriend. Although these are national averages, one group does stand out: Aboriginals. Aboriginal women reported spousal violence rates three times the national average for non-Aboriginal women, and twice the rate of Aboriginal men, according to a 1999 study by Statistics Canada. Worse still, because the study in question was conducted in English, it is very possible that the rates for Aboriginal, immigrant and visible-minority sectors of society are even higher than reported.

According to a 2002 national report by provincial and territorial ministers responsible for the status of women, the rate of sexual assault reported to the police has been declining. It is not clear whether the incidence of sexual assault has declined or fewer women are reporting because there are fewer support services in the community for them.

By leaving, the woman is not relinquishing any rightful claim to ownership of a home (which can be asserted later in legal proceedings), financial support or custody of children. As an interim emergency procedure, she may apply for welfare if private funds are not available, and/or may seek an order of support from the court.

Possession of the home is often an issue because the abused spouse will probably want to lock the abuser out. However, if a home is owned by the couple as joint tenants, then the wife is not legally entitled to change the locks on the doors without a court order. If the husband complains to the police, they may try to prevail upon the wife to let him in, unless she has a court order. Even if the man and woman do not own the house as joint tenants, a lockout may be difficult to effect. The police do not like to adjudicate between husband and wife as to who is entitled to possession of the home, although they may intervene if they are convinced that she has suffered abuse. To lock her spouse out, a woman usually needs a court order, which can be obtained in most jurisdictions only if physical abuse can be proven. This is not a quick or easy remedy, because the couple have to live together pending the hearing. A victim who resides in Saskatchewan, Manitoba, Ontario, Nova Scotia, the Yukon, Alberta or Prince Edward Island may have it easier because these provinces passed legislation to give legal support to such victims. This legislation is described in the next section.

THE CRIMINAL PROCESS

If a woman has been abused, she should call the police and charge the abuser as a criminal. In fact, this is sometimes the only way of forcing the man to realize the seriousness of his actions and his spouse's unwillingness to put up with continued abuse. In many communities, police are instructed to take positive measures such as removing the abuser from the home temporarily. Sometimes, police will lay charges themselves as part of an increasingly widespread policy of "zero tolerance." If the police will not act, however, the spouse should lay a charge herself with a justice of the peace.

The criminal process will not give the victim any compensation for the injuries she suffered. However, in the context of a civil damages suit, the criminal process is a wise first step because it helps to prove that the abuse happened. Otherwise, in the civil suit, the victim might be cross-examined on why she did not call the police. The criminal injuries compensation board might ask the same question.

As soon as possible, a woman should take the following steps so that she will have evidence later to present a clear case:

- Call the police and then get medical attention *immediately*. Report injuries to both police and doctors in detail, so that their reports will be complete and they will be capable of verifying the story at the trial.
- Write down everything that happened as soon after the incident as possible, and in as complete a form as possible, so that the victim will not have to rely only on memory.
- Have colour photographs taken of the injuries as a useful record.
- Keep track of any related expenses, including receipts and documents, any

time lost at work and any changes in physical and mental condition.

The victim should be prepared to see the case through to the end. Until the trial, there are often lengthy delays (many months or even a year), during which some women, fearing for their own safety, seek to withdraw the charges. However, withdrawing a charge is not so easy to do these days; once a woman has made a complaint, most jurisdictions will expect her to follow through and give evidence at the criminal trial.

SUSTAINING SPOUSAL ABUSE CHARGES

Over the years, society has opened its eyes to the shocking extent of wife assault and has sought to provide a woman with expeditious legal means of protecting herself from a violent husband. The zero tolerance policies in effect in some areas—by which police and Crown attorneys insist on police prosecution of all cases of wife assault—have provided more support for battered women. However, these policies have come under fire lately by people who say that some battered women, particularly those from racial minorities, believe that these policies can endanger their lives even more than the battering. A University of Toronto criminology study reported in 1996 that mandatory charging and "no drop" (of charges) policies are not necessarily a solution. A report by the Commission on Systemic Racism in the Ontario Criminal Justice System recommended in 1996 that Crown attorneys be allowed the discretion to make exceptions to the current practice of taking virtually all spousal abuse cases to trial. Abused racial minority women told the Commission that mandatory charging may prevent them from calling the police at all and might, therefore, be driving family abuse underground; the women have been left believing that they have "no choice or voice" about charging and prosecution decisions.

The legal system does not deal as effectively as one would wish with many of these cases. This unfortunate fact was highlighted for Toronto residents by a series of articles in the *Toronto Star* published in 1996, reporting that newspaper's eight-month tracking of 133 cases of domestic violence through the courts. The investigation found that 37 percent of the cases fell apart because the victim, often out of fear, either failed to show up in court or changed her story in the witness box. The study explored how other jurisdictions had managed to proceed with cases where the evidence did not have to include the testimony of the victim. The study revealed that almost half of the abusers broke bail conditions by harassing, stalking or moving back in with the victim. By the end of the eight months, 60 men were convicted, but of these only 23 were jailed; the other 37 received the legal equivalent of a slap on the wrist, usually a probation sentence of one to three years, often with no criminal record. In 29 percent of the cases, children witnessed the assaults.

One in four of the accused batterers was charged again within one year, and in 83 percent of those cases, with assault on the same woman.

The study noted that the courts in all cases relied on the victim's testimony and not on corroborative evidence such as photographs of injuries, 911 tapes, witness testimony or police testimony, which could secure a conviction without involving the victim directly. The new domestic violence courts in parts of Ontario and Manitoba encourage the police to gather other evidence in addition to the victim's testimony.

SENTENCING THE ABUSER

If the abuser is convicted, punishment can range from a "peace bond" to a fine to a jail sentence, depending on the severity of the assault and any previous convictions. A first offender is more likely required to sign a peace bond—a court order that obliges him to keep the peace and be on good behaviour for up to 12 months, and comply with other conditions that the court believes will encourage good conduct (for example, staying away from his wife). A peace bond under the Criminal Code is not a formal criminal sentence as such. A person who refuses to sign a peace bond when the court finds that the complainant has good reason to fear for her safety, is liable to a fine or jail term of up to 12 months. If a person signs a peace bond and disobeys its terms, which may include staying away from the complainant, he may be found to be in contempt of court; besides being liable to a fine or jail term, he may be jailed by the police immediately. The man may be fined or imprisoned for up to five years for assaults, ten years if he used a weapon or caused bodily harm, or 14 years if he endangered her life or her children's.

Sentencing in wife assault cases has been the subject of much public discussion. Many people are concerned that the sentences are too short to deter this behaviour. For example, a 1996 Ontario decision gave a man a five-year prison sentence for sexually, physically and emotionally abusing his wife for nearly a decade. The abuse included "some sexual contact with the family dog," being forced to perform in a pornographic movie, and being punched, kicked, slapped and threatened. The judge said that the abuse was "unspeakable . . . prolonged, brutal, sadistic and degrading." Such offenders rarely serve their full terms, however. Most are eligible for parole after serving one-third of their sentence, unless the court has ordered that at least one-half be served. All sentences are subject to statutory release of one-third and another one-third may in some cases be possible for good behaviour, on review by a parole board. This particular offender, therefore, may have only been in jail for one year and eight months.

In cases where murder or attempted murder is tried, the courts seem to apply more stringent sentences. In two cases of attempted murder that went before the Ontario Court of Appeal in 1996, the Court upheld the trial judge's sentences in both cases. In one, a 40-year-old common-law husband pleaded guilty to shooting his common-law wife three times in the head and once in the chest, and was sentenced to nine years' imprisonment in addition to the ten-and-a-half months he had spent in pretrial custody. The victim recovered. In the other case, the husband pleaded guilty to shooting his wife of 21 years in the neck, paralyzing her for life; she now needs around-the-clock nursing care. He was sentenced to ten years' imprisonment after 12 months in pretrial custody.

In a murder case, a 48-year-old man with a history of alcoholism and spousal abuse was convicted of the "brutal and unprovoked" murder of his wife of 25 years. The jury rejected his defence of intoxication. The trial judge sentenced him to life imprisonment without eligibility for parole for 14 years because the murder was of a spouse. The Ontario Court of Appeal revised the period of parole ineligibility down to 12 years, saying it was an error in law to sentence spousal murderers differently from any other murderer in the absence of specific legislation.

Saskatchewan was the first Canadian province or territory to pass innovative legislation to deal with domestic violence. The law is called The Victims of Domestic Violence Act, and has been in effect since 1995. It permits a specially designated justice of the peace to issue an emergency intervention order, without notice to the abuser, containing a number of possible terms: an order giving the wife exclusive possession of the home; a direction to the police to remove the abuser from the home or to accompany the victim to the home to gather up belongings; a restraining order to prevent the abuser from contacting the victim; or any other term thought necessary to ensure the protection of the victim and children. Within three working days, the justice of the peace must send all the papers to a judge, whose job it is to review the order and confirm it, or order a rehearing before the same or a different judge.

There is also the opportunity to ask for a non-emergency victim's assistance order. In addition to including anything available in an emergency intervention order, a non-emergency order may also include a prohibition from such places as the victim's residence, business, school or place of employment, as well as a compensation order for monetary losses, including loss of earnings, out-of-pocket losses for injuries sustained, moving and accommodation expenses and legal costs. The victim's address can be kept confidential at the victim's request, and the court may order a private hearing.

Other jurisdictions have special measures. Prince Edward Island, Manitoba, Ontario, Nova Scotia, the Yukon and Alberta have legislation similar to Saskatchewan's. In Alberta, there is leeway for the victim to get a restraining order by phone, and the victim is notified when their suspected offender is released on bail. Manitoba and the Yukon broadened the application of their law to include same-sex partners, and Manitoba's legislation includes remedies for stalking.

Elsewhere, the police can make use of Section 31 of the Criminal Code, which permits police officers to arrest a person if they have "reasonable and probable grounds" to believe that that person will commit a breach of the peace.

Specialized domestic violence courts, such as the ones in Manitoba and Ontario, facilitate early intervention in the cycle of violence, provide counselling and reassuring courtroom and support services for victims, provide counselling for offenders and give rise to more effective investigation and prosecution.

Victims are helped to get copies of bail orders and probation papers to show to police should harassment or another assault occur. Police, Crown prosecutors and judges get special training on treating victims with sensitivity and how to gather relevant evidence. Police are told to gather other forms of evidence (tapes of 911 calls, audio and videotapes of the initial victim statements, photos of the victims' injuries and the crime scene) that can secure a conviction without involving the victim directly.

Studies have shown that these courts can make a real difference in holding abusers accountable and providing safety for victims. The number of spousal abuse cases reaching the courts has increased, the average time from first court appearance to the conclusion of the case has decreased and there is a higher number of guilty verdicts.

BATTERED WOMAN'S SYNDROME AS A DEFENCE

There have been cases in which the abused spouse has been battered severely over long periods of time and eventually kills or maims her partner. Her defence is self-defence, on the basis that the history of abuse and fear of imminent danger from present and future abuse drove her to violence against her abuser. The precedent-setting case that established the right to use the battered woman's syndrome as a defence was *R. v. Lavallee*, which reached the Supreme Court of Canada in 1990. In that case, a woman killed her common-law partner and alleged self-defence because of her fear that he would attack and possibly kill her. At the trial, the jury acquitted her after hearing her evidence that the shooting was the final, desperate act of a woman who believed that she would be killed that night. She told of her ongoing terror and inability to escape the relationship.

In light of the Lavallee decision, the federal government decided in 1995 to review the cases of women imprisoned for killing their abusive partners to determine if they should be freed or retried, and to give them an opportunity to use the battered woman's syndrome as a defence. The inquiry, run by Ontario judge Lynn Ratushny, reviewed 98 requests and recommended that seven convictions be re-examined. The federal government freed two of the women, gave two conditional pardons and ordered a new trial for a fifth.

CIVIL SUIT FOR COMPENSATION

Suing for compensation for personal injury caused by spousal assault is a relatively recent phenomenon. A lawyer is needed to represent the person bringing the civil suit, whereas in criminal proceedings the lawyer for the Crown prosecutes the case. The victim will claim payment for the actual costs incurred, such as lost wages, and the pain suffered from the injuries inflicted. Another amount can be claimed as "punitive damages," an extra amount over and above the victim's proven losses that is intended to punish the abuser for his conduct. Punitive damages are not ordered if the perpetrator has been punished as a criminal.

Court orders for compensation have ranged from $15,000 to over $100,000, depending on the circumstances of the case. For example, in a 1995 Ontario case, during a four-month period and despite a restraining order, a husband had called his ex-wife continually during the day and night, left letters at her home, videotaped her through the bathroom window from a tree, threw a cupboard door at her (narrowly missing), threatened to abduct their child, stalked and threatened to kill her, and continually harassed her friends and professional advisors. He even hunted her down when she was out of the country and told her, "There is no way you can get away from me."

To try to escape from him, the ex-wife had to assume a new name and relocate to a different community. The wife was awarded compensation of about $105,000, which included $44,000 for her future medical and psychiatric care; about $6,000 for such items as an alarm system and repairs; $40,000 damages for invasion of privacy, trespass to the person, intentional infliction of mental suffering and emotional distress; and $15,000 for punitive damages for, in the words of Mr. Justice Kenneth Binks, the "calculated, devilishly creative and entirely reprehensible conduct of the husband." She also received an order for her husband to pay her solicitor and client costs; as the judge said, "There is no reason why the plaintiff should have to bear any portion of the legal costs when the actions of the defendant went far beyond the bounds of civilized behaviour."

In a 1996 Ottawa case, a husband who raped his wife and then helped another man do the same was ordered to pay her $30,000 in compensation for sexual assault, including $10,000 punitive damages. The wife had divorced him after 23 years of marriage and two children. She brought the claim for personal injury at the same time as the divorce action, which is often a convenient way of dealing with all the issues at once. She never brought criminal charges against her husband or the other man.

CRIMINAL INJURIES COMPENSATION

Every province and territory has a criminal injuries compensation board, which provides financial compensation to innocent victims of violent crime.

The process is relatively simple and informal. The incident must be reported to the police immediately after the event. A monetary award is possible, even if the abusive spouse was not convicted of assault, as long as it was his criminal behaviour that caused the injuries. The board may pay for drug prescriptions, medical bills, lost wages, and pain and suffering. Because every province and territory has its own rules, maximum payment levels and limitation periods for applying, it is wise for an abused spouse to apply as soon as possible after the incident, and find out how it works in her area. Ontario, for example, provides as much as $25,000 to a victim.

DIVORCE

A wife can sue for divorce on the basis of her husband's physical cruelty if an act of physical cruelty can be substantiated by witnesses or by medical or police reports. However, the divorce process is less complicated on separation grounds. Since a divorce is available after one year of separation, a woman may find it unnecessary to sue on the basis of cruelty.

When a battered spouse sues for divorce, she may at the same time seek an injunction from the court to prohibit her husband from contacting her. If he disobeys the injunction, the sheriff, through the court, will enforce the civil order; the police will deal only with infractions of the Criminal Code.

3. The Criminal Process: Consent and Credibility Issues

The issue that often arises when a man is charged with sexual assault is whether or not the woman consented to sexual relations. The law on this issue has evolved over the years. There used to be a legally accepted assumption, often used as a criminal defence, that if a woman had ever had sexual relations with anyone, her credibility was in question when she said she had not consented to have sexual relations with the accused—as if to suggest that any woman who is sexually active is more likely to have consented.

In 1976, the Canadian Criminal Code was amended. The jury was no longer permitted to hear evidence of the victim's previous sexual conduct, unless a judge first concluded in a hearing without the jury that the questions were relevant to the issue of the victim's consent. The victim could be questioned twice, once in front of the judge and again, if the judge approved, in front of the jury.

In 1983, the Criminal Code was again changed. It specifically stated that, in trials on sexual assault charges, the alleged rapist's lawyer was not permitted to bring out evidence about the victim's sexual activity with any person other than the accused, unless it came within certain narrow exceptions specifically set out in the Code to ensure that the evidence was relevant. Defence lawyers could not surprise a victim with these questions at the trial, but had to give notice in writing to the prosecuting lawyer of their intentions, with particulars. After notice was given, the judge would first hold a private hearing without the jury, and without the victim being required to testify, to determine whether questions about the victim's other sexual activities should be brought before the jury. The defence had to prove that questions about the complainant's past sexual activity were relevant to the defence. For example, the victim's answers might give evidence of the accused's honest but mistaken belief that the complainant consented. On the other hand, the defence could not ask questions meant to show that a sexually active woman was more likely to have consented to sex with the accused, or that her evidence was therefore less credible. For example, defence counsel could not ask the rape victim how many sexual partners she had had.

This 1983 law was struck down as unconstitutional by the Supreme Court of Canada in 1991 in the case of *R. v. Seaboyer*. The decision, written by Madam Justice Beverley McLachlin for the majority, said the law favoured the rape victim at the expense of the accused. However, writing for the minority, dissenting judge Madam Justice Claire L'Heureux-Dubé's opinion was that many judges decide what is relevant according to myths and stereotypes about the nature of women's sexuality. She referred as an example to the myth that a sexually active woman, because she has consented to sex with one man, may consent indiscriminately to sex with any man.

ACTUAL CONSENT

The current "rape shield" law, in effect since 1992, is based on the belief that the complainant's previous sexual history is rarely relevant, and therefore no longer admissible before the court to prove that a woman is more likely to have said yes to the accused, or is less worthy of being believed. In addition, a man may no longer excuse his conduct by saying he honestly believed that she consented; he must get her *actual* consent, and there must be evidence at trial to prove that she did consent. A goal of this law was to define consent so that the victim's prior sexual conduct would be rendered irrelevant.

Consent to sexual relations is now defined as actual consent. The participants in sexual activity must each agree and continue to agree. A woman can change her mind and say no in the middle of sexual activity or after foreplay. There is no consent if she says stop. It is no defence for a man to claim that she allowed him to go so far, he could not control himself. As a result, any woman who is pressured to go farther than she wishes should simply say *no*. The law is on her side: no means no, whether or not she has said yes in the past, to the accused or to anyone. A woman must voluntarily agree to the sexual act in question.

In 1999, the Supreme Court of Canada ruled on a challenge of this law, in the case of *R. v. Ewanchuk*. A 49-year-old man had been charged with sexually assaulting a 17-year-old woman during a job interview, when he refused to stop groping her when she said no; in fact she said no at least three times. The Alberta Court of Appeal in a decision rendered by Justice John McClung interpreted the woman's failure to struggle, scream or attempt to escape as "implied consent" and even commented that given how she was dressed, she was not in a position to complain (he said in his ruling that she "did not present herself in a bonnet and crinolines" when she entered his trailer for the interview). He also made light of the man's actions by commenting that they were "far less criminal than hormonal" and were "clumsy passes."

The Supreme Court of Canada unanimously affirmed that there is no defence of implied consent in Canadian law, that no means no and consent to sexual activity must be communicated and voluntary, in each and every instance of sexual activity. The Court overturned the man's acquittal and sent him back to the Alberta trial courts for sentencing. Madam Justice Claire L'Heureux-Dubé and Justice Charles Gonthier added a special comment of concern at the continued stereotyping of women implicit in the Court of Appeal's decision, stating that "complainants should be able to rely on a judiciary whose impartiality is not compromised by these biased assumptions." They pointed out that the Court of Appeal decision "ignores the law" that intended to do away with such stereotyping, namely, the 1992 Criminal Code amendments and the 1991 Supreme Court of Canada decision in *R. v. Seaboyer*.

The rape shield law is also clear in that the woman must be capable of giving consent. It is not consent if she is induced to say yes by someone who abuses a position of trust, power or authority. Nor is it consent if someone else purports to say yes for her. An accused person cannot defend himself by saying the woman consented when she was drunk. If a man has sex with a woman who has passed out, he is guilty of sexual assault.

However, in a surprising Supreme Court of Canada decision in 1993, the six-judge majority ruled a man innocent of sexual assault because he was very drunk when he assaulted a 65-year-old woman he knew. He said that he did not intend to do it. Three judges dissented, arguing that drunkenness is no defence because it is self-induced. As a result of this court decision, the federal government amended the Criminal Code in 1995 to prevent such a case from recurring. The amendment states that a person is criminally at fault when, in a state of self-induced intoxication that renders him or her unaware of or incapable of consciously controlling his or her behaviour, that person voluntarily or involuntarily interferes or threatens to interfere with the bodily integrity of another person.

What if a woman silently submits to sexual assault? Until 1994, the courts could assume that she agreed to sexual relations on the basis of the old adage, "silence means consent." A Nova Scotia man, found guilty of sexually assaulting his stepdaughter, had managed to persuade an appeal court to overturn the conviction on the grounds that she had passively submitted to him. But the Supreme Court of Canada in 1994 restored the conviction, ruling that the woman's lack of resistance did not mean she consented.

The media are banned from publishing the evidence from the private hearing. If the judge allows the defence to question the victim in front of the jury, he or she can also order that the testimony be kept confidential.

This evolution over the past 29 years of the rules applicable to questioning the complainant may seem technical, but it demonstrates the process by which change is effected and then challenged, effected and challenged again. Until there is consensus about what process is fair to both the accused and the complainant and still serves society, these changes are inevitable. Since the 1992 changes, the law in this area seems to have stabilized and the issue of consent has been dealt with in a more straightforward manner, in accordance with the law. A female victim's previous sexual history is not raised as often as a means of challenging her credibility. However, yet another accused has challenged the rape shield law. In *R. v. Darrach*, a man appealed to the Supreme Court of Canada both the trial and appeal court rulings that the rape shield law is constitutional and does not prevent the accused from making full answer and defence. He argued against the limitations in the Criminal Code on the use of a woman's sexual history as a defence in sexual assault trials. In October 2000, the Supreme Court of Canada dismissed his appeal and ruled that the rape shield legislation is constitutional.

However, issues remain. The battleground has shifted to challenge the complainant's credibility on other grounds, centred on the defence's demand for access to the victim's counselling and therapeutic records, which is discussed in the next section. And, notwithstanding the 1992 rules, the perception remains that a woman is at least partly to blame for a sexual advance by someone she knows. The courts show their ambivalence by their sentences: In a typical case, an Ontario teen accompanied a man she had just met to his room, where he forced intercourse upon her. The jury convicted him, but the judge sentenced him to only 18 months in prison, in contrast to the maximum possible sentence of ten years. With statutory and good behaviour remission of jail sentences, his jail term could be reduced to one-third, or six months in jail. In another case of sexual assault causing bodily harm, which the court said involved a very high degree of violence, cruelty and degradation, the sentence was 34 months' imprisonment.

4. Rape Victims as Complainants: Facing the Legal Process

THE COMPLAINT

A rape victim should press charges quickly, preferably immediately and certainly within 24 hours. She should call the police or a sexual assault crisis centre, whose staff members will often escort her to a hospital. It is important that the victim not bathe, use the toilet or change her clothes. Medical staff will examine her to ensure that there are no internal injuries and to collect physical evidence to be used at trial if she lays criminal charges. She will be offered emotional support and counselling by crisis centre staff. She should expect the police to question her

rigorously to ascertain if her evidence will hold up in court or be, as they call it, "founded." The legal process may take a couple of years, or more.

THE COURT PROCESS

I wish I could say that the legal system has figured out how not to re-victimize the victim of a sexual assault when she presses charges. Despite legislative changes and court reinterpretations of the law over almost 30 years, a woman who is ready to testify against an accused rapist must still be prepared for some rough challenges to her credibility. She faces this ordeal partly because the law supports the right of the accused to a full opportunity to defend himself, and one of the ways a defence lawyer chooses to defend the accused is to challenge the believability of the complainant.

The defence may try to suggest that the woman enticed the alleged rapist or that she is falsely accusing him, even though such accusations occur no more frequently than false reports of other crimes. Juries may also be less inclined to believe a woman if she submitted passively (as women are told to do, to avoid greater harm) or shows no sign of injury. The important issue of consent must be canvassed, and defence lawyers keep trying to find ways to cast doubt on the woman's story and her character. These challenges to credibility and character can make many victims feel as if they are on trial, and many women take this difficult experience into account when deciding whether or not to press charges against the rapist. It is generally acknowledged that the vast majority of sexual assaults on women go unreported to the police. More female victims of sexual assault than of other crimes were deterred by police or court attitudes from reporting the crime.

PUBLICATION BAN

One protection that a rape victim can usually count on is securing a publication ban to keep her name out of the media. However, even this protection was almost lost in 1994 when an Alberta judge dismissed sexual assault charges against a man and, at the same time, chose to rescind a publication ban because, he said, the complainant was "a liar, a perjurer and a prostitute." The Supreme Court of Canada set the Alberta judge's decision aside the next year, saying that the publication ban is irrevocable unless the complainant or Crown, whichever requested the ban in the first place, consents. The Supreme Court also said that the law was intended to create a climate where victims feel comfortable coming forward—a more important intention than unmasking potential perjurers. Had the Alberta decision stood, then every time an accused secured an acquittal, the court might have said that the complainant was lying and allowed her name to be published, as a form of punishment.

Around the same time, in 1995, a newspaper published the name of a complainant despite a publication ban, and the complainant successfully sued for damages; the court ordered the newspaper to pay her $12,000 damages for embarrassment and humiliation and $5,000 punitive damages.

COUNSELLING RECORDS

When the definition of consent was narrowed in 1992, the government hoped that this change would render irrelevant a victim's prior sexual conduct. However, defence lawyers now try, and often succeed in, a new strategy: subpoenaing the counselling and therapy records of the victim, who may have gone to a crisis centre or a shelter for advice and support. It is not clear what use these records would have in a trial except to create and perpetuate new myths.

Two such cases were challenged at the Supreme Court of Canada by several sexual assault crisis centres, supported by a number of women's groups. In 1996, the Supreme Court ruled that a rape victim's counselling records must be produced and may be admissible in evidence in some cases. In each such case, the court must review the balance between the rights of the accused and the right of the victim to privacy, but in the end it must order the records released if they are "likely to have relevance," particularly to the issue of consent. The Supreme Court also said records are relevant if they may reveal that the therapy influenced a complainant's memory. The request for their counselling records may further discourage rape victims from reporting the crime.

In response, some victims have chosen not to seek counselling, and some counsellors have stopped keeping records. Destroying records can create problems. In an Ontario case, the judge stayed the charges, saying the accused could not obtain a fair trial as no one knew whether the records contained relevant information. The appeal court sent the matter back to trial, but the Supreme Court of Canada in 1997 reinstated the trial judgment.

The federal government acted quickly to counteract the two 1996 Supreme Court of Canada decisions. In 1997, it passed legislation to restrict access to medical, counselling, therapeutic, psychiatric, school and employment records, as well as to diaries, journals and other personal records of complainants, in such sexual offence prosecutions as sexual assault, child sexual abuse, incest, prostitution, indecent acts and rape.

The justification for the legislation was clearly identified—to strengthen protection for complainants of sexual offences, to enhance privacy and equality rights for all complainants, and to deal with "an unwarranted invasion of a complainant's private and confidential records for improper purposes." The act set out a two-stage process for applications for access to a complainant's records. First, the accused would have to establish the likely relevance of the records to an issue at trial or to the competence of a witness to testify. Then, if relevance is established, the judge would review the records in private and reconsider their relevance. She or he would also consider the Charter rights of both the complainant and the accused, and decide the extent to which the defence should have access to the records. The act provides a detailed list of acceptable and unacceptable grounds for relevance and, therefore, access.

This new law was also challenged on constitutional grounds. In 1997, an Alberta court ruled the Criminal Code provision unconstitutional because it violated the right of the accused to a fair trial. In this case, *R.* v. *Mills*, the accused wanted access to all a teenaged victim's medical and psychiatric records and the trial judge, setting aside the recently passed Criminal Code section, ruled that a victim's right of privacy did not trump the right of the accused to a fair trial. The Supreme Court of Canada reversed the Alberta decision in 1999, upholding the constitutionality of the 1997 law.

TESTIFYING AT THE HEARING

Once they have registered a complaint, some complainants do not wish to testify at the hearing. Can a woman be forced to testify if she takes rape or assault charges to court? The simple answer is yes. A person, especially a victim, is expected to give evidence when she or he has witnessed a crime. Because our legal system is based on the assumption that a person is innocent of a crime until proven guilty, it is essential for citizens to be willing to give evidence. Although there are many ways to prove innocence or guilt, an eyewitness's testimony is the most helpful proof.

To promote fair trials and respect for court orders and the legal system, judges have the authority to charge and punish witnesses who refuse to testify. Marriage does not exempt witnesses from testifying against their spouses.

If a person is served with a subpoena and fails to appear in court to testify, she or he can be charged with contempt of court, punishable by a maximum fine of $100 and/or a maximum of 90 days in jail. If she or he appears in court but refuses to testify after the judge has directly ordered her or him to testify, the witness can be charged with contempt "in the face of the court" and fined up to $500 and/or a maximum of six months in jail.

Judges rarely charge rape or assault victims with contempt of court for refusing to testify—but it has happened. In 1984, two Ontario cases were reported. An Ottawa rape victim was sentenced to one week in jail for refusing to testify. An Orillia assault victim, although pregnant, was given a three-month jail sentence, later reduced to two weeks after an appeal, for not testifying against the man she planned to marry.

These contempt convictions occurred after the provincial government made changes to legal guidelines in response to public concern about the extent of violence against women. The Ontario attorney general's office told police to press charges (such as rape and assault) on behalf of battered women, who had usually been left on their own to press charges. Crown attorneys were also told that they could proceed with prosecutions against the women's wishes.

These policies are still in effect in many jurisdictions, although lately questions about their efficacy have been raised. The changes to the guidelines may not respect battered women's situations or respond to their needs, such as for more shelters and counselling. Sometimes police mediation or an immediate court hearing is more helpful than court charges in such circumstances because the problem is dealt with immediately, not many months later. Since witnesses are often affected by a real or perceived fear of reprisal by the accused, greater police protection for witnesses would perhaps encourage co-operation with the legal process.

5. Stalking

Although the police did not take stalking seriously for a long time, this offence represents serious intimidation, mostly to women, by former boyfriends, husbands and sometimes strangers. Stalking is often obsessive behaviour intended to frighten and harass the victim. It includes such actions as following the woman on foot or by car, waiting for her outside her home and leaving threatening notes for her in odd places and at odd times to make her believe that the harasser is omnipresent and watching her. The victim usually feels unsafe and isolated.

INTIMIDATION

Before 1993, the main legal prohibition against stalking was an obscure section of the Criminal Code, designed to deal with industrial disputes, that made "intimidation" an offence. The offence was defined as minor—a summary conviction offence—and carried a maximum penalty of $2,000 and/or six months in prison. Prohibited behaviour included persistently following a person from place to place; watching the place where a person lives, works, carries on business or just happens to be; using violence or threats of violence to a person or the person's family; and damaging a person's property.

But the law against intimidation did not fit the crime of stalking for three reasons. First, it left loopholes for stalkers, who could exonerate themselves by proving they had legal authority or justification for approaching the victim's house or workplace. A cab driver, for example, could say that he was waiting for a fare, or a market researcher that he was obtaining information for a study.

Second, the intimidation law put the onus on the victim to prove what was often unprovable—that the accused had followed or watched her with the intention of interfering with her legal right to come and go as she pleased.

Third, the law did not address the serious extremes to which stalking can go. For example, a secretary felt so threatened by a stalker shadowing her everywhere that she drastically curtailed her normal activities and eventually changed jobs to avoid him.

CRIMINAL HARASSMENT

To address these problems and deal specifically with stalking, the federal government in 1993 made "criminal harassment" an offence. This law prohibited conduct that causes people to have reasonable fears for their own safety or the safety of someone known to them. That conduct includes repeatedly following a person or someone known to the person being harassed; repeatedly communicating with a person or someone known to the harassed, either directly or indirectly; watching a place where a person lives, works, carries on business or just happens to be; and engaging in threatening conduct directed at a person or a member of the harassed person's family. It was no longer necessary for the victim to prove that the pursuer intended to harass her, or compel her to do or fail to do something. The possible punishment became more severe: While the judge could limit the sentence to a $2,000 fine or up to six months in jail in minor cases, more serious cases now carry a prison term of up to ten years. For example, a 72-year-old Prince Edward Island man pleaded guilty to a charge of criminal harassment for persistently following an employee in his car and parking in front of her home. He was sentenced to one year's probation on condition that he stay away from her, but within two weeks of the probation order, the police caught him again and charged him. This time, he was convicted and sentenced to 45 days on each of three charges of criminal harassment, for a total of 135 days in jail. This sentence appears to be no tougher than it would have been under the earlier law.

A more stringent sentence was meted out in 1995 when a stalker harassed his former girlfriend, saying that he was trying to drive her crazy so that she would kill herself. When he went so far as to slash her tires and burn down her cottage, he left her a note: "I want to take your life apart, piece by piece and you know I can do it." Then he tried to extort $5,000 and sexual favours from her. While no one was physically harmed, she and her family were terrorized. He pleaded guilty to criminal harassment, arson, attempted extortion, breaking and entering and possession of a stolen vehicle, and was sentenced to eight years in prison.

A stalking victim can also sue for compensation for damages in a civil court. In a case decided in 1995, a woman got an order that her ex-husband pay her $105,000 for stalking and tormenting her after their divorce to the extent that she had to move from her community and assume a new name.

The federal government passed legislation in 1997 to toughen the criminal harassment provisions. The law provides that a court, when imposing sentence on a person convicted of stalking while a criminal restraining order (peace bond) is in effect, must treat that violation as an aggravating factor. In addition, the law provides that people who commit murder while stalking, if they intended their victim to fear for her safety during the stalking, will face a first-degree murder charge, whether or not it can be proven that the murder itself was planned and deliberate. First-degree murder carries with it a mandatory penalty of life imprisonment with no eligibility for parole for 25 years. In addition, the new Firearms Act provides that a factor in issuing a licence to have a gun is whether a person has been convicted of criminal harassment in the previous five years.

Since then, in the 2000 case of *R.* v. *Bates*,

the Ontario Court of Appeal unanimously ruled that a trial judge was wrong in giving a suspended sentence to a stalker convicted of 11 offences against his ex-girlfriend including criminal harassment, assault, death threats, and failure to comply with bail terms to stay away from her. Instead, the Court ordered the man to serve 30 months in penitentiary and three years on probation (with counselling), and prohibited him from carrying firearms. Also in 2000, the Ontario Court of Appeal upheld the constitutionality of the anti-stalking law.

A 1997 study for the federal Justice Department, based on 601 criminal harassment cases under the 1993 law, concluded that insufficient police resources are spent on investigating criminal harassment cases and training police, and there is a lack of adequate victim services. In 2002, according to police statistics as reported by Statistics Canada, about eight out of ten victims of criminal harassment had some form of relationship with their stalkers, either as partners, friends, acquaintances or other family members. Females were most likely to be criminally harassed by a partner, while males were more likely to be harassed by an acquaintance.

When a woman believes she is being stalked contrary to the law, she should have someone witness the stalker's repeated conduct to help prove what happened. She should also ask the police to observe the stalker's behaviour and try to convince them to lay a charge. She should keep a diary to document the incidents, including the date on which they occurred and how they affected her; take photographs of the stalker's actions where appropriate and possible without endangering herself; keep any letters and notes sent; make copies or keep the original tapes of any messages left

on the answering machine; and give copies of all evidence to the police.

6. The Role of the Police

An innovative case involving a Toronto rape victim put the police on notice that they must warn potential crime victims so that they can take protective measures.

After being raped in August 1986, the victim, known as "Jane Doe," learned that local police had known about the danger to women living in her neighbourhood. Within a one-year period, numerous sexual assaults had taken place in a downtown area of the city. All the assaults involved white single women living in second- or third-floor apartments, where the attacker entered through a balcony door. The man who raped her (and at least four other women) was captured six weeks later. He subsequently pleaded guilty to all the charges in 1987 and was sentenced to 20 years in prison.

After the perpetrator went to prison, the victim sued the investigating officers, the Chief of Police and the Board of Commissioners of Police. She alleged that the officers had breached their duty as police and violated the Canadian Charter of Rights and Freedoms, which promises security of the person and equality rights.

The victim alleged that her Charter rights to security of the person were threatened when the police neither warned nor protected her, but used her, and other women like her, as "bait," without her knowledge or consent, to catch the serial rapist. She alleged that, in doing so, the police knowingly placed her at risk.

She also submitted that, when the police chose not to warn her, they breached the equality-rights sections of the Charter by acting wrongly on their stereotypical and discriminatory belief that women would become hysterical and scare off the rapist.

The police took the position that their decision not to warn the community was merely a "policy" decision, and left it to the courts to decide whether there was an error in judgment. Meanwhile, the rape victim asked for compensation for expenses she incurred, income she lost, inconvenience and pain she suffered, and loss of enjoyment of life. She stated that she suffered from serious bouts of depression and anxiety, requiring psychiatric counselling and therapy.

It took the victim three years and three court hearings simply to get the right to continue her legal suit. When the lawyers for the police challenged her right to bring forward a lawsuit at all, a judge, after hearing five days of legal argument in 1989, told her that she had a right to pursue her case against the police. The police lawyers then appealed, but the judge's decision was ultimately supported by three appeal-court judges in 1990.

In 1998, after a 39-day trial, the trial judge ruled in Jane Doe's favour and ordered the police to pay general damages of $175,000, special damages (for example, medical expenses) to date of $37,301.58 and future costs of $8,062.74 together with enough to produce $2,000 a year for 15 years for cabfare. The judge found that the police had violated Jane Doe's rights under the Charter, and compensated her accordingly.

The trial judge explained the police failed in their statutory duty to prevent crime and protect life and property, when they failed to warn Jane Doe and the other victims of the presence of a serial rapist in their neighbourhood. They were found to be "irresponsible

and grossly negligent." The excuse given by the police—that the women would become hysterical and scare off the attacker—was, ruled the judge, sexist stereotyping reflecting systemic discrimination in the force against women, and made the women into bait for their attacker. This represented a breach of Jane Doe's Charter rights to equal protection and equal benefit of the law. The decision was not appealed.

The Jane Doe case took so long to wend its way through the court system that even before the trial was held, police commenced issuing warnings to the community whenever there was a possibility of danger. The case made a difference even before it was finally decided.

In fact, a 1995 court decision applied the principle too, notwithstanding that the case at that early stage was not a formal precedent. The 1995 case involved a dangerous sexual offender, serving a life sentence for murder, who escaped from a minimum security prison and beat and sexually assaulted a woman who lived in the area. She and her family sued the offender as well as the federal government and Correctional Services Canada for negligence in not identifying that he would be a risk and in not reporting his escape quickly enough to the provincial police. After a 46-day trial, the court ruled that the prison officials should have known that a violent offender, who was in a state of some anxiety and who, to their knowledge, took out his frustrations by violently assaulting women, posed a significant risk to any woman he met in the vicinity of the institution.

The offender, the government and the government's agency were found liable and required to pay damages to the victim of $437,000, including pre-judgment interest, plus partial costs. (The government was ordered to pay "party and party costs," which ends up being roughly one-third to one-half of actual costs, and the offender was ordered to pay "solicitor and client costs," which is intended to be full indemnity for costs, but usually ends up being closer to one-half to two-thirds of actual costs.) The case was not appealed.

And in 1999, in another evolution from the Jane Doe case, a judge permitted an individual to sue the police for "malicious misfeasance" (the wrongful exercise of lawful authority) while in public office and their supervisors for negligence in supervision. An individual died when police shot him after he fled a pursued vehicle following a bank robbery and his estate was allowed to pursue the lawsuit against the police.

C. BY THOSE IN A POSITION OF AUTHORITY

1. Medical Devices

A manufacturer can be successfully sued if a person's health suffered because of a faulty medical device, and the manufacturer was negligent in its manufacture or design, or failed to adequately inform the doctors and public of potential problems. The doctor may be found negligent if he or she failed to warn the patient of possible risks. When the use of a device is voluntary, as in the case of most silicone breast implants and birth control pills, there is a heavy onus on the manufacturer and doctor to inform the patient of possible risks.

SILICONE BREAST IMPLANTS

An estimated 100,000 to 200,000 Canadian women have had breast implants, most of them made of silicone gel, although the trend seems to be towards saline implants. About 80 percent of these women chose to have implants because they wanted bigger breasts; the rest chose breast reconstruction, usually because of a mastectomy. While breast implantation has been practised since the 1960s, no serious safety concerns were raised until several years ago, when a series of lawsuits against manufacturers revealed that the silicone gel sac had sometimes leaked or ruptured, allowing the silicone to move to other parts of the body. In other cases, the sac itself moved—towards the woman's armpit, for example—or the woman suffered from infections. In many cases, the women were unaware of any potential harm when they opted for the implants.

Manufacturers of breast implants have a duty to ensure that the product is safe, and to warn women of potential dangers. If manufacturers break these rules, they can be held liable and ordered to compensate the victims. Similarly, a woman's family doctor and the surgeon who performs the operation also have a duty to warn her of possible risks.

A 1993 appeal case in British Columbia shows how the courts have treated the potential liability of the manufacturer, family doctor and surgeon. The plaintiff got silicone breast implants ten years earlier, at the age of 23, to rehabilitate and correct breast abnormalities. Within two years after surgery, she noticed a painful lump in her right breast. During further surgery to remove the implants, the surgeon discovered that one implant had ruptured, spilling silicone into the breast cavity; the silicone envelope could not be found. After the removal of both implants, her condition continued to worsen, and she eventually had to have a double mastectomy.

At the trial in 1990, the judge ordered the manufacturer, Dow Corning, to pay the woman compensation of $95,000, of which $50,000 was for pain and suffering and $45,000 for lost income. But the judge ruled that the surgeon who performed the implants was innocent of wrongdoing because the manufacturer had not warned him of the risks.

In 1993, the B.C. Court of Appeal upheld the award against Dow Corning. Dow Corning appealed to the Supreme Court of Canada, which in December 1995 affirmed the company's liability and imposed a heavy burden on manufacturers of potentially hazardous medical products to fully warn consumers of the risks.

The Supreme Court did not let Dow Corning off the hook by allowing it to blame the doctor as a "learned intermediary," because Dow failed to properly warn the medical community of the risks of post-surgical implant rupture through normal use. The Court was clear that manufacturers have "a heavy onus to provide clear, complete and current information concerning the dangers inherent in the ordinary use of their product." When the surgery took place, the manufacturer knew of between 48 and 61 reports of unexplained ruptures, yet its warnings did not change for more than two years afterwards. Dow also knew, before 1985, that loose silicone gel from ruptured implants can cause adverse reactions and travel to other parts of the body. The Court said that a manufacturer has a duty to keep doctors informed of the known effects of their medical products, even if the implications are not conclusive.

That Supreme Court of Canada decision will affect other liability cases involving medical products, but not every case against a manufacturer will succeed. Much depends on the circumstances and the informed consent of the patient. For example, in another case in 1993, the B.C. Court of Appeal upheld a trial judge's 1990 decision that a woman's doctors were not responsible for her breast implant complications. The woman had suffered from severe fibrocystic breast disease and had decided to have mastectomies and breast reconstruction with implants. Afterwards, she developed a severe infection and the implants were removed. She then had several more operations and new breast implants. The Court dismissed her lawsuit because the doctors had properly informed her about the risk of complications, including infection, and she had chosen to proceed anyway.

In Ontario, following the enactment of new legislation permitting class-action lawsuits, such a lawsuit was launched in 1993 on behalf of all Ontario silicone breast implant recipients. A similar lawsuit was also launched in Quebec. In a class-action lawsuit, the court permits one person and one lawyer to litigate on behalf of many others who have suffered similar injuries. This type of lawsuit significantly reduces expenses for the individual litigant. Individuals can choose to opt out of the class action and pursue their own claim if they wish. But if they do not opt out, they will be automatically included and will both benefit and be bound by any court judgment or settlement affecting all recipients. In each case, the court establishes the method of opting out and informs the public.

In the Ontario class-action lawsuit, a $29-million settlement was reached with Bristol-Myers-Squibb in 1995 for the benefit of both Ontario and Quebec women on behalf of present and future claimants. Women share in the settlement fund by receiving a lump sum—different for each woman and based on the severity of her illness, her degree of disability and her age at the onset of the symptoms—but will be able to reapply if their symptoms worsen. Part of the fund is to be invested and set aside for the benefit of implant recipients who develop first-time symptoms in the future. A deadline date for registering a claim was set by the courts, and advertised in the newspapers.

In 1998, a $22-million class-action settlement was reached with Baxter Healthcare for women who received its Heyer-Schulte implants between 1971 and 1984, which leaked and were said to cause autoimmune diseases.

Canadian women should not be misled by the huge awards given some implant victims in the United States, such as the $25 million ordered by a Texas jury in 1992. In Canada, personal-injury awards have always been far more modest because verdicts in product-liability cases are often decided by judges, who are usually swayed less by sympathy than juries.

BIRTH CONTROL PILLS

The way the courts treat breast implant cases follows the trend started by the case law dealing with injuries suffered by women as a result of taking birth control pills. Many years after the first birth control pills were available in 1961, some women suffered a stroke or other serious health problems that appeared to be related to the use of the pills.

In 1986, the Ontario Court of Appeal ruled that a drug manufacturer was negligent in failing to warn doctors and users of oral contraceptives of the serious risks associated with birth control pills. The case involved a woman who suffered a stroke about six weeks after starting to take the Ortho-Novum 1/50 oral contraceptive in 1971. She was partially paralysed, suffered some brain damage and became unemployable. The woman testified that she would not have used these birth control pills if she had been told of the risk involved. The Court decided that the manufacturer's failure to warn of the possible risks caused or materially contributed to the woman's injuries. She was awarded $606,795 for damages, expenses and loss of income, interest of $230,239 and legal costs.

Although the manufacturer's instructions to doctors and users followed the guidelines set out in the federal Food and Drug Act, in effect in 1971, the Court saw the instructions as inadequate. Information inserted in company products in the United States at the same time stated that an increased risk of strokes and embolisms was associated with oral-contraceptive use, but the Canadian package insert did not mention this association. During the lawsuit, the company acknowledged that it had been aware of at least 40 articles in medical journals that discussed the dangers of oral-contraceptive use. One study, described by the trial judge as the most reliable one available at that time, showed that 95 percent of the strokes among oral-contraceptive users would not have occurred if the women had not been taking the pills.

The trial court had decided in 1984 that the Canadian drug manufacturer had not carried out its duty under common law to warn of a dangerous product. According to the appeal court, the duty is greater in the case of oral contraceptives than in other medications because the use of contraceptives is voluntary—a more educated consumer can make a more informed choice—and because some users face unavoidable risks.

Once this case hit the news in 1984, the federal guidelines for warnings changed. Since 1985, Health and Welfare Canada has required drug companies to include a more strongly worded caution in packages and booklets, advising users of the specific potential side effects of oral contraceptives. The warning says, for instance, that the pills should not be used by women who have had a stroke, who have undiagnosed, unusual vaginal bleeding, blood clots, heart problems, cancer, jaundice or liver disease, or who are over 35, and that a woman should discontinue use if she suspects or discovers that she is pregnant. It also states that users of oral contraceptives should not smoke.

PACEMAKERS

A pacemaker is a medical device that controls the beating of a malfunctioning heart by transmitting electrical impulses to the heart through a lead—an insulated wire or wires inserted through an artery into the heart and affixed to the heart muscle. Unlike breast implants and birth control pills, pacemakers are not usually elective, but are mandated by the patient's state of health. However, the same liability rules apply: the manufacturer must take proper care in its design and manufacture of the product, and must keep doctors fully informed.

A class-action suit was approved by an Ontario court in 1995 for cardiac pacemaker recipients against a company that manufactured leads for pacemakers. Approximately 1,125 Canadians had been implanted with the leads, which were known to fracture in 16 percent to 25 percent of cases, allowing the wire to cut through the heart with disastrous results. Doctors gave evidence that surgically removing the lead from all such pacemaker recipients was riskier than continuing to monitor all patients with the leads. The number of patients affected and therefore entitled to compensation could not be ascertained, but the suit also covers patients with no present claims. The case was settled in 1997 and about 1,000 patients or their estates have shared $15 million in compensation.

2. A Doctor's Duty to Fully Inform Patients

In a precedent-setting case in 1993, an Ontario court ruled that a doctor who makes a mistake during surgery or other treatment must inform the patient, even if the patient asks no questions. The judge described the doctor/patient relationship as one based on trust, requiring absolute honesty and good faith between both parties.

The Ontario case involved a man who injured his back while working as a painter and continued to suffer pain for several years. He was referred to an orthopedic surgeon, who proposed operating on a particular disk in the man's spine. The patient consented. After the operation in 1977, however, he experienced even more pain.

The orthopedic surgeon had operated on a different disk from the one intended. A year later, while some doctors were reviewing the surgeon's records for the Workers'

Compensation Board, they noted his mistake and told him about it. But no one told the patient. Later the same year, another orthopedic surgeon operated on the correct disk but could not remedy the problem. He did not tell the patient about the previous surgeon's mistake either.

It was not until 1985, some eight years later, that the patient learned about the error. A law student who was helping him with an appeal to the Workers' Compensation Board read about it in the board's files and told him. The patient sued the surgeon who had performed the original operation in 1977.

When the case came to trial in 1992, the court held that the patient had undergone "unnecessary and fruitless surgery" because of the surgeon's error. The surgeon eventually admitted that he had made a mistake but declared that his obligation to inform the patient ended when another doctor assumed the patient's care. The judge disagreed. In fact, the judge held that, as a matter of principle, a doctor has a responsibility to tell a patient what happened, regardless of whether or not the patient asks.

The patient ended up with chronic pain syndrome (a long-term condition that resists treatment), was permanently disabled and could no longer work. The court ordered the doctor to pay the patient compensation of $135,000 for the stress of the operation, the disappointing result and the loss of any future benefits of employment.

The court also awarded the patient an additional amount to compensate for losses arising from the delay in his discovery of the error, which in turn delayed his taking action against the surgeon. The amount was equivalent to the interest he might have received if he had been able to collect the money earlier.

This specific amount was settled between the parties; the court directed the amount to represent about 13 years' interest.

This case extended the law as it affects the doctor/patient relationship. Previously, the law of disclosure required doctors simply to obtain a patient's informed consent to medical treatment, and to clearly warn a patient of any risks that the recommended treatment entailed.

The absolute honesty required in the doctor/patient relationship, as spelled out in the Ontario case, was confirmed in 1993 in a decision by the Supreme Court of Canada. The Court unanimously ruled that doctors must halt medical procedures once patients withdraw their consent, unless stopping treatment would threaten a patient's health or life. This case is significant because the Court took a strong stand: Patients have a right to "bodily integrity" and a right to decide what is to be done to their own body, rights that underlie the principle of disclosure.

The Ontario Court of Appeal took the law one step further in 1995 by awarding punitive damages to a 40-year-old woodcutter to be paid by the patient's doctor. Not only did the doctor make a mistake by operating on the wrong disk and failing to tell the patient, but he also tried to conceal and deny wrongdoing, did a second operation to correct the problem without telling the patient why and altered records. The Court ruled that punitive damages of $40,000 were appropriate because of the morally offensive, cold and calculating acts of the surgeon. In addition to punitive damages, the Court awarded the patient damages, past and future loss of income and medical costs of over $570,000.

3. Abuse of Authority

Another buried secret of human malfeasance has come out of hiding in the last few years. Some adults and children have come forward to reveal that, at a vulnerable age or during a vulnerable time in their lives, they were abused by doctors, teachers, members of the clergy, baby-sitters, scout leaders and others who held a position of authority or trust. Often, the victims tried to tell someone at the time but were not believed. As adults, many of them are laying criminal charges, suing for compensation or both. There have been public inquiries, especially when the allegations are about numerous incidents in one public institution, and in some of these cases, compensation has been provided by the public purse.

People like doctors, teachers and members of the clergy are highly respected professionals who are automatically trusted by most people who deal with them, partly because of the authority of their position. It is usually because of their position that some of these professionals are able to take advantage of vulnerable people.

In all cases, the professional governing body or employer will be responsible for limiting the offender's future opportunities for repeat offences. Ontario has a law that automatically revokes the licence of 24 different health professionals including doctors, dentists, chiropractors, nurses, massage therapists, physiotherapists, dieticians, podiatrists, and pharmacists if they have sex with someone in their care. The law also requires colleagues to report suspected perpetrators.

Thereafter, or at the same time, a health professional may be charged with a breach of the criminal law, such as sexual assault. A number of criminal offences focus on breaches by those in a position of authority. In addition, sexual abuse is now seen as a personal injury compensable in damages, and many civil lawsuits have yielded awards to help the victim pay for therapy and the costs of coping.

The damage to the victim is incalculable, and all a monetary award can do is assist her or him to pay for therapy and compensate for the loss of income due to continuing emotional trauma. Many victims bury their knowledge of what happened to them, and the memory reaches their consciousness only when they are adults, often in therapy for reactions or feelings that they do not understand. As a result, most jurisdictions have modified or extended the limitation period for the prosecution of sexual abuse cases, in recognition that such abuse often goes unreported or unacknowledged and sometimes even undiscovered by the complainant for many years. Generally, the limitation period will start to run once the victim discovers the connection between the harm suffered and the conduct that caused it.

Allegations against doctors in a variety of specialties have been the most common and, so far as I am aware, all cases reported have been of female patients sexually exploited by male physicians. The professional governing body will usually remove the doctor's licence to practise medicine in proven cases. In addition, awards of compensation have been made.

The leading case on sexual conduct as a breach of the doctor/patient relationship was in the 1992 Supreme Court of Canada case of *Norberg* v. *Wynrib*, in which a doctor gave a patient prescriptions for drugs to which she was addicted, and in exchange extracted sexual favours. The patient sued for compensation on the basis of sexual assault, negligence, breach of fiduciary duty and breach of contract. The trial judge and the B.C. Court of Appeal dismissed her case, but the Supreme Court of Canada allowed the appeal, and ruled that because of the power dependency relationship between the doctor and patient, an inequality existed that the doctor exploited. As a result, the patient was entitled to damages in the amount of $30,000. The majority found the doctor to have inflicted a tort of battery, and other members of the Court found him to be in breach of fiduciary duty (a fiduciary is a person in a position of trust). In this context, fiduciary duty can be found in the power exercised by the doctor and the vulnerability of the patient. This power imbalance calls into question the validity of any alleged consent.

In 1996, a 38-year-old Toronto woman was awarded $95,000 for the damage she suffered at the hands of her family doctor when she was between nine and 20 years of age. She was also awarded half of the cost of her continuing therapy, which her lawyer estimated at about $200,000. In a 1993 New Brunswick case, a woman was awarded damages of $50,000 for her doctor's breach of fiduciary duty to her, because he had a sexual relationship with her when she was 16. Even though the relationship was with her consent, the court ruled that it is up to the adult to control the situation and that the victim's consent is no excuse for a breach of a position of trust.

In several cases, the governing body has dealt more severely with the practitioner than has the court. For example, in a 1995 Quebec case, the Quebec College of Physicians found a plastic surgeon guilty of sexually assaulting a patient under anesthetic on an operating table, even though a court exonerated the doctor of a criminal charge of sexual assault.

Other authority figures have been accused of abusing their positions. For example, a choirmaster used his 16-year position in a church to sexually abuse choirboys, and the church that harboured him paid damages to the victims in an out-of-court settlement. A scout leader and elementary school teacher in Northern Ontario who was convicted of 71 counts of sexual assault over an eight-year period received a sentence of only two years.

The Supreme Court of Canada issued a strong message to teachers in 1996 when it reversed a trial and appeal court acquittal and convicted a 22-year-old male teacher of sexual abuse, even though the 14-year-old female student initiated the contact. The Court said teachers have positions of authority that require them to resist even the most persistent sexual advances.

Serious allegations have been made against priests in a number of religious orders for sexual abuse of children in their care, and settlements have been made to compensate many of these people for offences against them when they were young. The cases go right across Canada, with churches found vicariously liable many years later for the sexual abuse inflicted by priests and others, from the Mount Cashel orphanage in Newfoundland and Labrador to the Roman Catholic Church in British Columbia. All were ordered to pay compensation.

Authority figures have been punished for abuse of authority in other places. For example, a man who worked at a prestigious sports arena in Toronto for many years was discovered to be a predator who lured young, vulnerable, disadvantaged boys into engaging in sex acts with him. He pleaded guilty in 1998 to 24 counts of indecent assault and sexual assault over a 20-year period involving boys aged 10 to 15. The trial judge sentenced him to two years less a day plus three years' probation but the Court of Appeal ruled that the sentence was too low—the man was a pedophile who exploited the trust of young victims, premeditated his attacks and profoundly harmed the young men. The sentence was increased to five years in prison.

In another case, a psychiatric nurse was found guilty of professional misconduct for kissing a restrained female patient.

Allegations of mental and emotional abuse have even been made against orders of nuns. In one case, an Ontario woman is seeking $5 million in damages from an order of nuns for allegedly mentally and emotionally abusing her when she was a young teenager in their Toronto training school in the early 1960s. The woman stated that the nuns kept her in an isolation room as punishment, once for up to six months. In another, a group of women raised in a Newfoundland and Labrador orphanage in the 1950s alleged physical and emotional abuse by nuns.

An employer may be held responsible for an employee's abuse of position of power. In 1995, an employer was found liable for sexual assault committed by one of its employees, even though the employer had no idea of the employee's predilections. The B.C. employer was a charitable organization running homes for emotionally troubled children, and a member of its staff, who acted in the role of surrogate parent, sexually assaulted a child in one of its homes. The court's message to the employer was to supervise its staff more closely.

The same year, a Nova Scotia court ruled that the province was liable for $75,000 in damages for an employee's sexual assault on a 14-year-old girl at a government-operated reform school. The court stated that the school should have known better because other complaints were registered against that employee.

The sentencing principles codified in the Criminal Code include an open invitation to judges to increase sentences if the offender abused a position of trust or authority in relation to the victim.

4. Medical Malpractice

It is not necessarily malpractice if a doctor's treatment of a patient is unsuccessful, or if a doctor made an understandable error in judgment. There are no guarantees in medical treatment. But sometimes a doctor is careless in surgery, inaccurate in diagnosis, mistaken in choosing a drug or negligent in informing the patient of the risks. Patients who can prove the error or negligence can collect compensation from the doctor.

In every case, the person injured must be able to prove that the doctor was not acting according to customary medical practice, or that she or he was negligent, and did not act according to a reasonable standard of skill and care. The patient must prove that the doctor's negligence in fact caused the injury. The patient must also prove the appropriate compensation for loss of income, expenses incurred and pain and suffering.

Any lawsuit for negligence must be brought within a limitation period, which varies with the jurisdiction and the profession. For example, not only doctors but also nurses, dentists and other health professionals, as well as hospitals, are governed by laws that require lawsuits to be brought within a specified period after the negligence took place. An injured person should consult a lawyer as soon as possible after the injury takes place.

Sometimes, patients expect a doctor to know more than medical science. For example, the Supreme Court of Canada in 1995 ruled that a physician was not negligent because a woman contracted HIV through artificial insemination in January 1985. Neither the doctor, nor anyone else at that time, had known HIV could be transmitted through artificial insemination; nor was there any test available in Canada for the detection of HIV in semen or blood. The first article to reach the medical literature suggesting that particular method of HIV transmission was in September 1985. See also the section on AIDS and the Law in this chapter.

Many medical malpractice suits arise out of problems in surgery; a surgeon may inadvertently leave a sponge inside the body or operate on the wrong disk, or just make a mistake. In a 1989 B.C. case, a physician performed a vasectomy on a patient and cut an artery, which led to prolonged pain and other complications from which the patient never recovered. The court ordered the doctor to pay the man $53,125 for his damages and loss of income.

A unique lawsuit may arise if a woman is sterilized but nevertheless ends up giving birth to a child. This type of case provides an interesting example of how medical malpractice lawsuits take shape.

The patient does not win such a lawsuit simply because she became pregnant. In any operation, there is a risk of failure. The patient must prove that the doctor's negligence caused the birth of the child, and that the doctor did not exercise reasonable skill, care and knowledge.

Both the woman and her husband can sue and seek compensation for pain, suffering, inconvenience, mental anguish, "loss of enjoyment of life" (which includes interruption of sexual relations) and medical expenses. The amount of compensation might be reduced if the woman could have aborted the pregnancy—unless she is opposed to abortion. Her husband can seek compensation for "loss of consortium"—sexual and homemaking services.

How much compensation can the woman and her husband expect? The traditional legal approach is to look upon the birth of a child as a joyful event and to consider the parents as being adequately compensated by the intangible benefits of the child's presence in their family. But the courts are being called upon to recognize that some large families regard an additional child as a detriment, and that people need to rely upon contraceptive and sterilization techniques.

In Canada, there have been several "wrongful birth" actions, claiming that doctors' negligence caused unplanned pregnancies. Until 1985, only three cases were reported. In one, a Quebec mother was awarded $2,000 for loss of enjoyment of life, for pain, suffering, inconvenience and anxiety relating to the birth of her eleventh child and a subsequent second sterilization. The father was paid $400 for loss of consortium.

In another, an Ontario mother received $1,000 for mental anguish. The judge said it was "grotesque" to set a value on a human life and expressed concern for the child who would know that she or he was unwanted. In the third case, in Alberta, the method of sterilization (sealing the tubes with a silver nitrate paste) and the follow-up X-rays might have caused damage to the fetus, and the woman had a late, painful abortion. She received $5,000 for pain and suffering.

There was no compensation in any of these cases for a mother's lost earnings during pregnancy and child-rearing or for the cost of rearing a child.

Although a child born by mistake can also bring legal action through her or his parents, no Canadian court has yet compensated a child for the failure of sterilization. A Quebec judge indicated that the child's compensation was the "gift of life." A B.C. Court of Appeal case in 1995 ruled that, "there is no independent cause of action by an injured child for 'wrongful life.'" An obstetrician has a duty to warn a pregnant woman of the risks of childbirth and effects on the fetus, and she has the option to carry to term or not.

In a 1996 Ontario case, described as "wrongful pregnancy," the court ruled that the woman who had a baby after a failed tubal ligation was entitled to damages for the pregnancy, labour, delivery and second ligation procedure, which were quantified at $40,000. Child-rearing costs were not ordered because the couple chose not to abort or give the child up for adoption. Madam Justice Joan Lax summed up the law:

> The love, companionship, affection and joy which a child brings is thought to so outweigh the burdens that we bridle at the thought that the law could be so foolish as to regard this as a "compensable loss." . . . The responsibilities and rewards cancel each other out.

In a 1999 Manitoba case, the doctor failed to warn his patient against getting pregnant while taking anti-convulsive medication. The medication caused birth defects and the child would require constant care and supervision for the rest of her life. The court awarded $150,000 including the cost of future care. Again, no amount was awarded for "wrongful life" as the court considered it impossible to evaluate the child's disabled existence as opposed to non-existence.

Doctors can also be sued for treating patients without their consent. For example, when an unemployed, unmarried woman had an abortion, the doctor inserted an IUD against the patient's express wishes and without her knowledge. He also gave her a prescription for birth control pills. Within days, she went to her family doctor, complaining of spotting and pain, which continued for two years until an x-ray revealed the presence of the IUD. She had to have it surgically removed under anaesthetic. The court awarded her $12,000 in damages for battery and mental distress and anguish.

D. EVERYONE

1. Rights of Crime Victims

Crime victims have greater rights than ever before, but it is up to the victims to assert them. Victims can have an impact on the conviction of the accused perpetrator, on the severity of the sentence, and on if and when the perpetrator gets parole. Victims also have the right to claim financial restitution and compensation.

Unless there is a guilty plea, victims usually appear in court to testify about the accused's criminal behaviour. If the accused is convicted, he or she will appear in court for sentencing, at which time victims have the right to file a victim impact statement describing the harm done by the criminal behaviour and the losses suffered. If the victim is dead or unable to make a statement, then a spouse, relative, guardian or dependant may prepare the impact statement.

Victims may also have a right to limited information about when the offender may be released from prison. They are entitled to obtain from the National Parole Board or Correctional Services Canada such information as when the sentence began, its length and dates when the offender becomes eligible for unescorted temporary absences and parole.

Victims can usually obtain additional information, at the discretion of the parole authorities, but only if they can establish that their interest outweighs the invasion of the offender's privacy. Such information could include in what institution the offender is incarcerated, the date of any hearing, the date and type of release, the offender's destination and the conditions of release.

Under current criminal law, victims of sexual assault cannot force their assailants to undergo tests for HIV. However, in a civil suit for damages brought in 1996 by an Ontario rape victim, Madam Justice Ellen MacDonald ordered Paul Bernardo, an admitted rapist, to undergo an AIDS test.

The onus is on the victim to request all information in writing. Similarly, victims must take active steps if they wish to play a part in a parole hearing. They must contact a penitentiary, an office of Correctional Services Canada or the National Parole Board.

Written victim impact statements have been allowed at parole hearings for some time. While there are no statistics on their effect on parole applications in Canada, U.S. statistics indicate that victim impact statements increase the rate of parole denial from 50 percent to 80 percent.

At the moment, victims' relatives do not have an automatic say in the early parole of murderers, which is decided by a jury rather than by a parole board (although the government is considering a change in the law). The minimum sentence for first-degree murder is life imprisonment with no parole for 25 years, but a controversial section of the Criminal Code allows convicted murderers to seek parole after 15 years. The Supreme Court of Canada clarified that it is at the discretion of the presiding judge to decide whether permitting victim impact statements is relevant and proper.

In all Canadian jurisdictions, victims of crime can apply for compensation from provincial compensation boards. In Ontario, for example, compensation is available to victims of violent crimes if those crimes are offences under the Criminal Code (even if the offender is not prosecuted or convicted), if they occur in Ontario and if they result in personal injury or death. Ontario's Criminal Injuries Compensation Board, for instance, may award a lump sum of up to $25,000 to compensate for pain and suffering, as well as up to $1,000 per month for out-of-pocket expenses such as medical bills or lost wages from work as a result of the injury; however, applications must be made within one year of the occurrence. Claims may also be made by a dependant if the victim dies, or if a child is born as a result of sexual assault.

Compensation may also be available through the courts, which may order restitution for property damage as a condition of probation or as a term of the sentence. Amendments have been proposed to expand the scope of restitution to include damages resulting from personal injuries. In general, however, such orders are of little practical benefit to victims. Follow-up by the criminal system is rare, and even when a court makes such an order, victims must often hire a lawyer to enforce it.

In addition, in certain circumstances a crime witness may sue for damages for personal injury. In 1995, an Ontario court granted a witness to a crime, who suffered post-traumatic stress disorder, the substantial sum of $428,000 plus solicitor/client costs. A 14-year-old boy had travelled from his home in British Columbia to visit his aunt and uncle in Ontario. On the way home from the airport, his uncle stopped the car, supposedly to aid motorists in trouble, and his aunt was murdered. Later, it was found that his uncle had hired the killers. The nephew sued his uncle successfully.

Ontario, British Columbia, Manitoba and Prince Edward Island all have a victim's bill of rights. Ontario was the first and its law is one of the widest in scope and most strongly worded. For example, Ontario's law contains a set of principles stating how victims of crime should be treated by the criminal justice system: Victims should be treated with courtesy and respect; victims should have access to information about the investigation of a crime; sexual assault victims should have the opportunity to be questioned by a police officer of their same sex; victims should be advised when the offender is released, even on a temporary basis.

While the federal government does not have a victim's bill of rights as such, some of the 1999 changes to the Criminal Code benefit crime victims. For example, witnesses under the age of 14 and witnesses who have a mental or physical disability may have a support person present in court and close to the witness while testifying, if the judge is of the opinion that the proper administration of justice requires it. The judge may order that the witness and the support person not communicate with each other while the witness is testifying. Testifying outside the courtroom is available to witnesses under 18 and to witnesses who may have difficulty communicating their evidence because of a mental or physical disability, in cases of sexual offences, prostitution-related offences and all levels of assault and sexual assault.

2. Libel and Slander

Libel and slander are issues that can affect the ordinary person. A neighbour may spread false rumours in conversation or in writing. A family member may reveal secrets that affect another member's reputation. How can people deal with these issues?

A person's reputation is protected from harmful falsehoods under the law of defamation. A defamatory statement is a slander, if it is spoken, or a libel, if it is written.

Abusive insults that merely injure a person's feelings or cause embarrassment do not amount to slander. False accusations of criminal conduct, sexual impropriety, dishonesty, alcoholism, lack of mental competency or of being infected with a sexually transmitted or other communicable disease are slanderous.

For a person to be able to sue, the statements must have been made to another party. If that person repeats the slander, then he or she may also be sued; it is no defence that someone else provided the information and that the defendant repeated it in the mistaken, but reasonable, belief that it was true.

Truth is a defence to a defamation action. The defendant must not necessarily prove that each and every fact in the statement is true, but only that the whole of the statement is substantially correct. The defendant cannot succeed by showing that the plaintiff engaged in other conduct that was just as reprehensible.

Fair comments that are made in good faith on subjects of public interest are protected from legal action. However, the law affords no such protection to statements motivated by malice.

To be defamatory, the statements must have a tendency to lower the person's reputation in the eyes of the community. Therefore, the plaintiff's position and standing in the community are relevant considerations. The law protects a person's actual reputation—rather than the one she or he deserves or would like to have. Accordingly, the issue is not whether the plaintiff is a good or bad person, but whether she or he has a reputation to that effect.

If the defamatory statements do not refer to the plaintiff by name, it must be shown that the people to whom the statements were made would understand them to refer to the plaintiff. For example, in a case where an obituary notice was placed in a newspaper by a woman with whom the deceased had allegedly been having a sexual affair, the widow sued on the grounds that the notice was published out of spite with the intention of causing her emotional injury. She alleged that the notice contained words relating to the reputation of her late husband. The case was dismissed on a preliminary motion. The court found that the ordinary, reasonable person reading those words in the newspaper would not understand them as referring to the plaintiff; further, the words in the notice did not relate to the widow's own reputation.

The modern availability of instant and widespread communication over the Internet creates new defamation issues. In 2004, the Ontario Court of Appeal dealt with this issue in the case of *Barrick* v. *Lopehandia*. Lopehandia used the Internet to post what were found to be defamatory messages about Barrick Gold Corporation, which affected its business reputation. The Court noted the powerful impact of this newer form of communication, pointing out the potential damage by "its interactive nature, its potential for being taken at face value, and its absolute and immediate worldwide ubiquity and accessibility." As a result, the appeal court awarded general damages of $75,000 as well as punitive damages of a further $50,000 and an injunction to stop the defamatory activity.

DAMAGE AWARDS

Generally, a person is entitled to be awarded compensatory damages, whether or not any actual monetary loss has been suffered. In addition to compensation for the injury to reputation, damages for mental suffering and humiliation may be awarded. Finally, any resulting social disadvantage may be compensated, such as the plaintiff being refused admission to a club or being made unwelcome in a family or social circle.

Some circumstances that do not amount to a defence may nevertheless reduce the amount of damages awarded to the plaintiff. Damages may be mitigated if the defendant issues a public apology, for example. They may also be mitigated if the defendant can show that he or she had in good faith repeated statements heard from others, or that the plaintiff had provoked the defamation by previously attacking the defendant.

The court may take the character of the defendant into consideration when assessing damages. If the defendant is not someone whom others are likely to believe, the injury resulting from the defamatory statements may be minimal, entitling the plaintiff to an award of only nominal damages. On the other hand, if the defendant holds a respected position in the community, damages from the false statements may be higher.

Even if the plaintiff's reputation has been unaffected by the defamation, she or he may be awarded nominal damages to vindicate her or his position. For example, in a 1996 B.C. case a man was awarded $6,000 in damages against his common-law wife, who described him verbally as a "mad dog woman beater" and posted a public notice claiming that he physically abused her. He could not, however, prove that his reputation had been harmed, or that he had suffered any financial loss. The people in his small community knew both him and his common-law wife, and likely believed him over her.

Punitive damages may be awarded in exceptional cases, such as if the defendant consciously set out to harm the plaintiff, or the defamatory statements were especially repugnant. For example, in a 1996 B.C. case a lawyer was granted damages of $20,000 plus $10,000 in punitive damages to be paid by the real estate agent who defamed her reputation by falsely and maliciously accusing her of unethical conduct.

Although the right to trial by jury varies from one province or territory to another, libel or slander actions are usually tried by a jury. The jury's role is both to decide whether the defendant is liable and to assess the amount of compensation.

The largest libel award in Canada's history—$1.6 million—was upheld by the Supreme Court of Canada in 1995 against the Church of Scientology and its legal counsel. The lawyer had been televised outside the court building accusing a Crown attorney of misleading a judge and breaching a court order, accusations that were found not to be true.

In addition to claiming monetary damages, a person may also seek an injunction to restrain the defendant from continuing to make defamatory statements.

3. AIDS and the Law

The very best protection, legal or practical, against a person who knowingly, recklessly or innocently infects another person with the AIDS virus is prevention. AIDS—acquired immunodeficiency syndrome—can be transmitted by an exchange of blood or semen during sexual intercourse with an infected person, for example, or by a blood transfusion from a carrier.

If a person has AIDS or has tested HIV-positive, and has not advised his or her sexual partner of the risk, the law may punish him or her and warn others to be wary of this person. He or she may also have to pay financial compensation for the injury suffered if the defendant has the ability to pay and the plaintiff can prove that the defendant knowingly spread the infection.

PUBLIC HEALTH LAWS

In most provinces and territories, the only laws to protect the public against venereal diseases and AIDS are public health laws, which define AIDS as a communicable disease. Doctors with AIDS patients must inform public health officials, who in turn contact the AIDS patients and do their best to inform anyone with whom the patients admit they had contact. In some places, doctors are protected if they breach confidentiality, but there is no AIDS-specific law authorizing a physician to disclose this information to a patient's partner. Even so, the Canadian Medical Association has advised doctors that it may not be unethical for them to breach confidentiality by disclosing to the patient's spouse or current sexual partner the fact that their patient has AIDS, without the patient's consent but with the patient's knowledge, especially if the doctor knows that the patient refuses to tell his or her sexual partners. It is not clear whether or not the Canadian Medical Association's advisory will protect a doctor from a lawsuit.

By law, people with a venereal disease, such as syphilis, gonorrhea or genital herpes, are required to take steps to stop spreading the infection. They must seek medical treatment promptly and report their sexual contacts to public health authorities, who may order the contacts to be examined and treated if necessary. In Saskatchewan, for example, the law states that a patient must seek treatment within three days after suspecting an infection, and a doctor must report the name of the infected patient and names of contacts to public health authorities within three days; these deadlines vary from province to province. In all cases, doctors must insist that their infected patients complete the necessary treatment program.

CRIMINAL LAW

The Criminal Code has not been updated to make the reckless spread of HIV (the virus that causes AIDS) a crime. In an attempt to deal with HIV carriers who knowingly donate contaminated blood for transfusions, or who knowingly engage in unprotected sex, the courts have reinterpreted and applied other sections of the Criminal Code, with mixed success. Here are some of the possible criminal charges.

Criminal Negligence: The police may charge a person with criminal negligence if they can prove that the HIV carrier showed "wanton or reckless disregard" for life or safety by having sexual relations despite the risk, and indifferent to the risk, of transmitting AIDS. The maximum sentence for a person convicted of criminal negligence is ten years in prison if the negligence causes bodily harm, and life imprisonment if it causes death.

Assault: Assault is a possible charge, on the basis that the HIV-infected person touched another person without true consent; the plaintiff would argue that he or she consented only to safe sex. The maximum punishment for a conviction ranges from ten to 14 years in prison.

Common Nuisance: If the HIV carrier is promiscuous and behaving irresponsibly, the police may charge him or her under the Criminal Code as a "common nuisance." This charge describes an individual who "endangers the lives, safety, health, property or comfort of the public" or "causes injury to any person." If, in doing so, that person does an "unlawful act or fails to discharge a legal duty," he or she may be found guilty of an indictable offence and imprisoned for two years.

Murder: In 2005 an HIV-positive man, based in Hamilton, was charged with first-degree murder for causing the deaths of two women from AIDS; the man had had sex with them without informing them of his condition. While the case has not yet been decided, this is one of the few times when the perpetrator has been charged with murder.

A number of cases, in which criminal charges have been laid, illustrate the situation. In 1989, Criminal Code charges were used for the first time to deal with a reckless AIDS carrier, who was convicted of endangering the public and sentenced to one year in jail and three years' probation. The accused had pleaded guilty to the lesser charge of common nuisance, thus avoiding hearings on the charges of aggravated assault, bodily harm and criminal negligence relating to his relationships with two women. A later appeal by the man was dismissed.

In a 1991 Ontario case, 21-year-old Denver Lee pleaded not guilty to a charge of aggravated sexual assault after engaging in consensual intercourse with a 34-year-old woman, although he knew that he was likely an HIV carrier. He had shared needles with others when he took drugs intravenously and he had had sex with a man whom he knew was HIV-positive. Lee neither warned the woman nor practised safer sex by using a condom. The Crown argued that the woman had not given "informed consent" because Lee failed to warn her that he might be an HIV carrier. But the court ruled that Lee had not committed fraud with regard to "the nature and quality of the act of sexual intercourse" and had not committed assault in having unprotected sex with the woman; therefore, he was found not guilty.

In 1992, in another Ontario case, Charles Ssenyonga was charged with several offences, including "administering a noxious thing" (semen) with intent to endanger life, committing a common nuisance, aggravated sexual assault and criminal negligence causing bodily harm.

Ssenyonga was HIV-positive but had unprotected sex with three unsuspecting women. All three subsequently contracted the same rare form of HIV as the accused— a strain previously unknown in Canada— and one developed full-blown AIDS.

At the preliminary hearing, two of the charges were dismissed: "administration of a noxious thing" because there was no evidence to prove Ssenyonga intended to harm his partners; and common nuisance because the accused had not "offered himself to the general public" but had become attached to specific women.

Ssenyonga stood trial on two charges: aggravated sexual assault (sexual assault with injury) and criminal negligence. As in the Lee case, the Ontario court reasoned that, regardless of the fact the Ssenyonga was HIV-positive, there was no assault because the women had consented to unprotected sex; he was acquitted of this charge in April 1993. Three months later, Ssenyonga died, two weeks before the court was due to render its judgment on the criminal negligence charges, which were left undetermined. The judge refused to deliver a verdict, saying that criminal charges are a matter between the accused and the state. Unfortunately, the judge's decision meant that the trial did not set a precedent with respect to the issue of criminal liability when a person *knowingly* transmits AIDS.

The Ontario Criminal Injuries Compensation Board subsequently awarded $15,000 to each of the three women, but not without admonishing them for taking unreasonable risks. "Given the dangers of unprotected sexual activities," said a board member, "a reasonable person would require a much longer period of trust building." The size of the award was appealed by the women to the Ontario Divisional Court, which ruled in 1995 that the women should get the maximum allowed of $25,000 each, and that the Criminal Injuries Compensation Board was wrong in law in "demanding an unreasonably high standard of behaviour" from the women. The Court said the women were reasonable in accepting the man's claims that he was in good health.

In several other similar cases, particularly where the accused pleaded guilty, the nuisance and criminal negligence provisions have been used with some success. The sentences for such offences ranged from one to three years—until 1993 when the Newfoundland and Labrador Court of Appeal took a much harsher view in the case of *Regina* v. *Mercer*. When Raymond Mercer, then 27, had tested HIV-positive in 1991, the local medical officer warned him always to use a condom. But Mercer continued to have unprotected sex with his 16-year-old girlfriend and repeatedly denied that he was infected with HIV. He also had a brief affair with a 22-year-old single mother and assured her, too, that there was no need for him to wear a condom. Both young women eventually contracted HIV. The teenager became pregnant and had an abortion when she learned the baby might also be infected.

Mercer pleaded guilty to criminal negligence causing bodily harm and was initially sentenced to two years and three months in prison. But the Newfoundland and Labrador Court of Appeal stated that "his crimes were of monumental proportions" and increased his sentence to an unprecedented 11 years.

Then, in 1995, an Ontario court sentenced to 12 years a man who admitted raping a woman under particularly despicable circumstances. The judge had rejected a joint submission by the lawyers both for the Crown and the accused for a seven-year sentence, saying that it was "difficult to envisage a more dangerous threat than an unrestrained, unrehabilitated HIV-positive rapist."

In 1991, in the case of a man who donated blood knowing he was HIV-positive, the Ontario Court of Appeal upheld a conviction and sentence of 15 months in prison on a charge of common nuisance. Mr. Justice Patrick Galligan, speaking for the Court, stated that his "conduct verges on the unspeakable. It cried out for a sentence which would act as a deterrent to others and which would express society's repudiation of what he did." The Supreme Court of Canada upheld the conviction in 1993.

CIVIL SUITS

Criminal charges are not the only course available to those whose partner has knowingly infected them with the AIDS virus. They may also have recourse to the civil courts by suing for monetary damages as compensation for the harm done to them. A sexual partner who transmits the disease can be held legally accountable.

Under civil personal-injury law, the HIV-positive partner can be sued for compensation for the personal injury suffered. Claims can be made for payment for loss of income, medical care, pain and suffering. The basis of the claim is either negligence or assault. To prove negligence, an injured party must prove exposure to an unreasonable risk of harm, which could have been anticipated. To prove assault, non-consensual touching must be proven—that consent was given only to safe sex and not to sex that would bring on disease—and that it resulted in injury.

If a lawsuit is filed but not completed before the injured party's death, the lawsuit may be continued by the executors of his or her estate; if the suit is won, the payment will go to the heirs. The estate and dependants may also sue to claim for the loss of life. If the defendant dies, the case may continue against his estate.

A convicted rapist was ordered in 1996 to take an AIDS test at the request of the victim, who was suing him for damages in a civil suit.

INFECTION THROUGH BLOOD TRANSFUSION AND ARTIFICIAL INSEMINATION

A person can be infected with the HIV virus and be completely unaware of the danger to either themselves or others. For example, Kenneth Pittman was infected through HIV-infected blood transfusions after a heart operation. Even after the Red Cross found out that the blood given to him was from an AIDS carrier, and told his doctor, the doctor did not advise Pittman or his wife Rochelle Pittman, assuming that they were not having sexual relations. When Rochelle Pittman contracted AIDS from her husband, she sued the doctor and the Red Cross. The court awarded her over $250,000 to be paid 40 percent by the doctor, 30 percent by the Red Cross and 30 percent by the hospital in 1994. She died a year or two later.

In another case, a woman sued her doctor for negligence because she became HIV-positive from artificial insemination in 1985. At the time, it was not recognized that HIV was transmissible through artificial insemination. The jury at the trial awarded her $883,000, but the Ontario Court of Appeal set the decision aside and ordered a new trial, a ruling with which the Supreme Court of Canada agreed ten years later. Both appeal courts ruled that since the doctor was acting according to established medical practice, the jury would have had to rule that the standard of practice itself was negligent.

This case illustrates some of the difficulties and impracticalities of the present legal system. The aggrieved party was injured and struggled ten years through the legal system, only to be told at the end of the day to go back for another trial. The cost of the process was not revealed in the ruling, but suffice it to say that an individual litigant can rarely afford it. For the medical community, the case was probably an important precedent because it suggested that those doctors who do stick closely to established practice will not be found negligent. For trial judges, it was a guideline for how to instruct juries in such cases.

Some provinces have compensation programs in place for hemophiliacs who contracted the AIDS virus from contaminated blood transfusions, before proper programs were in place to screen blood and blood products for the HIV virus.

4. Sentencing for Crimes

To many Canadians, sentences for crimes often seem unduly short and criminals seem to serve less time than the judge orders. Opinion polls have revealed that a majority of Canadians believe that sentences are too lenient, and that two-thirds oppose parole. Public interest is heightened when a high-profile case hits the headlines, particularly when someone is attacked by a violent sex offender out on statutory release after serving only part of the sentence. But the back pages of newspapers contain many examples of sentences with which some Canadians may agree or disagree.

Some examples: A man was sentenced to eight years for passing himself off as a spiritual healer who promised to lift an alleged curse from a ten-year-old girl by giving his energy to her through sexual intercourse; he kept at it until the girl was 16, when she realized that he was abusing her and called the police. A stepfather also got eight years for sexually assaulting three children: his own son between the ages of two and seven, and his two stepchildren in their early teens, one boy and one girl. A stalker got nine years for breaking into a home, and drugging and molesting an 11-year-old boy who was home alone. Another stepfather was sentenced to 13 years for sexual assault on one child between the ages of five and 17, another child on numerous occasions from the age of five and his stepdaughter when she was 13.

On the other hand, a man described by the court as a 36-year-old "businessman" who raped his 12-year-old stepdaughter while drunk was handed only a one-year sentence. And, in 1996, an Ontario judge let a man off with a two-year suspended sentence and the requirement to perform 200 hours of community service for an "intrusive and painful" sexual act on his "defenceless" six-year-old niece. The court seemed to feel that this light sentence was appropriate because the man's family supported him, he had no criminal record and he suffered from osteoarthritis and other infirmities. The court said the sentence was also appropriate because there was "no violence" and the occurrence was isolated. There is no indication whether or not a victim impact statement was part of the proceedings.

Here's how the sentencing and parole systems work—the factors that determine how much time an offender spends in prison.

SENTENCING

Judges have broad discretion in imposing sentences and take into account numerous factors, including the degree of violence, the offender's record and typical sentences in similar cases. The Criminal Code of Canada sets out maximum penalties for most offences, but the vast majority of sentences are much shorter. For example, a 1993 Statistics Canada study revealed that while the maximum penalty for aggravated assault is 14 years in prison, the average sentence handed down was about nine months.

For the most serious crimes, the Criminal Code also sets out minimum sentences; all murder convictions bring automatic life imprisonment, for example. Even so, killers often avoid long prison terms, in some cases by pleading guilty to the lesser charge of manslaughter, which carries no minimum penalty. The Criminal Code now provides a minimum mandatory four-year jail sentence for anyone convicted of using a gun in committing a violent offence, including aggravated sexual assault, robbery and attempted murder.

In 1999, the Criminal Code was amended to increase the fine to $600 for the first offence of driving while impaired by alcohol, with a blood alcohol level exceeding 80 milligrams per 100 millilitres of blood, or refusing to take a Breathalyzer test. The law also made having a blood alcohol level over 160 milligrams of alcohol per 100 millilitres of blood an aggravating factor on sentencing and increased the length of the mandatory driving prohibition to one year minimum and three years maximum on a first offence, two years minimum and five years maximum on a second offence and three years minimum, with no maximum, on subsequent offences. The prohibitions are in addition to any term of imprisonment. The one-year minimum on a first offence can be reduced to three months if there is an alcohol ignition interlock program in place and the offender participates in it for the remainder of the one-year period.

Alberta toughened its impaired driving rules in 1999 to permit the government to issue an automatic three-month driving suspension to those charged but not yet convicted of driving over the legal limit, and to suspend drivers who refuse to provide a breath sample. In 2000, British Columbia passed a law that drunk drivers would lose their driver's licence for one year for a first offence, three years for a second offence and third-time offenders would lose their licence for their lifetime.

In 1996, new legislation took effect, as part of a thorough revision of the sentencing provisions of the Criminal Code, stating that the policy objectives of sentencing are to contribute to a "just, peaceful and safe" society. The principles of sentencing were codified and included deterrence, rehabilitation, reparations to victims, and separation from society. Among other changes, the law obliges judges to give reasons for the sentences they mete out, and now allows for conditional sentences.

The law requires a court to bring down more severe sentences when crimes are motivated by prejudice or hate based on race, national or ethnic origin, language, colour, religion, sex, age, mental or physical disability, sexual orientation or any other similar factor; when the offender abused his or her spouse or child; when the offender abused a position of trust; when the crime was committed as part of an involvement in a criminal organization. In 2001, evidence that the offence was a terrorism offence was added as an aggravating factor for sentencing.

Conditional Sentences: The conditional sentence provisions are meant to provide an alternative to incarceration in an institution. A conditional sentence is a sentence of imprisonment, but is served in the community under specified conditions. Certain conditions are mandatory; the sentencing judge has wide discretion to impose others.

A conditional sentence is available for any offence that does not attract a minimum term of imprisonment. If the sentencing judge imposes a sentence of less than two years, and "is satisfied that serving the sentence in the community would not endanger the safety of the community and would be consistent with the fundamental purpose and principles of sentencing," he or she may make an order that the sentence be served in the community. Conditional sentences have been imposed for a wide range of offences, including fraud, sexual assault and impaired driving. Typical discretionary conditions include observing a curfew or house arrest, abstaining from alcohol and non-prescribed drugs, performing community service, taking treatment or counselling, staying away from certain people or places, and not owning or carrying a weapon. Unlike in a sentence of imprisonment served in custody, one cannot earn early release from a conditional sentence by good behaviour. If the judge says a year, the full year is served.

If the offender breaches any of the conditions without an excuse, he or she can be brought back before a judge, who may take no action; vary the optional conditions; suspend the running of the conditional sentence and order the offender to serve a portion of the term in custody; or terminate the conditional sentence and have the offender committed to custody until the expiration of the sentence.

Dangerous and Long-Term Offenders: The federal and provincial governments have enacted stricter measures to protect the public from chronic violent offenders. An indefinite sentence is now mandatory for dangerous offenders. It is also a little easier for prosecutors to apply for a dangerous offender finding. They used to have to apply for a finding that an accused was a dangerous offender before the sentence was imposed. Now, if they give notice before sentencing that they will possibly apply, they have until six months after the accused is sentenced to actually make the application. At the time of applying, they must show that evidence that was not reasonably available at the time of sentencing has become available since.

The legislation creates a broader category of "long-term offenders." The criteria for finding that an offender is a long-term offender are as follows: a judge has deemed a sentence of two years or more would be appropriate; there is a substantial risk that the offender will offend again; and there is a reasonable possibility of eventual control of the risk in the community. The criteria for a substantial risk of re-offending are as follows: conviction of sexual interference, invitation to sexual touching, sexual exploitation, exposure, and all degrees of sexual assault; a pattern of repetitive behaviour, of which the offence for which the offender has been convicted is a part, that shows a likelihood of the offender's causing death or injury or inflicting severe psychological harm; conduct in any sexual matter, including that for which the offender has been convicted, that shows a likelihood of causing injury, pain or other evil to other persons in the future through similar offences. An accused who is found to be a long-term offender must be sentenced to prison for a minimum of two years, followed by supervision in the community for not more than ten years.

The offences that can trigger a dangerous offender application include any violent crime or dangerous behaviour except treason, high treason, or first- or second-degree murder. Long-term offender applications are available only for sexual offences.

PAROLE AND STATUTORY RELEASE

Under the parole system, prisoners are released early to serve the rest of their sentence in the community, subject to conditions imposed by the parole board. The possibility of parole gives prisoners an incentive to behave well in prison and offers a mechanism for supervising their reintegration into society. However, parole has long been controversial: the Law Reform

Commission and a parliamentary commission called for its abolition (except in the case of life imprisonment), but this proposal has not been implemented.

Most prisoners can apply for full parole after serving one-third of their sentence. In 1992–93, almost half of parole applications were granted. Of those who are turned down for early parole, most are automatically free to go under statutory release (formerly called "mandatory supervision") after serving two-thirds of their sentences. The exceptions are certain violent offences. About 17 percent of offenders on statutory release will commit a crime during this period.

A 1992 federal law tightened up some aspects of parole and statutory release. Now, violent or sex offenders are no longer automatically entitled to statutory release after two-thirds of their sentences. Furthermore, judges have power to delay parole eligibility for some offenders to one-half the sentence, rather than one-third.

NATIONAL SEX OFFENDER REGISTRY

On December 15, 2004, the federal government announced the establishment of the new national sex offender registration system, as a partnership of the federal government and all provincial and territorial governments. The new National Sex Offender Database will be maintained by the Royal Canadian Mounted Police (RCMP). The information in the database will only be accessible by accredited law-enforcement agencies and will serve more than 60,000 law-enforcement officials in every province and territory.

The database will allow police to conduct a search according to a full or partial address and the offence of a sex offender or both. Offence and registration information will be included, as well as pertinent identification data such as tattoos and other distinguishing marks. This will assist police officers in the immediate identification of possible sex offender suspects known to reside near the offence site.

Convicted offenders will have to register within 15 days following a court order for registration or release from custody. They will be required to re-register annually and within 15 days of a change of residence.

They will also be obligated to provide local police with information such as addresses and telephone numbers, names and alias(es), and identifying marks and tattoos. Penalties will be provided for failing to comply with a registration order or for not giving truthful information.

5. Damages for Personal Injury

In Canada every year, it is estimated that over a million people are injured and 12,000 accidentally killed. Personal injury victims and the families of those killed may suffer physical, psychological, vocational and financial problems as a consequence.

The victims or their survivors may be entitled to sue those responsible for the accident. If a person is injured, it is important to get the names, addresses and telephone numbers of anyone involved in the accident and any witnesses. To assist in proving the claim, victims should note the precise time and date and details of the incident, and keep a diary of injuries suffered and medical attention required for as long as the symptoms remain.

The purpose of an award of damages is primarily to pay for any health care costs not covered by medicare, to reimburse any other out-of-pocket expenses incurred, to replace lost income following the interruption or cessation of earnings and to compensate for the injury itself.

In most cases, particularly for injuries as a result of a car accident, the defendant is covered by insurance. The insurance company takes over the defence of the legal action and ultimately pays the plaintiff, if the plaintiff is successful. Usually the defendant's insurer reaches a negotiated settlement with the plaintiff's lawyer, either before legal action is commenced or at some point before the case goes to trial.

One of the first things a claimant or the claimant's lawyer must consider is the applicable deadline for making a claim. Limitation periods vary from province to province and depend upon the nature of the accident and the identity of the defendant. Often, when a claim is made against a governmental body, the law provides for either an unusually short limitation period for the commencement of legal action or for prior notification of the prospective defendant. For example, a person who sustains injuries from a fall on an icy public sidewalk may be required to give notice of the accident to the city as quickly as within one week from the date of the accident.

Personal injury victims frequently complain about the length of time it takes for a claim to be settled or tried by the courts. It is not unusual for a claim to take over two years to be resolved. Generally, the length of time increases with the seriousness of the claim, and until the matter has been finally settled or tried, the defendant has no obligation to make advance payments. Innocent victims whose injuries have rendered them unable to work may be left without a sufficient income.

Jury trials are rare in personal injury cases. Usually, a judge alone decides the defendant's liability and assesses the damages. Awards are normally in the form of a lump sum, which includes both losses suffered before the trial and an estimate of future losses.

In a small minority of cases settled out of court, typically where the victim is permanently disabled, the parties agree to a structured settlement—a combination of lump sum and periodic payments designed to cover losses for future care and lost earnings.

The onus is on the injured party to prove the losses suffered. With respect to financial losses incurred or special damages, the plaintiff's loss is the difference between what would have been his or her financial position up to the time of trial, had the accident not occurred, and his or her actual position as a result of the accident. With respect to lost earnings, the plaintiff may find the amount easy to prove by producing evidence of income since the accident. Sometimes, however, establishing what the victim would have earned if the accident had not happened can be problematic, particularly if the victim was self-employed, because the business may have been cyclical in nature or the plaintiff may not have kept proper records. As well, people who were unemployed or receiving social assistance before the accident may be hard-pressed to prove that they would have obtained a job and earned a certain amount, had the accident not taken place.

Similar considerations apply in cases where the injured party will remain unable to work following the settlement or trial. The length of time that the plaintiff will be disabled, and the amount of future income that will be lost, are even more difficult to establish accurately. The calculation of prospective lost earnings takes into account such uncertainties as the victim's pre-accident promotion prospects, considering her or his experience and qualifications, the likelihood of salary progression in that particular occupation and the effects of inflation and taxation. Actuarial evidence is commonly used to help the judge arrive at a lump sum that takes such variables into account. A 1998 Alberta case ruled that damages for lost income of women should be calculated based on male earning statistics and should not be based on historic wage inequities.

In addition to reimbursement for pecuniary losses, a personal injury victim is entitled to receive monies in compensation for pain and suffering, not just from the original injury, but from necessary medical treatment or indirectly from the accident. In one B.C. case, where an injured woman was rendered incapable of natural childbirth, she recovered damages for her physical discomfort during two Caesarean sections.

An injured person may claim for loss of enjoyment of life as well, whether the injury is temporary or permanent. This claim may include the inability to continue to participate in sports and hobbies or to engage in sex; or lost or reduced prospects of marriage, of having children or of pursuing an occupation, including homemaking. If the victim's lifespan is reduced by the injuries, loss of expectation of life is also compensable by damages.

Homemakers can claim compensation for loss of homemaking capacity. If a homemaker hired replacement services, she is entitled to reimbursement for those costs. If the homemaker's domestic tasks have been taken over by other members of the family, she may be paid compensation or, in some provinces, those who provided the services may be paid a direct award. Alternatively, if the domestic tasks are simply left undone or the injured homemaker continues to do them, but less efficiently, compensation is still payable, although the amount tends to be based upon the estimated cost of substitute services.

An injured person is under a duty to mitigate damages. A plaintiff who unreasonably refuses to undergo necessary medical treatment will face a reduction in the damages payable. Similarly, if the accident victim is incapable of returning to his or her previous employment, he or she may be expected to seek alternate employment or to take reasonable steps to retrain.

A successful plaintiff does not usually receive full indemnification for legal costs, because legal expenses are not completely reimbursed. Although legal costs are normally added to the amount of damages awarded or negotiated, the amount paid typically covers only a portion of the victim's actual legal expenses; the balance must be paid from the monies received by way of damages. The financial burden of these additional legal expenses often persuades the plaintiff to accept a settlement offer, rather than proceed to trial in hopes of a larger award from the court.

Once a lump-sum settlement is reached, or an award made, this amount is final. Even if the plaintiff subsequently finds the injuries more serious than he realized, or will be unable to work for a longer period than his doctors had estimated, he cannot later seek an increase in the amount of damages received.

Lump-sum awards used to be the most common form of compensation, but more structured settlements, providing periodic payments, are now the norm. They are often ordered in the form of annuities.

FATAL ACCIDENT CLAIMS

Close family members of a fatal-accident victim may be able to claim for their own monetary losses resulting from the death. These losses are generally based upon the survivors' interest in the deceased's income and domestic labour.

The deceased's income represents the amount of the victim's after-tax income that could reasonably have been expected to be available to the surviving dependants, after the deceased's personal living expenses have been deducted. Typically, the amount is calculated in the range of 70 percent of net income.

The period over which the loss is calculated depends upon numerous factors, including the joint life expectancy of the deceased and surviving spouse. In a claim by a child whose parent was killed, the period of loss usually runs until the child's majority, or beyond if the parent was likely to support the child during postsecondary education.

Claims by a parent whose child is killed are not as common because parents do not normally receive financial support from children. Nevertheless, the courts have recognized that in some families, with a strong cultural tradition of filial obligation, parents may reasonably have expected financial assistance from a deceased child. Thus, in one B.C. case, parents in a Chinese-Canadian family were awarded $175,000 in 1994 for their pecuniary loss on the death of their daughter, a university student with good prospects.

The loss of domestic labour or family work suffered by the survivors of the victim may take into account a broad range of tasks formerly performed by the deceased, including cooking, shopping, gardening, laundry, housecleaning, yard work, home repairs, vehicle repairs and even the preparation of tax returns. If the family includes young children, the additional labour of rearing them can form a substantial component of the claim.

The court generally assesses the loss of domestic services by referring to the cost of replacement services in the marketplace—for example, the cost to hire a housekeeper or nanny. Accordingly, a widower in Alberta was awarded damages for the loss of his wife's housekeeping services, even though he did not intend to hire a housekeeper to replace them; the court reasoned that the man was being compensated for the loss of housekeeping services, and how he used that compensation was not the court's concern.

Similarly, a widow may claim for the loss of her husband's family work. In a rather unusual example that went all the way to the Supreme Court of Canada, a widow was held entitled to compensation for the loss of her husband's work in renovating the house, which was half-finished at the time of his death.

Awards for intangible, non-pecuniary losses stemming from the death of a close relative tend to be modest. They are meant to compensate for the loss of the role filled by the deceased, rather than to compensate for emotional distress and grief experienced by the survivors.

The Manitoba Court of Appeal has established "conventional" awards, to be applied in all but the most unusual cases, of $10,000 each to a husband and young child for loss of a wife and mother. In other jurisdictions, the amount will depend upon the individual circumstances of the case, with careful regard to precedent. The Manitoba Court of Appeal ruled in 2000 in *Braun Estate* v. *Vaughan* that the "conventional" award for loss of guidance, care and companionship is not to be increased to take account of inflation. It is "a formal declaration or statement of sympathy, sanctioned by law, which recognizes that a wrong has been done," and "not an economic award intended to compensate for an economic loss."

The maximum award under similar legislation in British Columbia is $30,000, and in New Brunswick the award in a typical case is $30,000. Ontario awarded $25,000 in a similar case.

A survey of fatal accident awards since 1988 shows that, on the death of a wife and mother, awards typically fall into the range of $15,000 to $50,000 to a husband, and $10,000 to $35,000 to a child.

For example, in 1994 the family of a 30-year-old Ontario woman was granted $225,000 in total: $65,000 to her husband, $30,000 each for her one-year-old and three-year-old daughters, $35,000 for her five-year-old son, $20,000 to her mother, $15,000 to her father and $6,000 each to her five siblings. She was described as an "exceptional person, a loving wife and mother to her children, a devoted and best friend to her father and mother, and a thoughtful and giving person to each of her brothers and sisters."

In a 1997 Ontario case, the sum of $15,000 was awarded to the mother and $50,000 to the husband of a woman who suffered brain damage as a result of severe blood loss during negligently performed surgery. At age 21, she incurred permanent communication, perception and cognitive deficits.

In another 1997 Ontario case, the sum of $5,000 was awarded to the grandmother, $5,000 to one sister and $3,500 to the mother of a 16-year-old young woman who was catastrophically injured in a car accident. One leg was amputated above the knee, her intelligence was reduced by brain damage, and she was rendered permanently unemployable. The grandmother had raised the girl, but distanced herself after the accident. The mother had been minimally involved in the girl's life, except for a short period before the accident. The sister had been close to the injured girl.

These compare to the 1987 case of a B.C. working wife and mother, aged 32, in which the court granted higher awards: for loss of income, $100,000 to her husband, $17,500 to her 13-year-old daughter and $20,000 to her nine-year-old son; for loss of guidance, advice and comfort, nothing to her husband, $15,000 to her daughter and $20,000 to her son.

Awards in compensation for the loss of a husband and father can vary even more widely. In the 1994 case of a Nova Scotia husband and stepfather, aged 28, the court granted $22,000 to his wife and $20,000 to his nine-year-old stepson. In the 1990 case of a 48-year-old Manitoba trucker, however, the court ordered, for loss of future support, $204,172 to his wife, $3,011 to his 15-year-old son, and $5,862 to his 12-year-old son; for loss of guidance, care and companionship, $10,000 each to his wife and sons.

These awards give some idea of the wide range of amounts that have been granted over the years. No amount can compensate for the loss of a loved one, but financial awards are the only means a court has of dealing with the loss and helping the dependent survivors. Close relatives should not accept any settlement without the advice of a lawyer who is experienced in personal injury cases, and knowledgeable about the anticipated awards for different types of claims in local courts.

E. RIGHTS OF PERSONS SUSPECTED OR ACCUSED OF CRIMES

1. Detention and Arrest

POLICE

The police do not have the right to stop just anyone, at any time. They must have reasonable grounds for stopping someone, whether that person is on foot or in a vehicle. They may make random spot checks of vehicles under provincial highway legislation, but only for legitimate purposes like checking licences, registration and vehicle safety and making sure drivers have not been drinking.

"Detention" means that the police have assumed control over a person's movements and the person reasonably believes he has no choice but to comply with the officer's directions, or face legal consequences. Physical restraint is not necessary, so long as the person's freedom of movement is restricted. When the police detain somebody, they must tell the person why he is being detained.

Except where a serious offence is involved, the police may not arrest a person without a warrant. They must show the warrant, if there is one, or inform the person being arrested of the reasons for the arrest.

SECURITY GUARDS

An owner of property or someone authorized by the owner has the authority to arrest anyone whom they find committing a criminal offence on or in relation to that property. Store personnel and mall security guards can exercise this power of "citizen's arrest." However, they must turn the person over to the police right away.

2. Right to Counsel and Right to Remain Silent

The police are required to inform everyone who is arrested or detained of the right to speak with a lawyer (to "retain and instruct counsel") and give him or her an opportunity to do so. If legal aid duty counsel are available, information on how to contact them must be provided. Despite the popular notion that "you get one phone call," there is no rule in Canada that limits a detainee to a single phone call. A person has the right to keep trying if he or she cannot reach a lawyer on the first attempt. The right to counsel is not an absolute right to the lawyer of one's own choice. If a person's own lawyer will not be available within a reasonable time, he or she cannot refuse to speak to any other lawyer and then complain of being deprived of the right to counsel. Privacy must be provided for telephone calls to a lawyer or legal aid duty counsel.

The police must not question a detainee until he or she has had a reasonable opportunity to contact a lawyer. On the other hand, if a person does not make reasonable efforts to contact a lawyer, he loses the protection of the right to counsel, and the police may go ahead and question him. What counts as a reasonable opportunity and reasonably diligent efforts will depend on the circumstances. For instance, if someone is detained at night and there is no local legal aid duty counsel available, "reasonable opportunity" may mean when the lawyer's office opens in the morning. Once the person has spoken with a lawyer, the police may continue questioning her even if she says she does not wish to answer any questions. Although the police may question a detainee or arrestee, the person is not obliged to answer questions or give a statement. Adults are not entitled to have a lawyer present when the police question them, so long as they have had an opportunity to speak with counsel and get advice.

The police will sometimes place an undercover officer in the cell with someone who has been arrested, in the hope of obtaining information. The courts have ruled that this practice is permissible, so long as the undercover officer does not coerce, intimidate or manipulate the arrestee into giving information against himself. A person who is in police custody should avoid talking about how he got there with anyone but his lawyer, until and unless he decides to give a statement to the police.

The police may require a driver to submit to a roadside ALERT (Alcohol Level Evaluation Roadside Test) without consulting a lawyer. As well, provincial legislation may authorize the police to give roadside co-ordination tests without the person consulting a lawyer. However, a person is entitled to consult a lawyer before taking a Breathalyzer test. Refusing to take the test is a criminal offence; the lawyer's advice will be to take it. The driver should exercise the right to consult a lawyer, all the same, as the lawyer may provide further advice besides "take the test."

3. Search and Seizure

Ordinarily, the police may not carry out a search unless they have a search warrant. The Charter of Rights and Freedoms protects the right of the individual to be free from unreasonable search and seizure. This right is personal; the Charter protects persons, not places. The key question in deciding whether the right has been violated is, does the person have a reasonable expectation of privacy in the place being searched? One's own home is the place where the expectation of privacy is greatest. Still, a court has held that a teenager did not have a reasonable expectation of privacy in his own bedroom in a case where the rules of the home gave other family members free access. A police search of the room, with his mother's permission, was ruled not to violate his rights. There may not be an expectation of privacy in a friend's home. A search of an accused's girlfriend's home, which turned up drugs in a duffle bag he had left there, was held valid. A passenger in someone else's automobile has little, if any, expectation of privacy in the automobile.

The police may search a person on arrest without a warrant, and seize anything on his person or in his immediate surroundings. They are not required to give a person an opportunity to consult counsel before searching her. The purpose of this "search incident to arrest" is to ensure the safety of the police, the arrestee and the general public, to discover evidence or prevent its destruction and to prevent escape. The search must be reasonable and take place within a reasonable time. It must be carried out for a valid objective and not be conducted abusively. A search conducted merely to intimidate, or a search carried out in a humiliating manner, would be a violation of the rights of the person being searched. A strip search of a woman on a public street in Toronto gave rise to allegations of racism (the woman was a member of a visible minority).

Principals, teachers and other school officials have a responsibility to enforce school rules and to look after the health and safety of pupils. In fulfilling these responsibilities, they may search students and student lockers under certain conditions. The school official must not be acting as an agent of the state (for example, acting on instructions from the police). There must be reasonable grounds to believe that school rules have been or are being violated, and that evidence of the violation will be found on the student or in the location searched. Provincial legislation making teachers and principals responsible for students' health and safety can also provide a legal basis for searches. In one case, a principal received a tip that a certain student would be bringing marijuana to a school dance, hidden in his sock. The principal called the student into his office and, in the presence of a police officer, asked him to roll down his sock. The marijuana was found and turned over to the officer, and the student was arrested. The Supreme Court of Canada eventually ruled that although the police officer was present, the principal was not acting under his direction. The search did not violate the student's rights, even though he was not advised of his rights and given an opportunity to contact a lawyer beforehand.

4. Release from Custody

For many offences, the police will not take a person into custody, but release him with an appearance notice requiring him to appear in court or send him a summons later. The police can also release a person they have taken into custody, and may impose conditions on the release. Anyone who is not released by the police is entitled to a prompt bail hearing. The Criminal Code specifies that a person in custody is to be taken before a justice of the peace or provincial court judge within 24 hours if one is available, or as soon as possible after that. In practical terms, people arrested on the weekend and kept in custody are likely to spend more than 24 hours waiting for a hearing.

At a bail hearing, the presumption is that an accused person will be released from custody, unless the Crown can satisfy the justice that he or she should be detained until trial. The permissible grounds for detaining a person are to ensure the accused's appearance in court, to protect the public against further offences, or for "any other just cause" such as maintaining confidence in the administration of justice. While the first two grounds are specific, the last is fairly wide and flexible. A broad range of conditions can be placed on an accused who is released. Breach of the conditions can result in arrest, detention and further criminal charges.

The judge has the power to require "sureties," that is, persons who will guarantee that the accused will abide by the conditions of release and will appear in court. The willingness of a family member, friend or employer to take that responsibility, and his or her ability to persuade the judge that he or she can exercise control over the individual, may determine whether the person in custody will be released.

5. Assault Counter-Charges

Women who complain to the police that their male partner has assaulted them should be aware that some men use the tactic of laying an assault counter-charge against the woman. At one time, pressure would be put on women to withdraw assault charges against their partners. When governments and police adopted policies of charging and prosecuting in all cases, the new tactic of laying counter-charges developed. Women should not let this dissuade them from complaining to the police. However, they may need a lawyer to defend them against this form of harassment and intimidation.

6. Retaining a Lawyer

Normally law-abiding people may find themselves facing criminal charges, whether through a lapse of judgment, through someone else's mistake or simply through being in the wrong place at the wrong time. A great deal can be at stake: Liberty, reputation, employment, and the ability to travel to other countries can be lost or compromised by a criminal conviction. It is extremely important to get effective legal representation. While the initial contact will probably be with duty counsel, their role is limited. The accused person needs his or her own lawyer with criminal law expertise as soon as possible.

A person who cannot afford a lawyer should try to get legal aid. See Chapter 12.

CHAPTER 9

PROPERTY

⚖️

Introduction

Anyone with assets needs to know the legal implications of property ownership, the subject of this chapter. While it may seem like a dry area of the law, the concepts of morality, fiduciary duty and good faith have crept into property law. Vendors and purchasers of homes have a duty to act in good faith; so do bankrupts, insurance companies, collection agents, and computer users.

When cases deal with personal property, these broader issues are part of the context.

1. Buying and Selling a Home

The purchase of a home is a major financial undertaking. The home chosen may be a house, a condominium townhouse or apartment, or a co-operative. But if the property is being bought rather than rented, there are legal consequences to consider.

Some definitions may help. A house may be attached, detached or semi-detached, but it is located on a specifically defined and prescribed lot, which is, in fact, what is being sold and purchased. For example, the deed will convey "Lot 123 and Part Lot 124

on Plan 567 in the Municipality of . . ." and a recent survey will be part of the closing documents. In diagram form, the survey lays out the property description in detail, including the lot line and any fences, and positions any existing building within the lot lines. If the building is not properly within the lot lines, the survey should indicate this fact; the purchaser will then usually be reluctant to buy the property.

A condominium is usually either a development of adjoining townhouses or an apartment building. The area within the development that the individual owner uses as a residence is only part of what she or he "owns"; the condo owner also owns an undivided share of the "common elements," which may include the land, hallways, lobby, outer doors, outside windows and outside walkways of a condominium apartment building. Sometimes, one of the common elements is for the exclusive use of an individual owner, such as the backyard or front steps of a condominium townhouse unit. These are known as "exclusive use common elements." In Ontario, less common forms of condominiums exist: a common elements condominium corporation creates common elements but no units and its owners must own a neighbouring piece of land outright; a phased condominium corporation can be expanded by phases that add units and common elements to the corporation; a vacant land condominium corporation has no buildings; a leasehold condominium corporation holds a leasehold interest in the lands.

Some homes and apartments are owned as co-operatives. In these properties, the owners have shares in the corporation, which entitle them to live in a defined space.

A new form of property called "life lease" has evolved in conjunction with elder-care facilities. The purchase entitles the owner to live in the home or apartment for her lifetime or as long as she is mentally and physically capable of doing so.

DEALING WITH A REAL ESTATE AGENT

The sale of a home is a major undertaking. The vendor will usually hire a real estate agent or broker, who is licensed by the province or territory in which he or she works, and is subject to professional and ethical rules of practice. For example, a real estate agent must usually disclose any personal interest in a listed property.

The vendor will sign a "listing agreement" that usually gives the agent or broker the exclusive right to sell the property for a specified period, usually 90 days, and for a specified commission, usually 4 percent to 6 percent. The commission rate will usually depend on whether the vendor agrees to the listing broker also offering the property for sale on a multiple listing service. If anyone offers to buy the property during that period (and the vendor accepts), the listing agent/broker is legally entitled to the commission.

Vendors should read the listing agreement carefully; if it states that the agent receives the commission just for presenting an acceptable offer, the vendor should negotiate to reword the agreement to say that the commission shall be paid "only on completion" of the transaction. Otherwise, the vendor may find that the agent is entitled to the commission even if the deal falls through for any reason.

If the purchaser also has an agent, the vendor's listing agent shares the commission with the purchaser's agent.

Once the purchaser has chosen a home, it is up to him or her to present an "Offer to Purchase." There is often a period of negotiation before and after the offer is presented.

DEALING WITH A LAWYER

Purchasers should get a lawyer proficient in real estate to review the terms of the deal before it is signed because the offer represents a firm and binding agreement if it is accepted. Purchasers should also ask the agent and lawyer to calculate the cost of buying the home because there are additional and hidden expenses (particularly for new homes—such as GST) that are not apparent on the face of the agreement of purchase and sale. These include, for example, water and hydro meter, land transfer taxes, title registration disbursements, legal fees, survey (if required), new home warranty program registration fee (where applicable), subdivision grading and damage deposit. The purchaser will have to make a deposit or down payment on the property to be held in escrow (in trust) by the agent or lawyer pending the closing of the deal. In the offer, the purchaser may propose a method of financing the deal; for example, the purchaser may propose that the vendor take back a mortgage for part of the purchase price.

A lawyer may suggest that some of the following conditions be included in the proposed agreement:

- The right to have the property professionally inspected to ensure sound construction (for example, plumbing, roofing, wiring, insulation, heating, structure and imperviousness to water)
- A warranty from the vendor stating that the house does not contain any urea-formaldehyde insulation
- The right to a specified number of days to arrange financing, or the deal is off
- The right to inspect the house just before closing
- An up-to-date survey at the vendor's cost
- In the case of a new home, a warranty from the builder that the house will be completed properly
- A commitment that the down payment will be put in an interest-bearing account and the purchaser will receive the interest
- A list of "extras" to be included in the purchase price, such as draperies, fixtures and appliances
- The disclosure of any easements—that is, any right for anyone to have access to any part of the property (telephone or hydro may have an easement for cables and wires, for instance)
- The disposition of the deposit if a party fails to complete the transaction

TAKING TITLE

Soon after the purchaser and the vendor have signed an agreement of purchase and sale, the purchaser will need to consider carefully how to take title to the property. It is wise to consult a lawyer about the options.

Once the purchase agreement has been signed, however, the purchaser's lawyer must first ensure that the vendor has the ability to transfer good title. The lawyer will search through records at the appropriate land-records office to verify ownership, and will review prior deeds and mortgages, by-laws, zoning rules and registered restrictions that apply to the land.

The lawyer must also review the property's survey to ensure that all buildings are within the lot lines and do not encroach by mistake on a neighbour's property, the street or other rights of way. The purchaser should compel the vendor in the agreement of purchase and sale to provide an up-to-date survey. However, if the existing survey is out of date (that is, done prior to new construction or fencing on the property) and the vendor will not agree to pay for a new one, purchasers will sometimes arrange for their own in order to go ahead with the purchase.

Occasionally, a lawyer discovers a problem with the title and will ask the vendor's lawyer to clear it up. Most problems can be resolved. For example, if the purchase agreement lists a lot size of 15 metres by 45 metres, but the title and survey show that the lot is only 10 by 45, the purchaser will have to decide whether or not to buy the property, probably at a reduced price. In the rare case that the vendor does not have clear title to sell, the deal may be cancelled and the deposit returned.

Part of the lawyer's routine check is to make sure that there are no judgments or liens against the existing or previous owner that would affect title, and that the realty taxes and utility bills have been paid to date. If a problem exists, the lawyer will ensure that funds are deducted from the purchase price, thereby making the vendor pay these outstanding accounts. In the case of a condominium, the lawyer would also check such matters as whether any legal action is pending against the condominium corporation, whether the vendor paid his or her common expenses, the size of the reserve fund to cover contingencies, and review the by-laws and declaration of the condominium corporation to ensure that the purchaser knew the rules. For example, some condominiums prohibit pets.

At closing, the vendor will convey the property (transfer the ownership) to the purchaser; in turn, if a mortgage loan is helping to finance the purchase, the purchaser will sign a mortgage to be registered.

After closing, the lawyer will provide the purchaser with a "reporting letter" confirming all the details of the transaction and, in particular, that the purchaser received good title. In the letter, the lawyer certifies title, which means that if problems arise later on with title—problems that, with reasonable diligence, the lawyer should have discovered—the lawyer could be held responsible for any financial harm suffered by the purchaser as a result. In some places, title companies (effectively, insurance companies), rather than lawyers, certify title to a purchaser.

COST OF LEGAL SERVICES

The cost of a lawyer's services for the purchase or sale of a home will depend on a number of factors: whether the lawyer needs to prepare and register a mortgage or mortgages; whether he or she needs to clear up any problem with the title or survey; whether the taxes or utilities are in arrears; whether any municipal work orders are registered against the property; and whether the client requires extra attention and explanation. Many people shop around for the cheapest real estate lawyer without realizing that the job takes time and effort and that anyone who quotes an unreasonably low rate may also provide an unreasonably low quality of service. The best bet is to get a knowledgeable recommendation from friends who have actually dealt with a real estate lawyer.

DUTY OF GOOD FAITH

The purchaser owes the vendor the duty to act in good faith. Over the past ten years the courts have less frequently allowed purchasers who have changed their minds to get out of the deal with a technically correct but dishonest excuse. For example, in a 1995 Ontario case a purchaser tried to break the agreement after discovering that a construction lien had been placed in error against the property. Even though the vendor said he would get the lien removed, the purchaser refused to close and sued for the return of his deposit. The court said the purchaser wanted out of the deal for other reasons and was therefore not acting in good faith; accordingly, the court did not order the return of his deposit.

Most people assume that vendors have no obligation to the purchaser except to keep their contract commitments, which they will try to minimize. Caveat emptor—let the buyer beware—is the well-known expression that warns the purchaser to take care. But just as the concept of fiduciary duty has found its way into many other areas of the law, it now also obliges the vendor to be honest with the purchaser. In some circumstances, duties that used to be considered moral obligations have become legal obligations.

For example, a 1995 Ontario judge ruled that a vendor was liable to compensate the purchaser $18,000 to correct a problem that the vendor had denied existed. When the buyer had asked the vendor if the basement of the home was dry, the vendor had said yes. So the buyer went ahead with the purchase, only to find significant leakage after he moved in. Had the vendor said only, "See for yourself," he may not have been found liable.

In another 1995 Ontario case, however, a purchaser of contaminated land was held responsible for not being reasonably diligent in assuring himself of the property's condition. In this case, a carpet company bought a factory on land that it later found was seriously contaminated by varsol. The carpet company, which had previously been located just down the street, ignored a planning consultant's recommendation that the Ministry of the Environment be contacted for an inspection. While the vendor in this case did not actively divulge the truth about the contamination, it also did not conceal the problem: monitoring wells and pipes were reasonably visible on the property and should have made the purchaser inquire further. Vendors will be found liable only if they deliberately conceal a defect that is impossible to discover. In effect, the court in this case ruled caveat emptor. Therefore, purchasers cannot assume that vendors have an obligation to point out problems with their property, but should take defensive action to ensure that the property is what it appears to be and can be used for the planned purposes.

Fiduciary obligations also extend to the contractor hired to renovate or improve a property. In a 1995 B.C. case, a building contractor who took kickbacks and secret commissions from subcontractors was found to be in breach of his fiduciary duty to his homeowner client, who totally relied on him. He gave the work to subcontractors who had had difficulties in the past with completing work for the quoted price. The contractor had to pay the homeowner the extra $29,000 that it cost to complete the work.

2. Mortgages

A mortgage is a debt, and the promise to pay it is secured by ownership of real estate—a home, farm or commercial property. In the event of default, the mortgage lender may sell or take possession of the real estate. The mortgagor is the borrower; the mortgagee is the lender.

A married person seeking to place a mortgage on a matrimonial home usually will need the other spouse's signature on the mortgage documents to verify his or her consent. Before signing, that spouse should get independent legal advice.

Most mortgages stipulate a monthly payment that is a blend of interest and principal repayment. In a few cases, the monthly payment is only a payment of interest.

At most, a mortgage is usually for 75 percent of the property's value as appraised for mortgage purposes (usually a conservative value). The terms of the mortgage vary, and a mortgagee's choice of terms will depend on her or his prediction of future interest rates.

Mortgage payments of principal and interest are amortized (spread out in instalments) over a specified period. The longer the amortization period, the lower the individual payment, and the higher the final cost of the property.

Mortgage documents should be read carefully; they are usually long, technical and in tiny print, and too many people sign without reading because they assume that they know their rights and obligations. Later, they pay for their lack of attention.

For example, if a mortgage has a prepayment clause, mortgagors may assume that they can prepay at any time. But that is usually not the case: A prepayment clause may say that the mortgagor may prepay a stated percentage of the principal balance owing once a year and at a specific time (often the anniversary date of the mortgage); it may even stipulate, as a penalty for prepayment, that a mortgagor must give notice and pay a bonus of up to three months of interest. Rarely, however, does a mortgage allow mortgagors to prepay any amount at any time they want without notice or penalty, although in some cases the two parties may negotiate that term. If a mortgage bears a term of five years or less, the law does not require a lender to permit a borrower to prepay any amount.

MORTGAGE DEFAULT

A mortgagor who cannot meet the required payments will pick a course of action, depending on whether the property has any equity or whether the mortgage principal owing is more than the current fair market value of the property. The mortgage may be for more than the value of the home if the market value of the home has fallen. In such a case, the mortgagor will want to consider whether to let the property go by letting the mortgagee take over the home through foreclosure or power of sale (see below). However, if the amount received by the sale is less than the amount owed, the mortgagee is free to pursue the mortgagor for the difference because the mortgagor is "on the covenant." This expression means that the mortgagor promised to pay back the loan. The property itself was just security for the loan; the promise to pay the full amount remains.

If the mortgagor wants to try to keep the property, she or he can take steps that may help to keep the property or protect the equity already built up.

If the mortgagor misses one payment but knows she or he will be able to make good on it and meet subsequent payments, she or he should contact the mortgagee directly, explain the circumstances and request time to pay. This straightforward approach may often be successful. If she or he thinks that renegotiating with creditors or rearranging finances will solve the problem, she or he should seek credit counselling through a free government- or community-funded assistance program, and negotiate a more realistic mortgage repayment plan.

If the lender will not agree to the proposal or if the borrower is having long-term financial problems and doubts that she or he will be able to maintain the mortgage payments in the long run, the borrower should act to protect his or her equity. Perhaps she has a financial stake in the home from the original down payment, from the payments made towards the principal of the mortgage and from any increase in the property value since the purchase.

Here are some legal options that may be available, for discussion with a lawyer. Each province and territory has different laws governing mortgage default; the rules are usually so technical and complex that a mortgagor in default must seek legal advice in every case.

Power of Sale: If the borrower is unable to pay what is owed after a notice period specified in the mortgage document and/or by law (35 days after receipt of notice in Ontario, for example), the mortgagee is allowed to sell the property. If the selling price is more than the amount owed, the mortgagee must give the mortgagor the surplus after paying off any other debts against the property. The procedure is not court supervised because the mortgage document gives the mortgagee the power of sale. But the mortgagee can be sued if the borrower has good reason to suspect fraud—for example, if the mortgagee sells the property to himself, or a relative, or at too low a price, yielding no surplus.

Foreclosure: If the borrower is behind more than the specified number of days in a payment, the mortgagee can start a legal action suing for foreclosure and, if successful, will become the owner of the property. The equity that the mortgagor has already built up in the home will not be protected, and if the mortgagee sells the property for more than is owed, he is allowed to keep the surplus. However, if the property sells for less than is owed, the mortgagee cannot seek more money from the mortgagor.

When formal notice is received that the mortgagee is suing for foreclosure, the court on request may grant the mortgagor the opportunity to redeem the mortgage by paying what is owed and the mortgagee's costs to date. The formal notice to redeem may give the borrower time to catch up on payments and keep the property. For example, Ontario property owners have 60 days to sort out their finances, while Alberta farmers have a year.

Judicial Sale: Even if the mortgagee starts a foreclosure action, the court may convert it into a judicial sale, which allows the mortgagor to keep any surplus when the property is sold. The court supervises the sale.

REVERSE MORTGAGES

Reverse mortgages are a special form of loan created to assist older people to borrow against the equity in their home for living expenses, and yet still live in the home. The lender either pays the borrower a monthly amount, establishes a line of credit against which the borrower can draw or provides a lump sum. The mortgage is repaid when the house is sold, either because the borrower has died or has decided to move out. Before choosing this option, anyone interested should review the implications carefully with a lawyer familiar with reverse mortgages, and should be aware that not every province and territory allows for this arrangement.

3. Joint Assets

Joint ownership means that two persons (or more) have "paper" title to an asset—both their names are listed on legal documents identifying ownership. They may be spouses, business partners or just two people with a shared interest in one property.

This form of ownership can be compared to marriage: The joint owners become partners and are treated as if they are one under the law. During the "marriage," their interests are identical, with both entitled to use of the property and neither able to exclude the other.

Legal issues may arise if one or both of the parties want to separate their interests, or if one of them dies without leaving a will. How these issues are resolved depends on the type of property owned.

REAL ESTATE

If people (usually two) own property as "joint tenants" or "joint tenants with right of survivorship," neither one of them may sell or borrow against the property without the consent of the other. Any mortgage taken out will bind the whole property, unless the owners sign a clear agreement to the contrary. If one of them dies, the survivor automatically becomes the sole owner by right of survivorship. All that is necessary to register a conveyance (transfer of ownership) is proof of death. This survivorship right takes precedence over the deceased's will, and the property does not form part of his or her estate.

The words used to describe a joint tenancy with survivorship rights may vary in different provinces. For example, when the term "joint tenants" is used in Ontario, it is taken to include survivorship rights.

The other important type of shared ownership is tenancy-in-common. Any number of people can own a property together as tenants-in-common, each having a defined percentage interest. It is possible to sell or mortgage only the interest of one tenant-in-common in the unlikely event a lender can be found to do so. There is no survivorship right; if one owner dies, that owner's share is considered part of his or her estate and goes to the heirs named in his or her will.

A survivor may be surprised to find that the deceased has unilaterally severed the joint tenancy and removed survivorship rights. Under common law (outside Quebec), and in provinces where it is not specifically prohibited by law, a joint tenant can unilaterally convert joint ownership into a tenancy-in-common in order to own a separate interest. In fact, there have been cases where a couple's course of conduct has led a court to conclude that they intended to sever a joint tenancy, and so the deceased's heirs and not the surviving joint tenant got the deceased's share.

In one case, for example, a couple signed a separation agreement agreeing to sell their home and divide the proceeds equally. Meanwhile, the wife lived on in the home. Before it was sold, however, the husband died. The wife tried to keep all the sale proceeds to herself but the court disagreed, ruling that the couple's clear intention was to sever the joint tenancy, notwithstanding that the title was still made out to the husband and wife as joint tenants with right of survivorship. The husband's estate (left to his new wife) got one-half of the proceeds.

This is a complex area of law that must be arranged through a lawyer. If the jointly owned property is a matrimonial home, it is subject to special rules that may complicate matters further.

BANK ACCOUNTS

In most joint bank accounts these days, both joint tenants own the right to use all the funds in the account, unless the bank is given special instructions to the contrary. In most places, when one joint tenant dies, the remaining funds automatically belong to the survivor.

BONDS

If a person owns Canada Savings Bonds made out to "A and B jointly and the survivor," both parties must sign to cash them in. If one of them dies, the bonds will be transferred to the survivor.

DEBTS

Mortgages are often held "on joint account," which means that both parties are liable to pay. If one cannot, the other must or lose the property. When one joint tenant dies, the survivor becomes fully responsible for the loan, although the creditor will usually consider the value of the property before suing the individual survivor for compensation from her or his other assets. If the mortgage is life-insured, the insurance company will pay off the entire mortgage upon the death of either joint tenant.

Joint liability on credit cards and other debts will put the responsibility on the survivor if one partner dies and the deceased's estate has insufficient assets to pay the debt. Most wills specify that payment of debts is one of the estate's first responsibilities.

TRUSTS

Sometimes, property is owned by two or more people, but not everyone's name is on title. In this case, one or more persons are designated as trustees to hold the property for the benefit of all. The trustees have a fiduciary duty to manage the property in the interests of all the owners. When an owner's name is not on title but his or her interest is held by a trustee, that person is called in law a "beneficial" owner.

4. Collection Agencies

Some people feel harassed when a collection agency duns them for payment. While there are laws governing the behaviour of collection agencies, it is not harassment to be asked to pay debts. Creditors are entitled to seek payment of debts from people who owe them money, and they are entitled to hire collection agencies to do it for them. As long as they behave within the law, collection agencies may request payment of the account.

Most Canadian provinces and territories prohibit certain kinds of behaviour that are considered harassment. Generally, the following rules govern acceptable practices:

- The collection agent must first notify the debtor by letter that the agency has been hired to act on behalf of the creditor to collect the debt.
- The agent must ensure that the person being contacted is the true debtor.
- The agent must not start legal proceedings to collect the debt unless the debtor has been notified that such action will be taken.

- The agent must not threaten to take any action that cannot be legally implemented, such as threatening to involve the police.
- The agent must not make a collect telephone call to the debtor to demand payment.
- The agent must not telephone the debtor on a Sunday, a statutory holiday or any night between 9 p.m. and 7 a.m., and must not telephone the debtor so often that the number of calls becomes unreasonable.
- The agent must not collect more money than the amount owed.
- The agent must not contact a debtor's employer, spouse, relatives, neighbours or friends—except for the purpose of verifying the debtor's place of employment, address or telephone number—unless the person contacted is legally liable for the debt as a guarantor, for example, or else is an employer who is required to garnishee wages.
- The agent must not give out false or misleading information to others that may be detrimental to a debtor or the debtor's family.

Collection agencies are licensed by provincial governments. Licences can be revoked for improper behaviour, depending on how such behaviour is defined in each province and territory. The government department in each jurisdiction that protects consumers can provide more specific information.

In addition to provincial rules, the federal Criminal Code gives protection against criminal behaviour by collection agencies. No collection agent is permitted to threaten to cause bodily harm or damage to property if a person fails to pay a debt. If the agent threatens a debtor in this way, the debtor should complain to the police, who can lay charges of extortion or intimidation.

If an agent writes false statements about the debtor, knowing them to be false, the agent may be charged with libel. If the agent tries to enter the debtor's home without consent and without legal justification for the purpose of collecting money due, the agent may be charged with break and enter.

The best way for a person to avoid harassment is to pay bills on time or, when a collection agent gets in touch, try to co-operate in order to arrange a repayment schedule. Advice from a credit counsellor is an excellent idea.

5. Bankruptcy

For the year ended December 31, 2003, there were personal bankruptcies of 84,251 and business bankruptcies of 8,844 in Canada. In 1990, by comparison, there were 42,782 personal and 11,642 business bankruptcies.

This shows a dramatic increase of 96.9 percent in the consumer bankruptcy rate since 1990, and at the same time, a significant decline by 24 percent in business bankruptcies.

AVOIDING BANKRUPTCY

People who are considering personal bankruptcy should first consult a reputable credit-counselling agency to see if they have any alternative. While bankruptcy is no longer, for many people, the shameful thing it once was, it can affect self-esteem, credit record and reputation.

Creditors may prefer to have partial or delayed payments than to forfeit most of their money. If a person has a number of debts at high interest rates, such as credit-card debts, he or she may be wise to pay these off with a loan from a bank or credit union at a lower interest rate. He or she then has only one debt to worry about and one monthly payment.

In 1992, the federal government introduced a new system to make special rules for consumer debtors. An insolvent person whose total debts (other than a home mortgage) do not exceed $75,000 has the opportunity to make a proposal to pay the debts without actually declaring bankruptcy. In this simplified procedure, credit counsellors and a government-appointed administrator are available to help formulate such a proposal. The filing of this proposal stops all court proceedings.

If such measures do not work, individuals who are insolvent (having debt obligations exceeding assets) may indeed need to declare personal bankruptcy. In fact, a creditor can force into bankruptcy anyone who has $1,000 more debts than assets. People who do not agree that they are insolvent may challenge the creditor's request.

In 1997, new rules were again legislated to encourage reorganization rather than bankruptcy.

TRUSTEE IN BANKRUPTCY

Bankruptcy is a legal process that allows people to get out from under almost all of their debts. Federally appointed "official receivers" supervise the process. Most bankrupts require an officially appointed and privately paid trustee. In order to go bankrupt, a person must at least be able to pay the trustee's fee, which is often $1,200 or more.

The trustee takes control of most of the debtor's property—money, goods, land and even future interest in assets, such as payments made to a mortgage lender, or contingent interest in assets, such as an inheritance—and sells it to pay the creditors. The debtor can keep some things, including the basic tools of trade; if a computer or van is essential to making a living, for example, it will not be sold to help pay debts.

Once an insolvent person declares personal bankruptcy, he or she must answer questions from creditors about his or her financial affairs and inform the trustee of all assets and liabilities. The creditors can meet with the trustee and, after establishing their claims, can appoint their own inspectors to represent their interests.

To protect creditors from being defrauded by debtors, the trustee can void some transactions entered into before the bankruptcy declaration. These transactions include transfers of property up to five years before the bankruptcy, if the trustee can prove that the bankrupt was insolvent at the time of the transfer, or if the debtor knew he or she was about to go bankrupt and paid a close friend back a long-standing debt to the detriment of other creditors. The trustee may consider payments to relatives up to one year before, and to unrelated creditors up to three months before going bankrupt as fraudulent preference and can reclaim the money or property.

The trustee may even render ineffective a marriage contract between a bankrupt and his or her spouse. The federal Bankruptcy Act states specifically that any marriage contract providing for the future payment of money to the bankrupt's spouse or children does not take priority over the bankrupt's other creditors, unless the property was owned by the bankrupt at the date of marriage or the property can be proven to be owned by the spouse.

Once the debtor declares bankruptcy, unsecured creditors—those who have no security, such as property, to ensure the payment of the debt—generally have no rights other than to receive whatever the trustee in bankruptcy manages to salvage for them. If the debtor owed wages to employees, those employees are first in line to receive payment, the minimum amount and terms varying among the provinces and territories.

On the other hand, secured creditors—those who hold some property as collateral—can sell the property, if the debtor goes bankrupt. For example, if the debtor defaults on mortgage payments on a house, the mortgagee may take legal action to foreclose or sell the house to collect the debt. If the sale results in a surplus, the extra money may be available to unsecured creditors.

DISCHARGE FROM BANKRUPTCY

Three to nine months must usually pass before the bankrupt or the trustee can apply for an order of discharge from bankruptcy. This discharge releases the bankrupt from all debts in existence at the time of the bankruptcy, except for such things as support of dependants. But before and after discharge, the bankrupt still has certain obligations. In general, bankrupts can keep part of the wages earned during bankruptcy if they use the money to pay for family responsibilities (such as support payments for a spouse or

children), essential clothing, basic home furnishings and tools of a trade. In some places, bankrupts can keep a car used for business, books and instruments to practise a profession, and basic livestock and feed. They can also keep any compensation received in a lawsuit for injuries. However, the trustee can claim the rest of the money or property acquired during bankruptcy. (These rules vary slightly across the country; although the Bankruptcy Act is a federal law, some issues may be handled differently in each province and territory.)

A person will not be discharged from bankruptcy if the trustees or creditors believe she or he has undisclosed potential assets that could be used to pay debts. Alternatively, the discharge may be conditional on the bankrupt's having a continued obligation for certain debts or making certain specific payments from income. Bankrupts are occasionally called to account. For example, in a 1995 Kenora, Ontario, case a 39-year-old truck driver entered into a separation agreement with his wife that included a commitment to pay an equalization payment, with respect to their family property, in the amount of $12,290 within 21 days or over four years with interest. Five months after signing, the man went bankrupt and claimed that the debt to his wife was the only debt he had. The judge ruled that the man made the assignment into bankruptcy in a blatant attempt to avoid the debt to his wife, and that granting an absolute discharge in these circumstances would be unconscionable. The judge stated: "The Court must balance the interest of creditors in having their claims paid, the interest of debtors to have debt relief, and the integrity of the bankruptcy process." By integrity of the process, the judge meant that the process should not be abused. As a result, he made the discharge conditional on repaying the debt to the wife, but gave the husband the right to pay it at the rate of $100 per month and $2,000 per year, when he got his tax refund.

The court may issue a warrant for the arrest of bankrupts who are suspected of absconding to avoid paying. Until fully discharged, bankrupts must reveal their financial status if they go into business or apply for credit, or else they could go to jail. The discharge order releases bankrupts from all the debts that they had when they went bankrupt, except for such obligations as court fines, court orders to pay spouse or child support and debts arising from fraudulent activities. Even income taxes can be discharged.

In 1997, the federal government amended the Bankruptcy Act and made these changes, among others: Divorced spouses will get priority among creditors for payment of spousal and child support; students who go bankrupt and default on student loans will remain liable for payment for two years after going bankrupt; a debtor owing restitution payments for a sexual or physical assault will not be discharged of this obligation.

6. Insurance

Insurance is a way of protecting against some of life's risks. Basically, insurance is a written contract or policy whereby, for a fee called a premium, one party, the insurer, undertakes to compensate or indemnify another, the insured, against a defined type of loss, damage or liability arising from possible (specified) perils. The face value of the policy is the amount the insurer is contracting to pay if the insured has an "insurable interest." Some types of insurance pay the insured; if the insured's death triggers the payment, then the named beneficiary or the estate collects.

Because insurance policies contain a lot of small print defining the precise nature of the contract, an insured should read the policy, and not assume knowledge of its probable contents. The legal issues that most frequently arise in connection with insurance policies reflect a difference of opinion between the insurer and the insured as to whether the insurer must pay, or whether some reason buried in the fine print of the policy protects the insurer from responsibility.

Although there are many kinds of insurance, each with unique considerations, they generally fall into three categories: property insurance, such as home, car, jewellery and art, and baggage (travel); personal insurance, such as life, health, disability and accident; and liability insurance, to cover lawsuits filed against the insured by others. For example, an insured may be sued because of an accident in the insured's home, or a car accident causing personal injury.

PROPERTY INSURANCE

Automobile Insurance: Automobile insurance covers loss of or damage to the insured's motor vehicle, the damage caused by the insured to another's car, liability for the personal injury suffered by the insured or someone else, fire, theft and mischief. Most jurisdictions require any licensed driver to be insured to a prescribed limit. Many jurisdictions have some version of no-fault coverage, which means that persons are paid by their own insurer, no matter whose fault the automobile accident was. Where no-fault is the rule, an injured person is usually prevented from suing the one who harmed him, for certain kinds of losses such as pain and suffering. Ontario allows an individual to sue in limited circumstances including very serious permanent injuries. In Alberta the model is the minimum no-fault system. Drivers injured in accidents receive only modest accident benefits unless they are able to sue an at-fault party to recover damages for economic loss or pain and suffering. Quebec was the first North American jurisdiction to adopt a no-fault system in 1978 and permits no separate lawsuits for compensation, apart from the compensation provided by the government plan. The Saskatchewan and Manitoba systems are modelled on the Quebec plan. The no-fault system, in which a person gets paid according to a schedule of benefits, has been subject to numerous complaints of its inadequacy in dealing with the claims of persons who have serious and permanent injuries and unusual pain and suffering.

Auto insurance policies also usually cover anyone driving the car with the consent of the insured. Sometimes an insurance company denies payment, alleging that there was no consent, or the insured alleges that there was no consent; the actual driver may have to seek court intervention to resolve the issue.

Household Insurance: Household insurance is available whether a person owns or rents. Homeowners will have insurance to protect against fire and destruction of their home, theft of any of its contents and perhaps a floater policy to cover specified valuables such as jewellery, furs and art. Tenants will have insurance to cover loss of contents through fire or theft. Condominium owners will have a policy that protects against damage and loss within the interior of the unit; condominium corporations will have a policy insuring common elements. All household policies may include a liability component, which pays if anyone is injured on the premises, and a loss-of-use component, which pays the homeowner's hotel expense, for example.

The amount recovered from an insurance company is based on either depreciated cost (the amount for which it could sell, taking wear and tear into account) or replacement cost (the cost of replacing the item at current market value). A householder is wise to have insurance at replacement cost; even though it costs a little more than insurance at depreciated value, it is usually worth the extra expense.

If any money is owed on the property being insured, the insurance company should be advised to include a "loss payable" clause in its policy. For example, the insurer for a mortgaged home that was destroyed in a fire will pay the amount owed to the mortgagee first, before paying the homeowner.

Bank Deposit Insurance: The federal government, through the Canada Deposit Insurance Corporation, insures member bank and trust company deposits up to $60,000 per account, per banking institution. A person can have an individual account, a joint account and also a trust account with one bank and be insured for $60,000 for each. Some banks set up a number of separate banking corporations in which deposits are insured separately. As a result, customers of these banks can feel secure placing more than $60,000 with one bank.

PERSONAL INSURANCE

Accident Insurance: Accident insurance indemnifies the insured against injury suffered accidentally, and usually provides a lump sum to the insured's beneficiaries in the event of accidental death. The insurer will require proof that the injury or death was caused by an accident.

Life Insurance: Life insurance is to protect a person's dependent survivors. A man or woman with a dependent spouse and/or children usually has insurance that pays the face value of the policy on death, either to named beneficiaries or to the estate. A minor should not be named as beneficiary; instead, the minor's parent or guardian should be listed. For example, a man will name his wife to be the beneficiary absolutely or in trust for their children.

It is a good idea to name a particular person the beneficiary of a life insurance policy. If the estate, rather than a person, is named, the amount of insurance must be included in the value of the estate for probate purposes, which means that any tax or fee on the estate will be higher. The insurance company will usually pay out the policy proceeds to a named beneficiary very quickly, once the company is provided with a death certificate to prove the fact of death. It does not need to wait for probate to take place, which usually takes time.

Basically, there are two types of life insurance: whole life and term. Whole life policies usually require the payment of premiums for the insured's life or a pre-defined period. Whenever the insured dies, the payment is made to the beneficiary without limitation. Whole life insurance has a savings component, called "cash surrender value," that is returned to the owner of the policy if the policy is cancelled during the insured's lifetime. The insurance company calculates the cash surrender value based on an interest rate that is usually lower than the bank rate of interest on savings. The owner of the policy (who may be someone other than the insured) may borrow against the policy to an extent and still maintain the policy in force. If the policy owner fails to pay the premiums as required, some policies may pay the premiums out of the cash surrender value held in reserve. Whole life insurance policies are usually individual, and usually require a medical examination.

Term policies are pure insurance. They have no savings component and therefore no cash surrender value, but the premiums are usually less expensive than those for whole life policies. Term insurance usually comes in two types: reducing term or renewable term. Reducing term starts at face value and declines over the defined period of coverage, but the premiums stay the same. Renewable term is taken for a five-year period, usually at a fixed premium subject to renewal at the rates then in effect. Many term policies can be converted to whole life without further medical examination. Most group plans through employment or professional or business associations are term plans, and many are available without a medical examination. The beneficiaries collect only if the insured dies while premiums are being paid.

A variety of life insurance is mortgage insurance: If a person who owes money on a mortgage dies and has mortgage insurance, the insurance company will pay off the mortgage, leaving dependants with a roof over their heads (as long as they can maintain the other house expenses). Another variety of life insurance is called "universal life." It is a combination of term insurance and investment savings, which promises larger returns than a whole life policy and a way for tax-free retirement income, and is based on an investment of funds over many years.

Extended health insurance to cover extra costs beyond what the provincial government health insurance will pay is another form of limited personal insurance with defined benefits.

With any form of life and health insurance, the insured must be honest when filling out the application and giving medical information. Otherwise, the insurance company may disallow a claim in some cases. In a 1995 Saskatchewan case, for example, an insurance company refused to pay on a disability policy because the applicant had not revealed a number of symptoms that he had had medically checked; he was diagnosed with multiple sclerosis six months after buying the policy. Because of his material misrepresentation, the insured sued the insurance company unsuccessfully, even though his failure to report the symptoms was innocent because he had not thought them the sign of any disease.

Disability insurance is paid to a person who is unable to work for provable health reasons. Each policy has its own provisions; some policies pay only if a person cannot work at all, while others pay even if a person is able to work part-time at his or her accustomed occupation. These policies have limits and do not replace a person's regular income in full. They also usually include an elimination period—the amount of the premium will depend on whether the person must wait 30, 60, 90 days or more to start collecting.

People who wish to transform the proceeds from life insurance into a monthly payment, or who wish to convert a registered retirement savings plan fund into annuity payments, can deal with a life insurance company for this purpose. They should be aware that the life insurance industry has an insurance fund, called the Canadian Life and Health Insurance Compensation Corporation (known as CompCorp), which ensures payment of monies owing from insolvent life insurance companies. However, the fund has its limits; for example, an annuity is covered to a maximum monthly payment of $2,000. As a result, an annuitant would be wise not to take out any individual annuity to pay more than $2,000 per month.

LIABILITY INSURANCE

Liability insurance, which pays for injuries or damage caused by the insured person, is generally included in every automobile and homeowners' policy. For example, if someone slips and falls on a person's property and sues for negligence in not clearing the ice away, a liability policy will pay. If a driver injures a pedestrian, the automobile insurance liability policy will pay.

If an insured has difficulty collecting from the insurance company, she or he should approach a lawyer for advice. In a 1995 Ontario case, an insurance company refused to pay an insured homeowner for the loss of his wife's jewellery, valued at $11,060, because the policy said that coverage for jewellery was limited to $2,500 unless additional coverage was arranged. The homeowner had been dealing with the same broker for 25 years and relied on the broker to ensure his protection. The broker never told him about the limits of insurance for items such as jewellery, and he never read the policy. The court ruled that private insurance agents owed a duty to their customers to provide not only information about available coverage, but also advice about which forms of coverage they required in order to meet their needs. Therefore, the court found the broker liable for the difference between the appraised value of the jewellery and the $2,500 limit on the policy.

In another case, the insurance company cut off a person on long-term disability after four or five years, alleging that he was a malingerer. The man had been a bus driver for less than 16 months when he went on sick leave and then on disability pay, claiming to be completely unable to work on psychiatric grounds. The company doubted the man's mental illness, which was diagnosed as agoraphobia (fear of crowds), and treated him in a mean-spirited manner, sending him from his smaller community to Montreal for an assessment. The court agreed with the bus driver and ordered the company to reinstate his disability pay and give the man $11,000 in lost benefits and interest. But the trial judge, Madam Justice Judith Bell also stated that the insurance company's conduct was "so harsh, calculated, reprehensible, malicious and extreme as to be deserving of full condemnation and punishment," and ordered the company to pay an extra $7,500 in punitive damages.

7. Duties of Landlords and Tenants

A landlord is a person who owns property and leases it to a tenant. Both landlords and tenants have rights and responsibilities by law; these differ in every province and territory, but share basic similarities. In addition, the landlord and tenant are both bound by any lease agreement governing their arrangement.

In some provinces, a government agency regulates landlord/tenant relations. In others, contract law prevails, and the parties must either sort out their differences themselves or go to court.

A landlord keeps a key to the premises but usually must give notice that he or she requires access, usually 24 hours in advance, except in emergencies.

Good State of Repair: Landlords have a duty to maintain reasonable health, safety and repair standards. In every province, the landlord is legally obligated to keep the home fit to live in and in a "good state of repair." Generally, the landlord has these obligations even if the home is rented in an "as is" condition, and even if the lease has a clause saying the landlord is not responsible for repairs.

But there are limits: The landlord is not expected to renovate and modernize an old building to establish a "good state of repair" (a state undefined by most legislation). The building must be well kept for its age and type; it must be safe and reasonably comfortable. But a landlord may not need to paint at regular intervals, for example, as long as the walls can be washed clean.

Tenant Obligations: Tenants also have responsibilities. They are legally obligated to keep their residence clean and to fix any damage that they or their guests intentionally or carelessly cause. The landlord can sue if tenants fail to do so. Tenants must also perform such maintenance chores as changing fuses and fixing minor plumbing blockages; the difference between major and minor repairs should be discussed between the landlord and tenant.

If a major problem develops in the residence, a tenant should advise the landlord of the problem and give him or her a chance to repair it, before complaining to other authorities or suing. If the landlord refuses to make repairs, some of the following recourses may be available, depending on where the rented facility is located.

Tenant Recourse to Law: One recourse is legislation. Generally speaking, there are laws that set out the process for dealing with landlord/tenant problems. During this process, which usually takes place in some form of court, a judge may authorize repairs and order the landlord to pay the costs. If the tenant has already had the repairs done at her or his expense, the judge may order that the landlord reimburse the tenant, provided that the tenant proves to the court that repairs were necessary, the cost was reasonable and delay was inadvisable. It is usually not a good idea for tenants to withhold rent or set it off against cost of repairs without court approval; they risk being sued and/or evicted by the landlord for nonpayment of rent. Instead, tenants should ask the court to hold the rent money, order that a trust fund be established or demand that the rent be reduced by the amount spent.

The tenant is entitled to "quiet possession," which, if breached by the landlord, may entitle the tenant to a reduction in rent. For example, in one 1997 Ontario case, a tenant received a rent reduction because repairs to the building by the landlord over an eight-month period so interfered with enjoyment and use of the premises that the tenant had to wear ear plugs, keep the air conditioner off and door closed, and live elsewhere for periods of time just to get sleep.

Various authorities may offer tenants other recourses. If the problem creates a health risk, for example, a tenant might complain to the local public health authorities. Inspectors may order the landlord to make repairs if the premises are injurious to health—for example, if plumbing overflows and creates a neighbourhood sanitation problem.

If a local by-law is breached, the tenant could contact the municipality. For example, a broken security alarm sounding non-stop may breach a local anti-noise by-law.

If the problem is contrary to housing standards, a municipal building inspector may issue a work order requiring the landlord to repair. Broken and dangerous front steps, for example, are usually a breach of housing standards.

Fire inspectors may order the landlord to make repairs to fire hazards if, for example, the fire alarm system does not work.

If the lease is for property that is covered by provincial rent controls and the landlord discontinues a service, such as a pool, this may amount to a rent increase, and the landlord may have to reduce the rent by the estimated value of the service.

If the tenant knows the name of the landlord's insurance company, he or she might alert the company to a problem that could result in an insurance claim—for example, someone who slips and falls because of broken steps may try to sue the landlord. The company may ask the landlord to make repairs to prevent such an accident.

Landlord Recourse to Law: Landlords with difficult tenants have the right to bring eviction proceedings. Eviction is a legal process in which both sides have an opportunity to explain their position, and the court issues an order for or against the eviction. The grounds and the procedures are different in every jurisdiction. In general, landlords can try to evict tenants who fail to meet significant responsibilities. For example, a tenant must use the leased space only for the agreed purpose. If he fails to do so, for example, by operating a business out of a residence, the landlord can insist that he stop and if he continues, bring eviction proceedings. Similarly, a landlord may sue a tenant who continually has loud parties late at night causing the landlord to lose other tenants. A landlord simply cannot order a tenant to leave, although if a tenant leaves voluntarily on request, he cannot later complain.

In general, if tenants pursue their right to a safe home that is in reasonable repair, and the landlord retaliates by seeking to evict them, a judge will often refuse the landlord's request if convinced that the landlord is in breach of responsibilities to the tenant.

8. Copyright and Computers

Copyright is ownership of intellectual creations, which can include books, movies, records and tapes, photographs, computer programs and other works. A copyright owner has full control over sale, reproduction and distribution of the work, and can assign copyright or the right to publish or use in some defined way. Even though an unpublished work, such as a manuscript, does not require any formal claim on copyright, the creator is still wise to include the copyright symbol (©) before her or his name and the year of creation. Copyright lasts for the life of the creator and another 50 years following her or his death.

Copyright extends to patents, trademarks and industrial design, all called intellectual property. The rules for patents are slightly different. Whereas the creator of a book holds the copyright even without the copyright symbol, since October 1989 a creator of a patentable invention, such as a computer chip, must be the first to file a patent application in order to be the officially recognized patent-holder.

One modern form of copyright theft is "computer piracy" of software programs. The federal Copyright Act makes it an offence for anyone to sell, lease or distribute copies of any copyrighted work. Offenders are liable to a fine of up to $25,000 and/or six months in jail for a minor offence; in a more serious case, they may be fined up to a maximum of $1 million and/or imprisoned for up to five years. The law is designed to financially protect those who invest in the creation of software programs.

The Canadian Alliance Against Software Theft (CAAST), an association of software firms founded in 1990, estimates that the unauthorized copying of personal computer programs costs the industry at least $12 billion each year. CAAST has taken an active role in enforcing copyright laws as well as educating business computer users about their rights and obligations. Its antipiracy telephone hotline encourages people to report possible instances of software theft. Calls from reputable informants who are prepared to give evidence in court could bring many more convictions.

While it is difficult to enforce copyright of computer programs, it is not impossible. In 1993, the RCMP obtained a search warrant for the premises of an Ontario manufacturer of circuit boards. They discovered that the company's computers contained copies of four software packages it had not paid for, and charged the manufacturer with software theft under the Copyright Act. The company co-operated fully with the RCMP, corrected the problem and, after pleading guilty to four summary conviction charges, was fined $50,000.

In a major B.C. case heard in 1992 and released in 1994, the court awarded a software designer close to $1 million because another company had deliberately copied a design for hospital software, then tried to cover its tracks and intentionally misled the court throughout the trial. The award was for breach of copyright and lost sales, royalties and opportunities. In addition, the court ordered the computer pirate to hand over all copies of the software in its possession, to withdraw all copies of the software from the sites currently using it and to pay the costs of converting those sites to the copyright owner's product.

In 2000, a man who advertised software at discounts was convicted of software piracy and sentenced to pay a $7,500 fine and serve 12 months of house arrest, 12 months probation and 200 hours of community service.

The warning is clear. Anyone pirating software runs the risk of being charged and made an example to others as part of an ongoing deterrence process.

Photographs represent another area of copyright infringement. In one case, a photographer had taken a posed photo of then federal Member of Parliament Sheila Copps for a magazine cover. After the magazine appeared, the negative was returned to him and the photograph was his. Contrary to his copyright, however, a newspaper subsequently used a copy of the magazine cover to illustrate its story about Copps, without paying the photographer or giving him credit for the work. The photographer sued. The court agreed that his copyright had been breached and awarded him the $900 in damages that he had asked for as well as his solicitor/client costs.

Besides unauthorized copying of computer software, advances in technology have made it possible to copy and send music files over the Internet, and websites have been set up to facilitate the finding and transfer of music without any payment being made to the composers, lyricists, musicians or recording companies. Pictures and text are also easily copied and distributed. The loss of royalties to writers and musicians can be substantial.

The Copyright Act was amended in 1997. It now includes civil penalties up to $20,000 for each program used illegally. The software industry says the new law will act as a deterrent to pirates. Effective January 1, 1999, the law provides for a blank audio recording media levy. Manufacturers and importers of any "blank audio recording medium" must pay a levy on every unit sold. The money is distributed to authors, performers and record makers; this offsets losses to artists from unauthorized recordings of their material. Blank videotapes are apparently not covered by the Act.

In 2000 the federal government passed legislation to "support and promote" electronic commerce by protecting personal information that is collected electronically. Several provinces (including Manitoba, Ontario and Quebec) are also legislating the use of "e-signatures" to give a method of validating computer-generated signatures in place of originals on important documents. Electronic signatures cannot be used for wills, powers of attorney and negotiable instruments such as cheques and deeds.

Copyright law is a work in progress. The federal Parliament is continuing to review the Canadian Copyright Act to ensure that it adapts to the emerging issues raised by the current economic, social, technological and international environment. The Internet in particular represents a challenge and its international nature requires that Canada collaborate with other nations. The government is currently trying to bring the Copyright Act into conformity with the World Intellectual Property Organization Copyright Treaty.

In 2002, the federal government tabled in Parliament its five-year report, entitled *Supporting Culture and Innovation: Report on the Provisions and Operation of the Copyright Act*, which identified more than 40 issues for possible legislative action. Thereafter, the Standing Committee on Canadian Heritage launched a statutory review of the Act and reported with recommendations in May 2004. Among their recommendations were that the federal government ratify the WIPO Copyright Treaty; that the Copyright Act be amended to grant photographers the same authorship right as other creators; that the Copyright Act be amended to provide that Internet service providers (ISPs) can be subject to liability for copyrighted material on their facilities; and that the government amend the Copyright Act to allow for extended licensing of Internet material used for educational purposes. Whether and how the government decides to change the law remains to be determined.

9. Investment Losses

When an investor loses savings because of the bad advice of his or her broker, the investor wants to know whether he or she has any legal recourse. A broker can be sued in civil court for breach of fiduciary duty, breach of contract and negligence. Moreover, since 2004, there is a new Criminal Code prohibition on insider trading, carrying a penalty of up to ten years in prison.

The success of any lawsuit will depend on whether the broker failed to fulfill the responsibilities that he or she undertook, *not* whether the investor suffered losses in the stock market. It is the investor's decision to determine just how much reliance to place on a broker, and how much risk he or she is prepared to take.

It is customary for brokers to require a completed customer profile, which includes not only the customer's age, goals, net worth, income-earning ability, and whether he or she is a naive or sophisticated investor, but also identifies the level of risk he or she is prepared to accept. For example, a very conservative investor might limit investments to 100 percent fixed income instruments (e.g., bonds, GICs), while a very aggressive speculator might go for 100 percent growth stocks (e.g., Internet start-ups), and a moderate risk-taker may choose 50 percent fixed income, 25 percent blue chip stocks and 25 percent growth stocks.

There are three types of investor–advisor relationships, and the extent of the broker's responsibility in law will depend on which is contracted. In all cases, it is the responsibility of the firm to supervise brokers and ensure compliance within the guidelines you have set, and if they do not, the firm can also be sued.

The *managed-for-you* relationship gives the investment advisor the discretion to make *all* the decisions. She or he has a fiduciary responsibility, like a trustee, to know the client's needs and means, and act within the guidelines established in advance in accordance with the level of risk assumed. If he or she fails to make decisions within the parameters established, he or she may be found legally liable for the losses as damages for breaching his or her fiduciary duty, obligations in contract and negligence. For instance, if she or he knows the client is about to retire and will need to preserve capital to earn income on which to live, the broker should not invest in highly speculative stocks. Investors who lack knowledge, sophistication or time may rely on their broker for decisions.

The *advisory relationship* is most common, and it shares responsibility between client and advisor. While the broker gives advice, the client decides, and takes responsibility for the decision. The only exception may be when the broker permits the client to make decisions that do not accord with his or her stated objectives and pre-set risk guidelines.

The *self-managed* relationship puts all the responsibility on the client for making independent decisions. This is the structure for most discount services. As long as the brokerage firm carries out its instructions, the consequences are the client's responsibility.

CHAPTER 10

SEPARATION AND DIVORCE

⚖

Introduction

There have been extraordinary changes in family law over the past 30 years, and these seismic shifts in legislation reflect similar upheavals in social values.

Before 1968, for example, divorce was not available unless adultery, cruelty, desertion or another form of matrimonial misconduct could be proven in court. In 1968, divorce became available on the basis of three years' separation. Since 1986, however, a couple has been able to divorce after one year's separation, on the strength of a sworn affidavit attesting to the fact of separation.

Custody is another area of change. Forty years ago, the mother was assumed to be the natural custodial parent; 30 years ago, the father was more accepted as the custodial parent; today, the right is the child's—the child's best interests govern the custody decision. Access is no longer the right of the parent, but the right of the child. And the courts continue to grapple with the problem of custody and access when the custodial parent wants to move, and in high-conflict cases.

The law governing the division of marital assets has also shifted dramatically. In the early 1970s, the Murdoch case went through the courts and demonstrated how few rights to property a married woman had when her marriage broke down, unless her name was on the title to the property. Irene Murdoch, a farm wife who had been an equal working partner with her husband in running the farm, was told by the Supreme Court of Canada that she did not make a compensable contribution to the accumulation of marital assets, and was not entitled to share in the property she and her husband had accumulated.

It was only in 1978 that the first laws were finally passed requiring husband and wife to share some assets when a marriage broke down. Three or four years after that, however, in the case of *Leatherdale* v. *Leatherdale*, the courts showed once again that a married woman's contribution as wife, mother and homemaker was not acknowledged even as an indirect contribution to the accumulation of the family's assets. Since that time, all provinces and territories have passed laws that require an almost equal sharing of all the family's assets, including investments, pensions and businesses, whether a spouse made a contribution in the home or out at work or both. The specific rules vary to some degree in each province and territory.

Thirty-five years ago, when a marriage broke down, a married woman was limited to getting support. When property-sharing laws came into effect in the 1970s and 1980s, however, and women began receiving a share of property, the courts started expecting women to become self-sufficient soon after the marriage ended—even when they had never worked outside the home, and even when the property share was inadequate to support them. It took until 1992 to redress the unfairness of these expectations, when the Supreme Court of Canada ruled that they were unreasonable. Since then, court decisions have resulted in higher awards of spousal support and for indefinite periods.

As society's ideas about child support have evolved, so too has the legislation. Historically, child support has been low and difficult to enforce. In the 1980s, the provinces one by one established enforcement agencies to help collect both child and spousal support. Only in 1994, however, did the courts begin to recognize how inordinately low the payments usually were, and started to raise them. Since 1997, there have been legislated Child Support Guidelines, which has resulted in more generous child support awards for children.

At the same time as the spousal and child support awards have been increasing, governments have been cutting back social assistance, although the two are not officially connected as a matter of social policy and, of course, not all mothers on social assistance have a payor spouse or father to approach for support payments.

Even with the trend of a rise in support payments, Statistics Canada reported in 1997 that women and children who received support experienced a dramatic 33 percent median decline in their standards of living one year after separation. This contrasts with the situation of men paying support, whose lifestyle improves 20 to 25 percent. Statistics Canada had studied the tax files of Canadians with children who separated between 1987 and 1993 to obtain these statistics. In 2005, the federal government released for discussion a set of advisory guidelines on spousal support for the assistance of the courts and lawyers counselling family law clients. It is not intended to bear the weight of law.

Remarriage has become a newer area of legal concern. When divorce was uncommon, rules on remarriage were even more uncommon. Today, however, second and subsequent marriages occur so often that these issues arise in the courts.

And in 2004, the first same-sex divorce in Canada was granted by an Ontario court, soon after the Ontario Court of Appeal approved same-sex marriage. Whether or not all the laws applicable to heterosexual divorce described in this chapter will apply to homosexual divorce remains to be dealt with by legislators and courts. But where they are not held by legislators or courts to extend to same-sex divorced persons, court challenges can be anticipated.

The divorce rate has been dropping since the late 1980s. After the liberalization of access to divorce, the divorce rate had increased significantly in the late 1960s and through the 1970s and 1980s. In 1968, there were 55 divorces per 100,000 population; by 1982, there were 280. By 1997, this decreased to 225 divorces per 100,000 population.

A. RULES, RIGHTS AND RESPONSIBILITIES

1. Preparing for Separation

It is wise for spouses to think through the consequences of marital separation and plan for it beforehand. The first issues to deal with are custody of the children and possession of the family home. If the parties can reach an understanding on who will raise the children and where, the remaining issues often become simpler.

If the spouses agree on who will have custody of the children and remain with them in the matrimonial home, the next issue is obviously what this arrangement will cost and how it will be paid for. Who will cover the rent, the mortgage, taxes and other housing costs? Furthermore, how long will this arrangement last: until the completion of the school year, until the children have adjusted to the separation, until the children have reached 18 years of age or will it take longer?

If the parties cannot agree on the children and the home, both parents should remain in the home with the children until the decision has been made and financial arrangements concluded. This course of action is best because most jurisdictions expect that neither parent will wrest custody from the other without an agreement or court order. However, if one spouse is abusing the other, different considerations apply and a lawyer should be consulted.

Anyone who is having marital troubles and is considering separation should put money aside in advance to provide a financial cushion. He or she should also be wary of signing anything presented by his or her spouse without legal advice. This is not the time to cosign a loan or remortgage the house to raise money for a spouse's business or pay off the other spouse's debts.

The need for financial support should be considered realistically. Spouses who are not employed should investigate employment prospects and evaluate likely earnings. Then they should discuss with a lawyer the likely obligation of the other spouse to contribute to their support (and in what amount), and the likely obligation of the unemployed spouse to contribute to his or her own support and that of the children. If skills need updating, the unemployed spouse may have to canvass the training costs and the availability of courses, and may wish to commence a program while the marriage is still intact.

If a spouse is employed, he or she will have to consider whether the available income will be enough to meet post-separation needs, taking support obligations into consideration. An employed spouse who unreasonably reduces his or her income despite support obligations may be expected to pay based on his or her income before the reduction.

The parties should review the Child Support Guidelines to determine how much child support must be paid by the non-custodial parent and whether any of the children's expenses qualify as extraordinary expenses for which an amount over and above the chart amount under the Guidelines would be payable.

Information on the nature and specific value of the family's assets and debts should be gathered. A married person should not assume that he or she is entitled to a particular asset just because he or she used it or lives in it, or because one partner has said, "It's ours."

The parties should try to locate and put aside in a safe place copies of financial documents, such as income tax returns, annual statements of RRSPs, share certificates, bonds, deeds, mortgages, savings account passbooks, credit card statements, pension data, business financial statements and written spousal agreements.

If a spouse has received gifts and inheritances, he or she will need documents to prove ownership, in the event that the province or territory of residence does not require one spouse to share gifts or inheritances with the other.

If the couple have joint credit cards and want to ensure that they are not liable for both spouse's purchases, they should advise the companies to cancel the cards. If one spouse makes this decision independently, that spouse should notify the other spouse first; taking this action unilaterally can hamper negotiations because cancellation of credit cards is often seen as an aggressive act. Joint bank accounts are also a problem; if a spouse decides to close or empty a joint account, the other spouse may view this decision as an act of war. On the other hand, either spouse is legally entitled to remove all the funds from a joint account without the specific consent of the other party. Some people choose to take half of the contents of the account in order to avoid animosity. In any event, anyone who removes funds from a joint account may be legally required to account for the funds.

It is important to remember that there are time limits on the right to claim property and support payments in some provinces. Accordingly, a person should not wait too long after separating to resolve any outstanding issues, or at least to register a claim.

Spouses who have not yet separated should seek independent legal advice on whether the actual date of separation may affect their rights and obligations. In some provinces, the settlement depends on what the assets are worth on the actual date of separation; for example, a stock portfolio varies in value from day to day, but the value of a house is less likely to fluctuate so frequently.

Spouses who are contemplating separation should each consult a family law lawyer for advice on how provincial or territorial laws will affect their situation.

2. Separation Versus Divorce

The legal pros and cons of remaining separated, rather than proceeding to the final and complete break that divorce represents, depend in large measure on an individual's needs and goals. If the spouses agree to delay the divorce, temporarily or indefinitely, they continue to be legally married. This status may give one or both of them some advantages. A lot depends on what the separation agreement states. If the spouses are separated but have not entered into a separation agreement, other factors may be involved. Here are some situations to consider.

FINANCIAL SUPPORT

If there is a separation but no written agreement, and one spouse voluntarily pays spousal support to the other, there are no tax consequences: The payee does not have to declare any payments as income for tax purposes and thereby pay more in taxes; the payor may not deduct the payments from income and thereby reduce the tax payable. As long as a separation agreement does not exist, the parties can use the time to assess how much support is needed. As well, the payee can try to find some means of self-support, while still retaining the option of seeking partial or full support if necessary.

However, if the payee wants to be able to enforce payment, he or she needs an agreement or court order. Once an agreement is signed or an order is given, there is little difference between being separated or divorced. In either case, if the agreement or court order specifies periodic payments, the spousal payments will have tax consequences. See also the sections on tax consequences and support of children in this chapter. Child support payments on orders and agreements signed after May 1, 1997, do not have tax consequences.

HEALTH INSURANCE

Most health insurance plans allow spouses to remain on their mate's policy as long as they are not divorced. There is no need to inform the plan of any separation, or to change coverage during the period of separation. Once the couple are divorced, however, they are no longer "spouses" according to the insurance policy. The spouse who is being removed from the plan should usually arrange for other coverage three months before the divorce is finalized.

The spouses may agree to continue health insurance coverage during a long separation period. However, it is unwise to assume continued coverage, as the plan member may have the right to change to single coverage or to replace the legal spouse with a common-law spouse. In any event, the member usually cannot have more than one spouse at a time on a health plan.

DEATH OF A SPOUSE

If a spouse dies without leaving a will while the couple are separated, and there is no separation agreement, the survivor may receive the share of the estate that the law provides for the surviving spouse. However, there are circumstances in some jurisdictions that disentitle the survivor to the survivor's share.

If a spouse dies without leaving a will while the couple are separated, and there *is* a separation agreement, the survivor is almost always bound by the terms of the agreement. It may include clauses in which the parties give up claims to the estate of the other; it may provide that the survivor gets a lump sum on the death of the first spouse; it may provide that support is binding on the estate of the survivor.

If, on the other hand, the deceased left a will providing for the survivor that was signed *after* the divorce, or while the couple were separated and contemplating divorce, then the survivor may be entitled to collect—sometimes even if the separation agreement contains releases of any rights to benefit from the estate. Both parties should be careful here because divorce may invalidate a gift to a former spouse unless the will actually says the gift was specified in full awareness of the divorce. Once a couple divorce, a widow or widower has no right to claim against the estate of a deceased who dies without leaving a will; she or he can make a claim only if the separation agreement or the will provides specifically for the survivor.

Support is a different matter. If the couple is separated at the time one of them dies and the survivor was being financially supported by the deceased, the survivor may register a claim for support as a dependant under dependants' relief laws in all jurisdictions.

CANADA PENSION PLAN

If a spouse dies while the couple are separated, the survivor may apply to receive the survivor's pension under the Canada Pension Plan Act. Since November 2004, this includes homosexual survivors, for payments back to April 17, 1985, the date the equality rights provisions of the Charter of Rights and Freedoms came into effect. However, if the deceased was cohabiting with another person as husband and wife for at least one year before death, the CPP authorities must choose between the separated spouse and the common-law spouse.

In any event, whether a couple were separated or divorced, if they had lived together for at least one year before the death of one spouse, the survivor is entitled to apply to receive one-half the Canada Pension Plan credits earned during their marital cohabitation.

PRIVATE PENSION PLANS

About 43 percent of private pension plan members in Canada are entitled to name their spouse to receive a survivor's pension as a standard benefit. In most of these cases, however, a divorced and sometimes a separated spouse is not entitled to be the surviving spouse, even if the spouses agree, unless the member had retired and the pension

was being paid before the separation. In all cases, each party should check both the terms of the plan and the provincial pension laws, and consult a lawyer.

OTHER ISSUES

Some jurisdictions may set time limits on seeking rights as a separated spouse.

If the couple are separated but not divorced, and one or both of them live with someone in a spousal relationship, competing claims between the legal partner and the common-law mate may complicate matters and should be checked with a lawyer.

3. The Separation Agreement

When a couple initially decide to, or actually do, separate, the immediate concern is not the formal divorce, but the "corollary issues" of financial support, division of property, custody of and access to children, and other matters arising from the marriage breakdown. If the spouses can agree themselves by negotiating privately or working through lawyers, then the agreement can be incorporated by the lawyers into both the decree of divorce and the divorce settlement. The issues to be decided depend on the couple's circumstances.

SPOUSAL AND CHILD SUPPORT

Most agreements deal with support, and the amount of spousal and/or child support must be quantified. Usually, the payments are specified to be made on the first of the month, but if a payor is paid on a different date, or twice a month, or weekly, and wishes to write the cheques when paid, the agreement can state that decision.

The separation agreement often says that the spousal support payments are payable until the payee cohabits with someone else as a spouse, but sometimes the agreement states that the payments are to be varied only if the new spouse is actually providing financial support. The payments are usually payable either for the joint lives of the couple, or for the payee's lifetime (which means that the payments are binding on the payor's estate), or until a court varies them because of a change in circumstances. Child support payments are usually paid until the child reaches the age of 18 or—if the child is still in high school, college or university—even longer. The amount and the term will be stated, as will any added payments for school tuition and books, camps, day care and so on.

Most agreements provide for annual variations in the amount of spousal support to reflect changes in the cost of living as determined by Statistics Canada. Child support under the Child Support Guidelines is adjusted based on the payor's changes in annual income. Most agreements also contain a clause permitting either party to ask the other to vary the amount of support or, if they cannot agree, to ask a court to vary the amount if there has been a material change in the circumstances of a spouse or child. It is important to include a requirement of automatic annual disclosure of income by means of tax returns, so that if an increase is discovered in the future, the recipient will have a better chance of getting retroactive payments. The tax implications of spousal support payments will have to be dealt with as well.

Spouses should include in the separation agreement the consent of both parties to have the agreement made into a court order, so that the agreement can be treated as a court order for purposes of enforcement. In some jurisdictions, one party can register the agreement without the consent of the other, but it is still wise to include the clause in the agreement. If the agreement cannot be treated as a court order, the payee's only choice is to sue the payor for breach of contract and to get a court order that can be enforced.

Once support is settled, the couple will discuss insurance coverage to protect the support payments. They will also deal with medical insurance coverage, and dental and orthodontal expenses.

CUSTODY AND ACCESS

When the couple have children, the agreement will define which parent will have custody and which parent will have access. In some cases, the parents decide on joint custody; if so, the agreement should spell out, perhaps in a parenting plan, exactly how this arrangement will work.

PROPERTY SETTLEMENT

If the couple have assets, the parties will either divide them or take their value into consideration when determining a lump sum to be paid to one spouse. Assets include the couple's home, cottage, pensions, savings, bonds, furnishings and the value of any professional practice or business operated by one or both of them. Who will have possession of which assets will be identified, as well as who will pay which debts. And, of course, the agreement must specify who will pay the legal fees and who will initiate and pay for the divorce.

CAN AGREEMENTS BE SET ASIDE?

Once a separation agreement is signed, the court usually takes it seriously as a contract. The courts have in the past set aside agreements in circumstances that could be defined legally as duress or undue influence—both very serious allegations and difficult to prove. In recent cases, the courts have reinterpreted the law to expand the type of circumstances that will persuade a judge to, for example, order spousal support notwithstanding a separation agreement in which the claimant has released her rights to receive support, or to a variation of the amount, or to order payments after a termination date. In the cases, the courts have focused on the need of the claimant and the other spouse's ability to pay and found that the strict application of the separation agreement would make for an unfair result when there has been a radical change in circumstances.

The extent to which the courts will overlook agreements negotiated in good faith and with full disclosure became more limited with the Supreme Court of Canada decision in *Miglin* v. *Miglin* in 2003. In that case, the Court dealt with the appropriate threshold for judicial intervention in an application for spousal support when a separation agreement has a release clause.

Ms. Miglin asked the Court for spousal support in the face of an agreement containing a full release of spousal support.

In this case, the husband and wife had owned a lodge in northern Ontario as equal shareholders and ran it together as a family business, each drawing a salary. They had four children during their 14 years together and separated when the children were between two and seven and a half years of age. They signed a separation agreement, which contained the transfer of Ms. Miglin's interest in the lodge to her husband and a final spousal support release clause. The parties also executed a consulting agreement between the wife and the lodge that provided her with an annual salary of $15,000 for a period of five years, renewable on the consent of the parties. The husband would not renew the consulting agreement. Six months before the expiry of the consulting agreement, the wife applied for spousal support.

While the consulting agreement could be viewed as intended to provide spousal support, the court did not consider relevant the fact that the husband would not renew the consulting agreement. The court determined that the consulting contract reflected the parties' intention to provide the wife with a source of employment income for a limited time.

The trial judge awarded the wife spousal support in the amount of $4,400 per month for a period of five years. The Court of Appeal upheld the award of support and removed the five-year term.

The Supreme Court of Canada allowed the appeal, reversed the spousal support reinstatement by the trial judge and the Court of Appeal, and ruled that both courts gave insufficient weight to the agreement and support release signed. But the majority decision of the Supreme Court of Canada did not simply rule that "a deal is a deal."

The Court set out a two-stage analysis, within what it described as a "principled and consistent framework" to be applied in every case.

First stage: (a) if advantage was taken (and proven) of a vulnerable party, the agreement may be given little weight, and (b) if there was substantial compliance with the factors and objectives in the Divorce Act, including the expectation that the parties would try to settle their own affairs with finality, then the agreement would be given greater weight.

Second stage: (a) if unforeseen events changed the intended impact of the agreement it might be considered less binding (note that this does not mean "radically unforeseen," nor "strict foreseeability," but rather "the extent to which the unimpeachably negotiated agreement [could] be said to have *contemplated* the situation before the court at the time of the application.") (b) if the agreement is no longer in substantial compliance with the objectives of the Act, the court might ignore the agreement and modify spousal support.

The analysis is so complex and fact-driven that it will be difficult for lawyers to advise their clients as to whether a court will see fit to order spousal support in the face of a release clause in a separation agreement.

IF SETTLEMENT CANNOT BE REACHED

If the couple cannot agree on some or all of the terms of a separation agreement, they must go to court to have a judge decide the unsettled issues. The judge bases his or her decision on the laws of the province or territory and/or the federal Divorce Act. Each province has laws governing the division of property owned by a couple, rules to determine how much support should be paid to the dependent spouse and children, and guidelines to resolve custody and access disputes. Federal law decides whether a couple has grounds for divorce, and it can also decide support and custody matters. In a divorce case, the same judge will probably decide all the issues by applying the federal Divorce Act to matters of the divorce itself, support and custody, and the provincial laws that determine division of property. If no divorce action is underway, then custody and support will be governed by provincial laws.

4. Tax Consequences

Separation and divorce can have significant tax consequences. Spouses should be aware of the implications before concluding a settlement because tax problems can range from very simple to very complex. Here are some of the more common tax consequences.

SUPPORT PAYMENTS

Spousal: Periodic spousal support pursuant to a court order or a written agreement is taxable to the payee and tax deductible to the payor. Therefore, the spouses must first determine how much disposable income is needed and can be paid, and then calculate the tax payable in order to ascertain how much the recipient will actually receive and how much the payor will actually pay.

The one who receives periodic spousal support payments pursuant to an agreement or court order must declare these payments as income. She or he will pay tax on them similar to the tax on employment income. The one who pays support, on the other hand, can claim a deduction and, as a result, pay less tax. The calculation of the amount of tax payable will depend on a number of factors, including other income, personal tax credits, other tax credits, child-care expenses (a recipient of support who has no other income cannot claim these), other deductions, number of children and custodial status.

Child Support: Child support will also have the same tax implications if agreements or orders were signed before April 30, 1997, and are still in effect unchanged. The law was changed to exempt from tax implications child support payable pursuant to new orders and agreements made on or after May 1, 1997, or orders or agreements entered into by December 31, 1998, with retroactive payments pre-dating May 1, 1997. This is examined in detail in the section on Support of Children in this chapter. Under tax rules, in order for spousal support payments to be deductible the payments must be made pursuant to a written agreement or court order, and the parties must, in fact, be living separate and apart because of marriage breakdown. The separation agreement must also clearly state that the payments are periodic and paid at pre-determined fixed times (monthly, for example), and that they are for the maintenance (food, clothing, shelter) of the recipient or children, if applicable.

Third-Party Payments: Certain payments made to a third party for the benefit of a spouse may qualify as support payments for income tax purposes. Payments for utilities or rent, for example, may fall into this category. The agreement or court order must be properly worded for these payments to qualify.

PERSONAL TAX CREDITS

The spouse who has sole custody of a child or children may be able to claim a substantial tax credit for one child on the basis of equivalent-to-spouse status. This is a tax break for single parents. The other children's tax credits would be the same amount as they were when the spouses were married. If the couple each have custody of one child, or if neither parent has sole custody, it may be possible for each party to receive an equivalent-to-spouse tax credit for the child primarily in his or her custody, although the Canada Revenue Agency may review this if an order or agreement is in place that requires either party to contribute a specific amount to the support of a child.

PROPERTY TRANSFER

Any property transfers between married partners bear potential tax consequences, during marriage as well as in the event of separation or divorce.

Attribution Rules: There are "attribution" rules to watch for—under some circumstances, capital gains or income realized in the name of one spouse may be "attributed" to the other spouse as her or his income. The capital gains attribution rules continue to apply after separation until both parties file an election waiving them. Income attribution rules end on separation.

Matrimonial Home: A matrimonial home that was a principal residence for tax purposes can continue to have that status as long as neither party declares any other home as his or her principal residence. Separation agreements usually stipulate how long the spouses will agree on the matrimonial home having this status. Since there is no capital gains tax on the increase in value on the sale of a home used exclusively as a principal residence (one per family), as defined by the Income Tax Act, this stipulation is important where the parties owned more than one property that may be designated as a principal residence (such as a home and cottage) and each spouse is keeping one of the two properties. Thus, only one spouse will end up with the principal residence and be eligible for the capital gains exemption.

Tax-Free Rollover: Certain property can be transferred between spouses without tax consequences, if done according to a separation agreement. For example, the couple may wish to divide evenly their registered retirement savings plan holdings, and are permitted to make transfers by tax-free rollover. This means that, by signing forms approved by the tax department, a spouse can "roll over" to the other spouse sufficient RRSP funds to effect an equal division. When spouses do this, no tax is payable at the time of this transfer. However, if a person simply cashes some of his or her RRSP holdings in order to pay an equalizing amount to the other, then tax would be payable. In any event, when the recipient eventually cashes in the RRSPs, tax will of course be payable by the recipient. The RRSP rollover provision only applies on equalization of assets. It cannot be used, for example, to transfer a lump-sum support amount.

Lump Sum: When spouses agree on a lump-sum cash payment from one spouse to another, the payment itself has no tax consequences and is a net payment. However, if a spouse must withdraw from a business corporation owned by that spouse the funds to pay the lump sum, that spouse may have to pay taxes on the money withdrawn.

Most agreements should be reviewed by a tax accountant or tax lawyer, or by the family lawyer seeking the advice of an expert, to ensure that all tax implications have been taken into consideration. In any event, a couple should not finalize their divorce until property transactions are dealt with and the tax implications considered. Certain transactions between spouses can be done without tax consequences as long as the couple are still legally married; once they are divorced, this advantage is usually lost.

Tax Deductibility of Legal Costs: The cost of legal fees and disbursements incurred to obtain spousal and/or child support through either a contested court application or through negotiation of an agreement has been deductible for legal costs spent since October 10, 2002. The deduction is for the recipient, not for the payor.

5. Divorce and Annulment

GROUNDS FOR DIVORCE

Divorce has become a straightforward matter in the eyes of the law. Breaking the bonds of matrimony used to be almost impossible until 1967, when the laws were first eased to allow divorce on the grounds of a three-year separation, adultery or cruelty. In 1986, the laws were altered to make the process even easier. Since then, the only grounds for divorce has been marriage breakdown, which can be confirmed by proof of adultery, physical or mental cruelty or a one-year separation for any reason, even if only one spouse initiated the separation. Most people now petition for divorce on the basis of one year's separation; few choose to go through the effort and anguish of proving adultery or cruelty, unless they want to secure their divorce without waiting out the year of separation.

If the period of separation has been interrupted with any attempts at reconciliation, a divorce is still available, provided the reconciliation attempts totaled no more than 90 days. Reconciliation is generally defined as resuming a home life together and trying to re-establish a sexual and spiritual bond. A sexual rendezvous by spouses without reconciliation in mind does not interrupt the period of separation for the purpose of claiming a divorce.

Even if the couple have been living under the same roof, they may be able to get a divorce alleging separation. The court will look at a number of circumstances to determine whether the spouses have withdrawn from both the physical and the spiritual bond: separate bedrooms and no sexual relations, separate social lives, lack of communication, separate shopping and laundry arrangements, separate meals.

Adultery can be the grounds for divorce, even if the adulterous liaison commenced after the separation or was not the true cause of the marriage breakdown. The petition should name the involved party (formerly the co-respondent). Even in uncontested cases, adultery must be proven to a judge; evidence of the other spouse's relationship with the involved party and proof of opportunity for them to commit adultery must be provided. The court does not require eyewitness testimony or lurid photographs as proof. Investigators can be hired to find evidence that the two people stayed overnight together alone under the same roof, and most judges will presume from this evidence that sexual relations took place.

Parties are asked (at trial, or perhaps in their affidavit evidence) to confirm that they did not commit adultery just to get a divorce. To do so is considered illegal collusion, and the court would dismiss the request for the divorce. But collusion is rare, as are court dismissals of divorce petitions.

A divorce may be sought on grounds of physical or mental cruelty. Mental cruelty is generally defined as a tendency to inflict suffering on the feelings or emotions of another and an indifference to, or satisfaction in, the pain of another. To be considered physical or mental cruelty, the spouse's conduct must make continued cohabitation intolerable.

There is no simple definition or objective standard for what will always constitute cruelty. In most cases, fear of the cruel spouse is a common factor. Cruelty must be proven by corroborated facts (actual conduct). The courts have accepted different kinds of conduct as evidence of cruelty, including a refusal to have sexual intercourse, jealousy to the point of restricting a spouse's freedom, silent treatment, a domineering and supercritical attitude, physical abuse (abuse of a child has also been perceived as cruelty to the wife), abnormal sexual practice and passing on venereal disease.

The federal Divorce Act contains provisions that require a spouse to remove all barriers that are within his or her control that would prevent the other spouse's remarriage within that spouse's faith. Recalcitrant spouses who fail to remove these barriers may lose their right to oppose claims for property sharing and support. These provisions are particularly applicable to Jewish spouses who also require a Jewish religious divorce (a *get*), which is only available with the consent of the husband.

SUPPORT FOR DIVORCED SPOUSES

A court must consider many factors when making an order for spousal support in a divorce action. These factors include promoting the economic self-sufficiency of each spouse within a reasonable period of time; relieving the economic impact and hardship of the divorce; recognizing any economic advantages and disadvantages to the spouses arising from the marriage or its breakdown; apportioning between the spouses the financial consequences arising from the care of children, over and above an order for child support.

CUSTODY AND ACCESS FOR DIVORCED SPOUSES

If both spouses consent, the court may order joint or shared custody of children. But if one parent seeks sole custody, the court must consider whether the custodial parent will facilitate access to the other parent. The parent with access may have the right to request and receive information about the child's health, education and welfare. The court may order the custodial parent to notify the other parent in advance if the child's place of residence will change. If the custodial parent denies access to the other parent, the latter may go to court to seek custody.

PROCEDURE AND EVIDENCE

The petition for divorce can be filed immediately after separation, but if the ground for divorce is one year of separation, the divorce will not be granted by the court until the year has passed. If the spouses cannot agree on such issues as support, division of property, custody and access, they may have to wait longer than a year to get divorced; pretrial procedures must be completed, such as preparing documents, gathering evidence, and exchanging information and documents at examinations for discovery (the stage during which each party learns about the other's case). Sometimes, the parties will agree on—or the court will order—a severance of the issues so that the divorce can be granted immediately. However, the issues of custody, support and property will continue as a corollary relief proceeding.

In uncontested cases, the law allows proof of divorce grounds to be confirmed without requiring the spouse who is suing for divorce to appear before the judge. Sworn statements in affidavits will usually be used instead.

Without application, a divorce generally becomes final—and remarriage possible—on the thirty-first day after the divorce is granted.

Any dispute that goes through the courts takes time: most courts are overloaded and understaffed. Uncontested divorce cases can take at least three to six months to complete. Contested cases rarely take less than a year.

ANNULMENT

A divorce decree terminates an existing valid marriage on the basis of events that have arisen since the celebration of the marriage; an annulment declares that a marriage did not exist, that it was null and void from the beginning on the basis of facts existing at the time of the marriage. Divorce is a federal law and applicable across Canada, whereas annulment is governed primarily by the provinces and territories.

In the rare case that a spouse is so mentally incapable that he or she cannot understand the nature of the marriage contract at the time of the marriage ceremony, it is possible to get the marriage annulled. In this situation, it is not the spouse's mental illness, but his or her lack of mental capacity to consent—to understand the nature of the duties and responsibilities of marriage—that is relevant. In one case, a certifiably insane person was ruled to have contracted a valid marriage during a "lucid interval."

Most provincial laws make it clear that a marriage licence is not to be issued to any person who is mentally ill. Therefore, it is up to the spouse who is petitioning for annulment to prove the other spouse's incapacity at the time of the marriage on the basis of that spouse's conduct. For example, in one B.C. case, bizarre behaviour during the ceremony proved the husband's mental incapacity: He giggled throughout the ceremony, cartwheeled around the reception, sent his bride home and went to bed alone. A court will consider marriage entered into with a mentally incapable person as void from the beginning, with each person restored to her or his original status as if she or he had never married, even if the marriage was consummated.

Mental illness arising during the course of the marriage is not grounds for annulment but may be grounds for divorce.

If a spouse is capable of consummating the marriage but has wilfully refused to do so for at least a year, this behaviour is grounds for divorce. However, if at the time of the marriage the husband is incapable of sexual intercourse—defined in law as the inability to achieve complete penetration, whether or not ejaculation occurs—and his condition is incurable, the wife may be able to get an annulment. A decree of nullity declares that the marriage never existed.

In 1999, the B.C. Court of Appeal ruled against an annulment requested by a 65-year-old wealthy man. He claimed he was unable to maintain an erection on any occasion after his 22-year-old bride rejected him on their wedding night. His bride testified that they had had sexual relations a number of times during their five months of cohabitation. The Court said an annulment was only available if a spouse has an "invincible aversion" to the act of sexual intercourse. The Court also awarded the bride $1,250 in monthly support for three years and 10 percent of the man's "family assets," but none of a million-dollar apartment building he owned.

Other grounds for annulment include consanguinity (marrying a close relative), lack of parental consent when one or both partners are underage, duress (resulting from coercion and fear), mistake as to the nature of the ceremony, fraud or misrepresentation or bigamy. There have been few reported annulments in the law reports since the late 1950s, perhaps because it is now easier to get a divorce than an annulment.

6. *Matrimonial Misconduct*

A married person no longer needs to prove or even allege misconduct to get a divorce. Since the Divorce Act was amended in 1986, a marriage can be ended by simply proving one year's separation. It is therefore not legally relevant whether a spouse was nasty, abusive, adulterous, sexually unavailable, alcoholic, imprisoned or financially irresponsible. Although a spouse may petition on the basis of adultery and/or physical or mental cruelty, there is no advantage in choosing to divorce on grounds of misconduct, and trying to prove the case in open court is emotionally and financially draining.

The one-year separation method spares couples the trauma of giving evidence of misconduct in Divorce Court, as many were compelled to do until 1986. Until that time, the law required three years' separation, not one. This method also puts an end to cases where a judge could deny a divorce when she or he did not find the evidence of misconduct sufficient. In a 1980 case, for example, divorce was denied to a husband whose wife had had an abortion without his knowledge, and in a 1976 case, divorce was denied to a wife whose husband would not let her work outside the home. In each situation, the judge did not consider the defendant's conduct to be grounds for mental cruelty.

AND ADULTERY

Sexual intercourse between a married person and someone other than her or his spouse is legally considered adultery, even if sexual relations take place after the couple have physically separated, but are not yet divorced.

The law has changed completely in the area of adultery. Married people who commit adultery are no longer punished for it in the divorce courts. Adulterers pay no added amount of support and spurned spouses get no special compensation for their pain. The Divorce Act specifically says that the court is not to consider "any misconduct of a spouse in relation to the marriage." Instead, need is an important factor in determining support.

After separation, a spouse's casual sexual relations usually will not mean the loss of financial support; however, if a supported spouse lives with another partner, a court may end the paying spouse's financial obligation. Although, historically, most divorce support awards ended as a matter of course when the wife remarried or began living with another man in circumstances similar to marriage, the courts now often consider whether the new relationship in fact makes one partner financially independent of the other.

AND ASSET SPLIT

With respect to the division of marital assets, matrimonial misconduct is not generally a factor. For example, a spouse cannot argue for a larger share of the matrimonial home or other family property because the other spouse committed an assault or abandoned the relationship for another partner. Misconduct is not an excuse to make the errant partner leave the matrimonial home or the family business. However, several provinces say that gambling or reckless spending of family money may affect property division.

AND SUPPORT

Similarly, misconduct does not normally affect spousal support. Generally, the spouses will not pay more because of their bad behaviour or pay less because their partner behaved badly—even if their spouse left them, had an affair, was a slovenly housekeeper or engaged in immoral conduct. A rarely applied Ontario law is an exception. According to this law, if a court considers a spouse's conduct to be "so unconscionable as to constitute an obvious and gross repudiation of the relationship," the court may consider this evidence when deciding the amount of support. Spousal support largely depends on each spouse's income and needs.

AND THE CHILDREN

As for custody and access to children, the courts maintain that "children are not a prize to be awarded" to an innocent spouse, and so the past conduct of a spouse should not affect the decision, except when it is "relevant to the ability of that person to act as a parent." The court is supposed to consider only the best interests of the children. In some cases, when both spouses have equal parenting abilities, a court may withhold custody from the one who left the marriage for an adulterous relationship, if this factor is all that distinguishes the suitability of one parent from another. However, the courts do distinguish between adultery and promiscuous conduct, which is relevant if it affects the child. In one case, a mother described by the judge as "a person fond of male companionship" was denied custody because she left the child alone when she went out or took the child along with her late into the night.

A parent's ability to maintain a stable and satisfactory home environment is considered important. For instance, in a case where the mother was an alcoholic, the father got custody. In another case, both parents trafficked in illicit drugs, so a relative got custody. One mother did not receive custody because in the past she had frequently moved, and the judge decided that such conduct could be disruptive to the child. Providing a proper home life also includes the ability to provide proper discipline and the ability to keep all the children together in one home.

Even with the law minimizing conduct issues, divorce remains one of life's most stressful experiences. It helps if the spouses can distance themselves from each other's conduct and treat the divorce negotiations as a business deal. The one-year separation method may help them to focus more on financial and custody issues than on misconduct, at least in a court setting.

7. Do-It-Yourself Divorce

The justice system allows individuals to represent themselves in all legal proceedings, including divorce. A married couple should be able to represent themselves if they simply want a legal parting and can satisfy one of two conditions. First, they must both be self-supporting and have no children or property. Or second, they must have resolved their differences about custody, support and property, and have a properly executed separation agreement.

For a so-called do-it-yourself divorce, a

spouse must first obtain all the necessary forms (available in stationery stores and some provincial Supreme Court offices). Then, he or she must fill in the standard "petition for divorce" form, using the simple grounds of a one-year separation. Finally, he or she takes the completed petition for divorce and the marriage certificate (or a certified copy) to a court office to be formally issued with the court seal. The court charge for issuing the petition, which varies among the provinces and territories, totals $167 in Ontario.

Although a divorce petition is issued under the federal Divorce Act, the provinces may differ on some procedural rules. However, the basic process is as follows. If the standard divorce petition is issued, the petitioner will have to arrange for the other spouse to be served personally with the document. One spouse is not permitted to serve the other. A process server prepares an affidavit verifying proper service, and this is filed at the court, before the divorce can proceed. Process serving may cost about $60 or more, depending on the number of attempts made and the travel required. If his or her address is unknown, the court may agree to allow service on him of the divorce petition to be made by mail at his last known address, or through a newspaper advertisement.

If the spouses are co-operating, however, an optional process allows them to petition for a divorce jointly, and relieves one of them of the duty to serve the petition on the other spouse.

Once a spouse is served with the initiating document, he or she has 30 days in which to serve and file documents in response—60 days if he or she lives in another province or territory. If the respondent does not contest the divorce by filing the responding document within the required time, the petitioner is entitled to proceed with the divorce on an uncontested basis.

The petitioner prepares and swears an affidavit, and provides a draft divorce judgment and any other documents that the provincial Superior Court requires. Then, the Court will issue the judgment for a fee, currently $280 in Ontario for an uncontested divorce. Thirty-one days after the judgment is granted, the petitioner prepares and applies for a Certificate of Divorce, at a court cost in Ontario of $19. A person cannot remarry without this document.

Therefore, the total cost of a do-it-yourself divorce amounts to approximately $500 in Ontario for court costs and process-serving. The cost will be different in each jurisdiction. Hiring a lawyer or paralegal to handle an uncontested affidavit divorce will probably cost between $600 and $1,200 for fees and court costs, depending on which province or territory the spouses live in.

If the other spouse decides to contest the divorce or custody, support or property issues, then the petitioner would be unwise to continue with a do-it-yourself divorce.

Preferably, even before one spouse moves out, the spouses should resolve custody, support and access issues by agreement or court order. Both spouses should clarify any rights they may have to inheritances received. Are there family debts or loans that a husband or wife cosigned or guaranteed? The couple should decide who will be responsible for them.

Divorce ends marital rights to support and property, so the couple will have to deal with these issues within a specified time. In Ontario, for example, spousal support rights must be claimed within two years of separation, and property rights must be claimed within either six years of separation or two years of divorce, whichever comes first. Spouses should resolve these matters with legal assistance before seeking a divorce.

8. Avoiding Court: Mediation, Arbitration and Collaboration as Dispute-Resolution Techniques

Almost everyone in a conflict that threatens to erupt into a full-scale court battle wants to settle. However, settlement is often impossible, unless both parties choose to be reasonable and make the necessary compromises. A settlement cannot be forced, just as a person cannot be forced to be reasonable and fair-minded.

When a couple separate, they experience many confusing emotions. A person who fears for future security might find it difficult to be what the other party regards as reasonable; a person who comes to mistrust the motives of a formerly trusted partner may find it difficult to be what the other party may consider fair. Confusing and strong emotions can stall the negotiation process to the point where one or both parties decide that litigation is the only answer.

Sometimes, one of the partners goes too far in pursuit of a settlement, and makes too many concessions to get the other spouse's signature on the agreement. Buying peace at any price is usually unwise because the conceding partner may later regret it. No matter what the motivation for an agreement, once it is signed the signatories will likely be held to it. They cannot expect to get a settlement reversed because of second thoughts, unless the agreement is unconscionable in its impact on one of the parties.

Since emotions can run high during what is fundamentally a business negotiation over economic matters, a couple may be wise to seek the assistance of specialists in resolving disputes after a marriage breakdown to help defuse the emotional context, and aid the spouses in arriving at a resolution. Experts can be lawyers, social workers, psychologists, psychiatrists and occasionally accountants. Mental health professionals are particularly useful in resolving issues that relate to children, and their services are almost always preferable to court intervention in controversies over custody or access, except when compromise proves impossible. Family lawyers manage financial issues best, with the assistance of accountants in complex cases.

Mediation: Mediation is a helpful alternative means of resolving disputes when both parties are able to behave reasonably. The parties to mediation must be able to negotiate safely, voluntarily and competently in order to reach a fair agreement, and it is up to the mediator to ensure that they can. The couple usually meet with the mediator on their own. Their lawyers are involved only when the parties feel they need them, by private consultation outside the mediation meetings. The couple may feel empowered by a process that helps them to arrive at a resolution themselves, as long as the mediator can maintain an even balance and not let one side overpower the other. Power imbalances can occur in cases of physical or mental abuse; when one spouse wants to reconcile and the other does not; when one spouse is more wealthy, connected and educated; or when intimidation has occurred or is feared. Mediated settlements often prove to be more detailed and responsive to all the issues in the case than litigated settlements.

Mediation can be open or closed. If closed, everything said in mediation is confidential, and the mediator cannot prepare a report for the court. If open, everything said can be quoted by either party or the mediator, and if they cannot resolve matters themselves, the mediator can be asked to prepare a report and a recommended outcome. Open mediation, especially in custody/access disputes, is usually preferable because it avoids making the parties and children go through the process all over again if the couple cannot settle the dispute themselves in mediation.

Varieties of open and closed mediation have evolved. For instance, the parties may agree that the mediator can file a report to the court without recommendations; that the mediator may report to the lawyers in confidence but not to the court; that a mediation team, including a psychologist, psychiatrist or social worker and a lawyer, may be able to deal with all the issues.

The professionals who assist couples to reach a settlement are not magicians. If a person has always had trouble dealing with his or her spouse, chances are that the professionals will, too. If the couple were usually able to work things out together, then the open communication between them may facilitate the process.

Even if a couple choose mediation, it is wise for both spouses to have their own lawyers during the process, to advise them of their rights. The mediator and/or the couple should not draft the final document without the services of a family law expert, to avoid potential pitfalls. During mediation, it is better not to give up any rights, such as possession of the home or ownership of property, until an agreement is signed with legal advice.

In some places, mediation is touted as so important a solution that it should be mandatory. In other places, it is strongly encouraged. But mediation is not always feasible. Spouses who have been bullied or dominated during the marriage may not feel capable of holding their own in mediation, while rigid or abusive spouses may not possess the necessary flexibility to compromise. Cost may prove a barrier: paying for the services of a mediator as well as lawyers can add significantly to expenses, particularly if the case is not ultimately settled.

Arbitration: If mediation is not possible, there is still another option to going to court—arbitration. Arbitrators, who are usually either psychologically or legally trained, or both, will impose a solution on the couple. Both parties must agree in advance to abide by the arbitrator's decision, but one of them may appeal that decision to a court, in the same way that a person can appeal a judge's decision. Arbitrators are paid by the spouses, however, whereas judges are paid by the government.

Most provinces have legislation allowing for the arbitration of a wide variety of disputes, and these arbitration acts are also used to provide the rules for family law arbitrations. A controversy was ignited recently in Ontario over the use of (Muslim) Sharia law to resolve family law disputes; objections were made on the basis that the results would be unfair to vulnerable women. The Ontario government appointed former Ontario attorney general Marion Boyd to review the issue. In her December 2004 report, she recommended that arbitration using religious law should continue to be an alternative dispute resolution option for family and inheritance cases, as long as recommended safeguards were observed. The extensive list of recommended safeguards includes permission for the courts to set aside the arbitration agreement if (a) it is unconscionable or results in a party being on social assistance, or (b) if either party did not have or waived independent legal advice, or (c) if either party failed to receive a statement of principles governing their faith-based arbitration or was not first advised of Ontario law applicable to his or her situation. Boyd recommended new regulations to require that arbitrators provide written reasons for their decisions, certify that they have screened the parties separately for signs of domestic violence, and are satisfied that the parties are signing the agreement voluntarily. The report also stipulates that arbitrators must keep files and report their decisions annually to the provincial government.

The Ontario Government has not indicated at this writing whether or not it plans to implement the recommendations. The government would be wise to be cautious. The proposal makes inroads into the traditional separation of church and state. It takes away from vulnerable women the hard-won rights in secular family law, without the benefit of mandatory independent legal advice.

Collaborative Family Law: Collaborative law, the newest method of family law dispute resolution, uses lawyers but avoids court. It is mediation with a twist. Like mediation, spouses are directly involved in the negotiations, but unlike mediation, each has a lawyer at his or her side, acting as legal advisor, problem solver and advocate. The goal is to achieve a settlement in a non-adversarial, amicable and principled way. The four-way settlement meeting is the structural framework, with both spouses and their lawyers present at all meetings. Letters back and forth are minimized.

Both lawyers must be trained in collaboration, willing and able to work within its rules and principles. Before undertaking collaborative law, lawyers take specialized training in interest-based, non-adversarial negotiation skills to add to their legal expertise.

The parties sign an agreement at the outset that includes a commitment not to start or pursue litigation during the collaborative law process. To make this agreement effective, the lawyers who represent the parties in the collaborative process cannot be the ones who litigate for them if the negotiations break down. Each spouse must hire a new lawyer if he or she has to start court proceedings to resolve the case. As a result of this approach, everyone has a vested interest and a greater commitment to settling the case outside the adversarial rancour of the courts.

The participation agreement, which the parties and their lawyers are required to sign, includes rules of conduct *everyone* must follow—honesty, respectful communication, a commitment to act in good faith, and full financial disclosure. Parties are encouraged to set their own agendas and discuss issues with each other and both lawyers. Neutral professional experts (for example, mental health professionals for cases involving children, or accountants and valuators for financial issues) can also be added as consultants by mutual agreement. These experts then become part of the team. This interdisciplinary approach is fast evolving as the standard when the case calls for it. When a settlement is reached, it is incorporated into an agreement drafted by the lawyers and thereafter, if the parties wish, into a court order.

Collaborative law is *interest-based*, like mediation, because collaborative lawyers consider the focus on the family's complex underlying interests a benefit in finding common ground to achieve a fair settlement. Mediation is different because the partners negotiate directly with each other, normally with one neutral mediator present who tries to facilitate a resolution. It is often only after achieving a tentative settlement that the parties each go to their respective lawyers for independent consultation and the preparation of a legal agreement. This is when they may get information and advice that may change their minds. Another risk of mediation without lawyers present is that one spouse may dominate the process.

Both collaborative law and mediation differ from traditional lawyer-based negotiations in which the lawyers conduct the negotiations for the parties, who may or may not be in the room while the negotiations take place and may or may not have participated in the discussions. Collaborative lawyers and mediators often say traditional lawyers take extreme positions that reflect a party's very "best day" at a trial. They suggest that traditional lawyers' methods rely on the threat of going to court and that lawyers may not be able to settle until the parties are "at the courthouse door" after an expensive process that entrenches animosity.

The best process to select is the one that suits the personalities of the parties. Some couples need the court process and a court-imposed decision, particularly if one of the parties is uncompromising, abusive or unwilling or unable to see more than one side to the issues. In such cases, litigation may be the only way to resolve the impasse. Sometimes, the act of initiating litigation will itself encourage settlement. But litigation can be expensive, and the outcome is not guaranteed to satisfy the litigants. The

adversarial process can also be traumatic, because ordinary people are not used to summarizing and justifying their lives and expenditures from a witness box. In the end, however, the courts are a safety valve, imposing a resolution on disputes that are otherwise deadlocked.

It is worthy of note that even within the court structure in many jurisdictions, there is a built-in *settlement-minded* focus. For example, many Ontario courts require at least one preliminary "case conference" with a judge to try to settle as much of the case as possible before proceeding with any litigation.

Since 1999, seven local collaborative family law associations have been established—in British Columbia, Alberta, Saskatchewan, Manitoba, Ontario, Quebec and Nova Scotia—all of which have specific training qualifications for members.

B. PARENTING THE CHILDREN

1. Resolving Disputes

If divorce is difficult for parents, it is even more wrenching for children, who usually cannot understand why the marriage is ending and therefore place some blame for the breakup on themselves. According to a Statistics Canada study released in 1998, one in five children sees his parents separate before he reaches the age of five. The less conflict between the parents regarding child-care arrangements, the easier the process will be on the children.

If the parents are unable to resolve these issues themselves, they should seek outside assistance to help determine what is best for their children. Mediation services are available from psychologists, social workers, psychiatrists or other mental health professionals to facilitate a resolution by the parents themselves. Even if mediation does not help, the mediator/assessor may be asked to write an assessment report. Collaborative family law may also help, particularly if a divorce coach and/or child development specialist is part of the collaborative team.

The great advantage of these decision-making methods for the resolution of child-care disputes is that the parents themselves have an important voice in establishing the ground rules and choosing the professional to assist.

If parents are unable to decide their children's future themselves, then a court-imposed solution through litigation may be the only alternative. The guiding rule of law for the courts and assessors is, *What is in the child's best interests?* This seems such a simple concept, but it can be difficult to apply because the needs of children differ and are complex. When the parents live together, the test never arises: The parents can do what they want as long as they do not harm the child. When the parents separate and can agree on the child's care, there is no outside scrutiny of a child's best interests. When the parents disagree, however, the legal system must deal with the conflict.

In the context of litigation, an assessor may still be of assistance to the court in reporting on the family dynamics, any clinical problems, the needs of the child and the ability of the respective parents to meet those needs. To evaluate the child's situation, an assessor usually visits the child at home or has the child come to his or her office with each parent separately, and sometimes talks to relevant extended family. Sometimes, the assessment process may shorten or eliminate the need for a custody trial. If parents facing a trial do not consent to an assessment, the court may order one to be prepared. While this arrangement can confer a great deal of power on the assessor, in the right cases, assessments can be helpful and appropriate.

Some judges have expressed reluctance to automatically order assessments. In a 1993 Supreme Court of Canada decision, Madam Justice Claire L'Heureux-Dubé commented that expert evidence is not required in all cases to establish the best interests of a child. Similarly, a 1994 Ontario Divisional Court ruled that assessments should be limited to cases in which clinical issues need to be determined.

2. A Variety of Possibilities

While married, parents have joint custody of children. Dividing this responsibility on separation traditionally meant giving one parent custody and the other one access. Today, parents, lawyers and courts have conceived of a number of ways to share the children's upbringing, although custody to one parent and access to the other still remains one of the options.

Custody and access arrangements now come with a variety of names and can vary as much as the parents and children need. Imaginative solutions have been created by parents who want to have flexibility and yet, at the same time, maintain stability for their children after divorcing. Even if the terminology around custody and access changes, effective communication and co-operation between parents remains essential to make any arrangement for custody and access work, and a successful arrangement is possible even when the parents cannot get along as a married couple.

CUSTODY

The custodial parent is sometimes referred to as the parent with "day-to-day custody, care and control." This means that the child resides primarily with this parent, who has the daily responsibility for the child's care and the right to make all decisions on matters affecting the child, including health matters and medical treatment, schooling, extra-curricular activities, as well as religious upbringing and education.

The rights and obligations of the custodial parent are rarely scrutinized by the court. In the infrequent cases when a custodial parent has come before a court to justify his or her actions, the key issues have been religion and medical treatment (the right of the access parent to intervene in religious and health issues), and mobility rights (the right of the custodial parent to move to a different city with the child against the wishes of the access parent).

ACCESS

Basically, the access or non-custodial parent has visiting rights when he or she has the opportunity to fulfil the obligations of parenthood, to give the child care, attention, and emotional support and involvement. Orders and agreements for access can be either a general statement, such as "reasonable access" or "generous and liberal access," or quite specific, defining particular days and times, the pickup and delivery arrangements, telephone access and holiday access. In most cases, access takes place every other weekend, one mid-week evening and a precise share of holidays such as Christmas and school breaks. Some agreements specify the arrangement for Father's Day, Mother's Day and the child's birthday. Visits usually occur outside the home of the custodial parent.

Access arrangements can also include the right to information and consultation regarding the child's health, education and welfare.

Access is an arrangement between parents, and a court will rarely leave the children to decide when visits will take place. In a 1994 Ontario case, in fact, the court refused an access parent's request for an order that access be at the discretion of the children, aged 14, 11 and 8. The court stated that such an order would allow parents to abdicate their responsibility for such decisions and place the burden on the children.

The court will always order access for the non-custodial parent, unless compelling evidence shows that these visits would be against the children's best interests. The law is clear—unless access would be harmful, children should be allowed to know both parents, and benefit from their love, care and guidance. In several cases, access has been declared the right of the child, not the access parent; in one Ottawa case, two 11-year-old twin boys tried to sue their father for failure to comply with the agreement to visit in the divorce judgment between their parents. The boys were going to represent themselves in court, but the judge said they needed a lawyer; their application to legal aid was turned down. A child's right to access has not yet been decided in a court of law.

SUPERVISED ACCESS

Sometimes, access is made subject to supervision. For example, if a parent is unable to care for the child, another person may have to be present during the visits. In a 1994 New Brunswick case, the court limited a father's access to a four-year-old to two hours a week in a supervised setting because of the father's behaviour. He continually used profane and degrading language against the mother and, in the child's presence, had verbally and physically assaulted the mother (and was twice convicted). He also let the child sleep in the same bed with him, and was found to endanger the child's security and proper development and to place her emotionally at risk. The court ruled that the best interests of children are affected when they observe violence between their parents.

A British Columbia man convicted of strangling his estranged wife even applied to court asking for a study to see if it would be harmful for his three-year-old and five-year-old to visit him in prison. His claim was dismissed, and the supervised access he had while released, prior to his conviction, was stayed.

GRANDPARENT ACCESS

Increasingly, grandparents, who often play important roles in families, seek court orders for access. The laws in some provinces, including Newfoundland and Labrador, Quebec, and British Columbia, provide that a grandparent may apply for custody of or access to a child. In some provinces and territories, the law is less specific but allows for custody and access orders to be made to persons other than the parents.

Whether or not legislation specifically provides for a grandparent to claim custody or access, courts have held that the right of access is the right of the child, not of the grandparent. This means that only the child's best interests are relevant, not the needs or wants of the grandparents. And, since courts typically recognize the parents' authority to decide with whom their children will associate, a good relationship with the child's parents is still a grandparent's best bet for maintaining contact with a grandchild.

In a 2001 Ontario case (*Chapman*), the Ontario Court of Appeal reversed a trial court decision that had forced specific terms of grandparent access on an eight- and ten-year-old. The children were found to have negative feelings about their grandmother, due to parental influence. This was not a situation in which the children's parents were separated or divorced. The court ruled that the children had loving parents who were making decisions about the children's best interests as they had a right to do, and failure to see their grandmother was not proven to be detrimental to them. The court left it to the parents to decide the nature and frequency of any access.

JOINT CUSTODY AND SHARED PARENTING ARRANGEMENTS

Some parents agree on a joint custody arrangement. This means that the parents continue to share both decision-making and daily care, although they are no longer living together under the same roof. Physical arrangements vary. Some parents share daily care, the children living with both parents at different times but attending the same school and living in the same neighbourhood. Or, the children may live with one parent on weekdays and the other on weekends. Some families alternate weeks, months or longer periods.

"Equal time" is another evolving type of joint custody arrangement. It usually means that parents share decision-making and the children spend an equal amount of time living with each parent. For this to work, parents generally need to live in the same neighbourhood so that the children can go to school from either home and have the same friends.

It may also mean that the children reside primarily with one parent but spend weekends and some evenings with the other, and both parents make the major decisions. In most cases, parents are wise to draft a detailed agreement on how the arrangement will work in practice.

Joint decision-making works best if parents can communicate about their children without rancour and consult with each other in an amicable and reasonable manner.

If spouses can agree on joint custody, the court will likely approve the agreement and give it the same legal weight as any court order. Occasionally, the courts have varied a joint custody order to give one parent sole custody when joint custody has not worked for the family, and the parents have not been able to co-operate in the child's best interests.

Without the agreement of both parents, courts used to be reluctant to order joint custody, unless this arrangement had actually been in effect before the trial, although they did so in the rare case. Currently, there is a trend to "parallel parenting" in which high-conflict parents are given joint custody, with very defined and specific arrangements in place for every aspect of child-rearing and decision-making.

The question to be addressed is whether equal time or any other form of joint custody or shared parenting is in the best interests of the children. Can the parents put the children's needs first? Will the arrangement maintain stability and consistency for the children? Joint custody can be very satisfying to both parents and children if parents can co-operate and maintain a civil and tolerant relationship. Where they are unable to co-operate or where one parent behaves in a violent or domineering manner, joint custody can become a nightmare. When feuding parents focus on their rights, rather than on their responsibilities to their children, everyone suffers.

In 1998, a joint federal Senate/House of Commons committee on child custody and access called on the government to remove the terms "custody" and "access" from the Divorce Act and instead require parents to have "shared parenting," a term that is not equivalent to joint custody, but is a symbolic change intended to incorporate any and every child-caring arrangement. The committee recommended that parents be required to have written parenting plans in which they would work out the details of physical care and decision-making. The federal government introduced a bill to amend the Divorce Act to incorporate many of the committee's recommendations; the bill did not make its way through the legislative process before the 2004 federal election was called. The legislation has not been re-introduced.

If parents can agree in principle on a shared parenting or joint custody arrangement, but are concerned that they will not be able to agree on the day-to-day details, they would be wise to seek the assistance of a trained professional, such as a mediator, to help implement, mediate and arbitrate ongoing arrangements from time to time.

Decisions regarding children are never written in stone. Any arrangements that parents agree to or a court orders, including joint custody, may be reviewed later by parents or a court if there is concern that they are no longer in the children's best interests. If parents really co-operate, the winners in settling a custody dispute will be the children.

3. The Guiding Principle: The Best Interests of the Child

To resolve conflicts about custody and access, the courts rely on one guiding principle: the best interests of the child, an apparently simple but actually quite complex idea. Many factors must be considered before determining the child's best interests.

NO RULE OF THUMB

It used to be a rule of thumb that a child was best off in the mother's custody. But this guideline no longer stands: Current laws favour neither parent. A mother cannot assume she will automatically be awarded custody, although many judges consider it to be a "principle of common sense" for young people to be with their mother because she is often the primary caregiver, especially if she is nursing an infant.

FACTORS TO CONSIDER

When deciding custody, the court will review both parents' proposals for the children's upbringing and daily patterns of living. Judges will generally want to keep brothers and sisters together whenever possible, and will emphasize continuity and stability in care arrangements. The parent's ability to provide financial security and physical accommodation is a factor, but not given priority. The child's emotional relationship with each parent, and the extent and nature of each parent's previous involvement in the child's care, are both relevant. The child's relationship with extended family and a parent's willingness to co-operate in its continuation are also important. The court will take preservation of a religious, cultural and linguistic heritage into consideration. Will children be able to continue in the same school? Will they be allowed to have access to their friends? Will they continue to take extracurricular lessons? Will they be able to keep their pets? In some cases, a mature child's wishes are considered. The court must weigh all these factors.

When the parents are of different racial backgrounds, the best interests of the child may involve the choice of which parent can raise the child in his or her own racial culture. This issue was raised in a British Columbia case that went to the Supreme Court of Canada primarily on this issue. The court in 2001 declared in the case of *Van de Perre* v. *Edwards* that race was not the predominant factor in choosing the custodial parent; it said that race was only one of many factors to be considered. In that case, the child of an African-American man and a white woman was given to the mother to raise.

PARENTAL CONDUCT

The physical and mental capacity of the parent to meet the child's needs and provide a disciplined and loving upbringing is an important part of the court's decision; the conduct of the parent may also be considered. While a spouse who committed adultery will not necessarily lose custody, a spouse who "unjustifiably breaks up the marriage," according to the judge, may not be favoured. A spouse who abused a child, or the other spouse in the presence of a child, is unlikely to get custody; however, he or she may get access, depending on the circumstances, even if it is only supervised.

Occasionally, one parent has used custody claims as a bargaining tool to attempt to convince the other parent to accept less child support or to give up property rights. Since it is clearly inappropriate to trade off children for a financial gain, the courts will take into consideration that a parent was willing to do so, if this willingness can be proven.

Research has shown that ongoing conflict between parents often produces behavioural and emotional problems in children. Children frequently feel their loyalty is torn between both parents, and may even be exploited by one or both spouses in matrimonial warfare. Because such conduct directly affects the best interests of the child, the court may therefore consider it when determining custody and access.

WISHES OF THE CHILDREN

Courts tend to consider the wishes of children over the age of 12; sometimes, even younger children will be asked with whom they want to live. These wishes will not necessarily be granted, unless the court perceives them to be in the children's best interests. If one parent tries to buy the affections of the children or manipulate them with custody in mind, and the court sees

through these tactics, even a child's wish to live with that parent will not necessarily sway the court.

In a B.C. case, children in a joint custody arrangement expressed dislike for their mother's new partner and a desire to live with their father. Although he had a gender-dysphoric condition (he liked to dress up in women's clothing and considered himself to be a woman by nature), experts determined that this condition would not interfere with his ability to parent. The court therefore concluded that it was in the best interests of the children to be in their father's custody.

FACILITATION OF ACCESS

In making the custody decision, the court is mandated by the Divorce Act to consider whether the custodial parent will facilitate access by the non-custodial parent. Studies have shown that children who have ongoing involvement with both parents do better socially, emotionally and academically, particularly when the custodial parent supports the visiting arrangements. At this time, however, the law offers no effective way to enforce access visits.

4. Career Commitment

In many families today, both parents work outside the home, a fact that should put both parents on relatively equal footing in terms of the time they can contribute to their family and their suitability as parents. However, this is not the case. When considering custody, the courts may enter into a close review of the amount of time each working parent has available for the children.

In custody disputes where one parent can provide full-time care and the other hires a caregiver, the courts tend to favour the full-time parent. But when both parents work outside the home, the decision becomes more complicated, and much depends on the plans the parents are proposing.

In a 1988 Manitoba case, the court initially granted custody to the father because his new wife, with whom his eight-year-old and five-year-old had a good relationship, intended to stay home to care for them and her new baby. The mother, a business-woman, planned to rely on paid child care, which the judge concluded was not in the children's best interests. On appeal, the court overturned the decision and gave custody to the mother, concluding that there was no evidence the children would suffer any harm from the use of a professional caregiver. The Supreme Court of Canada refused leave to appeal, so the case ended there.

In a 1992 case, the B.C. Court of Appeal upheld a trial court decision to take custody of four children aged six, eight, ten and twelve away from the mother, and gave both custody and exclusive possession of the matrimonial home to the father. The mother had been primary caregiver until the separation, but wanted to retrain to become a dental assistant, and so would need baby-sitters when she was away from the home. In the meantime, the husband had worked outside the home throughout the marriage and spent little time with the children. However, after he broke his neck in an industrial accident and became a paraplegic, he became very involved with the children. He supported himself with Workers' Compensation Board and CPP disability pensions. Rather than retrain, he wanted to stay home full-time with the children.

The most publicized case in which a mother's career commitment affected custody was that of Judy Tyabji, then a high-profile member of the B.C. legislature whose marriage ended after she had an affair with then B.C. Liberal leader Gordon Wilson. In the ensuing legal battle with her ex-husband between 1992 and 1994, Tyabji was awarded interim custody of their three children, aged six, four and two. However, at a permanent custody hearing in 1994, the B.C. Supreme Court granted custody to the father, Kim Sandana. Although Sandana also worked full-time, the judge concluded that his job in a grocery store likely would not interfere with his attention to the children; he also noted that Sandana was less ambitious and aggressive than Tyabji and had been a more active parent. Finally, the judge regarded as relevant his interpretation of Tyabji's responsibility for the marriage breakup, as it implied that she would likely place her own interests ahead of those of her children.

Tyabji initially appealed, but proceeded instead with an application in 1996 to vary custody on the basis of a change in circumstances—after losing her seat in the legislature, she did not run for re-election and was employed only part-time, so she could spend more time with the children. She also argued that their health would be better in Victoria where she lived, than in Kelowna where her ex-husband lived, and that her ex-husband had not facilitated her access. The court disagreed with both claims. The judge decided that it was still true the children would benefit more from their father's "calmer, less aggressive lifestyle" and noted as well that Tyabji was involving, to their detriment, the children in the custody dispute. Later court proceedings over access issues did not alter the custody determination.

Any parent who loses a custody or access battle has three choices: accept the result, live with it and work on the relationship with the children in whatever time is available; appeal the decision, although an appeal court is unlikely to interfere unless the trial judge misapplied a principle of law or made important factual findings that were not supported by the evidence (such as finding that a parent was abusive to the child); or make an application to vary custody based on a material change in circumstances that affects a child's best interests.

5. Religion

Since the custodial parent controls the religious upbringing, a religious dispute can end up as a custody dispute. It can also end up as an application by the access parent for an order allowing him or her to teach the child religion during access visits, or by the custodial parent for an order prohibiting the access parent from teaching the child religion during visits.

Leaving such a decision to a judge is unpredictable; the court will not choose between differing religions. The only legal guide is the rule that the best interests of the child prevail over the wishes or needs of either parent. The Supreme Court of Canada reviewed the law in 1993, but inexplicably ruled on two similar cases in opposite ways on the same day. In one case, the Court said that the child's best interests meant what is shown to benefit the child; this ruling reaffirmed the rights of the custodial parent, who was assumed to be the best judge of what benefits the child. In the other case, the child's best interests were interpreted more broadly to mean what was shown not to

harm the child. This decision gave more freedom to the access parent.

In both cases, the fathers were members of the Jehovah's Witnesses, joining the church without the mother's involvement. The mothers had custody when the marriages ended, but then the fathers claimed custody or extended access so that they could provide the children with a religious education. The mothers objected and asked the courts to prevent the fathers from indoctrinating the children.

In one case, the Supreme Court concluded that the child could benefit from exposure to her father's religion, and that such access should be barred only if the benefit is outweighed by a clear risk of harm. Therefore, the father would be able to involve the child in his religion until the teachings were proven to harm the child— for example, if the child showed symptoms of trauma such as nightmares, bed-wetting or learning difficulties.

The other ruling rejected this "harm test" as an interpretation that put the child at risk, and said that the custodial parent is in the best position to decide what will contribute to the child's welfare. Accordingly, in these circumstances the parent with custody can limit the other parent's access. Arguing against the harm test, Madam Justice L'Heureux-Dubé said that with all the social, economic and emotional pressures facing single-parent families, the court should not add to their burdens by expanding the rights of non-custodial parents.

Because the courts may follow one or the other of these cases, parents having a dispute about religion need to seek legal advice where they reside before pursuing a course of action.

6. Mobility Rights

Mobility cases are often the most difficult to resolve; they arise when a custodial parent wants to move away from his or her city of residence for personal or career reasons, and the other parent objects because the move will affect his or her access to the child.

The courts have been stymied in their attempts to establish a rule of law that will give some predictability and consistency to decisions in this area. While mobility decisions are officially based on the best interests of the child, the meaning of this legal principle has been interpreted and reinterpreted by courts over the past seven years, with the end result that each case is judged on its own merits. Parents who cannot agree will have to seek a court ruling, and then perhaps bring or respond to an appeal.

No specific law prevents a custodial parent from moving with the children. However, even if a separation agreement or court order gives one parent the right to move, the other parent can still apply to court and ask a judge to order otherwise, arguing that the move is not in the best interests of the child. The children's best interests—not the rights of the parents—are paramount, and the law recognizes that what is best for children can change over time. Therefore, the parent who wants to move must prove that the move will benefit the child.

The difficulty is that the best interests of children can mean different things to different judges at different times. By 1990, when determining the best interests of the child, the Ontario Court of Appeal had ruled that the right to change a child's residence was too important a decision to be left to one parent, and could not be assumed a right of the custodial parent. However, while a custodial parent did not have an automatic right to move with the child, his or her views and wishes were entitled to great weight. Other factors the Court of Appeal considered included the reason for the move, whether the move offered any obvious benefit or detriment to the child (aside from reduced access) and whether the custodial parent would co-operate in restructuring the access to maintain a relationship between the access parent and child.

In these cases, courts also look at the nature of the relationship between the child and the access parent; the distance of the move; the child's views; and relevant legislation. The Divorce Act provides that courts must give effect to the principle that children of the marriage should have as much contact with each spouse as is consistent with their best interests, and the courts must consider the willingness of the person seeking custody to facilitate such contact.

The decision comes down to this: Does the custodial parent's reason for the proposed move justify the reduction in access?

If the court suspects that a proposed move is intended to frustrate access, the court will likely refuse it; however, the court will not draw this conclusion easily.

Many judges have made orders that have the effect of preventing a custodial parent from moving, at least when that parent wants to remain the primary caregiver to the children. While a court cannot stop a parent from changing cities, it can prevent the child from moving; an order for the child to remain in the jurisdiction may have the effect of transferring custody to the other parent, if the custodial parent chooses to move. If the move is for a second marriage to someone who lives and works in another town, a custodial parent may have to choose between the new partner and the children.

In most cases where the move has been denied, the court has held that the bond between the child and the access parent is too important to be interfered with.

The emphasis shifted in 1995 in the case of *MacGyver* v. *Richards*, when the Ontario Court of Appeal reaffirmed the right of a custodial parent (in this case, a mother) to decide whether a move was in her child's best interests. Madam Justice Rosalie Abella concluded that it is the custodial parent, and not the judge or the access parent, who must live with the daily consequences of caring for the child; she ruled, therefore, that a "presumptive deference" must be given to the needs of the parent who is the constant presence in the child's life. She pointed out that "the judicial perspective should acknowledge the overwhelmingly relentless nature of the custodial responsibility, and respect its day-to-day demands"; accordingly, the court should not interfere with the parent's capacity to make decisions.

She reasoned that denying the right of a move for economic reasons could force a mother and child into a life of poverty, just as denying the right to move with a new partner denies the custodial parent the right to get on with her life.

Appeal courts in British Columbia, Saskatchewan, Ontario and Manitoba have applied this case, deferring to custodial parents to make decisions in their children's best interests.

In May 1996, however, the Supreme Court of Canada took a look at this issue when deciding the case of *Gordon* v. *Goertz* on appeal from the Saskatchewan Court of Appeal. Although the Court's decision was unanimous in upholding the custodial mother's right to move to Australia with her seven-year-old daughter, the majority backed away from Madam Justice Abella's analysis, supporting the previous analysis that the best interests of the child must be determined independently of the interests of the parents.

When judges are determining best interests, the majority stated, they must look at the existing custody arrangement and the relationship between the child and the custodial parent; the existing access arrangements and the relationship between the child and the access parent; the desirability of maximizing contact between the child and both parents; the views of the child; the custodial parent's reason for moving, but only if it is relevant to that parent's ability to meet the needs of the child; the disruption to the child of a change in custody; and the disruption to the child of a move from the family, schools and community that he or she has come to know.

The minority of Mr. Justice La Forest and Madam Justice L'Heureux-Dubé agreed with the result, but their rationale was similar to the reasoning of Madam Justice Abella in the MacGyver case. They held that the notion of custody under the Divorce Act encompassed the right to choose the child's place of residence, although the non-custodial parent had the right to oppose such a choice by seeking a variation of custody. In the absence of explicit restrictions in the custody agreement effectively limiting the geographic location of the child's residence, they said a court must assume that the existing custody order or agreement was in the best interests of the child, and that the appropriate decision-making authority rested with the custodial parent.

The next month, in June 1996, a majority of a five-judge panel of the Ontario Court of

Appeal upheld a trial decision (*Woodhouse v. Woodhouse*) that refused to allow a mother to move to Scotland with her new husband and the children. While leaving the children in their mother's custody, the judge restricted the children's residence to certain parts of Ontario.

Currently, then, where does the law stand? Although the onus shifted briefly to require the access parent to prove a move would harm the child, the majority of the Supreme Court have held that the onus remains on the custodial parent to prove positively that the move will benefit the child. This ruling may help the access parent, but likely at the expense of the custodial parent. Because the law in this area is so fluid and dependent on the facts in each case, a parent considering a move should consult a lawyer before making any assumptions or final arrangements.

7. Denial of Access

Access orders and agreements must be made to work by both parents on a continuing basis. The custodial parent must encourage and facilitate the active involvement of the access parent; the access parent must be careful not to undermine the custodial parent. When they cannot sustain these lofty goals, the courts may be asked to step in to try to resolve differences.

Custodial parents can have many reasons for limiting the other parent's access or involvement, but they usually persuade themselves that they are acting in the children's best interests. Some custodial parents feel betrayed by the other spouse and react by involving the children in their anger and hurt; the children then express the

anger as their own to the access parent. Sometimes, custodial parents intentionally sabotage access to punish the ex-mate, or they may simply wish the schedule of visits to suit their own convenience. In a 1997 Ontario case a mother was found to have attempted to alienate three children, ages twelve, seven and three, from their father, to the extent that their mental stability was affected. She was in other respects considered a "loving and caring" parent, but one who "smothered" the children. The court also pointed to the "strong bond" between mother and children. The mother was allowed to retain custody, so long as she co-operated with the children's counselling and attended the sessions at the request of the counsellor; but the father was given the responsibility for the children's mental health, including choice of therapist, and also awarded extended access periods.

In another case, an Ontario court in 1999 awarded the father custody based on an assessor's report that concluded that unless the eight-year-old child was removed from the mother's care for a period of time, the father would have no meaningful participation in the child's life. The court stressed that it was in the best interests of the child to have involvement with both parents.

These cases demonstrate how wrenching it is for the court to deal with cases in which one or both parents engage in a tug-of-war over their children, and why sometimes the custody must be shifted to promote the best interests of the children.

Alternatively, the custodial parent may have good reason to worry about the access parent's behaviour and its impact on a child—alcoholism, abuse and an inability to take proper care are all valid reasons to wish to limit access. In some cases, the access parent may be using his or her time with the children as an opportunity to win them over as allies in a war against the custodial parent. As this manipulation can wreak emotional havoc on the children, who cannot cope with their conflicting loyalties to both parents, the custodial parent may wish to protect them from this treatment. Sometimes, however, these reasons for limiting access are used without foundation. It is up to the court to sort the situation out, sometimes with the help of an assessment by a social worker, psychologist or psychiatrist.

The legal options available to the courts are drastic ones, and must be balanced against the best interests of the child. Custodial parents who deny access can jeopardize their continued custody, if transferring custody is the only way to ensure reasonable access to the non-custodial parent. If custodial parents breach an order for access without excellent reasons, the court may find them in contempt, and may fine them or, in an extreme case, imprison them. Some of the parents have been jailed in the past up to ten days for contempt of access orders. Occasionally, a custodial parent may lose spousal support as punishment for denying access, if the loss of this income does not adversely affect the child. Child support is rarely cut off as a form of punishment because the child suffers as a result.

Access visits are not always perfect. For any number of reasons, children sometimes become upset before, during or after a visit to the other parent, and some custodial parents are quick to blame their ex-spouse. But a court will not deny access just because a child came home cranky, was given too much chocolate, did not sleep well or had the occasional nightmare.

Indeed, a court will deny access only in the most serious circumstances: abuse of a child; a child's emotional panic at the prospect of a visit, so severe that it will clearly cause serious damage to the child's health; a parent who uses the visits to brainwash a child against the other parent; a parent who is unable to care for the child, perhaps due to mental illness, alcoholism or severe disability.

These grounds must be proven—not always an easy task. For example, at one extreme, a parent who alleges sexual abuse by the other parent may run the risk of losing the child if the allegation is not proven. However, at the other extreme, a parent who is suspicious but reluctant to allege abuse may be labelled a poor parent for not raising these concerns immediately. There are many possible scenarios between these two extremes.

As sexual abuse cannot always be proven, access can sometimes be denied on other grounds. For example, in several cases the father was denied access, even though allegations of sexual abuse could not be proven, because the child's behaviour was permanently affected by the visits, and demonstrated significant problems in the relationship.

In a 1995 Nova Scotia case, the Court of Appeal terminated a father's access to his four-year-old daughter, who had told her mother about incidents that appeared to indicate sexual abuse. The child later testified at trial that the incidents were only dreams. However, the Court said that the father's spankings, which caused an injury to the child's anus, violated the girl both physically and emotionally. The Court added that the father's harsh and authoritarian style of parenting was harmful to a child he knew was emotionally fragile. A child abuse expert had recommended termination of access, and the Court of Appeal agreed.

An Ontario father lost his access to his three-year-old daughter since, despite a generous schedule, he failed to visit at least 70 percent of the time, with no explanation. The father's infrequent visits "allowed their attachment to wither away," according to the judge, who agreed with the mother's concern that the visits were so sporadic that the child was basically spending time with a stranger.

The law in some provinces imposes specific sanctions on a parent who wrongfully denies access. Unless the denial is justified, a custodial parent can be ordered to provide compensatory access and reimburse the access parent for reasonable expenses as a result of the denial. In addition, a custodial parent may claim court intervention when the other parent fails to exercise access (because of, for example, baby-sitting costs) or has not returned the child as ordered.

8. Separate Legal Representation of Children

Although children are not legally parties to their parents' divorce action, they are greatly affected by the result. If parents cannot agree on custody and the courts must decide what is best for the child, the children's interests are usually represented by their parents and their parents' lawyers. However, in some hotly disputed cases, neither the husband's nor the wife's lawyer can represent the child because the adults' interests may conflict with those of the child. Therefore, an independent lawyer for the child will assist in the decision-making process.

The role of the child's lawyer in a divorce action is not clear-cut. Does the lawyer represent the child's wishes, or what the lawyer regards as the child's needs and interests? This question leads to others. At what age are children capable of expressing wishes? Do the children know what they want, or are they being unduly influenced by the parent with whom they live? Even if children know their feelings, would fulfilling their wishes be in the children's best interests?

Sometimes one parent wishes an advocate appointed for the children because she or he believes the children will repeat what the other parent wants and express it as their own wish. It has been held by a court that it is inappropriate for one parent to retain counsel for a child as there is, at the very least, an appearance of bias that cannot be in the child's best interests.

A lawyer can play three roles:

- **Advocate:** The child must be old enough and mature enough to instruct the lawyer, who then represents his or her views. As an advocate, a lawyer may have to maintain confidentiality, whether or not this is best for the child. In some cases, the child may require this objective advisor.
- **Guardian:** If the child is incapable of giving instructions, the lawyer will act as guardian, representing the child's best interests as she or he sees them. Although this additional point of view may assist the court, it is questionable whether a lawyer is trained to play this role.
- **Friend of the Court:** The lawyer acts as a neutral fact-finder to assist the judge.

Whatever role the lawyer takes, the judge ultimately determines what is in the best interests of the child. Even without legal representation, a child's wishes have long been considered relevant. Although not often done, judges may interview a child privately in their chambers in order to find out what the child wants.

Some jurisdictions, including British Columbia, provide specifically for an advocate for children in their legislation. A lawyer appointed by the attorney general may assist at custody, maintenance or access hearings, or intervene at any stage of a court action to act as counsel for the "interests and welfare" of the child.

In other jurisdictions, such as Ontario, New Brunswick, and Newfoundland and Labrador, legislation provides for the right of a child to be heard, including through a spokesperson called different names in different places—sometimes "official guardian," sometimes "child and youth advocate" or "children's lawyer"—is specifically authorized as the children's separate representative. Appointed by the government, this person has a staff to assist in representing children's interests. In jurisdictions without specific legislation, the court still has the authority to appoint counsel to assist in determining the best interests of the child. Often the children's lawyer in the province fills this role.

In a 1999 Newfoundland and Labrador case a judge ordered the province's Justice Department to fund independent counsel for a four-year-old girl caught in a high-conflict custody dispute, which included allegations that the father had sexually molested the girl.

9. Abduction of Children

Parental abduction of children is a growing problem, contributing to the overall rise in child abductions. If a parent has real concerns about a possible abduction, he or she should consider preventive measures, including restricting access to and use of a passport for the child. When parents are separated, only the custodial parent may apply for a passport for the child, and must provide all legal documents that refer to custody of, mobility of or access to the child. Under some circumstances, the access parent's signature may be required.

If a court believes that one parent is likely to abduct a child or not return the child after an access visit, it can make orders to effect the return of the child to its place of habitual residence. It can restrain the issuance of a passport to the custodial parent or require either parent to deliver up his or her own passport and the child's passport. A court order may also prohibit border officials from permitting the potential abductor and/or the child from leaving the country. Canada Customs may be notified of a potential abduction and asked to facilitate enforcement of an order under its missing children program, called International Project Return.

CRIMINAL SANCTIONS

If parents do abduct a child under the age of 14, they can be charged with kidnapping under the Criminal Code in the following circumstances:

- They refuse to return the child after an access visit.

- They take and detain the child out of the city in which the child lives, contrary to an access agreement or order. This may apply to a custodial parent who breaches an agreement not to remove the child from the jurisdiction without the consent of the access parent.
- They remove the child from the lawful parent's charge without consent, even when the court has not issued an order for custody.

If abducting parents are found and convicted of kidnapping, they can be punished with up to ten years in prison. To avoid a conviction, they would have to prove that they took the child with the other parent's consent, or without knowing that an order was in place and therefore without intending to violate the order or deprive the other parent of the right to custody. Alternatively, the abducting parent would have to prove that he or she took the child to protect the child from "danger of imminent harm."

INTERNATIONAL ABDUCTIONS

A parent may decide to remove a child to another jurisdiction, often the parent's country of origin, hoping to be in a stronger position to obtain a custody order in his or her favour. If the child is under the age of 16, a custodial parent may gain assistance from the Hague Convention on the Civil Aspects of International Child Abduction. The Hague Convention is in force throughout Canada and has been ratified by many other countries, including the United States. A current list of the contracting states and signatories may be obtained from the federal Department of Justice.

The Hague Convention's primary objective is to implement the safe return of abducted children to the state in which they were habitually resident before the abduction. The term "habitually resident" is not defined in the agreement. In a 1994 case, the Supreme Court of Canada interpreted this term to mean the place the child lived before the breakdown of the marriage. One parent cannot unilaterally change the child's residence by surreptitiously relocating the child. A court must consider both the duration of the child's stay in a new place and the intention of the parent with the right to decide the child's place of residence.

The Hague Convention will not make custody decisions, but will enforce existing custody rights. Wrongful removal is determined in accordance with the laws of the state where the child was habitually resident. When the court finds that there has been a wrongful removal, it must automatically order the return of the child, unless the person opposing the return can prove the situation falls within one of the exceptions for which provisions have been made. If the child is found in a participating country, that country must co-operate in the return of the child unless one of the following exceptions holds true:

- More than one year has passed, and the country's court determines that the child is "now settled in its new environment."
- The parent attempting to obtain the return did not have custody at the time of the abduction, or consented or acquiesced to removal or retention of the child.
- The child would be exposed to grave physical or psychological risk if returned.

- The child's human rights or fundamental freedoms would be threatened if returned.
- The child refuses to return, and the court considers him or her old enough and sufficiently mature to have a say. (No age is specified in the Convention.)

In 1996, the Supreme Court of Canada considered the application of these exceptions and held that they must be interpreted narrowly. In that particular case, the father, who had interim custody, moved from the United States to Quebec with the child without notifying the mother. The mother subsequently obtained an order for custody in the United States, in the father's absence. One year later, the father brought a motion in Quebec for custody, and the mother responded by requesting the child's return under the Hague Convention. The father argued that the child was settled in her new environment; however, the Court held that it was in the child's best interests to return her to her mother.

In 1995, the Manitoba Court of Appeal held that the provisions of the Hague Convention were to be applied separately to each child. In this case, after the separation, the mother wrongfully removed two children from England where the family had moved and where the youngest child was born. The eldest child, who was adopted by the husband after the marriage, suffered from spina bifida. No one disputed that the return to England presented a grave risk of psychological harm to the elder child, who felt suicidal at the thought of going back. Nonetheless, the Court considered the children separately, without regard to their relationship to each other, and concluded that since the return to England did not expose the younger child to any physical or psychological risk, she should be returned while the elder could remain in Canada.

A British Columbia court ruled that a mother who removed her children from the United Kingdom to Canada put unacceptable pressure on them when she repeatedly told them that she would not return with them to the U.K. if they were ordered back. Not surprisingly, both children expressed a desire to remain in Canada. Even though the eldest, who was ten, was entitled to have her views considered, the court ordered the children back to the United Kingdom to the father. It held that the mother could not be permitted to create a situation where the children could suffer psychological harm, and then rely on that situation to uphold her wrongful removal.

In 2001, a Canadian-born Israeli mother of eight tried to find safety in Canada from Jerusalem's terrorist threats for her three youngest children. In response to a court application by her Israeli husband, the Toronto court found her to be in breach of her custody agreement and the Hague Convention, and ordered her to return the children—aged 11, 12 and 14—to Israel.

There have been a few cases under the Hague Convention in which Canadian courts have allowed a parent fleeing with a child to remain in Canada. In a 1999 case a mother fled California with her child to seek the support of her family in Ontario. The husband initially succeeded in gaining an order for the child's return to California. On appeal, however, the court found on the facts that there was evidence to establish the estranged husband had a history of significant spousal abuse and had put the child in danger due to his abuse of drugs and alcohol and his lack of basic parenting skills. The court agreed that, while the Hague Convention does not determine ultimate custody, it does allow some discretion in assessing the interests and circumstances particular to each child. Here it was found unacceptable to return the child to a violent situation that exposed him to physical and psychological risks.

Each jurisdiction in Canada has designated a Central Authority responsible for enforcing its obligations under the Hague Convention, generally the Department of the Attorney General or the minister of justice. A person claiming a child has been wrongfully removed should contact his Central Authority for assistance. If the Central Authority believes that the child is in another contracting state, they must apply to its counterpart in that state, who must co-operate to seek the voluntary return of the child.

If necessary, the Central Authority where the child is believed to be must take appropriate measures to locate the child; take measures to prevent further harm to the child or prejudice to interested parties; initiate proceedings to obtain the return of the child; and make arrangements for his or her safe return.

If the applicant cannot afford legal counsel, she may be entitled to legal aid. As well, some states do not charge the applicant with the costs and expenses of legal proceedings, including the participation of lawyers or advisors. However, the cost of legal proceedings does not necessarily include the expense of returning the child. A parent may be able to obtain some assistance from the Transportation Program of Abducted Children. Under this program, Air Canada and Canadian Airlines provide free return airfare for the parent and child returning to the state of habitual residence, assuming they fly there.

The costs to procure the return of a child, even with co-operation between states, can be substantial, particularly if the child must first be located. The person who wrongfully removed him or her may be ordered to pay some or all of the above costs. In a 1984 case, a mother successfully sued a father for damages when he abducted their child to Australia. Damages were awarded on the basis of an intentional infliction of emotional distress, a violation of her legal rights by the kidnapping of her two-year-old son and a breach of the Ontario Children's Law Reform Act.

If a parent cannot use the Hague Convention, and does not know the location of the child, he should seek the assistance of a lawyer in his jurisdiction and his local police department. The police department can report the disappearance to the Missing Children Registry of the RCMP, which will make international inquiries and notify Customs and Immigration Canada. Once the location of the child is known, the parent should contact the Canadian Department of External Affairs and request assistance in obtaining the names of lawyers in the area where the child has been taken. The lawyer can then initiate proceedings, requesting this jurisdiction to recognize the Canadian order or, if necessary, applying for custody of the child there and permission to bring him or her back to Canada.

These remedies are only as effective as the degree of co-operation between jurisdictions, including contracting states to the Hague Convention. Countries are sometimes less than willing to assist in child abduction cases. Some parents, returning to their country of origin with their abducted children, have been able to garner support from their local community and sometimes even the judicial system to prevent the children's return. Continued pressure at the international level is needed to protect the rights of abducted children.

C. PROPERTY DIVISION

1. Sharing the Assets

Until 1978, spouses had no right anywhere in Canada to claim, by virtue of their marital status, a share of any property accumulated during their marriage. It is a measure of the vast changes in the law of family property that there is now no place in Canada where a married person cannot claim a fair share of the family's assets.

There is no federal property law that applies across Canada; by constitutional law, property is a matter for provincial jurisdiction. All provinces and territories have laws that require spouses to share assets when a marriage breaks down, but the rules differ in every jurisdiction and can be complex to interpret. It is not possible to say simplistically that "everything is 50–50."

In fact, not all assets are shared in every jurisdiction; nor is every asset split equally. Sharing can mean getting title to a share of the assets, or it can mean a payment representing a share of the value. The treatment of the matrimonial home differs depending on where the spouses made their home. Legislation may mandate various exclusions and deductions from sharing. The authority of judges to exercise their discretion to vary legislated divisions also differs. However, the general direction of the law

seems to be to share the family wealth, and the onus is usually on those who do not want to share equally to bring their situation within the exceptions permitted by a province's legislation.

Generally, title governs ownership throughout Canada during marriage, and rights to share in property in the other spouse's name do not arise until separation, when the provincial and territorial laws come into play. Some of these laws permit a judge to take individual factors into account, such as the length of the marriage, the duration of separation, a spouse's contribution to assets in the other spouse's name, the contribution of each spouse to the marriage and welfare of the family, including as homemaker or parent, and any dissipation of assets by one of the spouses.

If all the assets are in joint names, each spouse has the rights of any titled owner of property. However, since one of the spouses usually has title to a greater share of the assets, the other spouse must make a legal claim to have a chance at receiving a share of the titled spouse's assets or a share of their value on separation. Negotiations often resolve matters, and the parties sign a separation agreement. However, if agreement cannot be reached, the claim must proceed through litigation, relying on the matrimonial property law in the jurisdiction where the spouses reside.

LIMITATION PERIODS

Most provinces provide time limitations, after the marriage breaks down, and the parties separate, within which a spouse must apply to claim a share of property in the other spouse's name. For this reason, spouses should either agree on a date of separation or be able to substantiate their chosen date. The date of separation is also important in many provinces because it is the date at which the assets to be shared are valued. It is important to check the law in each jurisdiction as limitation periods for sharing property may vary from 60 days to two years from the date a divorce becomes final. In the Yukon, application must be made before spouses obtain the divorce judgment.

If spouses separate and do not divorce, limitation periods may still apply, some allowing two to six years for a property claim. In Ontario for example, spouses have two years from the date of the divorce or six years from the date of separation, whichever comes first, to apply for the property division. Although some jurisdictions do allow for extensions, they do so only in very limited circumstances, so applications should be made before the last moment, particularly if one spouse suspects that the other will not agree on the date of separation.

PROPERTY-SHARING

The laws in most jurisdictions allow for extensive sharing of assets on separation. In general, the value of all assets, whether used for family or for business purposes, is shareable upon separation, subject to various deductions by each spouse: the value of property owned at the date of marriage, the value of property acquired by gift or inheritance, a damage award for personal injury and payments under a life insurance policy.

Some jurisdictions limit sharing to family assets. However, what constitutes family assets in these jurisdictions varies. These jurisdictions begin with the premise that only those assets used and enjoyed by the family are shared, such as the family home, cottage, cars, and that the court has a discretion to also require that business and other assets also be shared, especially where the non-titled spouse made a direct or indirect contribution to its acquisition. Quebec, for example, specifies pensions as family assets.

How these assets will be shared depends on the court, which means that entitlement is less certain and predictable.

In 1994, for example, the B.C. Court of Appeal overturned a trial judge's decision that awarded a traditional wife and mother in her forties, after a 17-year marriage and three children, a standard 50 percent share of the couple's main asset—the matrimonial home. The husband, a letter carrier, lost his job, defaulted in his modest child support payments and then cashed in his pension and kept all the proceeds for himself. The Court of Appeal upheld the trial decision that the home could not be sold until the children had moved out (the youngest was then eight) and gave the wife a 75 percent interest in it. In doing so, the Court acknowledged that, without the wife's contribution of her inheritances during the marriage, totalling $97,000, the couple would not even have this asset.

Even in jurisdictions with the most restrictive sharing of assets on separation, where normally little discretion is allowed in defining the family assets to be shared, a court may exempt from sharing property owned at the date of marriage, or property acquired by one spouse as a gift from the other spouse or a third party, or damage awards from personal injuries, proceeds of life insurance and personal effects. It is best for spouses who are separating to get legal advice on how the law in their jurisdiction applies the sharing of assets and their value. What is certain is that there is no *automatic* "50–50 sharing" as some people assume so it is essential to get legal advice tailored to an individual's own situation.

HOW SHARING IS ACCOMPLISHED

Whether or not spouses have their name on title to the assets and depending on the jurisdiction, sharing is accomplished either by dividing the assets themselves or a share of the proceeds from their sale, or by sharing the value of the assets.

2. Matrimonial Home

The matrimonial home is often a couple's main asset, and therefore receives special treatment and protection during the marriage and on separation. In general, a spouse is not allowed to sell or mortgage a matrimonial home without the consent of the other spouse or a court order—no matter whose name is on title. As divorce usually ends this limitation, a separated spouse should not wait until after divorce to register a legal claim.

In most jurisdictions, a married or separated person may (and, if fraud is suspected, should) put potential buyers or mortgage lenders on notice that a property is a matrimonial home by registering a document at the local registry office; thereafter, any dealings with the property will require the consent of both spouses.

Only on separation do many spouses realize the drawback of having permitted a mortgage to be registered against the matrimonial home. They may have agreed for the sake of a loan to benefit the partner's business, which may have no asset value for sharing purposes at the time of separation. Or, perhaps the mortgage was taken to pay off a partner's debts, on the understanding that the partner would be liable to repay the mortgage. However, if the mortgage attaches to the interests of both parties, both are equally liable unless they had an agreement to the contrary, preferably written, or unless the mortgage was signed without benefit of independent legal advice. A spouse who was not advised or not allowed to obtain independent legal advice may be successful in avoiding any obligation, but the victory could be at great expense.

Although most provinces tend to limit the shareable assets to those accumulated during the marriage, a number of jurisdictions provide that the entire value of the matrimonial home is shared—even if one spouse owned it and brought it into the marriage. (Certain jurisdictions provide further protection for the matrimonial home, as the next section on gifts and inheritances describes.)

Almost all provinces provide the right for a spouse to apply for exclusive possession of the matrimonial home and its contents on separation. British Columbia gives the spouses a one-half interest in the home as tenants-in-common on separation, irrespective of how title is registered. Newfoundland and Labrador goes even further: Notwithstanding how title is registered, on marriage a matrimonial home is deemed to be held in joint tenancy with rights of survivorship on death, and is not subject to division the way the rest of the assets are.

In a 1994 B.C. case, a woman was successful in retaining a matrimonial home registered in her name for herself and four of her six children still at home. She and her husband had separated in 1988 after a 20-year traditional marriage. It was not long before he stopped paying support, and at the time of the trial was $18,500 in arrears. The woman worked in a low-paying job and had the sole responsibility for the children, all teenagers. She paid all the expenses for the home, including the $20,000 mortgage taken out to pay off her husband's business debts. Considering these circumstances, the court ruled that the home, estimated to be worth about $150,000, should be entirely hers to ensure the security and independence of herself and her children.

3. Gifts and Inheritances

Even in provinces where most assets are shareable, there are still exceptions. Most jurisdictions allow spouses to exclude or deduct the value of assets that they received during the marriage by way of gift or inheritance from someone other than the other spouse, so long as the asset was intended to benefit the recipient alone. The rationale behind the equal sharing of assets accumulated during the marriage is to recognize the contributions of both spouses to each asset. Since spouses do not usually contribute to a gift or inheritance during the marriage, this type of asset is generally not shareable. The onus is on the spouse claiming the exemption to prove it. Some provinces value the property at the date it was acquired and some fix its value at the date of separation.

In those few jurisdictions where there is no specific provision for excluding or deducting gifts or inheritances, the law still gives a judge general discretion to determine if sharing such assets would be unfair or inequitable.

The matrimonial home is often treated as a special asset, which many provinces have protected from the claims of a spouse for an exemption from sharing the matrimonial home because it was purchased partly or entirely from gifts or inheritances received only by one spouse.

Since not only the rules but the definitions can vary from place to place, it is best for spouses to seek legal advice if any of the family's assets were originally received as a gift or inheritance. In general, the best way for spouses to ensure that a gift or inheritance remains their sole property is to either spend it on themselves during the marriage or keep it separate from other assets, particularly the matrimonial home. They can also enter into a marriage contract.

4. "Non-Family" or Business Assets

In addition to assets normally used by the family, other assets accumulated during the marriage may be shareable, depending on where the spouses reside. Some provinces and territories do not usually provide for an automatic sharing of business assets if they are registered in one spouse's name only. Spouses may be able to claim a share if they show they contributed directly or sometimes indirectly to the business, but they may have to make a case to a judge, who will then use discretion to decide whether the business assets should be shared, or whether the spouse deserves a greater than one-half share of the family assets instead.

A Nova Scotia case heard by its Court of Appeal in 1992 considered a couple's "matrimonial" and "non-matrimonial" assets after a 17-year marriage. The husband appealed the characterization of a number of assets, claiming that they were business and commercial assets and therefore not sharable. The Court of Appeal took a look at how the assets were acquired over the lengthy marriage, and concluded that those assets acquired using income diverted from family assets could be classed as matrimonial property. This category included the husband's stock investments. As this case indicates, the courts generally recognize that most assets accumulated during a marriage require a family's, rather than an individual's, contribution.

Sharing business assets is often a complex matter, especially when a spouse owns an operating business, real estate, a professional practice, a limited partnership or a trust. Sometimes financial statements do not fully disclose the true income and asset values; sometimes there are hidden assets. Professional valuators are often required to fix the value for family law purposes. In complex cases, however, it is frequently the valuation issues that cannot be settled and that push the parties to trial.

5. Employment-Related Assets

Aside from pensions and RRSPs, other employment-related assets may be shareable: severance packages; accrued severance allowance, retirement allowance or termination allowance (generally applicable to government employees); accrued vacation pay; some disability pensions; profit-sharing plans; insurance renewal commissions; accumulated sick leave, where available; pay equity settlements attributable to the marriage period; air travel points; and survivor benefits when a member spouse retires before separation. Spouses should consult a lawyer to see whether any of the above assets apply in their case.

6. Lottery Winnings

What if a spouse wins a lottery? Are the winnings shareable? Although this used to be an uncommon occurrence, more and more cases are coming before the courts as a result of the increase in government-sponsored lotteries. In fact, in recent years, the courts in almost all the provinces and territories have dealt with claims by married and common-law spouses to share in a partner's lottery winnings.

In one of the early cases, a 1995 Alberta court held that the winnings were shareable. In that case, it was found that the decision to play the lotteries was a family decision, and that therefore each member should share in the good fortune, no matter who actually purchased the ticket. Even if the purchase was not a family decision, the ticket-holder may be required to share the proceeds with his or her spouse if the ticket was acquired through joint family funds. On the other hand, if the ticket was a gift and the spouse kept the winnings separate from other property, then they might fall under the exceptions for gifts or inheritances, as previously described.

In two 1998 Alberta cases, and another one in 2004, when the husband received multiple millions in lottery winnings after separation, the court ordered the husband to pay the wife 25 percent of the winnings.

In a 2000 Ontario case when the winning ticket was bought prior to separation, the wife received the benefit of one-half of the winnings. The same result was ordered in a 2000 Saskatchewan case, when one of the spouses after dropping off the other spouse at work went to check the lottery ticket against the winning numbers, found she had won and promptly moved out. She was ordered to pay her partner one-half of the winning sum.

How the winnings are used is important. A New Brunswick case in 1991 held that, since the spouse who won did not make a point of keeping the winnings separate or acting as if they were hers alone, it was not inequitable to include them in the matrimonial property of the parties. For winnings to be excluded, they must exist in their original form or be traceable to the acquisition of other property that exists at the date of separation. The onus will be on the spouse claiming the exclusion to prove her or his case.

An important factor in the reported cases was the status of the parties' relationship, that is, whether or not they were separated at the time of the purchase of the winning ticket.

In any event, even if lottery winnings are considered one spouse's property alone, they could still be viewed as an income-producing asset and affect a spouse's ability to support herself or himself or pay spousal or child support. In some cases support awards are available in a lump sum; therefore, it may be possible to claim a lump-sum share of the lottery winnings as support.

7. Private Pensions

Most pension plans are shared in some manner as part of a divorce settlement, but pensions are complex and there are many traps for the unwary, so expert advice is essential.

The law recognizes that both pensions and RRSPs represent a diversion of funds from the family for the family's future benefit. Therefore, the value of the part of these family assets accumulated during the marriage is normally shared on separation.

Basically, there are two types of employer-run pension plans: the defined benefit plan and the money purchase plan. Most require the employer and employee to contribute. Both aim to build up enough capital to generate income to pay the monthly pension payment on retirement. In the defined benefit plan, the monthly retirement payment is fixed in advance, so the appropriate contributions to fund the payments are pre-determined. In the money purchase plan, the ultimate monthly payments are not predetermined; the employer and employee contribute to a fund, similar to an RRSP's accumulation of capital, and on retirement the employee purchases an annuity.

Defined benefit plans are gradually being phased out by employers in favour of defined contribution plans or group RRSPs. Over the last 15 years, the percentage of workers covered by defined benefit plans has fallen from 29 to 21 percent. When interest rates and equity returns declined, companies failed to adjust their funding assumptions, so there was insufficient funds in the private plans. Corporate balance sheets did not reflect the liability to pensioners, if there was a shortfall in the pension plan. The companies once assumed that if there was a surplus in the plan, the company would get the benefit. However, that changed when the Supreme Court of Canada in 2004 ruled in the *Monsanto* case that when there is a partial windup of a company, the pension surpluses must be distributed to the defined benefit plan members, and not to the companies.

Unlike most other assets, a pension is not "marketable"—the employee cannot sell it or pledge an interest in it by using it as collateral for a loan, nor can creditors access it to pay liabilities.

DEFINING PENSIONS AS PROPERTY

Some provinces specifically include pensions as shareable property. However, others leave the courts to determine whether and in what way a pension can be shared, and whether to consider it when determining spousal support or an unequal division of family assets.

SHARING THE PENSION'S VALUE

There are different approaches to sharing the pension's value:

Sharing Pension Credits: This option gives the spouse of a pension-holder his or her own separate pension plan, created by splitting off half of the spouse's pension. For example, provinces such as British Columbia, Saskatchewan, Manitoba, Quebec, New Brunswick, Nova Scotia, Newfoundland and Labrador, and the federal jurisdiction have laws that specifically permit this transfer of the pension credits in certain circumstances.

Receiving a Lump-Sum Payment: Some other provinces and territories give a spouse the right to a part of the value of a spouse's pension in the form of a lump-sum payment, actuarially calculated. Even in provinces with the shared credits option, the court might instead order a lump sum, especially if

the marriage has been short or the employee spouse is not close to retirement. This option also provides the parties with more of a clean break.

Dividing Pension Payments: The third option is for each pension payment to be divided when the pensioner receives it. The court imposes a trust on the pensioner spouse to hand over the other spouse's share each month as it is received. This option is chosen in provinces where the law does not allow the plan to split pension credits and where the employee spouse is close to retirement, or where there are no other assets to trade off against the value of the pension. This method of sharing the pension's value is also called an "if and when" division, because the payments are received only if and when the member spouse retires. This option can be risky because the spouse claiming a share has to wait for it and assume the employee spouse will stay in the plan and reach retirement. If the member spouse dies before retirement, the only payment usually available (except for the survivor's pension) is a lump sum representing the total of the member's contributions plus interest.

Although a province may provide for sharing of a pension, there can be many pitfalls if a spouse does not obtain an agreement or order that is in accordance with the pension legislation in the jurisdiction of the member spouse's pension plan, particularly if the member spouse predeceases the non-member spouse. Otherwise, the spouse claiming a share might end up having to make a claim against the other's estate. This happened in a case heard by the B.C. Court of Appeal in 1995. The couple entered into an agreement to share the husband's pension equally when the husband received it. They did so until the husband died and the pension plan refused to make any payments to the wife as the survivor. She successfully sued the husband's estate for damages, on the basis of the husband's failure to ensure that she would continue getting half the pension by maintaining her as joint and last survivor beneficiary. Fortunately for her, the estate had assets available to make good on her claim.

If the parties have agreed on an "if and when" division of each pension payment, but on retirement the member spouse takes the whole amount, the other spouse may still be able to obtain payments by registering a claim for spousal support. The court will usually consider the pension income when determining the support to be paid, but in some cases, will consider it unfair for a recipient to get both a lump sum based on the value of the pension and spousal support too. The courts call this "double-dipping." This issue was reviewed by a number of judges in different cases, all with different results.

The Supreme Court of Canada is the court to provide leadership when there are inconsistent results in the lower courts. The Supreme Court of Canada in the 1999 case of *Best* v. *Best* permitted double-dipping. However, in the Supreme Court of Canada's 2001 ruling in the case of *Boston* v. *Boston* the Court did not permit double-dipping, but said there were times when it was appropriate.

In the Boston case, the ex-husband challenged a spousal support order that required him to pay $2,000 a month to his former wife, after a 36-year marriage in which she was a homemaker who raised their seven children. Most of his income came from his pension benefits, the lump-sum value of which had already been shared with his former wife. At the time of their settlement, the husband had agreed to pay the wife $3,200 per month in spousal support, indexed annually to the cost of living. He applied for a reduction when he retired.

The larger portion of the pension, $5,300 per month, came from assets he retained on equalization, while the smaller portion, $2,300 per month, was earned since separation and not part of the equalization of net family property. The motions judge reduced the amount of monthly support from $3,433.12, indexed, to $950, unindexed. The Ontario Court of Appeal changed this to $2,000 per month, indexed. The Supreme Court of Canada allowed the appeal and reinstated the unindexed award of $950 a month.

The majority of the Court ruled that the husband's support must be calculated having regard only to the pension income that was not considered in the distribution of matrimonial property, and that the court should avoid double recovery "where practicable." But the court went on to say that double recovery cannot always be avoided, and the income from a pension may be ordered shared with an ex-spouse when the payor has the ability to pay, where the payee has made a reasonable effort to use equalized assets to produce income, and despite this, still suffers economic hardship. The Court made a distinction between support paid as compensation and support paid as a result of need.

Madam Justice Claire L'Heureux-Dubé and Mr. Justice LeBel dissented, regarding the situation as a straightforward matter of the assessment of the needs and means of the former spouses, and argued that "all income streams are relevant" in this assessment.

SURVIVOR'S PENSION

A person whose spouse dies while receiving a "joint and survivor" pension usually gets a survivor pension worth 60 percent of the amount the member received. A separated spouse may also be entitled to a survivor's pension, depending on a number of factors, including the date of separation, the date of retirement, priorities of competing beneficiaries (a new or common-law spouse, for example), the type of pension plan, the elections that a member spouse chose on retirement, the effect of any orders or agreements and the by-laws governing the specific plan.

To have a chance at a survivor's pension, a spouse must make sure the pension settlement is resolved before the divorce. Once divorced (and, in some jurisdictions, once separated), the non-member may lose status as a "spouse" for the purposes of the pension plan, and with it the rights to surviving spouse benefits or death benefits.

8. Canada and Quebec Pension Plans

In most provinces, spouses are entitled to share CPP or QPP credits accumulated during their period of cohabitation. The Canada Pension Plan Act provides for mandatory division of pension credits between spouses on marriage breakdown unless a province chooses to opt out and allow spouses to contract out of this equal sharing. At the time of writing, only three provinces, British Columbia, Saskatchewan and Quebec, had chosen to pass legislation to allow spouses to contract out of this equal sharing. It is important to check the law where the spouses reside. If there is no opting-out legislation in that jurisdiction, sharing the CPP credits is mandatory, whether or not the parties sign an agreement to the contrary. In a 1993 case before the Federal Court of Canada, the judge confirmed, despite the terms of an Alberta couple's separation agreement, that they were not at liberty to contract out of the pension credit split under the Canada Pension Plan because their province had no legislation allowing them to do so.

9. Unequal Division of Assets

A spouse who contributed directly or indirectly to a business in the other spouse's name, or who may get less because of the other spouse's unreasonable impoverishment or dissipation of the family's assets, may wish to claim more than the basic share allotted to her or him under provincial legislation. For a claim to be successful, a judge must be satisfied that certain criteria set out in the legislation are met.

A judge's discretion may be very broad when it comes to adjusting the division of assets—for example, in some provinces, judges are guided by such terms as "not just and equitable," "unfair" and "inequitable" to award a greater share to one spouse. In other provinces, the legislation limits unequal division or division of assets not normally shared, and guides judges by terms such as "grossly unfair or unconscionable." Although a spouse's conduct is generally not included as a factor, if the spouse deliberately dissipated an asset, or transferred the asset to a third party for less than it was worth, the judge may take this conduct into consideration.

In making an unequal division or a sharing of business assets in addition to family assets, the law in some provinces sets out considerations such as the following:

- A contribution, whether financial or otherwise, by a spouse either directly or indirectly to the acquisition, conservation, improvement, management, etc., of an asset owned by the other spouse
- The terms of an agreement between the spouses
- Any dissipation of the property by a spouse

A 1995 Ontario case effectively gave an unequal division in favour of the husband because of his disproportionate contribution to the home and family. The wife left the jointly owned home and for 17 years the husband paid all the expenses, including a mortgage, and fully supported the children, aged ten and eight at the time of separation. When the wife claimed half the home 17 years later, the court rejected her claim and ruled that the husband was entitled to the wife's interest. In 1994, the B.C. Court of Appeal reapportioned the husband's share of the matrimonial home in favour of the wife for several reasons: four of their six children lived in the house with her; his support contribution was minimal; she was paying the home's expenses, including the mortgage, which had been raised to cover the husband's accumulated business debts.

10. Effect of Bankruptcy

If a spouse is in precarious financial shape, each spouse should obtain legal advice from a bankruptcy specialist before drafting the agreement. If a spouse later declares bankruptcy, the terms of the agreement may be important if creditors claim that the division of property is a fraudulent conveyance.

For example, disputes with creditors are a potential problem when an unemployed spouse signs over his or her share of the home to the other spouse as some security in lieu of regular support.

D. SUPPORT

1. Support of Wives

Until recently, the history of spousal support has been the history of support for wives. The accepted convention for much of human history was that husbands supported wives—an understanding based on biological, cultural, economic, religious and practical realities.

Husbands and wives founded families in which the wives bore children and made a home, and the husbands provided an income. With few economic opportunities outside the home, women had little chance for economic self-sufficiency. Contraceptives were primitive or unavailable, so women had little chance to avoid having a large family. Servants were available only to the rich, so most women had to care for their own children. These practical, biological and economic realities took on the force of cultural and religious axiom.

The legal struggle has primarily been to define the support obligation of the husband as financial provider to the wife as family manager. (In the last 30 years, however, the law has changed so that husbands in need can claim support from wives with means, as the next section describes.)

FACTORS IN SUPPORT

The law came from a time and place when women were entitled to lifetime alimony (which literally means a "pension for food") only if the marriage broke down through no fault of their own; for example, if the husband was deserting, adulterous or brutal. A woman who was considered at fault for the marriage breakdown (because she committed adultery or deserted her husband, for example) could expect neither support nor custody of her children.

Even when Canada passed its first federal divorce law in 1968, conduct remained one of the factors in determining support, but it became less important. In determining support between 1968 and 1986 under the Divorce Act, the court considered the income, assets, reasonable needs and expenses of both the wife and husband. The effort has been to compensate a spouse who, in a marriage's traditional division of labour, took on most of the child-care and household duties, and therefore suffered the financial brunt of the separation.

Once property rights were established starting in 1978, the courts took the value of each spouse's share of the assets into account, and often reduced support payments on the assumption that the receiving spouse therefore had less financial need. Support—sometimes time-limited and often low—usually failed to take into account the inability of a woman who had worked only or primarily in the home to become self-sufficient after the divorce. Judges would assume that if a woman had a job, even a low-paying one, she could take care of herself financially.

After the 1986 amendments to the Divorce Act, the court was required to change the way it ruled in these cases. The amendments called for judges to ignore spousal misconduct and recognize any economic advantages or disadvantages to the spouses arising from the marriage or its breakdown; apportion between the spouses the financial consequences arising from the care of children, over and above an order for child support; relieve any economic hardship of the spouses arising from the breakdown of the marriage; and promote, as far as possible, the economic self-sufficiency of each spouse within a reasonable period of time. Nevertheless, many courts still interpreted the law as requiring them to expect (rather than promote) spouses to support themselves within a reasonable period of time.

COMPENSATORY SUPPORT

In this context, some wives claimed "compensatory support" as a lump sum (in addition to periodic support) to compensate for the overall capital financial loss that the marriage represented to them. When marriages lasted for a lifetime, a woman invested in her husband by, for example, working to put him through school; once she stopped working outside the home to raise their children, his improved income-earning ability was expected to be available for the family. Women usually took a secondary economic role in order to fulfil child-care and home-making responsibilities, even if that meant taking a less demanding position with lower pay or working only part-time. These sacrifices for the family usually reduced a wife's ability to be financially self-sufficient.

Courts across Canada were looking for the right way to compensate women, beyond periodic support, for the economic disadvantage of their traditional role in marriage.

The first cases to award compensatory support gave a lump-sum payment. In 1990, for example, a Unified Family Court in Ontario placed a dollar figure on the wife's future loss of earnings. The woman had been a nurse for the first eight years of her 21-year marriage. The court assessed the cost of the interruption to her career at $103,000, and ordered the husband to pay this amount to her in a lump sum.

But, in a 1993 case, the Ontario Court of Appeal moved in a different direction when it overturned a trial judgment awarding a woman who stayed home to care for the children $75,000 in compensation for future loss of income. The Court of Appeal termed the lump sum payment "crystal ball gazing," since it involved speculating about the future. The Court reasoned that the asset to be shared was the husband's uninterrupted career path. As his only means of paying was through his income from employment, the wife should share in this stream of income. Accordingly, the Court awarded her support of $1,000 per month indefinitely. Since this ruling, the courts have generally awarded indefinite periodic spousal support as compensation.

THE MOGE CASE

The spousal support case that gave direction to all Canadian courts was the 1992 Supreme Court of Canada landmark decision of *Moge* v. *Moge*. This case held that it was unreasonable to expect total self-sufficiency from a long-time homemaker, usually the wife, who quit working or never worked, and lost skills, income, seniority, benefits and opportunity in order to look after a family. Madam Justice Claire L'Heureux-Dubé, writing for the Court, stipulated that self-sufficiency was only one factor in the support award, and that this interpretation of support law had contributed to the feminization of poverty in Canada.

It all started when Andrzej Moge, a welder by trade who had been paying support to his ex-wife for 16 years, went back to court in 1989, wanting to stop the $150 monthly payments because he thought his ex-wife should have become self-supporting. He earned $2,200 gross per month. Zofia Moge was a part-time cleaner who had raised their three children, was earning $804 gross per month at the time of trial and had a Grade 7 education. Manitoba trial judge Joseph Mullally terminated spousal support with these words: "She cannot expect that Mr. Moge will support her forever."

The Manitoba Court of Appeal disagreed in 1990, saying that she could not be totally independent because her marriage had diminished her earning potential and she was entitled to a subsidy. The Supreme Court of Canada agreed.

Madam Justice L'Heureux-Dubé's decision drew on an important federal justice study, released earlier in 1992, that proved women suffer a significant and lasting reduction in their earning capacity when they interrupt their careers—even for a short time. The study concluded that the average woman of 35 who returned to work after five years as a full-time homemaker would lose $50,000 in future earnings. The amount of the loss would increase with age and length of time out of the work force.

The Supreme Court ruled that husbands are obliged to compensate their wives when marriage responsibilities erode their earning ability. This compensation, in the form of periodic or lump-sum support, may be in addition to a division of property and monthly spousal support. It is based on the wife's needs and the husband's ability to pay, and must be paid even if the wife works outside the home full- or part-time.

When courts are determining the amount of spousal support, the Supreme Court ruled that they should consider both the immediate and future impact when a woman leaves the work force, or works part-time, to care for children. What the Divorce Act requires, the Court said, is a fair and equitable distribution of resources to alleviate the economic consequences of marriage or marriage breakdown.

Relying on the Moge decision, courts across Canada began awarding spousal support in higher amounts, for longer periods of time and more frequently to women who assumed a traditional role of wife and mother in marriage. Courts have increasingly recognized economic disadvantage as a basis for awarding compensatory spousal support. Depending on the length of the marriage, the ages of the spouses and the relative income positions of the parties on separation, awards may be made for a fixed term or for an indefinite term. Courts are reluctant to limit the term of the award unless they can be satisfied that a wife needs assistance only in retraining and/or re-establishing her previous position in the work force in order to achieve economic independence.

However, even in similar cases, judges can come up with different results. In 1999, a 39-year-old wife with custody of two children asked the Ontario Court of Appeal to remove the five-year time limit imposed at trial on her spousal support of $30,000 per year. Her husband was a partner in a major law firm while she had a Grade 12 education and had not worked outside the home for the last eight years of the 13-year marriage. The appeal court found the lower court had placed too much emphasis on the wife's self-sufficiency in light of her need to supervise the children into their late teens. Instead of removing the time limit, however, they merely extended it for a further four years.

On the other hand, a nurse who gave up several jobs to accommodate her RCMP husband's postings was found by a Nova Scotia court in 1994 to have sacrificed her nursing career and to be at an entry-level position in the job market. Since she had lost her job security and her future was uncertain, the court refused to place a time limit on the duration of her support.

Spousal support has been extended to "top up" the modest income of secondary wage-earners in newer forms of traditional marriages. In 1998, in examining a 13-year marriage in which both spouses worked, an Ontario judge relied on the Moge case to conclude that the wife had been economically disadvantaged and was entitled to $400 per month in spousal support, with no time limit. He attributed the fact that the wife assumed the primary care for the parties' two children as one of the major causes of her income being half that of her husband's.

Courts recently have been more willing to make higher awards of spousal support. In the 1999 Ontario case of *Andrews* v. *Andrews*, a husband earning $200,000 appealed a trial court order requiring him to pay spousal and child support that left the wife and children with 60 percent of the parties' total disposable income. The wife was earning $5,000 per year and had responsibility for the parties' three children, two of whom had special needs. In upholding the trial-level decision, the Court of Appeal reasoned that her 17-year marriage had left the wife economically disadvantaged.

SPECIAL CASES

Generally speaking, courts have been unwilling to place a time limit on support awards to wives with limited education, low-paying employment, illness or disabilities. For example, in a 1996 case the Manitoba Court of Appeal ruled that ex-spouses who cannot support themselves due to health problems that occurred during the marriage are entitled to indefinite rather than fixed-term support. The 39-year-old husband, a Winnipeg police officer earning $55,000 per year, was aware when they married that his wife, 38, had multiple sclerosis, which was in remission during most of their 11-year marriage; it flared up just a few weeks before separation and made her permanently disabled. The marriage was childless and both spouses were employed. The Court required the husband to pay her $500 per month indefinitely; in addition, she received about $30,000 a year from disability pensions.

Ontario courts have now extended the husband's obligation to cases where the wives were in good health when the parties separated, but became disabled after their marriages broke down. In 1995, after a seven-year childless marriage, a wife, 43, was awarded $1,000 per month in spousal support for an indefinite period. She was diagnosed with multiple sclerosis two years after the couple separated in 1991, and could not work. The judge ruled that even if a wife's career potential, employability and income-earning capacity were not impaired

during the marriage, support is still appropriate if the wife is sick or disabled. The court based its decision on one of the stated objectives of spousal support under the Divorce Act: to relieve any economic hardship arising from the marriage. The husband earned $63,000 per year. Several other cases followed suit.

In 1999, the Supreme Court of Canada, in the Bracklow case, ruled that seven years of cohabitation followed by three years of marriage was sufficient to establish entitlement to support for a B.C. wife with a history of ongoing health problems. By the time of trial she was totally disabled and not expected to be able to return to work. The Court focused on the parties' financial interdependence during the marriage and the fact that the husband had looked after the wife's needs in the early stages of her illness. It concluded that divorce left her in a state of economic hardship. Having provided this guidance, the judge sent the matter back to the trial level for a determination of the amount and term of support. Taking into consideration the relatively short duration of the marriage, the trial judge awarded spousal support of $400 per month as of March, 1995, for five years, ending in February, 2000. (Mr. Bracklow had been voluntarily paying this amount as of May 1994.) The judge noted, however, that "unforeseen events" such as the wife no longer qualifying for disability pension or the husband losing his job might warrant a review of the order.

SUPPORT FOR HOW LONG?

Courts have increasingly set aside final agreements under the Divorce Act, to reinstate spousal support where need exists. In 1997 the Ontario Divisional Court in the case of *Santosuosso* v. *Santosuosso* threw out a 1987 final settlement that limited a 43-year-old homemaker to two years' support. During the marriage the wife occasionally worked part-time, but following separation she was unable to secure a full-time job due to the recession and her lack of skills. Her former husband was a full-time tenured professor. The Court ordered $500 per month support with no time limit, reasoning the agreement was based on the parties' expectation that the wife would be able to become self-support-ing. Her failure to do so was held to be a "rad-ical unforeseen change in circumstances."

In 2000, in the case of *Bailey* v. *Plaxton*, a wife who agreed to three years' support end-ing in 1990 found herself, after a sincere effort to establish herself in a career, in dan-ger of losing her home. She applied to court for support, including interim support pending the final disposition of her claim. Despite the fact that ten years had elapsed since her support ended, an Ontario judge awarded her $5,000 per month in interim spousal support. The judge found the wife's economic hardship arose from the break-down of the marriage and was allowed to make the order under the Divorce Act notwithstanding the agreement, which was only one factor. She held that the husband was well able to pay the support ordered, pending trial. An appeal by the husband was refused.

These cases indicate a willingness on the part of the courts to re-examine support orders and agreements to ensure their terms remain fair when there has been a radical change in circumstances.

LUMP-SUM SUPPORT

Lump sums are occasionally awarded instead of periodic or monthly allowances. Accepting a lump sum normally means accepting less money overall because of the security of getting the money immediately and all at once, and because it is not taxable. However, courts are reluctant to award lump sums if periodic support is appropri-ate, since lump sums require more specula-tion as to what the future may bring. Spouses should be wary of signing any per-manent settlement for lump-sum support simply to resolve matters quickly and per-haps to save legal costs. If unanticipated cir-cumstances arise, a wife may never be able to claim further financial assistance from her husband. Monthly payments have the advantage of allowing a spouse to apply to court for an increase if personal circum-stances change materially.

A lump sum may have appeal if a woman fears that her ex-husband will not have the money in the future or that she will have trouble collecting support payments from him. However, with support enforcement agencies in every jurisdiction now, collec-tion may be less of a concern.

If the spouse has a history of bad faith and refusal to pay support, a lump sum may be the only answer. In making one of the largest lump-sum awards in Canadian history to address chronic non-payment of support, Ontario justice John R. McIsaac in 1994 (in the case of Verdun and Verdun) awarded a 57-year-old wife $250,000 and stated it was "the only practical way to get deserved spousal support into the [wife's] hands, given the cavalier and twisted attitude of her husband towards his matrimonial responsi-bilities." The court was concerned that an order for periodic payments would "invite further contemptuous refusals to pay . . . . Litigation [would] be endless." The husband had failed to comply with an interim support order of $3,500 per month, saying that he could not afford to pay.

As a result of this trial, the woman kept the home and farm and her husband kept their business interests. Previous average lump-sum awards had been about $50,000.

LUMP SUM FOR RETRAINING

Wives who have put their careers on hold while raising a family may need retraining to contribute to their own support. Husbands have been ordered to pay a lump sum for such educational costs. If it is likely the spouse will be fully self-supporting after the training, any periodic support also ordered may be time-limited or subject to review. On the other hand, if, despite retraining, the wife is unable to become self-supporting and needs full or partial support, the courts have ordered continued payments even after retraining.

SPOUSAL SUPPORT ADVISORY GUIDELINES

Spousal support *advisory* guidelines were issued in 2005 for public debate by the federal government. They are intended only to provide a mechanism by which the fair *amount* of spousal support can be negotiated; they do not deal with entitlement, nor do they change prior agreements or court orders. The advisory guidelines approach traditional long-term marriages with children differently from medium-

length and shorter marriages, and those without children.

Spousal support is calculated by sharing the couple's income, rather than trying to meet budgetary needs. If there are no children, the critical factors are the gross income differential between the spouses and the length of their marriage. If the couple have children, the income-sharing takes into account the fact that child support is being paid and shares the couple's net income after these payments.

The guidelines are not binding. Individuals should not apply these complex guidelines without legal advice.

2. Support of Husbands

The obligation of spousal support after separation is reciprocal in all provinces and territories, as well as under the federal Divorce Act. Although in the majority of cases it is wives who apply for spousal support, husbands have applied for and obtained it as well.

The principles applied by the courts are the same as for the support of wives. In most cases, therefore, if a husband stayed home with the children and lost employability, seniority and other benefits, his working wife would have to provide support for him until he could become self-supporting. In determining the support obligation, the law recognizes that male and female roles in marriage cannot be stereotyped. Just as men are not the only financial providers for the family, so women should not be regarded as exclusively responsible for household management and child care.

Much will depend on whether the husband was economically disadvantaged by the marriage, why he is dependent, whether the dependency was caused by the marriage and whether he is able to contribute to his own support. In our society, in which men have traditionally been breadwinners, few husbands have a financial need for support or wish to assert it. As well, few men have reduced their income-earning capacity because of marriage. At the same time, despite equal pay laws, few wives have enough income to support themselves adequately, much less to support a needy husband.

In some cases, the facts make the decision to award support relatively straightforward. For example, in a 1993 Alberta case where the woman earned over $102,000 per year as a dentist in the armed forces, the couple moved a number of times to accommodate the wife's career, and the husband was not expected to work. The husband was awarded $3,000 per month until he completed his studies in a chiropractic college.

In a 1994 Nova Scotia case, a wife earning $102,000 per year in a senior broadcasting position, with interim custody of the two children, was ordered to pay her husband $1,500 per month in interim support. The husband had left secure employment in Alberta, where he earned $52,000 per year, to move to Halifax for his wife's job. In the three years since the move, he had been unsuccessful in finding employment in his field, and had been spending most of his time looking after the children.

In other cases, the facts are not so clear-cut. Often neither party is well-off. While the husband may need support, the wife's ability to pay may be very limited. In 1993, an Ontario court ordered a 46-year-old wife earning less than $26,000 per year and supporting two children from a previous marriage to pay a lump sum of $4,000 support to her 53-year-old husband who, forced to retire on a disability pension due to serious medical problems, later declared personal bankruptcy.

In a 1994 Ontario case, the wife, a registered nurse, was ordered to pay her unemployed husband $1,350 per month for two years, at which time he would have to prove reasonable efforts to become self-supporting.

Husbands are not always successful in obtaining support from their wives. A husband in the Northwest Territories who took early retirement because he was dissatisfied with his job and wanted to pursue a business opportunity was not granted support. The Court of Appeal ruled that the husband's decline in income did not result from the marriage, but from his decision to retire and pursue the business opportunity.

In 1995, Ontario judge Madam Justice Ellen Macdonald was unsympathetic to a husband's claims that he had suffered an economic disadvantage because he had looked after the children during periods of unemployment. The judge took a close look at the man's employment record, noting that he was often unemployed because either he was dissatisfied with his employment or his employers were dissatisfied with him. His wife urged him to seek retraining, but he refused. The wife did not encourage the husband to quit his jobs; the decisions had nothing to do with the family and were made unilaterally by the husband. Therefore, the wife was not required to support him.

3. Support of Children

Every jurisdiction in Canada requires parents to support their children after separation and divorce. Children's needs are not supposed to fall by the wayside after a couple split up. However, this is precisely what has happened since divorce became more common—child support has not always been consistent or adequate.

Problems in the past usually arose because of faulty assumptions and therefore arbitrary decisions about the financial needs of children, which were sometimes overstated by the custodial parent, understated by the non-custodial parent and arbitrarily defined by a court. The total income of the parents is often insufficient to maintain two households at the same standard of living that existed before separation, so it was unrealistic to expect a spouse to pay support based on an accurate assessment of need. Calculating a spouse's ability to pay based on income is often difficult, particularly for self-employed persons with incorporated businesses. Courts sometimes made unrealistic calculations of the tax impact of child support payments when they were taxable to the recipient and deductible to the payor. Some people were even concerned that if the monthly payments were too high, the payor would not pay or would quit working to avoid paying; but low requirements did not appear to improve the payment rate.

Lawyers and courts used to calculate child support case by case by determining the reasonable needs of the children, each parent's means, the extent to which each parent had the children in his or her care and was paying for their basic expenses, and the children's standard of living before separation

or divorce. A budget was prepared detailing the costs of the children's expenses, such as food, clothing, shelter, transportation, education, lessons, camp, pets and haircuts. In theory, the parents' lawyers or, if matters went to court, a judge would then prorate each parent's contribution to this budget.

In 1989, the House of Commons passed a resolution to eliminate child poverty in Canada by the year 2000. A major cause of child poverty is unacceptably low child support payments after marriage breakdown. In 1991, the federal Justice Department released a report for public discussion on child support. It concluded that the cost of raising children was seriously underestimated by judges, lawyers and the parents themselves, and that, even after support payments, about 66 percent of divorced women and their children had total incomes below the poverty line. When no support was paid, that figure went up to 75 percent. The report also found that the custodial parent's larger contribution of actual nurturing time went unrecognized in financial terms. The report suggested legislative guidelines for child support.

COURT-ESTABLISHED GUIDELINES

While the government studied the issue, courts were also grappling with the problem. In 1994, a special five-judge panel of the Alberta Court of Appeal, set up by its chief justice, Catherine Fraser, released a groundbreaking decision, called *Levesque* v. *Levesque*, in which the Court gave priority to maintaining the child's lifestyle, preferring that the parents reduce their own standards of living. The panel of judges created their own simple guidelines, with the parents' combined gross income as the most important factor. The Court decided that it was reasonable to spend 20 percent of the parents' combined gross income on one child or 32 percent on two children. Each parent was to contribute in proportion to his or her income.

This "Levesque litmus test," as it was called, was applied not only in Alberta, but by some courts in other provinces; even where it was not applied strictly, it triggered significant increases in child support orders across Canada.

GOVERNMENT GUIDELINES

In 1997, the federal government took the initiative and enacted formal Child Support Guidelines, which established fixed guidelines for the amount of support to be paid and abolished tax consequences for the payment of child support. This double-barrelled approach, aimed at improving the situation for children of divorce, became law effective May 1, 1997. The new rules apply only to orders or agreements for child support made on or after May 1, 1997, including amendments made after May 1, 1997, of agreements in force before that date. The federal government, which has jurisdiction over divorce law, was hopeful that the provinces and territories would apply the federal guidelines to provincial child support laws, which determine all child support issues in which the parents are not divorcing. All provinces and territories have now implemented guidelines for child support, most simply by adopting the federal guidelines. Quebec, however, chose to implement a different model for its provincial guidelines, particularly when adjusting for different lengths of time spent by the child with the non-custodial parent.

The guidelines do not contain a formula for calculating specific *needs* of children. The assumption is that the amount a family spends on the children is directly related to the means of both parents, and that this amount changes as the income of either parent changes. The guideline amounts are based on the income of the payor (typically the father), the number of children and the province or territory where they live. The income of the other parent is not regarded as relevant; the new law assumes that if the mother has income either through work outside the home or spousal support, the children will benefit. In Saskatchewan, for example, according to the tables in the guidelines, a father earning $40,000 would pay $328 per month for one child, $544 for two, $717 for three and $858 for four. These amounts also recognize that support does not simply double if you have another child, nor is it halved if one child is no longer dependent. In a change from previous law, these amounts are not taxable to the recipient, nor deductible by the payor. Every case that goes to court will have child support pegged in accordance with the guidelines, which take into account provincial variations in living costs. If all a parent wants is the guideline amount, the court is unlikely to inquire into the child's needs, the custodial parent's means or the non-custodial parent's assets.

ADJUSTMENTS

In many families one parent may feel that payments prescribed by the Child Support Guidelines are either too high or too low.

The law specifies a number of situations when adjustments may be made:

- **Extraordinary Expenses:** These must be both necessary and reasonable, and include such items as day care, orthodontic work and postsecondary education. A parent can ask the court to order that such "add-on" expenses be shared in proportion to each parent's income.
- **Special Provisions:** If the custody agreement includes unusual provisions that benefit the child, such as the transfer of the family home to the custodial parent, the guideline amount may be changed to offset that benefit.
- **Undue Hardship:** Either parent could plead undue hardship, if, for example, he or she is also supporting another person. However, a court will not make an adjustment that would leave the parent claiming hardship with a higher standard of living than the other household.

There are other considerations that may warrant an adjustment in child support payments:

- **Shared Custody:** Currently there is no specified guideline amount for families in which the children spend at least 40 percent of the time in each parent's care. To decide support amounts in these cases, the courts must take into account the increased costs of shared custody, the manner in which the parents share costs, and the circumstances of the family. This provision has created a lot of difficulty and is currently under review.
- **Consent Agreements:** Parents may make their own deals that differ from the law, but these may not be upheld by a court if the judge determines the needs of the child are not being met.
- **Other Possible Adjustments:** If a parent earns over $150,000 per year, or the children are over the age of majority but still in school or university, the court may consider both parents' income when fixing an amount. (For parents who earn over $150,000 a year, there is an optional formula in the guidelines.)

Unfortunately, such adjustments, particularly for add-on expenses, allow for discretion. The guidelines do not state what adjustments are appropriate. In order to arrive at reasonable amounts for their children, many parents are still forced to go to court. In June 1997, in one of the first comprehensive decisions under the guidelines, it took an Alberta court over 40 pages to interpret 12 questions in the case of *Middleton* v. *MacPherson*. Despite comprehensive decisions in several provinces, as each court across Canada put its own spin on the discretionary clauses in the guidelines, the promise of predictability for parents faded. Now children in some provinces get certain add-ons while those in other provinces do not, or may have different expenses covered.

By 1998, controversial high-income payor cases began to make their way through the courts. The Ontario case of *Francis* v. *Baker* was one of the first appellate decisions to consider discretion in the amount of child support for payors with income over $150,000, and the Ontario Court of Appeal decided that a high-income payor is permitted to pay no less than the chart amount based on her or his income. As this case made its way to the Supreme Court of Canada, lower courts continued to wrestle with comparative lifestyles of parents and children after separation. When the case was heard in 1999, the Court ruled that, based on Mr. Baker's considerable income (about $950,000 per year), he must pay the chart amount of support for two children of $10,034 per month. While conceding the amount was generous, the Court did not feel it was excessive or inappropriate, particularly once lifestyles for the children in the parents' two homes were compared. (Mr. Baker's net worth was about $78 million.) The Court said other cases would have to be decided on a case-by-case basis, and, while the courts have the discretion to either increase or decrease the chart amount for high-income earners, there is only limited judicial discretion to vary the chart amount of child support.

Shortly after the Supreme Court of Canada decided *Francis* v. *Baker*, the Ontario Court of Appeal chose not to apply any judicial discretion in the case of *Simon* v. *Simon* and ordered that the amount established in the guidelines chart should be imposed on NHL hockey player Christopher Simon, who earned about $1.4 million a year, for his five-year-old son. This amounted to $9,215 per month. The Court presumed that some of these funds would be set aside by the custodial parent for the child's future care and education.

But soon after, courts in Ontario again imposed discretion on the determination of the amount of child support. In June 2000, six months after the Simon case, the Ontario Court of Appeal heard the case of *Tauber* v. *Tauber*. The trial had been held prior to release of the Supreme Court of Canada decision in *Francis* v. *Baker,* and the trial court had strictly applied the chart amount from the guidelines and ordered a father

who earned $2.5 million a year to pay $17,000 per month to support his 18-month-old child. The Court of Appeal felt that this amount was inappropriately high because it was for a healthy child who did not need that much. Without ruling out the possibility that the Child Support Guidelines chart amount might still be upheld, the Court sent the matter back to a trial judge for a review of the "condition, means, needs and other circumstances of the children who are entitled to support and the financial ability of each spouse to contribute to the support of the children." The appeal court also ruled that the wealthy father should pay most of the mother's legal costs just because he was challenging a precise application of the guidelines. In 2001, the case was reheard and the father's child support order was reduced to $11,173 per month.

In an era when increasing numbers of families are sharing custody, the division of financial responsibility has become more complicated. The Child Support Guidelines states that the basic chart amount is only paid by one parent to the other if that paying parent has the child or children less than 40 percent of the time. Otherwise, if a spouse has the child for 40 percent of the time or more over the course of a year, the amount of child support must be determined by taking into account the table amounts for each of the spouses, the increased costs of shared custody arrangements, and the conditions, means, needs and other circumstances of each spouse and of any child for whom support is sought.

As simple as this appears on the surface, it is complex in practice. In the Ontario case of *Contino* v. *Leonelli Contino,* three levels of court made different determinations. The father had applied to reduce child support from $550 per month because he had the child with him 50 percent of the time. The motions judge agreed and reduced his payment to $100 a month. On appeal by the mother, the Divisional Court increased the father's payment to $688 per month. The Ontario Court of Appeal, in 2003, decided that the correct amount to be paid by the father was $399.61. The court noted that shared custody does not necessarily result in a dollar-for-dollar decrease in the amount of support required by the responding parent. Evidence of extra costs incurred by the payor must be available. The decision is discretionary. The Court of Appeal started with a set-off, this being the difference between what each parent would pay according to the chart, based on their income. Then they reviewed the mother's and father's fixed costs and applied a multiplier, adjusting the result by the actual spending pattern of the parents on the child. The Supreme Court of Canada gave leave to appeal in 2004; the matter is pending.

In 2005 the Alberta Court of Appeal made a significant change when it clarified the law of retroactive child support. The court ruled that it should be common practice for a payor to increase child support from the date of increased income, even if the recipient does not request (or even know about) the change. "Pay now or pay later," the court said, but the delay will no longer work in the payor's favour.

FINANCIAL DISCLOSURE

The new rules require a non-custodial parent paying child support to provide the custodial parent with annual financial disclosure on request. Similarly, a parent in

whose favour an order was made for extraordinary expenses or undue hardship can also be required to provide annual financial disclosure to the other parent. Any provision in an agreement or order that tries to limit a parent's obligations to provide this financial information will not be enforced.

This financial disclosure is designed to make it easier for a custodial parent to keep up-to-date on the other parent's financial status; however, if the non-custodial parent's income has indeed increased, the custodial parent will have to hire a lawyer to seek an adjustment in child support based on the financial information. It is important to include a clause requiring the automatic provision of tax returns annually in any agreement, or the recipient may have difficulty garnering back payments related to the payor's increase in income. There are special rules to help a court determine the income of shareholders or business owners who control their income in a way salaried earners cannot. For example, the court may include in a shareholder spouse's income all of the pre-tax income of his or her corporation.

OPTING INTO THE GUIDELINES

Child support out-of-court settlements and divorce orders that took effect before May 1, 1997, need not follow the guidelines. If a separated parent with an agreement or order made on or before April 30, 1997, wants to take advantage of the new law, both parties must agree on, or one party must apply for, a variation in the existing order.

Many custodial parents have not opted in to the new guidelines as they may be economically disadvantaged by doing so, particularly if they had generous arrangements in place or if they would have to go to court to fight for add-on expenses that used to be considered part of their child's accepted expenses. Many non-custodial parents do not benefit by opting in because they stand to lose the tax deductibility on the child support they pay.

HOW LONG DOES CHILD SUPPORT LAST?

How long child support must be paid depends on whether the order is made under federal or provincial law. A child support order made as part of a divorce judgment falls under federal law, which requires the non-custodial parent to support children as long as they remain in the custodial parent's charge and are unable, due to illness, disability, pursuit of reasonable education or other cause, to support themselves. There is no arbitrary cut-off age, but as a child gets older, proving dependency gets tougher. Support often extends to age 23 if a child is still in college or university. There is no age limit if a child is disabled.

Under provincial law, the maximum age to which child support must be paid varies from jurisdiction to jurisdiction and ranges from 16 to 19; the maximum age is higher in some places, if the child is in school.

Some cases illustrate the obligations of parents to support their dependent older children. In 1994, a Manitoba court ordered a father to continue paying support at $2,000 per month for his 20-year-old daughter who, despite diligent attempts to find employment, was still dependent; she had not been able to attend college because she could not afford tuition, and now she could not find a job. That same year, the Nova Scotia Court

of Appeal required a father to continue paying $100 per month for his 21-year-old daughter, and confirmed that, as a general rule, if children are over the age of 16, parents remain responsible for their support if they are bona fide students. This period of dependency will continue until the children reach a level of education commensurate with their abilities, which will enable them to join the work force at least at an entry-level position in the appropriate field.

In a 1995 case, an Alberta court ordered a father to pay support at $1,500 per month for ten months for his 28-year-old daughter, who had psychological problems and was a "destitute person" according to provincial legislation.

A parent may be ordered to support an adult child during his or her education, even though the child has broken off relations with that parent. In 1995, an Ontario court ordered a father to pay support for his 23-year-old daughter through medical school; however, it did hold that under some circumstances a parent may not be required to support a dependent adult child who deliberately turns his or her back on that parent. This was the case when a B.C. court in 2000 agreed to terminate a divorced father's support for his 19-year-old daughter. The court found that the girl's unexplained decision as of age 11 to refuse to have anything to do with her father ultimately constituted a unilateral termination of her relationship with him. It ruled that once she attained the age of majority (19 in British Columbia) her father was justified in discontinuing support.

4. Cost-of-Living Adjustments (COLA)

Until 1984, adjustments in support amounts to reflect changes in the cost of living were not part of the law. In 1984, however, an Ontario Court of Appeal case called *Jarvis* v. *Jarvis* upheld a trial judgment by Ontario justice George Walsh making annual COLA increases on a support order automatic, and, in 1986, Ontario legislation followed suit. Since then, cost-of-living adjustments have become more common across Canada, and are often calculated according to a clause in the order or agreement stating the method for the parties to follow. Child support paid under the Child Support Guidelines is not subject to a COLA clause as it is expected to be adjusted annually in accordance with the payor's income.

COLA clauses allow a recipient spouse to keep up with increases in the cost of living without returning to court. A court order or separation agreement should stipulate the date on which the increase is to be calculated each year. Statistics Canada provides figures for the calculations at no cost. When considering whether or not to order an automatic cost-of-living adjustment, the court may consider the circumstances of the parties—for example, a spouse's ability to support himself or herself and the likelihood of the payor's income keeping pace with inflation.

If it is not possible to obtain an automatic cost-of-living adjustment, or an existing agreement does not include one, a spouse may negotiate or apply to court subsequently for this adjustment; at the very least, he or she can request a one-time increase by going to court and claiming this as a change in circumstances. The onus will be on the spouse requesting the increase to prove that it is warranted—for example, he or she may have to produce statistics to show how much the cost of living has risen since the original order or agreement. The court will also consider the circumstances of the payor—whether that spouse's income is too unpredictable to keep pace with inflation, for example.

5. Enforcement of Support Payments

When a payor of support defaults, provincial and federal enforcement laws and agencies now help the recipient to find the debtor and collect arrears. But the extent of their help depends on the province or territory in which a creditor resides.

The most direct initiatives have been in Ontario, Quebec, Manitoba, Alberta, and Prince Edward Island. These provinces can require employers to automatically deduct all court-ordered spousal and child support payments from the payor's paycheque, in the same way that employers deduct income tax. Recipients do not need to apply for this action; it is usually part of the process when the court orders support.

The court order is filed for enforcement with the government enforcement office, which notifies both the payor and the payor's employer. The employer is required to deduct the appropriate amount—usually up to 50 percent of net wages—to make regular support payments and pay any arrears. The employer forwards a cheque to the enforcement office, which deposits the money and issues its own cheque to the recipient. Any employers who fail to make the required deduction may have to make the payment from their own funds. If payor spouses leave their places of employment or are laid off, both payors and employers must notify the enforcement agency within a specified time or risk penalties.

While the other provinces and territories do not automatically deduct support directly from the payor's income source, they all have enforcement agencies that can garnishee the payor's wages if she or he defaults. New Brunswick's legislation imposes a 3 percent surcharge on the debtor, to be added to the amount of support collected from any order filed with the court or any amount paid into court. British Columbia imposes an annual default fee. Since an order normally requires a payor to make support payments to the agency, the agency can start enforcement proceedings if and when the payor defaults. The recipient is not left to enforce it.

If the payor is not a wage earner but receives income from a business, investments or other sources, all jurisdictions are still required to enforce support orders, including registered support orders from other jurisdictions.

In addition to garnisheeing wages, an agency may garnishee bank accounts, register a lien against property or take the payors to court to disclose their finances and explain why they have not paid. At the federal level, funds can be seized from a defaulter's income tax refund, regular interest on Canada Savings Bonds, EI, CPP, Old Age Security and federal pensions.

In every jurisdiction, a defaulter can be sent to jail for failing to make support payments. Many provinces also provide for fines—for example, Ontario can order a fine of up to $10,000. A jail term or a fine does not cancel the support owed.

All enforcement agencies have the right to require the payor to deliver a financial statement with proof of income, as well as the right to demand copies of the payor's tax returns. If payors fail to deliver the financial statement or tax return, they can be held in contempt of court, or the agency can ask that an arrest warrant be issued, requiring payors to answer the charges in court.

INTERPROVINCIAL AND INTERNATIONAL RECIPROCITY

When a payor moves, either before or after a support order is made, reciprocal legislation in other jurisdictions provides a means of enforcing an order in another province or territory, without running into conflicts between the laws of various jurisdictions.

All provinces and territories have this reciprocal legislation, and will enforce the laws of other reciprocating jurisdictions. Most of the provinces and territories have signed on to the new Interjurisdictional Support Orders Act, which is intended to increase efficiency and reduce costs for families seeking orders across jurisdictions.

The goal is to help people to enforce orders not only in Canada, but in many parts of the United States and in some countries in Europe, Africa, the Caribbean, Asia and Australia. Quebec, however, will enforce orders only that conform with Quebec civil law, which is unique in Canada; the rest of Canada follows the common law.

Each provincial and territorial attorney general has a list of jurisdictions where reciprocal arrangements are in place. Once the support recipient (claimant) initiates proceedings, an officer of the court—usually the attorney general or a similar administrator—takes responsibility for transmitting the documents and statements of law for provisional orders to a similar official in the reciprocating state. The duties of such officers are set out in the respective laws in each jurisdiction. If an enforcement agency is involved, it will usually make the request on behalf of the support recipient.

If there is no order in place to be enforced, the claimant must first obtain a provisional order in her or his own jurisdiction, which can then be forwarded to the reciprocating state for a confirmation hearing. The proposed payor must be given notice of the hearing, and the opportunity to be heard. Once the order has been confirmed, it can be enforced as a registered order in the foreign jurisdiction. If an order for support has already been made in the jurisdiction where the claimant resides, and the payor moves, no confirmation hearing is necessary: Both parties are assumed to have been given notice at the time the order was obtained.

To be enforceable, all support orders must specify the amount of support to be paid, converted into another currency, if necessary. In some circumstances, one of the parents may appeal the order or ask that it be varied, according to the rules within particular reciprocating states.

This reciprocity is an important part of the enforcement process. Without it, a support award would be meaningless once a payor moved out of the jurisdiction.

OPTING OUT

Most provinces and territories will allow a recipient of a support order to opt out of enforcement through the agency and opt back in if a payor defaults in payment. A recipient may choose to opt out if the payor is reliable in his or her payments and it is more convenient to receive payments directly from the payor. Unfortunately, sometimes recipients opt out to enforce privately if their enforcement agency is not efficient at collecting arrears. This creates added cost for the recipient.

LICENCE SUSPENSIONS AND OTHER MEASURES

Despite the introduction of enforcement agencies, default continues to occur. For example, Ontario government statistics in 2004 indicated that 34 percent of payors were in partial compliance with support orders (where payments are being made but there are still arrears owing), a further 34 percent were in full compliance (paid up and no arrears owing), and in the other 32 percent of the cases, recipients were receiving no funds at all.

More provinces and territories have toughened up their enforcement capabilities, as has the federal government. For example, Alberta, British Columbia, Ontario, Saskatchewan, Prince Edward Island, Manitoba, Nova Scotia and the Yukon now have provisions to revoke, suspend or refuse to issue or reissue the drivers' licences of defaulting payors. If the payor needs a licence for employment, some legislation allows for a conditional drivers' licence that may permit the debtor to drive at certain times of the day. Manitoba and Ontario will also ensure that credit bureaus are notified when defaulters are a bad credit risk.

Sometimes defaulting parents try to get a court to wipe out their debt, and forgive payment of arrears, in order to get their drivers' licences reinstated. In one such case, an Alberta judge dismissed the father's application, saying that the man had deliberately put himself in a position where he could not pay.

In 1994, another Alberta judge found that a father of two who had been ordered to pay $300 per month in child support had paid virtually nothing for seven years. He pleaded poverty, but the court found that he had used his company to shield him from showing income. In fact, he was sole owner of, and a hard worker in, a very active trucking business, and the company paid his shelter costs, bought him a car and gave him a series of payments. The matter was brought to court by the Alberta director of maintenance enforcement.

Alberta's Justice Jean Côté was blunt in saying that he did not believe anything the man said, noting that "key parts of his evidence are wildly improbable" and contain "simple evasion and bafflegab." The judge commented that the man "has been making a monkey of the courts . . . with great deliberateness and total success." Finding the husband able to pay and guilty of willful default, and concluding that ordinary enforcement methods are ineffective, Mr. Justice Côté ordered him jailed immediately for 14 days and gave the director of maintenance enforcement authority not only to seize the man's financial books and records—with the aid of a locksmith and police, if necessary—but also to become the Receiver of all his property. A Receiver takes full charge of a person's assets, including operating any ongoing business.

As a result of frustration over defaultors hiding behind their corporations, provinces such as British Columbia, the Yukon and Alberta now have enforcement provisions to get at such corporations and make them responsible for payment of the debt. Ontario has also expanded enforcement measures, including allowing garnishment of 50 percent of funds in a joint bank account where one of the owners owes support arrears, and seizure of certain lottery winnings. Judges can now require a person who is financially connected to the payor, such as a current wife or girlfriend, to file financial information and documentation to enable the court to find and seize assets of the payor which may be sheltered by this person. In April 2000, amidst controversy, Ontario's enforcement agency began charging administration fees for processing paperwork such as statements of arrears and postdated cheques. As well, a charge of $400 was implemented for each "aggressive" enforcement process taken against a defaulting payor. For cases withdrawn from enforcement after October 31, 2004, a fee of $50 was added if a party opted back in. While most of these charges apply to support payors, not recipients, those charges that are levied against recipients will add to the financial strain on the very people the agency is set up to assist.

The federal government has a licence-denial scheme to authorize the suspension of passports and specific federal transport licences in cases where the payor has persistently breached support obligations. As well, federal legislation allows the government to garnishee federal public service employee pension benefits to satisfy support arrears.

TRACING THE PAYOR

In 1987, the federal government established a tracing service to help locate disappearing parents who failed to abide by support, custody and access orders and agreements. The federal government negotiated successfully with all provinces and territories to establish the conditions for the release of confidential information from the federal data banks. These data banks, which can be accessed only to secure information for the enforcement of support, custody or access orders or agreements, include the Canada Pension Plan's record of earnings; international social security records held by Health and Welfare Canada; Canada Employment and Immigration records; and social insurance number records. The federal government has now added the Canada Customs and Revenue Agency (formerly Revenue Canada) to this list.

A recipient cannot get the information directly from the tracing service. Instead, the provincial enforcement agencies obtain the payor's address and the name and address of his or her employer, and can access the federal data banks without court authorization. Within their jurisdictions, these enforcement agencies also have the power to obtain information from provincial and territorial government sources to locate defaulting payors. As with federal information, this provincial information is confidential and cannot be used for any other purpose. If a payor has moved to another province, the agencies are also authorized to co-operate with one another in exchanging such information.

E. VARIATION OF ORDERS

Circumstances change, and no support, custody or access order is carved in stone. If there has been a material change in circumstances, a party may apply to court for a variation of custody, access or support orders. Because the courts have not been able to keep up with the many variation applications in recent years, in some jurisdictions the matter may take some time to reach court for decision. Variation procedures can take up to one year or more between the time a lawsuit is started and an order is made.

1. Variation of Custody or Access

Whatever an agreement or court order says, the court always retains the power to review and vary custody and access arrangements to protect the best interests of children. This does not mean, however, that orders are easily changed. A variation in custody or access must be justified by a material change in circumstances that affects the best interests of the child. The onus falls on the parent alleging such a change to prove it.

It is not uncommon for custody and access variation applications to be made as a result of a custodial parent's decision to move, particularly if a move will affect access arrangements. Courts must balance the detriment to the child of reduced access with the child's overall best interests. This issue is discussed under the topic of mobility rights.

Alternatively, a variation in access may be sought, for example, if a custodial parent fears the children are being harmed through the access visits. In 1992, the Ontario Court of Appeal reviewed a mother's application for terminating access based on the father's behaviour. The mother had left the marriage shortly after the child was born because of the father's actions, which included threats to kill her. Despite the mother's application to deny access or require that it be supervised, the father was granted overnight and unsupervised visits. Over the next few years, the mother moved and the father followed, with the parties consenting to some access orders.

But with overnight access adversely affecting the five-year-old girl, the mother had the child examined by a doctor. On the doctor's advice, access was stopped because the doctor suspected possible sexual abuse, and when the Court concluded that the child had been sexually abused, access was cancelled. When the father appealed, Madam Justice Rosalie Abella of the Ontario Court of Appeal upheld the termination of access, finding that the continuing and unrelenting stress of the visits amounted to a material change in circumstances affecting the child's best interests. Since there was no chance that these circumstances would change, the Court decided that supervised access was not appropriate because it is only a short-term measure. Justice Abella concluded: "The [father's] biological link cannot be permitted to trump the child's welfare and best interests."

A New Brunswick court found ongoing domestic violence to constitute a change in circumstances. During the course of a violent relationship, the father had broken the mother's jaw, held a knife to her head and broken her eardrum when he hit her in the head. The three children, aged eight, ten and 11, had seen their father assault their mother on a number of occasions. Following one such incident at the end of an access visit, the mother refused to continue to let the father see the children, and moved to terminate his access. In 1994, the court found the mother in contempt of the existing order, but did not penalize her. Despite the father's conduct, the court was reluctant to deny all access, and instead ordered

access for one full weekend a month under strict terms designed to eliminate any contact between the parents. The father was ordered to abstain from the use of alcohol during visits and for 24 hours before, and to "refrain from any displays of anger, violence or threats in the presence of the children." The court did not say what would happen in the event of a breach. Presumably, the wife would return to court to ask again that access be terminated.

A material change in the circumstances of a parent, rather than a child, may not necessarily justify a variation in custody or access. The Saskatchewan Court of Appeal in 1994 reversed an order that changed custody of a seven-year-old from his father to his mother. At the time of separation, the mother, who was much younger than the father, decided the child would be better off with him. Several years later, having matured, remarried and improved her prospects and education, she applied for custody. By this time, the father's prospects had deteriorated; he was unemployed and on social assistance.

Since the trial judge found both parents able to meet the child's needs, the Court of Appeal held that there was no material change in the child's circumstances to warrant awarding the mother custody. However, in an interesting turn of events, the Court took it upon itself to order joint custody, based on the recommendation of a counsellor.

Sometimes, a variation is prompted by a child's request. As children get older, they may wish a say in decisions of custody. Depending on the maturity of the child, if the reasons for residing with the other parent can be established to have originated with the child and not the other parent, and the change is found to be in the child's best interests, a variation might be considered appropriate.

2. Variation of Spousal Support

A court may consider a variety of factors when determining whether there has been a "material change in circumstances" to merit variation of support.

Generally speaking, no variation application will be considered unless there has been an unanticipated change in the circumstances of either party. The courts have been reluctant to use their power to remedy a bad bargain if the original agreement was entered into voluntarily and with full knowledge; but in recent years, the courts have in fact made a number of such variation orders when the payee has been in great need, perhaps due to health problems, and the payor has had the ability to pay.

The onus is on the applicant to prove that the change in the circumstances or means of either party warrants a change in the support payment stipulated in the original agreement or court order. When considering an application to vary, the court starts from the premise that the original amount ordered was correct, based on all the circumstances at that time, and determines the varied amount with reference only to the change in circumstances. Even lump-sum "final" awards can be varied, but the court will do so only in special and unusual circumstances.

A court will consider a number of events as contributing to a material change in circumstances: substantial changes in the means and needs of either spouse, loss of a job, a salary raise, remarriage, a business reversal, or health problems affecting income or causing expensive medical care for a spouse or child. The inflationary erosion in the value of the support dollar will justify a variation when inflation has outpaced the recipient's ability to support himself or herself.

A situation in which an ex-spouse retrains but cannot find a reasonably paid job may qualify as a material change in circumstances. In 1997 the Ontario Court of Appeal extended the right to support for a 53-year-old nurse and longtime homemaker who, despite retraining to become a teacher, was still having difficulty finding full-time work. Mrs. Trewin was initially given three years of support; however, at the end of this time she was forced to encroach on her capital as she could not make ends meet. The Court noted that in some cases it might be totally unrealistic to expect 45- or 50-year-old women who have been out of the job market for many years to become self-sufficient, despite retraining.

Retirement does not always justify a reduction or termination of support. In 1995, a Newfoundland and Labrador court upheld spousal support of $300 per month for a wife who, during a 30-year marriage, had looked after the home and children, taking on some part-time clerical work once the children were all in school. At 57, the wife was able to earn only $14,400 per year, while the husband took an early retirement package from his $40,000 per year position. In confirming the support, the court found that although the circumstances of both had changed, it was impractical to expect the wife to become self-sufficient, whereas the husband, even with his reduced income, had the ability to maintain the monthly payments.

In a 1996 Prince Edward Island case, the wife of a 29-year traditional marriage, receiving $625 per month support, eventually gained employment and remarried, thus becoming "self-sufficient" according to the Divorce Act. Her former husband sought to reduce or eliminate his support obligation. By lowering her support to $400 per month rather than eliminating it, the court recognized that being economically independent and suffering no economic disadvantage as a result of the marriage were not necessarily the same thing. The wife had forgone years of generating her own pension in order to contribute to her husband's. If support were terminated, the court reasoned, the husband would be left to reap the benefits from this pension for himself.

If spouses or former spouses become financially in need and apply for an increase, they are not required to use up their assets first to supplement support and other income. The review of support will consider a spouse's needs in light of the standard of living enjoyed during the marriage. A spouse will not usually get more just because the other spouse's ability to pay may accelerate rapidly. If a payor spouse receives an inheritance or wins a lottery, the other spouse cannot seek to share it. However, he or she can ask for more monthly support, if needed, and the lottery winner could hardly claim insufficient income after investing the winnings.

Payors looking for a reduction in support cannot voluntarily assume an expensive lifestyle and then expect a court to adjust their support obligations so that they can pay for it. As one judge said of a husband, he "may, of course, live in such style and manner as he sees fit with the money remaining after he has first fulfilled his obligation to his former wife and his children. . . ." This husband was spending half his income on lavish rental accommodations with a common-law wife.

These days, support does not automatically come to an end if a wife remarries or lives with another man. Historically, courts held that support ended on remarriage because it was against public policy to support another person's spouse. This attitude went hand-in-hand with the assumption that a sexual relationship usually involved economic support. In a 1995 Supreme Court of Canada case, it was held foreseeable that a wife who was seeing another man at the time her support was negotiated would eventually cohabit with this person. The Court concluded that her cohabitation with this man did not create a sufficient change in circumstances to warrant termination of her support.

Even if a support provision stipulates that the payments end if the spouse cohabits with another person of the opposite sex, the facts supporting this cohabitation must be proven in a court application. When a former wife receiving support had her fiancé staying with her typically five nights each week, a New Brunswick court in 1994 found that there was no "cohabitation" and therefore ordered support payments to continue. The woman's fiancé did not contribute financially to household expenses, did not perform domestic tasks, ate few meals there, received his mail elsewhere, received few telephone calls, did not keep clothing and toiletries there and did not have a key to the home. They had not made any joint furniture purchases together and did not maintain joint bank accounts. She was not the beneficiary of his life insurance.

The Ontario courts have in several cases of legally valid "final" agreements under the

Divorce Act reinstated spousal support where the wife was in need and in fact suffering economic hardship due to a "radical unforeseen change in circumstances." In 1997 the Ontario Divisional Court in the case of *Santosuosso* v. *Santosuosso* refused to uphold a 1987 settlement that limited a 43-year-old homemaker to two years' support. She turned out to be unable to get a full-time job. The Court ordered her professor ex-husband to pay $500 per month support with no time limit.

In 2000, an Ontario court in the case of *Bailey* v. *Plaxton* reinstated support for a wife who had, in a 1987 agreement, accepted the termination of her support after three years in 1990. In an interim decision pending trial, the court ordered her ex-husband to pay her $5,000 per month.

In varying final agreements and orders, the courts are giving notice that the agreement must be fair to the parties or it will be re-examined carefully. In 1987 when both these agreements were negotiated, there was a view in many quarters of the legal profession and the courts that the law required a woman to be self-supporting as soon after separation as possible, and agreements and orders incorporated these views. This misapprehension was corrected by the courts starting in about 1992, and the willingness of the courts to revisit previous agreements and orders makes it clear that they wish fairness to prevail.

3. Variation of Child Support

Child support is never final, and can always be varied if the child is in need or there is a material change in circumstances. Even if one parent paid the other a one-time lump sum for child support, the recipient or the child can ask for more if the need arises; the law does not permit one parent to bargain away the child's right to be supported by the other parent.

Although some provinces have refused to allow variations in child support based on the coming into force of the Child Support Guidelines alone, Ontario courts appear to have now accepted that the guidelines constitute a material change in circumstances. This means a recipient can request a variation in child support without having to establish any other change in circumstances.

Either parent may request that the matter of child support be readdressed, if necessary. Circumstances of the parties or children may change over time, requiring the quantum of support to be reconsidered. While some circumstances, such as being laid off or becoming disabled, may be beyond a parent's control, the courts have been reluctant to adjust child support in cases where parents have voluntarily chosen a change in lifestyle that has a negative impact on their ability to support their children. On the other hand, if the children move to live with the other parent, the amount of child support will usually change.

For example, a Saskatchewan court in 1995 held that parents cannot escape their child support obligations by leaving their employment to continue their education. In this case, the father voluntarily left his employment six months after an agreement was signed and then applied for a reduction in child support because of his reduced income. The court was unsympathetic and rejected his application.

Remarriage may alter a payor's ability to support a first family, even though the needs of the first spouse and children have likely remained the same. The payor, often the husband, will want his first family to understand his current financial position and accept less; however, his first wife and children may be resentful and unaccepting, especially if he was the one who chose to end the first marriage. The custodial parent's new partner, however, cannot be expected to assume responsibility for the support of a spouse's children from a former marriage.

Mere evidence of a payor's remarriage will not mean that an order will be changed automatically, because remarriage does not always represent a drain on the payor. The remarriage must be shown to affect the needs and means of the parties.

While courts used to give priority to the needs of the first family as a pre-existing debt, judges now try to balance out the rights so that second families have a chance of financial survival. But the courts do not find it easy to achieve a balance because there is rarely enough money to maintain both families at their expected standard.

Much depends on the circumstances in individual cases. When children are involved, courts try to equalize the positions of the children in the two families.

When deciding whether or not to vary the amount of support, the court will want to accommodate the needs of both families as much as possible. Remarriage can mean a payor's expenses are higher if he or she has taken on financial responsibility for a new spouse and perhaps the new spouse's children. But if the new spouse has an income and uses it to share the expenses of their household, daily living will cost the payor less and he or she will have more disposable income from which to pay support for the first family.

A husband may not be successful in claiming that his new obligations are more important than his duty to support his first family, especially if he voluntarily assumes responsibility for stepchildren, to whom he does not have the legal responsibilities that he has to his own children. In 1996, an Ontario father applied to reduce or cancel child support based on his financial reversals and ultimate bankruptcy. He had remarried, adopted his new wife's two daughters and had two more children with her. Although both he and his new wife were employed, they went bankrupt.

The court found that the father had signed the agreement providing support for the children from his first marriage while already living with his future wife, aware of both his new support obligations and his future wife's income potential. The court stated that the deterioration in his financial circumstances was foreseeable and caused by his own mismanagement. He was not permitted to shift responsibility for his errors to the children from his first marriage by reducing their support.

The 1994 Supreme Court of Canada case of *Willick* v. *Willick* was a major variation case that also signalled a heightened awareness of previously inadequate support levels in awards. In this case, the Court looked at whether a significant increase in a father's income gave the mother a right to ask for more child support than the $900 per month for two children that had been negotiated in their 1989 separation agreement. The father's income had increased from $40,000 a year to $154,000 a year. The Supreme Court upheld the Saskatchewan trial judgment and increased support to $1,700 per month. In finding the $900 per month inadequate, the Court confirmed that, whether the parties agreed to the original amount or a court ordered it, a judge has a duty to be satisfied that reasonable arrangements have been made for the support of the children.

The Supreme Court also ruled that a variation of child support may be triggered by a material change in circumstances of the child or one or both of the parents. The Court recognized that the reasonable expectations of children are not frozen at the time of the divorce, but should correspond to their parents' financial means, not only at the time of separation, but in relation to any subsequent change in circumstances. Therefore, the children are entitled to benefit from a parent's improvement in lifestyle.

The Willick case was significant in its attempt to set a realistic amount of child support. Madam Justice L'Heureux-Dubé stated: "Children are our country's most important resource, our future. Their needs cannot be minimized on account of their parents' divorce. They are entitled to be looked after properly both before and after divorce."

This decision is also notable for its acknowledgement of the "hidden costs" in caring for children, such as the value of the housekeeping, child-rearing and nurturing work undertaken by the custodial parent.

F. REMARRIAGE

Remarriage presents its own set of legal issues and concerns. Sorting out priorities and competing claims among former and current spouses may be complex. The situation is made easier if carefully drawn legal agreements are in place—a separation agreement with a former spouse; a marriage or cohabitation contract with a present spouse. These contracts, which are taken seriously by the courts, may be useful in every case, but they are especially advisable if one spouse brings substantial property into the marriage, wishes to protect the inheritance rights of children from a previous marriage or has pre-existing commitments that must be acknowledged to take priority.

In a contract, spouses may write their own law by stating terms for property sharing, possession and control, spousal and child support, insurance protection and other personal financial matters that may arise during the marriage and after the marriage ends due to death or divorce. It is helpful for the spouses to state the circumstances under which the contract is written and to write the contract in the context of all the circumstances.

Without a contract, spouses are subject to the general law. In fact, spouses who remarry start over with the same basic rules as all other spouses. Here are the special considerations applicable to remarriage.

1. Property

If a remarried spouse owns a home that becomes the remarried couple's matrimonial home, the couple is subject to the property-sharing laws of their province. In many jurisdictions, the entire value of the home would be equally shared on marriage breakdown, even though one spouse brought it into the marriage. In others, only the value accumulated during the marriage would be shared.

No matter who owns the home, one spouse is not normally allowed to sell or mortgage it without the consent of the other spouse.

If property has been received by gift or inheritance from third parties, it is likely to be excluded from sharing, but the provincial laws on this point are complex. If the spouse put such a gift or inheritance towards the matrimonial home (for purchase, mortgage repayment or renovations), the home may still be shareable, nevertheless, in a number of provinces.

If a remarried spouse received a vested "joint and survivor" pension before death, the beneficiary is the person named on the date she or he retired with the first pension cheque. Under the terms of some plans, this person could be a former spouse, but only if the provincial law permits a former spouse to be named as beneficiary. On the other hand, if the spouse remarried before retiring, the survivor's benefits would normally go to the current spouse, again depending on the terms of the pension plan and the jurisdiction's legislation.

Honouring obligations to first spouses may become a legal minefield, as a 1995 British Columbia case illustrates. Pursuant to a separation agreement, the husband agreed to maintain his first wife as beneficiary of his pension by designating her as "spouse." Unfortunately, his pension was governed by the Canadian Forces Superannuation Act, which provides that a former spouse cannot be designated as a beneficiary. This left the second wife as the recipient on the husband's death. The first wife asked the court to order the second wife to act as trustee for the first wife and to pass on the pension payments when the cheques arrived in the mail. The court rejected this proposal and denied the first wife any claim to the pension. The second wife received the entire pension as the surviving spouse.

2. Support

SPOUSAL SUPPORT

If a separation agreement or divorce judgment provides for support payments to a former spouse, support must continue after the payor remarries. But these payments remain the sole responsibility of the payor. The current spouse has no legal obligation to help support the former spouse, although a current spouse's income may be seen as freeing up the payor's ability to pay by contributing to other expenses. A payor may seek to vary the amount of support if circumstances affecting his or her ability to pay have changed.

CHILD SUPPORT

Parents have the primary obligation to support their children from a previous or current marriage. Sometimes, a spouse voluntarily takes on the role of parent and financial provider to a stepchild; this role may lead to a legal obligation—even when the marriage ends—to continue supporting the stepchild if the biological parents cannot provide adequate support. This kind of support is called "in loco parentis."

In evaluating whether such a responsibility exists, an Ontario court held in 1995 that it was the step-parent's intention, not the attitude of the stepchild towards the step-parent, that was important. The onus to prove the husband stood "in loco parentis" to the stepdaughter fell to the second wife, who was claiming support from her husband for herself and her daughter. The daughter, her brother and two of the husband's children had lived with the couple before their separation. The wife claimed that the husband had treated her daughter as his own by taking an active role in her upbringing. Child support was refused, however, because the wife could not discharge the onus of proof required to show that the husband intended to treat the daughter as his own child. Similarly, another 1995 Ontario case looked at a casual and friendly relationship with a second wife's child. Although the husband baby-sat the child and took her to school and on outings, the court ruled that this behaviour did not constitute a settled intention by the husband to treat the child as his own.

In 1999 the Supreme Court of Canada in the case of *Chartier* v. *Chartier* held that, despite earlier Manitoba decisions, a stepfather who stood "in loco parentis" to his wife's daughter could not repudiate this relationship when the parties divorced. The Court held that the nature of the relationship is key to determining if a person stands in the place of a parent and, once this has been determined, a spouse cannot unilaterally terminate this role and escape liability for child support on marriage breakdown.

By the same token an Ontario court, relying on the Child Support Guidelines, in the 1998 case of *Boyle* v. *Boyle*, would not allow a natural father to escape liability for a share of child support simply because he had had no contact with his child for approximately ten years and had never been asked to pay support previously. In this case the mother and stepfather were divorcing and the stepfather brought the natural father into the action.

As noted earlier, the new partner does not take on any legal duty to share a spouse's financial obligations to a spouse and children from a previous marriage. This means that no court has a right to order a new partner to pay a specific amount directly to the spouse's former family to support their monetary needs.

However, the court will probably consider a new spouse's current and potential financial circumstances when recalculating the remarried partner's support obligations. If the new spouse is employed and contributing income to the household, he or she is also freeing up some of his or her partner's earnings to be available for support. Even if a new spouse is unemployed, as long as he or she has the capacity to work, his or her potential for paid employment will be relevant. The Child Support Guidelines specifically permit the consideration of total household income in determining whether a reduction will be made in the amount of support payable when the payor is arguing that he would suffer undue hardship if required to pay the full chart amount of child support under the guidelines.

3. Family Name

Some adults in reconstituted families choose to use the same surname, although there is no legal obligation to do so. Sometimes, they want their children to carry the new surname as well. Before proceeding to change a child's surname, a parent should consider how this change may affect the child's relationship with the other biological parent and whether this change would have an adverse impact on the child's sense of identity.

If a parent applies to a court for a child's formal change of name, the court will require the consent of the child's non-custodial parent, even though the rules differ from province to province depending on whether spouses are separated, divorced or remarried. However, a non-custodial parent does not have an absolute right to forbid a name change.

In many cases, a spouse may apply to the court to dispense with the other parent's consent if she or he can prove that it is fair and proper to do so. Judges will exercise their discretion after reviewing many factors, including the best interests of the child; whether the change will not "unduly prejudice" the other parent; whether the other parent has not contributed to the child's support, or disappeared for an extended period of time or is dead; whether the other parent is incapable of giving consent; and the reason for the desired name change.

In general, it seems that a non-custodial parent who wants to have control over the child's name must be actively involved in the child's life. In cases where the child and non-custodial parent have a good relationship, the courts have held that the child should continue to bear that parent's name.

4. Step-Parent Adoptions

Adoption by step-parents is a serious matter. Although an adoption order will normally include a change of surname (and possibly given name), it also changes the child's status and identity. The child will cease to be the child of the biological parent for all purposes, and the birth certificate will be changed.

Divorce does not affect the children's legal relationship with their non-custodial parent. It is natural for a step-parent to want to formalize a strong and loving commitment to the children of a new spouse. But if the children's other parent is involved in their lives to any extent, it is unlikely that a court will allow the step-parent to adopt the stepchildren without the natural parent's consent because adoption usually deprives the natural parent of any legal right to see the children. However, the law and the courts are challenging some of these traditional expectations of no access after adoption.

Courts rarely deny access to a divorced spouse, and will not allow an adoption to separate divorced families permanently. Manitoba and Saskatchewan permit a parent to seek visiting rights, notwithstanding an order for adoption by a step-parent and the custodial parent. British Columbia and New Brunswick laws allow a judge to protect access rights after an adoption order. Although the law in other jurisdictions does not specifically protect a non-custodial parent's access rights on adoption, courts have done so if they have felt that the circumstances warranted it.

In 1991, the B.C. Court of Appeal upheld a decision in a case where the biological father refused to give his consent to an adoption by a stepfather and the child's mother, who had raised the nine-year-old since he was two. The parents were both found to have caused access problems, and the father had not supported the child. The Court decided, under the circumstances, that adoption was in the child's best interests. However, even though the father lived in Montreal and the child in British Columbia, the two had developed a close relationship, which the Court found was also in the child's best interests. As a result, the Court held that the contact should continue and granted access to the father, in spite of the adoption.

Alberta and Ontario judges have also exercised their discretion to grant the natural parent access at the time of an adoption. In Nova Scotia and the Yukon, legislation allows a court to convert adoption proceedings to custody proceedings if warranted, thereby granting a step-parent and spouse custody instead of adoption status.

If the step-parent decides to pursue adoption proceedings, the non-custodial parent must receive notice of the adoption application and, in most cases, give consent. The judge will not compare the parenting talents of a step-parent and a natural parent: the natural parent's right to his or her children can only be displaced by his or her own neglect—dereliction of duty amounting to physical and/or financial desertion.

A court will usually proceed without the natural parent's consent only in extreme circumstances—if the parent voluntarily disappeared from the children's lives for an extended period; if she or he withheld financial support for a long time without justification; if the children do not know the parent at all; or if the parent is insane or incompetent. To help courts decide whether to dispense with a parent's consent, the law in Newfoundland and Labrador and the Yukon provides a definition of a "concerned" parent, which includes a parent regularly exercising (or attempting to exercise) rights of custody or access in relation to the child, and a parent regularly providing financial support for the child.

In addition to the biological parent's approval, the consent of the adoptive parent's spouse (the custodial parent) is also necessary in all provinces. The child's consent is required as well in all provinces, once the child reaches a certain age, generally age 12 or over. Judges may dispense with the child's consent if they consider it unnecessary, usually in situations where the child believes he or she is the natural child of a step-parent.

Although it is not always required in step-parent adoptions, the child-welfare authorities in most provinces may conduct a home study and report to the court whether the placement—even though to a step-parent—is in the child's interests. Once the adoption is completed, the child's birth certificate will normally be changed to the new parent's name and, if the parent makes a request, it is usually possible to change the child's given name or names.

Most statutes include the statement that for all purposes—including the child's right to inherit from the adopting parent—an adopting parent and child become related "as if the child had been born to that parent in lawful wedlock." The child "ceases to be the child of his or her existing parents," and the natural parent is divested of all legal rights and freed from all legal obligations to the child.

5. Custody

When a custodial parent remarries and then dies, there is no clear-cut rule as to whether the step-parent or the non-custodial parent gets custody. In any custody fight between the surviving natural parent and the step-parent, the key issue is the child's relationship with each. The natural parent has no ownership rights to the child, and the step-parent has no possessory rights. The parental figure who is a more integral part of the child's emotional and daily life is likely to get custody. Regardless of which person wins the case, the other is likely to have the right of access to the child.

If a divorced parent with custody wants to plan for the future care of the child in the event of the parent's death, she or he should reach an agreement with the ex-spouse or try to deal with the issue in her or his will by guardianship.

One hopes that the biological parent and step-parent can decide on custody without court intervention, but if a battle develops, a court application for custody must be made. In all provinces and territories, the court sifts through the circumstances of each case to find a solution in the best interests of the child. In addition to the factors customarily used to determine custody between parents, here are some other factors the court is likely to weigh:

- A desire to maintain continuity and stability in the child's life
- A reluctance to uproot the child
- Blood ties—considered important but not assumed to create a close bond of affection in every case
- The family setting—whether there are other children with whom the child gets along and whether there is a connection to a large extended family
- Preservation of a religion or bilingual heritage
- The child's wishes, if the child is mature enough to express them

6. Will Planning

A careful plan will minimize discord and enable everyone to feel treated fairly. Finding the right balance means having a clear sense of the needs of the children and a new spouse, as well as an understanding of what the law requires.

A person has the freedom to leave what he wants to whom he wants up to a point. For example, one cannot simply leave all one's property to the children from a first marriage and pass over the current spouse. In a 1998 Alberta case, the court intervened to provide for a widow when her late husband left his estate entirely to his children from a previous marriage. The parties were both elderly when they remarried and kept their finances separate. The husband had led his wife to believe he had no savings, when in fact he had substantial assets that grew in value during their marriage. After the husband's death, the wife's income was not sufficient to meet her expenses. The court ruled she had a "moral claim" and should continue to enjoy the lifestyle of the marriage, with an allowance for future contingent health care. The outcome might have been different if this couple had had a marriage contract.

It is best to plan a will and marriage contract with a spouse, preferably before the marriage. The two documents have different purposes and requirements. A will is a personal tool of disposal of assets after death and can be revoked at any time. A marriage contract is a mutually agreed-upon document outlining the obligations between partners and can only be amended by the court or both parties. To be valid, a will must state it is made in contemplation of a remarriage; otherwise marriage specifically invalidates a previous will in every province except Quebec (which does not have a set rule). In some provinces, including British Columbia, Manitoba, Prince Edward Island, Saskatchewan and Ontario, divorce automatically revokes a bequest to an ex-spouse, unless a contrary intention appears in the will.

If spouses are both in comfortable circumstances, they may use the marriage contract to release some or all rights to each other's property or support after death.

Such a contract could then override any provisions in family law legislation. In a 1996 British Columbia case, a couple in a second marriage had a marriage contract and, as agreed, the husband left the wife the matrimonial home in his will. The wife wanted more than this and contested the will, but the court dismissed her claim on the basis that she had adequate resources.

Care should be taken in naming an executor. If the bulk of the estate is to be left to the children from a previous marriage, and some assets and contents to a second spouse, it may be appropriate to name some or all of the adult children, plus the second spouse, as executors of the will.

If either spouse has support obligations from a previous marriage, these must be taken into account when planning wills. A failure to honour these legal responsibilities could cause a court to intervene with estate plans after death. Beneficiaries of insurance, pensions and RRSPs should also be considered.

Since second marriages generally involve estate planning, a will should be made with legal advice and should be reviewed every two to three years, or if circumstances change.

7. Rights on Death

In all provinces, if a remarried spouse dies, the former spouse who was receiving support at the time of death may apply for support from the ex-spouse's estate as a dependant, if the will does not provide for her or him adequately and if the terms of the separation agreement do not prevent the application. This decision is left to a court's discretion, and may involve the court choosing between the competing claims of former and current families.

If a spouse dies "intestate"—without a will—the estate will be distributed according to law. The current spouse will receive the estate, or a share of the estate if there are children. The law where the deceased spouse resided at death will stipulate the amount of the share. Normally, only the current legal spouse benefits from the estate under these circumstances.

If spouses are separated at the time one dies intestate, this may disentitle the surviving spouse to a share of the estate in some provinces. For example, in Manitoba if the spouses are separated and an application has been made to court for a division of marital assets or property has been divided, the surviving spouse is not entitled to a share of the deceased's estate on intestacy.

If remarried spouses want to leave their entire estate unencumbered to their present family, they would be wise to have an insurance policy that meets their financial responsibilities to their first family. Otherwise, for example, if a husband dies, his estate may have to continue paying support to a former wife, if the original order stated that support was for her lifetime. If the order did not state the duration of payments, the law may assume that payments will last only as long as both the payor and payee are alive, depending on the jurisdiction. However, if a spouse dies without ensuring support for either first or second family, the dependants may sue the estate for support.

CHAPTER 11

PLANNING FOR THE FUTURE

⚖

A. PLANNING FOR RETIREMENT

Retirement planning has always been difficult, but the reasons keep changing. In the 1990s, people could expect to be forcibly "retired" earlier than planned because of job loss, especially due to corporate and government "restructuring." Their retirement savings produced less interest than formerly because of the deep dive in interest rates, and therefore those planning for retirement had to save more to produce an adequate retirement income. The federal government was issuing dire warnings about the Canada Pension Plan's ability to meet its obligations, and in an effort to reduce the deficit reduced Old Age Security benefits.

These days, with most of the restructuring completed, an improved economy, and fewer younger workers, more companies want to hire older workers because their skills and experience are in demand. As a result, the style of retirement may be changing from a sudden withdrawal from the work force in favour of a change of pace, perhaps in type of employment or working hours. Governments are moving towards the removal of any mandatory retirement

requirements and changing the age when the pension payout starts. The federal government is also encouraging seniors to prepare for their own retirement by increasing the maximum allowable annual tax-deductible RRSP contributions to $16,500 by 2005, and thereafter indexing them to inflation. The Canada Pension Plan has been repaired by substantially increasing contribution rates.

At any time, many retirees are approaching their senior years with pre-existing commitments to others, including present and former spouses, children and parents. Where these are legal obligations, retirees must prepare for them or else their best-laid plans may be affected adversely.

1. Mandatory Retirement

When a person is forced to retire against his or her will, there are some legal protections in place.

Quebec law offers the best protection against forced retirement. The Quebec Labour Standards Act prohibits compulsory retirement based on age or number of years of service, regardless of what is stipulated in other Quebec legislation, a collective agreement, the employee's contributory retirement plan or "the common practice of his employer." The Quebec Charter of Rights and Freedoms also prohibits discrimination because of age, unless specifically permitted by law.

In every other jurisdiction in Canada, human rights laws protect workers from discrimination based on age, including harassment. However, there is an upper age limit in Saskatchewan (age 64), and in Ontario, British Columbia, and Newfoundland and Labrador (age 65). This means that in these provinces employers can have mandatory retirement rules and there is no law protecting those affected. In 2004, Ontario announced a review of this policy.

For reasons of public safety, workers are forced to retire at a certain age in some fields (for example, pilots and police at 60), regardless of their own physical or mental capabilities. This subject is also discussed in the section on Forced Retirement in Chapter 3.

2. Canada Pension Plan

Everyone over age 18 who has earned income in Canada and contributed to the Canada Pension Plan (CPP) or the Quebec Pension Plan (QPP) for certain minimum qualifying periods is entitled to a full pension at age 65 or, under certain circumstances, a reduced pension as early as age 60.

The amount of the monthly payments is based on contributions. In 2005, the maximum pension payable at age 65 was $828.75 a month. The maximum pensionable earnings in 2004 amounted to $40,500. The contribution of each employee and employer was based on a rate of 4.95 percent of earnings to a maximum of $1831.50 ($3663 for the self-employed).

A widow or widower of a deceased contributor may be entitled to receive survivor's benefits depending on the survivor's entitlement to a CPP retirement pension in his or her own right, whether the survivor is disabled, whether he or she has dependent children, and the age of the surviving spouse. In 2005, the maximum survivor's benefit for a survivor over age 65 was $497.25, and for those under age 65, $462.42.

While a person may be entitled to a survivor's pension, she may not be entitled to claim it at the death of her spouse, as Nancy Law, a 30-year-old Vancouver woman discovered. When her husband died at the age of 50, and their business subsequently failed, Ms Law applied for survivor's benefits. She was under 35 at the time of her husband's death, was not disabled, and did not have dependent children. As a result, she was found ineligible to receive benefits prior to age 65. Ms Law challenged the constitutional validity of the legislation. When the case reached the Supreme Court of Canada in 1999, the Court unanimously agreed with the lower courts and denied her survivor's benefits on the rationale that the CPP rule, although allowing differential treatment, was created to enhance the dignity of older people by maximizing benefits available to them on the loss of a spouse.

Surviving spouses aged 65 or older who are not entitled to a retirement pension of their own receive monthly payments equivalent to 60 percent of the deceased contributor's pension. Survivor's benefits are paid throughout the spouse's lifetime. They do not terminate on remarriage.

Since January 1, 1987, if a couple in an ongoing relationship are 60 years of age or over, they have been allowed to share a CPP pension received in relation to contributions made during the period of time they lived together. This means that a spouse who did not earn the right to a Canada Pension Plan can apply for a share of a partner's pension during his lifetime, which may give them tax savings.

The plan also allows for CPP/QPP pension credits earned during marriage (or during a common-law opposite- or same-sex relationship) to be split equally between separated or divorced conjugal partners. All such partners are entitled to claim a benefit representing the time they lived together, as long as it was for more than one year; if they are separated, they can apply after the qualifying period of one year's separation has passed, and if they are divorced, after the divorce.

Common-law and same-sex partners must apply within four years of the date of separation to be eligible. While the right to share is automatic after one year's separation, an application must be filed with Health and Welfare Canada. Health and Welfare Canada sends out application forms to parties to divorce proceedings, but otherwise, a form must be requested or picked up at one of its local offices.

In most provinces and territories, the right to share is automatic, even if separation agreements provide otherwise. In British Columbia, Saskatchewan and Quebec, however, spouses are permitted to give up this right in a contract.

If the separation occurred before January 1, 1987, the rules stating who can and cannot take advantage of this pension sharing are extremely complex; CPP administrators will determine whether an applicant stands to benefit.

The Canada Pension Plan was overhauled in 1997 following warnings that the plan would run out of money to pay benefits by 2015 when baby boomers began retiring. Increased funding was provided primarily through a jump in premiums from 6 percent in 1997 to almost 10 percent of insurable earnings in 2003. There were also changes in investment strategies akin to those used in large private pension plans, including entering the stock market. See also the section on the Canada Pension Plan in Chapter 3.

3. Old Age Security (OAS)

Old Age Security pension benefits are based on age and residency, not contributions. A person qualifies for a full OAS pension after residing in Canada for 40 years after age 18; a full pension was $473.65 per month for the April–June 2005 period (the amounts are adjusted quarterly). A person who is not eligible for a full pension may receive a pro-rated, partial pension after a minimum of ten years residence in Canada after age 18. OAS pension is payable at age 65.

Tax rules provide for the claw-back of benefits paid to individuals whose net income is above a certain level. The repayment amounts are deducted from the monthly payments before they are issued. In 2005, this level started at $60,806. The full OAS pension is eliminated when a pensioner's net income is $98,660 or more.

4. Guaranteed Income Supplement (GIS)

In addition to the basic Old Age Security benefits, those who qualify under an income test may receive a Guaranteed Income Supplement. However, if a person receives more than the stipulated maximum annual income, he or she will not be entitled to GIS benefits. This maximum amount depends upon the recipient's conjugal relationship status, and whether the recipient's partner also receives an OAS pension or Old Age Allowance. For the period April–June 2005, the stipulated maximum annual income for a single person was $13,512; for a couple, it was $17,616 if both partners were receiving an OAS pension and $32,736 if only one partner was receiving an OAS pension.

In 2005, the April–June rate for the maximum monthly GIS payment to a single person, or to a married person whose spouse or partner was not receiving such benefits, was $562.93. Each partner of a relationship received $372.79.

The married or common-law (opposite-sex or same-sex) spouses of pensioners, and the conjugal survivors of deceased pensioners, may qualify for an Old Age Allowance (formerly the Spouse's Allowance or Widowed Spouse's Allowance). The applicant must be between the ages of 60 and 64 and must qualify under an income test. The allowance for partners was a maximum of $840.32 in 2005; it ceases when the recipient turns 65 or if the parties separate. The allowance for surviving conjugal partners was $927.74 in 2005; it ceases when the recipient turns 65 or remarries.

5. Registered Retirement Savings Plans (RRSPs)

It is never too early to plan for retirement, and the federal government provides legal tax incentives to encourage retirement planning. A person may make tax-deductible contributions to registered retirement savings plans. While income earned by these plans is not taxable, funds withdrawn are taxed as income.

No later than at age 69, RRSPs must be collapsed; to defer taxes, the funds may be transferred to an annuity or a registered retirement income fund (RRIF). The receipt of ongoing income from these plans is taxable.

An annuity is usually purchased by paying a lump sum to an insurance company, which agrees in turn to pay the annuitant a regular sum each month for a defined period or for the rest of the annuitant's life. Some contracts guarantee payment for a specified number of years, so if the annuitant dies before the guaranteed period expires, a named beneficiary or the estate may be paid for the guarantee period.

The investments in an RRIF, on the other hand, are usually directed by the owner. The income from the investments is taxable. The deferral of the payment of tax until retirement represents a considerable saving.

In any year, people may contribute a maximum amount, depending on their income and its source. The federal government increased this amount to $16,500 in 2005. Any unused contribution in a year can be carried forward up to seven years. A married person may contribute to a plan for his or her spouse, who will own the plan. This may provide an RRSP for a homemaker who would otherwise not be entitled to contribute to an RRSP. The payment is tax-deductible to the contributor spouse.

It is wise to name a designated beneficiary of RRSPs to avoid access by creditors of an estate to these funds and to ensure that a surviving spouse is protected. The Ontario

Court of Appeal confirmed in 2004 in the case of *Amherst Crane Rentals Ltd.* v. *Perring* that creditors cannot access the proceeds of RRSPs that go directly to a named beneficiary after the death of the owner of the plan.

6. Reverse Mortgages

If pensioners are concerned about not being able to maintain their home, they can consider a reverse mortgage. (This is discussed in more detail in the section on mortgages in Chapter 9.)

7. Support Obligations

People who have been divorced or separated, and have support obligations, may find that retirement affects their ability to meet those obligations, and may be forced to seek a variation in their payments. Retirement does not automatically trigger a reduction or termination in support obligation, unless there is a prior agreement or court order to this effect.

Before the retiree undertakes any plan of action, she or he should first review the provisions of any separation agreement or court order to see if the document takes the possibility of reduced income on retirement into consideration. Some agreements contain a formula to define precisely what happens if the payor retires or experiences a drop in income. If support was decided by a court order, however, the order is unlikely to state that payments will automatically terminate on retirement. For example, the Ontario Court of Appeal in 1990 ruled that future significant changes in circumstances should be dealt with by an application to court to vary

support at the time of retirement, and should not be automatic because future circumstances are unpredictable.

If the separation agreement or court order does not address the issue, the retiree could try to negotiate a reduction with the other party. If negotiation fails, the payor may have to apply to a court for a variation.

If possible, spouses who anticipate ongoing support obligations should take preventive action. It is prudent to negotiate for terms in a separation agreement that provide for a potential change in income on retirement, preferably a formula that the parties can easily implement without the involvement of courts and lawyers. For example, the formula might simply state that the payor will pay the recipient a certain percentage of gross income, calculated by using the previous year's tax return or the current year's wage stubs. Alternatively, the agreement could set out the payor's income at the time the support was negotiated. This figure could help determine later whether circumstances had changed enough to justify a reduction in support.

An issue that is appearing more frequently is "double-dipping": Should a former spouse who has already received a share of the capital value of a member spouse's pension as part of the property settlement expect to be paid as well from the income stream of the pension once the member spouse retires? The courts have not approached this dilemma consistently.

The Supreme Court of Canada, in the 1999 case of *Best* v. *Best,* did not terminate a husband's spousal support payments at his date of retirement, but left it open for the wife to both share in the lump-sum value of the husband's pension and also receive support, which would be at least partly paid from the husband's pension income. The Court noted that the issue of double-dipping deserves legislative attention.

There was no legislative attention given to this issue, but another case made its way to the Supreme Court of Canada for consideration. In the Supreme Court's 2001 ruling in the case of *Boston* v. *Boston*, the Court did not permit double-dipping, but said there were times when double-dipping was appropriate.

Also see the section on private pensions in Chapter 10 for a full description of this case.

B. PLANNING FOR ILLNESS

While no one plans to become ill, it happens, and people are wise to consider the implications in advance and make realistic preparations, as far as possible. Otherwise, sudden illness or even gradual illness may create problems both for the sick person and any family members who are trying to help.

1. Income During Disability

Some careful planners, concerned that their savings may not provide enough income during long-term disability, arrange privately for income replacement insurance if their employer does not provide this benefit. In addition, the Canada Pension Plan will pay a disability pension to contributors who suffer from a severe and prolonged mental or physical disability that prevents them from pursuing any substantially gainful occupation. In 2005, the maximum monthly disability pension was $1,010.23. The disability pension ceases at age 65, when it is replaced by a retirement pension.

2. Power of Attorney for Property

In order to ensure that their property and income are managed properly and carefully, people are wise to appoint a close and trusted relative or friend to have a power of attorney over property. The person who gives the power of attorney is called the "donor," and the "attorney" (not necessarily a lawyer) can be any mentally competent person who has reached the age of majority and is prepared to take on the responsibility of carefully managing the donor's affairs without taking personal advantage.

A power of attorney document will not be valid unless signed and dated by the donor and witnessed, perhaps by a specific number of people. There may be restrictions on who can be a witness—for example, some provinces and territories do not permit the attorney's spouse or a person under the age of majority to witness the document. While only the donor can execute the power of attorney, he or she is wise to secure the attorney's consent to act in this role first.

The power of attorney can be revoked at any time, as long as the donor is mentally capable when executing the revocation. Whether or not the law in the donor's jurisdiction requires it, the donor should revoke this responsibility in writing, retrieve the original power of attorney document and notify anyone who may have a copy.

A donor should choose an attorney carefully. The position of attorney is one of trust, because the attorney has the power to do and authorize anything the donor might have done. Furthermore, any decisions the attorney makes about the donor's property are deemed to be made with the donor's consent.

All provinces and territories in Canada now allow "enduring" powers of attorney for property; this means that the power of attorney will survive the donor's subsequent mental incompetency, but only if the donor makes a statement to this effect in the document itself. Anyone relying on a power of attorney document should check its wording to be certain that it is effective notwithstanding any subsequent incapacity, since some jurisdictions made the enduring power of attorney law only in the mid 1990s.

Manitoba has had a law since 1996 that empowers people with mental disabilities to make as many of their own decisions as they are competent to do. The Vulnerable Persons Living with a Mental Disability Act also aims to curb their exposure to physical and emotional abuse. British Columbia proclaimed a similar law in 2000.

If the power of attorney is defined as general, the attorney has complete power to do everything that the donor could have done in financial matters, except make a will. If the power is specific, it may be limited to dealing with particular real estate or bank accounts, for example. An attorney for property cannot make personal care decisions, unless a separate personal care document—sometimes known as a "living will," "power of attorney for personal care" or an "advance directive"—is signed. (This is discussed in the next section.)

The attorney should have some familiarity with financial matters in order to manage the donor's affairs. Attorneys may also be asked to prepare accounts to show what they have done with a person's finances. An attorney claiming compensation for her work may also be held to a higher standard of care than one who receives no compensation.

An attorney has a legal obligation to act in good faith and for the benefit of the donor. If an attorney fails to do so, the power of attorney may be revoked in some provinces. In a 1994 Ontario case, a son, who had been appointed attorney by his mother, was called to account by her estate. On her death, her executors could not trace the assets of her estate. Although the executors had information that the estate was worth about $330,000 in 1991, they could find very little at the time of her death in 1994. Documentation indicated that the son, a beneficiary of only $10,000 in his mother's will, had used the power of attorney to remove approximately $250,000 from her bank accounts in 1992. Attorneys do not have authority to transfer assets into their own names, even if the intent is to avoid court and administration costs for estate planning purposes. If a donor wishes to allow his attorney the power to make gifts, he should specify this in the power of attorney.

Provinces have different rules about powers of attorney for property. In Ontario, for example, in order to be deemed mentally capable of giving a power of attorney, donors must meet certain conditions. They must know what property they have and its value, what obligations are due to their dependants and what powers they are giving. They must also recognize that the attorney must account to them for what she or he does; that they can revoke the power of attorney; that the value of the property may decline if mismanaged; and that the attorney could misuse this authority.

Powers of attorney should be reviewed regularly, especially if the donor marries, separates or divorces, or experiences any significant change in health or financial situation. Close relatives or business associates, if applicable, should be informed that a power of attorney for property exists, but they do not need to know the contents. Donors would also be wise to keep a list of the people who have copies with their own copy of the document.

As provincial laws may differ, a person should obtain legal advice before executing any power of attorney.

3. Power of Attorney for Personal Care (Living Will)

A living will is a type of advance directive; in essence, it is a power of attorney that provides for personal care. This document allows people to stipulate in advance a substitute decision-maker to make their preferred personal care decisions for them if they become mentally incapable. These decisions may be as personal as where a person will live, what he or she will eat and what kind of medical treatment he or she will have. Often, the direction is negative—that no heroic efforts are to be made to save the person's life if they will leave the person in a vegetative state.

Living wills were first given legal sanction in Canada in 1990, and since then they have received growing public acceptance. In the 1990 Ontario Court of Appeal decision that first sanctioned these directives, the Court permitted advance instructions to discontinue potentially lifesaving medical treatment, and ruled that "competent adults . . . are generally at liberty to refuse medical treatment even at the risk of death."

The case considered the actions of a doctor who, in an emergency treatment to save an unconscious patient's life, gave her a blood transfusion, despite a card in her purse expressly forbidding such transfusions

because she was a member of the Jehovah's Witnesses. Although the doctor took the position that he had a duty to save the woman's life, he was held to have acted improperly and to have committed the criminal offence of battery. The woman sued the doctor and was awarded $20,000 in damages.

While the courts struggled with this issue case by case, provincial governments gradually began to legislate the validity of living wills. At the time of writing, only New Brunswick and the Territories did not have such legislation.

Whether or not a power of attorney for personal care is approved in a particular jurisdiction, the document may be persuasive at least as a guide to a person's doctors. And whether or not a person chooses to put something in writing, the exercise of communicating her or his thoughts and wishes while in good health will help those who may be called upon to make such decisions for her or him in the event of serious illness. A person's doctor should be made aware of any living will.

Living wills are not mandatory. For example, long-term care facilities may find it useful to request such an appointment, but they cannot legally require it. As with a power of attorney for property, the donor must be mentally capable when making a power of attorney for personal care.

The choice of attorney for personal care decisions is very important. The person appointed should know the donor well and, preferably, hold similar values. The attorney must also have sufficient time and interest to take on this responsibility. It is important that the donor and attorney discuss the appointment. For example, the donor may want to specify different degrees of treatment, depending on the type or severity of an illness. He or she may also wish to vary instructions for treatment depending on whether the condition is temporary or permanent. Donors may wish to provide very specific instructions or conditions in writing, or simply tell their attorney what they want—either way, the attorney is obliged to follow the donor's wishes. An attorney for personal care should consider the donor's welfare and interests, and assist him or her, if possible, to have some independence, maintain contacts with family and friends, and consult, as appropriate, with the attorney and the person providing the personal care.

The attorney for personal care does not have to be the same person as the attorney for property and, in some cases, should not be, as these people perform very different functions.

A province or territory may have rules governing who cannot be appointed as an attorney. They may exclude a minor; a landlord; health care providers such as nursing home staff, a doctor or a nurse; or others who may be in a special position with the donor. They do not exclude a spouse or partner.

Donors may revoke a power of attorney for personal care as long as they are mentally competent. They should also review the document from time to time to ensure that the provisions are still appropriate.

4. Mental Competency Issues

When a person becomes incapable of managing his or her own affairs and making his or her own personal and health decisions, and has made no advance arrangements, it may be difficult, legally, to have someone else step in to act on that person's behalf.

A mentally capable person suffering a physical incapacity may still execute a power of attorney for property and personal care. If a person is mentally incapable, however, it is likely too late.

A close relative such as an adult child may have a legal basis for intervening in a parent's affairs if the parent is mentally incompetent in a legal sense—unable to make a judgment and understand the consequences of it. Under the law, mentally incompetent people are considered so disordered that they are a danger to themselves or to others and require care, supervision and control to protect themselves and their property.

If a person is generally of sound mind but simply not managing his or her affairs prudently, there is no legal basis to interfere.

Sometimes a person is not clearly mentally incompetent, or has intervals of competence. For example, it is difficult to assess the mental competence of someone with Alzheimer's disease, which weakens an individual's mental powers. People with this disease may be mentally competent in some areas and not in others, and their powers may vary from day to day. They may be able to take medication or cook their own meals, but lack the capacity to manage their financial affairs, consent to medical treatment or dispose of their estate by will. Each situation should be considered individually to allow the person to maintain as much autonomy as possible. British Columbia and Manitoba have laws to give these adults more control over their affairs to the extent possible.

The legal procedure to declare a person mentally incompetent and appoint someone to manage her or his affairs varies from province to province. Expert medical evidence is needed to prove a person mentally incompetent. Once incompetence has been proven, a committee or guardian—usually a family member but sometimes the public trustee—is appointed with broad powers that are subject to close court scrutiny and review. Any person appointed to manage the estate of a mentally incompetent person must keep proper records and account to the court. Several provinces have adult guardianship laws to protect vulnerable adults from mistreatment.

Upon the request of such interested parties as a doctor, hospital or relative, a court may appoint a guardian to provide medical consent to treatment. The judge must agree that the patient is mentally incompetent and requires the care, supervision and control of a guardian. This person may be a relative or a public trustee appointed by the judge for the patient's own protection.

In some cases, a similar order may be secured if someone is only temporarily incapable—perhaps because of disease or a drug habit. Whether temporary or permanent in effect, mental incompetency proceedings can be complicated and expensive. They are sometimes unavoidable, however, if the person does not have a living will.

In cases where a patient does not understand the necessity, risks or benefits of treatment recommended by physicians, and has not prepared any advance directives, treatment may be permitted with the consent of a family member, even though that person has not formally applied to be the patient's legal guardian. If the relatives cannot agree on the treatment, they may have to apply to court to solve the impasse.

Patients may have to be committed to an institution for protection and treatment if they endanger themselves or others. If a person has been certified as mentally disturbed by one or more physicians, every province allows authorities to detain the patient involuntarily for a limited time, although the length of time varies from province to province. Once involuntarily committed, the person may still have the legal right in some jurisdictions to refuse treatment without her or his consent.

Courts are reluctant to deprive a citizen's liberty on mental incapacity grounds. In the 1997 case of *Re Koch*, an Ontario judge overturned orders that allowed a husband to place his wife, who suffered from multiple sclerosis, in a chronic care hospital. During negotiations over a separation agreement, the husband took issue with his estranged wife's spending habits, alleging she exhibited an inability to manage her finances. The wife was forced to undergo a hearing and was declared mentally incapable of managing her financial affairs and property. In setting aside the finding of incapacity, the judge questioned the effectiveness of the evaluation conducted as well as the husband's motives. He concluded that "it must be remembered that the appellant has the right to spend her money foolishly if she desires. The right to be foolish is an incident of living in a free and democratic society."

The Ontario government amended its mental health law in 2000 to make it easier to force psychiatric patients to undergo treatment. The law includes community treatment orders, in essence a kind of parole for psychiatric patients after they are discharged from the hospital. The purpose of a community treatment order is to provide a person who suffers from a serious mental disorder with a comprehensive plan of community-based treatment or care and supervision that is less restrictive than being detained in a psychiatric facility.

5. The Right to Refuse and Discontinue Treatment

All people have the right to say no to any form of psychiatric or medical treatment, as long as they are mentally competent—that is, as long as they understand what they are doing and their consent is informed and voluntary. In fact, a doctor who treats a patient without the proper authority to do so risks being charged with criminal assault, battery or negligence.

In the rare court cases of passive euthanasia in Canada, adult Jehovah's Witnesses have been allowed to refuse a blood transfusion, even though refusal meant certain death. Similarly, cancer patients have legally refused to have surgery or start chemotherapy.

It used to be that patients could refuse to start a treatment, but could not discontinue it once in progress if doing so would threaten life. If doctors discontinued on the patient's instructions, the doctors could be charged with criminal negligence, homicide, attempted homicide or assisting in a suicide. Then the Quebec Superior Court extended the law to permit a terminally ill person to discontinue treatment by disconnecting a respirator, as long as doing so would not inflict death; nature would then take its course, and death would be caused by the underlying disease.

The 1992 case of "Nancy B." dramatically focused public attention on the tragic dilemma facing any mentally aware patient with an incurable disease who is kept alive by modern technology. At issue was not her life, but its quality. Nancy B., aged 25, was bedridden and paralysed from the neck down by Guillain-Barré syndrome. For more than two years, she had been connected to a respirator that did her breathing for her and kept her alive. She petitioned the Quebec Superior Court to instruct her doctor to discontinue treatment.

To disconnect Nancy B.'s respirator was to threaten her life. Had Nancy B. been able to do this herself, the court application may not have been necessary. To avoid criminal charges against anyone, Nancy B. applied for and got the Court's permission to turn off the respirator.

Nancy B. was able to communicate her instructions because she continued to be mentally competent. Instructions made in a power of attorney for personal care while the person is mentally competent should have the same force and effect.

The court applied the reasoning of the Law Reform Commission of Canada, which, in 1983, proposed changes, which were never made law, to give a person who is still mentally competent the right to refuse treatment even after it has started.

Despite the ruling in Nancy B.'s case, it would be unwise for people to assume that they have the unrestricted right to "pull the plug" for a friend or relative, whether acting on that person's instructions at the time or in an advance directive. If the person is not at death's door, anyone who causes his or her death—whether a doctor, spouse, family member or friend—could face murder or manslaughter charges and be liable to life imprisonment, even if the help was requested and the helper acted out of compassion. The helper could also be breaking the law against assisting someone to commit suicide, which carries a maximum penalty of 14 years' imprisonment, although prosecution has been rare in cases involving terminally ill patients who wished to die.

As every case is different, only a doctor should decide whether the termination of treatment would inflict harm or allow nature to take its course. Although the Canadian Medical Association's ethical guidelines state that doctors need not take heroic measures to keep incurable patients alive in the final stages of a disease, a physician might still want court direction in some cases.

6. Assisted Suicide

After the Nancy B. case, the British Columbia courts struggled with the case of Sue Rodriguez, a 42-year-old woman with amyotrophic lateral sclerosis (ALS—also known as Lou Gehrig's disease) who sought a court declaration that she be entitled to have assistance in committing suicide when her terminal condition was no longer bearable. In seeking this declaration, she argued that the sections of the Criminal Code that prohibited physician-assisted suicide should be declared invalid pursuant to the Canadian Charter of Rights and Freedoms.

It was only in 1972 that the offence of attempting to commit suicide was deleted from the Criminal Code, where it had been listed since 1892. Even before then, however, the common law had long held it an offence for a person to attempt to commit suicide. The woman faced a dilemma: While neither suicide nor attempted suicide are illegal in the Criminal Code, to "counsel, aid, or abet" suicide is still a criminal offence. She argued that she should not be forced to endure a life in which she would be totally dependent on others and then suffer a mentally agonizing death. However, at the time she would encounter these conditions, she would not be physically capable of committing suicide without assistance.

Both the trial court and the B.C. Court of Appeal dismissed her application. The B.C. Court of Appeal took the position that the broad religious, ethical, moral and social issues involved in a decision to permit physician-assisted suicide were properly a policy decision that should be made by the government of the day, rather than the courts.

Rodriguez then took her case to the Supreme Court of Canada. By the time the case was reached in 1993, her condition was rapidly deteriorating, and the Court noted that she would soon lose the ability to swallow, speak, walk and move her body without assistance. After this, she would need the help of a respirator to breathe and she would eventually be confined to bed. Her life expectancy was between two and 14 months.

The Supreme Court of Canada was split almost down the middle in their decision. Five justices held that her appeal should be dismissed, finding that the principles of fundamental justice required a fair balance between the interests of the state and those of the individual. The long-time prohibition against assisted suicide, they reasoned, was grounded in the state's interest in protecting life, and reflected the community's policy that human life should not be depreciated by allowing that life to be taken. They also noted that this protection was grounded on a substantial consensus, among western countries, medical organizations and the Law Reform Commission of Canada, that the best way to protect life and those who are vulnerable in society is to prohibit, without exception, the giving of assistance to commit suicide.

If such a "consensus" is apparent in western society, it was not apparent in Canada's highest court. The four dissenting justices, for various reasons, were prepared to allow

Rodriguez's appeal. Justice Peter Cory, one of the four dissenting judges, held that there was no difference between permitting a patient of sound mind to choose death with dignity by refusing treatment, and permitting a patient of sound mind who is terminally ill to choose death with dignity by terminating life-preserving treatment, even if, because of incapacity, that step has to be physically taken by another on the patient's instructions. Nor, he argued, was there any reason not to extend that same permission so that terminally ill patients facing death may put an end to their life through the intermediary of another. Since the right to choose death is open to patients who are not physically handicapped, he reasoned, there is no reason to deny that choice to those who are. Having lost her legal battle, Sue Rodriguez nevertheless won her personal battle by proceeding with an assisted suicide. To my knowledge, no one was charged with a criminal offence for helping her.

Doctor-assisted suicides continue amidst public debate. When Nancy Morrison, a Halifax respirologist, was arrested in 1996 and charged with murder in the death of one of her terminally ill cancer patients, thousands of people signed a petition urging the province to drop the case. Although a provincial court judge threw the case out in February 1998, saying no jury would convict Morrison, the Crown did not give up until December 1998, after its appeal to the Nova Scotia Supreme Court was dismissed. Dr. Morrison received only a reprimand from the Nova Scotia College of Physicians and Surgeons, after admitting she had acted "outside the accepted standards of medical care" when she administered drugs to hasten the death of her patient, Paul Mills.

Until Parliament decides to deal with these issues, the courts are left with the task. The Supreme Court of Canada in 1997 deferred wrestling with the moral and ethical dilemma of mercy killing when it sent the case of Robert Latimer back for a new trial. Latimer is the Saskatchewan farmer convicted of second-degree murder and originally sentenced to life imprisonment with a minimum ten-year sentence for taking the life of his 12-year-old daughter. She suffered from severe cerebral damage and physical deformities that had required substantial surgical intervention. She was in pain, and could neither care for herself nor communicate.

In December 1997, at his second trial, Latimer was again convicted. The trial judge stated in his reasons that he was influenced by the jury's wish for leniency as well as the public reaction following the severity of Latimer's first sentence. Relying on Section 12 of the Charter, the judge granted a rare constitutional exemption permitting him to replace the mandatory ten-year sentence with one of two years less a day, with only the first year to be served in jail. The Saskatchewan Court of Appeal disagreed and imposed the mandatory ten-year sentence. Latimer's case returned to the Supreme Court of Canada in 2000, and in January 2001, the Court dismissed Latimer's appeals against both the conviction and the sentence. He would not be eligible for parole for ten years, unless the federal government chose to grant him clemency by using the "royal prerogative of mercy" in section 749 of the Criminal Code.

In the meantime, patients, their doctors and their families are left to find their own ways to cope with the tragic dilemmas of terminal illness. With the increase in the aging population, the AIDS crisis and the technological improvements in medicine, the question of assisted suicide will arise more often.

C. PLANNING FOR DEATH

Planning for the inevitability of death may not be the most pleasant task, but it will benefit the next of kin and will set the planner's mind at rest. No matter what their age, all people with dependants and assets should have a will and plan how to meet their responsibilities.

A 1996 B.C. Court of Appeal case illustrates the devastating impact of not making wills. Although admitting paternity, William Eva had paid no ongoing child support to his daughter and had no contact with her or his granddaughter Michelle. He paid only $1,000 to Michelle's mother as part of an agreement made shortly after Michelle was born. When his daughter, her husband and infant daughter were killed in a car accident without having made wills, Mr. Eva was one of the three surviving grandparents who stood to share in his granddaughter's estate under intestacy rules. Although the trial judge ruled against Mr. Eva, on appeal the Court held that no amount of evidence as to his neglect of his daughter could alter the fact of his biological relationship as her father. Since estate legislation does not provide discretion to determine entitlement, he got a one-third share of the estate.

1. Planning for a Will

A last will and testament, usually called simply a will, is the document of instructions that a mentally competent person (called a "testator") signs to permit a trusted person (executor, sometimes called trustee or estate trustee) or persons to dispose of property in a specified manner on his or her death.

Planning carefully for a will ensures that an individual's wishes are respected after death and avoids leaving a mess for the family to sort out. Those planning their will need to think about who will need protection from the effect of their death; to whom they should leave their property; who should care for their children; and whom they should appoint to carry out their wishes.

Before meeting with a lawyer to give instructions, a person planning a will may find these guidelines useful.

PREPARATION

The person's preliminary preparations will save time and enable a lawyer to give informed advice, especially if the situation is complicated or estate planning is involved. Testators should take a list of questions to be discussed; a list of assets, such as property, investments, RRSPs, pensions, insurance policies and bank accounts; a list of debts; and copies of relevant documents, such as insurance policies and RRSP statements. Documents can help the lawyer identify property and verify ownership. For example, if both spouses are joint tenants, one spouse cannot bequeath the property to someone else in the will; ownership will automatically go to the surviving joint tenant.

Testators should also bring information on beneficiary designations on life insurance and RRSPs. They may name either their estate or a specific person; when a person is named, the proceeds pass "outside" the will and are therefore not governed by the will. A

---

lawyer should be consulted about the advantages and disadvantages in a particular situation. For example, if property does not pass through a person's estate, the court processing fees may be lower because they are normally based on the value of the assets that are governed by the will. As well, creditors may not be able to touch assets that pass outside the estate. Therefore, if a testator has significant debt and worries about leaving his dependants destitute, he may wish to name the beneficiaries of his life insurance policies and RRSPs outside his will.

Although there are no estate or succession duties in Canada at present, the impact of large hikes in court processing (probate) fees can be significant to an estate. In 1998 the Supreme Court of Canada (*Re Eurig*) held that Ontario's probate fee was unconstitutional, saying it was a tax in disguise. The government was given six months to pass necessary laws if they wished to try to pass a law justifying the fee. Ontario and other provinces, not wishing to lose this source of revenue, not only validated future charges, they backdated the law to try to avoid claims for reimbursement for charges from previous years.

With all the negative publicity on probate fees, avoidance plans have become very popular. For example, the testator may be encouraged to hold property in joint tenancy with right of survivorship. Property owned in this manner—with the other spouse or with third parties—passes outside the will and does not normally form part of the estate (except in exceptional circumstances). Think this through carefully and with legal advice. In a 1989 Ontario case, a husband died without a will, holding three properties jointly with third parties (various members of his family). The wife wanted a share of these properties as his widow, but since they passed to the joint owners by survivorship, they did not form part of his estate, so she had no claim to them. If a testator decides to hold her home jointly with an adult child and later wants to sell, rent or mortgage it, she will need that child's consent. Similarly, if savings for several children are held in a joint account with one child to avoid probate fees, there should be documentation to enforce that obligation on the testator's death.

Testators should also bring their most recent tax return, which is often helpful, especially if advice on tax planning is required. There may be a capital gains tax at death on assets that are worth more than their cost, except for a principal residence.

Marriage contracts or separation agreements are also useful because they may contain provisions binding on a spouse's estate. If the testator is preparing a will before marriage, the will must say so, or it may become invalid on a subsequent marriage. (Wills may lose their validity on marriage or divorce, depending on the jurisdiction where the testator resides.)

A list is needed of the full names and addresses of all beneficiaries, executors and guardians, as well as a list of any charities to receive a legacy, noting any specific purpose intended for the bequest. A charity may also be named in the event that none of the other beneficiaries survive to receive a share of the estate. A lawyer may need to consult with the particular charity to ensure that the terms of the legacy are appropriate. There may also be tax considerations to discuss.

Instructions about the desired funeral arrangements and organ donations, if any, should be prepared before the meeting. Even if testators include these instructions in their will, they would be wise to tell their next of kin ahead of time, as executors may not have access to the will immediately.

Finally, they should bring a list of any specific personal possessions, such as family mementos or heirlooms, to be left to certain beneficiaries. In some circumstances, a lawyer may advise the client to make a reference in the will to a letter that will inform the executors of such specific bequests. In this way, if the maker of a will has a change of mind, or if a specific personal possession no longer exists, the list may be changed without changing the will itself.

Mutual Wills: Mutual wills impose enforceable obligations on a surviving spouse that must be taken into account in any future estate planning. A B.C. couple who held all their property jointly made mutual wills to donate their life savings to a scholarship at the University of Manitoba. The surviving husband rewrote his will after his wife's death and decided not to follow through on this provision. Instead, he left only one-quarter of their $1.7 million estate to the university and the rest to relatives. A trial judge dismissed the university's claim to the entire estate, reasoning that the husband was not bound by the mutual wills as he received no benefit from his wife's will. The B.C. Court of Appeal disagreed, stating that revoking a mutual will after one party has died is tantamount to fraud.

EXECUTOR OR EXECUTORS

People making a will should choose an executor or executors they trust. Usually family members are chosen; often, when the estate is straightforward and the assets will be immediately distributed on death, one of the main beneficiaries can act as executor. If the estate is complex, the will could include instructions that permit the executor to retain the assistance of a financial advisor or other professional. Alternatively, the person making the will could consider appointing a trust company as executor, to benefit from its professional expertise. Perhaps the most effective solution for a person with a complex estate is to have two executors, one a professional and one a relative or friend. Be aware, however, that unless a will provides otherwise, all trustees, including professionals, must act unanimously. It is always wise to ask these people if they are prepared to act; otherwise, they may refuse when the time comes and someone else would have to be appointed.

Executor's compensation may be a factor in the choice. An executor is entitled to be paid by the estate for services rendered, which can be substantial. Family members (who may also be beneficiaries) often waive payment or reduce their fee, but the customary unofficial compensation in Ontario, for example, has been 2.5 percent on capital receipts and 2.5 percent on capital payments, 2.5 percent on income received and 2.5 percent on payments made, as well as a management fee of 0.4 percent per year on the average gross value of the estate.

Although it has been approximately 25 years since the Supreme Court of Canada provided any guidance on the matter of what is a fair and reasonable allowance for executor's compensation, the Ontario Court of Appeal considered three cases. Ultimately the Court ruled that the unofficial compensation approach is valid, unless there are special circumstances or provisions in a will specifically dealing with this compensation. A trust company, on the other hand, charges according to its own fee schedule, which is frequently higher.

It is wise to name alternate executors in case one or more predecease the maker of the will or are unable or unwilling to carry out their duties.

Most wills give executors complete discretion to do the job. However, if the will has no discretionary clause, the general law will apply and require the executor to make relatively conservative investments. Ontario, British Columbia, Quebec, and Newfoundland and Labrador have legislation to replace previously limited investment powers with a less restrictive "prudent investor" standard of care. This may significantly broaden not only the investment powers but also the level of competence to which executors and trustees will be held.

An executor or trustee is responsible for arranging the burial, gathering assets and investments, paying debts and taxes, and distributing property according to the will. If there are underage children and a trust has been established in the will, then the executor may be charged with the responsibility of managing the trust funds. An executor has the authority to act from the moment of death.

BENEFICIARIES

There are no restrictions on the choice or number of beneficiaries. If a person has several, it may be advisable to simply bequeath equal shares of the estate to "issue," a statement that would provide for children and, if the children predecease the testator, grandchildren.

The testator should decide on alternative beneficiaries in case any of those named predecease him or her. He or she should also remember that a failure to adequately provide for former spouses, stepchildren or children born out of wedlock, as stipulated in a separation agreement or marriage contract, could trigger a claim against the estate.

If any beneficiaries named are minors at the time of the testator's death, they become entitled to the bequest at the age of majority in their province, unless a later age is stipulated in the will itself.

If beneficiaries are minors, mentally disabled or financially irresponsible, a trust fund may be established by will, coming into effect on death, to provide them with investment income while preserving the capital.

If a husband and wife who left their estates to each other should die simultaneously, or in circumstances where it is impossible to determine who died first, the law in some provinces stipulates how their property is to be divided and whose will takes precedence. For example, Ontario law provides that when two or more people die simultaneously, the property of each person is distributed as if each person had survived the others. Since the law is not that clear in every jurisdiction, testators should stipulate in a will what they want to happen if they should die at the same time as any of their beneficiaries. A common provision in a will states that a person inherits only if he or she survives the testator by 30 days.

Beneficiaries may include a beloved pet. The owner may want to consider not only naming someone to care for the animal, but also providing financial assistance for this care. Local humane societies may be able to help. The Toronto Humane Society, for example, provides a "stewardship program" in exchange for a charitable bequest. The organization matches a pet with a suitable adopting family, conducts an annual check on the pet's welfare and provides free medical treatment.

Certain laws can interfere with intended distribution under a will. For example, matrimonial property legislation in a province or territory could prevent a person from leaving less to his or her spouse than that spouse is entitled to by law.

DEPENDENT CHILDREN

If children are under the age of majority, the testator should choose someone who is willing to act as guardian in case both parents die before the children are grown. One person may be appointed to be both personal and financial guardian, or separate individuals may be chosen for these different roles. For example, the executor could be the financial guardian, with someone else raising the children. There is a more detailed discussion on this topic in the section on guardianship of children.

The parent writing the will must leave the trustee instructions about the exercise of discretion in managing the funds on behalf of the children. Directions should state whether to provide the guardian with only the investment income, or to provide some of the capital as well, if the children need it for any reason or for specified reasons such as health and education needs.

There may be other dependants, such as parents or siblings, who relied on the testator. Provision should be made for them as well.

EXECUTION OF THE WILL

Once the will is prepared, it should be signed and witnessed at the lawyer's office to ensure that it is executed in accordance with rules established by law and is therefore valid and enforceable. The document must have two witnesses, present at the same time, who watch the testator execute the will and watch each other witness it.

A careful lawyer will prepare and have executed an affidavit of execution to be signed by one of the witnesses, confirming due execution. If the affidavit is signed when the will is executed, the trustee will not need to go hunting for witnesses when the testator dies, unless the will has been altered.

A beneficiary or his or her spouse cannot be a witness. If a beneficiary witnesses a will, he or she is thereby prevented from receiving anything from the will. A person who is asked to act as a witness should refuse if he is a named or possible beneficiary. In fact, independent, unrelated witnesses can help protect against claims of undue influence in situations where one person or relative is favoured over other family members. If necessary, the witnesses can take notes about the mental capability of the person writing the will. They can also engage the testator in some conversation to satisfy themselves that he or she is signing voluntarily, and understands the will's purpose. To prevent other questions being raised about undue influence, the person who is to benefit from the will should not pass along instructions for the will or accompany the testator to the lawyer when the instructions are given or the will executed. Certainly, the beneficiary should not be present in the same room when the will is executed.

As there is only one original will, the testator should decide where it will be kept once it is executed.

REVIEWING AND UPDATING A WILL

Testators should keep a copy of the will accessible and review it every two to five years to ensure that it is still current. With this copy, they should keep a current list of names, addresses and relevant account numbers with respect to bank accounts, life insurance policies, broker or investment dealers, employer pension or other benefits and RRSPs, as well as the amount and whereabouts of other investments such as Canada Savings Bonds and GICs. The location of tax returns and the original will's location can also be noted on this list.

If a person remarries after executing a will, the will is automatically invalid in all provinces and territories (except Quebec, where the law is silent on the effect of marriage), unless the will clearly says that it was made in contemplation of the remarriage.

On separation or divorce, testators should consult a lawyer about changing or making a will. Prince Edward Island, Ontario, Quebec, Manitoba and Saskatchewan presume that a divorce invalidates a bequest to the divorced spouse, unless the will specifically states otherwise. In British Columbia, legislation cancels a bequest to a spouse where a judicial separation has been ordered. But no change in the deceased's circumstances other than remarriage or divorce will raise the presumption that he or she intended to change the will.

2. Holograph Wills

If a will is entirely handwritten by the testator, it is called a holograph will—a handwritten, unwitnessed disposition of a person's property on death. Such wills are valid for the disposal of property on death in Alberta, Manitoba, New Brunswick, Newfoundland and Labrador, Saskatchewan, Ontario, the Northwest Territories and Nunavut, the Yukon and Quebec. In British Columbia, Nova Scotia and Prince Edward Island, a holograph will is valid only for members of the armed forces.

A holograph will must be written so that it clearly represents an intention to dispose of property on death. Here are some essential conditions:

- The will must be handwritten to be valid. If the testator uses a standard printed form, available at many stationers, a court may consider valid only those parts that are inserted in handwriting. The courts have had to examine many such wills, and although they have validated some, a person would be wise not to chance litigation by using these forms.
- A will should not be typed unless it will be formally witnessed according to the legal execution requirements. In 1984, the Supreme Court of Canada ruled invalid a typewritten letter signed by the deceased because the letter/will was not entirely in the deceased's handwriting.
- The testator should use pen and paper, even though the occasional exception has been recognized. In 1948, a farmer who was pinned under an overturned tractor wrote "all to my wife" in blood on

its underside, and the court upheld this declaration as a valid holograph will.

- The will should be written clearly, so that neither the handwriting nor the meaning has to be submitted to a court for interpretation. The judge may require proof that the will is in the deceased's handwriting.

- Witnesses are not necessary for a holograph will.

- The testator should state at the beginning that the will revokes earlier ones, and should date the document at the end.

- The testator should appoint an executor, and a guardian for any children under the age of majority.

- The person making the will must sign at the end of all writing, using her or his full name. Nothing should be added after the signature without the testator signing again after the addition. In 1995, children in Newfoundland and Labrador were unsuccessful when they tried to have a document in their mother's handwriting signed "Love Mother" upheld as a valid holograph will.

- Corrections, additions or deletions in the will can cause confusion. Unless the will is witnessed and the witnesses initial such changes, a court may find it impossible to determine whether the changes were made before or after the will was signed; changes added after the will is signed may make the document invalid. It is safer for the testator to rewrite the will and destroy the previous one, or consult a lawyer on how to ensure changes are valid.

- On marriage or divorce, a testator should make a new will.

An original will should be kept in a safe place, and the executor or next of kin advised where it can be found. A will should not be hidden. Copies can be made, but only the original document can be validated by a court. If the maker of a will stores it in a safety deposit box, she should ensure that a copy is available to help the executors prove they have authority to open the safety deposit box.

If the testator was mentally competent when a holograph will was made, courts will try to uphold his or her intentions, if at all possible. For this reason, a 1995 Quebec case upheld a will that the deceased dictated to his sister in 1954. She wrote it out, and then the deceased signed it. Although the form was questionable, the court found, on the evidence, that the will unequivocally contained his last wishes.

Normally, a testator revokes a will by tearing up the original and stating at the beginning of the new will, "I hereby revoke all previous wills. . . ." In a 1990 Ontario case, an 86-year-old man handwrote his will, stating that he wished to leave his house and money to a close friend. He then handed the document to the friend, stating, "Take this, I could kick off at any time." The friend tore up the will in the presence of the testator, but not on the testator's instructions. Two days later, the testator shot himself, and the friend found the pieces of the signed paper in a shopping bag in the kitchen, along with the garbage. The friend applied for probate of the signed paper, and the court held that not only did it satisfy the formalities of the law, but it also established the deceased's intention as to how he wished to dispose of his property.

In another Ontario case, in 1991, a woman had been making arrangements to change her will at the time of her death. She wrote to the trust company who retained the original, advising the company that she wanted to "cancel" her 1983 will and was arranging to have a new will drawn up. Although an officer of the trust company testified that the woman had advised him she had not yet revoked her 1983 will, on her death her copy of the 1983 will was found at her apartment with the words "Cancelled/Lily Downey" on it in her handwriting. This declaration, together with a letter to the trust company in similar wording, was held by the court to be clear, unambiguous evidence that the will had been revoked.

Once a testator decides to change or revoke a will, he should have a new will drawn up as soon as possible to ensure the estate is disposed of as he intends. If a will is revoked and not replaced, property will pass under a province's intestacy rules.

Although holograph wills are valid, lawyer-drawn wills are preferable because lawyers are taught what traps to avoid. And, although a lawyer's charge to prepare a will may vary, it is probably the least expensive legal service a person can buy.

3. Meeting Support Obligations to Dependants

BY AGREEMENT

Any contractual commitment that is binding on a person's estate may be considered a debt of the estate and take precedence over specific or general bequests. One of these commitments may be an obligation to pay support contained in a separation agreement or court order. If the agreement or order states clearly that payments to the dependant are to be paid for the dependant's lifetime, or that support payments are binding on the payor's estate, continuing the payments will be a definite obligation of the estate.

BY DEPENDANT'S RELIEF LAWS

If the payor was supporting the dependant at the time of the payor's death or had an obligation to do so, and the dependant can establish need, an application may be made under provincial dependants' relief legislation for support to be paid by the estate. If the claim is successful, these payments may come ahead of specific and general bequests.

The question of who qualifies as a dependant will depend, in part, on the facts in each case and the law in each province. A former spouse, current spouse and common-law spouse (and same-sex spouses in most jurisdictions) may qualify if the testator was supporting any one of them at the time of death.

While a separated spouse who gave up all rights to support in a separation agreement will not normally qualify as a dependant, a spouse with a nominal support award of a dollar per year was held to be a dependant in a 1982 Ontario case. In every jurisdiction, children are dependants not only if they are under the age of majority, but also if they are older than the age of majority and unable to support themselves because of a mental or physical disability. In some cases, a parent or sibling may also qualify. The amount awarded to any dependant will be based on need.

A person should obtain legal advice before considering whether or not to make a dependant's relief claim. She or he should also act quickly—if the claim is not made soon after the testator's death, the assets of the estate may be distributed and it may be too late. For example, in Ontario a dependant has six months in which to make the claim.

BY MORAL OBLIGATION

While most jurisdictions limit a dependent child to one under the age of majority, or older if unable to become independent due to a mental or physical disability, some jurisdictions allow more discretion. Adult children who have not been left a share of a parent's estate have applied under such laws to ask the courts to impose a "moral obligation" on a parent to share the estate with them.

More such claims have been made because of the 1994 Supreme Court of Canada case of *Tataryn* v. *Tataryn Estate*. The law in British Columbia gives a court broad discretion to make "adequate, just and equitable" provision for a spouse and children. In this case, the Supreme Court of Canada held that the law imposed a legal and moral obligation on the testator to his wife and sons. Despite the wife's substantial contribution to the family's assets during a 43-year marriage, the husband had left her with only a right to receive the income from his estate during her lifetime. He wanted only one son to get the estate on her death, but not the other. The Court ordered that the wife get ownership of the matrimonial home, the right to receive the income on a rental property and everything else outright. The Court awarded the sons an immediate payment from the estate of $10,000 each, and, on their mother's death, the sons were to get the rental property, divided two-thirds to the favoured son and one-third to the other son.

Relying on the B.C. legislation and the Tataryn case, in 1997 in the case of *Pattie* v. *Standal Estate* another B.C. court refused to allow an adoptive father to disinherit his 32-year-old son, whom he had not seen since the son was seven years of age. The son, who was found entitled to one-half of his father's $133,000 estate, had originally moved to Alberta with his mother when his adoptive parents separated; he was not well off financially. The court concluded that, unless there was a good reason to disinherit him, a parent has a moral obligation to provide for even an adult child.

Tataryn has been applied in other provinces, such as Alberta, Saskatchewan, and New Brunswick.

Ontario followed suit in 2004 when, for the first time since Ontario's Dependants' Relief Act was replaced by the Succession Law Reform Act (SLRA) in 1978, the Ontario Court of Appeal dealt with the issue of whether and to what extent moral or ethical considerations may be taken into account on a dependants' relief application. The Court of Appeal determined that when judging whether a deceased has made adequate provision for the proper support of his or her dependants, a court must examine the claims of *all* dependants, whether based on need or on legal or moral and ethical obligations, in dealing with the moral claims of an adult disabled child. The court considered not only the needs and means of the dependants who were actually making claims, but also the moral obligations of the deceased person towards other dependants who were not asserting need at the time.

In *Cummings* v. *Cummings Estate*, a 24-year-old disabled son and an ex-wife, on behalf of her 18-year-old daughter in school, applied for dependants' relief against the estate of their late father, who had remarried. Neither the second wife nor the first wife made any claim for support from the estate. The second wife was a joint owner by survivorship of the matrimonial home and cottage and beneficiary of the deceased's RRSPs. The deceased had left a trust fund of $125,000 for his son.

The court noted that if all, or substantially more of Mr. Cummings' estate had been allocated to the support of his son, then his second wife would arguably be in need. When he died, his testamentary estate was valued at $135,000, and his other assets (deemed by the law to be available for supporting a dependants' relief order) totalled $515,000: namely, a matrimonial home and cottage held jointly with his wife, and RRSPs naming his wife as beneficiary. The total net value of the estate, for dependants' relief purposes, was concluded to be about $650,000. The court did not want to disturb the second wife's ownership of the home, thus recognizing her moral claims. Instead there was an order for the setting aside of $250,000 for the children.

The result means that dependants' relief applications will be less predictable and more discretionary in the future. An application in 2004 for leave to appeal to the Supreme Court of Canada was dismissed.

4. Guardianship of Children

To avoid a court battle, parents should try to agree on whom to appoint as legal guardian of their children in the event of the parents' death. If each makes a will appointing his or her own choice as guardian, and the choices are different, the court will then have to make the decision for them. If the parents are in agreement and the guardian consents, the court order will be only a formality.

A person can be guardian of the child's person by having custody of the child, or guardian of the child's property, or both. The person with custody is in charge of the child's education and has responsibility to take care of the child, but has no obligation to provide for the child from personal funds. A guardian of the property, such as a trust company, has no authority over the child's person, but has the right to control the property, and the obligation to manage the property on the child's behalf for a fee. The executor of a will is usually given the right to deal with the child's assets.

If parents cannot decide on a guardian themselves, or have not designated anyone in their wills and there is no family member available to take charge, or if there is a contest between prospective guardians, the court will decide. Concerned with the child's welfare, the court will also consider the child's wishes, if they can be readily ascertained. The expressed wishes of the parents will also be considered, but other factors affecting the child's well-being (for example, the inability of a person with a disability to care for the child) may be presented to the court and override parental wishes. Basically, the best interests of the child will govern who becomes guardian, and the court will consider such factors as the emotional ties between the child and the proposed custodial guardians, their plans for upbringing and their own relationship. Before appointing a guardian of property, the court will consider the applicant's ability to manage the child's property, the merit of any proposed plans and the child's wishes.

If a non-parent applies to be a guardian while one of the natural parents is alive, the court will likely ask for the natural parent's opinion (and, in some provinces, his or her consent). In some provinces, the child's consent is also required, particularly if the child is 12 or older.

If the parents have voluntarily given up custody of their child to a third party, those custody arrangements will not be disturbed if they are in the best interests of the child. If, after one parent's death, there is a contest for custody between the surviving parent and the custodial party, it is likely that the custodial party will maintain custody.

Questions often arise over appointments of guardians when parents are separated or divorced. If a step-parent is appointed guardian by the custodial parent, and the non-custodial parent wishes custody, the court's intervention may be required.

In some jurisdictions, a parent may appoint a guardian by will; in other places, however, the guardian's appointment lasts only until the court decides who should get custody. The surviving natural parent may apply to the court to remove the guardian, but all decisions will in the end be based on the best interests of the child.

The legislation does not list necessary qualifications but, generally speaking, a guardian has the same obligations as a parent—to ensure that the child receives the necessities of life and an education. A guardian may resign his or her position with the court's permission. Guardians can also be removed by a court.

5. Providing for Children with Disabilities

How parents plan to provide for a child with a disability depends on a number of factors: the assets they have available, the nature of the child's disability and whether the child can live independently or requires either supervision or institutional care.

In a will, a parent should identify the child as in need of special assistance. If the parent bequeaths more to the child with a disability than to any other children, she should explain why in order to avoid a challenge to the will.

If the child is a minor or unable to manage money, the parent could consider establishing a trust to take effect while the parent is alive ("inter vivos trust") or within the will to take effect after the parent dies ("testamentary trust"). The trust should name the trustee or trustees, specify the extent of discretion available to the trustee and indicate whether the trustee is permitted to encroach on capital for the benefit of the child. A discretionary trust gives the trustee varying degrees of control, depending on the wording of the document. For instance, some testamentary trusts have allowed the trustee some flexibility to regulate the child's income so that the child might also qualify for government assistance. Trust issues are complex, and legal advice is essential.

The parent should name a guardian to make care decisions, particularly for a minor or adult with a mental disability. The will should also appoint a financial guardian (who may be the same person), even if the estate has few assets. The child may be entitled to government assistance payments and need someone to manage the funds.

Both parents should appoint the same guardians and trustees. They would also be wise to name an alternate or two, in case an appointee predeceases the child or is unable to continue in the role for any reason.

If the parents were divorced, the child is entitled, even as an adult, to receive support from the non-custodial parent. This right continues even after the death of the custodial parent.

In British Columbia, the Planned Lifetime Advocacy Network (PLAN) has organized another way for parents to provide for their children after their death. It facilitates the creation of surrogate families as support networks and offers estate planning advice to avoid institutionalization of children with disabilities.

6. Organ Donations

All the provinces and territories have similar laws about the donation of tissue or organs for therapeutic purposes—such as transplants—or for medical education and research. To give consent, donors ordinarily must be over the age of majority. Although a person may verbally consent in the presence of two witnesses, it is better to leave clear written consent and instructions. One simple way to do so is to sign the consent form provided on all provincial drivers' licences; the driver can specify the parts to be donated or just say "any useful parts." (Most legislation excludes the donation of skin, bone, blood or other tissues that the body can replace naturally.) People can also give consent in their will, but they should inform their executor ahead of time because wills are often ignored until after burial. They should also inform their next of kin and doctor so that their wish is certain to be respected.

Even without the person's consent, medical personnel may seek permission from certain other people when a person's death is imminent or has occurred. Quebec law permits doctors to remove organs with consent from the person's "consort or nearest relative." All other provinces and territories allow consent from a person's closest available relative; a spouse is considered the closest, followed by adult children, then parents and then adult sisters or brothers. In most provinces and territories, another adult next of kin may give consent as a last resort. Saskatchewan law specifies that a separated spouse is not allowed to consent.

If no next of kin is available, a person "lawfully in possession of the body"—perhaps a close friend—may consent, except in Quebec. The administrative head of the hospital where the prospective donor has died is not allowed to consent, except in Manitoba and New Brunswick. In Quebec, two physicians may remove a part for a transplant without any consent if they confirm in writing that it was impossible to get proper consent, that the immediate transplant might save a life and that the donor's death was first verified by two independent doctors.

Even when there is consent, most provinces and territories forbid the removal of a body part until the donor's death is confirmed by two doctors who are in no way associated with the proposed recipient, and are not participating in the transplant operation.

Minors are generally not allowed to consent to a donation of their tissues and organs. Exceptions may be made in Quebec, which permits consent from a minor "capable of discernment" if a parent also gives written approval, and possibly in New Brunswick, where the law does not specify that a donor must be an adult. In the other provinces and territories, the minor's parents or adult siblings may consent. Sometimes, a doctor may be allowed to act on a minor's consent if the doctor believes the child was legally able to consent—which would only be likely if the minor were 16 or 17.

In all provinces and territories, a mentally competent adult is allowed to donate an organ or tissue while still living—for example, some people donate one of their kidneys to a relative whose kidneys are failing. Quebec allows minors to donate an organ or tissue if the parents consent and the donation poses no serious risk to the child's health. Although people do not have to specify the person or institution to receive their donation, there is nothing to prevent them from limiting their consent in this way, or from limiting the use of the donation to therapeutic as opposed to research purposes.

D. SETTLING AN ESTATE

1. Intestacy

When there is no will, the estate is distributed according to the laws of the province or territory where the deceased resided. All jurisdictions assume that people prefer to leave their estate to the surviving spouse and children or grandchildren, but the allotment of shares varies.

Under most of the laws, distribution of the net estate (money and other property remaining after payment of debts) begins with a *preferential* share for the surviving spouse. Currently, the maximum amount of this share is $40,000 in Alberta; $50,000 in Nova Scotia, Manitoba, the Northwest Territories and Nunavut; $65,000 in British Columbia; $100,000 in Saskatchewan and $200,000 in Ontario. There is no preferential share in New Brunswick, Newfoundland and Labrador, Quebec, Yukon and Prince Edward Island. When the estate is worth less than the preferential share, the surviving spouse is entitled to receive the entire estate.

In places that award a preferential share, a spouse also gets part of any remaining estate as a *distributive* share. In places that do not provide for a preferential share—New Brunswick, Newfoundland and Labrador, Quebec, Prince Edward Island and the Yukon—the spouse is entitled only to a distributive share.

The amount of the distributive share also varies. In most provinces and territories, the surviving spouse receives all of the remaining estate if the deceased left no children. If there is one child, the spouse and child receive equal shares or one-third/two-thirds. If there are two or more children, the spouse usually gets one-third, and the children equally share the other two-thirds. (If one of the deceased's children has died but had children who are alive, these grandchildren of the deceased are entitled to their parent's share.) However, a spouse in Manitoba, regardless of the number of children, still gets half the remaining estate; a spouse in New Brunswick, Newfoundland and Labrador and the Yukon (which provide no preferential share) gets half of the estate, unless there are two or more children, in which case the share is reduced to one-third; a spouse in Quebec gets one-third of the estate and the children two-thirds (when there are no children, the spouse may get the entire estate).

A spouse claiming an interest on an intestacy should apply within a reasonable period of time. In 1995, an Ontario court considered the claim of an estranged wife to a share of a cottage in which she had released all interest to her husband in 1973. The husband died intestate in 1980. The court found that the wife's claim was extinguished because of the lengthy delay in applying.

Aside from laws providing preferential and distributive shares, many provinces also have family laws that may affect the distribution of the estate. In Ontario and Manitoba, for instance, the surviving spouse may choose to take half of the net family property instead of the preferential and distributive shares. In some provinces and territories, special rules also exist regarding the matrimonial home. In the Northwest Territories, Nunavut and Nova Scotia, the surviving spouse may elect to take the home instead of a preferential share, if the home is valued at more than $50,000. If the value of the home is less than $50,000, a surviving spouse may elect to take the home as part of a preferential share. In British Columbia, the interest of beneficiaries other than the surviving spouse in the home and furnishings may be held in trust for the lifetime of the surviving spouse, or for as long as the beneficiaries wish it retained.

If someone dies without leaving a surviving spouse, children or grandchildren, the rules of distribution become more complex. Generally speaking, the deceased's parents are entitled to the estate, followed by the deceased's siblings, and then any nieces and nephews.

Other factors may be significant. For example, all claims to any share in an estate are subject to dependants' claims for support. As well, the laws vary on whether estranged spouses get any share.

2. Meeting Property Obligations to Spouses

Many jurisdictions in the last few years have passed matrimonial property legislation to protect "disinherited" partners—partners of spouses who held all of the family's property in his or her name and who either died intestate or left nothing in his or her will to their surviving partner. These matrimonial laws permit a spouse to make a claim against an estate for at least the share of assets that would have been available on separation and divorce.

In Alberta, Manitoba, Ontario, New Brunswick, Nova Scotia, Saskatchewan, Northwest Territories, Nunavut, and Newfoundland and Labrador, the laws provide this right to share property on death. However, the provinces have different schemes for sharing. Some provinces, such as Alberta and Ontario, adjust the share of property downwards to take into account other property received by the surviving spouse as a result of the other's death, such as insurance proceeds or joint tenancy that passes by survivorship. Other provinces, such as Manitoba, Newfoundland and Labrador, and Nova Scotia, provide that a division of property rights is in addition to other benefits or assets received on death. New Brunswick allows a spouse to apply for the matrimonial home and contents, unless this share would be inequitable, whereas the matrimonial home in Newfoundland and Labrador automatically goes to the surviving spouse because it is deemed to be held in joint tenancy.

In British Columbia, Prince Edward Island and the Yukon, the property laws offer no specific provisions to protect spouses on the death of their partner. If a person in one of these jurisdictions has reason to believe his partner intends to disinherit him on death, and he cannot have property put in his own name, the only way to protect himself in advance is to consider leaving the marriage while the partner is alive and commencing a lawsuit to assert his rights as a separated spouse. If the partner then dies before matters are resolved, he can continue the proceedings against the partner's estate.

It is not uncommon for spouses in second marriages to wish to leave property on their death to the children of their first marriage as well as subsequent marriages. To ensure these wishes are carried out, they should incorporate their intentions into an agreement at the beginning of the marriage, and not leave them to be dealt with in a will. A wife in New Brunswick in a second marriage attempted to recognize her daughter's assistance to her and her second husband by leaving her husband a life interest in the matrimonial home, with the daughter (who was from the first marriage) to receive the home or the proceeds from its sale on the husband's death. The husband applied for an order under the Matrimonial Property Act, giving him title to the home. Although the trial judge was prepared to go along with the terms of the wife's will and deny the husband's application, the Court of Appeal was not. It found that the trial judge placed too much emphasis on the daughter's kindness and help to the couple, holding that these were the normal efforts of a family member. The Court would not allow the wife to circumvent the effect of the law by her will; however, considering the circumstances of the case, including the fact that the wife owned the home before the marriage, the Court ordered the husband and the daughter to share the net proceeds on the sale of the home equally.

Unless there is an obligation in an agreement to maintain insurance coverage to ensure support payments, when a person separates or divorces, beneficiary designations in wills, insurance policies, pensions and RRSPs should be changed in order to remove a former spouse as a beneficiary. A woman in British Columbia was forced to sue her sister's ex-husband to repay more than $67,000 in life insurance proceeds he received as named beneficiary on his ex-wife's insurance (*Roberts* v. *Martindale*). The sister was successful as she was able to prove that the ex-wife had intended to make the change and mistakenly believed she had done so. The 1996 ruling found the proceeds belonged to the ex-wife's estate.

Those provinces that provide for a sharing on death also impose a limitation period to apply. Limitation periods are generally six months, but in some places, this starts running from the date of death and in other places, from the date of probate. There are jurisdictions with a four-month limitation period and others with a one-year limitation period. This should alert potential applicants to apply as soon as possible after the date of death. It is possible in some provinces, in very limited circumstances, to obtain an extension to apply. However, it is best not to count on this, as the courts often reject such extensions, because they may hold up the distribution of the estate or may come after the estate has begun to be or has actually been distributed.

3. Contesting a Will

In order to contest a will, an interested party must act quickly to prevent the estate being distributed according to the terms of the document. He or she should consult a lawyer, who will immediately notify the executor and beneficiaries of the will, and inform the court and insurance companies that they must wait for the protest to be heard before they distribute the estate or pay proceeds from any policies. The lawyer will then help to decide whether or not any of the following legal grounds are available to contest the will.

SIGNATURE AND WITNESSES

The will may not be valid if it was not properly executed in front of two witnesses who were present at the same time and who also signed the will. (A holograph will is the exception.) The will may also be subject to challenge if a witness does not confirm that the document is in the same state as when it was witnessed, or if a beneficiary was a witness.

UNDUE INFLUENCE

The court may invalidate the will if it is proven that the testator unwillingly left a bequest to someone because he or she was forced to, perhaps by physical threats. If the testator decides to omit someone because of anger, or decides to include someone because of the beneficiary's devotion and love, the court will not consider the testator to have been under undue influence. However, if a beneficiary was present when the will was signed or passed along instructions to the lawyer, the court may invalidate the will on that basis.

In 1995, in the case of *Vout* v. *Hay*, the Supreme Court of Canada ruled that the onus is on the person who questions the validity of the will to prove undue influence. However, if there were suspicious circumstances, it is up to the person who wishes to rely on the will to disprove the allegations. He or she may have to prove, on a balance of probabilities, that the formalities of execution were followed, that the testator knew and approved of the contents of the will, and that the testator had testamentary capacity—was mentally capable—at the time the will was executed.

In this case, Clarence Hay, an 81-year-old bachelor farmer in Ontario, had executed a will in 1985 leaving his estate, then worth approximately $320,000, to Sandra Vout, a 27-year-old denture therapist. Vout and her mother were frequent visitors at Hay's farm and assisted him with various chores. Unfortunately, although Hay was in regular contact with his relatives, he never mentioned any relationship with Vout. Hay was beaten to death at his farm in 1988, and at one point the police suspected Vout of being involved in his death. Vout's statements about her involvement in the preparation of the will were conflicting; however, the evidence of the legal secretary who prepared the will indicated that Vout was present when Hay reviewed and executed the will, and might have coached him when he hesitated over certain provisions. In declaring the will valid, the trial judge, Mr. Justice Richard Byers found that "Clarence Hay, on the evidence, was not a befuddled, senile old man whose mind had been captured by Sandra Vout and who . . . was physically and emotionally controlled and isolated by those persons who stood to benefit . . ."; instead, the judge declared, Hay "made his will exactly the way he intended." When Hay's relatives appealed, the Court of Appeal ordered a new trial, but Vout appealed to the Supreme Court of Canada, which set aside the decision of the Court of Appeal, and upheld the validity of the will and Vout's entitlement to the estate, then worth about $600,000.

UNSOUND MIND

A will is valid if the testator knew what he or she was doing—and wanted to do it. A will may be challenged if a person suffered a serious mental disorder and lacked the necessary mental capacity to leave instructions for distribution of the estate. Even so, the will may be valid if the testator signed it during a period of lucidity. Determining unsound mind may be particularly difficult if a testator was in the early stages of Alzheimer's, or suffered from other diseases where mental capacity is known to be inconsistent. If the will is being challenged, the testator's doctor should be consulted.

DEPENDANT'S CLAIMS

A dependant may contest the distribution of financial worth by seeking support as a priority claim against the estate. Heirs are not always co-operative when claims are made by dependants. A son who "plundered" his deceased father's $900,000 estate to defeat the support claim of his father's common-law wife of 18 years was ordered to pay support. As a result of the son's refusal to co-operate in paying monthly support, an order was made for lump-sum support of $300,000, with $100,000 of this to be paid by a fixed date.

CLAIMS FOR SERVICES TO THE DECEASED

It is not uncommon for relatives or friends to provide personal care and other services to elderly people or people with disabilities, often expecting to be "remembered in the person's will." If they are not remembered, they may decide to bring a claim against the estate to ask to be compensated for these services.

Such circumstances arose in a Manitoba case in 1995. A sister-in-law sought compensation from a deceased's estate for assisting the woman during the last four years of her life by paying her bills, purchasing groceries and cleaning her house. The deceased had been blind for the last 20 years of her life. There was nothing in writing to confirm that the sister-in-law was to be compensated for her work, and she acknowledged that she had had no intention of charging for her assistance. She argued instead that the deceased had promised to put her in the will. The estate took the position that, since the two women had known each other for over 60 years, the work was provided out of love, affection and a sense of familial obligation. The court agreed with the estate, finding that, although the law will provide restitution in certain cases for services rendered in anticipation of a gift or legacy, particularly if services are provided by strangers, there are limits on when such restitution is available. On the facts of this case, the court found no evidence that the sister-in-law's services were not being provided gratuitously.

FACTUAL MISTAKE

Sometimes, a person leaves a child out of her will because she thinks the child is dead. If the child turns up and challenges the will, the court may decide that the parent would have wanted to include the child if she had not mistakenly heard that the child had died. On the other hand, if a parent knew a child was alive but felt that a sibling needed or deserved the money more, the court may not try to second-guess the parent's decision.

CLAIMS BY INDEPENDENT ADULT CHILDREN

Although most provinces allow only claims by adult children who continue to be dependent on a parent due to a physical or mental disability, provinces such as British Columbia, Quebec, Newfoundland and Labrador and Nova Scotia do not require such dependency in laws allowing for claims by children of the deceased. For example, the law in British Columbia gives the court broad discretion to make "adequate, just and equitable" provision for a spouse and children. In the 1994 case of *Tataryn* v. *Tataryn Estate*, the Supreme Court of Canada imposed an obligation on the estate of a deceased to give a property interest to the man's wife, and changed the distribution so that the favoured son had to share with the disinherited son.

In another case, a B.C. family challenged the will of a husband and father, described by the court as "harsh, frugal to the point of miserliness." During the 65-year marriage he beat and alienated his three sons and kept his wife on a tight budget. The man was a heavy smoker with a sizeable investment in tobacco shares, and he left $1.2 million, the bulk of his estate, to the Canadian Cancer Society. The family argued that this was a deliberate attempt to spite them. After a two-year legal battle, the B.C. Court of Appeal agreed, reduced the Cancer Society bequest to $450,000, and gave $1 million to his wife with a further $450,000 to his three sons, to be shared equally.

SUBSEQUENT MARRIAGE

A will may be contested if the testator married or divorced after the execution of the will without clarifying that the document was made in contemplation of the event. This legal ground applies even if the testator's new spouse died before he or she did.

4. Distributing the Estate

Executors, although named in a will, do have a choice as to whether or not they will assume the responsibility. If there is more than one executor, the remaining executors will carry on for the one who is unable or unwilling to serve. Many wills name co-executors or alternate executors to deal with the possibility that an executor may be unable or unwilling to serve.

An executor's first duties must be to examine the will and arrange for the funeral and burial of the deceased. The executor is entitled to obtain access before probate to the safety deposit box, but only to remove immediate necessities such as the will and deed to the burial plot.

If the will is nowhere to be found, the estate's lawyer will advertise for it and check the repository at the surrogate court, an optional place of safekeeping for wills. If a testator's intentions are clear, courts will attempt to uphold a copy or version of the will, even if it does not comply with the formalities of the law. In 1996, an Ontario court declared an undated and unsigned copy of a will to be a valid last will and testament where the original will was never found. A number of facts influenced the court: the copy was found in the deceased's apartment; the lawyer who prepared the will had no doubt that the will had been signed by the deceased and witnessed; the deceased acted as if she had made the will by telling the executor and beneficiary about it.

It can take at least a year to determine the assets and liabilities of the deceased, arrange for probate of the will—certification that the will is valid—and transfer the property to the heirs. A list of assets and their location, prepared by the testator, saves time, money and anguish, and ensures that property does not get lost. Otherwise, the executor may have to search the house to ferret out what the deceased meant by leaving "everything to my wife."

Before probate, the executor can ask the deceased's bank manager to exercise her or his discretion in releasing money from an account for the surviving spouse or for funeral expenses, but the executor must produce the will to persuade her or him to do so.

An insurance company will pay policy proceeds to a named beneficiary without probate, but a doctor's death certificate is required. If the estate is named as beneficiary, and the policy proceeds thus become part of the estate, an insurance company may pay part of the proceeds without probate to the beneficiary named in the will, usually if there is only one beneficiary of the estate.

The executors must locate and list the assets of the estate before the estate's lawyer can apply for probate. In applying for probate, the lawyer normally requires an affidavit by one of the original witnesses to certify that the formalities of execution have been followed. If an affidavit was prepared by the lawyer at the time the will was executed, it may already be with the original will. Depending on the condition of the original will, at least one of the original witnesses

may also have to swear in an affidavit that the will has not been altered. The condition may sometimes be a concern if a testator handwrote the will and made corrections, or made handwritten changes to the typewritten will. If a witness can prove that the changes were there when the will was executed, they are acceptable.

The document the executor receives to confirm the validity of the will and the right of the executor to implement the will is commonly called "letters probate." With letters probate in hand, the executor and/or lawyer arrange for the transfer of property from the deceased to the estate or beneficiary. The executor transfers stocks, sells properties, liquidates bank accounts, files a final income tax return (there are no inheritance taxes), obtains final releases from Revenue Canada, notifies the insurance company, the Canada or Quebec Pension Plan, the deceased's employer, creditors and debtors. Executors also receive proceeds and pay debts, which might include advertising for creditors. If necessary, the executor is also responsible for applying to court if there are any issues to be determined, such as interpretation of the will, claims by dependants or entitlement of a surviving spouse. Ultimately, executors must account to the beneficiaries and distribute the assets. If the executor is instructed to hold assets in trust for beneficiaries under the age of majority, he or she may also be responsible for investing certain assets and paying out income and/or capital for beneficiaries.

Before a will can be processed through the court, the executors must have a basic understanding of what the assets are and their approximate value. If this information is readily available, their job will be much easier and much less time-consuming. If executors have a reasonable basis for believing a deceased had life insurance, but searches of relevant documentation and inquiries of the deceased's employer do not assist, they can ask the Canadian Life and Health Insurance Association (CLHIA), based in Toronto, to make inquiries through its member insurers in Canada.

Most provinces have legislation allowing executors to claim compensation.

Aside from reviewing the will and applying, if necessary, for probate, the lawyer for the estate prepares the documentation necessary to transfer the assets, supervises any required passing of accounts through the courts, advises on any foreign taxes and duties, prepares beneficiary releases and represents the executor in any court proceedings. Lawyers generally charge a fee related to the size of the estate and how complicated it is to administer. If a lawyer does the executor's work, he or she is entitled to charge separately for it. It is common for lawyers to take over responsibility for some of the executor's work, such as advertising for creditors and transferring assets to the estate.

Executors may be allowed broad discretion to make decisions under a will; however, they must act in good faith and be fair in their treatment of beneficiaries in the exercise of their powers. If they are not, the courts may intervene. In 1996, in the case of *Fox* v. *Fox Estate*, the Ontario Court of Appeal removed the wife of the deceased as executrix because of her attempts to disinherit her only son, a residual beneficiary, because, in the words of Mr. Justice Patrick Galligan, "he dared to marry outside her religious faith." The son's first marriage ended with a bitter divorce, and his children were close to their grandmother. When the son later formed a relationship with his long-time secretary and advised his mother of their plans to marry, she was upset because the prospective bride was not of their faith.

The will gave the mother a life interest in 75 percent of the estate and the son a life interest in the remaining 25 percent, with the son to receive the residue of the estate on his mother's death. The terms of the will gave the mother very broad discretion to encroach on the estate funds for the benefit of the son's children. On hearing of the second marriage, the mother used her powers under the will to transfer the son's share to his children. The Court held this conduct in breach of the trust provisions in the will and removed the mother as executrix. So strong was the Court's disapproval of the conduct that it ordered costs in favour of the son to be paid by the mother personally, and not out of the estate. Leave to appeal to the Supreme Court of Canada was dismissed in 1996.

CHAPTER 12

ACCESS TO THE LEGAL SYSTEM

⚖

Introduction

This chapter is about the practical aspect of access to justice, for the legal system is the gateway to justice. The legal system has its own rules, which are managed by lawyers, judges and government administrators. Citizens have the choice to hire a professional to help them navigate the legal process or to represent themselves. This chapter describes hiring a lawyer, and paying the costs with the help of legal aid or contingency fees. It discusses whether a more appropriate option is to hire a paralegal. It analyzes the less costly and more efficient option of class actions, available in some cases. It tries to help those individuals who are self-represented, and also guides them through the Small Claims Court system. Alternatives to the legal system have evolved, and these other dispute resolution methods are discussed.

1. Hiring a Lawyer

No matter how much knowledge of the law you have, there is still no substitute for the advice of a good lawyer who is on your side.

Lawyers are trained to apply the law to the facts of each new situation, to negotiate to resolve differences and to advocate for a party by putting all the facts before the court in a way that best presents a client's case.

People sometimes ask how to choose a lawyer. Look for some of the skills and traits displayed by the best lawyers, who not only know the law and its procedures, but are skilful at problem-solving, legal analysis and negotiation. Look for a zealous bulldog for your interests, who is also practical and realistic in strategizing for a successful result. Look for integrity and empathy, efficiency and the habit of keeping clients fully informed.

Since you will, if you are sensible, take your lawyer's advice, be sure you have a lawyer whose counsel you trust. Because it is also impossible to know a great deal about anybody, you will have to rely on your instincts, but be sure to ask your friends for recommendations of lawyers whose work and reputation are known to them. You may also contact your local law society or bar association for a referral.

While the lawyer gives advice and makes recommendations, and should do so with an objective voice, it is the client who makes the final decisions and gives instructions when it comes to strategy and settlement. However, it is the lawyer who has the skill and experience in litigation, the courtroom and the preparation of legal documents, and it is the wise client who accepts reasonable recommendations. The client must be the one to determine whether he wants an aggressive lawyer or a settlement-minded one, or someone in-between. And the client must be the one to provide the needed accurate information about the facts and issues.

A lawyer should not act for both sides even if both parties agree, since it is a compromising influence that is likely to affect adversely the lawyer's judgment and loyalty.

If the client loses confidence in the lawyer for any reason, he should get a second opinion from another lawyer to test his instinct. If the client decides to switch to another lawyer, he should do so at as early a stage of the proceedings as possible, to limit the duplication of expense.

Lawyers generally specialize these days and the client should retain a lawyer with experience and expertise to deal with the client's specific problem. A real estate lawyer should be hired to close a house deal, an employment lawyer to deal with a wrongful dismissal, an entertainment lawyer to negotiate a recording contract, an intellectual property lawyer for computer and copyright problems, a corporate lawyer to incorporate a company, a tax lawyer to structure certain kinds of agreements, an estates lawyer to prepare a will and administer an estate, a family lawyer to do a divorce or a marriage contract. It can be very costly to hire a lawyer who lacks the experience to handle the case. Lawyers charge by the hour, and a less experienced lawyer may spend more time, resulting in a higher fee for the client. Also, the

lawyer may not get as good a result, which can add to this financial impact.

2. Legal Aid

The search for justice can be prohibitively expensive. Since 1967, legal aid has been the main option for those unable to pay full legal fees.

All provinces and territories now have some form of plan under which lawyers accept a significant fee reduction. The plans are usually funded through a combination (varying with the province) of government funds, lawyers' subsidy and client contribution.

In many provinces and territories, people in need of a lawyer apply to their provincial legal-aid plan for a certificate giving them the right to be funded, according to the provincial legal-aid tariff, for the services of a private lawyer of their choice who is on the legal-aid panel. This system of legal aid is often referred to as the "judicare" model.

In some provinces and territories, staff-salaried lawyers provide legal aid. This system is called the "public defender" model. In Saskatchewan, staff lawyers offer virtually all legal aid, and in Nova Scotia, Prince Edward Island, and Newfoundland and Labrador, they provide most services. Quebec has an extensive network of legal-aid offices throughout the province with salaried lawyers to act for litigants. But even in provinces that use this model, private lawyers are available at the choice of the litigant, particularly for cases where conflict of interest would otherwise result. For example, problems can arise when both parties in a dispute are using staff lawyers from the same office, or when a person is suing the province.

Some jurisdictions have both types of legal aid available. For example, most of Ontario's and British Columbia's legal-aid services are provided by private lawyers on certificates, but there are also clinics with salaried lawyers in some communities.

Whenever legal-aid plans become costlier than the government believes it can afford, some people suggest changing the system entirely to a public defender model, assuming it is less expensive than a judicare model. But Quebec's public defender plan is very costly. In its 1995 report, the National Council on Welfare preferred the public defender model for criminal cases, but acknowledged that Ontario's certificate system in family law probably costs the government less than a public defender system would.

Most provinces and territories, whether they have a judicare or public defender system, maintain duty counsel—lawyers paid by legal aid who assist unrepresented litigants with urgent legal questions "at the courthouse door," usually on a temporary basis.

All plans require the legal-aid client to repay at least part of the legal fees (depending on income), and/or to give the plan a lien on any real property the client may own (the legal fees remain as a debt registered against the property, to be repaid when and if the property is sold), and/or to repay fees from any money awarded in the lawsuit.

The provinces and territories vary in the types of legal matters they will subsidize, but none will pay for an action considered fruitless. Legal-aid officers evaluate the merits of the proposed lawsuit or the validity of a defence. In some provinces, only criminal actions are covered, partly because the federal government subsidizes criminal legal aid (although it has substantially reduced

this subsidy since 1992). The reduction in transfer payments to the provinces for social assistance has also affected funding available for legal aid.

In fact, immigration and refugee law was initially paid for by some provincial plans, partly because the federal government promised subsidies. However, the federal government has cut back these subsidies and left the provinces to cope with the expectation that provincial plans will pay for legal aid in these areas. For example, the number of legal-aid certificates for immigration and refugee issues in Ontario increased from 1,610 in 1989 to 15,247 in 1991. However, for the 2003–2004 fiscal year of the plan, only 10,191 certificates were granted for immigration and refugee cases.

Lawyers have tried to maintain the legal-aid system for the benefit of the public, and in British Columbia, Ontario, Quebec and Manitoba, lawyers have had disputes with their provincial governments over funding. British Columbia and Manitoba lawyers almost went on strike; Quebec lawyers did so in 1995.

A person's entitlement to legal aid depends on financial status, which is assessed by legal-aid officers. Those on welfare or at a low-income cutoff point can usually expect aid, as long as their province's legal-aid plan pays for their type of legal problem. For example, a legally aided client in Ontario with a family of four cannot exceed a yearly income of $29,352, or he or she will be required to pay all his or her own legal costs.

The courts are displaying concern about the impact of reduced legal-aid availability on individuals, particularly with respect to criminal charges, and how this will affect access to justice. In a 1996 Alberta case, a court stayed proceedings against an unrepresented person charged with a criminal offence, and ruled that people charged with criminal offences have a constitutional right to a lawyer. Mr. Justice Alexander Andrekson said a person who cannot afford a lawyer and cannot adequately defend himself must be provided with a government-funded lawyer or the case will be stayed. His decision was reversed by the Alberta Court of Appeal in 1997, although the stay was continued since the accused had been before the courts for five years.

Also in 1996, Ontario judge Mary Hogan stayed charges against an unrepresented man who could not afford either counsel or an expert witness, saying, "to proceed . . . would adversely affect the fairness of the trial."

In 1997, the Ontario Court of Appeal ordered the legal-aid plan to issue a certificate to a person accused of a criminal offence, who had limited English skills and a Grade 7 education, to assist him in his appeal of a 15-year conviction.

The Criminal Code in fact has some provisions that empower judges to appoint counsel for an unrepresented accused. If the accused person is mentally unfit, the judge must appoint counsel. If the accused is an appellant before an appeal court or the Supreme Court of Canada, the judge may appoint counsel. If the accused is charged with a sexual offence, he is prohibited from personally cross-examining witnesses under the age of 18, so the judge must appoint counsel to cross-examine child witnesses.

If the legal-aid plan will not pay for counsel assigned by the court, the fees and disbursements of counsel must be paid by the provincial attorney general to the extent that the accused is unable to pay.

In addition, the Youth Criminal Justice Act provides for appointment of counsel to represent a young person at any stage of proceedings if the young person is unable to retain counsel. The Ontario Court of Appeal has ruled in a 1999 case that in order to determine whether the youth is able to retain counsel, the court may inquire into the ability to pay of the young person's parents.

A judge may appoint counsel in a custody case in some circumstances. In 1996, Justice Stong of the Whitby, Ontario, court extended the right to counsel to include a child custody case. He relied on the Charter right to equal protection and benefit of the law to order the attorney general to provide counsel for a mother defending a father's application for sole custody of their child. The mother, although she was on social assistance, had been denied a legal-aid certificate. The father was represented by counsel.

Then in 1999 the Supreme Court of Canada, in a landmark ruling, unanimously declared that the New Brunswick government was under a constitutional obligation to provide the mother with state-funded counsel so that she could respond to a custody application by the government in child protection proceedings. In doing so, the Supreme Court of Canada overruled both the trial court and the New Brunswick Court of Appeal. Interveners before the Supreme Court included the attorneys general of Manitoba, British Columbia and Alberta, the Women's Legal Education and Action Fund, and the Canadian Bar Association.

The mother was indigent and receiving social assistance when she applied for legal aid, but her application was denied since custody applications were not covered under the New Brunswick legal-aid plan at that time.

The Court stated that the principles of fundamental justice in Section 7 of the Charter of Rights and Freedoms required the mother to be represented by counsel at the custody hearing. Section 7 guarantees every parent the right to a fair hearing and states that, for the hearing to be fair, the parent must have an opportunity to present her case effectively, and be represented by counsel. The Court said the government's wish to control legal-aid expenditures was not sufficient justification to permit them to breach the mother's Charter rights to a fair hearing.

Several of the judges noted that the case raised gender equality issues since women, especially single mothers, are disproportionately affected by child protection proceedings.

In 2000, a mother in British Columbia fighting a complex child protection proceeding relied on the New Brunswick case to seek a higher payment for her counsel than the amount allowed under legal-aid rules. She asked the court to order her lawyer to be paid at the legal-aid tariff rate for all preparation and trial time, not just the limited preparation time allowed in the legal-aid tariff. The court acknowledged her case was likely to require extensive preparation and that the legal-aid cap on her lawyer's time could impact on her ability to be fairly represented. Her application was ultimately turned down due to insufficient objective evidence on the preparation time actually required. The court left the door open to future claims by others for court-ordered legal aid.

In 2004, the Supreme Court of Canada ruled that trial judges may award costs before the trial is held. In the case of *British Columbia* v. *Okanagan Indian Band*, the court identified three criteria to justify such an award: the litigation could not proceed otherwise; the claim must obviously have merit; the issues raised transcend the individual litigant's interests, are of public importance, and have not been resolved in previous cases.

Legal aid is supposed to provide help for financially strapped litigants, but the slashing of legal-aid budgets in the 1990s by provincial governments has left many people vulnerable. If a person cannot get legal aid, he should first appeal the decision. Most plans have an appeal process in place. Then what legislation and recent case law exists should be used as persuasion. Student legal aid under the supervision of professors is often available from local law schools. Prepaid legal insurance, although usually limited in scope, is available through some unions and employers.

3. Contingency Fees

Contingency fees are a way to pay lawyers with a percentage of the proceeds of the litigation instead of providing fees on a pay-as-you-go basis. It is legal everywhere in Canada. If the individual has a good case, this may represent the only way he will be able to get his case heard. Contingency fees are useful only in those cases where the litigant hopes to receive a substantial sum of money at the end of the case. From this sum of money, the lawyer in personal injury and civil damages cases, for example, will get paid a percentage of the proceeds of the litigation. Contingency arrangements are usually not available in family law cases.

Contingency fees are usually anywhere from one-quarter to one-half of the proceeds of litigation and are most useful in personal injury lawsuits. British Columbia sets a maximum of one-third for legal fees in personal injury and wrongful deaths arising out of motor vehicle accidents, and 40 percent on any other personal injury or wrongful death claims.

4. Class-Action Suits

A class-action suit is a helpful court-supervised procedure allowing a number of claimants, whose cases raise common issues, to share the costs and the risks of what is often expensive and time-consuming litigation. They are particularly useful in product liability cases. While a claimant may receive less in compensation than if she sued on her own, the fact that the legal costs are shared often means that the person nets more in the end.

Class actions have been brought in Canada by patients who contracted hepatitis C from tainted blood, by persons implanted with faulty cardiac pacemakers, by victims of train and subway crashes, by victims of condominium developers and by Bre-X shareholders, among others. In a landmark 1998 case, the first wrongful dismissal class-action suit in Canada was settled on behalf of employees who lost their jobs as a result of large-scale corporate restructuring, and, through the settlement, received compensation.

The rules regarding class actions are not standardized across Canada: Ontario, British Columbia, Alberta, Manitoba, Quebec, and Newfoundland and Labrador currently have class-action legislation in place. In the other provinces and territories, it may be possible to have a "representative" action but these are not governed by as clear-cut a set of rules.

The idea behind a class action is to deal with a number of similar cases through one legal action. Basically, to qualify as a class action, the suit must satisfy the following requirements. First, there must be a "cause of action"—a legally recognized harm resulting from the actions or inactions of a defendant or group of defendants. There must be an identifiable class of two or more persons. There must be common issues and a class action must be shown to be the best way of resolving those issues.

A representative plaintiff or defendant who would fairly represent the interests of the whole group must be identified. That representative plaintiff must not have a conflict of interest with any other potential claimants.

The first step is to retain a lawyer who has some experience in class-action suits. The lawyer must be prepared to wait to be paid because, unlike in most litigation, lawyers representing clients in class actions are usually not paid their fees until the case is tried or settled. While class actions are more economical than individual lawsuits, they are still expensive. Usually, expert evidence is needed, and the litigation can be lengthy.

Lawyers will usually expect the claimants to at least contribute to the out-of-pocket disbursements. In the end, if the claimants win, the lawyer can charge a percentage of the award, known as a contingency fee, which is subject to the court's approval. If the case is lost, the lawyer only gets what has been paid for disbursements.

If the lawyer takes on the case, the next step will be to appear before a judge for an order certifying the lawsuit as a class action.

The judge then decides if the proceeding meets the requirements of a class action and ensures that a litigation plan is in place.

Any eventual award received is usually shared by both the claimants and other unknown members of the class. The court will establish rules to advertise the existence of the class action so that possible qualified claimants may come forward and have an opportunity to claim a portion of the judgment. Class members can opt out; usually a person opts out because she prefers to bring a separate lawsuit. Those who want to be included must register in the court-prescribed manner.

5. Hiring a Paralegal

Paralegals form an integral part of the legal system as support services for lawyers. However, they differ significantly from lawyers with respect to training, expertise and accountability, and should be used with care as a separate resource. A 1998 survey conducted on behalf of the Canadian Bar Association by its Ontario branch disclosed that three in ten Ontarians believe lawyers and paralegals are subject to the same amount of regulation, when this is in fact far from the truth. While many paralegals or law clerks do work under the supervision of lawyers, many others operate independently of them, often without any regulation or any liability insurance to protect them in the event something goes wrong. Paralegals currently handle uncontested divorces, traffic offences, small claims court and landlord-tenant matters.

There is a perception that paralegals are significantly cheaper than lawyers, partly due to the fact that they are only qualified to handle the most basic of legal matters.

Without regulation, continuing education requirements and liability insurance, their costs of carrying on business are able to be less than those of lawyers. While the initial cost may be low, the long-term cost of any mistakes may be higher.

Paralegals should not be representing clients in court or at other hearings on anything but the most straightforward and non-contentious matters. Unlike lawyers, they are not trained to interpret legislation and legal cases and, without regulation, have no ongoing obligations to maintain any particular skill level. For example, if a paralegal prepares a will or a divorce petition, he cannot provide legal advice. The size of an estate or a family's assets may seem small; however, the legal issues arising from these may be quite complicated and require the services of a lawyer.

6. Representing Yourself

If a person cannot afford legal counsel, and cannot secure legal aid, there is no class-action suit or contingency fee arrangement available, and a paralegal cannot handle the type of case, self-representation may be the only answer. There is no law requiring litigants to hire counsel. And with the cost of legal services beyond the reach of many, a person may feel he has no choice but to represent himself. (The Ontario Civil Justice Review, conducted in the late 1990s, found that an average case including a three-day trial costs a litigant $38,000, and an average award is $58,000.) Even so, try to consult a lawyer, a clinic run by law students or a paralegal to get background help with a strategy, drafting documents and procedures or just coaching from the sidelines.

In the 1990s there was a significant increase in the number of self-represented litigants, coinciding with a significant decrease in the nationwide funding for legal aid. In 2005 Ontario introduced waivers of most court fees for eligible low-income people involved in civil, small claims and family proceedings.

It is unwise to try to be your own lawyer in any criminal case, since your liberty will be at stake. (See the section on legal aid earlier in this chapter for instances of when a court may *order* a lawyer appointed in a criminal case.)

If a person has no choice but to represent herself, here's a game plan to help in, by way of example, a family law case, which is the type of case in which people are more often self-represented.

PREPARING THE CASE

Plan carefully. Think about all the issues that could be affected by the case: spousal and child support, custody, division of property, debts and pensions, health and medical insurance, life insurance, postsecondary education for the children and tax consequences. In determining what the lawsuit is intended to accomplish, consider your income and budgetary needs. Gather information and documents on the family's assets and debts. Try to find and keep in a safe place copies of important documents: tax returns, RRSP statements, any stocks, bonds and savings accounts, deeds, mortgages, credit card statements and pension information.

Try negotiating first. A court fight may be avoided if the parties can talk to each other reasonably, and work out an agreement. If an intermediary will make a difference, consider a religious leader with a connection to the family, or a respected relative or mutual friend. Try to agree on division of household contents, cars, family photos, CDs and other items. Custody claims are difficult if both parties want sole custody, but if you can agree to share time with the children, the details may be worked out by the parties.

A mediator, an expert trained in conflict resolution, may be able to help. However, this service can cost between $60 and $300 an hour and may be out of reach, although some professionals charge on a sliding scale basis in relation to the client's income. Many courts provide their own mediation solutions, in the form of pretrial hearings and case conferences.

Consider getting expert help. A consultation with a family law lawyer is advisable. Expect to pay $100 to $400 an hour, depending on location and experience. A knowledgeable family law lawyer can give you detailed advice on your rights, the merits of your claim and how the court process is likely to play out; she could also review any documents served on you and advise you how to prepare your own. Your spouse's lawyer may be willing to tell you the rules that apply or give you the necessary forms, although he has no obligation to do so and your spouse may not want to pay him to do so. Check your local library for books of legal precedents.

Watch other cases. If your case is not settled prior to trial, spend some time sitting through other cases at a family court hearing that is open to the public. (Not all are.)

IF YOU ARE SUING

Educate yourself on the court process. Ask the court office, a lawyer or paralegal about the rules for completion of certain stages in the proceedings, and what forms to file at what stage. Be aware of limitation periods for bringing lawsuits. For example, in Ontario since January 1, 2004, most court actions must be started within two years from the day the injury, loss or damage, as a result of an act or omission, is discovered, although family law cases are governed by different rules.

Do the paperwork. Write down what you are claiming and why. If you need support, prepare a budget (get forms from legal stationers, lawyers or paralegals). If you want custody, summarize the children's needs and why you are the better parent to meet them. Also, think about who your witnesses will be and whether they will attend voluntarily or whether you must subpoena them. Get the forms for a petition or application for divorce from a book, lawyer, paralegal or the court. Take the completed document and the marriage certificate (or a certified copy) to a court office to be formally issued with the court seal. You will also need to arrange for a process server (check the Yellow Pages or ask a lawyer for a name) to serve your spouse with the papers; you are not permitted to do it yourself.

IF YOU ARE BEING SUED

Do not ignore legal documents. If you are served with papers, do not just hope the problem will go away. If you do not take the required steps by the stated deadlines (filing a document, say, or showing up in court), then an order may be made without your knowledge—and without your side of the story being heard. If you fail to respond to claims for money, property or costs and an order is made against you, it can be registered as a lien against any property you own, or your wages or bank account can be garnisheed.

Stay put and do not do anything rash. Do not move house (unless you are at physical risk) or change the custody of the children; you might hurt your case, or find yourself unable to reverse an arrangement that you thought was temporary. Don't sign anything or cosign a loan agreement or any other financial undertaking with your spouse without seeking legal advice first.

IN COURT

Be brief. The judge will usually try to give you the basic information you need about the court process. However, courts are busy; do not count on getting much of the judge's time.

Once you are at trial and your turn comes, briefly explain to the judge the point of your case and list the documents and witnesses who will be presented. Your spouse or his lawyer can cross-examine you and any witnesses. After your husband presents his case you can cross-examine him and any of his witnesses. The goal is to challenge the truth of what he says. Both parties then summarize their cases.

Judgments are usually made at the conclusion of the hearing, or released later if the decision is reserved. If the decision goes against you and you want to appeal, you'll need to file a notice of appeal usually within 15 to 30 days.

7. Small Claims Court

Small Claims Court is the most expeditious legal route to get judgment for a claim ranging up to about $10,000. Every province has different maximum limits in its Small Claims Courts, and the claimant must usually abandon a claim for any amount over the maximum. If the claim is just over the limit, abandoning the extra amount is often worth doing.

People who sue in these courts usually represent themselves because a lawyer's fees could add up to more than the amount of the claim. When the plaintiff is running the case without counsel, the judge will often act as a guide to help the plaintiff present enough information to help him or her make a decision. Here are the basic steps in preparing a case for Small Claims Court.

GETTING READY

The first step is to gather all the evidence that proves the claim, including any written documents (preferably originals). This evidence must be kept to show the judge. If there is no evidence in writing, it would be helpful to have a witness who can testify from personal knowledge that the money is owed. Otherwise, it will be the plaintiff's word against the defendant's.

The plaintiff should write out a detailed, accurate summary of the facts and use it to prepare a concise statement of claim to serve on the defendant.

FILING THE SUIT

Next, the plaintiff completes the claim form provided by the Small Claims Court office and files it at the office. A fee will be required, the amount varying across the country. In some places, the Court arranges for the defendant to be sent the notice of claim; in others, the plaintiff is responsible.

After being notified, the defendant will have a certain period of time in which to respond (often around 20 days). If the defendant believes that she does not owe any money, she can submit a statement of defence with the reasons for her belief. If, on the other hand, the defendant admits the debt, she can pay the money. If the defendant thinks the plaintiff owes her money, she can make a counterclaim.

If one party fails to respond, the other party can apply to have a judgment issued in default. If the claim is disputed, the case will proceed to trial.

PREPARING FOR TRIAL

The Court will advise the parties of the trial date. In some places, a "pretrial" will be scheduled. This is a discussion with a judge to try to facilitate a settlement.

If no pretrial settlement is reached, all witnesses will need to be notified of the trial date. To ensure that the witnesses will cooperate and attend, it is often advisable for the plaintiff to ask the Court to issue a summons (subpoena) ordering them to attend. The Court may charge a small fee for this service.

It is a good idea for a plaintiff to sit through a few Small Claims Court cases to become familiar with procedures.

ATTENDING THE TRIAL

The plaintiff should count on spending the whole day in court, waiting through other cases. When his turn comes, he should briefly explain to the judge the point of his case and list the documents and witnesses to be presented. Then, the plaintiff takes the witness stand and tells his story. The defendant can cross-examine the plaintiff and any witnesses. The defendant then presents her case, and the plaintiff can cross-examine her and any witnesses. The plaintiff has the last word and can present reply evidence, which is new evidence to respond to any new issues raised by the defendant. Both parties can then summarize their case.

ENFORCING THE JUDGMENT

If there is a judgment against the defendant and she does not pay up, the Court can be instructed to issue a writ of seizure and sale against property such as a home, car and RRSP. In some provinces, garnishment can be issued against wages and bank accounts.

8. Alternate Dispute Resolution (ADR)

Alternate dispute resolution methods—such as mediation, arbitration, collaborative law and some variant of them—are replacing adversarial trials as the method of choice in resolving disputes. To "settle out of court" is an attractive option for many, and it is certainly the best approach if both the process and the result are fair.

Mediators are trained to assist parties in resolving their dispute themselves; they focus less on legal rights than on finding a workable compromise. Depending on the legal issue involved, the mediator may be trained as a mental health professional, a lawyer, an accountant, an engineer, among others, and usually operates outside the court process.

Arbitrators operate within legally defined rules and are usually trained as lawyers. They are akin to judges in that their role is to hear the evidence and impose a solution on parties who have agreed in advance to abide by their ruling, although parties are able to appeal the arbitrator's decision to a court just as a trial judge's decision may be appealed to a court of appeal. Arbitrators are paid by the parties and so this method may be more expensive than going to court, where a judge's salary is paid by the government.

In some jurisdictions, judges are now fulfilling that role by conducting case conferences and pretrials. (The same judge cannot also conduct the trial if the case does not settle.) In fact, there are many retired judges who are privately retained as mediators and arbitrators. One group of retired judges offers more than mediation and arbitration—the group also offers mediation-arbitration (if mediation doesn't work, a solution is imposed), mini-trials and private arbitration appeals from trial judgments and arbitral awards.

In some cases, each party will have her or his own lawyer involved in the process or behind the scenes, to ensure that her or his legal rights are protected, and to draft the resulting agreement. In some cases, the lawyers alone will assist the parties in a collaborative process (see Chapter 10). If the matter does not settle in mediation and the case goes to court, then it becomes important whether the mediation was open or closed, so it is wise to resolve this before the mediation starts. If mediation was closed, everything said is confidential and cannot be used for any purpose in court. If it was an open mediation, then parties and the mediator may quote what happened in the mediation sessions and the mediator may write a report and recommendations for a court.

Mediation has its risks and downside. In a successful mediation, both sides must agree on a resolution. In some cases, one party is stubborn and will not compromise, so a mediated solution will be at the expense of the more reasonable party. If approached with caution, mediation can be a useful first step. However, if it is not successful, both parties may have spent so much money in attempting settlement that they may no longer have the means to go to trial.

The advantage of a trial to resolve disputes is that an enforceable decision is made after evidence is heard according to the rules of evidence, and there is a possibility of getting an order for compensation for costs. In a mediation, the rules of evidence do not apply and anything goes if the mediator permits it. A mediated solution that results in a written agreement is not enforceable unless the parties agree to incorporate it into a court order and, as the parties consented to the order, it is not appealable. And mediations rarely result in costs agreements with the justification that the parties settled the case.

While ADR provides a satisfying way to resolve disputes for many people, the evolution of law is not furthered by this means. When a judge makes a decision in court he is required to give his reasons for decision, and they must be based on law and legal precedent. In turn his decision adds to the pool of precedents to assist in the determination of future cases.

On the other hand, it is clearly beneficial to resolve disputes in a way that a court is unlikely to do, with a win–win result fashioned to meet the parties' needs rather than a winner-take-all approach. And ADR is a private and confidential method.

In some places, these alternate methods are mandatory; in others, they are voluntary.

ENDNOTE

⚖

Our law continues to change as society's values change. While lawyers, judges, legislators and litigants play a significant part in this process, the general public also has an important role to play. Citizens should be a part of the law-making process, both as individuals and as members of groups with particular interests.

Public opinion does and should influence and effect change, and citizens can find ways to make their views known about proposed or needed legislation: They may write a letter or forward a petition to their government representatives; they may write, fax or e-mail a letter to the editor of their local newspaper; they may call in to a phone-in show and add their voice; they may attend a public meeting; they may make a submission to a legislative committee studying a bill; they may participate in party politics; they should vote in elections; they may even stand for election.

Every contribution to reaching a consensus makes for a more vibrant democracy. Every act of participation in the law-making process ensures that individual views are taken into account. The law is not "written in stone." It only appears to be immutable until it is reworked and transformed into another version of itself.

INDEX

⚖️

right to security of the person, 199–200
Chartier v. *Chartier*, 326
Child care, 80–4
  and best interests of child, 279–80
  child-care leave, 45
  disputes, 274, 278–9
  number of spaces, 82
  subsidies, 81, 82
  taxation of costs, 83–4
  types and standards, 80
Child labour, 84–5
Child pornography, 173–4
Child poverty, 308
Child support, 129–31, 308–13
  age limit, 130, 131, 313, 351–2, 361
  connection to child poverty, 308
  court-established guidelines, 308–9
  death of payor, 130–1, 351–2
  disabled children, 130, 351, 354–5
  divorced or separated parents, 130,
    258–9, 308–13, 325–6
  enforcement, 257, 314–19
  financial disclosure by non-custodial
    parent, 312
  government guidelines, 254, 255,
    309–12
  interprovincial and international
    reciprocity, 315–16
  "Levesque litmus test," 308–9
  licence suspension, 316–17
  owing to surrogate mother who
    reconsiders, 29
  paternity suits, 28
  preparing for, 255
  provisions in marriage contract, 94–5,
    98–9
  and remarriage, 268, 322–3
  retroactive, 312
  and shared custody, 310, 311–12
  statistics, 254
  step-parents' obligations, 325–6
  tax implications, 257, 262
  time limits, 313
  unmarried parents, 25, 28, 110
  variation, 309–14, 322–4
Child tax benefit, 83, 91
Child welfare
  fetal rights, 13
  laws, 116–17, 118–19
Child-welfare authorities
  and abandoned children, 118
  and adoption by step-parent, 328
  and teen abortion, 33
Childbirth, 11–36
  abortion, 16–24
  choice, 11–31
  concealment of, 166
  consent, 16–17
  fetal rights, 11–16
  midwives, 25–7
  paternity suits and support, 27–8
  single unattached mother by choice,
    24–5, 30
  sperm donors, 24, 30–1
  surrogate motherhood, 28–30
  teen abortion, 32–4
  teen contraception, 31–2
  teen pregnancy, 34–5

Children
  abandonment, 118–19, 165–6
  abduction, 287–91
  access *see* Access, to children
  adoption *see* Adoption
  adult, 130, 131, 313, 351–2, 361
  best interests of *see* Best interests of child
  child support *see* Child support
  of common-law relationships, 105,
    110–11
  custody *see* Custody
  death of both parents, 347
  with disabilities, 130, 351, 354–5
  and discrimination in
    accommodation, 137–9
  disinherited by mistake, 361
  as employees, 84–5
  female genital mutilation, 173
  financial support *see* Child support
  guardianship, 92, 348, 353–4
  and guns, 177
  harming an infant, 165–6
  incest *see* Incest
  legal representation in divorce suits,
    286–7
  molestation, 169, 170–2
  mother's duty to protect, 12, 13, 14
  parental duty of care, 92, 99, 116–20,
    129–31, 166
  parental liability for acts of, 119–20,
    176–8
  parental liability for injuries, 119
  parents' denial of medical treatment,
    121–3
  of parents who die intestate, 356
  paternity, 27–8
  physical abuse, 116, 120–1, 285–6
  possession of tobacco, 153
  prostitution, 123, 172–3
  religious and moral upbringing, 95,
    121–3, 173–4, 281
  and remarriage of parent, 268, 322–3
  rights under international law, 117–18
  sale of, 15, 29, 128
  school attendance, 84–5
  school-related injuries, 181–2
  sex among *see* Teenagers and
    sexuality
  sexual abuse of, 166–70, 207–8, 285–6
  sexual exploitation of, 123, 170–4
  support *see* Child support
  support of parents by adult children,
    131–3
  surname *see* Names, of children
  testimony in court, 171–2, 212
  tried in adult court, 178
  unborn *see* Fetal rights
  of unmarried parents, 24–5, 28,
    110–11, 112
  violence in schools, 175–6
  wishes considered in custody
    disputes, 279, 286–7, 319–20, 353–4
Children's Aid Societies
  attempt to act as guardian of fetus, 13
  intervention when child abandoned,
    118
  intervention when child physically
    abused, 120

intervention when parents refuse
  medical treatment, 121
right to seek support from parents,
  129
right to supervise parents, 116–17,
  119, 166
and teen abortion, 33–4
Choice
  of child's sex, 11, 15
  to continue or abort pregnancy, 16–17
  to have a child or not, 11–31
  over how to give birth, 25–7
  single mother unattached by, 24–5, 30
  of surrogate mother to keep child, 29
Chronic violent offenders, 221
Cigarette advertising, 153–4
Citizenship
  fetal rights, 14–15
  and marriage, 90–1
Civil Code of Quebec, 1, 31
  name after marriage, 97
  rights and duties of spouses, 93
Civil rights, 146–62
  access to government files, 146–7
  access to medical records, 149–50
  Breathalyzer tests, 155, 228
  constitutional rights, 157–60
  gun control, 160–1
  jury duty, 156–7
  non-smokers' rights, 151–5
  ombudsman, 150–1
  prostitution, 161–2
Civil suits, 222–7
  Jane Doe case, 200
  libel and slander, 212–14
  limitation periods, 168, 208–9, 223,
    372
  personal injury, 201–2, 202–3
  self-representation, 372–4
  small claims court, 3, 373–4
  spousal abuse cases, 190
  stalking cases, 198
  against transmitters of AIDS virus, 218
  victims of child abuse, 168–70
  against violators of publication bans,
    195
  "wrongful birth," 209–10
Class-action suits, 369–70
  against breast-implant
    manufacturers, 202–3
  over gay rights, 143–4
  pacemakers, 9
  against tobacco industry, 154
Clubs, and sex discrimination, 139–40
Cohabitation contracts, 107–10
  children, 110
  death, 109
  property, 104, 107–9
  support, 109
Collaborative law, 374–5
  family law, 272–3, 274
Collection agencies, 239–40
Collective agreements, 43, 46, 47, 58,
  64–6, 68, 73, 331–2
Common-law relationships, 103–15
  children, 105, 110–11
  custody of, 112
  contracts *see* Cohabitation contracts

and career commitment, 279–81
changes in laws, 24–5, 253
children in marriage, 92
children of unmarried parents, 24–5, 28, 110–11, 112
child's best interests, 110–11, 274, 276–80, 327, 353
after death of both parents, 353–4
death of remarried custodial parent, 328–9, 354
after divorce, 265, 275
factors to consider, 278
granted to step-parent, 328
if a parent is a smoker, 152
joint custody or shared parenting, 276–8, 310
after marriage breakdown, 268
and matrimonial misconduct, 268
mobility (moving) rights, 282–4
parental conduct and, 278–9, 280
and religion, 281
right of defendant to counsel, 367–8
self-representation, 371
separation agreements and, 259
variation of orders, 318–20

D

Damages
for abuse of authority, 206–8
duty to mitigate, 224
for fatal accident claims, 225–7
incest, 168–70
for infection with AIDS, 217–18
libel and slander, 213–14
for medical malpractice, 209
for personal injury, 201–2, 203, 222–7
for sexual abuse, 168–70, 206–7
for spousal abuse, 190
in stalking cases, 198
for violation of publication ban, 195
for violations of Charter rights, 200
Dangerous offenders, 221
Darrach (case), 193
Day care, 80–4
Death
of a common-law partner, 107, 109, 110, 115, 333, 351–2
of a former spouse after divorce, 330
intestacy see Intestacy
planning for, 344–56
guardianship of children, 92, 348, 353–4
organ donations, 345–6, 355–6
wills see Wills
after remarriage, 328–9, 354
of spouse during separation, 257–8
and support obligations, 257, 330, 351–2, 357–8
support of adult children, 130–1, 352–3, 361
support of children with disabilities, 354–5
Debts
joint liability, 239, 256
in marriage, 92, 101–2
after marriage breakdown, 102, 256
Decree of nullity, 266

Deductions from taxable income
equivalent-to-spouse status, 262
marriage, 91
spousal support, 261–2
Defamation see Libel and slander
Default on mortgage, 236–7
Democratic rights, 157, 158, 159
Dependant's relief laws, 351–3, 360
Dickson, Mr. Justice Brian, 17, 76–7
Disability
insurance, 246, 336
pay under workers' compensation, 50–1
pension under CPP, 50, 336
Disabled persons
definition, 59
discrimination against, 40, 55–7, 136
evidence in court, 172, 212
spousal support, 304
Disadvantaged groups
affirmative action, 6–7, 158–9
constitutional rights, 158
employment discrimination against, 55
employment equity for, 57–62
Discipline of children, 120–1, 285–6
Disclosure of confidential records, 126–7
Discrimination
in accommodation, 137–9
because of ethnic or national origin, 139
because of financial status, 136
because of marital status, 138–9
because of race, 139
because of sex, 138
against single parents, 138–9
against visible minorities, 138
because of religion, 134, 135, 138
complaint procedure, 135–7
alternatives to, 62
direct, 134, 137
in employment see also Employees, rights
because of age, 38, 72–5, 331–2
because of disability, 40, 55–7, 136
because of drug dependency, 39–41
because of ethnic or national origin, 39, 55
because of family status, 38
because of marital status, 38
because of pregnancy or childbirth, 38, 41
because of race, 38, 55, 79–80
because of religion, 38, 55, 57–8
because of sex, 38, 41, 51–4, 58
because of sexual orientation, 38
bona fide occupational requirement, 54, 137
harassment other than sexual, 79–80
inequities in pay related to, 51–4
against mentally handicapped persons, 38, 80
sexual harassment, 76–9
against single parents, 38
systemic, 57
union help in battling, 62

via personnel records, 37–9
against visible minorities, 55, 58, 59
freedom from, as basic human right, 134
indirect (systemic), 51–4, 57–61, 134, 135, 137, 186–7, 200
in public services (sports, clubs), 139–40
remedies, 57–8, 59–60, 62, 136–7
on basis of sexual orientation, 140–5
Dismissal see Termination of employment
Divorce, 263–5, 267–73
access to children after, 265, 268, 275–6, 284–6
arbitration, 271–2
and bankruptcy, 243, 300
based on cruelty, 191, 264
changes in laws, 253–4, 263–4
child support after, 130, 308–13, 325–6
compared with separation, 256–8
contrasted with annulment, 101
and custody of children see Custody
death of a former spouse after, 330
denial of, 264, 267
"do-it-yourself," 268–9
grounds for, 87, 191, 263–7
legal procedure and evidence, 265, 268–9
legal representation of children, 286–7
mediation of disputes, 270–1
property division see Property, division on marriage breakdown
rate decreasing, 254
and remarriage, 321, 324–30
same-sex, 145, 254
statistics, 254, 273
support after, 265, 300–18, 325–6
tax implications, 261–3
and wills, 257, 345, 358
see also Access; Separation
DNA evidence
as evidence of paternity, 28, 31, 110
in wrongful conviction cases, 7–8
from young offenders, 180
Doctors
abuse of authority, 206–7
birth control information, provision to teens, 31–2
breach of contract, 31, 207
breach of trust, 207
duty to fully inform patients, 204–5, 210
liability for unsafe medical devices, 202
maternity leave for, 44
medical malpractice, 204–5, 208–11
medical records, 149–50
obligation to report patients with AIDS, 214–15
regulation of sperm donors, 31
sexual assault of patients, 206–7
and teen abortion, 33
Doe, Jane (case), 199–201
Domestic violence see Spousal abuse
"Double-dipping," 298, 335–6
Doulas, 26

Intimidation (criminal offence), 197
Investment losses, 251

J

Jane Doe (case), 199–201
Jarvis v. *Jarvis*, 314
Job and benefits protection, 46
Job interviews, permissible questions,
　37–9
Joint bank accounts, 239, 256
　garnishment to enforce child support
　　order, 317
Joint custody or shared parenting, 276–8,
　310, 311–12
Joint ownership, 100, 237–9, 291
Joint tenants, 99, 237–9, 344–5
"Judicare" model of legal aid, 365, 366
Judicial sale, 237
Juries
　duty, 156–7
　in libel and slander cases, 214
　in personal injury cases, 223
　screening of jurors, 157

K

Kaufman, Fred, 7–8
Kidnapping, 160–1, 287–91
Knodel, Timothy, 141

L

La Forest, Mr. Justice Gérard, 2, 57, 283
Labour laws, 41–5, 62–8
Labour relations boards, 65–6
Lac Minerals (case), 5–6
Landlords
　definition, 247
　discrimination, 137–9
　duties, 247
　eviction proceedings, 248–9
Latimer, Robert (case), 343
Lavallee (case), 184, 189
Law, as healing agent, 5, 9–10
Law, Nancy (case), 332
Lawyers
　child's lawyer in divorce action, 286–7
　choosing a lawyer, 364–5
　collaborative, 272–3, 374–5
　contingency fees, 368–9
　dealing with insurance companies,
　　246–7
　in discrimination cases, 135, 136
　in dismissal cases, 66–8, 71–2
　distributing an estate, 362–3
　in family law, 255, 256, 258, 263, 270–3
　in foreign adoptions, 128
　home buying and selling, 232–4
　legal aid, 365–8
　maternity benefits, 44
　mortgage default, 237
　and preparing a will, 344–6
　probating a will, 362–3
　representing unborn children, 12
　right of accused to counsel, 227–8, 367
　trusts, 354
Lax, Madam Justice Joan, 210

Leatherdale v. *Leatherdale*, 253
LeBel, Mr. Justice, 298
Lee, Denver (case), 216
Legal aid, 3, 365–8
　availability, 366–7
　coverage of immigration and refugee
　　law, 366
　"judicare" model, 365, 366
　"public defender" model, 365, 366
Legal costs
　as barrier to justice, 3–4
　buying or selling a home, 234
　class actions, 369
　contingency fees, 368–9
　and damages, 224
　government ordered to pay, 7, 368
　hiring a paralegal, 370
　representing yourself, 268–9, 370–4
　small claims court, 3, 373–4
　tax deductibility, 263
Legal insurance, 368
Legal system
　abuse of, 3
　access to, 3–4, 7, 364–75
　　alternate dispute resolution (ADR),
　　　373–4
　　class-action suits, 369–70
　　contingency fees, 368–9
　　denied by government, 366–8
　　hiring a lawyer, 364–5
　　hiring a paralegal, 370
　　legal aid, 365–8
　　self-representation, 268–9, 370–3
　　small claims court, 3, 373–4
　handling of domestic violence cases,
　　187
Legal trends, 4–10
　aboriginal justice, 5
　accommodation of disabilities, 56
　adoption disclosure, 126–7
　collaborative family law, 272–4
　common-law couples, 104
　environmental law, 4, 8–9
　mandatory mediation, 271, 375
　midwifery laws, 25–7
　parallel parenting, 277
　protection of vulnerable witnesses,
　　171–2, 197
　regulatory negligence, 9
　same-sex rights and responsibilities, 4
　specialized courts, 9–10
　therapeutic jurisprudence, 9–10
　time limit on support, 304–5
　unions, 66
　whistle-blower protection, 10
　wrongful conviction, 4, 5, 7–8
Leshner, Michael, 141, 144
"Levesque litmus test," 308–9
Levesque v. *Levesque*, 308–9
L'Heureux-Dubé, Madam Justice Claire,
　84, 114, 192–3, 274, 281, 283, 298, 302,
　324
Liability
　AIDS carriers, 216–17, 217–18
　doctors, 202, 205
　of employers for actions of
　　employees, 208
　insurance, 246–7

joint liability for debts, 92, 101–2, 239,
　256
　of manufacturers of medical devices,
　　201–4
　of parents for child's acts, 119–20, 176–8
　of schools for injuries to children,
　　181–2
　of vendors of property, 234–5
　vicarious, 39, 119–20, 176–8, 208
Libel and slander, 212–14
Licence suspension, for default on
　support, 316–17
Liens, for child support, 315
Life insurance, 245–6
　beneficiaries, 344–5
　and marriage, 99
Limitation periods
　for child support, 313
　for claims against an estate, 358–9
　generally, 372
　for personal injury suits, 223
　for sexual abuse cases, 168, 170, 206
　for sharing of property after divorce,
　　291–2
　for spousal support claims, 304–5
　for suits against health professionals,
　　208–9
Living wills, 337, 338–9
Long-term offenders, 221
Loss of consortium, 209
Loss of enjoyment of life, 200, 209, 224
Loss of homemaking capacity, 224
Lottery winnings, sharing of, 295–6
Lovelace v. *Ontario*, 61
Lump-sum awards, on divorce, 263, 297,
　301–4, 306, 320

M

M. v. *H.*, 142, 143
Macdonald, Madam Justice Ellen, 211,
　307
MacGyver v. *Richards*, 283
Malpractice, medical, 208–10
Mandatory mediation, 271, 375
Mandatory retirement, 72–5, 331–2
Mandatory supervision, 222
Manslaughter, 27, 160–1, 165, 170, 182,
　219, 341
Manufacturers, duty to issue warnings
　about products, 202, 203–4
Marijuana, 159–60
Marital status, discrimination on basis of,
　38, 138–9
Marriage, 86–102
　annulment, 100–1, 266
　assumptions and expectations, 87,
　　93–4
　beneficiary designations, 91
　breakdown *see* Divorce; Separation
　children, 92
　citizenship and residence, 90–1
　common-law *see* Common-law
　　relationships
　consent to abortion and vasectomy,
　　16–17, 90
　consent to get married, 88, 266
　consummation of, 90, 100–1, 266

O

Old Age Allowance, 334
Old Age Security (OAS)
    and common-law couples, 104, 333
    retirement planning and, 333
    same-sex couples and, 145, 333
Ombudsman, 150–1
    privacy commissioner as, 147, 148
Ontario Human Rights Commission, 40,
    56–7, 74, 78
Organ donations, 345–6, 355–6
Orphan's benefits under CPP, 50
Outplacement counselling, 71
Overtime pay, 43–4

P

Pacemakers, class-action suits, 204
Paid leave
    adoption, 45
    child care, 45
    fully paid leave, 46
    maternity, 44–5, 63
    parental, 45
    paternity, 44
    preventive, 14
    sick leave, 63
Paralegals, 370
Parallel parenting, 277
Parental leave, 45
Parents, 116–33
    abduction of children, 287–91
    adoption *see* Adoption
    of children killed in fatal accident,
        225
    conduct and custody, 278–9, 280
    consent for teen's abortion, 32–4
    consent to child's medical treatment,
        31–5, 121–3
    consent to teen giving birth, 34
    consent to teens' marriage, 89
    consent to teens' use of
        contraception, 31–2
    discipline of children, 120–1, 285–6
    duty of care to children, 92, 99,
        116–20, 129–31, 166
    harm to infants, 165–6
    liability for child's acts, 119–20, 176–8
    liability for child's injuries, 119
    religious and moral upbringing of
        children, 95, 121–3, 173–4, 281
    sexual exploitation of children, 123,
        172
    single *see* Single parents
    supervision by Children's Aid
        Societies, 116–17, 119, 166
    support by adult children, 131–3
    see also Access; Child support;
        Custody; Mothers
Parole, 218–19, 221–2
    victims and parole hearings, 210–11
Part-time employees
    benefits, 41, 64
    definition, 63
    Employment Insurance, 48, 64
    maternity leave, 44, 63
    minimum hours, 63
    notice of termination, 64

pension plans, 64
rate of pay, 63
sick pay, 41, 43, 63
statutory holidays, 63
vacation pay, 47, 63
Passports
    denied to child support defaulters,
        317
    married persons and, 91, 97–8
Paternity
    leave, 44
    suits, 27–8
    surrogate motherhood and, 29
Patients' rights, 205
Pattie v. *Standal Estate*, 352
Pay equity
    back pay for federal workers, 53–4
    and the Charter of Rights, 54
    minority group members, 55
    women, 51–4
Paycheques, garnishment, 314–15
Peace bonds, 187, 198
Pension credits, sharing, 258, 297, 299,
    333
Pension plans
    beneficiary designations, 91, 142,
        334–5, 344–5
    common-law relationships, 105, 115,
        333
    defined benefit, 296
    and dismissal, 71, 73
    divorce settlements and, 258
    Guaranteed Income Supplement
        (GIS), 333–4
    money purchase, 296
    private, 64, 296–9
    RRSPs *see* Registered Retirement
        Savings Plans (RRSPs)
    survivor's pension, 141–5, 258, 297,
        299, 324, 332–3
    see also Canada Pension Plan (CPP);
        Old Age Security (OAS); Quebec
        Pension Plan
Personal Information Protection and
    Electronic Documents Act (PIPEDA),
    147–8
Personal injury *see* Injury
Personal insurance, 245–6
    accident insurance, 245
    life insurance, 245–6
Personnel records, 37–9
    confidentiality, 148
Pets, provision for in will, 347–8
Photographs and copyright, 250
Piracy of software, 249–50
Pittman, Kenneth (case), 218
Planned Lifetime Advocacy Network
    (PLAN), 355
Police
    custody, 227–8, 229
    detention by, 227
    duty to warn potential crime victims,
        199–201
    handling of domestic violence
        complaints, 185–6, 189
    questioning by, 227–8
    search and seizure, 228–9
Pornography, child, 173–4

Poverty
    child, 308
    discrimination on basis of, 136
Power of sale, 237
Powers of attorney
    for personal care, 337, 338–9
    for property, 336–8
Pregnancy
    discrimination on basis of, 38, 41
    job safety issues, 14
    maternity leave, 44–5
    support by spouse (contract), 98–9
    and teenagers, 34–5
Preventive leave, 14
Priests, abuse of authority, 207
Principal residence
    common-law partners and, 104, 107, 108
    see also Matrimonial home
Principals, right to search students and
    lockers, 229
Privacy
    and adoption records, 126–7
    and AIDS, 214–15
    federal law, 147–8
    and government records, 146–7
    medical records, 149–50
    and police searches, 228–9
    and sexual assault victims, 191–6
    of sperm donors, 31
Privatization
    of the legal system, 5
    of public resources, 8
    of public-service jobs, 66, 151
Probate of a will, 345, 362
Product liability, 201–4
Property, 231–52
    buying and selling a home *see* Home
        buying and selling
    common-law relationships and, 104,
        107–9, 112–15
    disposal on death *see* Wills
    division on marriage breakdown,
        87–8, 94, 259–60, 267, 291–300
    bankruptcy and, 241–3, 300
    Canada and Quebec pension
        plans, 258
    employment-related assets, 295
    gifts and inheritances, 257, 293–4
    lottery winnings, 295–6
    matrimonial home, 87–8, 235
    "non-family" or business assets,
        294–5
    preparing for, 255–6
    private pensions, 258, 296–9
    sharing assets, 291–3
    unequal division of assets, 292–3,
        299–300
    inheritance rights of unborn children,
        11–12, 15
    insurance, 243–4
    intellectual, 249–51
    joint ownership, 237–9, 291, 344–5
    landlords and tenants, 247–9
    liens against, 315
    in marriage, 91–2
    marriage contracts and, 94
    matrimonial home *see* Matrimonial
        home